Ellis Island Interviews

. . . .

FEB - 2013

BULLARD SANFORD
MEMORIAL LIBRARY
VASSAR, MI 48768

FEB -- 2011

Ellis Island Interviews

In Their Own Words

Peter Morton Coan

Checkmark Books™
An imprint of Facts On File, Inc.

BULLARD SANFORD
MEMORIAL LIBRARY
VASSAR, MI 48768

Ellis Island Interviews: In Their Own Words

Copyright © 1997 by Peter Morton Coan

All rights reserved. No part of this book may be reproduced
or utilized in any form or by any means, electronic or
mechanical, including photocopying, recording, or by any
information storage or retrieval systems, without permission
in writing from the publisher. For information contact:

Checkmark Books
An imprint of Facts On File, Inc.
11 Penn Plaza
New York NY 10001

Library of Congress Cataloging-in-Publication Data

Coan, Peter M.
Ellis Island interviews : in their own words / Peter Morton
Coan. p. cm.
Includes index.
ISBN 0-8160-3414-1 (hardcover).—
ISBN 0-8160-3548-2 (pbk.)
1. Ellis Island Immigration Station (New York, N.Y.)
2. Immigrants—United States—Interviews. 3. United States.
Immigration and Naturalization Service—Officials and
employees—Biography. 4. United States—Emigration and
immigration—History. I. Title.
JV6455.C53   1997
304.8′73—dc21
97-2892

Checkmark Books are available at special discounts when
purchased in bulk quantities for businesses, associations,
institutions or sales promotions. Please call our Special Sales
Department in New York at (212) 967-8800 or (800) 322-8755.
You can find Facts On File on the World Wide Web at
http://www.factsonfile.com

Text design by Cathy Rincon
Cover design by Nora Wertz
Printed in the United States of America

MP FOF 10 9 8 7 6 5 4 3 2 1
(pb)   10 9 8 7 6 5 4 3 2 1

This book is printed on acid-free paper.

*For my daughters Melissa and Sara,
and for all the courageous souls
who passed through the Golden Door.*

On the boats and on the planes
They're coming to America
Never looking back again
They're coming to America

Home, don't it seem so far away
Oh, we're traveling light today
In the eye of the storm
In the eye of the storm

Home to a new and a shiny place
Make our bed, and we'll say our grace
Freedom's light burning warm
Freedom's light burning warm . . .

. . . .

—NEIL DIAMOND,
FROM THE SONG "AMERICA"

Contents

. . . .

Acknowledgments

. . . .

I am grateful to the National Park Service, which operates the Statue of Liberty/Ellis Island Monument, and to those who so capably help to keep its memory alive: Diana Pardue, chief curator; Dr. Janet Levine, oral historian; Paul Sigrist, chief oral historian; and Kevin Daley, photographer.

Special thanks go to Peter Hom of the Ellis Island Oral History Project for helping me find and select immigrant interviews for possible inclusion in this book. His advice, research assistance, and overall cooperation were invaluable. I am particularly grateful to Barry Moreno who, along with Jeff Dosik, heads the Ellis Island Research Library. Moreno's extraordinary knowledge of the history of immigration and Ellis Island are apparent in the Foreword. I also want to thank Dr. John Parascandola, historian at the U.S. Public Health Service in Rockville, Maryland, for his statistical help.

Finally, this book would not have been possible without the fine and determined efforts of my agent, Carol Mann, and my editor, Hilary Poole, who did a masterful job, and editorial director Laurie Likoff, whose belief and support have been unwavering. The other key unsung heroes at Facts On File, and I thank them all, are: Lisa Milberg, director of marketing; Kate Moore, publicity manager; Paul Conklin, director of sales; Sarah Muir, trade sales manager; and Antonio Gomez, director of electronic media. I would also like to thank Facts On File chairman Mark McDonnell for his vision and commitment to the project.

—P. M. C.

Foreword

. . . .

Though the recorded history of Ellis Island goes far back to early colonial times, the small island only emerged out of local obscurity onto the stage of American history in 1892, when it became the headquarters of the federal Immigration and Naturalization Service (INS) for the New York area—a location that dominated the scene of worldwide immigration to America's shores. Like the "slender thread" of Irish folklore that holds up the key elements of social existence, so Ellis Island, as small as it was, became America's slender thread for the peopling of the nation. The federal government endowed Ellis Island with a significance that changed lives.

The overall immigration statistics for the island are impressive. More than 12 million immigrants, or "aliens," as they were called, underwent immigration processing or detention at Ellis Island from January 1, 1892 until November 12, 1954—a span of sixty-two years. During those years, the island was the scene of more human dramas than one can imagine. They involved not just foreigners trying to enter the United States but foreigners already living here, who found themselves on Ellis Island for special inquiry and possible deportation as enemy aliens during the First and Second World Wars. The INS regularly issued warrants for their arrest and deportation.

But Ellis Island's heyday, 1892–1924, covered the years when the immigration laws of the United States were comparatively liberal. The federal government created the INS, originally called the Bureau of Immigration, and opened Ellis Island and other immigrant stations at seaports throughout the United States as landing depots to weed out undesirable immigrants. Those depots on the East Coast included Baltimore, Philadelphia, Providence, and Boston, and on the West Coast, Angel Island in San Francisco Bay (whose principal function was to exclude Chinese aliens).

The federal law was straightforward. The INS was required to enforce the Chinese Exclusion Act of 1882, the Contract Labor Law of 1885, and the Immigration Act of 1891. The latter piece of legislation excluded all mentally disabled persons, paupers, and those who might become public charges. It excluded those suffering from a "loathsome or contagious disease," as well as those convicted of a felony, an egregious

*Late 1980s photograph of Ellis Island on a misty day. In the foreground are the
still abandoned buildings of the contagious disease wards on what was known as Island Three,
where Dr. James Baker performed his medical experiments and electroshock therapy on
immigrants and U.S. naval personnel from 1949 to 1951. Island Two contained the general
hospital wards and lunatic asylum. Only the main building containing the Registry Room on
Island One was renovated from 1984–90.*

(NATIONAL PARK SERVICE: STATUE OF LIBERTY NATIONAL MONUMENT)

• • • • • • • • •

crime, or a misdemeanor involving "moral turpitude." Anarchists were added to the list of unacceptable aliens in 1903. Illiterates faced exclusion beginning in 1917.

The processing of aliens began as steamships entered New York Harbor. Boarding division inspectors and physicians from Ellis Island met the ships by cutter and examined first- and second-class passengers aboard the vessels. A few of these people were occasionally detained for further processing at Ellis Island, but the majority were released and were saved a visit to Ellis Island because they satisfied immigration officials of their comparative wealth, social standing, good health, or that they were simply temporary visitors.

By far, the greater number of passengers traveled in steerage or third class. These passengers were all required to go to Ellis Island for more extensive processing. Experience taught the INS that steerage passengers intended to remain in the United States but, often, were poor, illiterate, and in ill health.

When a steamship had docked, usually at a West Side Manhattan pier, steerage passengers were crowded aboard a ferry by INS men and taken directly to Ellis Island. They were carefully tagged, not just with their own names, but those of the steamships on which they had traveled. This was important because multiple steamships arrived on any given day, and immigrants often spoke no English and were frequently confused, angry, or fearful.

At Ellis Island, men were separated from women and children at once. They were lined up separately for inspection. Line inspection was medical in nature and was conducted by physicians of the U.S. Public Health Service, the agency that ran all federal immigrant hospitals. The inspection team was composed of "eye men," whose task it was to examine immigrants for signs of vision disorder such as cataracts, conjunc-tivitis, or trachoma. These diseases would almost certainly cause an alien to be excluded and returned aboard the next steamship to his country of origin.

The next set of doctors inspected aliens more generally. They observed demeanor and watched for signs of mental retardation, neurosis, or insanity. Aliens were examined for signs of pregnancy, physical deformities, favus (a contagious disease of the scalp), and goiter. Physicians devised a quick method for identifying aliens suspected of health problems. They simply chalked the chest of an alien with a letter of the alphabet denoting a suspected ailment or condition. H was for heart, K for hernia, Pg for pregnant, X for mental illness. These marks resulted in the alien's being detained for further examinations, and the issuance of a medical certificate, cosigned by three doctors.

The immigrants waited in long lines, frequently extending one flight upstairs, to enter the Registry Room or Great Hall. There, they were questioned by an immigration inspector assigned to interrogate the alien passengers from a particular steamship. The inspector worked from a long list of names, but was well armed with documents pertaining to each immigrant case, including the freshly written medical certificates. Other documents may have included telegrams from an alien's relatives or friends, cables from foreign police agencies requesting detention of a newly arrived alien, or other personal information that could affect the immigrant's future.

The inspector was assisted by a clerk and an interpreter. Thirty-two basic questions were asked of each alien concerning name, age, country and city of origin, occupation, whether the alien was literate in his own language, whether he understood English, the amount of money he carried, his final destination, and so on.

Alerted by an immigrant's demeanor, responsiveness, and excitability, inspectors often asked additional questions, which varied from immigrant to immigrant, such as: Are you an anarchist? Are you a polygamist? Sometimes they chatted further with other family members, watching for signs of inadmissibility. If an alien was suspected of being inadmissible, or if further paperwork was needed for admittance, he was put in detention.

Detention was a scary time for immigrants. It could last hours, but often lasted days, weeks, even months. Women and young children traveling alone were always detained until a male relative came for them. Penniless aliens were detained until someone could bring them money or vouch for them financially with a bond. Alien seamen and stowaways were detained until they could satisfy inspectors that they were admissible. Ill people or pregnant women were often detained for hospitalization. Criminals or others clearly undesirable were detained for immediate exclusion.

The first thirty-two years of Ellis Island's history, from 1892 to 1924, were the classic years when the "golden door" was open with few restrictive laws. The second period, 1924 to 1931, was different. Quota laws were introduced in 1924, which greatly restricted the number of immigrants who could enter the United States annually. The U.S. Census of 1890 was used as the basis of foreign quotas. Each nation was given a 2 percent quota based on that census. This tended to favor old immigrant nationalities, such as the British, Germans, Irish, and Swedes, over the new immigration wave of Italians, Jews, and eastern Europeans.

But the INS's work at Ellis Island really began to change when the processing of aliens was gradually assigned to U.S. consulates abroad. By 1931, the new system was in full force. This completed the island's

third phase, a downward slide until 1954. When the primary function as an immigration processing station to the U.S. eroded, immigration levels dropped dramatically from a high of 1.2 million in 1907 to approximately 25,000 in 1932. Now all questioning and medical examinations had to be completed at American consulates abroad, before immigrants could be granted a visa allowing them to enter the United States. As a result, Ellis Island—from 1931 to 1954—was used chiefly for law enforcement purposes, as a place to detain suspect aliens as well as those under warrant for arrest and deportation. Some of these aliens were criminals in Europe. In addition, the Second World War and its aftermath saw thousands of German, Japanese, and Italian enemy aliens, as well as refugees, detained at Ellis Island.

In 1939, the U.S. Coast Guard established a training base on Ellis Island, and in 1941, the FBI set up an office. Ellis Island remained the New York headquarters of the INS until 1943, when the Department of Justice moved the administrative offices to Manhattan. The U.S. Public Health Service closed the main immigrant hospital buildings on the island in 1951. Then, on November 12, 1954, the INS closed Ellis Island completely, under orders from U.S. Attorney General Herbert Brownell, abandoning the island for good in March 1955, and leaving the General Services Administration as the last surviving federal presence at the former immigration station.

—*Barry Moreno*
   Librarian and Historian
   Ellis Island Immigration Museum
   Statue of Liberty National Monument
   National Park Service
   U.S. Department of the Interior

Passage to Ellis Island

. . . .

Give me your tired, your poor,
Your huddled masses, yearning to breathe free,
The wretched refuse of your teeming shore,
Send these, the homeless, tempest-tost, to me:
I lift my lamp beside the golden door.

—EMMA LAZARUS ("THE NEW COLOSSUS")
INSCRIPTION AT THE BASE OF THE STATUE OF LIBERTY

The ocean was amazing. They all re-member that. The vast expanse of gray, angry water that seemed to go on forever. By and large, they came from nondescript farm villages and hamlets tucked away in forgotten European prov-inces and sleepy border towns routinely compromised by twisted ideology, plunder, and hate. It was a hopeless predicament that left many without economic wherewithal and no recourse but to look elsewhere for freedom and livelihood. It was a question of survival more than anything else. A prag-matic decision that had less to do with lofty goals and grandiose dreams, and more to do with keeping one's family intact and finding a realistic answer to a basic question: Where do we go from here?

They heard the talk. About a place where streets are paved with gold. A place

where all men are free. A place of compas-sion. But what about cost? Not just money for the passage, but the emotional toll. For most, the grandparents would have to be left behind, not to mention the cousins, uncles, aunts, friends. The same was true of the wives and young children. The men would have to go it alone and send for their families later. Lucky were those whose families were not divided.

The immigrants came in waves, and they came by boat (or plane in the fifties), with nothing but the clothes on their backs, a pocketful of dreams, a flimsy suitcase or trunk, and some crumpled bills carefully stashed away. They came to a country where they did not speak the language. They had little or no formal education. The men who traveled first were met by a distant relative or in-law who had come before them, and would vouch for them upon arrival. Many had never met this in-law or relative. Some had no one to vouch for them at all. But they came just the same, these lowly carpenters and peddlers and farmhands, many of whom were illiterate, yet in their character and spirit they possessed the constitution of generals; the intestinal fortitude of kings. It was a blind mission requiring a persistence and determination many people today hope to find in self-help books and audiotapes. For them it was second nature. Many of the children, who came with their mothers later on, would see their fathers for the first time in the shadow of the Statue of Liberty.

Their cross-continental trek was like a test of Darwin's theory of the survival of the fittest, because they were more than fit: They were driven—by pain and fear and hopelessness; by poverty and hunger; by religious persecution; or the simple need to survive. These things they had in common, as well as the hope of a better life. They all shared a common destination: Ellis Island. They would all wind up in the Great Hall or main hall—the Registry Room, as it was properly termed. Truly, these were brave men, as were the women and children who followed in their wake. They were, in large part, the gene pool from which America grew.

The stories you are about to read are the firsthand accounts of the last surviving original immigrants who came through Ellis Island's mythical Golden Door. They describe in detail the life they left behind in Europe—why they emigrated, what they endured, and what became of them after their arrival. These immigrants are literally the last of a dying breed, and this book is a testament to their courage and conviction, the last opportunity to capture on record this crucial piece of America's past before it is lost forever.

. . .

Ellis Island was the major federal immigration facility in America between January 1, 1892 and November 12, 1954. During those years, more than 24 million people were processed for immigration in the United States, of whom more than 12 million came through Ellis Island. But this does not include more than 4 million first- and second-class passengers who avoided Ellis Island entirely and were discharged at Manhattan piers after having been processed on the boat in New York Harbor by Immigration and Naturalization Service (INS) inspectors who were based on Ellis Island.

Therefore, between 1892 and 1954, more than 66 percent of the people who immigrated to America came through the Ellis Island station. That percentage was highest—71.4—between 1892 and 1924. The three years of greatest immigration influx were 1905 to 1907, when Ellis Island received as many as 5,000 immigrants per day. But when new quota laws took effect in 1931, the numbers dropped precipitously. The purpose of Ellis Island, and the INS, was not to welcome visitors but to find reasons to reject them.

Today, according to the Statue of Liberty-Ellis Island Foundation, "more than 40 percent of the U.S. population, or over 100 million Americans, can trace their roots to an ancestor who came through Ellis Island." Immigration statistics go back as far as 1820. The height of immigration was between 1820 and 1931. That means the majority of today's Americans are the offspring of pioneering ancestors from that period.

Examination of the statistics shows that seven country groups dominate the genetic blueprint of American stock. The seeds of America are seeds that belong to predominantly white northern Europeans. Essentially, America is a country born of (in order of immigration influx between 1820 and 1931)

THE HIGH TIDE OF IMMIGRATION—A NATIONAL MENACE.

An anti-European immigration cartoon published in 1903, expressing sentiments some now hold toward Asians, Latinos, and Haitian "boat people."

(NATIONAL PARK SERVICE: STATUE OF LIBERTY NATIONAL MONUMENT)

Germans (5,918,294), Italians (4,664,594), Irish (4,586,246), Austrians/Hungarians (4,133,976), English/Scottish/ Welsh (3,441,091), Russians (3,342,326), and Swedes (1,214,786). There is a common misconception that most immigrants to Ellis Island were eastern European. This is not true. Most were Italian—notably southern Italian—or northern European.

. . .

Ellis Island evolved out of scandal. Castle Garden was the first immigration station in the United States, from August 1855 to April 1890. Its original name was Castle Clinton, named after New York's first governor, George Clinton. In actual fact, it wasn't a castle at all, but an old fort at Bowling Green,

along the Hudson River in lower Manhattan, where people actually used to bowl.

Castle Clinton was built in 1811 to defend New York from British attack (though no shot was fired from there) and used as a jail for British prisoners during the War of 1812. In June 1824, Castle Clinton was renamed Castle Garden, when New York City leased the fort and turned it into a fashionable drinking and entertainment establishment. By the 1840s, the fort was roofed over, and Castle Garden became a popular theater where P. T. Barnum often staged his outrageous acts. By 1855 it had become an immigration station run by New York State.

Prior to 1855, anybody who came to America got off a boat and took their chances, as did the Irish who fled their

The Ellis Island station as it originally looked before the 1897 fire.

(NATIONAL PARK SERVICE: STATUE OF LIBERTY NATIONAL MONUMENT)

homeland on coffin ships during the potato famine that lasted from 1845 to 1849. Millions of Irish immigrants arrived on U.S. shores, and the government felt it had to do something. In August 1855 Castle Garden was designated an immigration depot. Approximately 8 million immigrants from northern and western Europe were processed there. In fact, two out of every three persons immigrating to America between 1855 and 1890, or nearly 70 percent of the incoming population, passed through this facility.

The purpose of Castle Garden, like Ellis Island after it, was to deny entrance to aliens deemed undesirable. This category included prostitutes, conmen, Chinese "coolies," and "any convict, lunatic, idiot, or any person unable to take care of himself or herself without becoming a public charge."

Furthermore, immigration officials were unabashed in their preference for white northern Europeans. There is no known proof that this was written policy, but the attitude prevailed. "Politically correct" was not a concept in those days. Put another way, if you weren't white northern European, and especially if you were black, Asian, or Hispanic, you were likely to be detained with an eye toward deportation. For instance, blacks—primarily from Africa and the West Indies—totaled less than 2 percent of the immigrant influx into Castle Garden (as well as Ellis Island).

When it came to racist exclusion, Castle Garden was successful.

It was not successful in its second purpose. That was to protect bewildered white northern European immigrants from the unsavory characters who roamed the wharves

Original 1910 photograph, never before published, of Annie Moore (1876–1923),
the first immigrant to Ellis Island. She was married to Daniel O'Connell. She is pictured
here with her infant daughter, Mary Catherine, 18 years after her arrival at Ellis Island—
January 1, 1892, the first day of business.

(NATIONAL PARK SERVICE: STATUE OF LIBERTY NATIONAL MONUMENT)

· · · · · · ·

exploiting gullible newcomers with false promises of jobs and housing. Frequently immigrants found themselves fleeced of their money and personal possessions. Prostitution was rampant, as was corruption inside Castle Garden itself.

In fact, complaints about abusive behavior by immigration officials toward immigrants were widespread. This included charges of sexual misconduct, political patronage, and excessive profits from the sale of railroad tickets. In short, Castle Garden had become a den of sin, a con man's Shangri-la, the inside no better than the outside. The situation got so bad that Congress initiated an official investigation, and on April 18, 1890, the immigration center was closed. The empty building eventually housed the New York City aquarium (1896), which was later moved to Coney Island (1940). It was renamed Castle Clinton and declared a national monument in 1946.

In 1890 when it closed Castle Garden, Congress created the Bureau of Immigration, or what later was known as the INS. The federal government, in effect, took control of immigration from New York state and, during the next two years, from 1890 to 1892, processed more than 1 million immigrants at the Barge Office in Battery Park, which was the federal customs office in New York.

The Ellis Island Immigration Station was consumed by fire June 14, 1897.
The buildings were made of Georgia pinewood. There were no casualties. Nobody
knows what caused the fire. The very next day, Ellis Island Immigration Commissioner
Dr. Joseph Senner said, "The buildings were a tinderbox . . . and good riddance," and ordered
the construction of fire-proof buildings made of brick.

(NATIONAL PARK SERVICE: STATUE OF LIBERTY NATIONAL MONUMENT)

Ellis Island as it appeared in the winter of 1911. In the foreground are the contagious disease wards on Island Three run by the U.S. Public Health Service. (In the early 1920s the ferry slip between Islands Two and Three was filled in with excess dirt dug while building the New York subway system.) Island Two, the middle island, was the site of hospital buildings for immigrants, also run by the Public Health Service. Island One had the main ferry slip, which still exists, and the main building, plus a powerhouse, laundry, bakery, carpenter's shop, kitchen, greenhouse, railroad ticket office, money exchange, detention building, incinerators, and a post office.

(NATIONAL PARK SERVICE: STATUE OF LIBERTY NATIONAL MONUMENT)

In the meantime, the U.S. secretary of the Treasury, who oversaw the Bureau of Immigration, sought a place to build a new receiving station. He wanted a site on an island in New York Harbor so that immigrants, upon arrival, would not once again be easy marks for seedy, opportunistic characters. In addition, a relative or close friend would have to vouch for them.

The first choice was Bedloe's Island, where the Statue of Liberty had been built only four years earlier (1886). But the statue's architect, Auguste Bartholdi, was horrified and declared the idea a "monstrous plan . . . a desecration." Eyes shifted to Governor's Island, but that was already inhabited by the Coast Guard. Instead, attention turned to a small island a few hundred yards north of Bedloe's, and 1½ miles west of Castle Garden off the coast of New Jersey, which had been used as an ammunitions dump. That state had been petitioning the federal government for removal of the powder kegs. That speck of land, of course, was Ellis Island.

It was originally called Kioshk, or Gull Island, by Native Americans in the 1600s; Gibbet Island in the early 1700s when criminals were hanged there from a gibbet, or gallows tree; and later Oyster Island, because of abundance of the shellfish. It wasn't until the early 1780s that the island was bought by the merchant Samuel Ellis from whom it got its present name. New York

State bought Ellis Island in 1808, using it as an ammunitions dump until June 15, 1892, when the immigration facility, built at a cost of $500,000, officially opened its doors. Annie Moore from Ireland was the first immigrant admitted (the last, in 1954, was a Norwegian merchant seaman).

Five years later, in 1897, the main building and much of the rest of Ellis Island's wood structures were destroyed by a fire whose cause has never been determined, and the Barge Office was reenlisted as a processing station. By 1900 the new "fireproof" Ellis Island complex had been constructed, of stone instead of wood. But fire was the least of its troubles.

The corruption that plagued Castle Garden had been carried over to Ellis Island. Inspectors forced immigrants to pay bribes, and young girls to give sexual favors; railroad ticket agents inflated the price of passage and pocketed the difference; clerks at the money exchange wantonly lied about international currency rates. The atmosphere of graft and sin became so overt and untenable that news reached President Theodore Roosevelt, who, in 1901, ordered a major cleanup and replaced the top Washington officials in charge, including the commissioner of immigration.

By 1903 two more islands were connected to Ellis, creating a landmass that looked like the letter E. The dirt from the digging of the New York City IRT subway, which opened in 1904, served as landfill to create Island Two, which housed the hospital administration as well as the contagious disease wards, and Island Three (facing the Statue of Liberty due south), the site of the psychiatric wards. Island One, as it was known—the original island—housed the main receiving building, which contained the Registry Room. Eventually the docking area between Islands Two and Three was filled, creating a rectangular shape with one port, which is how Ellis Island looks today.

. . .

This book grew out of the EI Series of the Ellis Island Oral History Project. Though immigrants had been interviewed on audiotape for inclusion in the Oral History Museum since the 1970s, the EI Series was different. Because many of the original immigrants were old and could be gone by the end of this century, the series—begun in 1990—was a final attempt by the museum to reach out and find them, to secure basic information about them and record their stories before it was too late. More than 1,700 original immigrants were located and volunteered to come forward. Many were discovered by word of mouth, or volunteered as the result of publicity of the project in local newspapers.

The interviews were audiotaped at the Ellis Island Oral History Recording Studio or at the immigrants' homes, which were often nursing homes. The interviews were conducted by oral historians Paul Sigrist or Janet Levine, employees of the National Park Service. Interviews outside the EI Series, or done before 1990, were conducted by other National Park Service personnel. Either way, the immigrants were asked a standard set of autobiographical questions, including their origin, why they came to America, on what boat they traveled, what they endured, and what subsequently became of them. Since all of this was public information, I had complete access to it.

Over the course of more than four years, I pored through hundreds of interviews and thousands of transcript pages to find the most compelling stories and winnow them down to the 114 immigrants finally selected for this book. I was looking for an even mix of nationalities, men and women, across a span of years, from before World War I to after World War II. The idea was to get a representative sampling of the immigrant experience as it related to the one thing they all had in common: their passage through Ellis Island.

The task was daunting. Most of the immigrants were old (some more than 100 years old) and their memories at times unreliable. When a transcript was incomplete, I reinterviewed them in person or by phone to fill in gaps, confirm facts, and complete anecdotes, which often led to new anecdotes and new sources of information. In some cases, the immigrant had either died or could not be located. I also interviewed many immigrants whose stories never made it into this book. Invariably they were peers of the subject and came through Ellis Island about the same time. The goal was to gain a comparative tone and feel for what it was like *then*, and whether the subject's story was truly representative or unique. The research that went into the correct spelling of foreign names, cities, and towns was a task unto itself. Sometimes I found that the person identified in a transcript as the subject's father was really the husband or brother. I had to, in a sense, be a detective and piece together what they were trying to say, all the while preserving the integrity of their voices and stories.

The complete transcripts with additions and corrections (some more than 100 pages) were then condensed to an average of fewer than 15 pages. I edited to avoid redundancy, and moved material only when necessary to preserve chronology, so that their stories would make sense. But at no time did I put words in their mouths. These are their stories, both sad and inspiring.

Stories where the emotion was strongest tended to be the most accurate and telling. Jewish people, due to the pain of their persecution, tended to have the most to say. I therefore let the stories go where the emotion took them. Some stories centered around the "old country"; others ended at Ellis Island; while still others extended through the assimilation process in America. It depended on the material.

Each chapter covers a nationality. The chapters proceed according to immigration density—greatest to least. The immigrants in each chapter appear chronologically, in order of the year they immigrated. In this way, one can look up one's ancestry and have a very real sense of what one's forebears probably experienced firsthand. That is the purpose of this book. To give a balanced portrait, I also included the stories of Ellis Island employees and what they experienced on the receiving end of this vast influx of humanity.

Except for public figures and a few well-known immigrants or Ellis Island employees who gave permission for their names to be used, I have changed the names of each immigrant to protect his or her privacy.

The names of immigrants were often Anglicized at Ellis Island, and since the majority of immigrants in this book came here as children, many of their names were Anglicized when they registered at public school. First names like Rolf became Ralph, Margarethe became Marge, Benedetto became Benny. Last names like Wallik became Wallace, and Fogelman trimmed to Fogg.

Most had never been on a boat, much less seen a major city like New York with its towering skyscrapers, the tallest of which, at the turn of the century, were the 278-foot towers of the Brooklyn Bridge, and later in 1913, the F. W. Woolworth building (792 feet) in lower Manhattan. And each nationality had its own idiosyncrasies in the personal effects they transported with them. Italian immigrants took their feather mattresses and bedding; Russians, their samovars; Jews, religious artifacts. Some immigrants didn't even know their birthdays, since they came from provinces that kept no birth records, or because their birth certificates were left behind or lost during passage. Many figured out their birthdays in

*An 1879 newspaper cartoon depicting the discrimination against
blacks (far left), Native Americans, and, in particular,
the Chinese, which led to the enactment of the
Chinese Exclusion Act of 1882*

(NATIONAL PARK SERVICE: STATUE OF LIBERTY NATIONAL MONUMENT)

. . . .

association with religious holidays. This is particularly true among the Jews. A few of the immigrants in this book even came here on the same boat on the same day.

Common in the interviews was the surprise, upon arrival, at seeing a black person for the first time; eating white bread at the Ellis Island cafeteria; tasting a stick of chewing gum; the wonder of toilets that flush, showers that gush, and "those strange yellow things" called bananas sold from small boats in New York Harbor and raised in a basket on a rope to the steamship. Then, of course, there was the Statue of Liberty, the legendary lady—some adults knew of it, some children read about it in school in Europe. Many knew nothing. But when they saw her majesty—unmistakably, undeniably, before them, it was like a physical affirmation—proof that America and freedom in all its magnificent wonder was, in fact, *real*.

Real, too, were the imminent name tags, long lines, medical examinations, and detainment cells. For many, the joy and wonder upon release was best captured in the Barry Levinson movie *Avalon*, in which an immigrant arrives in Baltimore to Fourth of July fireworks.

For others, Ellis Island meant deportation. The reasons for immigrant rejection were medical, moral, legal, even racist. The Chinese, for instance, described by periodicals in the late 1800s as the "Yellow Peril," were barred at all cost. Historians, in retrospect, surmise that their large numbers, and their reputation for honesty, obedience, and hard work did them in. They worked for little pay. They were not drunkards. They were family people. In short, they were an employment threat to white people.

. . .

Today, Ellis Island is perceived with great romanticism. Wistful feelings are evoked by its Wall of Honor, where people have paid

good money (and continue to pay) to have their families listed among the more than 500,000 names inscribed in steel. Most names deserve to be there. Some don't. And while there is nothing wrong with trying to see the past in a positive light, the reality of life at Ellis Island was not always positive. The "immigrant experience" had its dark side. Still in shock, trauma, or depression from the long boat ride, many immigrants endured verbal, physical, even sexual abuse from opportunistic guards, medical staff, and even fellow immigrants.

Though 355 babies were born into U.S. citizenship on Ellis Island, more than 3,500 immigrants died there, including 1,400 children. There were also three known suicides. So, while for some Ellis Island and its famous kissing post may have been known as the Isle of Hope, others knew it as the Isle of Tears or Hell's Island.

Though long denied but suspected, electroshock treatments were, in fact, administered at Ellis Island to immigrants, as well as coastguardsmen and merchant seamen, from 1945 until 1951, when the U.S. Public Health Service closed the hospital wards on Ellis Island. In the medical community, electroconvulsive therapy (ECT) was commonly used by doctors at that time for treating psychosomatic illness. Lobotomies were also a common treatment, although there is no conclusive proof that these were performed at Ellis Island.

Read the firsthand account of Dr. James Baker, who was a psychiatric resident-in-training in 1942 and later became the director of the neuropsychiatric service at Ellis Island from November 1949 to March 1951. I interviewed Dr. Baker over the course of two days at his home in Florida. Dr. Baker describes, in graphic detail, how electroshock was performed on immigrants, coastguardsmen, and merchant seamen, and how Ellis Island, in its waning years, became a virtual laboratory for experimentation and the treatment of psychological and physical disorders that are common today, but then barely known. The story of Dr. Burton Field, then a dental intern, confirms that shock therapy was used at Ellis Island as early as 1945, four years before the arrival of Dr. Baker, who dramatically expanded its use.

Historically, however, immigrants were regularly used as guinea pigs for psychological tests, even medical experiments, since the turn of the century. In fact, the U.S. Public Health Service was established at Ellis Island, and a cure for conjunctivitis, or "pink eye," which then led to blindness, was discovered there. Barry Moreno, the Immigration Museum chief librarian, explains: "Psychological testing was developed at Ellis Island. Eugenics was a movement in the early part of the twentieth century." (According to *Webster's Dictionary*, eugenics is "a science concerned with improving a breed or species, especially the human species, by such means as influencing or encouraging reproduction by persons presumed to have desirable genetic traits.") The U.S. Public Health Service, which staffed the hospitals on Ellis Island, actively engaged in developing tests to study the intelligence of races and compare them. These results were given to the U.S. Congress and were used as arguments in favor of restricting immigration. So eventually the Immigration Act of 1891, and the restriction or quota laws of the 1920s, developed out of the successful debates to exclude more immigrants of supposedly less intelligent races. Northern Europeans were considered the most intelligent, or desirable.

"Medical testing and treatment at Ellis Island throughout the twentieth century shows medicine in action, patterns of treatments and cures that included shock therapy, mostly on soldiers, during and after World War II, who had mental problems as a result of the war. This was typical. In the early part of the century, contagious diseases like tuberculosis prevailed. The layout of the contagious disease wards gave patients plenty of sunlight and fresh air, and, of course, isolation from other patients. Mental testing and shock treatments were all part of different stages in medicine. The study of different and unusual strains of bacteria were evident here as well. Different races and deformities could be observed. This was quite a place to look at different racial types that were unknown before in the U.S. It was not a time of modern medicine, so a lot of things were tested out and experimented on," states Moreno.

. . .

Today, immigration has resurfaced as one of the nation's hottest and most contentious issues. A recent CNN/*USA Today*/Gallup Poll found a majority of Americans—63 percent—want to cut back on immigration. Not unlike a century ago, Americans view immigrants as a threat to their well-being, competitors for jobs and money, and contributors to crime. "The very things they said about the Irish and the Italians and the eastern Europeans and the Jews coming in," said one scholar, "are word for word the same accusations being leveled against Hispanic and Asian immigrants coming in today."

In 1996, nearly 750,000 people became citizens of the United States. Nationwide, the INS will detain or deport 30,000 criminal aliens in 1997. Today, 22.6 million people, or 8.7 percent of the U.S. population are immigrants, more than at any time since World War II. Of those, 4 million are here illegally, and many more try to enter the country and fail. Recently, one man from the Dominican Republic was found floating in a Long Island marina near Kennedy International Airport, having fallen from a jet after stowing away in the plane's wheel well.

. . .

Once free, most immigrants cushioned the shock of their new venture by settling in enclaves that were geographically similar to their ethnic homes. The Scandinavians headed for the cold climate of the northern Midwest; the Irish tended to congregate near water—the sea and the Great Lakes; the Jews, the Lower East Side of Manhattan. They often endured horrific housing conditions and, outside those enclaves, blatant prejudice, frequently just a block or two away. Still, they were grateful for their new-found freedom, and made every effort to assimilate into American culture. They found work, learned English, became citizens, and were proud of it. With few exceptions, immigrants in this book did not voluntarily return to their homelands from America—America *was* their home. Some even volunteered to serve in the U.S. armed forces during World War II.

But in their advancing years, many went back to visit—as if on some pilgrimage to make peace with their past. Some walked away cleansed. Others found painful memories remained. All discovered that things had changed, for better or for worse. Even their children, who once repudiated their old world ways, had to recognize the unique part they played in history for having passed through Ellis Island. They treasured the notes, letters, and pictures they saved, and the audiotapes they made, to pass down to future generations. Some of the immigrants in this book even outlived their children; such was the purity of their character, the strength of their stock.

They were not all commoners, either. There were the soon to be famous as well: Bob Hope, Claudette Colbert, Frank Capra, Samuel Goldwyn, Rudolph Valentino, Edward G. Robinson, Lee Strasberg, Otto Preminger, Al Jolson, Irving Berlin, Arthur Tracy, Elia Kazan, Isaac Asimov, Kahlil Gibran, Henry Roth, Igor Sikorsky, Xavier Cugat, Knute Rockne, Father Edward Flana-

Rudolph Valentino

(NATIONAL PARK SERVICE:
STATUE OF LIBERTY NATIONAL MONUMENT)

gan, Baron von Trapp, Victor Borge, Abe Beame, John Kluge, Meyer Lansky, Charles "Lucky" Luciano, Nicola Sacco and Bartolomeo Vanzetti, and Bela Lugosi, who would go on to become Hollywood's Count Dracula and who, perhaps, had the most bizarre tale of them all.

Barry Moreno tells the story: "Bela Lugosi was an illegal alien who had jumped ship. Lugosi was a Hungarian stage actor born in Lugos, Hungary. In October of 1920, he was a crew member aboard a steamship called the S.S. *Graf Tisza Istvan.* The ship had sailed out of Trieste, Italy and arrived in New Orleans on October 27, 1920. Lugosi jumped ship in New Orleans, meaning he got a pass from his captain, went into town, and didn't return to the vessel. He was involved in left-wing politics, and that may have been a part of it. He was reported as missing to the police and INS officials. They were then, of course, on the lookout for him. He was an illegal alien seaman.

"Then he disappeared for about five months. He came to New York. He settled in a Hungarian community on the Upper East Side of Manhattan, which was then a poor community. He knew no English. The INS eventually tracked him down to a boardinghouse at 109 West Ninety-third Street, and he surrendered at Ellis Island. He was inspected March 23, 1921."

The recorded questions and answers of that interrogation below are typical of what every immigrant who came through Ellis Island experienced. Note, however, that Lugosi lied about his nationality and language in case Hungarian police, due to his left-wing politics, had put him on a list of radicals, which meant he would have been deported. The "red scare" in 1921 had INS officials wary of any immigrant from Hungary because of that country's communist or Bolshevik past. Lugosi was interrogated by Inspector John Richardson.

Name?—Bela Lugosi.
Age?—Thirty-eight.
Marital Status?—Single.
Calling or occupation?—Sailor.
Are you able to read?—Yes.
What language?—Roumanian.
Write?—Yes.
Your race or people?—Roumanian.
Last permanent residence or country?—Italy.
City or town?—Trieste.
Nearest relative or friend in country from whence came?—No one.
Final destination?—New York City, New York.
By whom was passage paid?—Member of crew.
How much money is in your possession?—$100.00.

Have you ever been in the United States before?—No.
Will you ever return to the country from whence you came?—No.
Length of stay in U.S.?—Permanent.
Do you intend to become a U.S. citizen?—Yes
Have you ever been in prison or Almshouse, insane asylum or supported by charity?—No.
Are you a polygamist?—No.
Are you an anarchist?—No.
Do you believe in or advocate the overthrow by force of the U.S. government?—No.
Have you come to the United States because of solicitation or Offer of Employment?—No.
Were you previously deported this year?—No.
What is your condition of health—mental and physical?—Good.
Are you deformed or crippled?—No.
What is your height?—Five feet, ten inches.
Complexion?—Dark.
Colour of hair?—Brown.
Colour of eyes?—Black.
Country of Birth?—Roumania.
Town of Birth?—Lugos.

. . .

Though Ellis Island closed November 12, 1954, the INS didn't move out until March 1955. The federal government then transferred jurisdiction to the General Services Administration (GSA), which dealt with surplus government property, which is what Ellis Island had become. The GSA was charged with providing upkeep of the island, which it didn't do, and with trying to sell the island, but the offers were deemed unsatisfactory.

On May 11, 1965 President Lyndon Johnson attached Ellis Island as a national monument to the Statue of Liberty, and turned maintenance of the island over to the National Park Service. Nevertheless, the is-

. . . .

Interior of an abandoned building, one of twenty-four such structures that remain on Ellis Island.

(NATIONAL PARK SERVICE: STATUE OF LIBERTY NATIONAL MONUMENT)

·   ·   ·   ·   ·   ·   ·   ·   ·

land remained in a state of abandonment, neglect, and decay, visited by looters and the ghosts of more than 12 million immigrant souls who once roamed its cavernous halls. It remained in that state for nearly thirty-two years.

It wasn't until 1986, and the renovation of the Statue of Liberty, that attention turned to the main building at Ellis Island. Private sector fund-raising, spearheaded by Lee Iacocca, chairman of Chrysler Corporation, and businessman William Fugazy, brought in more than $165 million, the largest restoration project of its kind in American history. On September 10, 1990, Ellis Island reopened to the general public as a museum and receives 2.5 million visitors annually, one of the top tourist attractions in the world. Despite this, the remaining twenty-four buildings on the island—the old hospital ward buildings—rot in the salt air, off limits to tourists. In fact, the World Monument Fund recently named Ellis Island, and six other historic sites nationwide, to a new list of the world's 100 most endangered landmarks.

At Ellis Island today, some of the visitors sit on the benches of the Registry Room and stare. Their eyes well with tears; they are choked with the emotion of what it must have been like; what their ancestors must have endured.

You are about to find out.

The main building at Ellis Island as it looks today.

(BRIAN FEENEY, NATIONAL PARK SERVICE:
STATUE OF LIBERTY NATIONAL MONUMENT)

1

· · · · · · · · · · ·

Ellis Island Employees

(MORE THAN 700 BY THE MID-1920s)

Photo of the Public Health Service staff in front of the immigrant hospital in 1924.
The years prior to World War I and just after saw the greatest influx of immigrants,
and thus demand for medical and surgical attention.

(NATIONAL PARK SERVICE: STATUE OF LIBERTY NATIONAL MONUMENT)

Dr. James Baker

· · · · · · · · · · · · ·

BORN APRIL 16, 1914 IN LEWISTOWN, PENNSYLVANIA
PSYCHIATRIST AT ELLIS ISLAND 1949–1951

*Of German descent, his great-grandparents originally immigrated to America in
the 1860s. When he was seven years old, his father—who was in the paint and
lumber business—fell three stories to his death while working on a building
project. Raised by his mother and her parents in Lewistown, he eventually
graduated from medical school at Temple University in 1940. He was first
stationed on Ellis Island for three months (July–September) in 1942, as part of
his psychiatric residency training. He then trained as a flight surgeon, but instead
became a commissioned medical officer of the U.S. Public Health Service, serving
in several of their hospitals. He returned to Ellis Island as director of the
neuropsychiatric service from November 1949 until March 1951, where he
instituted the extensive use of electroconvulsive therapy (ECT) on immigrants,
Coast Guard personnel, and merchant seamen. In 1966 he went into private
practice, then retired in Florida, where he makes his home today. In 1987 he
suffered a stroke, one month after his wife of fifty-two years, Marjorie, died of
lymphoma. He lives with his youngest son, Barry, who helps look after him.*

My first tour of duty at Ellis Island
was part of my psychiatric residency training. I was twenty-eight,
married. My wife, Marjorie, and I, lived in
Manhattan Beach in Brooklyn near the
Coast Guard station. I would take the BMT
subway, and then the ferry to Ellis Island.

At that time, our cases were mostly
coastguardsmen and merchant seamen. Our
immigration cases were people who had not
been adequately screened from the consular
offices in Europe. They either had epilepsy,
a convulsion, or started hallucinating aboard
ship, or had a criminal record that wasn't
discovered until after they left, and was discovered en route to America. Then, the
Board of Inquiry [in the main building, Island One], would send them to us.

We'd do a psychiatric portrait of a patient, including psychological testing, a
physical, and an electroencephalogram

(EEG), if that was necessary, because we had
to do that on the mainland. At Ellis Island
we didn't have an EEG machine. We would
present the case to the other residents and
everyone would comment on it, and there
was no appeal from our certification. If we
certified an immigrant as "mandatorily excludable," there was no appeal, and they
would be deported.

Often it would involve a small child,
who had a convulsion, and then the whole
family would have to go back. Epilepsy was
mandatorily excludable. So was a psychopathic personality, all the psychoses, such as
schizophrenia. Practically any overt mental
illness was mandatorily excludable. We
would provide whatever treatment was
needed, but then they were automatically
shipped back, unless we diagnosed that
there was no certifiable disease present, but
that was seldom because there was a certain

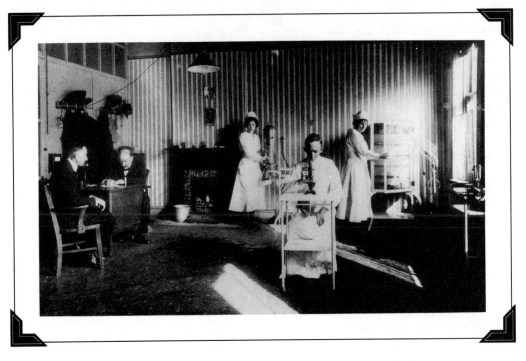

Medical staff, circa 1918. There were fifteen medical buildings on Ellis Island.

(NATIONAL PARK SERVICE: STATUE OF LIBERTY NATIONAL MONUMENT)

screening by immigration, and usually they wouldn't send us an immigrant unless there was a definite problem.

But it wasn't limited to just immigration cases. We saw the acute nervous breakdowns of Coast Guard personnel and merchant seamen. They hadn't necessarily seen any action, but they had a problem that had become so manifest, they were shipped from their station on vessels in the New York area to Ellis Island. Any ship that came into New York with a U.S. merchant seaman who had a questionable problem got sent to us. We were the only psychiatric service in the area. The marine hospital on Staten Island didn't have a psychiatric service.

The immigrants at that time were mostly from the Slovak countries in Eastern Europe. They were really undesirable people. To put it bluntly, we wouldn't want

them in this country, because they would be a strain on our resources. We would have to use an interpreter. We were dependent on how much usable information we could get, because the interpreter was accustomed to making sense out of what the patient said, and we didn't want it that way. If the immigrant didn't make sense, that's what we wanted to know.

We had six residents in training, and we would see, in 1942, a daily caseload of twenty to thirty patients assigned to each of us [a mix of immigrants, Coast Guard personnel, and merchant seamen]. I would say a fourth of the cases were immigrants. But that didn't mean they all came in. Some of them would be there for various lengths of time. Some of them would be there for treatment, some of them [Coast Guard personnel] would be transferred to Veterans

Administration (VA) hospitals. The merchant seamen went to state hospitals.

We ran a 200-bed acute psychiatric treatment service. We weren't a long-term treatment facility. The psychiatric ward was all of Island Three. Contagious diseases and medical administration was Island Two. I didn't handle contagious disease.

On Island Three, there were six psychiatric wards, or buildings, although they all looked like one building. We'd run pretty close to full census—the 200 beds. To have any leeway, we had to have about fifteen free beds. So we had about 185 beds filled. We worked at full capacity, and this was also true during my second tour of duty there.

Reserpine was the first psychoactive drug, and the only one we had at the time,

but it had serious side effects, though it benefited some schizophrenics. In fact, we didn't use Reserpine very often in '42, because of the side effects, and we didn't know that much about it. We didn't use shock treatment until the second time I was at Ellis Island [1949].

What we did use was hydrotherapy. There was often a condition called catatonic excitement, where the patient would get into a frenzy of activity. Prior to shock treatment, the only thing you could do was put them in sedative water packs and cold tubs, and hope. With the cold pack, it rapidly became skin temperature and had a sedative effect on patients. That was an old form of hydrotherapy or physical therapy for treating patients, particularly in their excited

A 1951 postcard of Ellis Island from Dr. Baker's photo album. The buildings at the top were the psychiatric wards (Island Three), Dr. Baker's domain. The buildings closer in, once separated by water and called Island Two, were the contagious disease wards. In the foreground is a rear view of the main building, Island One.

(COURTESY OF DR. JAMES BAKER)

phase, or if a patient became excited in relation to a delusion. Float tubs could also be used, with water flowing around them at a fixed temperature—lukewarm, because it was possible to lower the body temperature to an undesirable level if you use too cold a water. So while we called them "cold packs," they really ended up being at skin temperature. We might order a flow tub for an hour. The nurse or the hydrotherapist would be with them. We had four or five flow tubs with a hydrotherapist and a couple attendants there constantly.

But many of these catatonic excitements ended up with a fever getting out of control, and they ended up dead. Fortunately, I didn't see many of these cases in '42. It was probably in 10 percent of the cases where they [the patients] went on to die, but that was still a pretty high number. They died because their temperature would just keep shooting up. The body got to where it could not maintain temperature regulations. The temperature would shoot up to 105, 106, or 107, and the patient would just expire.

From Ellis Island, as part of my residency training, I then spent six months at the New York Psychiatric Institute up near Columbia University. The institute had nothing to do with Ellis Island or the Coast Guard. Each night, from Manhattan Beach, I would take the BMT subway to the Eighth Avenue subway [to the institute].

At the institute they had hydrotherapy, six to eight tubs. But mostly I did insulin therapy. The institute had a whole insulin therapy ward that would have maybe fifteen patients in various stages of insulin coma. The therapy was mainly used for schizophrenics, who didn't respond to other treatments. If we gave insulin therapy, the patient would go into a deep coma for not more than an hour, and that altered state was therapeutic to them; then it would be terminated.

But they didn't always respond. Most of them responded rapidly to the termination by injection of glucose. But not all of them did. It would be a prolonged coma, even death. So getting them out of the coma was the problem. Frequently they wouldn't wake up when we injected them with the glucose solution. Others were so slow in responding, we were on needles and pins. I had one patient die on my supervisor there, and then I had to deal with the relatives.

Shock [treatment] was fairly experimental at the psychiatric institute. They were doing it for the first time. They were just playing with it, and everybody was leery of it. Some of the staff were reluctant to use shock therapy, even though it was being widely used in spite of the opinions of some of the staff. They viewed it as a punitive procedure. So my first experience with real shock was when I went down to Fort Worth, Texas [in July 1947].

I had become clinical director of the U.S. Public Health Service hospital there, a 1,000-bed facility. At Fort Worth, they were using shock full blown. During the war, the West Coast navy would send, by the trainload, a couple of hundred patients to us at a time—right into the siding of the hospital. We had a shock line of about 100 patients a day for shock treatment, and we found that it was a very effective method for treating schizophrenia and depression.

Only a certain category of patients were eligible for treatment at U.S. Public Health Service hospitals—merchant seamen, the Coast Guard, and, like at Ellis Island, they took in whatever they wanted to study there.

One of the studies was on Thorazine. I was one of the first to use the drug Thorazine. We were one of the first to experiment with it. It was better than Reserpine because it didn't have the side effects. Up until then, we just used psychotherapy. Besides Reserpine, we had no psychoactive drugs. We had electroshock treatment, which even then was in its infancy. But that was about it.

The U.S. Public Health Service, which at that time was a commissioned uniformed service and historically had been part of the armed services in time of war, selected Fort Worth Hospital to be one of the original places that Thorazine's effectiveness was to be evaluated. It was a new drug made by Smith, Kline and French.

We found that patients seemed to benefit, even the schizophrenics, with Thorazine. We tried shock and Thorazine, but it seemed to be the shock that made the difference rather than the Thorazine. And we didn't want to contaminate what we were doing and not have a clear picture of the benefits. Earlier we had combined the two, but then we separated the treatments to better evaluate them.

At Fort Worth, we were able to discharge 80 percent of the patients as markedly improved, or recovered, as a result of electroshock therapy or Thorazine. Electroshock treatments were a very effective method for treating schizophrenia. In fact, it was the only method we had at that time that proved effective, as opposed to insulin therapy, which was much more dangerous, and to a lesser degree, hydrotherapy, which we also did at Fort Worth. A lot of people since have gotten mixed up on the fact that electroshock therapy is punitive. That's ridiculous. Fortunately, shock therapy is now coming back into the picture as an effective treatment.

We also had two or three cases treated with lobotomy. At that time, it was called the "ice pick operation," because you went in above the eyeball and severed the connection to the frontal lobe. [Gestures.] But after that, the patient wasn't the same. Maybe they weren't reacting with delusions, but they acted like a psychopath, who wants instant gratification, which is all they understood. I remember one patient [after the

lobotomy], the patient had a distant look. He wasn't interested in anything that didn't strike him. He was more like an animal. Very primal, primitive behavior. He seemed perfectly happy, but you got the impression the smile had no humor. Of course, that's true of the schizophrenic, they may smile, but you get the feeling that there's a lot of hostility behind it.

Lobotomies were for intractable patients, who didn't respond to any kind of treatment. It was widely used for a short time. I don't remember whether we used lobotomy on any cases at Ellis Island or not. I don't think so. Most of the cases that didn't respond from Fort Worth we would transfer to a Veterans Administration hospital after six months, sometimes three months, depending on how they responded.

I was then transferred from Fort Worth to the U.S. Public Health Service Hospital in Lexington, Kentucky [July 1948]. I became clinical director there [chief of the acute psychiatric service] for a little over a year, and in 1949, returned to Ellis Island as the director of the neuropsychiatric service.

I had two assistant directors. I had three staff psychiatrists and six residents in training. I had maybe fifty nurses covering all the wards and shifts. There were three eight-hour shifts. But there were no quarters for nurses on the island. There were three nurses to a ward. We had six wards. I would estimate about eighteen nurses worked the day shift and then rode the ferry.

When working, I always wore a uniform. We'd take our uniform coat off, and wear a white coat over the uniform shirt and tie. As the director, I was on call twenty-four hours a day, seven days a week. I didn't serve as a duty officer, but I had to be there to make a decision.

I reported to Washington because the hospital commanding officer [CO] there [on Ellis Island] didn't want to get mixed up in what he didn't know anything about. The

Mental examination of an immigrant by two Public Health Service surgeons and a psychiatrist, circa 1926

(NATIONAL PARK SERVICE: STATUE OF LIBERTY NATIONAL MONUMENT)

CO lived across the hall from my wife Marjorie and me in a building that faced the Statue of Liberty. His name was Dr. Reed. He never got involved in the psychiatric stuff. When paperwork would come through [on a patient], he wouldn't even look at it. [Laughs.]

He also had a drinking problem. And when he was drinking, he was quite paranoid. I knew if I drank with him to go slowly, but he would say when he was drinking, "You know what they used to call me in the army? The Green Hornet." Meaning the guy who searches things out, and makes a sting. A troubleshooter. I later found out his army career wasn't that impressive. They [the U.S. Public Health Service] eventually dumped him. But he was my boss, and he didn't want to get involved. In fact, if a congressman would call, he would say "Dr. Reed isn't here now, would you call Dr. Baker?" So I dealt directly with Washington [with the commanding officer of the hospital division of the U.S. Public Health Service] most of the time. [But even then] we'd tell them what was recommended and what was needed.

That's the thing I always liked about Ellis Island and the U.S. Public Health Service [in general]. We could be good doctors, but we weren't having a line person dictate our treatment. There was no commissioner on Ellis at that time [the commissioner title was abolished in 1940]. In fact, there was practically no one on the island then, except Pete, the electrician, and the maids, and the people that did the cooking.

By 1949, the top administration officials of the Immigration and Naturalization Service [INS] had already moved completely offshore to [new offices at] Fifty-ninth Street, near Columbus Circle. For immigration cases, we'd call up to Fifty-ninth Street. We'd talk with them and find out what they wanted to do about a certain patient. We only communicated to Fifty-ninth Street as it related to immigrants. They would just call us and ask what our diagnosis was on a patient. There wasn't any mandatory communication.

For the diagnosis, we used psychological tests. When I first came to Ellis Island in my residency, the Rorschach [test] wasn't too much used. The second time I was there we used it quite a bit, and we used the personality inventories, such as Minnesota Multiphasic Inventory [MMPI].

We also used electroencephalograms [EEG]. For instance, we would occasionally have a merchant seaman who was incapacitated with anxiety neurosis, but usually it would be a psychosis or a convulsive seizure. Frequently, they would be sent to their ship's medical doctor, and he would immediately get an EEG. And not knowing how to use the EEG, he [the ship's doctor] would be quite confused, if he [the seaman] had a negative electroencephalogram. But we knew that you had to have a series of electroencephalograms before you could establish a diagnosis, unless you were lucky and got a diagnostic reading the first time. But you usually only got that when you had an electrical activity buildup that was preseizure.

Electroconvulsive shock therapy was at Ellis Island before I became director in '49,

but I was the one who really expanded its use. [Author's Note: ECT was, in fact, first used at Ellis Island in 1945; see the interview with Dr. Barton Field.] It was up to us to decide what treatment to give them [the patients]. They [Washington] didn't get into that. In fact, we wouldn't have wanted them in that. They knew about it. We made no secret of it. They considered ECT something that was entirely out of their bailiwick.

In 1949 they were still sending the immigration cases, as well as coastguardsmen and merchant seamen. The immigration cases were the same [as in 1942]. Most of the cases we saw were cases of either acute depressions with suicidal threats or other self-destructive implications; the schizophrenias; and epilepsy. The immigration cases wouldn't get to this side of the water if the condition had been detected at the other end [in Europe], because they wouldn't have been approved for a visa. Most of the immigrant cases were a psychiatric illness, or they had a nervous breakdown aboard the vessel they came over on, or they had a convulsive seizure. A large number of cases were where tuberculosis wasn't uncovered or diagnosed at the consul. Those we didn't have anything to do with because that was contagious diseases.

So, we would get patients referred to us as a result of lax investigation by the consulates in Europe. Also, sometimes when you move a personality from a home environment, they may manifest symptoms in a strange environment that they don't show at home. That's my only explanation of how they [European consulates] could not have diagnosed it beforehand; or there were inadequate medical records. Some of the immigrants had a previous breakdown and it wasn't noted. There was no history. And we solicited data that confirmed there was a breakdown, but it wasn't noted in the record.

I would say we got five to ten new admissions per day. We may have gotten

*Dr. James Baker in full uniform at Ellis Island,
June 1, 1950, after having earned his third stripe
to full commander.*

(COURTESY OF DR. JAMES BAKER)

more, depending on a ship coming in. Coast Guard and merchant seamen made up about 75 to 80 percent. And immigration cases were 20 to 25 percent. We were running near full capacity—more than 90 percent full for the 200 beds. The bulk of immigrants were diagnosed and returned; [approximately] 5 percent [of the 20 to 25 percent] were admitted for treatment. Coast Guard personnel and merchant seamen were usually held, because we knew there was a problem, because there was a [written medical] history. And we'd try as rapidly as we could to decide what additional information we needed to make an accurate diagnosis. So they were there to be treated. But only short- term treatment like six weeks on average. The longest we kept patients was three

months. Also, occasionally I'd get a call from the ship [commanding officer] inquiring about [the recovery status of] a seaman. But nobody really kept tabs on the immigrants once they were held for treatment.

From the boat, the immigrants would have an immediate immigration hearing on Fifty-ninth Street. I don't know the mechanics of that, but I do know that frequently they were sent right from the ship to us. And there was a heavy fine if the captain concealed anything that had developed on the boat. Because the captain [on behalf of the shipping company] didn't want to have to pay the cost of sending the immigrant back. All the immigrants I saw came by boat. I can't remember one that came by plane.

Probably 95 percent of the immigrants we saw were going to be mandatorily excluded or deported, because we wouldn't get the cases, unless there was probable cause that they were excludable. We didn't put them right back on the boat, because they had to be diagnosed first as mandatorily excludable, and because the boat wouldn't accept them. The captain of the ship wouldn't accept them, because he didn't have adequate medical facilities on the ship. And many of these immigrants came over on boats that didn't have adequate medical facilities, [much less] psychiatric treatment. And a lot of them freaked out on the ship and that's how we got them. The captains, who were forced to pay for the return shipping cost, they didn't want any problem aboard their ship.

Many of these immigrants that we certified as mandatorily excludable had epilepsy. There was no problem in treating that [for the return trip], we just gave them an adequate dose of an anticonvulsant and shipped them back, and what was done when they got back to their country, we had no control over. The acutely depressed and acutely disturbed [schizophrenia], we'd treat them until they had recovered enough to be deportable.

The captains mainly were afraid of taking the immigrants who had psychoses; that they stood clear of. Suppose he [the immigrant] wrecks the cabin? Suppose he's able to break out of the cabin? I could appreciate their situation, because they would assume responsibility [for the immigrant]. But we never sent anyone back who was dangerous. We'd treat him until he wasn't dangerous.

I remember one immigration case I diagnosed down in New Orleans [at the U.S. Marine hospital in 1951, Dr. Baker's post after he left Ellis Island]. I diagnosed him [the immigrant] for a type of schizophrenia, and they [the shipping company] wouldn't take him back on ship, because it didn't have a doctor on it. I had to escort the immigrant back to London, even though he had recovered, and I told them he was well; but they wouldn't have any part of that.

With immigration cases—we'd make the diagnosis, hold them about a week, and then, if they could be deported, we told immigration [on Fifty-ninth Street] what the diagnosis was, had a formal medical hearing at the hospital with the immigrant present, and they were deported. Otherwise, they were held and given treatment. If an immigrant had schizophrenia, they were excluded without appeal. Period. But they would get treated, get shock therapy, so that they could be deported. Some were too sick to deport.

Cases that were mandatorily excludable, and resulted in deportation, were any history of a psychopathic tendency as evidenced by antisocial behavior. If they had a prison record they couldn't get in. If they were homosexual they couldn't get in. Any mental illness, particularly the schizophrenias, the overt psychoses; like maybe a patient would have an organic psychosis, such as chronic brain syndrome, which was evidence of senility. Alzheimer's wasn't diagnosed in those days. It was only diagnosed at an autopsy. But the patients who were having early Alzheimer's symptoms wouldn't be admitted. We didn't have too much of a problem other than convulsive seizures with the neurological disorders. They were self-evident most of the time. Maybe some cases slipped through.

Usually if there was any reason for suspicion at the immigration hearing [on Fifty-ninth Street], the immigration service would get us any records that were available. But on the psychopathic side, sex offenses— maybe somebody had talked too much aboard ship and there was reason to believe this guy's not straight—there would be a preliminary immigration hearing, and they would send them to the hospital for a fuller evaluation.

You had to be very careful, because a lot of these immigrants didn't speak enough English. It was rarely that they did. And many of the Orientals—they'd just dummy up when they got in a stressful position, and they didn't answer anything. So you had to be very careful. You would suspect that an individual was mentally defective, and then you'd get a history that contradicted that, if you could get them talking. We'd usually have to work through an interpreter, and that's where we had much of our difficulty.

We had one girl who was with the language department at the City University of New York. She was a crackerjack at appreciating what we were driving at. And anytime I could use her, I did. [Laughs.] But the trouble with most of the immigration interpreters, they would talk with a patient and the immigrant would talk a long string, and then the interpreter would come out with "He says, 'Yes.'" They tried to make sense out of them, and that wouldn't be what we were driving at.

In the wards, the patients were all together [immigrants, coastguardsmen, and merchant seamen], depending on what type of custody they needed. It depended on how disturbed they were. We had two "close custody" wards: one ward for the suicidal, and one ward for the acutely disturbed—patients who displayed an overt psychosis and were in close custody. We had more staff available on these wards. Then we had a "medium custody" ward; that's where we were afraid immigrants might try to escape. Then we had three "open" wards, where freedom was less restricted, and the patients required less supervision.

However, we had one Chinaman, in one of the open wards, who tried to swim to the Jersey shore, and he drowned. I don't know of anyone who ever made it, because the currents were really vicious. But we retrieved the body. I don't remember what he was in for. But he was about to be deported. We had treated him, and now he was in an open ward, because we thought he wasn't much of a risk.

But Dr. Reed got into it. As soon as he saw that [the Chinaman] was Catholic, he said [the Chinaman] is not dead. I said, "Oh, he's quite dead." But Dr. Reed insisted on giving him artificial respiration till the priest could arrive and give him last rites. So the priest arrived from the mainland and gave last rites to a dead body.

If somebody died, we would call immigration, notify them—we didn't have to call Washington—and then they would call the coroner's office. I don't think we had a coastguardsman or merchant seaman die. Of the immigrants, the Chinaman was the only one I can recall. [Author's Note: According to official statistics of the U.S. Public Health Service in Rockville, Maryland, fifty-eight immigrants died on Ellis Island in 1949. No statistics are available for 1950. However, according to Dr. John Parascandola, the service's chief historian, "It would not be inaccurate to assume that a similar number died in 1950, before the hospital closed in 1951." Dr. Baker maintains there was only one fatality that he's aware of while he was director, and can't explain the statistic.]

We didn't have a female problem. We didn't have woman sailors. There might be an occasional immigrant woman, but mostly it was men and children. We had to have almost a separate facility when a woman came along. Everything had to be kept separate.

We would do twenty to thirty ECT's per day, depending on the day. There was one building where it was done. It was done [on a floor] over the close custody wards, because these were patients who were manifesting acute psychotic symptoms or acute depression, who had limited movement, and we moved these patients upstairs for the treatment, and then moved them back. Thorazine was only effective in the psychoses—the schizophrenias. There was enough evidence then [for] limiting Thorazine to the psychoses. ECT worked best in depressions and the schizophrenias [psychoses]. Of course, we'd use the shock treatment for acute depression right away.

The success rate wasn't as high as the 80 percent at Fort Worth, because those were young guys in the service. It was a younger age group. At Ellis, I'd say 60 to 70 percent responded to treatment, because the immigrants, were older—in their thirties and forties. We didn't have any really old immigrants.

In terms of a hierarchy of the cases—all of which were considered mandatorily excludable—were the psychoses or schizophrenia being number one. Epilepsy, number two. The acute depressions, three, and the criminals, or homosexual deviants, number four.

We wouldn't give the homosexual deviant ECT. There's nothing that that would do for the homosexual. I considered it [homosexuality], then and now, an untreatable condition. We kept immigrants for two or three days to a week, then sent them for deportation, especially if they had epilepsy.

The criminal we would diagnose as a psychopathic personality, and if he wasn't showing any other manifestations, we'd send him back. These were people who had a felony record [in Europe]. The depressives were best treated with ECT. The epileptics were given a daily dose of Dilantin, sometimes twice daily, depending on how frequent the seizures were, to control them. We didn't use ECT on the epileptics. For the schizophrenics, we tried Thorazine; if it seemed to work, we'd continue it. If it didn't work, we would stop it and try the ECT.

In 1949, we used electroshock in combination with a new drug, Intercostrine. This is a curare-like preparation, which minimized muscle movement, the convulsive part of a seizure. In fact, often it amounted to no more than slight movement of the mouth, and bare movement of the extremities, so that it reduced the complication of severe contractions, because they could produce fractures. But we also had to titrate [monitor] the effects of the Intercostrine, because it seemed to vary from day to day, and from patient to patient, as to how much you needed to get the desired curare effect.

Curare was first used by an aborigine tribe. It's a plant that has a paralytic effect. The aborigines made a crude extraction of curare to use in their poisonous arrows and, at that dosage, it killed the people that were hit. Curare was just around, and somebody had the idea that it might help to give mild doses with the shock treatment, and that's how it got started.

Curare has the effect of paralyzing the muscle system. It can be deadly, but we didn't use deadly doses. We just used it in doses that would minimize the muscle contractions that came on with the electroshocks. So we would give an immigrant an injection of Intercostrine and then administer the shock. We found that there was an optimum period between giving the Intercostrine and the shock. We usually waited a full ten seconds and then gave the shock, although it would vary, because some days it would seem to be more effective.

Sometimes we would wait fifteen seconds. Other times, to have the desired effect, we would wait six to eight seconds. Effectiveness could only be determined by observation. We'd start out giving a standard dose and then vary that depending on what we saw in the patients. If we saw slight muscle twitching in the extremities, that would be the desired effect. But if the extremities were too flaccid, we were probably getting a little too deep, too much curare effect. Sometimes the treatment wouldn't be effective, and we couldn't tell because we wouldn't get a recognizable seizure. So we just had to play it by ear.

We were using this treatment mainly for schizophrenic patients as well as depressions and acute depressions. It was very effective for acute depressions and catatonic schizophrenia. But we almost never used hydrotherapy and the flow tubs anymore, because shock treatment was so much more effective in controlling the excited stages of catatonic excitement. In fact, there was one ward devoted completely to hydrotherapy, but we renovated that and made it into beds.

Before electric shock therapy, we had a drug that was injected to produce a convulsion. I forget the name of the drug, but it caused an anxiety reaction in patients, and they would be apprehensive about further treatments. You didn't have that with shock treatment, or you had it to a lesser degree. Patients would be reluctant to receive electroshock treatment, but it would be on the basis of their reluctance of [having anything done] to them.

We didn't tie them down or strap them down. That's what you didn't do. Places did do that, but we found that just by riding with the patients' motions, not fully restricting them, you were apt to avoid fractures, which was the danger. The complications were that, with a heart convulsive seizure, you'd get a spinal compression fracture.

What we'd usually have is someone up at the head of the table administering the treatment, who would protect the head and neck, with one person on each arm and leg, and one person on each side restricting a patient's movements, but gently; not a rigid restriction, because that caused fractures.

For the shock, we'd have padded electrodes on both temples and put a little pressure on the contact so it would be good. And then, with the shock machine, you could set it. I forget what amperage we had to use to get effective response. We didn't go to the top of the scale, it was probably in the medium range. Then they started making these machines with a device called the Go-issando Effect, which sharply increases the [amperage of the] current, but it didn't increase it all at once with a bang. Supposedly that was developed because they [patients] showed less acute amnesia after the treatment. I think maybe the manufacturer was doing some wishful thinking.

The patients usually didn't remember having the electroshock administered. They knew something happened to them, because other patients would tell them, of course. We made no bones about telling them that they were on shock treatment. And some of them were even able to appreciate it, while they were on treatment. We'd give between fifteen and twenty treatments before we stopped, because we found that by giving a fewer number of treatments, the patient was more apt to relapse even though they had a good initial effect.

We found that giving shock daily produced a pronounced amnesic effect, and that the amnesia was more apt to be prolonged, doing them daily. We found that the best interval was three times for the first week and then drop off to two a week thereafter for the balance of treatments—six to ten weeks—but it all depended on the type of case we had. For example, with catatonic excitements we would have to give maybe two or three a day, until we controlled the excitement and then back off to the less frequent treatment.

It was all experimental. It was dealing with a particular patient, and what they were showing, what their main problem was. Today, I don't know whether you could even say there are fewer complications. [Laughs.] We had gotten electroshock treatment to where there were very few complications.

Today, you can give a patient a pill like Valium or, if they're reluctant, an injection of medication. And that's so much easier, simpler. Many of these drugs are equally effective, if not more effective, with the schizophrenias, although they can be addictive, unlike ECT. Nobody ever asked for more shock. [Laughs.] There was such a thing as giving additional shock treatment, at a later date, if the symptoms recurred, but then you just go for the briefer period and stop the treatment.

The amnesia bothered the patients a good bit, the fact that they couldn't remember and felt a little confused. Usually that would disappear after a period. The more shock treatments you gave, the longer it took to dissipate, and the more the patients would react to it. They found it disturbing, because they couldn't use their minds for recalling things, and that is disturbing to a person. But, as I say, we're talking about a transient effect. We even had the problem of having hysterical reactions, where the patient claimed they couldn't remember when it wasn't so. We had ways of proving to ourselves that they really could remember, and we could use reassurance, and we wouldn't get into an argument with them, "Yes, you can; no, you can't." That sort of thing. We'd just reassure them. We didn't have too many cases of hysterical conversions on the amnesia problem, but it did occur.

In our dosage testing we discovered, with ECT, seldom would less than eight treatments be effective. Most of them required twelve to twenty shock treatments for it to be effective, because if you treated them less than that, they [the patient] would improve temporarily and then relapse. So we learned to use more frequent [shock].

Depending on what we were dealing with, we usually set a patient up the first week for three treatments, and then, depending on how much he improved, decide whether to continue for another week on three treatments, or drop him to two, and maintain the two, from there on out, until the end of treatment. Acute depressions were inclined to respond to less shock treatment than the maximum of twenty. They would be most improved by twelve. The schizophrenics, you would have to keep them on shock treatment longer. The Thorazine would stop their hallucinations and delusions. You might get a remission, but with the older cases, they have to remain on a maintenance dose of Thorazine from there on out. The schizophrenics had the poorest prognosis for recovery [because they had] too much [mental] deterioration already. The paranoid and the catatonic [schizophrenic] responded fairly well to Thorazine, or if it didn't retract it, ECT. ECT generally worked. For the catatonic excitements [like the depressives], we had to institute ECT from the beginning.

The first treatment, they would recover their memory in as little as thirty minutes to an hour. The second to third treatment would probably be an hour. By the twentieth treatment, it might take them a couple of weeks to fully recover their memory.

We were always trying, experimenting, with psychotherapy, but at that time, there weren't any other treatments. So there wasn't anything in those days besides Thorazine, ECT, and psychotherapy. There was some literature at that time to guide us, but we soon learned that we couldn't take what the [salesman] from the drug company might think that he knew [about how to treat psychiatric disorders]. Then we'd find out he didn't know what dose was effective and so forth.

I wrote the service a detailed letter about the future of psychiatry. They had asked for it. I expressed in there that I thought most of these things were going to turn out to be organic, or genetic, or a predetermined inheritance, and that we just had insufficient knowledge of brain chemistry. I don't know if we ever did a nationality study, but it seemed like the Latin Americans [immigrants] were more prone to depression. But we were too busy with what we were doing to do any studies.

But there were special study cases. A special study case would be if we were interested in a particular [ailment], like the National Institutes of Health does [today]. They have cases, free [of charge], that they're interested in studying. I remember one that we had on Ellis Island. Her name was Margaret. I don't wish to identify her further. She had a case of catatonia, where she withdrew into the womb, almost, and assumed a fetal position. I admitted her mainly because I didn't think she would get the treatment outside at that time, and her father happened to be the administrative assistant to the Surgeon General. So her father, Paul, called me, and I said, bring her up here, we'll admit her as a special study case. She hadn't manifested anything up until that time, so her family didn't know what to do with her. She was a citizen of the U.S. She stayed with us [Marjorie and me], because we had plenty of room. And fortunately we gave her shock treatment, and she responded beautifully and never had another episode. I know this, because I talked with her father three years ago.

. . .

There were only four families living on the island. The medical officer in charge [Dr. Reed]; the administrative officer, who was married, with no children, had an apartment; one of the residents, who had two kids; and me, my wife Marjorie, and our five-year-old son, Bill. The other medical staff members came out by ferry, including the nurses who worked in staggered shifts.

Back then, the Ellis Island ferry departed to and from the Battery, near Governor's Island ferry, not Fort [Castle] Clinton like it is today. There was no traffic from the New Jersey side, just a bunch of docks and ships—very commercial. It was all from the New York side. An occasional Coast Guard boat would pull into the ferry slip. But that would just be if they had emergency business on the island, like bringing a patient.

We lived in a two-story building, plus a large attic and unfinished basement. There were two apartments with a common hallway. The other apartment was Dr. Reed's, who lived right across the hall from Marjorie and me and Bill. We had four bedrooms, one bath, and a very large living room, dining room, and kitchen. And they were well furnished. We had a black kitchen stove, a shipboard stove, and it worked on 230-volt, two-wire direct electric current, as did the lights and everything else. That was the only type of current we had. So we had to improvise on Ellis Island. We had a shipboard refrigerator. The other electrical appliances were nonexistent. We made them work.

For example, the mixer. You'd have to hook a lightbulb in a parallel circuit, and as the mixer had more load on it, the lightbulb would get brighter, and then it would slow down. The same thing with the sewing machine. The radios, small radios, were much easier to work. Back in those days, television was just coming out, and we wanted a television set, but couldn't figure out a way to work it.

I finally solved that by taking the rotary converter that I used for giving the shock treatments. The hospital had purchased a rotary converter so that we could give shock treatments, because the shock machine was AC current, 110 to 115 volts. The rotary converter changed the current from DC to AC. I found that the rotary converter would work with the television. So after we finished our daily shock treatments, I'd take it up to my quarters and run the television off it. Then I would bring it back in the morning and hook it up to the shock machine. It was a small thing. It was not difficult to carry. But very expensive. That's why I didn't get my own, because it would have cost as much as the television set; and 12½-inch television sets weren't cheap then. Fortunately, they had bought a heavy-duty converter that had more capacity than the shock machine used, or I wouldn't have been able to run the television off it. At that time, a 12½-inch set was a large set. In fact, I think that was the only size tube they had.

The only trouble was, we had current surges. The rotary converter wouldn't regulate the current, or stop surges. The whole island was working off the same current. Pete, the electrician, had his own generator plant. But the trouble with that was Pete didn't have an automatic control on his generator. As the current would surge, say about the time they cut off the stoves in the kitchens after breakfast, lunch, and dinner, it would blow out a fuse in my television set. So I found a place [in Manhattan] where I could buy fuses [for the television set] wholesale, and we scheduled ECT after breakfast was finished, so it wasn't a problem. We'd start about 8 A.M., and we'd be through by 11 A.M., which is when the patients had to be back to their wards. If a patient needed two or three treatments in a day, we'd do it in the afternoon; but that was very rarely.

From our living quarters, we had a front-row seat to the Statue of Liberty across the harbor. It was right in our backyard. We had a front seat for all the maiden voyages of the steamers. It was a very pleasant location, but with some drawbacks, mainly the damn ferry. [Laughs.] The Ellis Island ferry only ran at fixed times and quit completely with the 10:45 trip from the mainland.

I remember [Marjorie and I] running with our tongues hanging out to catch that ferry many evenings, and particularly if we went to a New York show. Often you didn't get to see the last curtain, because you had to leave to make the ferry. So we didn't go to many shows.

At that time, our son, Bill, was in kindergarten. But there was a complication. There was a kindergarten on Governor's Island that Bill could go to, but we had a three-month infant boy at the time, Barry, so certainly Marjorie couldn't supervise Bill getting there, and I couldn't.

So we enlisted this patient of mine, Tom Trimble, a burned-out paranoid schizophrenic, to take him [Bill] over to the school on Governor's Island and escort him back. When we talk about a burned-out schizophrenic, particularly the paranoid, this means they no longer react to their delusions, except in a more acceptable fashion. They're no threat to themselves or others, it's just that they still have their delusional system. It's there, but they don't react to it. And I realized that he was that type of case.

There was little alternative. He [Tom] had kind of attached himself to us. He was one of the first people we met there when we got off the boat. I thought he was an employee [laughs] because he said, "You're the new doctor?" I said, "Yes." He said, "Let me help you with your things." And he apparently had freedom. So he loaded our suitcases onto a hand truck, put them in our quarters, and said he'd be back to see if we needed anything else. But he turned out to be a patient! He was on the open ward. Of all the patients, he was there the longest [two years].

He was very friendly with the nurses, and usually Tom would take Bill with the nurses on the ferry that was leaving when he went over to school, and a lot of them [the nurses] were on the ferry when he came back from school. But there were also a couple of male nurses you weren't sure which side they batted from. Tom wouldn't have anything to do with them. He told my son to stay away from them. "Don't get around those people," he'd say. He didn't give Bill any reasons, just told him to stay away.

His [Tom's] delusion was he thought that people were trying to make him into a homosexual. That was his big thing. He thought there was a plot out to try to turn him into a queer. He was perfectly content to stay with us, because I think he saw us as family and it was his God-chosen duty to look after us. [Laughs.] He wasn't a religious man at all. But he had this fixed delusion. He was like part of the family.

Tom had been a merchant seaman. He had shipped on high-octane tankers during the war, because they didn't screen you too much. [Laughs.] But he was well trained in a lot of things, I found out. When we were away for a few days one summer, we came back and Tom says, "I have a safe place for you to go if there's an atomic [bomb] attack." I said, "Where?" He said, "I'll show you." And in our basement, which was unfinished, he had dug out the big rocks, and filled it in with concrete. I said, "Where the hell did you get the concrete from?" He said, "Immigration had some of it left over, and I just borrowed it. It was from a previous job, and it was just sitting there, and they weren't using it." I said, "I didn't ask you to do this, and I hope you don't get in trouble for doing it." He said [in a Forrest Gump voice], "I won't get no trouble." [Laughs.]

The day before I left I discharged him [Tom], because he didn't want to go over to the Staten Island Marine Hospital ward there, and I didn't think he needed to. In fact, I didn't think he needed to be there [Ellis Island]. The last I ever heard of Tom, he was supposed to go to downtown Brooklyn and check into the St. George Hotel. The St. George was very popular with seamen. I called to see if he had checked in. He had never checked in. But I wasn't surprised. He could have registered under a different name. I don't know what happened to Tom. He had his seaman papers. He may have been shipped out.

There was also lots of kitchen help who worked on the island for years. They were a group of women, older. Many of them were married. The husbands did maintenance-type work. They came over as part of that influx of Irish immigrants that came to this country in the late 1800s and apparently never got beyond the island. They turned out to be such good workers that the Immigration and Naturalization Service hired them. So Ellis Island became home to them.

A lot of them had considerable misgivings when they heard the island was going to close. One of them, a woman named Nora, even wanted to work for us, until she found out that I was being transferred to [the U.S. Public Health Service] New Orleans [laughs], and wasn't staying in New York. Nora was a maid, as was Lillian. Lillian was a colored girl, but she lived in New York City. Many of them were eligible for civil service retirement. What was unusual was the affection they had for us, even though we had been there on the island just a short time. This Lillian wrote my wife for years. She would send her a Christmas card and put a note on it. I imagine she's died.

[Author's Note: The U.S. Public Health Service officially closed the hospital wards at Ellis Island in the fall of 1951. However, as it wound down, a skeleton medical staff remained to support the INS in the main building on Island One.]

I drove the first car that was ever on the Ellis Island ferry. When I was leaving, I brought my car over and drove around the hospital to my quarters, and loaded my family up, and went back on the next ferry.

I was also the first one to land a helicopter on the island. This was during my residency in '42. I knew how to fly a helicopter, because I earlier had training as a flight surgeon from the School of Aviation Medicine [in Pensacola, Florida]. I took off from Floyd Bennett Field in Brooklyn, and I landed between the second and third islands [the water was landfilled], between the two medical wings, quite close to where I later occupied quarters. I had no flight plan that covered legal landing there, so I didn't tarry too long. I landed mainly because it was there, and I wanted to do it. [Laughs.] Nobody knew what rules to apply to helicopters, because helicopters were new then, so most anything went. Patients streamed out to see what was going on.

Other times, I'd do harbor patrol just to fly the helicopter and look around New York. Sometimes I'd have a mec [mechanic] with me, and sometimes I'd fly it alone. The purpose of harbor patrol was to see if there were any oil slicks, or evidence that vessels were dumping their holds, and if there was any unusual debris on the water. I never caught a vessel doing that, but . . . [laughs] one time I was flying up the Hudson River toward the George Washington Bridge, and I thought, "What the hell? I can go under this easier than climbing." So I flew under the bridge. Then I turned back, and the only thing I wanted to do then was get out of there. My God, it was reported in the papers [the next day] because someone saw me . . .

I enjoyed my tour of duty at Ellis Island. I have never regretted my station there. In fact, I haven't regretted anything that I did, or didn't do.

William "Bill" Baker

· · · · · · · · · · · · ·

BORN AUGUST 21, 1944
LIVED ON ELLIS ISLAND FROM 1949–1951

He is the son of Dr. James Baker. A graduate of Duke University in 1966, he received his M.B.A. from the Wharton School of Business in 1968. Today, he is a marketing executive at IBM, and lives with his wife Ruth and their two children in Oakton, Virginia.

I was five years old when we first moved to Ellis Island. My father was a psychiatrist there for the Public Health Service. I remember the first night we came and having no idea where I was. I actually remember the ferryboat ride when we arrived from New York. It must have been around ten o'clock at night and just the newness and being in the dark on this ferry with this island out there that I could barely see.

I remember the two-story house we lived in. As a little kid, it seemed like a spacious house. I remember the configuration of the living room, kitchen, dining room, and being so fascinated by ferryboats and tugboats that I converted our living room into my version of New York Harbor, with cardboard boxes for ferryboats and ropes across the furniture.

I remember watching "Howdy Doody" on our first TV and how we always had problems with the electricity. None of the appliances would work. Everything out there was 220 volts as opposed to the normal 110 volts. So my father had to specially rig all the appliances to get them to work.

I remember one particular evening when there was a very severe storm. To me it seemed like a hurricane. The waves were crashing over the seawall and I was very scared the island was going under with us

Six-year-old William "Bill" Baker as Hopalong Cassidy at Ellis Island, Christmas 1950. The costume was a Christmas present.

(COURTESY OF WILLIAM BAKER)

on it. I remember my mom trying to comfort me and taking me up to the attic and looking out the dormer window and just watching the huge waves crashing over the seawall as she tried to reassure me. I remember another night there was a huge fire on the New Jersey side. It must have been old warehouses and it just seemed like the entire Jersey shoreline was engulfed in flames for hours. I remember watching it in the middle of the night, this awesome sight.

My mother viewed Ellis Island as an experience. My father viewed it as an adventure. It certainly was an unusual situation, and it did have its frustrations. Shopping was a little awkward. My mother did all her shopping at the army base on Governor's Island. That's where we went for most things. We ate all our meals at home. Maybe once or twice in the cafeteria, but since this was a hospital environment, I was restricted to a large degree in terms of where I could go and what patients I could be around. I was not allowed on the side of the island where the Great Hall was. I don't recall what all the reasons were, contagious diseases or something.

But it was fascinating, living where we did and being able to view the skyline of New York City and the Statue of Liberty from our backyard. I remember watching the great ocean liners; the *Queen Mary*, the *Queen Elizabeth*. I could recognize them by how many smokestacks they had and the fireboats that would escort them with long shooting streams of water. To me that was just a very fascinating experience, and to ride the ferryboat to school on Governor's Island, which was an army base.

I went there for kindergarten and first grade. I had to make the trek into Manhattan on the Ellis Island ferry, which was incredibly slow. I remember that. I remember always being embarrassed by the Ellis Island ferry. It was the worst of any of the ferries in New York Harbor in terms of being slow and ugly. It was an awful army-green-colored boat and it seemed to take forever, but I was fascinated by it. Then, from Manhattan, I would take the ferry out to Governor's Island and walk to the other side of the island to get to school. I was escorted by one of my father's mental patients, a relatively harmless one, named Tom Trimble. He was a merchant seaman who was there at the Marine Hospital and I can think of a couple others. One of them was Charlie. I remember Tom always telling me to stay away from Charlie, "Watch out for Charlie. He was crazy."

Tom was my only real playmate. Every once in a while I was able to entice one of my schoolmates to make the trek over from Governor's Island. I was also friendly with the maintenance workers and the guys that ran the ferry. I would help them close off the gates and tie up the boats. I would watch every move they made as they docked. The captain would let me put my hands on the steering wheel. But my real buddies were these mental patients who also did work around the island. They let me tag along. I remember the big incinerator on the island and following these guys on their rounds and watching them dump trash into the incinerator. I remember just being fascinated by little things, like these sticks that they used to nail garbage on the ground and stick it in their sacks. At that point in my life I probably aspired to be a trash picker-upper. There really wasn't much to do. So I just appreciated other things about the island like the boats and the scenery.

Ellis Island was in its closing years. There were not a lot of people on the island compared to its heyday. There were a small number of patients and nurses and the people that ran the hospital. Probably half the island was active because it didn't appear that there was a whole lot of activity on the immigration side.

*Marine Hospital Service doctors standing outside the Barge Office in Battery Park in 1899.
After the fire at Ellis Island in mid-June 1897, the Barge Office was once again temporarily
employed for immigration purposes until the new "fireproof" Ellis Island buildings were
completed, and the station was reopened on December 17, 1900.*

(NATIONAL PARK SERVICE: STATUE OF LIBERTY NATIONAL MONUMENT)

I remember my father would take me on tours of the hospital, various wards; particularly on Sundays when he was the only doctor and he would make his rounds. I remember the long hallways we had to go down that sometimes got flooded by rain. I remember the offices and the nurses and one nurse named Miss Brave. She was almost like a second mother to me. She was the head nurse. She lived on Long Island somewhere. And I became attached to her, and she became attached to me like an aunt or a grandmother.

When we left in 1951, the Public Health Service had made the decision to close the Marine Hospital. We left for my dad to take another assignment. I don't remember leaving, but I do know we were the last family that was a resident on the island.

* * * * * * * * *

Dr. Burton Field

· · · · · · · · · · · ·

BORN AUGUST 26, 1921
DENTAL INTERN AT ELLIS ISLAND, 1945

*He was a dental intern at Ellis Island for five months, from May to
September 1945. Dr. Field, who worked in the Marine Hospital
(of the U.S. Public Health Service) four years before the arrival of
Dr. James Baker in 1949, corroborates that electroshock therapy was used at
Ellis Island in 1945. In fact, the nurse who assisted in giving the shock
treatments later became Dr. Field's wife. She has since died.*

My father was one of the first plastic surgeons in Philadelphia, and a professor at the University of Pennsylvania. So despite my lousy grades in undergraduate school, I was being pushed into medical school. This was in 1942, when the United States entered World War II, and I went up to see the dean, and he said, "Well, young man, are you following in your father's footsteps?" And I said, "No, sir. I'm going across the street to the dental school." And he literally fell off his chair.

During the war, since we were technically army privates, we had to march on Sunday after working in the clinic five days a week. And we used to drive the sergeants and the lieutenants crazy because we pooped out with our packs in half an hour. And they said, "Well, get up and march, or we'll shoot you." And we said, "Fine. Go ahead. Shoot us." And they said, "Boy, it's easier to go back to France than to put up with these kids."

I was in dental school all day long. I studied half the night. Then on Saturdays we had to march on Franklin Field, which was the university stadium for football and track and field, so there was very little free time. They condensed four years of study into thirty-six months, to rush us so we could get shipped overseas.

When I graduated the dean presented me with my diploma and there was an officer standing next to him. He said to me, "Here's your orders, lieutenant." And I looked at him and said, "Well, I have my diploma, keep your orders. I don't want them." And he looked at me and said, "We'll see you Monday morning at the hospital in uniform, lieutenant." Of course, Monday morning I showed up at Ellis Island. I didn't have much choice. It was that, or take a gun and go to France. Two of my classmates and myself from the dental school, and two or three from the medical school, were all stationed here for the U.S. Public Health Service.

We served the Coast Guard, the merchant marine, government employees, and we had to take care of emergencies for immigrants and prisoners of war. While on duty one day, a German prisoner of war was brought in with a loose cap on a lower molar. And he took the cap off and handed it to me. It was a stainless steel shell, that covered a missing tooth on a bridge supported by the two neighboring teeth. And I looked at it and said, "Well, you want the shell recemented so the tooth functions?" He said, "Yes, the shell had a capsule of cyanide in it which I was supposed to swallow if I was captured. But when I was cap-

· · · · · · · ·

tured, I dumped the cyanide and decided not to swallow it." So he wasn't a real good Nazi. [Laughs.]

I was a dental intern, a junior dental officer with one stripe, and I had a senior dental officer with two and a half stripes. And then we had M.D.'s of various ranks in the medical department. Our office was in the Marine Hospital. It was three or four chairs; two dentists; two or three female dental assistants, two assisting, and one doing secretarial work.

There were no facilities for us to live on the island. I rented an apartment at Seventy-sixth and Amsterdam, and took the subway to the ferry and then here in the morning and then back in the evening, five days a week. I believe I took an eight o'clock ferry. And then I left work for Manhattan about 4 P.M. The required hours for our daily duty included the time we spent, back and forth, on the ferry.

We did basic dentistry, minor surgery, fillings, cleanings, X rays, and examinations. And, as I mentioned before, emergencies for the immigrants, the employees, and the prisoners of war. For the coastguardsmen, the merchant seamen and, the government employees, their dentistry was a little more thorough. I cannot remember how extensive, whether they were entitled to porcelain or baked-on metal jackets, or dentures or partials, but all the basic treatment was included at no charge.

In my recollection they were state-of-the-art facilities. They were not antiquated. That was, of course, in the days of standup dentistry with a belt-driven drill for making holes in the teeth. There were no fancy air turbines or fancy suction. It was much less comfortable for the patient because of the extremely slow speed of the drill. So the patient's head would vibrate regardless of the degree of pain, and hopefully there was none with the local anesthetic. We used lidocaine, commonly called Novocaine, with epinephrine, commonly called ad-

renaline. And that produced good local anesthesia. I do remember that merchant seamen would bring us bottles of imported liquor from Europe, or silk stockings for the nurses, figuring that would get them better care, or a sooner appointment, because at that time those were precious commodities.

We were permitted to go to any part of the island. I made a couple visits to the immigration center out of curiosity because of my parents' heritage. My parents came from Kiev about 1898, and they were children at that time, so they came with their parents.

I remember the vastness of the Great Hall, and the emptiness when there were no human beings in it. It was awesome. There were not a lot of immigrants at the time because this was during the war, so a lot of the rooms were vacant. My other trips were to assist with, quote, "shock therapy" in the psychiatric wards. "Shock" was a common term for electroconvulsive therapy, ECT, because there were no tranquilizers at that time. So when these soldiers came back, it was a very common treatment to get them out of their depression. We would tie them down on cold, barren tables with straps, put the electrodes on their heads, and give them a very light "electrocution." And it helped quite a bit. To what degree, I cannot tell you.

That was a very depressing experience. I would be called on to assist the doctors if I was not busy and they were shorthanded. The electroshocks were given in a small building behind the hospital over toward New Jersey. The idea was, the sooner a soldier could be rehabilitated, the sooner he could be transferred to active duty or another hospital facility for further treatment.

I met my wife at Ellis Island. She was a nurse and she assisted the doctors in the shock therapy. Her name was Irene Sabo, which is an abbreviation for the Hungarian *S-z-a-b-o*. She was inspecting bomber sights for Hoover Vacuum Cleaner Company in North Canton, Ohio prior to going into nursing. Bomber sights were instruments which would help the B-29's and the other planes more accurately locate sites to be bombed in Europe. And she was working in a sterile room for accuracy, and there she would examine them before they would be shipped out to the planes. And the opportunity to get in the U.S. Government Nurses Cadet Corps came up, and she decided this would be to her liking. The pay was terrific. You got room and board and fifteen dollars a month. And she became enrolled in Massillon State Hospital in Massillon, Ohio. She rotated to various other hospitals so she could experience the different categories of nursing. Her last station was Ellis Island, and this is where I met her in the spring of 1945. I don't remember what her duties were, other than to assist with the shock therapy.

I met her in the cafeteria. I was wearing my uniform, of course. It was the khaki officer's uniform with the black epaulets, cap, khaki shirt, and black tie . . .

The war ended during my term at Ellis Island. V-J Day was September 15 and the dental department was closed very soon afterwards. I was transferred to the Staten Island Marine Hospital, which was a much larger operation than the one at Ellis Island, and my wife joined me.

I did not learn a lot of dentistry at Ellis Island. I was told many times, "You're an officer first, a doctor second," which was certainly a shock after putting in eight years of school. Of course, that was not enforced in the medical corps like it was in the infantry. It was definitely lax compared with the infantry. Our unit was more like "M.A.S.H."

Rita Bellmer

. . . .

BORN JANUARY 27, 1920

She was born in Ridgewood, New York, the daughter of Martin Bellmer, who was chief of Mail, Files and Records at Ellis Island from 1919 until the island closed in 1954.

My father was born in 1892 in [the] Williamsburg [neighborhood of] Brooklyn. His mother and father had come to this country as immigrants from Germany. His mother came over as a teenager, and she worked as a waitress at a restaurant called Neiderstein's which was well known at the time. And that was where she and my grandfather met. They were married, lived in Williamsburg, and then they moved to Ridgewood, Brooklyn.

My father worked in the U.S. Postal Service on the mail trains right after he was discharged from service after World War I. Then he went to work for the Immigration and Naturalization Service in Mail, Files and Records until he was promoted to chief. He was in charge of the ship manifests. These were the records of all the ships that came into port, and all of the people who were aboard the ship. And there were occasions when he had to appear in court with a manifest to verify the time of entry or departure of an immigrant for legal purposes. He also installed a new system of keeping names to help prevent misspelling and help facilitate identification of names because of the complication of foreign names and foreign sounds.

He enjoyed his work. I'm not too sure if he enjoyed all of the daily ferry rides back and forth. There were also times when the weather was bad, there were fogs, and the ferry couldn't leave the slip, and all of the workers had to stay on the island overnight. This happened a number of times.

As a youngster I came over to Ellis Island quite frequently. I would come with my mother. At Christmastime, there was always a Christmas service. A member of the clergy conducted it, and it was for the participation of all the immigrants. They sang Christmas songs and carols, and they had a gigantic Christmas tree at the end of the Great Hall. The families of the employees were invited out.

It was fascinating. I didn't have any sense of fear or apprehension about the immigrants or about coming here. That was his job. There was no thought about differences of nationalities or any such thing. It was just taken for granted. It was exciting to take the ferry ride and to go where Daddy worked. His office was off a balcony. He did not wear a uniform but he had to carry his badge and his identification. I wasn't allowed to talk to the immigrants. Even at Christmas. I was upstairs where the offices were. The service was conducted downstairs, and I was upstairs on the balcony observing and singing along.

I had his name put on the Wall of Honor. I felt that my father had given so many years of service all of his working life on Ellis Island. And even though he did not come to this country as an immigrant, I felt that I wanted to have his name there as a kind of memorial to him. And then last October my son and his wife and youngster were here to visit, and they saw it, and they took a picture of my granddaughter with her finger on her great-granddaddy's name.

Joseph Gallo

· · · · · · · · · · · · ·

BORN JANUARY 24, 1927
IMMIGRATION AND NATURALIZATION SERVICE EMPLOYEE 1947–1954

He worked in multiple capacities for the Immigration and Naturalization Service (INS) at Ellis Island from 1947 until it closed (1954), although he remained on until 1955. He was a detention officer, a statistical clerk, a process server, and an armed guard. He married in 1955 and worked for the next thirty-four years as a customs agent until he retired. He died in 1995.

My parents both came through Ellis Island from Naro, Sicily. My father was one of thirteen boys and the only one that migrated to the United States.

He was courting my mother in Sicily, but they married after they arrived here. My mother came in 1912 when she was eighteen and was released to her mother who

· · · · · · · · ·

BULLARD-SANFORD MEMORIAL LIBRARY VASSAR, MI 48768

was already here. My father came in 1913 when he was twenty. I have three brothers and two sisters.

I got out of the service July 20, 1946. My dad had a fruit and vegetable business, and he asked me to run it for him. But I didn't care for it. The margin is pennies, and you work a hundred hours a week. But for my dad, that was his life. He says, "Well, if you're not going to work for me, go into the government." He felt that going into the government you had a job, security. I took a civil service exam, and I did fairly well. I was also a disabled veteran, which meant I had preference over the GI or anyone else. I was called by INS July 1, 1947, and ended up working for the government for forty-two years.

I started off in the main office at 70 Columbus Avenue as a GS-1 clerk. My salary was disgraceful, thirty-eight dollars a week. I came to Ellis Island in October 1947. I didn't know anything about Ellis Island. When they used to say Ellis Island it was like you were on a government blacklist, like you were exiled, because nobody wanted to come to Ellis Island. When I first came from the main office, they thought I was with Internal Affairs to see if anything was wrong. They were suspicious. But once they got to know me, I had the run of the island. When I say run of the island, I mean I wasn't restricted.

I became very popular. I ran the softball team. We had our own immigration softball team. The aliens used to manicure our field. And we used to play other government agencies: the Post Office, the U.S. attorney's office, Internal Revenue. We formed our own league. The government bought us equipment, they bought us uniforms. It was real nice.

A lot of the immigrants did work on the island. They worked in the kitchens under the supervision of an immigration officer. They did all the cleaning. They loved enter-tainment. It was very boring for these people to just sit around. So they would watch us play softball. There were benches, but they weren't allowed to play. This was strictly government employees. And we had to show our I.D. before we played.

I was with Immigration and Naturalization and we played against U.S. Customs, and we were rivals. The Post Office was a soft touch. The aliens used to bet money. They would say to me, "Hey, Joe, who's good tonight?" And I'd say, "Well, we've got competition tonight. It's an iffy game." And they'd say, "Do you think we're going to win?" I said, "Look, don't bet heavy." [Laughs.]

The way these aliens used to gamble! Sometimes it got out of hand, especially the card playing, and we had to take the cards away from them. They used to cut an orange in half, and they used to bet to see how many pits were in half of the orange. They used to go to the windowsill and bet on which raindrops dripped further down. This was especially true of the Chinese. The Chinese were big gamblers. They played blackjack, poker. And we allowed it for a while. We felt that as long as it kept them occupied we were happy, because there was less trouble for us. But then it got out of hand. There were fights. Occasionally we had to lock them up. Some got out of hand so bad that we used to cuff them and incarcerate them in the government prison on West Street, the Federal House of Detention.

It wasn't just the Chinese. We had all different types. We had the Italians, the Germans, the Russians. All types of Russians. The way it worked was I used to get their passport papers, and I used to check them. If there was a problem I would give them to BSI, which they used to call the Board of Special Inquiry. These were immigration inspectors, and they had their own court. There were three men on this court. Now sometimes we used to get letters or telephone calls from an agency in Europe saying that this guy was a communist, or this guy was bad, watch him. This agency, I forget the name, kept track of all the things that were going on, and they let us know. So if a letter came in, it would be given to the Board of Special Inquiry and they'd say, "Joe, when this person comes in I want you to hold him until we have a hearing." And when he got off the boat or the plane, I would tell him to sit downstairs until he was ready for his hearing. Aliens used to wait two, three days sometimes. And then they'd go before this board, which would decide whether they let them in, or set bail, or deported them.

The immigrant aid societies or agencies were also involved. They had offices in the Great Hall. Each nationality or ethnic group had its own agency. There was Italian Welfare. They used to handle all the Italian people. Then we had the Czechoslovakian agency. They used to handle all the Czechs. HIAS handled the Jews. So anybody who was being held for a particular reason, these agencies used to interpret for these people. And the agencies had lawyers that worked at no fee to the immigrant. And the lawyer, the interpreter, and the immigrant would go before the Board of Special Inquiry and the lawyer would say, "I'm representing John Doe . . ." Now, there's no way that this interpreter from the agency could finagle what the immigrant was saying because we had people on the board who understood the language. But the board never let them know.

Our offices were little cubicles on the second floor off the Great Hall. These were the people who handled all the different problems on the island. And we used to keep records. We had folders and binders as big as your arm. And every day we used to get all the immigration papers from all the aliens coming to the island, and we had to record them—name, date of birth, etc. If the papers were in order, I took them to the Board of Special Inquiry office and gave them to Ed Clark, a beautiful man. He was in charge of all the inspectors. We became friends. And I'd say, "Eddie, we've got ten cases . . ." or whatever. He'd say, "Okay, Joe," and hearings would be scheduled. Every alien had a hearing.

Ed Clark was the number one man on the board. Then you had a fellow by the name of Russ Danielson. There would be a stenographer taking notes. You'd have three people, you'd have a stenographer, you'd have the alien sitting down, and then you'd have the interpreter, the lawyer, and the person from the welfare agency. And they would go through a routine of questions.

We always had interpreters on hand. Most were employees, and occasionally outside interpreters. There were cases sometimes where I couldn't talk to the person. And I says, *"Capice italiano?"* And I'd say, "Well, talk to me in Italian." And if I didn't understand him, then I didn't want to be involved because I didn't want to steer the guy wrong. So what I used to do is call this gentleman that worked at Italian Welfare, this fellow by the name of Frank Triversa, who was a beautiful man. He spoke everything to everyone. And I used to pick up the phone and say, "Frankie, I've got a little problem." He'd say, "What is it, Joe?" And I'd say, "I need an interpreter for this dialect. I don't understand it." I spoke fluent Italian, but there's fifty to a hundred different dialects in Italian. You got the Roman, what they call *Alta Italia*, which is the high Italian. You could talk to me in *Alta Italia*, and I couldn't understand beans. But this fellow, this guy was beautiful. He knew all in all dialects, and when I was in trouble, I called him.

The hearings were very emotional. The aliens didn't know what to expect. Suddenly they were standing before a judge, a panel of people who decided whether they entered the United States or faced deportation. Very rarely did I see them make errors in that respect. I mean, most were released. Either on bond or bail. Some were held on bond because we didn't want them to become a public charge to the United States. So we asked their relatives to put up a $500 bond, so if anything happened and they became a public charge, they would take it right out of the bond. But most of them were released on what we called ROR, released on own recognizance.

After the hearings I would get the documents back, and Ed would say, "Okay, you can release him." And he'd give me a release form. And I'd go downstairs and I'd call out "Mr. So-and-So," and release him. Or I would release him or her to the agencies. I'd say, "Look, this person is being released, could you see that somebody meets them on the other side, the New York side?" We didn't let these people out blind. So the agencies used to make the arrangements. They would call relatives or friends of the immigrant, and say, "Your friend, or your cousin, or your aunt is being released. They're going to be on the two o'clock ferry." And they'd be waiting on the other side, so these people wouldn't be lost in New York.

If the alien came in with gold, or a wristwatch, or money, which they were only allowed to keep so much, they were held by Tony Galetta. Tony was the agent cashier on Ellis Island. He handled all the personal properties of the aliens. He used to confiscate them and give them a government receipt until they left.

One case I'll never forget as long as I live. There was a young lad, a seventeen-year-old German. He stowawayed on a Pan Am flight. We picked him up at Kennedy Airport and they brought him to Ellis Island. This kid was a snake. When I say a snake, I mean this kid had every girl. [Laughs.] He could maneuver you out of . . . But he never gave

us any trouble. He was a worker. We would say, "Here, take this pail of paint and brush—go paint this." And he'd work like a dog for you because he was happy to be here knowing that he wasn't going back to Germany.

But we couldn't deport him. We couldn't deport him because Germany wouldn't accept him. We were stuck with him. The only good thing about that was Pan Am paid the tab. We used to bill Pan Am every month. And they used to send a check, and they'd pay his tab.

INS did everything to try and get rid of this man. Eventually, he was adopted by a family in Texas when he was twenty-one years old. They heard about his story and went through the legal formalities. He was detained at Ellis Island for four years! That's the longest anyone was ever held.

The reason Pan Am paid was because they had to. They were responsible for him. They had two choices. They either paid his room and board, or they had to deport him. Same thing with any ship. Any ship that brought in stowaways or anybody that jumped ship, or anybody who had illness—whether the reasons be legal or medical—the steamship company was responsible. See, that was another part of my job. I was a process server. I used to notify the agencies, who notified their lawyers and got a signature. The agencies didn't pay the lawyers 100 percent. They paid like 25 percent. If a case cost a thousand dollars, they'd pay $250. Then I would serve the summonses on the airlines and the steamship companies. So I wasn't that popular with them.

We had quite a few cases of TB. We used to isolate the aliens ourselves. We used to send them to the U.S. Public Health Service hospital, which was on the other side of the island. And we had rooms where they were kept isolated until we got enough paperwork to get rid of them, otherwise they'd never be allowed in the United States. Then there were cases of glaucoma. Those immigrants weren't allowed in, or if they came with venereal disease.

In fact, there were a lot of Cuban prostitutes at that time, Cubans, even Italians. There was an Italian girl that was picked up in New York as a prostitute and was here illegally. We brought her to the island and then we couldn't get rid of her. She was another case in point where we couldn't get documents on her. But you can't just put a person on a plane or a ship and say, "Here, Italy, this is your body." They wouldn't accept them, unless you had proof, a birth certificate, something. We eventually let her on bond because she was more damaging to the people here than . . . She was offering her wares on Ellis. [Laughs.] And we were a close-knit population. The men had a ball. She made more money on Ellis Island than she made on the streets of New York.

Otherwise, I didn't have much interaction with the Public Health Service hospital. If a person was sick, I would call up and say, "Doctor, this is Joe Gallo. We're sending John Doe over. He's got this . . ." And we used to send a gurney, a wheelchair, or stretcher, and take them over, unless they were bedridden. When you got off the ferry at Ellis Island there was a connecting bridge. We used to go to the right. The medical people that worked for the Public Health Service went to the left. We were Immigration and they were Public Health.

I remember the Coast Guard used to tie up their boats with the ferries, because they used to eat in our cafeteria. I think we paid, like, fifty cents for a meal. And we used to get a fairly decent meal. I mean, we got a meal that was worth two, three dollars outside. The food was good because it was cooked by immigration people. The cafeteria had seating for about forty, and we were allowed a half hour, forty minutes, for lunch. And it was well kept. It was very clean. The aliens used to clean it. But they

couldn't eat there. They had their own cafeteria. The only aliens that used to eat there were the people that served. We had aliens serve us. They were behind the counter. And you went with your tray . . . you ate, and then you paid. There was a man at the door, and at the end of the meal we gave him a meal stub, a chit, and you paid him. That's the way you got out. Nobody ever went ashore to eat because the food was good and the price was right because it was subsidized by the government. You also had to be on call for emergencies.

Don't forget, we had a lot of people who resented being held. "Why ain't I getting examined?" Or, "Why ain't I going before the Board of Special Inquiry?" "What am I doing here?" And then two people get together and the next thing you know they're throwing punches. And you're in the middle, and you're trying to be the good guy and you end up getting belted. But we had enough help during the day. It was at night that we didn't have the help because we ran this place with only thirty-five, maybe forty detention officers. And remember, at that time, we handled approximately two thousand aliens a day.

The aliens ate between 4:30 and 6:30. And then they were allowed to stay up until 9:30, 10:00 o'clock, and lights out. But they never went to bed. They used to just congregate. The only people that went to bed were the families, because they had their own separate rooms. They had places to go and be comfortable. We tried to keep the families together. You couldn't expect a family of four with kids to live in dormitories. Also, European families were very close-knit. The children hung onto the mother. The mothers and fathers were strict. The kids were the least of our worries.

Single people stayed in the dormitories. It was not divided by sex. They mingled. We didn't care. Our job was to detain them, see they got serviced, and that there's no problem. The big problem was not to create a problem. Most of them, 85, 90 percent, you had problems.

George Foreman was the chief of detention, the superintendent. He was in charge of the island. The king of the hill. But he was an oddball. I mean, the guy knew his job. There's no way in the world I can dispute that. He had a big responsibility and he appreciated the work you did because he knew everything was up to par. But he never smiled. Everything could be perfect and the man still walked through the office with a frown on his face. [Laughs.] I'll never forget this story. George had his own car, a government-issued car, and it was stolen on the Manhattan side of the ferry. It was a black Buick, a nice car, and he tried to blame the theft on one of our detention officers. "I want it back," he said. "You stole it!" He was blaming everybody and everyone. But then it turned out the car wasn't stolen at all. His son had borrowed it. He was so embarrassed he didn't know what to say. I think he wanted to crawl under his desk. But that's the type of man he was. You were wrong until you were proven right.

I lived [at] home. Nobody lived on the island, not even Mr. Foreman. I came every morning on the Ellis Island ferry. I worked the 8 A.M. to 4 P.M. shift. But it was inconvenient. If you missed it, you were stuck at least an hour. And they never paid any overtime. It was an old-type ferry, but the service was excellent. There were no cars allowed on that ferry, and it carried the employees of not only INS but of the national Public Health Service. So in the mornings that ferry was really mobbed because you had at least a hundred people that worked on the island at that time. Once the midnight shift came on board, the ferry stopped. And then it started again at 5:30 A.M.

I wore a uniform. It was olive green with a black tie. In the summertime we wore short-sleeve shirts. Wintertime we had long coats because it got cold out there. We wore a hat. We were all examined by the chief. Before we went on duty he briefed us about what went on during the night shift. He'd say, "Look for this problem," or "Check this," or "Watch this guy." And then we briefed the shift that came after us.

Most of the women were secretaries. There was one woman named Evelyn Franco, a black woman, but a beautiful woman. She had a responsible job. She was the middleman between my office and the Board of Special Inquiry. But for the most part women had secretarial jobs. We had a lot of what they call "searchers." Searchers used to look for misplaced files. And we used to call and say, "Look, we need . . ." and they would scan through all the files and find it.

One time we had Jimmy Durante here. He gave a show for the aliens. He was the only celebrity that came to Ellis Island and gave a show. But otherwise the aliens, they supplied their own entertainment. They had radios. I don't remember television, but they might have had it. There was no entertainment at all in the Great Hall except at Christmas, we put up a tree. Somebody would buy little gifts. For the Jewish people they had Menorahs for Hanukkah. We used to try to make it as pleasant as possible for the holidays. It's not easy to be locked up during the holiday, especially for children. When I say "locked up," I mean they couldn't go anywhere, but they were not in jail. "Detained" was the word we used. Of course, for them it felt like jail.

If an immigration inspector felt an alien couldn't be released at the airport, they brought them to Ellis Island to let the Board of Special Inquiry decide. The same was true for displaced persons. The poor people. After the Second World War, they were brought in by the boatloads. They were detained until their papers were cleared. Many of them got in. There were many communists, or people that were in jail in Europe and they got in through the Displaced Persons Act in 1947. That was a big thing.

The act said that if a person didn't have a country to live in, they could come to the United States. We didn't know where to put these people, so they all came here. Ninety-nine out of a hundred were released because we couldn't send them back to their home country. Most of them came from behind the Iron Curtain; not so much the Italians, French, British. These people came in on quotas. See, all those countries were allotted a quota every year, so they weren't even mentioned in the Displaced Persons Act. It was for people behind the Iron Curtain who came from countries that didn't want them, or for the incorrigibles. Castro emptied his jails and sent them to us. But some of them were caught, stopped. They went before the Board of Special Inquiry and were put back on the plane or the ship and sent back.

Same thing held true with the war brides. We had a big influx of war brides after 1947 to maybe 1950. While the GIs were in Europe, they married everything and everyone. The British, French, Italian, everyone. And these girls used that as a way to get into the country, because that was the fastest way to get into the country, because you didn't have a quota. You were the bride of a GI.

I was in charge of that project, and I used to handle all their papers. And they used to come in, we used to hold them here until the GI would call and say, "Mr. Gallo, you got Mrs. So-and-so?" And I'd look at my file, and I'd say, "Yeah, she's here. She's waiting to be picked up." They come out to Ellis Island, they'd have to identify themselves as a GI, the husband on the marriage certificate, and take them home, these beautiful girls. I mean, these were outrageously beautiful girls. All different types. And they married some bum. [Laughs.] And I used to talk

to these girls and say, "You know, by law you're supposed to live with this GI." I think at that time it was mandatory that they had to live with the GI for at least a year. And then they scat. They leave. But that was the fastest way to get here. Nine out of ten brides ended up on Ellis Island, just to be processed and to be picked up by the groom.

Two months before the island closed, the government spent like two or three hundred thousand dollars to put in a new sewer system for Ellis Island. I mean, it was a big operation. They were doing a lot of fixing. And no one had an inkling about the island closing until this general came along named General Swing. He was the commissioner of Immigration. He didn't even come to the island. He stood across the harbor on the Manhattan side where the ferry was, pointed, and said "Close it."

At least 250 people lost their jobs just like that. I was in shock. The whole staff was in shock. I mean, you had people here fifteen, twenty, thirty years. When they found out that Ellis Island was closing, they just couldn't believe what they were hearing. I thought we had a good operation. A place where you could hold people and take care of the problems that existed in immigration. I mean, today . . . I wouldn't want to work in immigration today. It's a whole different game. But this general said, "Close it," and that was it. The government did try to transfer us to other positions. The only thing they kept here was detention until we moved to a new facility at 641 Washington Street off the West Side Drive.

The island closed in November 1954. Before it did, we had more or less a pre-Christmas party. But it was sad because we were like a family, a close-knit family. I remember cleaning out my desk. My God, what a sad feeling. I loved it here. I always looked forward to coming to work because you had people you loved to work with. Every day was something different.

Mel Berger

. . . .

BORN JULY 14, 1929
COASTGUARDSMAN, DECEMBER 1951–MARCH 1954

*Born in Mount Carmel, Pennsylvania, he chose the Coast Guard because "I
knew I was going to be drafted and I wanted to select where I wanted to go." He
was stationed at Ellis Island from December 1951 through March 1954. Today,
he lives in Levittown, Pennsylvania, having spent nearly forty years as an
elementary-school teacher.*

I was at Cape May three months, having completed basic training, when I was transferred to Ellis Island. We went across New York Harbor, past the Statue of Liberty, the first time I had ever seen it, and we arrived at Ellis Island. I remember the day, December 29, 1951. There was an aura of mystery about the place. I didn't really know what to expect. I didn't know what kind of facilities there were, nor how long I was going to be there. It was just a matter of going along with the tide, so to speak. Whatever would befall me, I was more or less ready to accept. I was kind of young [twenty-two] and somewhat eager, and it was just really an adventure.

It was a relatively new station for the Coast Guard, so that the total would be maybe sixty, seventy personnel. I was a seaman. Shortly after I arrived, I was given a job to work in what was then called a ship's store, or canteen. It used to bother me to say it was a ship's store because I wasn't aboard a ship. But at any rate there was no ranking for that type of work. So if you wanted that kind of job you knew that you wouldn't be elevated in rank and you stayed a seaman, but you had that job, and it was sort of a security-type thing, and I accepted it.

When I first arrived, the island was more or less just opening up to the Coast Guard, and they had not yet established a store. One evening I walked into the operations room, and that room was in disorder. Desks had been moved in. And a young ensign found out that I was a college graduate, and he literally jumped off the desk he was half-reclining on, and said, "I can use you." He said, "Mel, I intend to open up a store and I need someone to be my assistant. Would you like the job?" And he and I together opened up that store.

It was located in a rec hall; a building that held a gymnasium/auditorium near our barracks. And in the rear of that building were a number of rooms, and it was there we established the store. We sold handy items; soap, toothpaste, cigarettes, immediate necessities. And then we enlarged upon it. We got clothing, shoes, jewelry, watches, and snack food.

Our store was open to the immigration side of the island. Most people who were employed there would come over to the store. And I think Friday was payday, and they would line up to buy cigarettes. That was the big item that we sold. So the Coast Guard and the Immigration and Naturalization Service shared the ship's store.

The immigration building was opposite the ferry slip from the Coast Guard. That is, the ferry slip was in between the Coast

Guard buildings and the immigration building. So the immigration process at that point was taking place in the main building, the Great Hall, and we were on the other side of the island. I can recall only one occasion that I went over there. It was as part of a tour by the Coast Guard.

The rec hall wasn't used very much. In the daytime it wasn't used at all, but in the nighttime they set up folding chairs and showed movies. On occasion, a service organization would entertain the troops with quiz shows. I distinctly recall one group that came over. They asked for volunteers. I went up on stage. And I was asked a question to which I didn't know the answer. And the question was: "What lady recently traveled from the United States to Europe?" When I was in the Coast Guard I wasn't following news. So I hesitated to give an answer because I just didn't know. But before I had a chance to say anything, one of the personnel from the quiz show walked behind me and whispered the answer to me. [Laughs.] And I said, "Mrs. Roosevelt." For which I was given a prize of seventy dollars.

The hospital, prior to the Coast Guard coming, was a marine hospital. The marines had it, abandoned it, and the Coast Guard decided it was a good place to have a station. Once the Coast Guard was established, there was no further use of those buildings as a hospital. They were used as barracks for the men stationed there. The wards became barracks. Large rooms filled almost exclusively with rows of double-tiered bunks for forty, fifty men. There were no medical facilities operating at that point. It was purely a Coast Guard area.

We ate in the basement of the main building. That was the commissary, the kitchen, and the room for eating. I'm very selective when it comes to eating and I didn't enjoy everything they had. We had beans or spaghetti quite regularly, and I didn't care for their beans or spaghetti. We

had potatoes every second or third day. I didn't care for their potatoes. There were times I went on the chow line and I couldn't see anything that appealed to me until I got to the end. So I'd fill up with a bowl of ice cream, and that was my meal. Holiday times didn't seem to be much more special than any other times.

The main function of the Coast Guard on Ellis Island was to guard the piers of New York, and Hoboken, [and] Jersey City. I did that for four months. Two or three men would go out in forty-foot Coast Guard boats, land on some designated pier and stay there for five or six hours to make certain that all the people who came onto the piers to work were bona fide. I didn't really know too much what I was looking for, but I think it was being cautious about sabotage. And I don't recall any incidents that happened when I was in the Coast Guard, but it was a precautionary type of thing. It was making certain that the people who worked on these piers were not going to sabotage anything in New York Harbor.

We used to ride the ferry into Manhattan on what we called our "liberty." When we were no longer assigned to duty, we could either go across to the mainland, or stay in the Coast Guard area. Most of the fellows wanted to see the sights of the town. I must have been there maybe two months before I got up enough nerve to go to this strange place called New York City. I felt I'd get lost. Having been brought up in the country, I didn't have much knowledge of large towns, much less New York. And I did manage to get lost that first visit. Later on with friends, I would go to places like Carnegie Hall and Broadway to see quiz shows and musicals. We were always dressed in uniform. In the summertime it was white, and in the wintertime it was gold or navy blue. There was a steady stream of coastguardsmen going out each evening on liberty and then coming back at night. Nobody ever went to New

Jersey, but then there were no ferries to go there.

We never went to the Statue of Liberty, even though we were so close to it. We never went there because there was no direct way to get there, unless you wanted to swim. I didn't have any desire to go. To me the impressive part of the statue was seeing it from the outside, and it was there for me to see every day and night. I often remarked that I was so close to the statue that she shone her light down upon me every night when I went to bed. It wasn't until years later on a trip to New York that I visited the Statue of Liberty for the first time.

For recreation, I remember we had one tennis court and one baseball diamond with no backstop. It was just an open area where we played ball in back of the barracks. We played softball, but nothing organized in the way of competitive sports.

We were not allowed [to have] guests on the island. Nobody could come. I had my dad come to New York, but he only got to see Ellis Island from the ferry. And I had my wife there shortly after we were married. She came to visit me one weekend, but she was not allowed onto the island.

I met my wife in college and she knew that I was going into the service, and she was certainly not against that. But it was while I was in service that we decided we would get married. I had signed up for three years' duty, five years' reserve, but I was in the Coast Guard two and a half years. At that time the Coast Guard came up with a plan, due to budgetary reasons, to allow X number of men to be discharged six months early. So we were married in June of '53, and it was in the spring of '54 that I was discharged along with a lot of other men. [He pulls out a newspaper from 1954 with the headline: "2,000 Coast Guard Men Get Early Out."] That's 2,000 nationwide, not just Ellis Island. There was no party or celebration. The discharge came pretty much as a surprise. So when I left, the Coast Guard was maintaining a presence there at Ellis Island.

Part I

ITALY

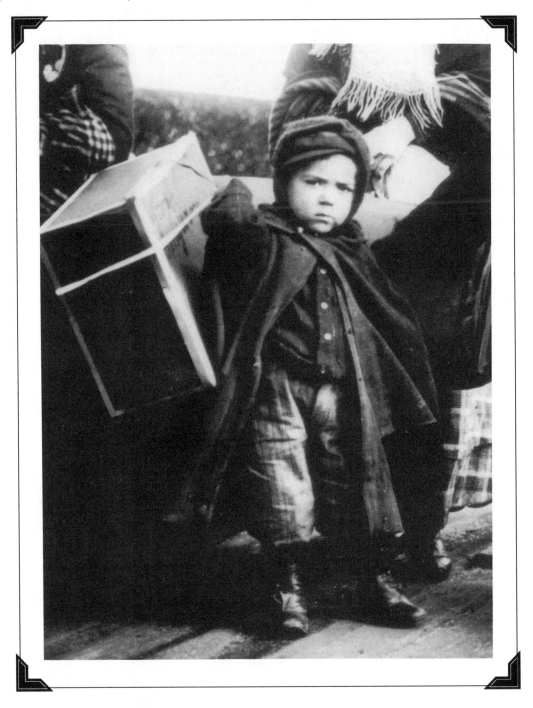

Young Italian immigrant carrying his own baggage, Ellis Island, 1926

(NATIONAL GEOGRAPHIC SOCIETY, NATIONAL PARK SERVICE: STATUE OF LIBERTY NATIONAL MONUMENT)

2

Southern Italy

(APPROXIMATELY 3.3 MILLION IMMIGRANTS, 1892–1954)

Mario Vina

· · · · · · · · · · · · ·

BORN AUGUST 3, 1896
EMIGRATED 1909, AGE 11
SHIP UNKNOWN

He came from the southern Italian village of Frosolene. His family settled in Middletown, Connecticut. He remembers Presidents Taft and Teddy Roosevelt marching in parades through town. A welder much of his life, he served in the National Guard in New Mexico in 1916 and fought against Pancho Villa. He also served in France during World War I and was shot above one eye. He married in 1921, but his wife has long since gone. Now 101 years old, he lives near his daughter and son-in-law in Lenox, Massachusetts.

*I*n Frosolene, people were farmers, and there was a few that made cutlery and things like that. It had three churches. Once or twice a year, we used to have a big feast for Saint Anthony with fireworks. The whole town used to participate in that. We lived in an apartment on the second floor above a wine shop, a saloon. It had an open fireplace. As a boy, I used to love to walk to St. Mary's Church, which was nearby.

My mother used to make very good tomato sauce, and she used to make lovely bread. We used to go to the mill and grind the grains. Then she'd take it to a place in town where they used to cook it in the ovens. For water, we had to carry it in buckets from the main fountain to the house. We had no plumbing. My mother came from this village. Her father, my grandfather, lived there and her brother lived there. My grandfather made cheese.

My father, when I knew him, was working in the forest cutting down trees. Then he came to America. He became a molder in a cast iron shop in Middletown, Connecticut. Why Middletown, I have no idea. He had no relatives or friends in America. I was small at the time. I had a sister, and my little brother was about a year old when he left. I don't remember anything about my father until I saw him in New York.

To make money, my mother took care of an old lady who lived a couple of doors down. I went to school in a one-room schoolhouse that was for first, second, third grade, altogether.

We were supposed to come to this country in 1907, two years before we finally did. My father sent cash to my mother to buy the boat tickets. But my grandfather fell off a horse and got sick. My mother spent the money on doctors. She wouldn't leave him when he was sick. He died at ninety-seven.

In 1909, the year we came, my father got smart. He sent no cash, just the paid tickets. I was glad I was going to America, but then I was sorry I left all my friends. I remember my mother had a great big box, like a trunk, and she packed a lot of stuff. Somebody came and picked up the trunk and we didn't see it until we got to Ellis Island.

From Frosolene, we went by a stagecoach, horse and carriage, to the railroad. I was so excited. I had never seen a train before. We got to Naples and went on the steamer. We stayed overnight on the boat and left the next day. This was in June 1909.

· · · · · · · · ·

INS ferry that transported immigrants between Ellis Island and Battery Park from 1904 to 1954. On the far left is Castle Garden, the former immigrant receiving station from 1855 to 1890 run by the state of New York. When this photograph was taken, in 1940, Castle Garden was the site of the New York City Aquarium, before it was moved to Coney Island.

(NATIONAL PARK SERVICE: STATUE OF LIBERTY NATIONAL MONUMENT)

I had never seen a boat before. I had never seen the ocean. I had never seen Mount Vesuvius, which had erupted a couple of years before. I was amazed.

On the ship I was separated from my mother and put in with the men, the men's section. I didn't like that, and I started roaming around the boat till I found my mother. She said, "I don't have enough room for you to sleep here." But there was a lady sleeping nearby. She had room and I stayed with her. It was a big room. Of course, we didn't come first class. We came in steerage.

I didn't get sick, but my poor mother was sick all the way over from Gibraltar for two weeks till we got to this country. She was sick every day. A lot of people were. The ship was crowded. My only objection was that none of the crew spoke Italian, yet everybody on the ship was Italian. So we had to have an interpreter all the time.

One day I went to the kitchen and asked the cook to get some chicken broth for my mother. He was very nice, I got acquainted with him, and I used to go up there and help him in the kitchen washing the pans, scraping them. In return, he used to give me food I could take to my mother. Take a roast chicken, things like that. I used to take it down to her. I used to go to the forward deck, sit there, wonder what everything was all about.

I just loved the ride. I was sad when it ended. But then I said, "Well, this is it. This is America." I could see the New York skyline. There weren't too many tall buildings then. We were on the boat two overnights when we landed. It was around the Fourth of July. I remember seeing fireworks from the boat. We were all examined on the boat. If anybody was sick, they had to stay.

Then we ferried to Ellis Island and we all got separated, and that's when the trunk came back. They put name tags on us. We were fed sandwiches, which was new to me. We were checked again for eyesight, our ears, our heart with a stethoscope. We all passed the examination, and then we were told to stay in one place until we took the ferry to Battery Park. It was from the ferry I remember seeing the liberty statue. I had seen pictures of it in different books in Italy. I thought it was a beautiful monument, one of the most beautiful things I've ever seen.

When we got to Battery Park, there were two men walking down some stairs and, all of a sudden, my mother spotted him, spotted my father. She says, "It's Papa!" I looked. I had forgotten what he looked like, you know. My mother hugged him, kissed him. He hugged me and patted me on the back. He had come with a friend of his.

Then we went to Middletown by train and when we got there he had a present for me. A baseball bat and glove, which I had never seen before. "What are these for?" I asked him. "You play with these," he said. "It's a game. It's called baseball."

Paulina Caramando
. . . .

BORN JANUARY 19, 1912
EMIGRATED 1920, AGE 8
PASSAGE ON THE *DANTE ALIGHIERI*

She was an only child from the village of Santa Maria di Licodia. The daughter of a strict Sicilian father, her family settled in Lawrence, Massachusetts, where her father became a railroad worker. She married an Italian plasterer and had two sons, one of whom died of leukemia. She divorced, and later married a farmer who also had two sons, both of whom eventually succumbed to AIDS. Now eighty-five, she lives in Salem, New Hampshire. "I always say thank God my father decided to come here because during the Second World War our house in Sicily was bombed," she said. "One of my cousins and three children were killed. My father went in and found them in pieces . . . Please, dear God, I have suffered enough heartaches. I don't want any more."

I was there during the First World War and I remember all the people in northern Italy came down to Sicily because there was fighting in the northern part. That's where my father was for years. In the army.

The town was poor. We hadn't had enough to eat ourselves. But we had to help those people that came because they didn't bring anything with them. Just their lives. They ran away because they were in fear of dying there. I remember there was a little boy my age that didn't know where his mother was. He was all alone. I remember one woman, she gave birth to a baby. One of the villagers took her in. She didn't know whether her husband was alive or dead.

We cooked on burners where you put wood under the parts. We would go in the woods and collect sticks because over there there was hardly any lumber, any trees. All the trees were fruit-bearing trees, so they didn't cut those down. We would collect sticks and sell them so we could buy flour for bread, and we'd use the sticks to fire our pots. We had no running water. There was a fountain with faucets in the town where we used to wash our clothes. We had these rocks, and we would use that for a scrub board. The streets were cobblestone. We would also fill clay jugs with water to take home. People would [carry] it on their head. And everybody had a donkey and they'd take their animals down there to water them. To go to the bathroom, we'd dig a hole in the garden. That's all there was. Not even an outhouse. You just squatted down and that was that. Can you imagine living that way today? It was very bad.

My mother and father both came separately to the United States around 1902. I don't know if they came through Ellis Island. They never spoke about it. But they met and got married here. They were young, seventeen, eighteen. He got a job in the mills in Lawrence, Massachusetts. They lived there for a few years. In fact, before the First World War broke out, my father always had the intention of going back, so he sent my mother back, and I was born two months after she got there. My mother was twenty-six. My father was here with his younger brother. So then the war broke out, I always remember this, my father used to say if you didn't go back to fight for your country they wouldn't let you back in. My father said, "They didn't even give us a

chance to get off the train." They grabbed them, and into the army they went, both of them.

During the years he was in the army, I saw him maybe three or four times, that's all. They'd let him come home once in a while. When he came out, I was about seven years old. I wouldn't even go near him because I was shy. I didn't know the man.

My father got a job in the village tending, watering, gardens or orchards. They belonged to rich people who lived in the city, but they had these big gardens, and people would work to take care of them. That's the only work there was. They picked oranges that were then sold and shipped. I remember the great big piles of oranges. Oranges were plenty there. They used the donkeys to move the oranges they picked, and the olives. The olives were shaken from the trees and taken to a mill and pressed into oil. Same thing with the grapes. Workers would pick enough grapes to make wine for themselves and then sell the rest.

It was mostly red wine they made. Even my father made his own wine. He'd have it in the cellar in barrels, and it would have to ferment, and you could smell that all through the house. We lived in a four-story house and you could smell that all through. The four tenants that lived in the place made their own, too. Everybody made it.

My father always wanted to come back [to America], especially after what he went through in the army. He talked about it. The fighting. I'd sit there with my mouth open every time he started talking. He was injured, his foot. He got shot there. He told stories of these young kids in the army, seventeen, nineteen. And this one young fellow, he was so scared, he didn't want to fight. This was in Austria, way up in the Alps. So you know what the commander did? He shot him.

So my father wanted to get back here as quick as he could. He had his sister here, too.

were coming also. We were all together. And it was heartbreaking. They were crying. The steamship company wouldn't let them on the boat. They were turned away.

I remember on the boat my mother and I were so sick. The men and women weren't together at night. You know what I mean? The men and the boys were in one section, the women and the girls were in another section. So in the morning the first thing my father would do was to come down below and take us up on [the] ship, where we'd lay out there on blankets half-dead. [Laughs.] At least we'd have fresh air up there, you know. I remember, we'd have to hold on to the railing, the way the boat would rock, and go up the stairs.

The first-class people, all the rich people, were way above. I'd look up at them, they were all dressed nice, and we were like a flock of sheep down below. Oh, it was terrible. Twenty-two days. And sick, so sick. I could smell coffee. To this day, I could never get used to drinking coffee, never. I never drank coffee in my life.

The next thing I remember was when we got to New York Harbor. These small boats came along the ship selling things. They'd have a basket, lower the basket down with a rope. My father bought some bananas. I never saw a banana in all my life. Of course, he knew what it was. And he brought the bananas up, and he peeled it, and gave me one. I tasted it. I didn't like it at all. And that's the best thing I like now.

I remember going into this great big hall, and they took our clothes. We had to strip. We had to take all our clothes off. The men and women separate. They gave us a blanket. It was the first time I ever saw a naked woman. It was quite an experience; my mother was holding me. We took showers, and then wrapped ourselves up in the blanket and come out and wait for our clothes.

They took our clothes to fumigate them, delouse them. When we got our clothes

A woman physician from the Public Health Service (PHS) examining a female immigrant at Ellis Island, circa 1905.

(NATIONAL PARK SERVICE: STATUE OF LIBERTY NATIONAL MONUMENT)

As soon as he got enough money we made passage. We took bedsheets and some clothes. But I remember in particular I had a doll that I loved, and my mother says, "No, you can't. We have no room for it." I had to leave my doll, and that broke my heart. [Laughs.]

We crossed by boat from Sicily into Italy. Then we went to Naples. I don't know what happened, but we were there a week, maybe two weeks. And we slept in this big hall of the steamship company.

We were examined there. My father had a friend with his wife and a little boy that back, I remember going into this big room where they had not bunks but hammocks, because I remember wondering if Ellis Island was a place for soldiers.

Our clothes were all wrinkled. My father said, "We'll change when we get back on the boat," because we had to go to Boston from there. I became a citizen because at the time

children under twelve automatically became citizens.

So we got off the boat, my aunt was waiting for us. And the first thing my aunt did when we got there, she took me to a store, and bought me a new pair of sneakers and a dress which I still have somewhere.

Peter Mossini

. . . .

BORN JULY 8, 1898
EMIGRATED 1921, AGE 22
PASSAGE ON THE *PESARO*

He came from a large family, dirt poor, in the seaside village of Santa Teresa di Riva. Uneducated, he was forced to labor at a young age. Unskilled, he followed his eldest sister to western Pennsylvania and worked the coal mines for eighteen dollars a week. He worked the Pennsylvania Railroad, scraped through the Depression, and bought a sanitation business on the cheap in 1934. He sold it and opened a bar and restaurant that he ran until he retired.

In them days, there was two classes of people in Sicily: the rich and the very poor. My family was very poor. I never went to school. I started working from before I was ten years old. My father and mother, they send me to work to make maybe ten cents a day. I was working in a lemon factory. I work from one o'clock in the morning to about two in the afternoon the next day. Eleven, twelve hours. Them days, if you make ten cents a day, that was a lot of money. There was no time for play. For fun, I play boccie or soccer maybe. But we no have a ball. So we used a lemon.

My father was also working in the factory and my younger brothers did, too, later on. My mother no work because we had a

big family, you know. Eight children. And there was no work for the women. Even if they wanted to work, there was no work. So my sisters stay home. We had only two bedrooms. Today, if you got four children, you got four bedrooms. Them days, if you had four boys, they all had to sleep in the same room or if you had four girls, same thing.

To feed the family in winter, my father would buy a hundred kilogram of dried beans. My mother would soak them the night before and the following day get some macaroni and that's how we fill the family. And naturally, she baked her own bread. The flour came in fifty, seventy-five pound bags, and she bake maybe sixteen, eighteen loaves of bread each week. The oven was outside the house, a communal oven.

The first few days the bread was pretty good because it was soft, but after a week the bread was like a rock and many times I remember we had to soak the bread with a little water and rub it with garlic and that's what we were eating. That and fish. Fish was cheap.

The day before Christmas we always had fish and on Christmas day, maybe my father go to the butcher shop and buy a couple pounds of pork, you know, and we mixed sauce and we have a dish of spaghetti. Over here, even my own children or my grandchildren, you buy steak, cost you five dollars a pound and they say, "Who wants that garbage?" Over there, if you had a piece of fat you was lucky and boy, it tasted good, too. There was no gift. There was no money. What gift? You was lucky if you can buy a loaf of bread.

We never miss church. We was all baptized, confirmed. Madonna Mount Carmel.

Immigrants in steerage upon arriving in New York Harbor, November 1920

(NATIONAL PARK SERVICE: STATUE OF LIBERTY NATIONAL MONUMENT)

A big church. The church, I would say, was three miles from where we was living. So we walk to church because there was no transportation. I'll be honest with you, my first pair of new shoes I had on my feet, I was sixteen years old. Every time I got a couple penny, I had a place in the wall where I put the money. And there was a shoemaker. He was making a pair of shoes for himself. And when I see that pair of shoes I ask him how much they cost. He says, "Sixteen lira," and I try them on my feet. Now I says, "I'm going to go get the money." I went home, and got the money from the wall. My piggy bank. I went back and I says, "Now you're going to make another pair for me." He says, "A lot of work!" I says, "I'll stay all night with you." We stayed there all night and he work all night to make the shoes.

I wanted to come to the United States because my father did. The first time my father come was in 1901. He went to Pennsylvania and he was working in the coal mines. Every once in a while, he send a few dollars. He was there about five or six years. Then he come back to Sicily. The last trip he made to the United States was in 1912. He stay one year. But there was no work, and he just had enough money to pay his fare and come back to Sicily. By that time, the family started to get a little big. So we no starve, my brothers were working. So we all pulled together.

During the First World War, I was in the army, and I held to my idea about coming to America. Then, in 1919, my sister Josephine came. I was very close to her. She was the oldest one in the family and I respected her like a mother, because she was like a mother to me. She came by herself and she got married. She was doing very well over here. And I wanted to build myself a new life, better myself. Eventually, all my brothers and sisters came to United States.

So I saved my money because my father, he couldn't afford to pay for my trip. I don't remember exactly what I pay. As soon I got out of the army, I apply for the passport. That took about four, five months, because they started closing the immigration.

I took a little suitcase and I had just a few pairs of socks, couple of handkerchief and couple of underwear and a couple of shirts. There was me, my cousin—he was only sixteen years old, I guaranteed for him—and this friend of mine. He was about nineteen. They're both dead now. And we left from Naples the nineteenth of March 1921.

The boat was *Pesaro*. A German boat. Italy got it after the First World War and there was no cabin, no first, second, or third. There was just one class in them days. Steerage. One floor. One room. There was bunk beds. And in the morning, you had to get up because the crew had a firehose and they washed the floor.

I remember as soon as we left Naples they gave you a pillowcase. Inside that pillowcase you had your aluminum dish, your fork, knife, spoon, and a metal cup. When it was time to eat, we lined up and got our stuff. We ate twice a day. They gave you a cup of soup, piece of meat, piece of bread, and cup of coffee. Then we had to find a place to sit down because there was no dining room. This was a troop transport boat.

When we reach New York, I thank the good Lord. It was early morning, the Fourth of July. We was on the deck like a bunch of sheep. Everybody had a suitcase, dragging their suitcase, and I remember the first meal they gave to us at Ellis Island. They give a sandwich, white bread with a piece of cheese and a piece of ham and it tasted so good. It tasted like a nice piece of cake. That was something new for me. I never seen sandwiches in Sicily. They examined if you had lice in your head. If you did, they shaved your hair. I remember that. There was a lot of bald people. And if you had some kind of disease in your eye, they send you back.

We left that night by train from Pennsylvania Station in New York. We went to Portage, Pennsylvania. It's between Altoona and Johnstown. Western Pennsylvania. My sister Josephine lived there with her husband.

Them days, the train stopped every station for the people who worked in the coal mine and the railroad and the factory, every station. By the time we got to Portage, no one was on the train. Just us—me, my cousin, and my friend. We didn't know where to go. None of us spoke English, and it was April, kind of cold. We had the Italian clothes on, very light, because Sicily's warm like Florida. And we see an old man inside the stationhouse. He was making a fire with coal to keep the station warm. He sees us with our suitcases.

"Hey, where you going?" he asks us. We don't know what the hell he says. "*Italiani?*" Oh God, my heart went. He spoke Italian! We say, "*Si, si!*" Then he asked us where we supposed to go and we give the name of my sister and my brother-in-law. He says, "Oh, yeah. I know them." He got in touch, and then my brother-in-law come, thanks to God.

This was the trip.

Angelina Palmiero

BORN SEPTEMBER 8, 1913
EMIGRATED 1923, AGE 10
PASSAGE ON THE *GIUSEPPE VERDI*

She came from San Cataldo in central Sicily. During the Depression, she became a seamstress in a dressmaking factory in Brooklyn where she met her husband, an American-born Italian. She married at nineteen. In 1959, she bought a dressmaking factory, had twenty-eight employees, and eventually sold it in 1969. "The Jewish people owned the factories, the Italian people worked," she said. "We tried to make ourselves Americanized as much as we could at the time. Now, thank God, we're all one. I hope so."

My grandfather was a ranch foreman. He would take care of all these men that worked. They picked olives and almonds, and then they would have to crack them. I remember going to a place where they would crack them with a little hammer, the almonds, all by hand. I had three sisters. I was the baby of the three. They got us kids to take the almonds out of the shells and put them in a burlap bag. We wanted to get into the burlap bag because they said the bag was going to America.

I used to visit my grandparents at their farm, but we lived in the town. I remember I was in school when Mussolini came into power, and they took us out of school, and they made us march all around the town with flags. Our school was upstairs from a prison. There was an open yard with an iron

*In the main building, around 1910, the Money Exchange at Ellis Island run by the
American Express Company, which got the exclusive contract to exchange currency in 1903.
Prior to then, immigrants exchanging money were often cheated by clerks.*

(STATE HISTORICAL SOCIETY OF WISCONSIN, NATIONAL PARK SERVICE:
STATUE OF LIBERTY NATIONAL MONUMENT)

walk all around. The prisoners would be in the yard, and from way up on the railing we would talk to the prisoners, all us kids. I went up to the third grade . . .

We were a loving family. My mother babied me a lot. My two sisters babied me also. I was spoiled. I was a tomboy. I was a spoiled brat until I was ten, eleven years old—until we came here. But we weren't bad off, because my father used to send money from America. My father left when I was about four years old. I really didn't remember my father that good. So when we came here, he was pretty much unknown to me.

My mother never worked, but she always had enough money. My father was a very good provider. In fact, everything he made here he sent to her. She exchanged the dollars into Italian money, and then she changed it to American money when we got here because she had some money left. But she was afraid to spend some of the money, because people over there didn't have much. She didn't want to show that she was doing better than them because her husband was in America. She had a lot of compassion for the people there, and sometimes if she bought something extra for us, she'd say, "Don't tell anybody that I bought this," so as not to make them feel bad, you know. She lived very well in Sicily. In fact, she lived better there, while my father was here, than when we got to America.

Just before we came, I remember they used to make a fire in the middle of the street, and it was like a feast. And the fellows would run down the hill and jump over the fire, and see who could jump the highest. I was standing there watching them, and one of the fellows stretched his arms out and hit me right in the eye, and I got a black eye. My mother was scared because we were going to leave for America and what if they wouldn't let me pass with my eye, with the black eye I had. When we left from Palermo, my eye got better. But she cried for a week.

My oldest sister was thirteen years old. She went to a dressmaker to learn how to make dresses. She made all our dresses. When we came here we all looked like Jacqueline Kennedy, all dressed up with georgette dresses, a thin material that you have to wear over a slip. My sister wore high heels. And my mother bought straw hats for all of us with cherries on them. We had to get rid of all our clothes when we came here, because they were too dressy. My sister had to get rid of her high heels, and she cried for six months because she couldn't wear her high heels at fifteen years old.

I remember that we didn't pay anything to come to America. My father was here before the war, the First World War, and there was something that if he came to Italy and served in the Italian war, we would get free passage to America. So he came to Italy. He went to war there. After the war, he came right back to America. This was 1919 . . .

We didn't pack too much because my mother had a sister in New York, and my father, his brother and his wife were living in Pittstown, Pennsylvania, which was about eleven miles outside of Scranton. My aunt told us not to pack too much, and I remember we left a lot of stuff, but we brought all our good clothes. We bought two trunks. That's all, nothing else.

There was a big sendoff at the train station. That morning my two grandfathers and my grandmother came, and I was telling my mother the night before, "Oh, tomorrow everybody's going to cry, and everybody's going to do this." But when the train came, I was the one who cried the most because I didn't want to leave my grandfathers and my grandmother. I knew them all my life and they were very good to me.

My mother was very excited. She didn't care who she left behind. It wasn't like today where you have a plane, and you go back and see your father. She knew that once she left she'd never see him again. It was very hard on her, but at the same time, she was excited.

It took us about seven hours to get to Palermo. It was a very long ride, which now I hear it's about an hour and a half by car. We went to a hotel and we stayed there about three days. I had been to Palermo before, but I was never in a hotel. And we went to the opera, and we went to a movie theater, which was brand new. They were just starting the movies. I remember that night they didn't know how to work the cameras. They didn't know how to set everything up, so we all had to go back to the hotel.

One day we went sightseeing in a horse and carriage. Friends of my mother took us around Palermo. We went to a park. I remember riding along the water, which I never saw. My town, San Cataldo, was in the center of Sicily and we never saw an ocean before, never mind boats. [Laughs.] So when I saw that big boat, I was really amazed.

All I knew about America was that I wanted to go there because my father was here. But America meant nothing to me whatsoever. They used to say there was big buildings in New York. And to us a big building was maybe three stories high . . .

We left the 26th of August 1923. I don't remember much about the boat because within a couple of days, I had swollen glands. I had a fever and my mother brought me to the hospital on the boat, and they left me there.

It took thirteen days to get to the United States. I know that because we got here on my birthday. My mother started kissing me and hugging me because it was my birthday. And somebody yelled, "The Statue of Liberty, the Statue of Liberty!" We all ran to the railing to see, and everybody was praying and kissing and happy that we were coming up the Hudson. But then we docked in the harbor. Ellis Island was too crowded. There was quite a few boats from other ports. Each boat had to wait their turn. I don't remember how many days we anchored, but it was quite a few days because my father used to come with the tugboat. And that's how I saw him for the first time, from all the way up on the railing looking down. I remember he bought big bananas from vendors on the tugboat. They would put the bananas in a pail and lifted it up to the ship. I didn't know what bananas were. "Don't eat it like that," he shouted. "Take the skin off."

When we got to Ellis Island, I went one way and my family went another. I don't know what happened to them. They brought me to the hospital. I was there for twenty-three days.

My sisters, with my father and mother, went to Pennsylvania. My father had to pay a $250 bond that he would return to get me.

I wanted my mother. I was crying when they got me. There were two men that brought me into the hospital. I was kicking and screaming and after a while I got tired, and they put me in there with this girl who was older than I was. She must have been about thirteen, fourteen. "Me Jew," she said. She didn't speak Italian. I remember we got a kick out of the sliced bread in the morning when they brought us breakfast, and we would both talk with our hands, and try to make each other understand. She only stayed about a week with me, because then I was left alone in there.

Nobody told me anything. Nobody explained, nobody ever said a word to me for twenty-three days. Just the nurse that came in and took my temperature. She gave me medicine. That's all I saw was the nurses. At night I used to pick up the gate. There was a gate that came down, and you pick it up. I would pick up the gate and walk to the end and go look out to the water and see the boats and the Statue of Liberty and the Staten Island ferry.

During the day I slept a lot. From the hospital window, there was a big yard. The hospital rooms wrapped around. If I didn't sleep, I would watch all the birds, the seagulls—by the thousands. They used to feed them. They used to throw food to them.

At night was the only time I would run away from my room, because during the day I was afraid they would holler, the male and female nurses, whoever was there. They would holler if I'd try to get out, but I never stayed in bed. I had two lumps, the size of walnuts in my throat. They said it was contagious, but I think they forgot me after a while.

Then my mother got a telegram to come and get me. I remember standing in front of the judge by myself in the big hall. I was ten years old. There were thousands and thousands of people in there. I remember him sitting up high. "All right, you sit there," he said. I sat there . . . My father had to find me amongst all those people, but I knew him after having seen him from the ship. I knew he had gray hair. He was only thirty-three years old. There was nobody there with gray hair at that time who looked thirty-three years old. So I knew that it was him.

I didn't know where he was taking me. But I remember that we took the ferry to Lackawanna Station in New Jersey, and then the train to Scranton. He bought me a chocolate bar, a Hershey chocolate bar. That's the first time I ate a Hershey chocolate bar. He bought it on the train. And he was telling me about my mother, where they were, and my sisters. And, of course, I was crying that I wanted to be with my mother.

When I got home, there was a really big feast and I asked my mother what happened, and she said she didn't know anything. The next day, they made sure that I enrolled in school, and they had me go in the first grade. I was too smart for the first grade, you know. But I couldn't pronounce the words properly. Like the A here, was "ah" there, you know, C, "chi." So it was different. And there were no other immigrant kids in my class, so the kids used to make fun of me, call me "dago." Call me all different kinds of names. And, for a while, I wouldn't go to school no more. I stayed home. Then I was sent back, but I didn't go much. I only had three years of schooling in America.

What I learned I learned all by myself. I kept in contact with books. I worked on my English. I promised myself I would never have an Italian accent, because I was afraid of what I went through as a kid. I always made sure my words were perfect. I read a lot of books. There was nothing else to do in Pennsylvania but read.

My parents were very strict. I wasn't allowed out of the apartment at the time. We lived in a four-room apartment in a house, and we three girls slept in the same room. I couldn't go to a movie unless my mother or father took me. And my mother started to have babies, one every year, and she could never take us. My father went to work, so he didn't have time to take us. He worked for the Edison Company, digging the streets to put the new wires. I remember he worked on Thirty-fourth Street [in Manhattan] putting the wires under the ground.

I wasn't allowed to go anyplace. Maybe three or four girls from the neighborhood, we would get together and put records on. That was the only enjoyment I had. Never, never be near a boy.

One sister met the fellow next door and she got married when she was sixteen. The only way she met this boy was because he lived next door. My eldest sister, the dressmaker, went to New York six months after we got to Pennsylvania and got married right away. So at thirteen I was left with my mother. I had to help her with the babies. She had six. One died, but she had five living. I was like a little mother. I had already quit school, and no woman worked in Pittstown. It was a very small town. No woman could go to work whether they were willing or not. Only men were allowed to work.

So, when I was sixteen, I came to New York. I told my father I was going to see my aunt. I never went back.

Rosa Vartone

. . . .

BORN APRIL 4, 1901
EMIGRATED 1924, AGE 23
PASSAGE ON THE *DUILIO*

She was born in Calabria, raised in the country in Laurignano outside Cosenza. She never went to school. From the time she was twelve, she picked olives in the orchard, grapes in the vineyard, until she married and came to America with her husband, who died young. Forced to raise a son and a daughter on a domestic's salary, she never remarried. Now ninety-six, she lives in New York.

It was my mother, my father, my grandmother, my two brothers, and me. My dad's name was Carmino. In English they call it Carmine. He was a construction worker. My mother, she used to do nothing. She would stay home. My father was a tall, husky man. He was good man, a good father, but he was strict with me, especially with me, because I was oldest and I was pretty. I had long hair.

I used to work on the farm. I used to work in the country a lot, you know. A lot of girls working in nearby fields. I used to pick olives, grapes. I started when I was twelve years old. And I got paid. But I always give money to my mother. And he was afraid, my father. Maybe I fall in love with somebody, you know. And he would punish me. He didn't want me to go to church on Sunday morning, the big church in Cosenza. That's where all my friends used to go, all the younger people. My father, he don't want me to go. He insisted I go to the church in the village, in Laurignano, where all the old ladies go. Even there, I had to go with my mother. He was very strict with me.

To this day, I don't know how to write and read. I know just a little bit because my father, he don't want me to go to school.

There was the teacher in the town, but my father, he don't want me to go to school. He said because I was a woman I don't need to be writing and reading. The boys, yeah. He used to push the boys to go to school, but not me.

I feel bad, I feel bad. Then when I started to get big, you know, I told my mother that I like to know how to read and write. She says, "But Papa don't want you to go to school." So what I used to do, when I go to work, I used to take a book with me in my pocket. And then I asked my friend, "Do you know how to read?" And I used to say, "How do you say this? How do you say that?" I could read more than I write. This was accepted in this town. A lot of the girls weren't educated.

I remember when I used to sleep with my grandmother, I take a prayer book in my pocket. She know how to write and read. And she used to teach me a little bit. She says, "I'll learn you, I'll teach you." That's how I know how to read. I read my prayer in the morning and at night. My father never find out.

He want me behind lock and key. Sometimes they used to get together someplace—a young boy, a young girl, you know. And I wanted to go, too. "What are you going to do over there?" Papa says. "Well, we'll all be together," I says. "No, no, no," he says. He don't let me go. Then my grandmother, one time, she says, "I got to say something." She said to Papa, "She's good enough to work in the fields. How come she's no good to enjoy herself a little while?" He say, "You mind your business. She's my daughter."

It's amazing I met my husband. His name was Michael. He was here in America for seven years, and then he come back when he was nineteen. He was born in Italy. I knew Michael as a child. We almost grew up together. He know my mother, my father, everybody.

One day Michael went shopping with his mother and they stop at my house. We talked. They left. He went to the town to play *boccia*. He used to go in the saloon and drink, and meet his friends. My father was there. My father like nobody, but he liked Michael. "I see your daughter," Michael says.

"Yeah, she get big."

"I thought she was married."

"No," my father says. See, back then, the parents marry off their children. So Michael says to a friend who knew my father, "You better tell Carmino, I'm going for his daughter. I like her. She's very nice."

So my father, he ask me if I was interested in marrying Michael. I says, "No." So he says, "No? Why?"

"I don't know," I says. "He no come over here to marry me. He come over here to marry somebody else." Which was true. He was interested in another girl named Rosario. I knew this.

"If you don't marry him," my father says, "forget about it. Make believe there's no man for you, alright?"

I was crying. I feel bad. So then my grandmother, she says, "No, Rosa. Say yes. He's a nice man. We know how he is. We know his family and all."

So again I said, "I don't know."

Then everyday Michael keep coming to my house to visit and one day I confront him. I said, "But you come to marry Rosario."

"No," he says. "I'm here for you. I marry who I want to marry. Will you marry me?"

I said, "Yes."

We were married within two months. This was 1924. I remember my wedding. It was in my house. No hall. A big dinner. Everybody happy. Michael wanted me to wear a veil and a white dress and everything, you know. But my father, he don't want it. He says, "Why? You don't need it, why?" I got married in a velvet dress, a green velvet dress I had.

Two months after the wedding we come to America. We live at my mother-in-law's house. We were one room. But our bed was all closed with a canopy. A little privacy, that's all.

I liked being married at the beginning, but then everybody was disappointed when Michael said he would take me to this country. I feel a little bad for my mother and my grandmother and my father and my brother, you know. I'm going to leave everybody and I don't got nobody in America. My husband used to say, "But you got me."

All people talked was, "America, America, America." My father, he said, "You want to go with Mike to America?" I says, "Well, he's my husband. I got to go with him. I can't stay here by myself." So he says, "You're going to feel sorry if you go over there."

"Why?"

"Because you're used to being outside in the field. Over there, you got to stay in the house all day. You never see the sun. You're not going to like it." And to tell you the truth, in the beginning when I come over here, I didn't like it. I felt like I was in jail. I miss everybody. I was crying every day, you know. And then I get used to it.

Mulberry Street, 1900

(NATIONAL PARK SERVICE: STATUE OF LIBERTY NATIONAL MONUMENT)

We took a trunk. Some clothes of mine and Michael's. And we take a suitcase, that's all. We took the train from Cosenza to Naples. I never was in Naples. I never was in anyplace. It was dirty, Naples. I didn't like it. Then we take the boat. We had a little cabin. Third class, all the way down.

Nine days on the boat. It was terrible. Nine days I was sick. Nine days I don't eat nothing. I was sick every single day. The weather was bad. The boat was swaying left and right and left . . . A lot of people were sick. They used to come with the milk. They used to come with big containers of milk, and a little cup. "Anybody want some milk?" As soon I take it, I throw up right away. The ship doctor give me an injection. He give me some pills, but they no help me. Every morning they used to come, and say, "C'mon, c'mon, go outside, get fresh air." Otherwise the people sat down there, they sat on the floor. It was bad.

When we reach over here, everybody shout "*Statua Liberta, Statua Liberta!*" But because the boat stopped, I felt better. That's the only thing I knew. When we got off, I told my husband I was hungry. He say, "Well, it's about time you told me you're hungry."

They made us open the suitcase, the trunk to see what's what. Then we stand in line. Everybody. There was a woman, I never forget. She gave me a towel and says in Italian, "Take off your clothes. Take everything off. Socks, everything. You got to take a shower." I go take a shower. They fumigated the clothes. I feel ashamed. I feel bad. But we was all women. My husband was with the men. It was crowded.

Michael was a citizen, so they say he could go. But I had to stay overnight. They couldn't find my name on the list. I don't know why. Michael says, "I'm not going to leave her. I stay here. We leave together

tomorrow morning." I slept on a cot in a room. It was all women. Everybody was speaking Italian. Nobody speak English.

The next morning, in New York, we take a cab to some cousin's house on the Lower East Side. First Avenue. Michael's cousin. Where he lived for seven years when he was here. We stayed for three or four months, then we find an apartment.

Michael worked for a shoemaker. He was shining shoes, then later fixing shoes. I used to work in a factory that made men's pants. So we made a living. I used to go shopping on First Avenue. All the pushcarts. All the Italian people. But I was afraid at the beginning, you know. I wanted to go back in the apartment. But then I get used to it, and I thought, "So this is New York. Oh, my God."

We had a son and a daughter. During World War II, Michael went into the service, the American Legion. He come out and he get sick. He had a stroke. He was a veteran so he was in a government hospital for two years. He was forty-four when he died.

I was thirty-eight. I had to raise and support my children by myself. Thank God I had the relief, government checks, because Michael was a vet. And then I used to do a little work here and there, housework and all. A domestic. They don't give you much. But I get along. I get along still today.

After thirty-three years, I went back to Italy. I wanted to take my mother over here, but she don't want to come. She don't want to come. And I didn't want to stay. I don't like it. Everything looked different to me, because I get used to over here. I don't like it no more. My father was dead. My mother was still alive.

Mama says, "Come back over here." I says, "No, Mama. Then I got to go work in the field again, Mama." I says, "I can't do it no more." You know?

Regina Rogatta

BORN OCTOBER 20, 1923
EMIGRATED 1928, AGE 4
SHIP UNKNOWN

She was born in Ribera in the province of Agrigento. She grew up in Astoria, Queens. After graduating from high school, she studied at the Katherine Gibbs Secretarial School and became a secretary. She has one son from a previous marriage, two grandchildren. She remarried in 1978. "I've had a full, good life here," she said. "And I'm very grateful to my gutsy parents."

The town was a typical Italian town. Family members all lived very close together. My uncle Lawrence lived nearby with his children, and we would spend all the holidays together. It was a very loving childhood that we grew up in. My grandmother lived with us. In the end, she had a stroke. She owned the house, and then the house was passed down to my father.

My father spent most of his time going back and forth to America because there wasn't enough work there for a carpenter. Practically all of the Rogatta family were carpenters, and they were master carpenters. And he'd come back and forth every couple of years. That's why all my brothers and sisters are spaced two years apart. My mother became pregnant every time he came. [Laughs.]

It became too burdensome for my father to keep coming back every couple of years. You know, that boat trip was no joke. And monetarily, it wasn't feasible for him to be spending all this money. Then my uncle Lawrence told him one day that he should take the whole family back with him, because my mother had gotten very sick. Someone told her that he wasn't coming back, that he had found a woman. And that wasn't true. This person made up the story.

But my uncle says, "This time it's just a rumor." He says, "Go back with him and make your life over there, because next time it might come true."

We went to Palermo. I don't remember the trip. Lawrence escorted the five of us to Palermo, and then we came to America from there. I was the youngest. The oldest was twelve.

I was told about a terrible storm. When we hit the Strait of Gibraltar, there was this terrible storm that broke out. It lasted three days. The water was so rough that the waves, my sister tells me, almost capsized the ship. She said that it went over the ship, actually. She said they saw the whales. First they thought they were sharks, but it was whales because everybody was screaming in Italian, "Whale. Whale." But she said that these old women were throwing their medallions in the water and getting down on their knees and crying, just praying to God to calm the waters. See, that I don't remember, but they tell me about it and four of them said the same thing, so it must have been a horrendous thing because I blocked it out completely.

We weren't in the hold. We were in a cabin. The captain and the people in the next cabin used to look out for us because we were five children by ourselves, you know. So my uncle must have spoken to the captain and told him to keep an eye on us or whatever, because we were treated royally. My sister said the captain used to take us into the dining room and he used to tell my brother, "Eat, eat," he says, "because if you don't eat you'll die." He was throwing up all the time, and he couldn't stand to eat anything.

There were a lot of people, all class of people. Some just came with what they had on their backs. They didn't even have baggage. And they were throwing up, and if you wanted to faint, there wasn't room for them to faint. They couldn't lie down on the floor. There was no space.

I remember New York Harbor. It was the most beautiful sight in the world because we didn't die in that storm. We were alive. [She is moved.] We made it. We were in America, a free country. We would be reunited with our parents.

I remember being disgusted by the water. We were used to the blue Mediterranean, and here I see this monkey green, dirty water, you know. "Where are we?" you know. It looked so dirty compared to the beautiful blue waters of Italy.

My sister said there were hordes of people, and then this doctor and the nurses. They were standing on the steps. And they would watch people because there were such hordes of people, they didn't have time to examine each and every one. Just by the looks of them, they would pull people out from the crowd, and then they would examine them. But we came through without any problem at all. The only thing, they said they examined our heads to look for nits, and we were clean, so we were sent right through. And we were healthy-looking. You know, we all had nice rosy cheeks. [Laughs.] We were lucky. There were many that were sent back. And my sister said some of them were jumping off the boats because they were told to go back, and they were committing suicide. Just the thought of that voyage going back and not being able to stay in this country. We were the lucky ones.

My father came to meet us at Ellis Island. Oh, my goodness. I'm all choked up. I can see that almost vividly. We were in this big room. And they call your name out. And when they called "Rogatta," [very moved] my father came running through the turnstile, and he squatted on his knees with his arms outstretched, and the five of us ran into his arms, and we were kissing and hugging. We were so happy to be together. He said, "We're all together now. We'll never be apart again."

Josephine Sorvino

. . . .

BORN MAY 20, 1920
EMIGRATED 1932, AGE 11
PASSAGE ON THE *ROMA*

She was born in southern Italy in the farming village of Comparni near Calabria. Her first name was changed to "Sunday" at Ellis Island because she arrived on a Sunday. She has two children, two grandchildren, and lives with her husband in North Merrick, Long Island, where she spends her days writing, and has already finished an unpublished novel about her immigrant experience. "I thought America was like a heaven," she said, "full of kings and queens and princes, and everybody was so rich."

I had one brother. He was almost five years old when we came here. At the time, it was just my mother, my brother, and I. My father was already here. He came here first in 1921. He had not seen my brother, his son, until we came here in 1932.

I had a great-grandmother who lived two doors away from us. She and I was constantly together. We used to take walks to her land. She owned a beautiful piece of land that was sloped. It had olive trees, and it was surrounded by hills and mountains. During the evening she came over to our house, and we sat by the fireplace, and she told me so many stories, so many fairy tales.

I remember, well, she told me about Cinderella. She told me about Moses. But one thing I do remember is when we left Italy. A few days before, she and I took a walk to her land and she was very, very sad. She said, "Ah." She said, "You're going to America now. Some day you will remember me. But," she said, "remember when you get there, when you reach the Battery, there is a row of fountains there. But do not drink out of it. Because if you drink from that fountain you're going to forget all about us."

So when I arrived at the Battery I was looking for the row of fountains, but I didn't see the row of fountains. So I thought, I guess it must be okay. She also wanted me to write and tell her about the Brooklyn Bridge, because she had heard about the Brooklyn Bridge, but she died before I saw the Brooklyn Bridge. Today, when I'm driving along, many, many times I think of her. The words echo in my memory. "You're going to America now. Some day you will remember me."

Elda Torini
. . . .

BORN SEPTEMBER 25, 1927
EMIGRATED 1947, AGE 20
PASSAGE ON PAN AMERICAN AIRLINES

She was born and raised in the winemaking town of Vittoria in southern Sicily. She was engaged when she came to New York by plane, to join her husband-to-be, Vini Spagone, who was present during this interview. They live near Hartford, Connecticut.

I remember when Mussolini came to my town. I was young. Vittoria was a very good place for wine, and he was impressed by this big fountain of wine, you know. But it was not scary. Everybody was free, everybody kept open doors. Nobody's scared. We used to go to the beach. I never was afraid.

My father was a winemaker. He worked for a vineyard. He was about six feet tall with dark hair. When he died, he still had dark hair. And he was a nice-looking guy, nice educated. He liked music, he liked operas. My mother, she's old-fashioned way. She like cooking and sewing. She lives in Florida now. He and my mother used to get along all the time good. They were married about forty-eight years.

Our house was right in the town. We were city people. My grandparents, my father's mother and father, used to live with us. I was very close to them, more so than my sister. But then she was eight years younger than me. I had one sister.

My grandfather used to cook my breakfast in the morning and take me to school every morning. I was very close with him. I don't even want to go to my mother, I want to stay with him all the time. My grandmother, too. My grandfather was a tall guy, but he was blind. Something happened, they took it out, and he was blind. But he knew where to go. He was a very smart guy. He used to tell me so many stories because he was in America, too.

He show me so much affection, you know. Sometimes we used to go to the store for a haircut. He used to take me, because my father was working all the time. He used to buy me a grinder on the way, mortadella in a small bread. I used to love that, you know. And then he says, "Okay, now you sit over here, and I want you to read this book." So I started reading, and then all of a sudden I got tired. I figure my grandfather can't see. So I skip a couple of paragraphs. And he said, "Doesn't sound right. Go back where you come from." So I had to do it all over again. My God, I couldn't fool him at all, you know.

My grandmother went to church all the time. She say, "You got to come with me."

When I was hungry, she had a bread inside there [she gestures inside her blouse], and she'd say, "You hungry?" She used to put it underneath her blouse all wrapped up. She say, "You hungry? Here, a piece of bread." [She gestures again.] "A piece of cheese?" [She gestures again.] "You thirsty?" [She gestures again.] And she gave me a little bottle of water. Everything I wanted. I remember that.

My mother, she wanted me to go to school, and that's how I could have a good education. I didn't graduate from school because I got married. I was going to finish my school. That was 1947. I had to drop out school. My husband and I, we are first cousins. My husband visit us in Italy, and that's where we meet each other. But I never met him before.

My husband came to see his parents, his aunt. I invited all my friends from school to my house for a party. He came. And somebody came with an accordion, another came with the drum, another came with the violin. They started playing. So that night we had a good time, you know, we danced, and I guess we fall in love. I had long hair, long nails. I was good-looking. [Laughs.] Now I'm old.

VINI: My parents were Sicilian. My father came from Vittoria, and my mother came from Siracusa. They came here. I was born and raised in Hartford, Connecticut. I always heard the stories that my father told me about Italy, how the food grows and how everything was so nice, but there was poverty there because those were the days before a lot of progress was made.

I joined the navy. I was part of the Sixth Fleet in the Mediterranean right after World War II. I was aboard the light cruiser *Huntington*, and the home base happened to be in Naples. It came to the point where I was able to get a two-week leave to go visit my aunts down in Vittoria, Sicily. I went down there. Elda was my first cousin, but I had no intentions of getting serious with her. The courtship actually began after I left. I wrote a letter to my father, I says, "Pa, you know them well because it happens to be your sister, the mother." And I says, "Do you think that maybe they might be interested in my getting serious with your niece?" Because it's not an everyday thing that cousins marry. But they were very delighted about the whole situation. I wrote to her about joining me in America.

ELDA: I wrote back. I say, "I don't think I want to go to America. I got everything here. I got to finish my school." But I think it over, and my mother said, "If you go to America you'll be better off." So I wrote him again and I said, "Well, before I decide, I want to see you again."

VINI: I saw her about nine months later, because I was at sea, going from Philadelphia to Naples, back and forth. We were still little kids, really. I wasn't even twenty-one. I was in the navy until my twenty-first birthday. I got in at seventeen. So as far as emotions go, I really wasn't that serious about it.

ELDA: When he came, he stayed about two weeks. But we never went out by ourselves. We go with my mother, you know. [Vini laughs.] That was the old-fashioned way.

VINI: We had your grandma, too.

ELDA: We had a big party before I left. All my friends from school, they all came, they all cry. We all cry, because they don't want to leave me. But I made up my mind, that's it. And my mother, she was so happy that I come here. My father, he feel the same way.

I just took a suitcase with a few nightgowns and underwears, just clothes. My mother gave me a couple of sheets. That's all I had. I had to go to the consulate for a passport, vaccinations, and the paperwork. In Palermo they had a consulate. Just in case he didn't marry me when I got to America,

my parents deposited $500 so I could come back to Italy. That was the law then.

My father paid for my passage from Vittoria to Messina across the straits to mainland Italy. I went by train to Rome. That was the first time I'd been to Rome. I never was in Rome before. I just went to the airport. So I didn't see nothing. Years later, my husband took me on vacation there to see it. [They laugh.] Then I flew from Rome to Lisbon to New York. On Pan Am, Pan American. There were fifty girls coming here, all on the same plane. All a similar age. Going to marry or meet their boyfriends who were soldiers or in the navy. Nobody else was in the plane. Just us fifty girls.

But the plane had trouble. One motor was out of control because there was a big storm. So we stopped in Lisbon one night. The next day they took us, and we stopped in Canada. Me, I was sick like a dog on the plane. Oh, my God. I thought I would never make it here. The first time I'd been in a plane. I mean, I had never been more than eight miles from my house and here I was going to America . . . From Canada we were supposed to go to Idlewild, the international airport. That's where I was supposed to meet my husband. But we landed at LaGuardia. One of the girls was met by her boyfriend, and he gave her a mink coat. I thought, "Wow! A mink coat!"

VINI: We just missed each other.

ELDA: I thought, "Oh, my God. What am I going to do?" . . . Then I was taken with all those girls to Ellis Island, but we didn't know where we was going to end up. We started crying. We got in the ferry. Suitcase, all ripped up, three days being up and down. We carry everything, and we got to this place. And there was a big, big room with all the beds and they say, "This your bed, this your bed." Oh, my God, we started to cry . . . In the morning, a breakfast like I never saw in my life. The dining room was full of all kinds of foods. Pancakes, French toast, sausage, bacon, and all kind of Danish. Unbelievable! But me, I didn't want to eat because the black men, they served, and I was scared. I never saw any black people. So I didn't want to have nothing. A lady who worked there said, "You know, you'll be here for a couple of days, you should eat." I said, "I don't care. I just want my boyfriend. I want to get out of here."

I finally sent a telegram to my mother-in-law.

VINI: I was waiting with my father and a friend of the family at Idlewild, the international airport. And we waited and waited, and we didn't see anything happening. We spent the whole night at the airport. Finally, we found out that they were being held on Ellis Island, and we were instructed to go down to the Battery, which was where the ferryboats from Ellis Island bring the people. I was worried, because my father, he came through Ellis Island a long time ago and he

says, "My gosh, I hope she's going to be all right there. I hope it's not going to be bad." On top of it, there was a snowstorm. This was the end of December 1947. The snow was about twelve inches high.

ELDA: So I was sitting there reading a book when that lady says, "Elda Torini." I says, "Yeah!" I'm screaming. "We got good news for you. Your boyfriend is coming . . . The ferry leaves at three o'clock. But when you get there, don't move. Stay with everybody else . . ."

When I got off the ferry, I spotted him. She said, don't move. And it was snowing, it was freezing. I had never seen snow in my life. And I was wearing a spring coat and high heels. I didn't find no boyfriend to bring me a mink coat. [Laughs.] But when I saw him, I says, "I don't care," and I broke away and ran in the snow to him . . . We went to Hartford. A few days later, January 12, 1948, we were married.

3

. . . .

Northern Italy

(APPROXIMATELY 620,000 IMMIGRANTS, 1892–1954)

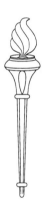

Italian immigrant at Ellis Island

(NATIONAL PARK SERVICE: STATUE OF LIBERTY NATIONAL MONUMENT)

Carla Martinelli

. . . .

BORN JUNE 3, 1896
EMIGRATED 1913, AGE 16
PASSAGE ON THE *COLUMBUS*

*She came from the poor village of Pietragalla near Potenza. She emigrated with
her father, brother, and sister, seeking work. All the men in her family were
barbers, including her husband, an immigrant Italian, whom she met here.
They settled in Newark, New Jersey and raised three children. The years have
taken a toll on her memory.*

Pietragalla was a small village. My parents and grandparents all grew up in this village. There was nothing there. Just a church. I used to sing in the church. I was practically living in the church. We go to church all the time, very religious . . . Very poor. Not much people in the village. The young people wouldn't stay there. People work on the farm because there was nothing there, no work. People, they go to the other towns to work, or they farmed vegetables, olives . . . They grew for their families, not to sell.

My *papà mia* was a barber. He went to America twice, back and forth. I was young. He went to get work. Make money. I forget the dates . . .

I went to school. I went to fourth grade, and then I don't want to go to school no more. We had a different school for the boy, and different for the girl. We didn't go together like here. I didn't like school. We had a little store, and I worked with my *mamma mia* in the store. We all did. My five sisters and my brother . . . I used to go to the fountain in the village and wash clothes. Beating the clothes with a stone and the water. All the villagers did this. People carried fresh water in jugs on their head. That's all we had at that time . . .

When I was sixteen, I was supposed to marry a man in Italy, but I didn't want him. My mama tell me, "Either you marry this guy or you go to America." But I told her, "I don't like him." She say, "Then you go to America." That's why I came to America. There was nothing in Italy, nothing in Italy. That's why we came. To find work, because Italy didn't have no work. Mama used to say, "America is rich, America is rich . . ."

My mama didn't come to America. *Papà mia* didn't want her to come and scrub floors. At that time, ladies scrubbed floors. He says, "Your mama not coming here to scrub floors . . ."

We left in 1913. Me, *papà mia*, my brother Rocco, and sister Carmella. A girlfriend from my village also came. I forget her name.

We did not bring much here. I had an old dress, this and that. I wore a long dress with puffed sleeves, white, and a kerchief I had . . . All I remember about the boat was the water coming in, the waves, and sitting there down below, way down in the ship. Sitting on the floor eating. *Papà mia* gave me macaroni. "You've got to eat! You've got to eat!" he say.

When we get to New York, to Ellis Island, I say "God bless, God bless." We passed the examinations and everything was all right. One of my uncles, he was a lawyer, and he was up in the balcony. And he came down. Then we got in the ferry to New York. Then to Brooklyn. I had an aunt, one of my mother's sisters, in Brooklyn. She had extra two rooms. One was for my brother and my father. And one for me and Carmella . . .

Soon after, I went to work. It was a bread factory. They were making the bread in a big factory in Brooklyn. One of my uncles brought Carmella and me there. My father became a barber. My brother, too. It was a barbershop in Brooklyn. My whole family were barbers. My grandfather was a barber. Later, my husband was a barber, my brother-in-law was a barber. All the men . . . Then we moved to the Bronx. After I got married I moved to Newark . . .

I wrote mama all the time, though. After I came here I wanted to go back. I wanted to see my *mamma mia*, and, in 1948, I went to Italy. I went back. To visit. For the last time.

Amelia Giacomo

. . . .

BORN APRIL 28, 1909
EMIGRATED 1916, AGE 5
PASSAGE ON THE *CASERTA*

She came from Lucca near Florence, one of seven sisters and two brothers. She met her father for the first time when she arrived at Ellis Island. They settled in San Francisco. In 1941, she married a Michigan salesman, and in 1961, started an import business that was eventually taken over by her son and purchased by Hallmark. "I had a good life," she said. "I'm delighted I came. It was wonderful, . . . the dreams of my parents really did come true."

My dad decided he had had enough of poverty, and with eight children, he wanted them to have a better home, a better life, and America was known as the Land of Opportunity. My father was a gardener for a wealthy doctor. The doctor financed him, and he went to San Francisco with my older brother. They left in 1912 and they got a job with Italian Swiss Colony in San Francisco. They farmed the land and sold the produce, and they got room and board there, and a stipend. And the stipend they saved so they could send for us—me, my mother, my six sisters, and my brother, who was sixteen years old.

We were scheduled to come to America on the ship *Anconia*. Our passports were ready. But my brother had not gotten his military waiver. And we could not leave until he did. So we had to postpone the trip. And we were all real disappointed and real upset because we didn't know when it would come. Two weeks later it came, but as I say, we had canceled passage on the *Anconia*. And then we found out the *Anconia* was torpedoed and sunk—no survivors.

I've been a fatalist ever since. I give my mother a lot of credit because, through it all, even when we found out about the ship being torpedoed, it had no effect on her at all. She said, "If we're destined to be there, we're going, and this is what we're going to do."

We boarded the ship *Caserta* instead. In Genoa. And then it went to Naples and filled up. The voyage was a harrowing experience. It was during the war. We had a lot of safety drills. And, naturally, we came steerage, and believe me, it leaves a lot to be desired. I remember this officer on the boat. One of my sisters reminded him of his daughter, so we got to do galley duty as a family. We peeled garlic, we peeled pota-

toes, we cleaned vegetables, and he gave us first-class food. We really lucked out.

I also remember, when I got on the boat, my mother took a liking to this gentleman because he was so knowledgeable about Ellis Island. We knew you could be deported or detained if something was wrong with you. It was well known what you had to go through, so it was important that we all stay healthy and all be examined. He spoke Italian. Well, one day, we took a walk on the boat. I was only five years old. And he said, "You know what? When you get over to Ellis Island they're going to examine your eyes with a hook," and he says, "Don't let them do it because you know what? They did it to me—one eye fell in my pocket."

Marianne Riga

. . . .

BORN AUGUST 30, 1913
EMIGRATED 1920, AGE 6
PASSAGE ON THE *DANTE ALIGHIERI*

She came with eight members of her family from Turino, Italy. They were detained at Ellis Island for ten days. They settled in Woodcliff Lake, New Jersey. After graduating from high school, she worked as a comptometer operator (using an adding machine) for Dunn & Bradstreet. She has two daughters and three grandchildren, and lives in New Jersey with the man she married sixty-six years ago. "My father felt America had been very good to him, and I feel the same way," she said.

My grandmother had come to the United States prior to World War I, sometime around 1914. At the end of World War I, her husband, my grandfather, passed away. She was now left with two young teenage sons she had left in Italy, and two older sons, one of whom was my

father. She decided to return to Italy to live. She came back and found Italy in a terrible, devastated condition, and she couldn't reconcile to it because she had become used to the American ways. She decided to sell the property she owned in Turino, which was the apartment house we lived in. So she sold the property and she said to my father, "Come with me to the United States. You can do better in the United States. I will pay your passage, and you come with me."

In January 1920, we sailed to the United States. There was my grandmother, and her two young sons, my uncle John and his bride, my aunt Mary, and my mother and father, my brother Aldo, who was four years old, and myself. I was six years old. We came together.

I remember that my grandfather, my maternal grandfather, was accidentally killed a week before our sailing date, and my mother was very upset. She was so terribly weak all the way across because of the loss and because she was leaving all of her family behind.

My father was very glad to get away. [Laughs.] We had a very hard time in Italy during the war. My father was working in a government machine shop, he was a machinist, so there was never the threat that he was going to be enlisted, but conditions were very bad. There were days that we didn't have anything to eat. And I remember my parents talking about standing for hours on line to get a loaf of bread.

We left from Genoa. I remember going into the dining room to eat and there was a storm at sea, and things in the dining room sliding around and having to hold on, you know. I remember them serving us tea, which was very strange to us 'cause we never drank tea. We were only used to coffee.

I remember it was a cabin and we had like four bunks, for my mother, my father, my brother, and I. My mother became ill from seasickness. She was the only one. She was very weak when we came, and we had a long crossing, about two weeks. She couldn't hold food down and she couldn't stand up and she had to lay in the bed all the time.

I remember getting into New York Harbor and my father running around to the cabins and saying, "Come up. Come up. We're going to see the Statue of Liberty." It had no meaning to me. But it did to him!

We were put on a ferry to Ellis Island. They put my mother on another ferry and took her to an isolation hospital on Hoffman Island. [Hoffman Island, off the coast of Staten Island, had a quarantine facility.]

My first vivid impression of Ellis Island, of being in America, is when they tried to remove me from my father to send me with the women while he and my brother stayed with the men. I was absolutely frantic. My mother was gone and now they were taking me away from my father! Of course, my father refused to let me go, but he spoke no English. One of my uncles did and he went to the authorities to see what could be done.

It was finally settled that my father sign some papers whereby he assumed full responsibility for my welfare and that's when I was told I could live with him and Aldo in the section with the men.

I was greatly relieved. My father was very watchful of me because there were all types of men, all nationalities, all walks. We were in this huge room, and it was filled with men! Some of them were not being let in for whatever the reasons.

My father had sisters in the United States, and when one of them came to visit, he said to bring a harness to him the next visit. He put the harness on me and tied me to the belt of his pants, so that I could only wander a certain distance. That's how he kept me for the whole time we were at Ellis Island.

Of course, the first night my father refused to take me into the sleeping area. The authorities would come and take Aldo and I and my father in the evening after we had our dinner. And they would bring us to some building that they were still working on. And we were put in a room with three single beds and a lavatory. And they would lock us in, and we would spend the night there. In the morning, a guard would unlock the door. By that time, we would be up and dressed, and take us back into the main room again.

We took our meals with everybody else. I remember the white bread. We hadn't seen any white bread. It was a novelty. It was on the table for everybody to help themselves.

We were there ten days, all told. We were very fortunate because we would get visitors every day. And they would bring us something. Little toys. I remember my brother got a mouth harmonica and I got a little doll, a mirror, and a comb. So Aldo and I would pass the time with whatever items they brought to us.

We didn't see my mother until the day before we left. They brought her from the hospital on the ferry to us, and then, when we were all together, we were finally processed, and we left. We were brought to my grandmother's home. She had already rented a large apartment for all of us. It was in New York City on Thirty-seventh Street. I remember the apartment because it was huge compared to the two rooms we had lived in in Turino. It was like being in an auditorium. What a big place to live, you know?

We stayed with grandmother a very short time, until my mother and father found an apartment. My father got work relatively quickly as a machinist. I remember we moved somewhere on Ninth Avenue because I remember the elevated trains! Ninth Avenue at that time had elevated trains.

We had a cold-water flat. [Laughs.] I think that's what they used to call it. We had a kitchen and two bedrooms, and I don't think there was any kind of a living area. We lived in the kitchen.

I started school. I have very little recollection of the school, except that I would sit there and not realize what was going on at all. I remember one day, my father refused to have any other papers except American papers, newspapers. He was going to learn English and he refused to have any Italian papers in the house. I would look at the papers he would buy. It was a paper that ran a lot of pictures so that it would help him to understand what he was reading. It was like a revelation to me to be able to look at those words, and I *knew* what it meant. To this day I can still remember that.

We stayed for about two and a half years until we moved out to northern New Jersey. To Woodcliff Lake, which was very Italian. And that's where I grew up.

Nina and Edward Hemmer

. . . .

BORN DECEMBER 30, 1913 AND JULY 18, 1912
EMIGRATED 1925, AGES 11 AND 12
PASSAGE ON THE *PRESIDENT WILSON*

The Hemmer family heritage is Slavic. Their mother died young, and the two siblings were raised by their father's sisters in Fiume, Italy near the Yugoslav

. . . .

border on the Adriatic coast. In America, their father became a very successful banker on Wall Street. They grew up on Central Park West in Manhattan and attended private school. Despite speaking broken English when he first arrived, Edward became the first student in the history of New York state to get 100 percent in the advanced Regents tests. "They had a special committee see if they could take off a point in grammar," he said. "But they couldn't find anything wrong with my English."

NINA: I was born in Hamburg, Germany because my father was a coffee merchant. And even though his home city was Fiume, Italy, he traveled, and Mother traveled with him. So I was born in Hamburg.

EDWARD: Well, he meant to settle first in Le Havre because the ships carrying coffee came from Brazil, the transatlantic ships, stopped in Le Havre. But he didn't like Le Havre so he moved to Hamburg. I was born in Le Havre.

NINA: There were so many changes at the time. My mother died in 1916 in Hamburg. She was twenty-six years old. I was only two years old. She died of tuberculosis.

EDWARD: It was very common, worse than AIDS today. Before she died, we were shipped to an orphanage in Fiume, just outside town. We were there about two months, so that we wouldn't hear any of the commotion. The talk of the funeral. So we were completely out of her death. Years later, when I asked my father about Mother, he would say, "Oh, let's not talk about foolish things."

I almost died in 1918 from the Great Plague. More than 1 million people died in Europe at the end of the war from dysentery. In those days, they didn't know how people got it. But now we know it came from the human fertilizer they used on vegetables. I was bleeding internally for a month, but I came through. And then, for another month, I was only allowed to eat chocolate and rice, chocolate and rice. [Laughs heartily.] Pudding. I enjoyed that. And cod liver oil. I loved cod liver oil. They had to hide it from me.

We were brought up by my father's two sisters. So our lives were mostly concerned with living with our aunts. We never knew any relatives on my mother's side. We lived in a modern apartment building. Two apartments on each floor and probably four floors. We had a full bathroom. We each had our own room.

Life was very different from America. For instance, children never played in the streets. The streets were absolutely deserted. They had to play at home or in school. You didn't have street crime and so on. Very, very safe. If we went out we were always accompanied by one of the aunts. And we had this park. It was once a prince's private park, and every day our aunt took us there to play. Not in the streets or down by the port. In winter, when the park was closed, we played along the harbor. The weather was not so cold there. I remember when we ran out into the street to touch snow. It was such a rare sight.

NINA: But the economy in Italy was horrible, incredible inflation, and because of this, Father left after the war in 1919 to come to the United States. But again we were separated from him. We didn't see very much of him when he was home, but he was very interested in the children. I still remember him teaching me the "Our

Father" when I was a little girl in a youth bed. You know, he stood over me and he always said to me, "God is greater than your father." You know, for us he was almost a god. Not our aunts. They were more in a subservient position, you know. He told them how to bring up his children. They didn't have very much authority as far as making decisions. He made all of the decisions and they carried them out.

EDWARD: This is where we see things differently. I didn't particularly like it when he was around because to my mind he was dictatorial, very dogmatic, especially the way he treated Nina, very repressive. For instance, she had to say her prayers. He didn't bother with prayers with me. He also insisted she play two hours of piano every day whether she had a calling for it or not, because that was the thing to do for a middle-class family. The girl must learn how to play the piano, things like that. So I was very happy when I was alone or when I was in the park.

NINA: Father spoke five languages, so he was able to get a job in the Italian Commercial Bank in the Foreign Department on Wall Street. He was very interested in the arts and music. He met some of the people from the Metropolitan Opera House and he lived with some of the tenors in furnished rooms. By 1925, he became very lonely for his family and that's when he wrote to the aunts for us to come to the United States. And because our aunts were our only mothers, we didn't want to be separated, so he said, "You come!" In addition, it would have been very difficult for Father to take care of two teenagers, so he said, "Well, then, all four of you come together." Aunt Irma went to the Immigration Council, and the Council said, "You're out of you're mind if you think four people can come from one country!" But he said, "Bring the papers anyway, and we'll put it through for

whatever it's worth." Then he noticed that my aunts were born in Austria, he was born in France, I was born in Germany. And he said, "That's the solution to our problem. Each of you will come on a different quota." The two aunts on the Austrian quota, Edward on the French quota and I on the German quota. That settled it.

EDWARD: I didn't want to leave because I had a girlfriend.

NINA: Aha!

EDWARD: I wrote poetry. She was at the railroad station when we were leaving. That broke my heart. I was dreaming that I would come back on my own and marry her.

NINA: I was heartbroken, because I had quite a few friends. And also each year we received an award if you were at the top of your class, and I always received a beautiful certificate, or book, some kind of an award. And now we were going to a different country where I didn't know the language and I would no longer be head of my class, you know. At the same time, I was very excited. I really missed Father, so I was really looking forward, and he promised us all kinds of things. He said, "When you come here, you will go on horseback, and you will go sailing in the rivers around New York." He promised us all kinds of very interesting experiences.

EDWARD: The only ideas I had of America was the book *Uncle Tom's Cabin*, which I read in Italian. I knew about slavery, about the West—the Indians and so on. We also had a lot of books, romances for kids. Jules Verne, in Italian, I remember. So I had all these great romances and adventures that fueled a lot of dreams in my life.

NINA: It was very disrupting to pack and break up your home. We took, of course, our clothing and some pieces of china that were very special. A blanket or two made from real good wool.

EDWARD: There were a few personal things. Of course, there was pressure to leave things there, but our aunts accommodated us kids. I brought a lot of things [laughs] that I now wonder why I was so attached to them, like greeting cards—they were very romantic in those days—and a few toys. My tin soldier . . .

NINA: I was hoping he wouldn't bring those soldiers because when we played together at home, I was German and he was French, and he would always decimate my soldiers, kill them all off . . . [Laughs.]

EDWARD: We left from Trieste on the *President Wilson*. I believe we came first class. I remember eating in the dining room, and all the dishes would slide off the table because we had ten days of maximum storms. Just unbelievable. Looked like Everest mountain in the sea.

NINA: There were some very poor people with us on the journey, and they would sit on the floor all day long, they were so frightened. And some of them must have been ill because I developed an infection in my eye, which was a very serious and a traumatic experience for me. [Laughs.] Aunt Irma took me to the ship's doctor, and the doctor said, "Oh, this is very serious," you know, "and unless we can clear this up you will be sent back." At that time, people who were sponsored, as we were by my father, didn't have to go through Ellis Island. But we had to on account of this infection.

EDWARD: It's hard for people to understand today what it was like to be on a boat then in a storm like that. Tremendous noise. It sounded as if the boat was heading for rocks. The great waves would smash, the noise tremendous, and I thought we would flounder at any moment. They posted "Captain's Messages" up. At that time, it was Morse code received from other ships in the ocean, saying, "SOS. We are floundering!"

"Help!" I would go up on the captain's deck because I had friends there and I enjoyed the sight, this wild sight, of the ship going way, way down under the sea and then lifting up. And the waves rushing right up to the captain's bridge, a terrifying scene but, as a boy, I enjoyed it, and I wasn't sick.

NINA: The ladies were not allowed on the deck at all. Then, one day, the captain announced we were entering the harbor of New York City and that there was a marvelous statue there that would greet us, and they invited us to come up to the deck. That was one of the happiest days of my life—January 25, 1925. I could see Brooklyn buried in snow.

I remember the Great Hall, and I remember how we had to stand on line in order to see the doctor. There were hundreds of people just from our ship, and hundreds more from other ships. And, of course, Father wasn't there because he wasn't allowed to come until they decided whether or not I would be allowed to remain. But then they examined me and they said that the infection had been cleared, thanks to the doctor on ship, who put drops in my eyes every single day in the infirmary. So, of course, that was another tremendous high, to think that I could [laughs] see Father, you know. We could be united with him after six years.

EDWARD: There was one thing that I resented very much as a kid. They asked the boys and the men to form a line and take out their penises. The doctor went from one man to the other. I didn't know . . . I was brought up very conservative. I resented showing somebody my penis. [Nina laughs.] And besides, they didn't tell us what they were looking for. Now I realize they were looking for sexual diseases, but a twelve-year-old boy? That was ridiculous. I remember being very puzzled and very indignant at the same time.

Angelo Falcone

· · · · · · · · · · · · ·

BORN (IN THE U.S.) OCTOBER 11, 1917
EMIGRATED 1929, AGE 12
PASSAGE ON THE *ROMA*

*After graduating from high school in Astoria, Queens, he was a tile worker and a
waiter at the Pierre Hotel, where he met his wife. They married in 1941. Drafted
in the U.S. Army, he became a sergeant and later a spy for the Allies behind
enemy lines in Italy. "I'm not bragging, but I've killed a few people while I was
in civilian clothing behind the lines," he said. "I even carried ammunition for the
Germans so I could get Mount Casino before the Allies took it. One time, I went
too deep, nearly got blown up. I was captured. Wounded. I wound up in a
hospital in Naples. I got shock treatments to revive me. Then they exchanged the
wounded. That's how I got back. I still have nightmares about it . . . I feel proud
that I have done my part for this country." He lives with his wife in Brooklyn,
New York. They have two children and five grandchildren.*

I was born in Astoria, Queens. I remember being very cold. My father used to go on line to get coal, stand a couple of hours on line. My parents brought us over to Italy, me and my two brothers, thinking it wouldn't be as bad. My father had property over there. I was the oldest. I was five years old.

We went to Cremona, near Milan. It's in northern Italy. That's where my father was from. My youngest brother, Alvin, they put him up in the mountains with my mother's folks. He was about a year old. They split us up. I never saw him. Me and my other brother, Mario, who was two years younger than me, we stayed on a farm with my grandparents, my father's folks, which included my uncle and his wife. My father owned the land. And my uncle and my grandparents were living on it. Then, my father and mother returned to the United States to make a living. My father was a chef, a cook, at some top hotels in New York. They wrote me letters to tell me they were all right.

My grandmother was a little woman. A nice old lady. She wore a black dress all the time. But my uncle, he was a tough guy. He was one tough hombre. He was married. His wife owned a bakery in town. In the mornings, I used to plow the corn and wheat fields with Mario. My uncle used to be in front with the oxen, and I was right behind with the plow. Four o'clock in the morning, we'd work. My grandmother used to come out with a bowl of cornmeal. We lived on cornmeal and milk three times a day. I was six then, Mario four.

We worked till about seven o'clock, [then I would] get on my bicycle and go to town and get bread for my uncle's wife, bread that he wouldn't even let us eat. Then I went to school. After school, I come back and we go pick the corn. I also had to go to church every day, because my grandfolks were very religious. Sometimes in the morning, sometimes late at night or in the afternoon. There was no time for play.

· · ·

By 1929, it was getting a little too rough with Mussolini. My father was afraid for me because they start you young in the military there and I was now twelve years old. Mussolini and the Fascists had come into power and you had to join the Blackshirts. Mario and I became Blackshirts: We had no choice. It was sort of a Fascist version of the Boy Scouts. We actually had to wear black shirts. Not all the time. Not when we worked on the farm. But when we went to school. We went on a trip with other kids who were Blackshirts, and we sang songs, propaganda songs. It was getting a little bit too far, you know.

I did an awful lot of crying. I remember crying so many times. I wanted to go back with my parents, you know. My uncle was working us so hard, no time for anything. And I didn't like this military business. I wanted to get away before I got drafted.

After it was decided we would return to America, Mario and I were reunited with my little brother, Alvin. I remember the day. Mario and I were picking wheat. We were working on the wheat field. We were cutting and tying it up. My uncle came. He said, "Here's your brother." I looked at him. He was about six years old. I didn't know him from Adam. I said, "Hi. How do you do?" He was so quiet. He never said a word. He was scared. Strange place, strange people, you know. "These are your brothers," my uncle said to him. He didn't even answer us.

It wasn't easy to get out of Italy then. But we had American passports. My father paid a woman from the town, a woman named Toma, to escort me, Mario, and Alvin back to America. Toma was coming with her daughter.

We went to the main town by horse and wagon, and then from there, a dilapidated car to Genoa. It was the mayor's car. You could hear it ten miles away. In Genoa, we boarded the *Roma*. But because Toma was responsible for us, she was very strict. We couldn't go up on deck. I remember they had movies on the boat. I'd never seen a movie. But she wouldn't let us see it for some reason.

We were in a big cabin. Way down, I remember, down pretty deep. About a dozen people in there. My two brothers, Toma, her daughter, and some others. I remember most people didn't go to the dining car because they were sick. I know I wanted to go up on deck, but Toma was afraid we'd get lost. I could hear music up there. I could hear the sound of an accordion and everybody singing, you know. So we stayed in the cabin, or not far from it, until it was time to go up and eat.

When we got into New York Harbor, that was exciting, the horn blowing. The Statue of Liberty. Amazing. We'd never seen nothing like it. I didn't have to plow the fields no more, I was thinking. Free in America! It's a feeling that is very hard to explain unless you actually went through it, by golly. Beautiful.

But a lot of confusion. When we got off the boat, more confusion. I had a sack and a dilapidated bag. I remember an officer outside the main building at Ellis Island said, "You go in that big room, and you sit on that bench, and you wait there." Good thing the guy spoke a little Italian. Most of them spoke English. I was scared stiff because, you know, I'd never seen that many people. I was on that bench. Alvin didn't move at all. We didn't want to get lost in all that confusion. And even Toma, she stood there waiting, waiting. "*Aspette, aspette.*" They checked our bags. Then we got examined—ears, eyes, hair for lice—we were all healthy.

We were there a couple of hours when my folks came in. My mother and father. My first thought was, "Are you sure they're your parents?" It had been so many years. I heard my father say, "My kids are coming, they're Americans." My mother went bananas. She was an affectionate woman anyhow. Oh, boy. Everybody crying. Oh, Christ! I get tears even thinking about it, for God's sake.

Part II

THE BRITISH ISLES

4

. . . .

England

(APPROXIMATELY 1.3 MILLION IMMIGRANTS, 1892–1954)

Abraham Beame (Birnbaum)

· · · · · · · · · · · ·

BORN MARCH 20, 1906
EMIGRATED 1906, AGE 3 MONTHS
SHIP UNKNOWN

Born in London, he was an infant when he passed through Ellis Island with his
mother and two brothers. He grew up in the tenements of the Lower East Side.
Despite this, he rose to become mayor of New York City from
January 1974 to December 1977.

My father's name was Philip Birnbaum, but my father changed his name to Beame when he got his citizenship papers. My father and mother were born in Russia, but they lived in Warsaw. He was a Socialist, a very liberal person who fought against any kind of oppression. He was opposed to the czar and his rules. And he was involved with a group that opposed the czar and the cossacks. Well, one day he apparently got word of the fact that he was under surveillance and the police were going to arrest him. So he packed up to go to America and told my mother, who was pregnant with me, to go to her sister in London with my two brothers, and that when he got to America he would send for her. That's how I was born in London.

When my mom, her sister, and I came to America, we lived on the same street on the Lower East Side of New York. At the time, my father operated a restaurant with his brother. That restaurant eventually closed, and then when I was twelve or thirteen years old he was a paper cutter in a factory which cut stationery paper—three-by-five index cards.

We came to America in June or July of 1906 when I was three months old. My earliest recollection is being five or six years old, going to school and living on the Lower East Side. We all lived in tenements. They were known as railroad flats. You had a living room, a kitchen, and one or two bedrooms. I remember we used to sleep three to a bed. I slept with my two brothers. The tenements were heated by coal. But you had to buy your own coal and your own ice to put in the icebox. Vendors would come around and we would buy from them. The apartments were lit by gaslight. The toilet was down the hall. You shared them with the other apartments. I remember one place I lived where the toilet was an outhouse in the yard. Years later I would jest that my father never paid rent because we constantly moved. [Laughs.] We lived on Pitt Street, Essex Street, Orchard Street, Rivington Street, Delancey Street.

They were hustling, bustling areas, but there was always a very warm feeling among the people. Most of them were Jewish immigrants. And they all belonged to associations or credit unions, *noxia*, they called it in Yiddish, where they could borrow money without interest. So the *noxia* were very important. And although my father was very well learned in the Hebrew and Jewish tradition, he was not orthodox at all. I was never brought up that way. Religion was incidental.

I remember going on a vacation trip to Goldberg's farm. That was in Brooklyn. [Laughs.] It wasn't done for our sake. It was done for my parents' sake, so they could take a rest. I remember we used to have what we'd call block fights. One block would fight with another block. They'd throw bottles and milk cans from the roof. I was involved in these things as well as everybody else, and one day I slipped and hit my head against a curb. And do you see this? [Gestures to his head.] I still have the mark where the stitches were, but I didn't go to the hospital. On the corner of Stanton and Rivington Street, there was a drugstore called Kohler's. And I remember standing on a chair while the pharmacist, this drugstore owner, stitched me. [Laughs.] If it were done

in a hospital, it probably wouldn't be as evident as it is now.

But the important thing in those days were the social clubs. And the purpose of the clubs were both social and athletic. We joined the University Settlement on the Lower East Side. That's the oldest settlement in the country. Eleanor Roosevelt was involved at one time or another. It recently celebrated its hundredth anniversary, and Attorney General Louie Lefkowitz and I were both honored. It's also the place where I eventually met my wife. Several of my friends met their wives there.

Part of the purpose of the settlement houses was to keep the kids off the streets. It was the difference between becoming a rowdy and growing up to be a criminal, or becoming a good citizen. And there was a

Immigrant family in a typical "railroad flat" or "cold-water flat" in a
tenement building on New York's Lower East Side

(NATIONAL PARK SERVICE: STATUE OF LIBERTY NATIONAL MONUMENT)

lot of rowdiness at that time. You had to be careful in those days. If you were Jewish and you walked into a non-Jewish area, you might have been attacked, or vice versa. There was always that kind of situation. Racial situations in New York are not a new phenomena. They always existed to some extent. So we'd have block fights, and you had to be careful where you went and when.

The University Settlement offered social activities, athletics. We used to play basketball there. They would put on shows. In those days I was pretty good at recitation, and I recited there and I won some prizes. I read poems like "Gunga Din," "Billy the Kid," and an interesting thing happened. There was something called Boy's Week. And I was asked to recite poems on WOR Radio located in Bamberger's Department Store in Newark. I recited them on the radio, which was in its infancy.

I remember when I went to school I was on the 100-yard relay race team. And to show our prowess, in those days, we rode bicycles. I took a friend of mine from the social club and rode with him on the handlebar. He was heavier than I was, but I rode from the Lower East Side to Times Square and back. [Laughs.] I couldn't do that in a million years today.

Bob (Leslie Townes) Hope

. . . .

BORN MAY 29, 1903
EMIGRATED 1908, AGE 5
PASSAGE ON THE *ST. LOUIS*

Born in Eltham, Kent, England, he grew up in Cleveland and went on to become one of America's most beloved performers of stage, screen, and film. He started out in the early 1930s in New York radio and Broadway shows, living in an apartment on Central Park West and Sixty-sixth Street. He married singer Dolores DeFina (Reade) in 1934, and in 1937, moved to California. He is most famous for his "Road" pictures with Bing Crosby and Dorothy Lamour and his film The Big Broadcast of 1938, *from which the tune "Thanks for the Memory" soon became his theme song. He has entertained American troops overseas in every U.S. conflict since 1942. The recipient of virtually every type of award imaginable, he is listed in the* Guinness Book of World Records *as the world's most decorated entertainer. In 1992, Hope contemplated giving five million dollars to establish "The Bob Hope Family History Center" at Ellis Island, but negotiations weren't successful, and he withdrew the offer.*

My family came to America from England around 1908. Yes, we landed here in April of 1908. We left from Portsmouth or Southampton. I think it was Southampton. My father, who arrived the previous year, was a mason, a stonemason, and he had a job possibility in Cleveland. Building construction. I remember getting the vaccination for the steamship before we left, and trying to run away from the doctor. He caught me. I don't remember much about the trip itself. I was about five years old, for God sake! We were only at Ellis Island for a few hours. But I do remember standing with my mother and five brothers on the boat as it entered New York Harbor for the first time, and seeing the lights and the Statue of Liberty. It was early morning. I was wearing knickers and a cap, and it was cold. My nose was running. I was just a kid. I didn't know what was going on. And I remember looking up at my mother after we passed through inspection. We smiled and kissed and hugged each other because we had achieved this great thing, this rite of passage . . .

Years later, after I made it in show business, vaudeville, I guess I was in my late twenties. I was doing some sort of publicity thing in New York—down near the harbor. I just remember staring out over the water to Ellis Island and the statue, and remember feeling very grateful, very lucky, and saying to myself, "Thank you." Thanks for the memory. That was the first song I sang in the movies with Shirley Ross and it was such a hit, I just kept on doing it. But emo-

Bob (Leslie Townes) Hope, one of the most famous Ellis Island immigrants, passed through Ellis Island in 1908.

(NATIONAL PARK SERVICE:
STATUE OF LIBERTY NATIONAL MONUMENT)

tionally, when I hear it, I think of that day we arrived at Ellis Island. I don't think, in all my years, I ever told anyone that . . .

Thomas Rogen

· · · · · · · · · · · · ·

BORN APRIL 28, 1902
EMIGRATED 1909, AGE 7
PASSAGE ON THE *CARMANIA*

Like something out of Charlie Chaplin's life story, he was raised in abject poverty near the rat-infested docks of the Thames River. His father, who was Polish, had the income of a tailor but the dashing good looks and personality that found favor with women. Rogen is a graduate of the City College of New

· · · · · · · ·

York and is proud of that fact. Today, he lives alone in an apartment on the
Upper West Side of Manhattan. He has outlived both his wife and his two sons.

My parents were born and raised and married in Dobrzyn, a city in northwest Poland, a very short distance from Germany. When I was about nine months old, my mother took me to England. My father went first by himself trying to get enough money for steamboat passage for my mother and me. My father got a job as a tailor. But it was very poorly paid. He was gone about three or four years before he saved up enough money and we could join him. We moved to a slum neighborhood in London.

We had no money to speak of. My time in England was a period of poverty, great poverty. At that time, gas was used for lighting. There was no such thing as electricity, certainly not for us. And sometimes we had no money for the gas. We used to put a penny, a big English penny into the meter, and many is the time that I'd watch the light flicker and then go out, and we'd just sit in the darkness.

My father was a very jolly, convivial person. The ladies loved him because he was so handsome. And my mother didn't like that at all and showed it by the way she spoke to him. As a matter of fact, they were constantly bickering with each other. She'd be jealous of him and suspicious of where he was going and what he was doing. My whole childhood, when they were together, they used to quarrel bitterly. She would accuse him of all sorts of infidelities. I remember that very clearly.

We lived near the docks on the banks of the Thames River. I used to watch the ships from my window moving up and down the Thames. I became so interested in boats that later on, when I had lots of money, I bought a forty-two-foot sailboat which I still have but I can't use it anymore. I'm too old and there's no one but me. Everyone in my family is dead, including my wife, even my two children. My two boys and I, the three of us, used to sail from Florida to Maine.

What I remember most was going to school in England and being constantly assaulted by non-Jewish kids. I encountered a lot of anti-Semitism. I used to have long curls which my mother didn't remove for quite a while because she was so religious. But then she finally cut them when the other boys began to jeer at me mercilessly. On my way to school in England, they constantly would bother me, punch me, and then let me go. Of course, today they might use knives or guns. Then they just used their fists to show I was persona nongrata.

We lived in just a one-room apartment with a wood-burning fireplace. My father would buy small packages of wood. We didn't even have a clothing closet. I remember seeing my father's old clothing—trousers, coats—hanging on nails that were driven into the wall. We were desperately poor in a desperately poor neighborhood. I remember my mother going to the toilet outside in the yard somewhere, the outhouse. There was no inside plumbing. My mother used to fetch pails of water from a well and bring them into the house. She used to scrounge from the neighbors. We didn't have money to buy anything.

The fireplace was rather large, but that was for heating. My mother did her cooking over a kerosene stove, which was very temperamental. It never worked properly. I remember once it caused us to have a fire in the place. We were burned out to the point where I had no clothes. All my clothing was burned.

Funny, I don't recall much about food. I don't recall eating meat. But there must have been chicken, because I can't imagine a Jewish person going without chicken. I remember bread, of course, was sometimes quite scarce. I remember going for two days without any food at all. We were very poverty-stricken. Bread was our staple. We all slept in one room, in one bed.

We had one relative in London, my uncle Aaron, my mother's brother. He used to bring us bananas. That I remember. And, of course, there were rats in our neighborhood. I remember once he somehow trapped a rat and killed it and then wrapped it in a towel and performed a mock service over the rat. He was a character. Kind of a joker. My father was a wise guy, also, so they got along. I never saw my grandparents. The only recollection I have is a photograph of my grandfather standing up against a brick wall in a hospital gown. That's all.

My father decided to come to America when he was offered a job by a cousin who owned a cigar factory in New York. He became a cigar packer, not very skilled labor. He would pack the cigars in boxes and then nail up the boxes. Incidentally, because of his unhappy life with my mother, twice he left home and went to travel to Chicago where he knew somebody. So he came to America not just for the job, but to get away from the domestic situation. I never discussed it with him. When I think of the things we never discussed, I'm curious about how incurious I was. My situation with my father was not one of complete affection. It was a strange thing. I felt a bit awkward with my father. Possibly because of the constant bickering between him and my mother.

After my father left, things got worse. My mother never worked outside. She wasn't the type to get a job. I don't know how we got along. I suppose he sent money. There was no other source of money. She just kept the house very clean. She was

fastidious about that. I do not recall my father writing a letter to us, but if he had, I would have been the one who wrote back because I'd been in school and could write. I was the amanuensis. I was the one who was given the task of writing letters to relatives in America. The phrase they always used to describe America was "the golden land." And so my parents looked at America as the place where there was every kind of opportunity to rise and make something of yourself. To me, America was just a name. I knew nothing about it.

My father went first, presumably to pave the way for our passage to this country. He worked for this cousin as a cigar packer, a very menial job. But he apparently did raise enough money to get us on a steamship. We were very destitute. I remember wearing frayed clothing, cast-off clothing from neighbors. [Laughs.] I remember having shirtsleeves that were stiff from the snot of the kids who wore the shirt.

I remember very distinctly traveling on a railway train from London to Liverpool. My mother, me, and my younger brother, Charlie. The three of us. It was a very black day. The sky was completely overcast, the sea was absolutely black. I remember that clearly.

I remember that the railroad tracks continued on to the dock, where we embarked on the ship *Carmania*. I remember the name of the ship. My mother brought a rolled quilt filled with feathers that she carried with her from Poland. I remember that. There were some other odds and ends, packages—but we had no such thing as baggage or valises. Just bundles and boxes, that's all.

I had seasickness every day. My mother was okay, but that's what I remember most. Throwing up into a jar so as not to disgust the other passengers. We didn't travel steerage, strangely enough. We had a cabin. There was an upper berth in which I slept,

Transfer ferry bringing immigrants to Ellis Island in 1910

(NATIONAL PARK SERVICE: STATUE OF LIBERTY NATIONAL MONUMENT)

and my mother was down below, with a ladder to climb to the top. I remember being rousted out of bed every day by the person whom I called the nurse, who was really the cleaning lady who put things in order. She'd hustle us out. I'd go on the deck with my little jar.

Funny, I don't recall seeing the Statue of Liberty. Certainly, nobody pointed it out to us. I remember seeing little tugboats going in all directions, loud tootings and hootings and so on.

The one thing I remember about Ellis Island was confusion. A lot of movement and people, women wearing babushkas, those kerchiefs and boxes and bundles. I remember officers, officials with blue coats and brass buttons going back and forth. Rows of benches in a big hall with kids running in all directions . . . After Ellis Island, after being processed—we were out the same day, we did not stay overnight—we took a boat to New Jersey, where my father met us. My mother had a sister who lived in

Jersey City, and I thought, "We're finally on land."

Strangely enough, the one thing that struck me was the width of his trousers and how loose they were, flopping around his legs. That struck me at that time about him. He didn't pick me up or kiss me or show any affection for me, you know?

I remember walking up the street to where my aunt lived, and hearing kids on the other side of the street yell, "Greenhorn! Greenhorn! Greenhorn!" How they knew I was a greenhorn I don't know.

We stayed with her for about a month, while my father looked for a place for us to live. We came to New York City. He found a small two-room apartment for us on 114th Street and Lexington Avenue; then later on, a three-bedroom on 121st Street, a lively, noisy, immigrant neighborhood with lots of Italians, Jews, and Irishmen.

I remember an Irish lady, Mrs. Doyle, living on the fourth floor, we were on the second. I used to play with her son, a boy about my own age. He called himself Eugene Muggins Doyle. He adopted the name Muggins, a real Irish-looking guy. But Mrs. Doyle was a big, burly, husky Irish woman and took a great liking to my mother. She loved my mother and used to take her around. "Mrs. Rogenstein, I'll look after you," she said. "I'm your friend." And so on, and she remained a friend of my mother's all the time that we lived there.

It was important to have friends because of the anti-Semitism. It was not just in London, but in New York, too. I remember every time I went to school I passed across a churchyard and would get held up by other kids on my block. Kids were very conscious of their own block and strangers on their block. It was very common that if a stranger came they'd walk up to him and grab him by the scruff of his clothing, and

say "What block? What block?" And then they'd punch and slap you around. It happened to me very often. It was unpleasant but I had no choice.

It wasn't until years later that we had electricity. I remember this was like a great event for us. And I figured I'd have all sorts of bulbs of different-colored lights. I remember when they first installed the electricity. I can remember the guys drilling with their long drills as they passed wires through under the apartments and through joists in the floors.

My parents continued their tense relationship here and right up until the bitter end. My father remained the gay blade. My mother was the opposite. The more he persisted at being himself, the more she hated it. Every once in a while my father would shout and curse in Polish, but as a rule they didn't. My mother spoke Yiddish, but she would fight in Polish. I remember that. Eventually, my mother began to speak English fairly well, and my father went to night school to improve his English. I think they took pride in becoming Anglicized as quickly as possible.

In fact, because of the anti-Semitism, when I became an adult I changed my name from Rogenstein to Rogen. I regret that now. My parents and brothers kept their original name.

All in all, I'm very glad I came here. How glad? In 1932, my wife and I visited England and I came across a cousin of mine who had remained there. He was a house painter. And as soon as I saw him, he was my age and about my size, I thought, "Here, but for the grace of God. Am I thankful," because had I remained in England, the moment I turned fourteen I would have had to go to work. My parents would have insisted on it. Forget college. I would have been like my cousin, a house painter.

Sara Miles

. . . .

BORN NOVEMBER 22, 1899
EMIGRATED 1920, AGE 20
PASSAGE ON THE S.S. *OLYMPIC*

She grew up in poverty in the farming village of Bishop's Waltham.
She settled in Schenectady, New York.

I loved school. I loved geography. I always wanted to travel. I got the urge to travel because of geography in school. But we were poor people. My mother, my father, my brothers, and I worked as laborers on a farm. We worked the cows. And when a cow freshens that means she has her calf, and the calf can't take all the mother's milk. So the farmer, the landlord, would give us the extra milk, which was a wonderful thing because we never had milk. My mother would take the milk and make rice pudding. She also had a box of shredded wheat biscuits, which was quite a treat for us. And on the back of the box was an advertisement about Niagara Falls. That was my first knowledge of America. I had a dream that one day, some day, I would visit Niagara Falls. I didn't know how or when, but I never lost that dream.

My mother grew up in Bishop's Waltham. She had ten children, and all of them lived but one. I was the only girl in a family full of boys. I was more a boy than a girl actually. [Laughs.] I was also the eldest child. None of the kids could get educated. But my mother kept the house clean and saw to it we had enough to eat on such small wages. We were allowed two pieces of bread and butter for "high tea." If the slices were a little bigger than the others, we would [laughs] fight over who was going to get the big slices.

We lived in a brick house with four bedrooms, a kitchen, and a drawing room, which was for company. We didn't use it. Only for special company. There was no electricity or telephone. But there was a fireplace for heating. My little brothers used to roast in front of it in winter. And more than once when I'd gone to bed—I was the only girl, so I had my own bedroom—my father would throw his big overcoat on top of me so I wouldn't get cold. I can still feel that coat.

But we did have a great garden, and we all liked vegetables. We all had our chores to do. We had parsnips that we planted in the fall so we had them in the spring. Green peas always had to be planted, so we had them for Easter Sunday along with new potatoes. That was tradition.

In the summer, we would get up at four-thirty in the morning and walk two miles to pick strawberries, so we had enough money to buy shoes for school in September. In fact, one Christmas my mother had no money, so my grandmother gave me a shilling to go down to the village store and get each of the boys a chocolate candy. We had no Christmas tree, no Christmas ornaments. But we did have a nice piece of beef. My father got it from the landlord farmer. One of his men butchered it. We had meat on Sunday, but Christmastime we had meat for two or three days because the farmer gave us a very generous portion of beef.

When World War I came, my father enlisted in the Red Cross. He worked in a hospital about twelve miles from where we lived. We had bicycles to visit him. My father couldn't help medically, but he could clean the soldiers up and help that way. I was sixteen, and the hospital used to throw out a lot of meat because the men couldn't eat it. So my father told my mother to send me and one of my brothers down there, and with special permission, they would give us some of the meat to take home so it would not be wasted. It was wonderful.

But then, one time my dad said to me and my brother Frank, who was three years younger than me and closest in age to me, "Tomorrow I want both of you to go to the docks and watch the wounded soldiers come in. I want you to see what those men are going through." I never could get that out of my mind. Lots of times I thought, "How terrible"—men right from the battlefield with dirt and mud and blood. Everything. But he wanted us to see firsthand the tragedies of war so we would be grateful for the little we had.

My mother and father were going to come to America. My father had two brothers there—my uncles. But my mother wouldn't come. So I said, "Well, I'm going to go someday. I'm going to write and ask my uncles if they'll send me money so I can come." And they did.

It took quite a while to get a letter across at that time. But they sent me the money. Both of my uncles lived in Fultonville, New York. I promised them I would work until I paid them back. And I did. I went without a lot of things a lot of girls would like such as pretty clothes. I just gave up everything so I could pay that money back when I got here. I waited until the war ended.

In the meantime, I worked in the village store and saved money. I also paid my parents. We all had to. That was the only way all of us could live. The bigger kids had to earn money and pay them.

I was excited about coming here. I didn't realize what it meant. You don't stop to think. You're too young to think what it might mean. My brother Frank came with me. He was an ordinary sort of Englishman. He just got it in his head because I was coming. I said to him, "Now, I'm going. You're not backing out at the last minute, because if you do, it's too bad, because *I am going*, and that's it!" He backed out once, but he finally committed.

There was an agency in the village where we bought the tickets. I don't remember how much they cost. But I do remember that Frank and I were so dumb we didn't know we needed a visa and had to have it signed. We also didn't know we had to pay to get it signed. We rode our bikes into the village and between the two of us, we barely had enough money, almost to the penny, to get that signed. [Laughs.]

My mother and father borrowed a car and drove us to Southampton. The ship was the *Olympic*. We were going up the gangplank when I realized I hadn't kissed my mother good-bye and I ran back. I didn't think they'd let me go back, but they did. [Laughs.] It wasn't a big farewell, because I was planning to come back. I promised my mother I would be back in two years.

We traveled third class, which to me was very nice. I had one little trunk, and one suitcase the people gave me from the village store where I worked. We were in a cabin with four other people. We had good meals, too. It was a beautiful boat. But we got seasick. That wasn't so good. I remember getting out of bed and going up to the deck for air trying not to slip or slide or fall. But everybody was sick, so they didn't care where you vomited. It was terrible.

I think the trip lasted six days.

The first thing I saw in New York Harbor was not the Statue of Liberty, but a billboard for Lipton's Tea. "Welcome to America." [Laughs.] My cousin was supposed to meet us in New York. There was some sort of mixup and my cousin never showed. We didn't have fifty cents. I belonged to the Girl's Friendly Society, who I appealed to for help at Ellis Island. Of course, Frank was with me so there was nothing she could do, but there was a security guard on the boat who was very nice and he gave us five dollars, gave us our breakfast and put us on a milk train to Fultonville, New York. Later on, I wrote him a letter and returned his five dollars and thanked him. He wrote back and said, "I had faith to believe that you would do this."

We got off the train, and there was a drugstore. We asked if anybody knew where my uncles lived. That started the ball rolling because everybody was looking for us. [Laughs.] One uncle had a farm, where he bought and sold meat. Frank stayed with him. My other uncle was just a plodder. He did garden work and he was good at it. He worked for quite a well-to-do estate, and I stayed with him.

I got a job in Fultonville running a machine that made gloves and stockings. Fultonville was quite a place for silk. They had bundles of silk and dyed it. It was a very prosperous little town. The woman who taught me how to run the machine, also owned the business. "Oh," I said, "the machine goes so fast." She said, "Before you get through, it won't go fast enough." [Laughs.] But I liked it.

Less than two years later, I went back to England for three or four months, and lived on the farm with my mother and father. I got my old job back in the village store so I had enough money to get back to America. My dad was always sorry that he didn't go, although my mother wasn't. A few of my brothers eventually came to America. But I kept my promise to my mother that I would be back in two years.

I returned to America and came through Ellis Island again, this time by myself. I returned to Fultonville and got married. I met my husband in church. He was an American. Frank, meantime, worked the farm with my uncle and then went back to Bishop's Waltham. He married his childhood sweetheart, brought her over here, and they went back on the farm to live.

I know I've been much happier and content in America than I ever was in England. When I've been back I've seen how the people are happy in the sadness, because they don't know any different. But I couldn't go back because I know the difference. That's all. My brother Frank died. His wife is still living. My husband and I had my parents come over one summer. They loved it, but they wanted to go back home. Home was England. Older people realize that.

And yes, I did live my dream. I eventually did get to visit Niagara Falls.

Vera Winston

. . . .

BORN SEPTEMBER 6, 1910
EMIGRATED 1922, AGE 11
PASSAGE ON THE S.S. *CEDRIC*

She was born and raised in poverty near the docks in Liverpool during World War I. Her father was a dockhand. When he died prematurely at forty-nine, her

. . . .

family—without means of support—decided to pursue America's "streets of gold." But once here, they experienced a far different fate. Her family separated. She was put into a New Jersey orphanage with her younger sister and brother and eventually became a household domestic, like her mother and older sister. She married twice but did not have children. Today, she lives in Bayonne, New Jersey near her sister Sally, who also came with her from England. "In a sense, my childhood stopped in England," she said. "It has been a hard life. But I still think this is the greatest country. That's why everybody wants to come here."

My mother and father were Irish. They both came from County Louth. He was about six feet with gray eyes and light brown hair. He was very quiet. He worked on the docks in Liverpool as a longshoreman, unloading bags of cement off the ships. Heavy labor. In those days they didn't make bags. They were like flour bags of burlap. And the cement powder was inhaled as you worked, and that's what got into his lungs. It's like the people who were in the mines. He died when he was forty-nine.

My mother had brown eyes and was a real brunette. She had very fine features, and she was quiet, too. Like most Irish, she was very fond of step-dancing. My father, too. That's how they met. She was very young when she married, I think about fifteen or sixteen.

They had ten children. My oldest brother Patrick, my sister Kathleen, Tommy, then John, then Margaret, myself, and Sally. Three others died. My mother had twins, and they only lived a short time. The third one was my brother Lawrence. He died of the flu. It was the time of the great influenza epidemic. But being at war with Germany, they used to call it the German measles. We had different doctors see him. I can remember laying at the foot of the bed, the doctor was there, but my brother didn't survive. He was dead at his pillow.

My first memories are of Whitley Street, which was near the docks and the warehouses. We didn't have toilets where we lived. The toilets were outside in the backyard. And then from there we moved to Vauxhall Road. We lived in a big house. When you walked in the front part it was a store. And then there was a section where we kept the coal for the hearth, the fireplace. There was very little heat. But that's where my mother cooked. And we had a big iron pot where she used to boil clothes in. Outside was a small backyard, where the toilet was. We had two rooms on the first floor and then two rooms on the upper floor. So we all, more or less, slept together. I slept with my sisters. The three of us in one bed.

For fun, we used to play "push broom." We would set the broom a certain way to keep it from falling towards us, and hit it. We had rhymes and songs we'd sing. And when people bought cherries in the spring, we used to save the pits, we wouldn't throw them away. We called them "cherry wops," and we used to hit them up the rainspout of the building. We made use of everything. We saved broken dishes. We used to play house with them, or make believe it was a store and you were selling. We didn't have any toys. I think the only thing we ever had was a top with a string. Birthdays were not celebrated. We used to look forward to Christmas, but all we ever got was an orange in our stocking and maybe a piece of candy. We never had any Christmas trees. People didn't have it then. People were very poor. Liverpool was predominantly Irish. They came over from Ireland because they couldn't make a living. That's why my father came to Liverpool.

During the war, I remember seeing American soldiers walking on Vauxhall Road. And the kids, especially the boys, would run after them. And the boys would sing "Yankee Doodle Dandy," praising them to the sky. We also had to cover our windows at night so the light couldn't shine through. You know, blackouts. Because planes were new then, and there was a fear of air raids.

When I was about nine, I was Miss Work, a workaholic. I loved scrubbing floors, believe it or not. [Laughs.] And I liked reading especially. I had one book. It was called *The Legends of Ireland*. I read that book so many times that I knew it from cover to cover, and that was the only book we had in the house. My parents didn't encourage our education, we just did it on our own. My father didn't read. My mother used to have to read the newspaper for him because he couldn't read it. I don't think he was embarrassed because there were so many people like that in those days. On the other hand, my parents came from the same area in Ireland, so you'd figure if she learned to read why didn't he? But we would never say anything about something like that. There was a certain etiquette. For instance, we did not address our parents as Mom and Dad or Pop. We'd say, "Yes, sir. No, sir. Yes, ma'am. No, ma'am." Very strict. You just had to behave. If we did something wrong we got fanned on our hiney. We got hit. There was no such thing as getting away with something. So we would behave because we didn't want to get hit.

Then, around 1920, my father died. I remember him being laid out in a casket, and I even dreamed about it before it ever happened because he was sick. For my mother, the larger issue became, how would we live? She had no skills, and there was no

work. That's when I started to hear talk about America.

. . .

My mother had a brother in America, but we didn't have much contact with him. She also had a sister in Boston. She just had a picture of her, and my oldest sister Kathleen used to write to her and felt that coming to America was the best thing to do. She was encouraging my mother to come because my mother had no way of making a living in Liverpool. And, of course, all we heard were glowing stories about this country. How you could pick gold off the streets. But my mother never discussed coming here. It just all of a sudden happened. We were going. She sold the furniture. The only thing she brought with her was a Singer sewing machine with a foot pedal. Heavy as it was, that's what she brought. That I remember. I took maybe two outfits. There was no fanfare, no good-bye parties. We just slipped off into the night—Margaret, my mom, me, John, and Sally. The five of us.

I don't recall getting on the boat. But I do remember the name—the S.S. *Cedric*. All five of us were in one room with two wooden bunk beds. There was no porthole. We traveled third class. I remember going up to eat. They had a dining room. And I remember getting so seasick I couldn't go. I was throwing up all the time. There was a little Swedish girl. She was on the boat. She said to me, "You better get up and play, otherwise you're never going to get better." So I figured, well, I'd try it. So I started running around and playing with her and the other kids, and I didn't get seasick any more. The sailors on the ship put up a rope so we could have a swing.

We all had to take baths in this big tub. And they had a disinfectant called CN that they used. The minute they poured that into water it would discolor it green. I remember my sister Margaret and I, the two of us together in the tub. I felt something at the bottom of the tub. So I reached down and found a ring. It turned out it belonged to an Irish girl on the ship, and was given to her by her boyfriend who was with the Sinn Féin. They were against the Black and Tans, who were the English soldiers.

To pass the time, we used to do the step-dancing we learned in school. Some people would sing. We danced and sang because during the trip it was St. Paddy's Day, which is how I remember the month we came—March 1922. Sometimes we would go up on deck, but it was cold and the water was rough. I had a fear the ship would sink like the *Titanic*. My father had a brother who lived in Belfast, and he worked on the *Titanic* when it was being built in

England. And he had said that he wrote on the interior boards of the *Titanic* slurs like "Down with the Pope" and that sort of thing. And that "God punished it. That's why it sank." I prayed there were no slurs on the boards of the *Cedric*.

Ten days later, we got to New York. Everybody wanted to be on deck to see the Statue of Liberty. Although now if I see it, I'm more in awe of it than when I was a little girl. We took the ferry to Ellis Island, but when you're with your mother you don't pay much attention to details. I just remember the main hall, and that we stayed overnight, and that it was crowded. My mother's brother met us. I had never seen him before. All I knew was that he was my mother's brother and that we were in America.

Sally Winston
. . . .

BORN JULY 18, 1918
EMIGRATED 1922, AGE 3
PASSAGE ON THE S.S. *CEDRIC*

*She is the younger sister of Vera, and picks up the story of
what became of them once they arrived in America through the eyes of a child.
Sally, like Vera, never had children.*

I only have one memory of the boat ride. Only one. I remember water, sitting on somebody's lap, and then the bare, bright light of a lightbulb dangling near the bunk beds. I remember that bulb.

At Ellis Island, I remember this great big hall and people, and I remember somebody holding me and it just seemed like so many people. And I remember being frightened, like I wanted to get away

someplace. That was the feeling I always remembered.

Then we got to the house. My mother's brother's house in South Orange, New Jersey. I don't remember how we got there. I just remember my sister Katherine coming to see us. And eating mashed potatoes. I loved mashed potatoes. Katherine would make a hole and put butter in it for me. I remember the sewing machine because to me it was such a big thing the way it was crated, but I don't know whatever happened to it.

The next thing I remember I was at St. Joseph's Orphanage in Jersey City. I was first put in at St. Joseph's with my sisters Mary and Margaret. [Margaret was there only temporarily, before becoming a domestic like her mother.] I remember it being a big dormitory, many beds. And I remember being taken care of by a nun named Sister Ambrose. She was nice to me, but she was also wicked. I don't imagine she was bad. She was just tough. She treated everybody tough, that I remember. To me she was like a force of vengeance. I stayed out of her way. I never got in her way because if you were wrong, that was it. I was also one of the youngest children ever there. I was kept away from the older children because I was young. I was about four years old. I remember this damn parrot that used to call me. It had my name down because I guess I used to play with it a lot. I remember being sick and in the infirmary by myself. They used to bring the parrot in to keep me company.

We were taught to read. We were taught arithmetic. We were taught penmanship so we should have good handwriting. We were taught the regular schoolwork and given religious training. I made my first communion at St. Joseph's. We didn't wear a uniform, we wore a dress. Nothing fancy. Our hair was kept short to prevent lice. But if you had it, they put kerosene on your head to kill the darn things. I must have been about seven at that time.

I did not see my sisters very much. We were kept separate. I used to run and try to sneak to Margaret, but I used to get pulled back and not allowed to go. My mother worked at the orphanage initially. She worked in the kitchen. I used to sneak in to see her. My mother would have to turn me around and send me back, because I wasn't

allowed to do that. It was very regimented. We got punished when there was something wrong, but I wasn't beaten.

I was at St. Joseph's until I was seven, and then I was taken out of there to live with my older sister, Kathleen. She lived on Thirtieth Street and Ninth Avenue in New York City. She was married and had a little girl, my niece, Frances. She had a house full of boarders, and she was the superintendent, her and her husband, Jim. The boarders were mostly her husband's brothers from Ireland.

I remember vividly my mother's sister, my aunt Maggie. I never liked her because she wasn't nice to me. She tried to rule the roost, everything her way. She was kind of rough, but she would visit me when she had the day off. She'd take me on the Fifth Avenue double-decker bus. We'd go up to Grant's Tomb and back. Every time she came we took the same ride, so I used to hide down in the cellar. My sister's husband, Jim, used to follow me down to the cellar. He was kind to me. One time, I hid in the coal bin. He wanted to know why I was there. I says, "I don't want to go on that bus ride again."

I didn't realize that I wasn't born here until I was about twelve years old. And I got mad at the person that told me I wasn't. He says, "You were born in Liverpool, England." I said, "I was not! I'm an American." He says, "You were born in Liverpool, England, Sally." I said, "No, it can't be." So what do you do with a twelve-year-old kid when you tell her she wasn't born in this country? I thought he was being mean. I had no memory of Liverpool. To me this was my country. This was my home. So I had no conception at that age. But I finally had to accept it, and realized that I wasn't born here.

My older sisters had their lives. Vera and Margaret had to go their way because of circumstances. They were eight to ten years older than me. It was circumstances that brought all this about. My mother wasn't around that much. But to me, she was always a tall woman. She had white hair. Her hair was white as far back as I can remember. But she wasn't that communicative. She

was stern in her own way. In later years she became a little more mellow, but I felt sorry for her. As I grew older I felt she was a very unhappy woman, because somewhere along the line her boat didn't come in. She was not a happy woman.

Arthur Bergman
. . . .

BORN MAY 27, 1914
EMIGRATED 1923, AGE 9
PASSAGE ON THE *FRANCONIA*

He grew up in a crowded Liverpool tenement, one of eight children, during World War I. Today he lives in Tamarac, Florida with the woman he married in 1940. They have five children and fourteen grandchildren. "I think the nicest thing my parents ever did was when they brought us to America," he says. "Otherwise, I would never have met my wife."

My parents came from Russia and met in London, which is where I was born. I came from a family of eight children. When I was three years old, we moved to Liverpool. It was during World War I. The Germans were bombing London with zeppelins. In those days they didn't have planes. They used zeppelins, blimps. We moved to Liverpool to get away from the bombings.

When I was nine years old, living conditions in Liverpool were worse than during the Depression in America. The house we lived in was on 48 Kensington Street. It was a narrow building, about eighteen feet wide, with three floors. My father had a furniture store on the first floor, and on the third floor we had a shop to cut and fix furniture. The ten of us lived on the middle floor.

Fortunately, my father had some relatives in St. Paul, Minnesota, and my mother had some relatives in New Jersey and New York. But my parents didn't have much money. They certainly didn't have enough for a family of ten to travel from England to America. Fortunately, the relatives in St. Paul, Minnesota sent for my oldest brother. We had seven boys and one girl in our family. I was the second youngest child. And my oldest brother came to America and went to live in St. Paul. He got there in wintertime and he couldn't stand it, because in England you don't get severe winters like you do in Minnesota. So he decided to move to New Jersey, and fortunately he got a job. There was a big corporation years ago called the Durant Motorcar Company, and he became a foreman. He sent money for another brother and got him a job at Durant. The two brothers then sent for another brother, got him a job at Durant, and about eight months later the three of them sent for the seven of us; my mother, my father, four boys, and my sister. The whole process took about a year and a half. We arrived in July of 1923.

We took the *Franconia* from Southampton to America. The trip lasted about nine days. We traveled third class, not steerage. And it wasn't too bad. It was clean. Small cabins. The accommodations were nice, much nicer than the house that we lived in. I certainly remember the voyage because we all got seasick. I was nine at the time. My younger brother was seven, and he was the only one who came down every morning and ate his breakfast.

We were excited about coming to America. We heard about the Woolworth building, which in those days was the tallest building. We thought the streets were lined with gold. We read all the stories. It couldn't be any worse than in Liverpool because when my brothers sent over five pounds a week to our family—the pound in 1923 was five dollars, today it's about $1.80—we lived pretty good.

I don't remember much about Ellis Island. I learned more about Ellis Island when I visited last year, than I remember when I was actually there. I guess because I was so excited about coming to America. The most exciting part was seeing the Statue of Liberty. Everybody was on one side of the ship waving. I thought the ship was going to turn over. Also, because we were English-speaking, we went through pretty quickly so it was easy for us. We had heard the stories of immigrants who spent days and weeks there, but we went through the same day.

Of course, my brothers met us, and it was a very joyous occasion. We were so grateful to be all together again. My broth-

ers had an apartment set up for us in Linden, New Jersey, which is not far from Ellis Island. We took the ferry to Manhattan and then the train to Linden. It was a six-room flat for ten of us. [Laughs.] It was above a tavern and six months later we moved to Newark and I went to school there. I mean, I was ten years old then so you adjust. I eventually lost my British accent. All of us did except for my older brothers, because when you're young, you lose your accent. But the point is, anything was better than Liverpool. The Depression didn't even bother us. At least you could eat here.

My parents loved America. Absolutely loved it. Don't forget, my mother had sisters and a brother here. And my father had relatives in Minnesota. Plus, Newark was a melting pot. If you were Jewish, there was a Jewish area. If you were Polish, you went to the Polish area. If you were Italian, you went to the Italian area.

We were Jewish. My father was a very religious man. As kids, we went to Hebrew school. Saturdays we used to go to the temple and we were all bar mitzvahed. My parents wanted to be American. They accepted the American ways. And we had lots of friends who came over from England that didn't have a place to stay. I would wake up in the morning in my bedroom and suddenly find somebody sleeping.

. . .

Six years ago, my wife and I went to London and took the train to Liverpool. I remember as a kid the Lime Street Station in Liverpool, and we took a taxi and I said, "Will you take me to 48 Kensington?" They used to have trolleys on Kensington and, of course, the trolleys were gone. But the skinny house at 48 Kensington was still there. After sixty-nine years.

Stewart Wickham
. . . .

BORN OCTOBER 8, 1901
EMIGRATED 1923, AGE 21
PASSAGE ON THE *BERENGARIA*

*He was born in northern England, in the small town of Ashton-Under-Lyn,
in Lancashire. He twice tried to enter the United States with his sisters before
succeeding. He became an insurance salesman for Metropolitan Life in 1929
and retired thirty years later. Active in local charities, today he resides with his
wife of sixty-one years in Oil City, Pennsylvania. They have two daughters and
four grandchildren. "I love England," he said. "But I am very grateful to the
United States. I have had a wonderful life."*

My father died when I was five years of age. He left six of us. At that time there was no welfare, or food stamps. Everybody had to go to work, or you just didn't eat. I was the youngest child, and the only one who didn't have a job.

Then one Saturday morning when I was ten, I was playing marbles, and a man came. He said, "Would you like a job?" I said, "Yes, I would." So he took me to the farmer who said, "We want a boy delivering milk after school or Sunday mornings." I said, "Well, I'll take Sunday mornings to start." I remember running home to my mother, very proud of course, and saying, "Mother, you don't have to work any more. I've got a job." [Laughs.]

I received four pence, which was about eight cents, for the work. Then they put me on every day after school. Saturdays I used to clean the harnesses after delivering the milk. I was working steady on the farm when the war came. The government took me off of the farm and put me into a plant that made small parts for guns, working from six in the morning to eight o'clock at night, and to four o'clock on Saturday afternoons. Those were long hours.

In the meantime, I had an Uncle Sam who lived in the United States. He lived in Lawrence, Massachusetts, and he joined the United States Army, and he came over to England with the United States troops. Any troop who had relatives in England, the army would give them a furlough. So he came to stay with us. And he told us about the United States, all the good things. He said he had a nice home, a good job, and I said, "Well, I'd like to come to the United States sometime." But my mother was still living, Father was dead, my grandparents had died years before, and I didn't want to leave home. My mother wanted to live until I was twenty-one. Plus the war was on, which had a terrible effect on people—lining up for potatoes. We had one egg a month, no bacon. We had food stamps, powdered milk. It was hard on the old people. So my mother died when I was nineteen.

I had a job then as an apprentice in a tool-making plant. I finished my apprenticeship, but I realized that I didn't want to do that kind of work. I wanted to be a salesman, but there were no opportunities. Then, in 1923, I read the Ford Automobile Company was paying five dollars a day in the United

States and I thought, "My golly, why don't I go to the United States?"

I wrote to my uncle. He said he had a friend in Beaver Falls, Pennsylvania. "This friend is a preacher," he said, and "he'll help you if you ever come."

Me and my two sisters, Hilda and Nellie, left England at the end of September 1923. My two older sisters and brother were married. So there was just the three of us left. So we decided to sell off the home, the furniture, and come to Beaver Falls, Pennsylvania. We came aboard the *Scythia*, a 22,000-ton ship owned by Cunard. I left my girlfriend and her father and mother on the dock in Liverpool. I remember the goodbyes. [Laughs.]

By seven that night we were in thick fog. The fog siren was going all night long. We were supposed to be in Ireland by nine o'clock the next morning, Sunday morning, to pick up passengers. But at eleven o'clock Sunday morning we still hadn't arrived in Ireland. Hilda, Nellie, and I were walking along the deck when we saw something coming towards us. And then I realized it was a ship. It turned out to be the *Cederic*, the White Star liner, heading right for us in the fog, and it hit us; not in the middle though, otherwise it would have cut us in half.

Our ship tipped to one side and came back again. Everybody was scattered all over the deck. There was a big hole in the ship. We hadn't had a lifeboat drill because it was too foggy. So they announced for us to get our life belts, and we lined up. They let the lifeboats down level with the deck. The women and children got in first while they examined the damage. My sisters said to me, "Stew, if we're going down, we're going down together." You could hardly see the water, but you could hear it lapping against the side of the ship. But we didn't go down.

We returned to Liverpool. The passengers and crew were divided up onto different ships that went to Philadelphia, Boston,

Southampton, and Canada. There were more than 100 of us that got on the boat to Southampton. There, we boarded the *Berengaria*, which was headed for New York. It was a big 52,000-ton German ship used during the war, and taken over by the British. So we left Southampton. And it was crowded. It was booked up in the first place, but they crowded us in. One week later, we arrived in New York Harbor. They let everybody off except the passengers from the *Scythia*. We remained there for three days until a ferry brought us to Ellis Island.

We all lined up in the hallway. There were chairs on each side. I was told to go on one line, my sisters on another. And they opened a door to a cage and pushed me in with other fellows. Everybody was quiet. When the bell sounded, we went down to eat supper. We sat at long tables. Workers cut bread, but you couldn't touch it until another bell sounded, and then we all grabbed a piece. They poured something in bowls for us.

Sitting next to me was an old man, a Scotsman. I was trying to take care of him when he saw two women crying and waving. "Are those your sisters?" he asked. And I waved back. They'd already had their dinner, and we all left together. They put us up on a balcony and we sat there. Just sat there. Me, the Scotsman, and my sisters. We could hear all kinds of activity going on below.

At 9 P.M., a guard came and said, "You can't stay here." But he was also handing out milk and crackers to my sisters. I held out my hand. He said, "We don't give it to men." Then he said, "You follow me." So the Scotsman and I followed him. He took us to an empty room with beds hung on chains from the ceiling. The room had big doors. He gave us a black blanket, a piece of soap and he said, "Now, you get settled because we're going to open the doors and there's going to be a lot of people coming here." I didn't know what to do. I thought, "My God, how many people are going to come in here?"

I covered myself with the blanket. I figured I'll sleep with my clothes on. I tied my shoes together by the laces, wrapped it in a towel and made a pillow out of it. Sometime later, immigrants poured into the room. There was arguing until about two or three o'clock in the morning. A lot of these people couldn't speak English. It was sad. "Stewart," the old Scotsman said, "Let's get up early because when all these people get washing we're going to be in a mess." And that's what we did. A lot of them were still sleeping when we got up. Bodies were everywhere.

We went down for breakfast. Back to those long tables. They were scooping soup from a wagon. And then they put us together with special badges on. The people that had come from the *Scythia*. And they put us all together in a cage, a long one, my sisters included, and we stayed there until lunch. The long tables again. And then they said we were moving, but nobody would tell us where we were going. It was just guesswork.

We were at the docks when I saw my luggage being roughly loaded onto a steamer, including a box with a china tea service I had brought and I thought, "Well, there goes the china." But it must have been packed pretty good, because I still have it. [Laughs.]

So I asked a guard, "Where are we going?"

"Well, you're going back on the *Berengaria*."

Officials in Washington wouldn't permit us to come in because of the quota. It was full. The choice was to either keep us for another month, or send us back to England. They decided to send us back to England. But the crew on the *Berengaria* were nice. After we boarded, they said, "You can eat anything you want, because we know what you've gone through."

Once in England, most of the people didn't come back again. They'd had enough, including the Scotsman. But we had no home. We'd already sold it, so we didn't know what to do. So we stayed in South-ampton, and they put us in hotels for two weeks until the next boat and then we came back again. In those days, the boats left every other Saturday and got to New York on a Friday.

We took the *Berengaria* back to New York. By this time the crew had become almost our relatives. And once again, everybody got off the ship except us, the passengers from the *Scythia*, the few that remained. They wouldn't let us off because Washington had all the reports, and we had to wait for them to come in. My sisters and I thought, "My God, what are we going to do? Are we going back to Ellis Island?"

Two days later, it was morning, they let us off the ship, and we were free to go to Beaver Falls.

Harry Weston

. . . .

BORN MAY 16, 1921
EMIGRATED 1925, AGE 4
PASSAGE ON THE S.S. *OLYMPIC*, CUNARD LINE

Born in London, he came through Ellis Island as a child, then returned, coincidentally, for Coast Guard training there from September through December

. . . .

1941. He remained in the service until 1945. After the war, he married his childhood sweetheart from Brooklyn and worked for the New York Telephone Company until his retirement in 1983. Today, he lives in New Jersey with his wife of fifty-two years, Claire. Golf, day trips to Atlantic City, and a close-knit family fill their days. They have two grown children and one grandchild.

My father was the youngest of fourteen children, and they all lived in London. My grandfather had a strange trade. He was a gold beater. In other words, he'd take a nugget of gold and pound it with a sixteen-pound hammer until it was tissue-thin, four inches by four inches. It was used for signs and placed in store windows. He also did a lot of work for Ringling Brothers and Barnum and Bailey's Circus in London. He put gold leaf on all their wagons, saying "Barnum and Bailey's Circus."

There were so many stories about him. He was a tall, thin man with a little goatee. He liked his half-and-half—half beer and half ale. And he would walk down to the pub and have a good time with the boys. And he belonged to the volunteer firemen. One time [laughs] my father's sisters came into the kitchen in the middle of the night, and there were eyes peering at them in the dark. There was a lot of screaming and scurrying around, and what happened was, my grandfather had been to a fire at a chicken house and he brought home a couple of chickens that were roosting on the back of a chair.

My mother had relatives in America. They had been writing letters to my parents about how beautiful America was. My mother was the adventurous type. My father had a good job making instruments for Hawks and Sons in London. He was a drum maker. And he didn't want to come. But, of course, my mother persevered, and we came over to America May 28, 1925. I had a brother, but he died in 1918. He had fallen into scalding water and died. We arrived on my father's birthday.

The only thing I remember about coming across is that my parents had given me a rubber ball. The rubber ball was laying on the floor of our cabin, and it rolled back and forth under the bunk beds as the ship swayed. I don't really remember much else.

The S.S. *Olympic* left from Southampton, because in London the ships did not come up the Thames. We took the train to Southampton and boarded the boat. I would imagine it wasn't first class. I would imagine it was probably the cheapest way possible.

My earliest memories in America are of my grandmother's apartment, which was a railroad room on Tenth Avenue and Forty-sixth Street. The neighborhood was called Hell's Kitchen. On Tenth Avenue there were railroad tracks. And coming down the railroad tracks were freight trains with cattle in them. And in front of the freight train, in front of the engine, was a man wearing a big cowboy hat riding a white horse leading the train and the poor animals to the slaughterhouse on forty-second Street.

The other thing I remember were the parties. My mother had a lot of relatives in New York. And they used to make bathtub gin. My uncles would make it, stir it up and they'd have some wild parties at my grandmother's house.

At first, my father took any job he could get. Then he got a job with Gretch, a manufacturer of musical instruments. He didn't like it that much. I mean, it was a job. But it gave us an income and we moved to Flatbush, [a part of] Brooklyn. It was a lovely neighborhood then. An upper-middle-class neighborhood of doctors and lawyers. And so, my school, P.S. 152, was sort of silk stocking, so there weren't that many immigrant children. I remember my father would come home from work and he'd always have a cup of tea. Always had to have the cup of tea. He wasn't one of those men that went to the local bar with the boys. He would come home at six o'clock. He was very punctual. And my mom would have his cup of tea ready, and they'd sit there, and he'd smoke, and they'd have tea and talk.

Just before the Depression, I remember how worried my parents were because they didn't have a lot of money. What few dollars they had, they put into a bank. But they didn't know anything about it. Nobody gave them any advice. They saw a bank nearby with the word "America" in the title, and they figured it was safe. Of course, what happened was the bank collapsed, and they lost all their money. It took years before they recovered from that.

When I was nineteen years old, the Second World War was starting. A lot of my friends waited to be drafted, but I volunteered. I didn't like the army. I liked the sea, boats, the navy. Maybe it's the English heritage. But at that time the navy was a six-year enlistment. The Coast Guard was a four-year enlistment. I chose the Coast Guard. So I went down to the recruiter, signed up, and was sent to Ellis Island for six weeks training on September 4, 1941. It was the usual stuff—marching, short order drills, rifle drills, things of that nature. And it was one of the better things I did, because I thoroughly enjoyed my tenure in the service.

I had a friend who was a tugboat captain there. And on Ellis Island, they would give us inoculations against various diseases. And what they wanted you to do was to move your arms around a lot to keep the circulation. So they would put us in these long twelve-foot rowboats with oars and have us row to help circulate the inoculation. The tugboat captain and his crew would see us out there in New York Harbor,

a bunch of kids rowing, and he would come by and purposely speed up, swing the fantail around, and create huge waves. We were bouncing around, falling in the bottom of the boat. And these men were laughing at us.

We lived in barracks. Very large barracks. There was a boxing ring in one corner of it because of a man named Marty Sevorino. That was his real name, but his boxing name was Marty Servo. He had two championship fights with Sugar Ray Robinson, who was champion at the time. And he used to train in there. He was in the Coast Guard. And occasionally Jack Dempsey would come over and Servo and him would fight. One time they had some British seamen come in for a boxing match and there was yelling and screaming—you know, British against the Americans. I enjoyed that. I was rooting harder for the Americans than I was for the British. [Laughs.]

But the coastguardsmen were more into basketball than boxing. In fact, we had a team. Our coach was a Lieutenant Mazzada. And we weren't very good. So he would take us on this pleasure craft the Coast Guard owned and we'd go to Sand Street in Brooklyn, which is right near the Brooklyn Navy Yard, and we'd play basketball there, or in Staten Island. We played a bunch of high school kids. They ran our legs ragged, they were so good. [Laughs.] We looked like nine-year-olds, running up and down the court.

After I completed training, I was assigned to the laundry. We did the laundry for the kitchen and for the hospital next door. There was a big press, and I would run the sheets through the press, and then I would have to fold them. They taught you how to fold them and that's what my assignment was. Then we'd go and have basketball practice somewhere.

We stayed clear of the hospital. We never went upstairs because we were never allowed there. That's where they interned enemy aliens. We always stayed downstairs. But there was something going on up there. They had German and Italian seamen who were picked up by the Americans from their ships and brought upstairs for internment. I don't know how long they stayed there or what happened to them, but I know they were up there, because you could see them above our quarters. Only once do I remember that they came down. It was in our parade ground, and they let them walk around, but there was all kinds of security to make sure they didn't escape. So the active Coast Guard and the interned enemy aliens were kept separate.

After December 7, the whole atmosphere on the island changed completely. The lackadaisical, happy-go-lucky times changed. I was home on a weekend pass. I was in Brooklyn, and all my friends said, "You've got to leave." I said, "Why?" And they explained that Pearl Harbor had been bombed, and that all servicemen had to return to their barracks. So I dressed in my blues, took my shaving gear, went to lower Manhattan and got the Coast Guard ferry back to Ellis Island. The one thing I noticed immediately was that there were a lot of civilians, men, suits, ties, hats, with Orientals, many Orientals, and they kept them segregated from the seamen.

When I got back to the base, I was walking through the corridor. And the thing I'll always remember is that on one wall there was a large amount of luggage stacked high—very fine luggage. And of course, what it was, the men that were dressed in those nice suits were all FBI agents, and they had rounded up Japanese citizens. The thing that always amazed me was how, only hours after the declaration of war, they had picked up all these people. There were tons of them. Our duty was to make sure they didn't run away—guard them, not that they could go anywhere. They

stashed them someplace on the island. A lot of secrecy. I've often wondered what they did with them.

After that, we were taken by boat to parts of [New] Jersey, the seaports, where ships were being loaded with ammunition, and we would stand guard. I would see them load all kinds of shells and bombs and military equipment. Then, just prior to Christmas, I was assigned to a ship out of Staten Island called the CG83. It was an 83-foot patrol boat. And we went down to the Gulf of Mexico on antisubmarine duty to protect the Mississippi River, because there were a lot of tankers and ships being sunk there by German submarines. A lot of terrible things were going on. Then I was assigned to an LST, which is a 307-foot supply ship, LST meaning Large Shipped Tanks. I was an electrician first class by then and we loaded up with cargo, and went through the Panama Canal and crossed the Pacific. We stopped on the island of Bora Bora for fresh water. Doesn't that sound romantic? It wasn't. [Laughs.] And then we went on to French New Caledonia, down the Great Barrier Reef, to Brisbane, Australia. From there we hopped from one invasion spot to another, eleven ships in a convoy. We supplied the marines, the army, and all the Australians. We'd land the ship, and huge doors would open. A big ramp would fall down, and then tanks, trucks, and supplies would roll out. We stopped in Milne Bay, Finschhafen, Lae, Salamona, Hollandia, the Admiralty Islands, Manus Island, Sausapor, Biak.

Just before the invasion of the Philippines, I was sent home. I literally hitchhiked from New Guinea to the United States. I was with ten other men and we got to the airport in New Guinea, and said, "Who's going east?" And we found a marine pilot and flew with him to Guadalcanal. Then we hitchhiked [on] a navy plane to Hawaii, then San Francisco. Soon after, I was transferred to Boston and boarded the Coast Guard ship *Mohave*, which was a 247-foot craft. I did convoy duty from Newfoundland to Greenland. Then the war ended and I went back to Brooklyn. It was quite an adventure.

Helen Clinton

· · · · · · · · · · · · ·

BORN FEBRUARY 9, 1915
EMIGRATED 1951, AGE 36
PASSAGE ON THE *MAURITANIA*

She was born to a middle-class family in a resort town on the east coast of England. She survived the Nazi blitz of World War II, and married a man who owned a successful car service in London after the war. Despite their comfortable British life, they emigrated to America with their son and daughter. Today she lives alone in a Florida condominium near her sister and remains close to her children.

It was my two sisters, my two brothers, my mother, my father, and me. We lived in Clacton-On-Sea, a small seaside town with nice beaches, boating. A very nice way of life. We lived in a three-bedroom attached brick house, part of a row of six to eight attached houses. It had a thatched roof. We had coal stoves in all the bedrooms, the living room, or "front room" as we called it, and a big coal stove in the kitchen.

We went to school. We always had lots of sports and lots of friends, all kinds of games: rounders, which was similiar to cricket, marbles, hopscotch, you name it. And, of course, we had the beaches, swimming.

My father was about five [foot] six, quite a good-looking man and very good with the family. He was a house decorator and a painter, and he owned a business with his father and brother. He loved darts, he loved dominoes, he loved sports. But mostly, he loved boats. In fact, he and my grandfather were coxswains of the Lifeboat Institution, and they used to volunteer with lifeboats and rescue small ships.

My mother had blonde hair like me and my two brothers. My two sisters were darker, dirty blonde. My mother was an absolute dear. She was kind, thoughtful. She liked to do things for people. A good mother. If someone were having children she was always there to help. In a small town you did this kind of thing.

The church was important to us for both religious and social reasons. It was called St. James Church. We went there for Sunday school. My mother belonged to the guild of the church and there was a guild meeting every Tuesday. We used to go to parties at the church. We had Sunday school outings. Our grammar school was next to the church and we learned the basics: reading, writing, and arithmetic. The teacher taught us needlework. My favorite subject was sports—gym class, but we were always dressed. We wore a navy blue skirt with a white, long-sleeve blouse with a yellow and royal blue tie. That was the school uniform.

We had other family in Clacton. I had an uncle, my father's brother, and his wife. They didn't have any children. They liked to play whist, sort of like bridge. And, of course, there was my grandfather, my father's dad, who was well into his eighties. He dressed up like Santa Claus at Christmas. [Laughs.] He was a generous, honorable man. You had to do the right thing with him. And he loved what he did, his volunteer work and going out in the big lifeboats. My grandmother died before I was born, so he lived alone, ten minutes away from us by the sea. He had a daughter, [my] aunt, that lived a few doors up the road that kept an eye on him.

My other grandparents on my mother's side came from Cambridge, the university town. My mother was born and raised there. My mother met my father when she went on a holiday to Clacton-On-Sea with her sisters because the town had very nice dance halls, ballrooms.

In fact, that's how I met my husband. I was a very good ballroom dancer. And my husband came from London with a friend, also on holiday to Clacton. And he came to this particular ballroom one night, asked me to dance, and that's how it started. He was a beautiful dancer, which I liked. And we got to know each other and he went back and I was still there and then I eventually went to London. We dated off and on for three years until we married September 3, 1938, a year [from] the day World War II broke out the following year.

They dropped the first bombs of the war on Clacton-On-Sea. So my family moved to Cambridge. In the meantime, there was the blitz in London. By this time my son, David, was ten months old, and we were bombed out in London. We lived in the West End, and the Germans dropped bombs very close to our apartment and shattered everything.

The Germans were in France. They had control of France, right across the coast of England. And they were bombing from the French coast. We called them "buzz bombs." And you didn't know when these bombs were coming, even the attack guns, or the B-2 planes. They were so quiet. They'd come along, and you'd think it was just a plane, and all of a sudden it would drop the buzz bombs. That was the frightening thing about them. We could take the blitz because you knew what was happening, and you knew when to take shelter, but you didn't know that with the buzz bombs. That's how the Germans killed so many people.

So my husband took me to Cambridge, because my mother had gone there to be with her family. So David and I stayed with my mother for a couple of months, but I felt that I was needed in London with my husband, so I went back. He served with the fire department in London, which took a beating during the war. During one rescue, he broke his leg very badly. He was on crutches for a year until the end of the war. So I joined him, and we moved to Maida Vale, which is about five miles out of London. My younger sister eventually joined my husband and I because of the bombing in Clacton-On-Sea. But even in Maida Vale it was frightening because you could hear all the guns and you want to protect your child. So when the buzz bombs came, the first thing my sister and I did was go to David's crib, and wrapped him up in a blanket. Then all of us would just lay on the floor and pray we would survive.

London police had evacuated a lot of places that were dangerous. They got most of the children out of London. Many times the buses and trains couldn't run, and they really didn't want you on the street. So sometimes I used to take the baby to the

Underground and sleep the night there. A lot of us did that.

We survived on food rations. We got two ounces of butter a week, and a certain amount of sweets, meat. If you were pregnant you got a little more meat. And then if you were desperate, there was always the black market because you had a lot of Americans and other nationals. Fortunately for me, my elder sister had married a Canadian who was in the office of the Canadian embassy, so I was able to get extras for the baby, as well as [laughs] nylon stockings, which we all liked very much.

After the war, like everybody else, we went back to London to rebuild our lives and pick up the pieces. My parents went back to Clacton-On-Sea. Everybody wanted to go back where they belonged.

My husband wanted to come to America. He had close friends who had moved here from London. And although he had a nice business and we had a nice home, they were saying how wonderful it was in America. And he thought we should come. He thought we'd have a better life in America. I was happy in England. I had plenty of family and friends and we were very close. I had a great life.

So I protested, but not all that much, because I loved him and because there was a great deal of austerity in England after the war. I looked upon it as a new adventure. It meant leaving my family. I went down to Clacton with the children and told them about our decision. My mother, of course, was very upset. It never occurred to her, or my father, that we would want to leave England. But my husband was set on leaving. He was enthused and after a while I became enthused. We had no intention of coming back. If you immigrate, you immigrate. You're there to stay. And if you have young children and they've got to be schooled, you can't keep running back home. They've got to be schooled in one

place. I think that's very important. So I only came back for vacations.

We went to the American embassy and did all our medical exams, tests, everything, for us, the children, and I must say they were terrific. [Laughs.] I remember the nurse said to me, "Do you mind if I open all your clothes? I want to see if you're pregnant." I said, "I've got news for you. I'm not pregnant." Our lawyer said, "Tell everything like it is, and you'll never have a problem. You don't have anything to hide anyway." And that's what we did, and he was right. The whole process took a month before we had clearance from the American embassy.

My parents came to London and we had a big celebration before we left. I had my two sisters and brothers-in-law, and we all got together including my husband's family, of course. And they were all very sorry to see us leave. [Laughs.] It wasn't an easy departure. My mother was devastated. His family was upset, too. But my husband always said that "We'll go, and we're going to like it. And we'll come back again to see the family, never fear." So that was kind of how I felt. I thought, we'll see them again. My family said, "If you can't get to us, we will get to you." And I thought that was wonderful. That gave me a little more heart to go.

So we sold our furniture. As I say, we had a nice apartment, so neighbors were lining up at the door to buy our furniture and I hated to do it. But we did bring with us a lovely set of English china from the family. We packed two big trunks, and left from Southampton on the *Mauritania*. That was the first time I was on an ocean liner. We were accustomed to steamers, smaller ships, that used to do holiday runs from London to Clacton-On-Sea. We had a big pier there, and tourists used to visit, particularly in the summer, or the next seaside town called Friton. The actor Douglas Fairbanks had a house in Friton.

We had a nice cabin for the four of us, and I was feeling a bit under the weather. I had caught a bad cold and my arm, where I had the vaccination, was acting up. One day, my husband and the children wanted to go up on the deck and I said, "Well, I'll stick around the cabin and read a book." When the steward came, she said, "Don't you feel good?" I said, "No, I've got this cold. Plus, my vaccination here is acting up a bit." She must have passed that information on to the ship's doctor.

We arrived in New York in June. The trip lasted six days. And when we got in, the ship's doctor told my husband there was a doctor coming aboard to examine me. My husband said, "Why?" I remember the steward saying, "She's fine. She's just had a cold, nothing to warrant a doctor." But the American doctor came aboard anyway, examined me and said, "You look like a fine healthy girl to me. What's your problem?"

"I don't have a problem," I said.

"Well, they mentioned something about your arm."

"It was just bothering me, that's all."

"Well, they passed the buck to me."

Now, that conveyed nothing to me, so I said, "Oh, well, that's all right. We'll be off in a minute."

"No," he said, "You stay put."

I asked somebody what that meant, and they said, "I don't think you're getting off the ship right away." So, of course, my husband and I couldn't believe this. Why couldn't we get off the ship? I mean, if there was something wrong with me, fine . . .

We had to wait until everybody was off the ship. We naturally thought we were going to be detained for an hour. Our friends were waiting for us at the dock in Manhattan.

Two hours later they said, "We're taking you to Ellis Island." That didn't convey anything to me, either. And then the heavens opened up. It started to pour. My little Susan was crying. Our friends, as we later found out, were in a terrible state. And we had these four men escorting us by boat over to the island. The crew was standing at the gangplank, and I said, "Well, why can't we just go back? Put us back on the ship."

"No," they said.

"Well, I'm going back to England," I said. "I've had enough of this." A terrible thing to say, but I was devastated. I turned to leave and they grabbed me and pushed me onto the deck of the ship. My husband got into a fight with one of them. The two children just watched this. And I thought this was the most disgusting thing I had ever experienced in my life.

When we got to Ellis Island, they said, "We're taking your husband." And they put him in a jail. Then they said, "But we're giving you a private room."

"Where else would you put me?" I said, not understanding the situation.

"Well, most of the women and children are all together, but they don't necessarily have private rooms."

My husband was put in with all the men. Not very nice. He didn't like that setup at all. He said it wasn't right. "But what can I say?" he said to me. As long as I was looked after, it didn't bother him.

In the meantime, my friends didn't know what to do, what to say. My family was ready to fly over. And the days passed. And each morning the bell would ring at eight o'clock and we would go down for breakfast like convicts. The hall there for eating was the most disgusting thing I've ever experienced. At dinnertime the bell would ring . . .

It wasn't until day twelve that things started happening. We used to talk with other English, who also didn't know why they were there. One of the girls was a model, a lovely girl, here on a modeling assignment.

"How long is the assignment for?" she had been asked.

"Well, I really don't know," she said. "I don't know how long it will last."

"That's not good enough," they said, "we'll give you time to find out." And they put her on the island.

One day, I had to go into New York for a medical exam. They took me with two Swedish girls, lovely girls, who also didn't know why they were being detained. I told the doctor about my arm and my sniffles, and the next thing I knew I was being stripped from top to bottom. So I said to him, "Why? You've got all this paperwork from the doctors at the American embassy, the English embassy, the ship's doctor. What more do you want?"

"Well, this is something we have to go through," he said. "It's not my fault."

He was more interested in the two pretty Swedish girls in the examination room next door. He left me alone to strip and examine them. He was in there for a long time. [Laughs.] I laugh about this now, but I wasn't laughing then. I think we were there for a couple of hours, and then we were taken back to the island.

Another day, they asked if they could put a cot in my room for the wife of the Swedish ambassador and her little boy. I said, "That's fine with me." The room was big enough. She was an awfully nice lady, and our kids played together. And I said, "Why are you here?" She said, "Why are we both here? I don't know." Imagine, even the Swedish ambassador's wife!

But the guards were very nice. Men only. I don't recall any woman guards. One of them said to me, "You know, that's what happens. They take somebody off of every ship, every plane, so they can keep the island open." I spoke with two women, fortyish, who had been there for three months and still didn't know why.

My room was in the Great Hall off the third-floor balcony. I would come out of my room and look down for my husband in the morning, and he would be standing there looking up, waiting for me and the children to come out the door. The kids didn't know what it was all about. Heck, I didn't know what it was all about. To me, Ellis Island was something frightening, a place where they put all the criminals. But we weren't criminals. It was very frustrating.

Finally, one day a guard pointed out the governor of Ellis Island. So I made a dash through the crowd and grabbed his arm and said, "I have to talk to you."

"Well, what is it about? Are you English?"

"Yes." And I explained very quickly what had happened.

"Well, when you're called on the loudspeaker, bring your husband and children to my office."

I got the call about an hour later. I went in with my husband and children.

"We owe you an apology," he said. "You should have been off before. Your papers were in with Displaced Persons, and I hope you won't hold this against the United States. We wish you all the luck in the world."

I didn't say this, but I was thinking, "You've got to be joking! After all we've gone through for twelve days that's the best you've got?" My husband couldn't believe it, he was so upset. We took our papers, called our English friends Nettie and David Martin. They had lived in Maidavale. They met us on the Manhattan side and then we all went to West Orange, New Jersey, where they lived.

The first thing my husband and I did was write to our families to tell them exactly what happened. My parents were worried sick. My sisters were beside themselves. I know when we got letters back from them, they just couldn't believe it. Nobody believes things like this when you tell them.

You couldn't bring money out of England in those days. I think we came here with something like £200, which would be about $500 in those days. That was all we were allowed to bring, and that was not going to take us far. We had working papers. We had everything. There was no reason at all that we couldn't get a job.

In England, we had known some show people. My husband had drivers who serviced them. They lived in New York and they asked us to call them when we arrived. And we did. He got a job as a chauffeur which got us a roof over our heads. I did cooking for this family who lived in Bay Head, New Jersey. They had somebody come in to clean house. It was the family of Paul Hay, who had a seat on the stock exchange.

I loved it there. We were back at seaside. And they had a big house right on the water. We lived in separate quarters, a nice little apartment. And they were delighted with us. We felt no prejudice. They loved our British accents. In fact, they would say,

"Keep talking. We like to hear you talk." Plus, they didn't have any children, so they loved our kids. There were lifeguards on the beach because of the huge waves and right away my husband went to them and asked if they could teach our children to swim. He made an arrangement with them, and the lifeguards were glad to earn some cash. So Susan and David were taught to swim. We stayed with them for two years, bought a car and moved to Long Island.

Do I have any regrets? I had a nice life in England. My husband had a nice business. My family was all around me, and that's what makes you happy. But no, I don't regret coming here. My children loved it. They didn't know it any other way. The only one who knew it another way was me. But I'm lucky. I'm blessed with five lovely grandchildren . . . It could have been worse.

5

. . . .

Ireland

(APPROXIMATELY 1.1 MILLION IMMIGRANTS, 1892–1954)

A young Edward Joseph Flanagan (1886–1948), later known as Father Flanagan, the founder of Boys' Town, next to his brother (right) and other Irish immigrants on the steerage deck of the R.M.S. Celtic, arriving in New York Harbor from Ireland in August 1904

(NATIONAL PARK SERVICE: STATUE OF LIBERTY NATIONAL MONUMENT)

Joseph McGrath

BORN DECEMBER 21, 1900
EMIGRATED 1921, AGE 20
PASSAGE ON THE *CELTIC*, WHITE STAR LINE

The son of a Galway farmer, he emigrated alone to Portland, Maine, where he still lives today. He was a longshoreman, and an Erie Railroad worker. In 1930 he married his wife, Doris, who died in 1975. They had ten children, although three died in infancy. He has twenty-four grandchildren and thirty great-grandchildren. "Coming here, I lived through the Depression and the hard life, but we were happy," he said. "There was a contentment. If you're a millionaire and you're not happy, what good is it? Money is not everything. We have to have it, of course, but it's not the key to all our happiness in this world."

I was raised in Derry Loughne, seven miles west of Galway, in County Galway. My father was just a farmer. We used to raise potatoes and oats and wheat. There was a mill in Galway there. You brought it in and they ground it for you in Galway, and they'd mix that with white flour. My father owned the land, and his father before him. My niece owns that today, the same land where I was brought up. But there's nothing there but the foundation. They built all these nice modern houses now.

My father used to go to Galway two days a week selling turf. And my mother, of course, used to make butter and eggs. We didn't live in luxury, but we had plenty of common things—fish, potatoes, bread, tea. We ate fish and potatoes mostly. Fish was very plentiful in my time. In fact, there was a whole street in the city of Galway they used to call the Fish House. You'd walk along the street and there were barrels of herring and mackerel, and they'd be selling them by the dozens. Different types of fish.

In our house, we used to have gaslit lamps on the wall. The roof was thatched.

People had horses, and that's how they used to do their business in Galway. The standard of living was poor. And the wages, of course, were very poor. And the price of cattle was poor. And the standard of education was poor. For example, in my time, when I went to school, there was Jimmy the schoolmaster and his wife—there were two. And you'd have a hundred kids there, and they took care of the eight grades. Them days when you went to school, I used to walk three miles from my village in Derry Loughne to Spiddle, and we wouldn't have nothing hardly to eat again until we came home at four in the afternoon. They let us out at three o'clock but it used to take us an hour to walk the three miles to get home. Now they have transportation, electricity, automobiles, there are no horses on the streets, they have lunches at the school. So it's a different Ireland, you know?

I was brought up learning more Gaelic than English. My school was half Irish and half English. So we learned both. It's a funny thing, but if you went about six miles outside Galway, all they spoke was Gaelic. But in the town of Galway itself, it was all English. So the Irish language was pretty well eliminated there. But nobody speaks Gaelic anymore.

We were brought up as Catholics. My area was practically all Catholic. My father wasn't a religious man. He never went to church. He went to church maybe at Christmas or Easter and that's it. But my mother was a religious woman. In the public schools, they were allowed to teach catechism there. But we were forbidden, for example, to know Irish history. That was forbidden to be taught in the school, Irish history. Because Ireland was controlled by the British government in my day, and I suppose they figured, if they told young people about all the atrocities that were committed, from Cromwell on down, that would rouse them to rebel. So it was forbidden.

They were harsh times. I remember around 1918, it was the time of the flu epidemic, influenza. I was eighteen or so. The doctors had very little knowledge about it. The doctors from Galway were claiming that it was the air from Galway Bay that was affecting so many people. All those who was able to sweat was able to survive. So people drank extra brandy and scotch to sweat. In one town I went to there was a blacksmith. He had thirteen kids. His two eldest boys—twenty-four and twenty-two, and a daughter, thirteen—I saw them buried in one square hole. People were dying and quick.

The doctors, of course, would forbid you to go to the wake or to the funeral except if it was immediate family for fear you would be contaminated by the deceased. They were very much afraid of it. It's said the flu epidemic started in France where thousands of soldiers were buried. I remember, for example, I was with my oldest brother. We were planting one day in the field. We could see Galway Bay. It was about a quarter of a mile from our place. But I could see layers of fog coming from the ocean. And when it hit

me, I could swear I'll never forget. And the smell of it was like a dead carcass. Two days after that, I heard them say people was dying all of a sudden. That was the beginning of it.

That was also the time of the Black and Tans. I remember near Galway one time, there were three English officers of the Black and Tan wounded there. Any English soldier that was killed, they'd kill ten of the others for it. And it was indiscriminate, because lots of times some of the innocent got killed who had nothing to do with the uprising. They used to have blank bullets. But nobody knew whether they had blank bullets or the real bullets. And the rule was that they tried to make a person run before they'd shoot him.

The Sinn Féin at that time, the Irish Republicans, were cold-blooded murderers. They were fighting for a free Ireland. A lot of the Irish constabulary got killed because they were working for the British government. The objective was good, to get Ireland free, but the method was poor, that's the thing.

In October 1919 I went to East Galway where they had a tremendous lot of potatoes to dig. We used to go there to dig potatoes because the wages were better. I stayed there for a year and a half. Then one day I went to visit my mother in Galway and she said, "Joe, as long as you don't want to live at home, you ought to go to America. It will be better for you than to be in East Galway. You're working, and you're not getting much wage." Which was very true. And then that's the time I wrote to my uncle in Portland, Maine. He sent my passage, which in them days was $125. The 100 dollars was for passage. The other $25 was "landing money." When you came to this country you paid that $25 for transportation to go where you wanted.

I came alone. Two of my brothers came later, but I was the first of the family to go live with the Yanks. Everybody in America, we used to call them the Yanks. And I bought a blue suit before I left. I had it tailor made in Galway, and I remember distinctly I paid eight pounds and two shillings for it. At that time one pound was equal to five dollars. So the suit cost about forty dollars. It took me about four months workin' the farm to save for that suit.

I also had an extra gray suit for the trip. There was forty of us from Galway on the boat, so we grouped together because we all spoke Gaelic. We went on the train from Galway to Dublin. In Dublin we had to go to the American consul to be examined. That's the first time I ever saw Dublin. But I was not interested in Dublin that day. [Laughs.] I had only one thing on my mind, to pass the test. If you said you were coming to America for a steady job, that would disqualify you right away. So I told them I was coming to America to visit my uncle. I passed. From Dublin, we went to Holyhead, England. And from Holyhead, England we took the train about three hours to Liverpool. We didn't sleep that night. And boarded the boat the next day at nine o'clock.

We left the 16th of April 1921. There was a lot of English people going to Halifax. The boat went to Halifax first. It was the White Star Line. The *Celtic*. It would take eight days to New York, but nine days on account of stopping in Halifax.

I had a wonderful time on ship. There was three decks. Those who danced was on the middle deck. They had music, Irish music and dancing, very good. And the food was very good and fine. We were in second class. The first class, for example, I remember the bells would ring in the morning. We knew that was for first class, and we'd have to wait till nine o'clock for our breakfast, the second class. They had a beautiful dining room on the boat. The *Celtic* was quite a big

boat. The food was good, solid food—marmalades and juices, meat. And they had a bar for those who wanted to take a drink, but we didn't have much money. We were young and we were happy. And although we were strange to each other, we were all looking for the same objective, to land in this country. So we had a nice time. I enjoyed it. The camaraderie.

I slept in a bunk bed in a cabin. Two beds on each side and the space between there was a washbowl where you'd shave yourself, and a window you could look out. But over me, I was on a lower bunk, and I remember there was an Englishman, a very stocky fellow, a middle-aged man. He was sleeping above me. I was afraid the bed would break and he'd fall down on me. I mean, he was a heavy man. I was in with three Englishmen. Of course, that's the time of the Black and Tans and all that. But they were very nice to me. My blue suit, for example: This Englishman, well-dressed, showed me how to wrap it up so it wouldn't get so wrinkled. I mean, the common English people were nice. So even though there were Black and Tans, ordinary English people, ordinary like myself, they didn't have a say in politics anyway. [Laughs.] My brother once said to me, "I'd rather work for an English boss than for an Irish boss."

I remember coming into New York Harbor, it was Saturday night, and we had to wait there until Monday morning to go to Ellis Island. But the astonishing thing for me were the lights at night. I was brought up in the country. A dark night, you could hardly see the road, pitch dark. And now here was this glare of lights along Manhattan. New York Island. There were beautiful sights. I remember this big sign flashing on and off, "Lipton's Tea and Coffee." [Laughs.]

I don't remember anything about Ellis Island. All we wanted to do was go, get tested, pass, and get out. They put us on a boat and brought us to South Station in

Boston. Of those forty Gaelic, I know at least one didn't make it. He was the one that was calling the dances. Very well dressed. I heard that he didn't pass. It was TB, or some disease. Only two came to Portland, myself and this man Flaherty. Most everyone else went to Boston, some of them New York.

But myself and Flaherty, we would become friends for life. He died many years ago. They put us on a horse and buggy and drove us to North Station, and then a train to Portland. My uncle, my father's brother, met me and Flaherty.

I remember, my uncle brought me down to the store in Portius Mitchell. Port Mitchell. And, of course, in them days, they used to have a lot of ships there. There was twelve hundred longshoremen. Seventy percent of them were Irishmen from Galway. So it was common that everybody had a pair of overalls and a jumper, and that's the first thing my uncle did was to get me and Flaherty down to Portius to buy a set of overalls and jumper.

At the store, I saw these red apples. I thought they were painted at first. Because in Ireland the apples are green. Even when they're ripe they're green, but I never saw anything like these. So beautiful. And big. Laid out like an advertisement. It was so attractive, so beautiful. And I bought one. I can still remember how good it tasted.

Martha O'Flanagan

. . . .

BORN JUNE 15, 1903
EMIGRATED 1925, AGE 22
PASSAGE ON THE S.S. *BALTIC*

Now ninety-four, she lives in a nursing home in northern New Jersey. "I remember my first St. Patrick's Day here," she said. "It was the parade, and my cousins gave me a green dress to wear and I said, 'I'm not going to wear that green. I'm not going to wear green in the United States!' They laughed at me."

The fields are no greener anywhere in Ireland than in County Roscommon. It's an emerald green. A color of green you cannot find in this country or any other country. It had a lot of heather and a lot of fields. There was lots of farming.

I always said to my mother that father was the handsomest man in the west of Ireland. He was about six foot tall, and he had auburn hair and very light skin. He was a farmer. My mother had the real Irish dark hair. You have to be Irish to have dark hair. This notion that Irish people have red hair is not true. We got the red hair from the Danes when they invaded Ireland in 1014, and they married Irish girls. That's how we got all this red hair.

I grew up in a thatched cottage, walls of stone they were. I loved growing up on the farm. I wouldn't change it for another thing because it was the most beautiful place, the nicest environment to be brought up in. I

. . . .

was the baby. I had three brothers and they were much older than me. It wasn't hard work because there was such a crowd of us. There were six of us. And everybody chipped in and helped with everything. I helped my mother bake the bread—great, big Irish soda bread, and pancakes for breakfast. The kitchen was big, and two medium-sized bedrooms, I would say. But the kitchen was as big as two or three rooms put together. It was a great big kitchen with an old-fashioned fireplace and it had a thatched roof on it. In that fireplace we heated our kitchen and did our cooking with turf fire, or peat. Hay. We had to dig for it with a tool called the "slane." We picked it up into sods and put the sods out into the hot sun until they're nice and dry and hard, and you can make a beautiful, blazing fire. Me and my mother used to help in the hay fields.

We had three barns and we grew everything: potatoes, turnips, cabbage, beets. In fact, we grew everything so we could feed the family in winter. I had to help dig the potatoes with my father and the three boys, and I helped to plant them, also. Planting potatoes is not easy work. We had to use this tool called a "steeve" to make the holes, then put the potatoes in. Then the potatoes come up. And we had different varieties of potatoes in Ireland: "Irish Whites" a white, long potato; "Peelers," a reddish potato; and "Elephants," a long potato, the most delicious, and the first potato people usually digged.

Of course, we also had lots of chickens and mother was always making roast chickens, boiled chicken, chicken fricassee for the whole crowd of us. We also had eight cows and a small horse. I used to take care of the horse. The day I left Ireland I sure was in tears leaving my horse, and my dog, Beauty.

I remember all the time going to dances on Saturday nights and we had fiddles. Every house in Ireland it seemed had a violin or a fiddle or perhaps an accordion or a flute, the old-fashioned flute, the big one. And

everybody was able to play some kind of music. I didn't play any instrument but I always sang with the group.

When they got older, two of my brothers left the home. Of course, when the boys grew up in Ireland, and the girls, too, they usually went to England or the United States to continue their livelihood. One went to England to work on a big farm over there. My oldest brother, Thomas, went to America. He was a motorman driving the trolley cars on the West Side and East Side of New York. He was going to come back to Ireland, but then he got pneumonia and just never returned. I missed them a lot because we were real chummy. With the two boys gone, it was hard, rough work on a farm. The youngest of my brothers, Dominick, stayed. He was my pal.

But when Thomas left, I wanted to come to America. I wrote this letter to him, and he said, "Whenever you want to come, Martha, let me know and I'll send you your passage money for the boat." He sent me $200, I think.

My parents didn't want me to go. My mother always said, "Martha, if you like the United States, you may stay. And if you don't like it, you should come home. You'll find yourself a nice Irish boy and get married." Oh, and I said, "Is that so? How do you know I want to be bothered with any Irish boys? Maybe I want someone in Canada or someplace!" [Laughs.]

I wanted to come in the worst way! I also had several cousins here. And I was so glad when one of them said I could stay until I got work. One of my aunts had twelve children.

I got my passport, and I went up to Dublin on my bicycle to get my visa signed and came back home. I told my father and mother all the stories about Dublin. I didn't like Dublin. I didn't take a lot of stuff with me. My father didn't come to the town the day I left for United States. Dominick, my mother, and me—the three of us—we traveled in an Irish jaunting car, like a horse-drawn carriage, from our house out in the country to Ballyharny, the nearest town. My father just didn't want to be bothered. I know he was farming. It was a nice, sunny day and he had work to do on the farm. So the three of us went.

They took me to County Cork, that's where I got the boat, the S.S. *Baltic*. I was twenty-two. I traveled with a lot of boys and girls my age. An awful lot of Irish people embarked to Boston. Before I went on the boat, the doctor examined me. My fingers had warts on them. But he said it was nothing and gave me some kind of medicine.

The S.S. *Baltic* was beautiful. I didn't want to get off. I didn't want to get off because I loved the blue waters. I would have loved to stay out mid ocean. I was with another girl and her brother and her sister. The four of us traveled together from Ireland to the United States. She had been here ten years, and she had gone home on a visit to see her family, and now she was returning. We used to go up on deck and go dancing and [laughs] we used to dance all the Irish dances up on deck. We had a great time!

I didn't get seasick. I was too busy dancing on the deck. Old-fashioned Irish dances. And we saw the captain, shook hands with him, a lovely man, and the second mate and we were greenhorns from Ireland and we didn't know anything. [Laughs.]

The trip took eight days. At Ellis Island all I remember was that there were hundreds of people, and that they gave only a small amount of food to the immigrants coming in. Arrangements were made for Thomas to meet me at the pier. But he couldn't come because he had to work that day, so a cousin did and brought me to Astoria, in Queens, and they made a big dinner for me.

I remember getting on the subway and I said to my cousin who was taking me out to Astoria, "Look, you mean all them kind of people I have to ride on the subway with?" He said, "You'd better make up your mind because you'll be riding every day. You're going to get a job. Who knows where you're going to be working and you have to be prepared for it." He said, "Don't you worry about anything because you never know who you're going to meet or who you're going to see here! This is America."

I did miss Ireland. I missed Ireland so much. I missed my mother and father and Dominick. I wrote to them constantly. But I never saw them again. I never went back to Ireland. I always wanted to go on a trip, take a trip to the old country, but I never did. I promised my mother I would, especially after my father died. He died of pneumonia one year after I was here at Christmas. So it was my mother and Dominick left, the two of them. And I missed them. I still miss them.

Marjorie Kellhorn
. . . .

BORN MAY 28, 1906
EMIGRATED 1925, AGE 18
PASSAGE ON THE S.S. *PRESIDENT ROOSEVELT*

She grew up in a comfortable, two-income, middle-class family in central Ireland.
Like so many others, her family emigrated in stages. She lived most of her life as

a domestic. Now ninety-one, she wonders, to this day, whether she made the right decision. "I've gone back to Ireland since," she said. "And I saw people in my age bracket and they're all very comfortable, so I don't think we did any better here than we've would have done if we stayed in Ireland. I think anybody who makes it in their own country should stay there. I may be wrong, but that's how I feel."

My father came to America first when he was sixteen years old. As a matter of fact, he was one of the men working on the Brooklyn Bridge when it was built. I don't know what year that was. But he was a carpenter by trade. My father came back in 1914, and I remember being very excited. I was about eight years old. He brought us back lots of toys for my younger sister and I. I had two older sisters, but they were already in America. He was going to take us back with him, but the war was on and he couldn't get back. He was too old to be conscripted, but there were no boats going back and forth.

I was born in Offaly, King's County, right in the center of Ireland, in the midlands, between Tipperary and Westmeath. There were three distilleries in our town. My father worked in one of them, and did carpentry work on the side. He had a nice temperament, although he could swear a little. He had a fair complexion, very fair, with blue eyes and blondish, wavy hair. My mother was a little taller than he and very good-looking, brunette. There was a beautiful hospital where my mother was a nurse. Tellamoore Hospital, it was. And the Grand Canal ran through the town from Dublin and boats came through locks and delivered the Guinness beer to the pubs, and peat moss back up to Dublin, or by horse-drawn carriages.

We lived right near the Grand Canal, near the locks on the canal. Our house only had two bedrooms, a kitchen, and a little parlor. At that time, people in Ireland didn't have big houses. We were an average middle-class family. The kitchen was very square with a large fireplace. No stove. Cooking was done over the fire with iron "pot hooks" from which you could hang a pot and there was a way of letting it down close to the fire to cook faster, or raise it up to simmer. To each side were harps where you could hang your teapot or your kettle.

I remember my mother's bread and stews and soups and her rice puddings. Tapioca rice puddings, and Jell-O, those were our desserts mainly. 'Course, we had all fresh vegetables from our garden like celery, parsnips, carrots, turnip, cabbage, very much cabbage, onions, and of course, potatoes was the main dish in our house.

We always stored our potatoes. We put them in a dark place and put peat moss over them and covered them. Sometimes we left them outside in a pit, dug the pit and covered it with peat moss and wooden planks. That's how most people saved their potatoes for the winter.

The fireplace was the main heat. We'd light a fire there in the early part of the evening so the house would be warm by the time we went to bed, for my sister and I. We shared the same bedroom. We also used to put hot jars if the bed was cold; boiling water in jars and place them underneath the bed. There was no electricity. Electricity didn't come till 1922 or '23 to the average home. Up until then, only companies like the distilleries and our church had electric and steam heat.

We did not have steam heat in our school, so we had to bring a certain amount of money each month for coal, for fuel. We had several classrooms. It went up to eighth grade. There was a partition that divided the boys from the girls. I walked less than half a mile. Not far. We had Gaelic books, which I didn't like very much because I found it very difficult to understand the Gaelic language. Gaelic was like our second language but we only had that one day a week for half an hour, so most of the time I escaped. [Laughs.] My parents spoke Irish, not Gaelic. We were more modern. Gaelic was spoken mostly in the west of Ireland, near Galway.

Our school was part of the church. It was a Catholic school. We were taught by nuns. I remember we had a very lovely music nun. Her name was Sister Mary Antonio. I think there was some Italian in her. She was just one of the most beautiful people I've ever met, but very strict. If you didn't know your lessons or you were late, you got slapped—"Hold your hands out," she'd say, and slap you with a big, flat ruler, sometimes a pointer. So you always remembered, if you made a mistake you paid for it. It was a little cruel, but at the same time you learned, and you knew. You paid for your mistakes, and I think that's what's wrong today. People don't believe in hitting, they don't believe in slapping. That's wrong. You don't hit people to hurt them, you hit people to remember. Like my father would say, "You'll remember the day." If we didn't do something right we would get slapped.

Church life was also very strict when I grew up. We had to obey certain laws. We had prayers three times a day in school. We had prayers when we first went in, prayers at noon, and prayers at three o'clock before we left. All of my grandparents died young, before I was born, except my grandmother, my mother's mother, who was a lovely lady. I remember her because she taught us our prayers for church.

For fun, we played jump rope, marbles, jacks, and what we called rounders. It's like baseball here. The nearest beach was in Dublin or Galway, which was quite a distance at that time because people did not have cars. Our main transportation was bicycling. We also had a donkey and cart, and a pony and trap, that was for local traveling, about two or three miles. For longer distances you'd have to take a train. So people usually stayed within two, three miles of where they lived.

During World War I we had rationing, which affected us very much. You had to specify a certain store to get your supplies. And, of course, my mother was at the hospital the day they came to give the rationing book, and I picked the most expensive store in the town. [Laughs.] It was Egan's. They had everything and, of course, my mother was furious 'cause it was very expensive. It was mostly for sugar, tea, the things that Irish people like the most. Meat was hard to get. But, like most people, we had our own chickens, pigs. We couldn't get white bread, we had to eat black bread, the flour was unbleached, black. Not very appetizing. There was one girl I knew whose father worked for a bakery, and she'd have white bread for lunch in school and we had black bread, and I was very jealous of that.

In America, my father had two brothers and two sisters. We corresponded with them all the time and he would talk about them. My father loved America, that's why he wanted to go back. But my mother absolutely refused, and she certainly never wanted me to come here. But at that time, everybody had the idea of coming to America. The people were leaving, boatloads and boatloads, you know, and I just got the same urge.

Unbeknownst to my mother, I wrote to my two sisters in New York. They did domestic work. And my sisters paid my expenses to come here. My father knew, and he was anxious for me to come. I finally told my mother and she kind of got reconciled to it. But she was unhappy when I left, and I promised her I'd either come home or take her over there because she didn't want to be separated from all her daughters.

There was very little to pack in those days. I brought just one large suitcase. It was filled mostly with gifts for my sisters and relatives. I took Belleek, that's Belleek china. I bought it in Dublin and wrapped it very careful so it shouldn't break. I also brought a statue of our Blessed Mother, and it didn't break.

Saying good-bye was very hard, very sad. A lot of my cousins came to the train station to see me off. My parents, too, of course. And I was young. I was eighteen. And that's what worried my mother. I was not mature like the children are today.

I took the train to Queenstown in Cork. I had a letter from a hotel man in our town, who was a big friend of my mother's, recommending me to go to Brady's Hotel, which I didn't go to 'cause the group I met on the train were all going to Hennessy's Hotel. I remember Mr. Hennessy, the owner, talking about the *Titanic*. He said that people who went on the *Titanic* had stayed in his hotel, and one man had a dream that something would happen. "Don't be foolish, go! Nothin' can happen to a big ship like that," people said to him. But he didn't go. I'll never forget that, listening to him tell that story.

We spent three days in Queenstown being examined by doctors. Our clothes were fumigated. They put all this stuff in your hair for lice. It was routine for everyone. There were many sent back. Several people had been turned away for heart murmur. One fellow had something wrong with a finger and he was turned down. I had some marks on my side from a sickness called "shingles," but there they called it "wildfire," and I was marked from it and it looked like a burn, and I was worried I would be turned back because I was also asthmatic. I had spasms. When I got a cold it stayed longer than the average person, and I'd wheeze a lot, but I passed. When I see these people coming in illegally today, it kind of annoys me because it wasn't easy at that time. It was very difficult, you had to be well.

I didn't know anybody else on the boat, only who I met. There were mostly Germans on board, but also Greeks, Russians, and Polish people. Not that many Irish. The Irish were mostly from the west of Ireland 'cause it's poorer—Mayo and Galway, where the land was not productive and very rocky.

I was in steerage. There was two bunks, like double-deckers, and I had a roommate, a girl. There was only two classes on this boat, steerage and first class. Most of the English ships had first, second, and third, but not this one, not the *President Roosevelt*. My father had advised me not to eat much, "leave it go for a day or so," but of course I was so hungry by the time I got on the boat that I ate everything I could get. By the second day I was so sick I didn't eat anything for the rest of the week.

It was a shame because there was a gorgeous dining room on the ship. There was a bar, a recreation room; not a large boat but a beautiful boat. It had everything. As sort of a souvenir they handed out bands to everyone, little bands to wear around your hat or your hair, with the "S.S. *Roosevelt*" embroidered on it. I've kept it all these years.

There was lots of dancing on deck. I met several Irish fellows who loved to play music. They never took lessons but they all could play violin or accordion. And then, of course, there was a lot of people playing shuffleboard, which I had never seen.

I left April 10 on the boat. I landed here on April 17. It was 1925. We came in the dark and docked in the harbor overnight. And, of course, from the boat I could see the lights of Manhattan and it was very exciting. I could hear the seagulls . . .

The next morning we got on a tender to go to Ellis Island and I was like everybody else: I was excited, but I didn't know what to expect. There were an awful lot of people. I can still remember that very large receiving hall. They examined me all over again, but I was not there more than three or four hours.

Mr. Grimes, from one of the travelers' aid societies, followed me up to see that I was in the right place, which I thought was wonderful. I was looking for one of my sisters, but I didn't know what she looked like and then she had called out my name . . .

She took me to my other sister's apartment on the Lower East Side. A lot of Germans and Irish and Italian. Mostly German and Irish. She had five rooms there, two bedrooms, kitchen, dining room, and living room. She had electricity, running water, everything. I couldn't believe it.

I stayed with her for about a month. I got a job at Macy's, but I didn't take it. Instead, I took a governess job I got through my sister's neighbor. The girl I replaced had been a governess for this little boy. His name was George Compton. His father was professor of English at City College and the Comptons were going to Cape Cod for the summer. And that summer happened to be a very hot summer. A lot of people died in New York from the heat in 1925. I worked for them for a year, saved my money.

In the meantime, I wrote my parents steadily, and the following year, I paid all their expenses to come to America. My mother, she didn't like giving up her nursing job and her pension, but she wanted to be with her children. She came together with my father, and my brother, who was nine years old. They came on the same liner I did, the *President Roosevelt*. They landed here about three or four days before Christmas. My sisters and I met them at Ellis Island.

We were called in by the doctor. My father had become a sick man. He could not work, so they would not let them in. So I spoke to Mr. Grimes again from the travelers' aid society. He came down with me and he thought I might need a bond, you know. The bond was $500. My sisters and I, what little money we had, we pooled together. But it wasn't enough.

The next day, Christmas Eve, Mr. Grimes came down and gave me $500 to show to immigration officials so my parents and my brother could pass through and then give it back, which we did. Can you imagine a man trusting strangers with $500? He was a wonderful guy to do that. My sisters and I had to sign a paper that my parents would not be a burden to the country and that my brother would be sent to school until he was fourteen years old and provided for. They moved into my sister's apartment.

Two years later, on the 22nd of May 1929, my mother went to get my father a cup of tea. She was about to give my father a match to light his pipe. He smoked a lot. She put the match in his hand, but he was dead. He died of heart failure. He was only fifty-seven years old.

Emanuel "Manny" Steen

· · · · · · · · · · · ·

BORN JUNE 23, 1906
EMIGRATED 1925, AGE 19
PASSAGE ON THE *CARONIA*, CUNARD LINE

Born in Dublin, one of eight children, he came to America with a twenty-dollar bill tucked in his shoe. His story is a classic.

· · · · · · · ·

He became a successful manager of electronic stores in Manhattan during the advent of radio. He is still married to Mary, his wife of sixty-nine years. They married in 1928. Proud parents and grandparents, they live in River Edge, New Jersey, "very grateful for what we have."

My parents were married in Glasgow. They weren't Scottish people, but they were married in Scotland in 1894, and they lived there. My father came to Glasgow from London. And before London he came from Turkey. He had escaped from the Cossacks in 1891 during a pogrom in the Ukraine, in a village near Odessa. His parents and most of his family were massacred. My father and his kid brother escaped. They hid out and they took a ferryboat to Constantinople. They worked there for a short while, got a job aboard a merchant vessel as seamen, jumped ship in London, which was typical of the time. A few years later, they came to Glasgow. My father was about nineteen, twenty. His kid brother was about fifteen, sixteen, and they got work in Glasgow. My father lived in a boardinghouse. That's where my father met my mother, and he fell in love with her. I wasn't around yet. But three of the children were born there.

My mother had a separate adventure. She and her parents were from a village near Warsaw, Poland. In the 1880s, refugees from Poland and from eastern Europe walked across Europe to the port of Hamburg and immigrated to, they hoped, America. What did happen was there were sea captains with boats totally unseaworthy. They promised to take these refugees, supposedly for twenty dollars, to America. You had to provide your own food and bedding. They

(Left) Nineteen-year-old Emanuel "Manny" Steen in Dublin, 1925, just prior to coming to America. The back of the photo is a postcard.

(Above) Manny Steen, now ninety-one, and his wife Mary during a visit to Ellis Island in 1997. The couple has been married for sixty-nine years.

(PHOTOS COURTESY OF MANNY STEEN)

supplied water and toilet facilities. So they crowded these horrible little vessels in the port of Hamburg and set sail for, ostensibly, the United States. Once they got out in the harbor everybody got seasick. They couldn't care less where they were. These captains of these illegitimate boats dumped a load of refugees on the east coast of Scotland during the night in a little seaport. They just dumped them and they said, "This is America," and they took off. The people didn't know any different. They couldn't speak any English, and here were these peculiar-looking men in kilts. They had never seen anything like it. I mean, men wearing skirts. They thought they were in America.

The Scottish government was very nice. They permitted these people to stay. My mother's family was one of the families that were dumped there, and the Scottish government agreed to permit them to stay, provided they did not become an economic burden to the government. They agreed to be self-supporting. There's a big Jewish settlement in Aberdeen and Edinburgh, and finally they made their way to Glasgow, which was an industrialized city. And they rented a huge apartment, like a seven-room apartment, and her family lived in two rooms and rented out the others. This was typical there. But also in the United States, in New York, down on the Lower East Side. That's the way they made a living. When my father and his kid brother went to Glasgow, they went to the Jewish section. They got a room to stay in and there my father met my mother.

After a few years, after the three children were born, a depression set in Glasgow, which was a big shipbuilding port. So my father took a ferry from Glasgow to Dublin, and he got a job in Dublin. And as soon as he saved a few dollars, he got an apartment and he brought the family over, and the other five children were born in Dublin.

In those days you took a job at anything, as I did when I came to America. I mean, I worked for twenty-five cents an hour when I came to America. Anything. It didn't make any difference. I have my father's marriage application and he was twenty-four at the time and it said his occupation was "aerated bottle washer." He cleaned seltzer bottles. My mother is listed as twenty-one and a seamstress, whatever that meant.

From that apartment in Dublin, we moved to a house when I was about six, which is what I remember. All the children then were born by midwives at home. The midwives wore a shawl and a bonnet and carried a black bag. Children were not born in hospitals. That was only for very wealthy people. We were five boys and three girls, and I remember waking up one morning and all the boys were chased out of the house, and my mother was screaming and crying and here I'm on the sidewalk in front of the house. It was a residential, working-class neighborhood in the south part of Dublin, called South Circular Road. And I was terrified. I mean, my mother never cried. But she was in childbirth and I didn't know that. And then my sisters shouted, "Come on in and see your baby brother."

The house was part of a row of narrow, adjoining red-brick cottages. In front was a small garden and fence. The house was one floor with two front rooms, a parlor, and dining room. Then the kitchen and four bedrooms. There was a long, narrow backyard, and behind that backyard an alley lane, where everything was delivered, such as coal for the winter. The coal would be brought up the lane and dumped in our backyard.

But remember, we were eight kids. My father and mother was ten. My bachelor uncle was eleven and my grandmother, my mother's mother from Glasgow, lived with us. Twelve people! My grandfather died in Glasgow. I never knew him. The boys slept four in a bed, toe-to-toe. The girls slept three to a bed. It was rather crowded, but it didn't feel that way because everybody was in the same situation.

There was one tap, running water if you wanted to take a bath. But there was no toilet, just an outdoor john. And each room, of course, had a potty. My job as number seven in the family was to empty the potties. I remember that because it was a terrible job. The youngest one always got that dirty job, you understand. There was no central heating. Each room had a tiny fireplace and an hour before we went to bed, one of us would light the fireplace in each bedroom with a few pieces of coal. We were poor people, not dirt poor. There are different levels of poverty as I see it now. We were poor but we ate.

My first recollection of my father, he was working in a sweatshop as a tailor making about six dollars a week. I used to walk about three or four miles and bring him his supper in a tin can. My mother would make a soup in the bottom layer and the one on top would be a little meat or potatoes. He worked from sunup to sundown, I mean twelve-, thirteen-hour days. And he would stop and eat his supper, and I would take the can back home.

My mother used to cook herrings. The Irish were great herring eaters, both fresh and salt herrings. It's really funny when you think about it because salt herrings you associate with Jewish people, but no. The herrings were salted and pickled so they would keep. Salt herring on potatoes was a very typical Irish dish, because it was cheap. You could feed a family on it until your belly was full, so that took care of your needs.

About two miles away, in an area of Dublin called Clanbrassil Street, was the Jewish section: a Jewish butcher, shoemaker, draper, bakery, etc. And I used to go there on Friday. The entrails of a cow were considered garbage food for cats and dogs.

Humans did not eat the liver, the heart, lungs, and all that stuff. My mother was too embarrassed to ask, so I used to go in. She said, "Tell him you want two pennies' worth of meat for the cat and the dog." God forbid you said humans. We were going to eat this stuff. I'd go in there and the butcher would take a big knife and cut off maybe half a liver, throw in a heart, a couple of lungs, and she'd say, "Don't forget to ask for a couple of soup bones." That was it. The butcher would put it all in a newspaper and I'd have an armful of stuff for about two pennies, three pennies. And my mother would make a kidney stew. Boy, we fed the whole family for two or three days on that.

My uncle Jack contributed to the family. He worked. I don't know where. I don't know what. You didn't ask. He was just there, you know. He loved the kids. I remember sitting on his lap, and he would tell us stories. He always wore a shirt and a tie, neat as a pin, and had a derby hat. A real character. To this day, I don't know anything about him. He was just part of us.

The community was Orthodox Jewish. Very religious. Not many people realize this, but there is such a thing as an Irish Jew. It was a small Jewish population, and everybody went to synagogue. The synagogue near us was jammed every Saturday. There was another one on Clanbrassil Street in the primary Jewish quarter, the main synagogue in Dublin, a beautiful structure called Englisher Synagogue. It was very high-class. On Saturdays, the big shots wore fancy suits, and tall hats like Prince Albert, we called them. In our temple people wore working-class suits. I was bar mitzvahed there.

When World War I broke out, it was 1914. Ireland was neutral and the British government was short of metals. Another uncle of ours, who lived in the neighborhood, had gone into what they called the waste trade business, which included scrap metal. He had a contract with the British government which needed scrap metal for ammunitions. So he approached my father, that it would be better than working in the sweatshop. My uncle taught him the business. In Ireland Gypsies were called tinkers and my father opened a shop and bought scrap metal from the tinkers.

But what happened was the 1916 revolution broke out and there was holy hell. I remember it fairly well because I was ten and I remember hearing all the shooting. Around the corner from our house were British military barracks, the Wellington Barracks. I remember the name. I used to play with the soldiers and the tanks in the barracks. The rebels took the general post office and a couple of the main hotels. I remember my mother went out to the backyard to get a bucket of coal and some sniper took a potshot at her. Next morning we found a bullet hole in one of the windows. After that, we moved from Dublin to the town of Sligo, in northwest Ireland, right on the border of Donegal.

Shortly after we moved, my mother died of kidney disease. That was 1917. I remember when they came to take her away in a horse-drawn ambulance. Soon after, my grandmother died.

I went to a Catholic seminary in Sligo called Somerhill College, as a day student. We were the only Jewish family that ever lived in that part of Ireland. I enjoyed life very much there. It was lovely, wild country. I was there until 1919. The war was over. My father's contract with the government stopped and he came back a man of means. Because of the war, he had done very well. We came back to Dublin. He bought a small factory that made trousers and walking britches, with about ten workers, and bought a duplex apartment right in the heart of Dublin. The family remained intact, ten of us now.

We had about eight bedrooms. We had the second and third floors in this apartment house. It was a big place. My father bought it completely furnished. Downstairs were two stores, a greengrocer and an iron monger, or hardware store. The people who previously lived there were going to America so my father bought the whole thing lock, stock, and barrel. And behind the apartment building was the rear entrance to the factory.

I was entering college, Saint Andrew's College in Dublin. I was fourteen. But the college system was different there. You didn't have to graduate high school to go to college. You could start college at six years of age and go right through. I was studying pre-med. That was the ultimate direction.

I went there, and in 1921 my father died in an accident. He was eating at a friend's house, and they were joking and kibitzing, and he choked on a piece of meat. By the time the horse-drawn ambulance came, he was gone. I remember the day. It was a Saturday, and I was home doing my homework when the police came, and it was a terrible shock.

My uncle Jack assumed command of the family, so to speak, and he said, "We can't go on." My father had lived it up and, after he died, we discovered there weren't any reserves and I had to stop college. So I took a crash course in wireless telegraphy. I had to have a trade. I took the Postmaster General examination from London and passed. Now I had a certificate as a wireless telegraph operator, Morse code.

So my uncle says, "The economy is nothing, we're all going to America. That's all there is to it. You'll apply for a passport and a visa . . ." Which I did. We had no money. Ireland was going through a terrible state. By 1921 civil war broke out, and it was awful. There were street ambushes and killings and murders. Unemployment was rife. So he thought coming to America would be the panacea.

UNITED STATES   MAIL STEAMERS.

Steerage Accommodation Unequalled for Ventilation, Light, and Care for Passengers' Comfort.

Passengers cannot do better than take their Tickets from our Agents before leaving home.

BRITANNIC.   CELTIC.   GERMANIC.   ADRIATIC.   BALTIC.
REPUBLIC.   OCEANIC.   GAELIC.   BELGIC.

THESE WELL-KNOWN, FAST MAIL STEAMERS SAIL FROM

LIVERPOOL TO NEW YORK,

EVERY THURSDAY,

GERMANIC,	Thursday, Aug. 31	BRITANNIC,	Thursday, Oct. 26
CELTIC,	,, Sept. 7	GERMANIC,	,, Nov. 9
BRITANNIC,	,, 21	CELTIC,	,, ,, 16
GERMANIC,	,, Oct. 5	BRITANNIC,	,, ,, 30
CELTIC,	,, 12		

Calling at QUEENSTOWN on the Following Day.

These splendid, full-powered, First-class Iron Screw Steamers are among the largest and most powerful vessels afloat, and are distinguished for the shortness and regularity of their passages, and the completeness and comfort of their passenger accommodation.

SALOON PASSAGE, 15, 18, AND 21 GUINEAS EACH BERTH,

According to State Room selected, all having equal Privileges in Saloon. Children under Twelve Years, Half-Fare. Infants Free.

Return Tickets, available for one year, issued at Reduced Rates.

These rates include a Liberal Table and Steward's Fee, without Wines or Liquors, which can be obtained on board. £3 Deposit is required to secure Cabin Berths, the balance to be paid the day before sailing. Luggage will go on board with the Passengers in the Tender that leaves the Landing Stage for the Steamer on the day of sailing.

STEERAGE FARE to NEW YORK, BOSTON, or PHILADELPHIA,

Six Guineas (£6 6s.) including a plentiful supply of cooked Provisions.

Children under Eight years Half Fare, and Infants under 12 months £1 1s.

The Steerage accommodation in these Steamers is of the very highest character, the rooms are unusually spacious, well lighted, ventilated, and warmed, and passengers of this class will find their comfort carefully studied.

Passengers will be provided with Berths to sleep in, each adult having a separate berth; but they have to provide themselves with a Plate Mug, Knife, Fork, Spoon, and Water Can, also Bedding,—all of which can be purchased on shore for about 10/-. MARRIED COUPLES, WITH THEIR CHILDREN, WILL BE BERTHED TOGETHER. FEMALES will be Berthed in rooms by themselves.

BILL OF FARE.—Each Passenger will be supplied with 3 quarts of Water daily, and with as much Provisions as he can eat, which are all of the best quality, and which are examined and put on board under the inspection of Her Majesty's Emigration Officers, *and cooked and served out by the Company's servants.*

BREAKFAST AT EIGHT O'CLOCK.—Coffee, Sugar, and fresh Bread and Butter, or Biscuit and Butter, or Oatmeal Porridge and Molasses.

DINNER AT ONE O'CLOCK.—Soup and Beef, Pork, or Fish, according to the day of the week, with Bread and Potatoes, and on Sunday Pudding will be added.

SUPPER AT SIX O'CLOCK.—Tea, Sugar, Biscuit, and Butter. Oatmeal Gruel will be supplied at 8 p.m. when necessary.

LUGGAGE.—TEN CUBIC FEET will be allowed for each adult Steerage Passenger, and 20 cubic feet for each adult Saloon Passenger, free; for all over that quantity a charge of 1s. 6d. for each cubic foot will be made. Steerage Passengers must have their luggage ready to go on board the Steamer on the morning of the day of sailing.

Passengers are landed at the Government Depôt, Castle Garden, New York, where they can purchase Tickets for, and receive every information respecting the departure of Trains, Steam-boats, &c.

These Steamers run in connection with the Erie Railway from New York—the shortest and best route to the West, North and South-Western States; and **Passengers are Booked through at low rates, to all parts of the States, Canada, Aspinwall and San Francisco**, also to Australia, New Zealand, China and Japan, by the Pacific Railway and Mail Steam-ship Company.

All passengers are liable to be rejected, who, upon examination, are found to be lunatic, idiot, deaf, dumb, blind, maimed, or infirm, or above the age of 60 years; or widow with a child or children; or any women without a husband with a child or children; or any person unable to take care of himself (or herself) without becoming a public charge, or who from any attending circumstances are likely to become a public charge, or who from sickness or disease, existing at the time of departure, are likely soon to become a public charge. Sick persons or widows with children cannot be taken, nor lame persons, unless full security be given for the Bonds to be entered into by the Steamer to the United States Government, that the parties will not become chargeable to the State.

ALL STEERAGE PASSENGERS embarking at Liverpool must be at the Office of the Agents, 10, Water Street, Liverpool, not later than 6 p.m. of the day before the advertised date of sailing, when the balance of the passage-money must be paid, or the deposit forfeited.

All Steerage Passengers embarking at Queenstown must be at the Office of the Agent at Queenstown (Cork) not later than Six o'clock p.m. of the day before sailing when the balance of the passage-money must be paid, or the deposit forfeited, and all Passengers will have strictly to conform to the Rules laid down by the Company. In order to meet the requirements of the Government Emigration Officer, Contract Tickets will be issued for the Noon of the day previous to the advertised date of sailing

AN EXPERIENCED SURGEON IS CARRIED BY EACH STEAMER.

STEWARDESSES IN STEERAGE TO ATTEND THE WOMEN AND CHILDREN. NO FEES OR EXTRA CHARGES

Classic advertisement for Irish emigrants. All ships departing from Irish ports were required to sail to England. Passengers then boarded another vessel to New York.

(NATIONAL PARK SERVICE: STATUE OF LIBERTY NATIONAL MONUMENT)

In the meantime, my brother Lou, who was a year and a half older than me, had gone to America the year before. He was a wild one. He was a nice chap, but he just didn't behave. He [had] a wanderlust. He had Gypsy blood in him, so to speak. My father was still alive then, and [Lou] said to me, "Listen, don't tell Pop, but I'm running away." So he ran away with the Gypsies, the tinkers, and he traveled Ireland and finally wound up in New York.

While we were waiting for our visas, we paid off our tickets in installments. But we didn't go all at once. That same year, after Lou went to New York, my brother Henry went. Then my sister and my kid brother came. Then in 1924, another sister, Eva, and two more brothers. Finally, in 1925, I came with my sister Bertha. Everybody was already here, but they were scattered. It wasn't a unified family. My brother Lou was now a cowboy up in Wyoming or something; one of my sisters married some chap from London and moved there, etc.

I was nineteen. I had no ties and looked forward to America as an adventure. My brother Lou was writing, telling me all about the wonderful things he was doing as a cowboy and how he was with Barnum and Bailey's Circus as an equestrian. I knew so little about America. For me, America was cowboys and Indians and streets paved with gold . . . I only had the good news, you understand. What I did know was poverty wages were big wages for Ireland. I remember this bank manager in Dublin was getting like twenty dollars a week, and that was considered great. In America you said, "I raise my boy to be president." In Ireland you said, "I raise my boy to be [a] bank manager," because that's the highest you could realistically hope for.

I bought a secondhand cardboard suitcase for two dollars, which I later donated to the Ellis Island Museum. All I had was a suit of clothes, an extra handkerchief, and a pair of socks. I also had my stamp collection in there, a crummy little collection of stamps, and a few family souvenirs. I didn't fill the suitcase. We were required to have twenty dollars to show financial independence. Would you believe it? When I came through Ellis Island I had twenty dollars. I had it in my shoe so I shouldn't lose it or, God forbid, lose it gambling on the ship.

I left from the port of Liverpool with my sister Bertha. We had cousins in Liverpool, so we stayed overnight with them and boarded the *Caronia* the next day. The ship was jammed. We came third class. It was four bunk beds in a cabin. Two up and two down with a tiny washbasin. Toilet was down the hall, a shower, and they served three meals a day. The men and women were separate. My sister was with some other women in their cabin.

It was the first time I had ever been on a ship that size, know what I mean? There were no amenities, none. But you could hear the second- and first-class passengers having a great time up there. But we didn't care, I mean, it was ten days. A ten-day ride. I was a good sailor, so I had no trouble. But a lot of people were sick. As a matter of fact, I came down one day for breakfast—nobody. The whole dining room was me.

The food was very plain. You didn't have a choice. They gave you a menu but you didn't have a choice. You just ate what was on the menu, and it was all right. I mean, as far as I was concerned it was very exotic because after my mother died my sister Bertha did the cooking, and she was probably the world's worst cook, you know what I mean? She was a great gal, but she was a terrible cook, and so this stuff tasted great to me, you know.

I arrived in New York Harbor August 1. It was a Wednesday, Wednesday morning. I remember about six o'clock I heard the lookout say, "Land ahoy!" Everybody rushed up on deck to see land, the first sign

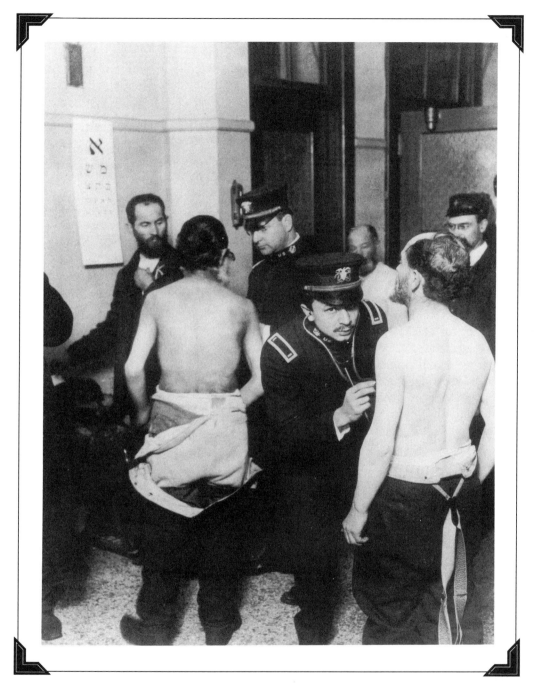

October 1907 photograph of Jewish male immigrants receiving a medical examination from
U.S. Public Health Service doctors

(NATIONAL PARK SERVICE: STATUE OF LIBERTY NATIONAL MONUMENT)

of America. I remember rushing up. I couldn't see a goddamned thing. I mean the horizon was the sea. Then, as we sailed closer, New York slowly emerged, as though it were coming out of the sea. And the first thing I saw was the Woolworth building. That was the tallest building in the world at the time. So the first thing you saw sticking out of the water was the top of the Woolworth building. And as we proceeded, of course, the building came out of the water. [Laughs.]

Everybody was cheering, "America!" My God, everybody was yelling and crying and kissing, and who could remember? There must have been two thousand people on that ship. You weren't aware that this was a historical moment, but it was. As we came in, of course, Manhattan Island started coming up, and the Statue of Liberty. Everybody knew what the Statue of Liberty was. I mean, there it was. I didn't understand too much about it. I knew about it in vague terms.

The boat anchored mid harbor, and then they tendered us from the ship to Ellis Island by the hundreds, suitcases in hand. The ferry had to go back and forth a few times, and we landed. Of course, the wharf and the whole area there was not like it is now. There was no grass or nothing. The main building was grimy on the outside. We got off the ferry and went right into the main building. That day there must have been three, four ships. Maybe five, six thousand people. Jammed! And remember, it was August. Hot as a pistol and I'm wearing my long johns and a heavy Irish tweed suit. Got my overcoat on my arm. It was the beginning of fall back home, see. And I'm carrying my suitcase. I'm dying with the heat. I never experienced such heat. During the day that hall became so hot and all they had was a couple of rotating fans, which did nothing except raise the dust. I just wanted to get the hell out of there.

Immigration officials slammed a tag on you with your name, address, country of origin, etc. Everybody was tagged. They didn't ask you whether you spoke English or not. They took your papers, and they tagged you. They checked your bag. Then they pushed you and they'd point, because they didn't know whether you spoke English or not. Understaffed. Overcrowded. Jammed. And the place was the noisiest, and the languages, and the smell. Foul, you know what I mean? But I was nineteen. You can stand a lot at nineteen. Then we had to go through the physical. I think, frankly, the worst memory I have of Ellis Island was the physical because the doctors were seated at a long table with a basin full of potassium chloride, and you had to stand in front of them, and they'd ask you to reveal yourself. They gave you what we used to call in the army a short-arm inspection. Right there in front of everyone, I mean, it wasn't private! You were standing there. And the women had to open their blouse. This was terrible.

I had to open my trousers and fly, and they checked me for venereal disease or hernia or whatever they were looking for. I was a young buck. I was in good shape, you know, but just the same I felt this was very demeaning, even then. I mean, it's terrible with women, young girls, and everyone, you know. And we had to line up in front of them . . . Years later I just thought they didn't have to do it that way. But this was the height of immigration. We were coming in by the thousands. And again, you're not aware this is historic, and this is something you're going to tell your grandchildren about . . .

Afterwards, we had customs immigration and we had to show our financial security of twenty dollars. I didn't realize until sometime later, but what happened was a lot of the guys on the ship were gambling. Some of the guys lost their twenty dollars. But there was a little racket there, you see. There was a wire fence and you had to go through the customs officers there. Now in order to go through, you had to show your twenty dollars. But a little further back on the fence there were a couple of guys making money. They would loan you the twenty dollars. Cost you two bucks, follow me? And they would loan you a twenty-dollar bill, and you'd go to the gate and come through the gate, and the guy would be there to take the twenty-dollar bill back from you. Cost you two bucks. For two bucks you could show twenty. Whether the guy was splitting it with the guard I don't know.

I almost died of thirst. Couldn't find the fountains. Could hardly find the men's room . . . Finally, Bertha and I got through, and my brother Henry was supposed to claim us. Our claimant. You had to be claimed by a responsible person. But Henry didn't show up, so we're waiting. They wouldn't let us on the ferry until we were claimed, and it's four o'clock and the island closed at five and the staff went home. So they shipped us over to the depot on the other side of the island, the ferry building, and we were held there in a group pen for unclaimed, but okayed, immigrants. I don't know how many because you're concerned about yourself. You couldn't be less interested. Bertha and I were wondering what the hell we were going to do. We didn't have Henry's phone number. We didn't know where he lived. Are they going to send us back?

Now it's five o'clock, and they're closing up. So I explained all of this to a guard who called up HIAS, the Hebrew Immigrant Aid Society. The idea was we would be turned over to HIAS, who would be responsible for us. About fifteen minutes later this little, short chap came in and the funniest thing was, knowing we were Jewish, he insisted upon talking Yiddish. We didn't speak Yiddish. We spoke English, a little Gaelic, but I did understand German from some college courses I took.

So we got along, and he took us by ferry to Battery Park, and we started walking to HIAS headquarters on Lafayette Street. Bertha and I were dying. It's hot. We've had nothing to eat, just a little water, and we're getting a little weak, and he's in a hurry because it's pushing seven o'clock, and this is a chore, and he wants to get home, follow me, follow me.

He takes us to the subway. I had never seen a subway. We knew there were such things as underground trains, and we go down the steps to the noise, the flashing lights. In those days there was no air conditioning. They had little fans in the trains. And I remember sitting in the subway car with my suitcase and Bertha, and this guy who paid no attention to us whatsoever, and we're dripping! I must have lost ten pounds that day. And those days I was only about 130 pounds.

It was just one or two stops, and we got off. It was one floor up. We could barely climb the stairs. And we came to the HIAS office, and he took off. There was a woman there. *"Will sassem?"* she asked. Do you want to eat? And she took us into a dining room with long wooden tables, nothing fancy, and brought out a big bowl of cold soup, a milky substance, with some green things floating in it. "Bertha," I said, "what do you think this is?" "I don't know, eat!" It turned out to be spinach soup. I'd never seen it before, but it was cold and it was wet and it was delicious, and she brought in a big pile of fresh pumpernickel and a big pile of butter and, Jesus, we ate everything.

When we got through, Henry comes in the door. I hadn't seen him in four years. He had gone to the island, traced us back. "Where were you?" I asked. The boss wouldn't let him off. Henry was a tailor. The boss said, "You want to get off? Don't come back."

We took the subway to a three-room apartment on 118th Street and Third Avenue in East Harlem. In 1925, East Harlem was a mixture of Italian and Jewish. About fifty-fifty. No blacks. And it was a very friendly neighborhood. Everybody more or less knew each other. As soon as we arrived, Henry said to me, "Get those long johns off and throw the goddamned things out. They stink like hell," and he loaned me a pair of BVDs. Oh, boy! It was like getting out of jail.

He had an icebox, I had never seen one, with a big chunk of ice in there. That was a tremendous novelty. And a modern cooker, and a bathroom with a shower. This was the height of luxury, you know what I mean?

Next morning, I'm up bright and early. It's like seven o'clock and Henry is up, too, and getting ready.

"Where are you going?" I asked.

"I gotta go to work."

"What will I do?"

"Today you take off," he says. "Tomorrow you get a job."

"All right." He's the older brother so he's the boss. I was accustomed to accepting authority, see. So I said, "What'll I do?"

"Take a trolley car and go downtown. Take a look around."

"What's a trolley car?"

"Tram. That's what they call them over here. Trolley cars."

"How much it costs?" because in Ireland we had a zone system. You go from one zone to the next, you pay so much for each zone. "No, there's no zone," he said. "One fare all the way."

"How much?"

"A nickel."

"What's a nickel?" You know, I had never seen a nickel. I didn't know what he was talking about. So he goes in his pocket and he takes out a coin, a five-cent piece.

"That's a nickel."

"Why do they call it a nickel?"

"Figure it out. I gotta go to work," and he took out another one. "See this one here, the little one. That's called a dime."

"Why?"

"Look, I can't stand here all day arguing with you. That's five cents. This is a dime. Two of those nickels make one dime, see? You go downtown. It will cost you a nickel, follow me? Ten cents will get you back and forth, follow me? But remember, only pay one nickel each way."

Then he hands me a quarter, the big shot. Not the most generous act he ever did in his life. He was a tight bugger. Anyway, he says, "That's a quarter. That's a quarter of a dollar. Twenty-five cents." So anyway, now I had twenty-five, ten cents, and a nickel, and he said, "Go downtown and take a look."

So I go to the corner, and the trolley cars were open trolley cars. And it's bright, sunny. The trolley car stopped, and I got on, and I sat down, and the conductor, he had a big, leather pouch, and he came over. The conductors on the Third Avenue trolley were all Irish immigrants. And he says, "What are you doing, young fella?" And I, at that time, spoke with a brogue. And I says, "Just taking a ride downtown."

"Is it Irish you are?"

"Aye," I says.

"When did you get here?"

"Yesterday. I just got off the boat!" [Laughs.]

"Why didn't you tell me that?" he says, "I wouldn't have charged you the nickel." He sat down beside me, and there was nobody else. It was about ten o'clock and he's pointing, giving me a free tour all the way down Third Avenue. He's pointing out the buildings, the Singer building, and I was fascinated. Hey, America is a great place. I'm here one day and this guy is giving me a royal reception.

I got off at City Hall Park where the trolley terminated. I saw City Hall. I was feeling very adventurous. Here it's a beautiful day, and I'm wearing thin underwear, and I'm beginning to feel comfortable now, and I walked across a park, and I looked up and there's the street sign. It says "Broadway." Well, I want to tell you, that was one of the most exciting moments of my life. Broadway! I'm only one day in America and I'm on Broadway! I mean, it may sound like nothing to you, but I got so excited. It's a wonder I wasn't killed, because the traffic was going in all directions, and I was so confused, watching to the left, to the right.

I started walking down Broadway to the Woolworth building. What an exciting experience to see that bloody building. When I looked up, it was a funny thing, the building looked like it was teetering forward, you know what I mean? Of course, it wasn't falling, but I had a feeling of hallucination that the building was going to fall down so I kept going to Battery Park, where I had come across from Ellis Island the day before. "How do you like that?" I thought. "One day in America and I'm right back here where I started from."

Fantastic! I walked across the park and sat down on the bench and nobody was bothering me. No one could identify me as a foreigner, you know, and everybody's acting like I'm a full-blooded American.

There was a guy with a pushcart selling hot dogs. Now I knew about hot dogs from watching American movies in Dublin. I knew that the people ate this thing here. They didn't have hot dogs in Ireland. They had sausages. But it was only five cents, so I figured I would speculate. I asked for a frankfurter and he gave me a frank and he wanted to put all the stuff on it. "No, no, no," I said. And the people there were buying. They were scooping mustard on it, and I was accustomed to English mustard, like Colman's mustard, that'll burn your guts off. So I said, "How can these people eat with all that mustard on there?"

I didn't have anything on it. I ate it, and it tasted nice. It was garlicky, you know, and it had a nice taste. And there I was eating my hot dog and taking the world in with my eyes and I thought, "I got it made," you know. I walked further, and I saw a guy selling ice cream sandwiches. Nickel a sandwich. I speculated once more, and I had a ball. It was a great feeling. Absolutely.

I felt like I had the world on a string. I mean, this was my day, see what I mean? Well, I figured I had to remember how to get back. And I was trying to remember different marks of identification to make sure I got on the proper trolley car. I finally got back to East Harlem, and it was late afternoon when I got back, and my brother came home, and I told him about my day. He thought it was dull and dumb, but it wasn't to me. It was one of the most exciting days. And that was my first day in America.

Stephen Brady

BORN JULY 19, 1914
EMIGRATED 1927, AGE 12
PASSAGE ON THE *PRESIDENT CLEVELAND*

His father and two older brothers came here first in 1926. He came the following year with his mother and four younger brothers. He went to college at night, shoveling rock from boats during the day for the National Gypsum Company.

He eventually became head of the purchasing and transportation department and, in 1970, started a refuse collection company now run by two of his sons. Retired in 1986, he and his wife Ann have four children, and thirteen grandchildren, and live in Naples, Florida. "I think the opportunities in this country are just mammoth," he said. "I mean, where in the world would a greenhorn like me get a chance to do what I've done."

We lived right on the sea. Our house was built on stilts about two feet high, and on a spring tide we would get water close by the house. The tide came in and went out right to our front door, actually. We were not more than maybe a hundred feet from the sea itself. The railroad tracks ran between our house and the sea. It was a bay, really. The house had six small rooms, all on one floor. We had a coal stove in the kitchen. It was a large kitchen. We had a small farm. We raised chickens. I cleaned out the henhouse all the time. We also grew potatoes, brussels sprouts, beans, and we had about 250 laying hens, so we sold a good deal of what we raised.

I was born in Raffeen in County Cork. When I was about four years old, the family moved to Monkstown about two miles away and we built that stilt house. Monkstown was a parish seat which takes in Raheen and Drumbilla. I went to school in Drumbilla with my six brothers. I had a sister, but she was born in New York City after we came here in 1927.

My father was in the British navy. He was a master rigger. In fact, when he came to this country he was one of the people who worked putting up the steel in the Empire State Building, the Chanin building, and all the big buildings that went up in the late twenties. He went to sea between Liverpool and Argentina. He would be away for two, three months at a time. And that was one of the real regrets that I have that I didn't see him, or get to know him even. I remember when he would come home for a visit

he would kick his bag, like a duffel bag, off the train and we'd pick it up, and we'd walk home from the station. But it was a period of my parents' life that was kind of regrettable in a lot of ways, because they didn't have a normal husband-and-wife life, put it that way. My father, when he was home, used to go fishing every night catching what he called "goodill."

My mother was very close to her mother, my grandmother. And she used to go see her once a week, which was a long ways away. She walked, it was a very lonely road, and spent the day with her mother. My grandfather was caretaker of a Franciscan monastery close by their home. He was really a very accomplished man when it came to horticulture. I seldom saw my grandparents on my father's side. Only once that I recall. They were living in Cork City, which was about ten miles from where we lived. I was about ten years old. And I went by donkey and cart to buy cornmeal that we used for chicken feed.

I was about six when I started school. We had a one-room schoolhouse. One side was the boys and one side of the room was girls. It was divided by a wall. I went from the first to the fifth grade there. It was a national school. A national school was a Catholic school over there. And I remember this family named Johnson were not Catholic, they were Protestants. And I remember they were let out to play during the catechism quiz, and I wished I was a Protestant then. [Laughs.]

There were two teachers. There was a woman who had the lower classes, and a man who had the upper classes. And he was a mean individual. He thought nothing about taking out an ash cane and bopping you with it across your fingers. He didn't touch the kids whose fathers were home. It was the ones whose fathers were away at sea or out of the country that got hit. The girls were treated a lot better. And, of course, if you were Protestant you didn't get touched.

There were a lot of Protestants in the area. The Protestants, generally speaking, were wealthy by our standards. They owned the farms. They came to Ireland from England. Going back into history, they got land grants from the king of England. They made no bones about taking the land away from the Irish who owned it.

It was unjust when you get right down to it. And there was constant friction. For example, we had goats, and a lot of people there had goats. And they'd round up our goats and lock them up from time to time, because they were grazing on their property. And they felt they had the right to do it, and we didn't feel that way, and we let them know it. There's never been any reconciliation, really. The Protestants had the wherewithal to hire people, and a lot of the Irish Catholics went to work for Protestants or they didn't eat. For example, to make extra money, my oldest brother Michael and I used to caddy on the golf course in Monkstown. The Monkstown Golf Club. He was nine years older than me. I would say I was closer to him than anybody else because he bailed me out every time I fell behind. He would take the heavy bag and I would take the lighter bag. I always say, when the Jews and the Arabs make up, so will the Irish.

I'm not saying who was right, who was wrong, but they had a disagreement among themselves, the Irish did. One wanted a free-state form of government, the other wanted a republican form of government. I remember Michael and I were going to go to confession in Monkstown, which was the nearest church. It was dark, a Saturday night, and we followed the railroad tracks. Well, we didn't get very far when there were shots fired over our heads. The man who was shot and killed was a soldier in the free-state army who was patrolling that area. Of course, we ducked back into the house as fast as we could. So there was actually real violence going on between the free state and the republicans.

My father wanted to come to America because things were so bad in Ireland that there was no prospect of jobs. I mean, Ireland was just stripped of its youth all the time. People couldn't find work, and they knew there was work in Canada, New Zealand, Australia, and America. There was no reason for them to stay. I remember this one man, the only one I knew who had a job, he would ride his bike over a mile, get into a boat, row across the bay, and then ride a bike to another building where he was a watchman, and that was the only work I knew of that was available in Ireland, which was a pretty sad situation.

I always tell the story that my mother wanted to take the family to America and my father wanted to take the family to Australia or New Zealand, and they compromised. They went to America. [Laughs.] He was very much influenced by England. He thought there'd be better opportunities in Australia or New Zealand. But my mother had sisters and brothers in the United States and, as I say, they compromised and did it her way.

My father and Michael left in July of 1926. The idea was to accumulate enough money to get the rest of us over. My father would send home the money to Ireland. Then in October of that same year my brother Patrick came. And by the following March of 1927, there was enough money to bring my mother, me, and my four younger brothers. It was a pretty damn tough existence. Patrick went to work for the New York Telephone Company. He was only sixteen or seventeen. And Michael, who was two years older, went to work for Seaman Brothers, a big food chain supplier. My brothers and my father lived with an aunt, my mother's sister, in the Bronx. She had a couple of rooms, and she rented it out to them.

We couldn't take very much with us. Just a few bags with our belongings. We got a donkey and a cart, and went to Queenstown. I know that night we left Queenstown it was midnight. We boarded the ship then. We were kind of excited about it. We were looking forward to seeing our father, my brothers, and so on. And the people of that town, little as it was, they were all family. That's what it really amounted to. Every time I used to caddy on Sunday morning on the golf course, I'd see these liners come in and you knew there were people getting on them you were never going to see again for as long as you live. [He is moved.]

We left Ireland on the 5th of March 1927. We had to go to the baths and be sure we were clean and no lice. A tender took us out to the ship, the *President Cleveland*, a 17,000-ton liner. We came way down in the bilges on the ship. We were steerage. Lucky to get out. The first landing was Halifax, then Boston and then New York. The restrictions going into Canada were not as rigid as it was going into the United States. A lot of people used to immigrate through Canada and spend some time there, and then come into this country.

The first day out of Queenstown we had some real rough weather. Everybody got sick. And us being down in the bottom of the boat didn't help, either. It was hot and it was bunk beds. My youngest brother got very sick. So being the oldest of the youngest, I had to watch out for them pretty much. I remember this German kid with this big German family tried to push one of my brothers down the stairs of the ship. Let's just say it wasn't my brother who fell down the stairs.

It was in the morning, about eleven o'clock, when we arrived in New York. My father, Michael, and Patrick were waiting for us at the dock. One thing about Ellis Island, we were cleared before we got there. We didn't set foot on the island. My father and brothers were at the dock when the ship came in. We could see them from the ship. It was pretty damn exciting to see them, I'll tell you.

6

. . . .

Scotland

(APPROXIMATELY 600,000 IMMIGRANTS, 1892–1954)

Clare Conrick

. . . .

BORN DECEMBER 31, 1895
EMIGRATED 1902, AGE 6
PASSAGE ON THE *CALEDONIA*

She was born in the country village of Dunoon near Glasgow.
She came through Ellis Island during the height of immigration. Sadly, at 101
years of age, time has stolen much of her memory. She says she married a
Native American who "worked for the health department," or "sold records in a
record store," or "worked in a furniture store." She is not sure.
She lives in a nursing home in Manhattan. She outlived her son and daughter,
but she has two grandchildren who visit her.

We lived near Glasgow on a street called New City Road. I remember the house because I remember a neighbor, whose name was Mrs. Olifant, and we were very naughty and we called her Mrs. Elephant. That was not very nice. I was reprimanded for that, and I thought that was funny, but it wasn't funny to the teacher. So I got punished. I had to stand up in front of the classroom and hold my hand out, and she slapped my hand. After that I behaved myself.

We had a housemaid that came in, and I think her name was Lizzie, and she helped us with the [house] work. I liked Lizzie because when she was off, she used to take me out at night to meet her gentleman friend. I liked that because the gentleman friend always gave me sweets, candy, and she'd take me out and I met all her gentleman friends.

We had a big family. My parents were very busy. We had eight children. Six girls and two boys, as well as uncles and aunts who lived nearby. My father's parents lived near us. We lived in a house. I never knew what apartments were like. I had never seen an apartment till I came here . . .

I remember, we never wore socks. I never owned a pair of socks till I came to America. We wore long stockings that were knitted by hand. Grandma, "Bubba," we called her, used to knit stockings, and they were so warm. Mother would teach us to knit, you know. She taught us to knit stockings because in the wintertime we didn't wear socks like the children do here. We had to be warm, so I was taught to learn to knit stockings. I liked that because then I was very proud when I knitted something.

My father was a carpenter, and he made very interesting tables, something he had learned from his father. Grandpa was a carpenter, too. There was one table that was so beautiful, a mahogany table, but it was sort of inlaid with different patterns. And you know what we did with the table? We were very naughty in those days and made believe there were spirits rising from the table.

Grandma was just a housewife, but she did charity work. She took us to a show called the Hippodrome, and it was like going to a circus. I loved it because she gave us each a bag of candy. But then I was told there's diabetes in the family, and I should not have too many sweets. "Don't be a pig,"

Natives of Scotland, John D. Third and family came aboard the S.S. Caledonia *and arrived September 17, 1905. Their sponsor was a friend named John Fleming (not in photo), who lived in Anniston, Alabama, where they settled. From Ellis Island, they headed south by train.*

(NATIONAL PARK SERVICE: STATUE OF LIBERTY NATIONAL MONUMENT)

she told me. "Don't eat too many starches and sweets. When you grow up to be a young lady and you have children, you don't want your children to inherit your diabetes."

I was not allowed to have it. Well, one time, during Yom Kippur, when we had to atone for sins, fast, and go to shul, I was in a waiting room. We were brought up religious, orthodox. I took three gumdrops from the table, and God punished me, because when I went out of the waiting room my gumdrops rolled down the gutter. So I got punished right away. [Laughs.] I never became diabetic, nor my children.

My brothers, my sisters, my parents, and my grandparents—all came to America together. We left Lizzie behind. I remember

my mother, who was very religious, took her English candlesticks for the Shabbat . . . We sailed from Glasgow. It was a big family, and we had good passage, we had cabins. There were about four people in the cabin with me. It was in a good place. I remember the steerage people down below, poor people who couldn't afford better. There were a lot of people who couldn't afford the trip, and the charity organizations paid for them . . .

I remember the plum pudding on the ship. I loved that plum pudding. And very good vegetables, and soup, and chicken . . . There were some people who couldn't tolerate the rocking of the boat, and they became seasick. We thought, how stupid, to get seasick. It was so much fun on the boat. But they were older people, and later on I had sympathy for them.

. . .

New York City! I was so excited. My parents said, "Don't make so much noise. You're not the only one that comes in here." [Laughs.] To think, I came to America! I had never seen tall buildings in Scotland, and when I saw the the Statue of Liberty I thought it was the most wonderful thing. I took pictures of it. I used to dream about it. I said, "Oh, we read about it in the history books, and now we see the statue." That impressed me, because it was something I read about and I thought I would never see it.

At Ellis Island, it was such a big fuss because some reporters came in. There were a lot of reporters. And we said, "Why are the reporters here?" The newspaper was called the *World Telegram*, I think. That was the name of an old newspaper. They took pictures of us, especially the Scottish men from the boat. They were wearing kilts, you know. And the men [the reporters] laughed at that costume when they came here. Then they [the inspectors] fingerprinted us and we had to take blood tests to see if we were in good enough health to be admitted. There were a lot of people who were not in good condition, but we were just a bunch of brats. We were in good health, every one of us . . .

My folks got a place out in Brooklyn in a place called Flatbush, way out near Coney Island. I thought it was so funny that people ate corn on the cob out in the street. I said, "What a strange land this is. They have corn on the cob, and they eat it in the street." I thought, "That's a very crazy way of living." But we did the same thing later. [Laughs.] . . .

The schools were very particular because they gave you a physical examination first. And, you know, it sounds funny, but they examined your head. I hate to tell you, but some people, they had vermin in their heads, and we never heard of such a thing. We said, "How does this happen?" They said, "Well, some homes, they are not very clean, and the children are allowed to do what they like."

We were examined for something in the head called nits. If you had nits you could have vermin. It sounds funny, but when I tell my children about it now they say, "Are you sure about that?" I say, "Yeah." They looked through our hair with a pencil. We had measles, and mumps, and all the childhood diseases, but we were in good health.

We weren't dressed like American children. We had long, they call them gaiters, because we were afraid of catching cold. We were not used to the American climate. So we were bundled up. Then we said, "Oh, how stupid." Afterwards, we learned to wear long stockings like the American children. But at first, we were very stupid, and Mama and Papa didn't know what to dress us in, but we learned. We learned to wear long stockings. Mama, Grandpa, Grandma used to knit stockings for us, homemade stockings, *zucken*, they called it.

Then we went on the streetcar. They called it a trolley. I never saw so many people out in the street, and the little private houses. It was very impressive, you know. I liked America as soon as we got here.

I stayed in school till about the eighth grade. I went to graduation. My school work was good. Some of us went to night school to learn typing and stenography. Others went to work, and I liked to work with the American people because they were so different. I worked in a store, and it was called Landay Brothers. It was a music store, and I loved it. And I loved the elevators, and we had an elevator man, a black man. My first black man. He was very funny. We'd say, "Willie, are you going up?"

"I ain't goin' down."

"You goin' down, Willie?"

"I ain't goin' up."

Marge Glasgow

. . . .

BORN JANUARY 23, 1906
EMIGRATED 1922, AGE 15
SHIP UNKNOWN

She came to this country alone when she was fifteen years old and worked as a domestic in Newark, New Jersey. She went on to own two very successful dress boutiques that helped "put my six children through college." Her husband was a German electrician she met at church. Today, they live in rural New Jersey, and though "it's hard to keep track," she says, they have twenty-eight grandchildren and great-grandchildren. "I have medals for dancing," she said. "I have my costume. From when I was eight till about twelve, I did all that Highland dancing in Scotland. The sword dance, the Highland fling. I loved to dance. I loved to have fun."

My family is Catholic, devout Catholics, and this particular town, Motherwell, was like Belfast, Ireland. There was such fighting between the Catholics and Protestants. I used to feel sorry for the priest coming around on sick calls on his bicycle and being disrupted and having things done to it. My religion was so strong that I think that's why I wasn't so in love with Scotland. Also when we had a May procession, my mother would dress us up in a pretty white dress and a veil, and these people would stop and pull our veil off and molest us along the way. Scotland is a beautiful place, and I've been back many times, many times. But it wasn't nice living.

I was never afraid. I didn't hold any animosity towards Protestants. This girlfriend and myself, we used to love to go to all the churches. We'd go to the Salvation Army, too, because they had a band. Anything that had music we would follow, just dancing, Highland dancing, and parading, and go and stop and enjoy the meetings, and go in and listen to the prayers, and do everything and come out.

My father was a puddler. He worked at a steel furnace. He used to work just with his pants on and a towel around his neck, and I used to stand and watch him and bring his beer, and he would turn that steel around, and it's red, red hot. And then pull it out and put it on rollers. And I would be standing just a few yards away from him, watching him do that. It was a good job to have. It wasn't one of the highest-paid. I think it was a little low class. But I was very proud of my father. It was just his great sense of humor.

He liked his drink. He had a little clay pipe. The men in Scotland smoked little clay pipes, and my father always smoked a clay pipe. But he loved to have a drink, and I loved to help him come home, staggering home. Across from a little Baptist church on the corner was the pub where all the men congregated. And that's where my father used to go on Friday night and come out singing all the way home. And I'd be waiting for him. We'd love to see him come home, you know. Of course, my mother was ready to beat him over the head with something.

. . . .

Motherwell was a nice little town, but after the war, I wasn't too content there. I just knew that there was something better, and [I wanted] to get to United States [where] I could make a better living. I felt I was at an age where I had to start earning money and making a career for myself, and I didn't see any possibilities in Scotland.

My whole idea was to get to United States, and work, and help to bring my family. Eventually, each one would come, because there were many people migrating, so I was very insistent and, of course, much to my parents' dislike, they were afraid to let me go at a young age. I had no relatives in America. But we did have neighbors who had young girls working in a factory [in New Jersey] making good money and I thought I could work, get a job and send money home to my parents.

It wasn't easy for me to convince my parents that I was capable of going over and taking care of myself. But I was determined. No matter what obstacle came up I always found a way out of it. For instance, a professional man—a priest or doctor—had to sign

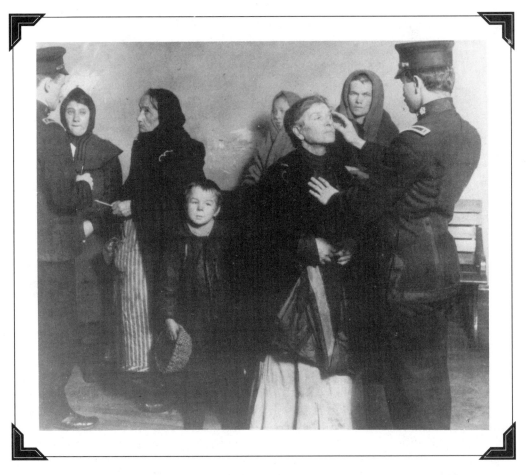

Peasants being inspected for trachoma or cataracts in 1905 during the height of immigration

(NATIONAL PARK SERVICE: STATUE OF LIBERTY NATIONAL MONUMENT)

certain papers, and the expression that my mother got from our Catholic priest was, "You're daft." My mother said, "You don't know this girl, what a determined person she is." So I said, "Well, don't worry. I know another Baptist minister, and he will sign it for me."

I finally got my way. My mother got me a pretty outfit and I left home. My father and brother took me to the boat. I don't remember the name.

It was a ten-day journey. In the cabin with me was a young mother with a little baby. When the mother was sick, I would help with the baby and get the bottle heated and take care of it. The journey over, I began to have regrets about leaving home. I was feeling very lonesome, sorry for myself, crying all the time. I don't remember if I went to Ellis Island alone or everybody went, but I was always afraid of Ellis Island. I had heard stories that if they keep you at Ellis Island they go through your hair looking for bugs. My mother was always scaring me with that. Anyhow, when I followed an attendant with my luggage [at Ellis Island] I thought, "Oh, my God, I'm going to be here." I remember they took all my clothes off and made me shower, and wrapped all my beautiful clothes in a duffel bag, which hurt me so much to see them being rolled up, you know, and put in a duffel bag and put away.

I remember the Great Hall, and the desks there with men. I don't know if they were doctors, judges or what, questioning the people, you know. And that's when I was very scared, to be all alone in that big building being questioned. So I was really crying hysterically and sobbing so hard that the doctor came to me. They had doctors there examining everybody, and he put his arms around me and said, "Please, please, don't cry so hard. We're trying to help you. We only want to help you. We won't hurt you. We're helping you." And I said, "Perhaps the people didn't come to get me." And he said, "No, that's not the reason." He said, "You have something in your eyes that we have to test [trachoma], and it will take ten days to test. It might be a disease. But we are also investigating other people. You'll be taken care of. Everything will be fine."

So I sort of calmed down, and then a nurse came, and she took me. I was in the hospital there. She said, "Come with me." I was still a kid, fifteen. I followed her on her rounds, and she was very kind to me. She consoled me so much that I felt better. Then she put me to bed in a room next to her.

The next morning everything was calm and nice. The nurse was still taking care of me. She took me outside to sit and see all the boats go by. I sat there and I wondered, "Will they let me into United States, or will they send me back?" I so much wanted to live here in United States.

Then, after lunch, somebody came and they brought me some flowers. There was a young man maybe eighteen, and he was always walking around. The nurses were admiring my curly hair, fixing my hair, I had auburn hair. They were fussing, teasing me, that I might be coming over to give Mary Pickford competition. This young man brought me a box of candy, and the nurses were so friendly, they even asked if I would like to get employment through one of the doctors, maybe as a mother's helper. I spent ten days there and every day was better than the [last]. It was such a pleasure. They were extra kind because they felt sorry for me, I guess, that I was alone and coming to a country not knowing anyone . . .

I was admitted, of course. But I always had problems with my eyes. The day I was leaving I was standing in line with others, and I remember putting my hair all inside of my hat, and one of the nurses came over, took my hat off and said, "Don't hide that beautiful hair!" I said, "I thought I might look older, it might help me get through." The doctors were most kind, saying good-bye and that if I wanted a job to be sure and contact them, but I couldn't do that because I had to go to the people who sponsored me. So my entrance to United States was very pleasant. It was wonderful.

The people who sponsored me were very kind. Then I discovered, when I went with them, that I was too young to go to work. I had to be sixteen to work. So my decision then was to go as a mother's helper. There was a lady who had a millinery store in Newark, New Jersey. I took care of her little girl, and I lived there. Then my brother came over. He came over about two months after I arrived. My sister came after that, and within a year, three more of my family came over, including my mother and father. I went to Ellis Island to meet them. That was nice, wonderful, because I introduced them to all my friends. It's been so long ago, I bet none of those people [friends] are alive.

I worked for that one lady taking care of the little girl. I wasn't paid too much. In the meantime, my sister was working for a family in Montclair, New Jersey, which is a lovely section. She told me somebody was looking for a girl to work. So I went there personally on a Saturday morning to apply for the situation. I met a Mr. Quigley, who was a judge, Michael J. Quigley. His family lived in Newark. He was a handsome, handsome man, and he came to the door, and I said that I came to apply for the job. He took one look at me and laughed. Then his wife came, and she said, "Mike, that's not very nice. Ask the girl to come in." So I went in. They were looking for a cook. They had six children of their own, and he said, "Now we have another one." So I got the job.

There were two girls, a girl in college and a girl in high school, by a previous marriage.

Then there were two children, maybe nine and eleven, and there were a set of twins, nine months old, who had an English nurse. They had a real nurse take care of them. They were a wealthy family. So I was hired, and I worked for them and loved them, and loved the family, the children. That was my home, really. I was with them for two years, till my mother came. My father came before my mother.

The Quigleys took the best of care of me. They paid attention to the company I kept, you know. My sister and I, we would go to New York to Scottish dances, Irish dances. Anything that was dancing. And Michael Quigley says, "You be sure . . . I want to know when you come home and who you come home with," you know. He took care of me like a father.

He loved my Scottish brogue. Once in a while he would ask me about my father. I would tell him a funny story that my father told me, when Michael Quigley had company. Sometimes he'd have the mayor of the town. He would come in the kitchen and say, "Marge, do you mind coming in here and telling the mayor the story your father told you?" And I would tell him the story. And they would all laugh!

One story I used to tell. There were a lot of Irish people who came over to Scotland to work in the steel mills. Some people had them, the Irishmen, as boarders. So my father used to tell how this woman had a boardinghouse and all these boarders, and one day one of them died, and she asked somebody else to go upstairs and carry him down. After a person dies, it seems, the last thing they have is a BM. So this man carrying him said, "Well, if he can shit, he can walk." And he dropped the corpse.

7

· · · · · · · · · ·

Wales

(APPROXIMATELY 53,000 IMMIGRANTS, 1892–1954)

Agnes Howerbend

· · · · · · · · · · · · ·

BORN APRIL 19, 1907
EMIGRATED 1912, AGE 5
PASSAGE ON THE *CAMPANIA*

*She was born in the north Wales hamlet of Blaenau Ffestiniog on the rugged
Atlantic coast. One of four children, her family settled in the Welsh community of
West Winfield, New York, outside Utica, where she lives to this day. "My heart
is in my homeland," she said. "I feel so near and dear to the people there. But
God bless America, it has been good to us."*

The town was carved out of a mountain; rows of houses and streets with iron fences, and sometimes you'd see sheep coming down from the mountain and going along the street near the sea. One day, I remember there was a woman who left her gate open. These two sheep went right in and ate up all of her flowers. [Chuckles.] But around our home the last recollection I had was when we were getting ready for the trip. I was getting dressed, and my parents said why don't you go in the yard and play awhile. And I looked up at the mountain, and there was this one sheep way up on the top clinging for his life. That's what I remember.

We lived in a stone house, a large house. Our grandparents, my father's family, lived in a smaller stone house down the road, almost a replica. We had, of course, a small farm, and there was a barn. Inside, I remember only that there was slate floor in some parts, and a great big fireplace and oven.

My father was a quarry man. He worked in the quarries, and he kept a hired hand to take care of the farm. I can remember my father and the other workers. They never took much time for dinner, but they always came up and sang. That was the big thing over there, a song. In fact, Wales is known as the Land of Song.

My grandfather was quite a tall man, good man. He loved to sing, too. I used to say to him, "You shouldn't do so much singing because you'll get all tired out." With a smile he'd say, "Well, I suppose I'll sing until I die." And that's what he did. There was a group of people called a Band of Hope that he used to teach in singing. People invited the band to their house for supper and they'd give a concert in the evening. One night, Grandfather sang until eleven o'clock before he said, "Well, now I've got to go to bed." And so he went, and the next morning they didn't hear anything out of him, and this lady went up and found that he had passed away.

I remember another night when a man came to the door. He had a basket in his hand and some knives in it, and he talked to my father. He wanted to know if he could leave the basket on our porch while he went up on the mountain, and my father said yes. But as my father was talking with him he looked down and saw some blood on a knife. The man said, "Why don't we take this basket to the barn?" and my father said, "Yes, that would be all right." So they went down to the barn, and on the way down, the man said, "My wife is up on the mountain, very, very sick."

"Well," my father said to him, "You go right back then."

"Will you come up there with me?"

"Yes, just as soon as I finish a few chores here. I'll be right up. But you go ahead."

My father, of course, suspected something and instead of going up the mountain, he ran down to the next village and got the police who went up there. And they found the body of a woman. The man had killed his wife. They caught the man. And that was the first tragedy ever in that part of the country, and it became local legend.

. . .

Both my parents wanted to come to America. Father thought that he didn't want to see his sons working in quarries because he said that was a very dangerous job. And my mother, who was a very calm person, had two sisters here for some years, but she was anxious to see them again. I don't think I knew a thing about America.

We were great friends with the people next door to us, the John Davis family. We used to go there often, and they're the ones that got our place, our stone house, when we left. For years after, I communicated with them by letter until I saw them again in 1975 when I went back to visit. Nothing changed.

I remember Father had a great wooden box built filled with quite a lot of dishes my mother took from Wales. Very pretty. Little dishes, sugar bowls, pitchers. Rose-colored. I remember we brought tongs from our fireplace, and a copper kettle we used to put on the fire.

We left from the port of Manchester. I don't remember how we got there. But I know we left in March of 1912 because Father had tried to get passage on the *Titanic*, and it was filled, so we couldn't get in on

that. And praise the Lord we didn't. The *Titanic* sunk the following month.

Instead, we came on the ship *Campania*. At breakfast time, this man would come around and hit a big drum, and that was our call for breakfast. As kids, all of us got seasick, so my father would take us out on deck for fresh air. In fact, we ran into a very bad storm for a few days. People became very frightened. And my father had met and befriended this minister, and one evening the sea was so rough, the minister came to our cabin, knocked on the door and asked if my father would come out and pray with him for the people in the lounge. The storm was so great, I remember getting burned on my arm when they were pouring tea. The next day as it turned out, two people had died. I don't know how they died. But I well remember Father at the funeral on deck, each one of us in hand. I turned around and they were throwing the caskets overboard into the ocean. Some people were throwing flowers. I remember that vividly.

The trip took nine days. My two aunts met us there, my mother's sisters. At the harbor in New York, my aunts came on board and stayed with us children while my father and mother had to go to be examined on Ellis Island. I thought they had left for good, so I cried and fell on the floor and kicked and squealed and hollered. [Laughs.] I can see my aunt now as she looked at me wondering just what to do. But my parents came back finally, and things were all right. Father had two suitcases that he was carrying when he came off the ferry with my mother, and this man came to him and said, "Would you like me to help you carry them?" So Father gave one of the suitcases for him to carry. And in that suitcase were all the presents that we'd received, parting gifts from friends and relatives, as well as bibles and religious artifacts. Well, Father gave it to the man to carry, but we never saw him again. He walked off with it.

James Grouse
. . . .

BORN FEBRUARY 9, 1904
EMIGRATED 1913, AGE 8
PASSAGE ON THE *CAMPANIA*

His family immigrated to America, settling into a Welsh community in
Utica, New York. After graduating from high school, he apprenticed
in the printing business and stayed with it until retirement. A lover of music,
he remains active in the local Welsh church choir. "I think singing is an inborn
thing with the Welsh," he said. "Although I wouldn't say every one.
I know Welshmen who sing out of tune."

I came from north Wales, in a small town called Talysarn. Slate quarries were the industry and, of course, farming, sheep breeding. There was a copper mine not far from where I lived. When I was six, we moved from Talysarn to a small town called Nantlle because that's where the quarry was that my father worked.

My father was almost six foot, strong. He had a mustache. He was very cautious about anything he did. There was nothing else in that village but the slate quarries. And you'd go up there when you were young and have a steady job. But it was a dangerous job. My father used dynamite to break big chunks of slate off the mountain. My mother wasn't too pleased about that, so he changed once in a while, and made slate roofs. He would cut the slate with the grain just like a piece of wood, and get a nice piece. Then his bosses would put him back to blasting again and my mother would really put up a fuss because my father's partner, a worker, died. After a blast, a piece of slate hit him on the head and killed him. After that my mother says, "I

don't want you up there at all." So that was the end of that.

In the meantime, one of my father's brothers had come to this country, and he was writing back to my father saying what a wonderful place it was, and so it got my father itchy. He wanted to come over here. He spoke English fairly well. So after writing back and forth, we decided to come to America. Mother was not at all sold about it because she couldn't speak English, and she had family close by who lived on a farm. She was one of twelve children, so she had lots of brothers and sisters. But she had only two children, me and my older sister Ellen, who was two years older than I. My mother also liked the village. She knew everyone and everyone knew her. So she never really cared about living in this country but, of course, she had to come.

There were many farms in Wales, which they called *yffridds*. I can't tell you why they called it that. And there were mountains near this *yffridd* where my mother was born, and they raised sheep, hundreds of them. Ellen and I used to watch them in the spring, the little lambs, jump around marshaled by the sheep-dogs. And then there was shearing time. It was all hand-sheared in those days. Nothing electric. Even the homes were lit by kerosene lamps. It was a sort of community thing.

Church was the center of that community. There was only one. Presbyterian, I think. I wasn't too keen about it because the sermons lasted two hours, and by that time you get fidgety. But my father was a religious person. He tried to tell me it was only for two hours in one whole week, but that wasn't true. We had church meetings, and Sunday school, and prayer meetings for people who were sick. It wasn't overdone, but it certainly wasn't two hours a week.

Education was a very important thing, even in those little quarry villages. You had to go to school. We spoke Welsh. I didn't learn English until after we came to America. But the problem was, after you got through grammar school, there was nothing for you to do except work in the quarry, unless you had an uncle in Liverpool or London, where you could go and work in the city. I didn't have such an uncle. Most didn't. One reason we came to this country was because my father didn't want me to end up working in a quarry.

So it was my father's decision to come here. I mean, my mother concurred because of the poor future for us. But they didn't have to come to America. They could have gone to England, to Liverpool. My father went to Liverpool to work for a while. But he was concerned about my sister and I. And then we kept getting letters from my uncle who painted this rosy picture of America—despite the fact he had some menial job—to the point my father finally bought the boat tickets. My uncle lived in Utica, New York. He was married with kids.

I was like my mother. I didn't want to come to America. The day I found out we were going, I jumped a stone wall and hid behind a tree. I didn't know anything about this country. All I knew was that I was going to leave my friends behind.

We left for America in September of 1913. I remember my mother had a trunk with a curved top on it. Inside were mostly kitchen stuff—knives, forks, dishes, but also presents that her family gave her, and lots of linens. I didn't take anything that I know of. I mean, I didn't have anything to bring.

So it was my father, my mother, Ellen, and me. I was eight years old. We took a train to Liverpool and boarded the *Campania*. It was an awfully big boat. [Laughs.] I remember that. I remember being afraid of falling off the gangplank when we boarded. We didn't go first class. It was second class. There were bunk beds along the wall. But my mother never got out of the cabin. She was seasick all the way. And the trip seemed to last forever. My poor mother. She wished she was back home.

I teamed up with some little Jewish kid. A nice kid. Neither one of us was seasick. But we were eating all the time and running around the deck until we both got sick. Sometimes the seas were so rough we couldn't go up on deck, and if they lifted that hatch up, water would pour in. In the dining room, there were long tables, and the dishes would go flying all over the place.

I don't remember seeing the Statue of Liberty. Later, my father told me about it. He had bought postcards that he showed me. When we got to Ellis Island, my father knew somebody who worked on the docks, and he vouched for us as we went through. We didn't have to stay there. I don't remember whether we were examined or not, all I remember is walking along with the other passengers and seeing a huge crowd of people off to one side, fenced in, men with handlebar mustaches, a lot of Welsh people, people who were being detained, and I wondered why.

Then we boarded a train to Utica, and my uncle was waiting for us at the station.

Randall Peat

. . . .

BORN OCTOBER 3, 1894
EMIGRATED 1914, AGE 19
PASSAGE ON THE S.S. *BALTIC*

*He was born in Colwyn Bay in north Wales on the shores of the Irish Sea.
His father died when he was one year old. The youngest of seven children
abandoned by their mother, he was raised by his grandparents. Today he lives in
a nursing home in upstate New York. "God gave me every inch of the United
States of America to live in," he said. "And I have lived here now eighty-two
years. I wouldn't want to live no place else."*

I was born at home. In those days there were no hospitals. Home was Colwyn Bay, a small resort town right on the beach of the Irish Sea. In the summer, thousands of visitors poured in, and the town would triple in size. They were English tourists exclusively; people from Manchester, Birmingham, Sheffield, the manufacturing towns. In time there were many hotels—the Welsh Hotel, Colwyn Bay Hotel, Marine Hotel, and they were occupied.

My father was a miner. There was a large quarry nearby. And one day there was a terrible storm off the sea. My father was at work in the quarry with the others, when a large fall came right from the peak of the quarry and buried him, killed them all. I was only a year old. I was taken to my grandfather and grandmother. They kept me. They brought me up.

My mother went to work. She did housework. She became a maid in one of the mansions. See, the town also had wealthy people who lived all over England, and who came to Colwyn Bay to retire, to be near the beach and the sea. Ships came in and [gestures] Ireland was over there, Scotland was over there, England was over here, and

Wales was over here. So there were two distinct classes of people in the town. Rich was rich and poor was poor.

The miners worked for very low wages, maybe five dollars a week. That would be the best they could do. In south Wales they mined for coal. But in north Wales they mined for slate and limestone. They would blast the limestone with the dynamite and create this great pit. A gang of people then filled trucks, took it to the mill to be crushed, and ships came from all parts of England and other countries to pick up the slate and limestone. Obviously, the work was dangerous. The men were always afraid of loose stones. They would be washed down, and they would always keep an eye on it, but they were too late for my father. And there were no hospitals, no pension, nothing. And so my mama had to go and take care of herself.

She was from a mining town a couple of miles from Colwyn Bay. She came from a family of miners, except my grandfather, my mother's father. He was a farmer. I lived with him and my grandmother. They were common, ordinary, hard-working people. Wealth was not on their mind. Wealth was out of their reach. If they could make a living, that is about all they could expect for the rest of their lives. My grandfather rented the farm. He didn't own one inch of it. Like all the other farmers.

What happened was, centuries ago, the people with money were granted the farms by the British royal family. They took the land from the people who owned it. These people were then forced to become tenants on their own land and pay rent. They would be lucky if they just made a living.

So my grandparents rented this land. They raised cows, pigs, horses, and grew oats, barley, and wheat to fatten the animals before they were sent to slaughter. There was an auctioneer who held a livestock sale once a week in town. And that's how they lived. They didn't live to make money, they lived to exist. The lord of the manor made the money, everyone else was a slave to him.

That's why I'm in the United States. As the saying goes: "... with Liberty and Justice for all." Well, you couldn't find liberty or justice for the Welsh farmer, or the Irish farmer, or the English farmer. My grandparents paid one English pound per acre. The ground was fertile, rich in minerals, but you would have to work like heck if you were to try to get one pound out of an acre of land. We used to say, "You are Welsh, you were born Welsh, and you'll always be Welsh. Don't give in to the English." Well, when you think of it, was anybody more grabby, more advanceable, than the English? Newfoundland, Canada, Australia, New Zealand, etc., all belonged to the English. On the other hand, there was no visible resentment between the local people and the English who vacationed there. They didn't show any hatred, because they depended upon the English for income, to keep it going. They needed them.

. . .

As time went on, year after year, there was always one child who moved out and went to work. Two boys ran the farm. My job

was to clean the barn and plow the land with a team of horses, and put the [seed] in. We used to sow seed by hand. From one end of the field to the other, backwards and forwards, all day long. And then you'd have a cultivator, pulled with a team of horses, to bury the seed.

Like every other farmer, we lived from hand to mouth. You could not make money on a farm. It cost too much rent. And if you didn't pay it, the attitude was, "Get out!" So my grandparents, who I considered my father and mother, lived as cheaply as they could, and saved every bit of bread, meat, everything for the next meal. My grandmother used to bake her own bread. She would save all the crusts, and in the morning, the same way you would have oatmeal in the United States or in England, we would just pour boiling water on these crusts and put a spoon full of pig's fat in the bowl for flavor. And that's what we ate instead of oatmeal. Everybody would eat a bowl of that, no complaints.

For dinner many times, my grandmother had nothing for us to eat. So she'd boil an egg and split it in half and give one half to me and one half to one of my brothers. That, with a cup of tea, was our dinner.

Despite this, we had only one way to live and that was happy. We didn't expect to make money and to be rich. We made the best of what we had. My grandmother used to pass down my brother's shirts, and if they were well worn, she'd patch them up, sew them up. And that's how we got our clothes. If anybody outgrew a suit, I would get that suit. The same with shoes.

School, I'm sorry to say, was all English. We could not speak a word of Welsh, not while we were in school. The teacher of the class was very demanding. She'd always have a big stick, and she'd wallop the heck out of you for the tiniest error. If you misspelled a word, she'd flog you. And if she didn't, the headmaster would flog you. It was miserable to go to school in those days.

Amongst ourselves, the Welsh, we spoke Welsh. But when there was English around us we wouldn't think about talking Welsh. We'd talk English. The English made you understand, "We are the supreme people. You do as we tell you." There was this feeling inside of you that you were conquered, conquered by the enemy, and the enemy called themselves English. They had the first word to say and the last word to say. The Welsh would keep their mouth shut.

There were three things in the family that counted more than anything else in the world. First was the home, second was my grandfather's work as a farmer. And the third was the chapel. There was no church, it was a chapel. There was only one church, the Church of England, Episcopalian. The Welsh chapel was Baptist, and it was taxed, with donations going to the Church of England. So we were Baptists. But the practice of it was very hushed up, secretive. When we were in the house and the family was around the table, we did not talk very loud. We spoke in whispers because we were performing a duty, a holy duty. The good Lord was feeding us. The good Lord was right there with us. That was the meaning of the thing. In chapel, you could do what you like, that was yours, your choice, and the clergymen were Welsh.

For fun, we played horseshoes, cricket. But mostly we had to work. There was no playing about. There was work to be done. It had to be done. It took two or three days to sow the grain. On those days we stayed out of school. But the headmaster knew. We had to notify him, "I'll be absent for three days. We are planting wheat . . ." And he knew those were jobs we had to do.

For Christmas, we certainly didn't have money. We would have a simple, home-cooked dinner, and maybe we got an orange. The prayer was, "May Father Christmas bless you and give you this orange," that was about the size of it.

. . .

I finished school when I was fourteen and I made up my mind that I wasn't going to be farmer. I got a job in a supermarket six miles away in the town of Abergele for fourteen shillings, or three dollars a week. I had to pay for my room and board. I lived in a boardinghouse, a room in the back, up on the third floor. I drove a horse and a two-wheel cart, delivering orders from the supermarket. They didn't have automobiles in those days. I had to carry the groceries myself, but my job was to deliver that order to the home. I would go without drawers, just the pants, the shirt, I was afraid to spend the money. I was living a secret life inside myself. My goal was to set foot on U.S. soil. It took me three years to save enough money to come to the United States.

I got the idea one day at Sunday school. A young fellow had just arrived from New York, where he had been working for four years in a stable, taking care of horses. His name was Dave Lloyd. I got to know him. I was asking him questions about America. And he was telling me all about it. One Sunday afternoon we were coming out of the church and he said to me, "I am going back to America. I can't find a job here that's worth a thing. Why don't you come with me?"

"I'd like to, but I haven't got enough money."

"How much have you got?"

"About twenty pounds."

"You've got enough, and if you run out of money, I'll give you $100. Come with me to America. That's the place for you."

So we went to the travel agent in town, and he said, "Within two weeks I can reserve passage for both of you to go to America. What class do you want to travel?"

"We'll go second class," Dave said.

"Why?" I asked. "Why not third? It's cheaper."

"Because if you go third, that's steerage, and we'll have to go to Ellis Island, and they'll examine us. But if we go second class, they'll examine us on board ship. They'll let us go straight from the ship to the sidewalk. It's worth the extra five pounds."

And that's what we did. We gave the agent a pound towards the ticket, and the next day, I got my money and paid fifty dollars for my passage.

I didn't tell my grandparents a thing. It would have been too hard to say good-bye to them at the age they were in. I knew they were much better off if I didn't say anything. I decided to write them when I got to America, which I did.

I took a small trunk with just my clothes. We took a train from Colwyn Bay to Liverpool. It took about an hour, fifty miles. The ship was the *Baltic*. We stood on the platform waiting for the ship to board among people from countless nationalities. People from Czechoslovakia, Yugoslavia, Ethiopia, Egypt, Jews, Germans . . . I was so surprised.

It was a rough journey. We shared a cabin with three other men, who were Scotch and English, and that was fine. But I became seasick. I remember saying to Dave, "I'm so sick I could jump into the water and stay there." He said, "Come with me," and we went to the bar and he gave me a glass of whiskey. "Take this," he said. "Drink it." And I drank it, and my seasickness went away. I got over it with whiskey. It was the first time I ever drank the stuff. But it wasn't the last. I was pretty loaded throughout most of the trip.

Eleven days later, we got to New York. We landed on April 1, 1914. April Fools' Day. Immigration officials searched our belongings and examined us on ship. They also wanted to know how much money we had. If we didn't have enough, they wouldn't let us land. "You've got to have money," some-one said, "you're not going to live on no relief."

We got off the boat at 9 A.M. and took the Delaware and Lackawanna Railroad to Utica, New York via Scranton and Binghamton. It was cheaper that way. We arrived in Utica at four in the afternoon. Dave had suggested we go there. I didn't know anything about it. He had an uncle and an aunt who worked there in the coal mills, the Utica Coal Company on Francis Street.

His uncle met us at the station. He was driving a car, which I never saw before. And he said to me, "I'm going to take my nephew to my home, but I'm going to take you to the Williams Hotel on Blandina Street—all the Welsh people are there." When I got to the lobby, I saw a row of Welshmen sitting around. I told the manager behind the desk that I just arrived from Wales and would be staying for a week or so. He listened, then shouted, "Hey, you men! Anyone want to hire a man just arrived from Wales? He can milk a cow, feed a pig, drive a horse, he can do anything. Anyone want to?"

"I know someone who could use some farm help," one of them said.

"Well, I don't want to work on a farm if I can help it," I said. Then, an old man sitting at the very end of the row came up to me and said, "Young man, heard you don't want to work on a farm, do you?"

"No sir, not if I can help it."

"Well, I'll hire you. You can work for me. I'm a superintendent of Borden's Condensery in Waterville. About twenty miles from here."

I didn't know what he was talking about, but I said yes. He took me to a boardinghouse, and I started work at 7 A.M. the next morning, shoveling coal. When Saturday morning came, he said to me, "Young man, it is customary for you to go to church on a Sunday, isn't it?"

"Yes sir," I said.

Immigrants from the German steamship Princess Irene *on
on a West Side Manhattan pier, 1911*

(NATIONAL PARK SERVICE: STATUE OF LIBERTY NATIONAL MONUMENT)

"Well," he said, "Take tomorrow off then. Down the street is a Welsh church, a large congregation. You can get acquainted with the group."

On Sunday morning there was eleven o'clock mass, and the head deacon came up to me. I introduced myself, and he said, "You and I can sit together in the back pew and talk." And we did. We talked about the old country, and the farms, and the horses and buggies that were still there, not this strange new thing called the automobile. Then he got up, the congregation had assembled, and he spoke before them.

"I'm sorry to say we have no minister this morning," he said. "But there's a young man who just arrived from Wales, who I'd like you to meet . . . Come on up, boy!"

So I walked down the aisle, up to the podium, and he introduced me. Then he handed me a book of hymns and said, "Carry on." I was scared to death. You have to remember, I was nineteen years old. But I opened the book. I was familiar with the hymns, every one of them. And I started singing. The congregation joined in. And after the hymn was sung, I turned to the deacon and said, "Now what?"

"Go ahead, carry on!," he said. "You're doing all right."

So I read a chapter from *Pilgrim's Progress* in Welsh, finished, and said, "What now?"

"You're doing all right," he said. "Carry on!"

So I read for another twenty minutes, closed the service and people came rushing down, shaking hands with me, praising me.

And so it went along. I attended mass every Sunday. I came to know everybody. And they, me. I got promoted to working in the milk plant, capping bottles. And then one day, about three years later, I was at

Sunday mass when somebody came up to me.

"Hello, Randall! How are you?"

"Am I supposed to know you?" I asked.

"Why, yes! I'm Billy Davis. I used to go to kindergarten with you in Colwyn Bay, remember?"

"Oh yeah, little Bill, I remember you . . ."

And then he said, "There's a young girl who just arrived last week. She's also from Colwyn Bay. She was inquiring about you . . ."

Her name was Florence. She was about twenty-two. Within six months, we married—had one daughter and lived together for sixty-two years.

Dave Lloyd, meantime, worked in the coal mill with his uncle. But he didn't like it.

The pay wasn't enough. He heard there were better-paying jobs in Milwaukee. So he quit, went to Milwaukee, and became an ambulance orderly. We corresponded at first, and then I never saw him again.

But you know something? To this day, I am still requested on occasion to give a short sermon. There's no Welsh church in Utica anymore. No Welsh minister. That fizzled out. But there are still plenty of Welsh people. And if there's a funeral, I'll be asked to say the Lord's Prayer. The Twenty-third Psalm, "The Lord is my shepherd, I shall not want . . ." But I'll say it in Welsh and then I'll conclude with: "Honor thy father and thy mother that thy days be long in the land which the Lord thy God giveth thee."

Part III

NORTHERN EUROPE

A mother and son, tagged, having just arrived from northern Europe, circa 1910

(SHERMAN COLLECTION, ELLIS ISLAND IMMIGRATION MUSEUM)

8

. . . .

Poland

(APPROXIMATELY 1.5 MILLION IMMIGRANTS, 1892–1954)

Larry Edelman

· · · · · · · · · · · ·

BORN JANUARY 5, 1910
EMIGRATED 1920, AGE 10
PASSAGE ON THE *CELTIC*

*His father came here first, and his family followed. After graduating from high
school, he attended New York University briefly, then became a window trimmer
for Alexander's, and then Hearn's, department stores. He owned a merchandise
packaging business for ten years, ending up as a book salesman for Simon &
Schuster. His first wife passed away in 1973, leaving one son. He remarried in
1975 and retired to West Palm Beach, Florida, where he is active in B'nai B'rith
and the Anti-Defamation League, and plays numerous games of bridge.*

Kovel was a large village [that] had a
central railroad depot, and therefore it was important for the Germans to capture that. At the time, my
mother was the sole support for all of us; for
me, my brother, and my sister. Before the
Germans occupied us, she worked in a laundry, and her fingers became all infected and
they had to operate. Then they made gloves
that fit her where she was able to keep on
with her work. It was a hard life.

She also did smuggling for others, [for]
which she got paid. When I say smuggling,
it was money where she hid it on herself and
made the trip to another city to deliver it.
She did that for a while, until the war broke
out. My older brother worked making cigarettes by hand, and I used to help him by
cutting the edges . . .

My father had gone to the United States
about 1911, 1912. After a while, he sent us
tickets to come to the United States. But by
that time, the war broke out, and we were
not able to leave. And, of course, we had
relatives. We stayed at my father's parents'
home. We lived there, and my mother had
a sister in the same town. I never knew my
father until I came here.

My grandfather, he wrote—scripted—
the Torah. He was able to write that. In fact,
when we left there to come here, he made a
pair of *tefillin* for me. That's the part where
you say your prayers, and he wrote the
prayer for it inside, which I used when I
became bar mitzvahed here in the United
States. It was one of the few things I brought
with me.

I remember the rabbi of the town. I recall
that he lived across a bridge, and we went to
his house—we had a synagogue there, and for
the holiday prayers. And we also had lunch
there after the prayers. They only took one
child of the family to go to school. I went to
Hebrew school, but never anything else. My
sister went to school there because she was
older [than] me. I was the youngest. My brother
had to work because he was the oldest.

· · ·

I remember when the Germans came into
our town. There was hand-to-hand combat
outside of the city, and we could hear yelling. We were in a room with the shades
down, you know, a blackout room. But towards morning I vividly saw one soldier on
a white horse coming through slowly. Then,

from all sides of the city, the German army, the soldiers came in. We were scared, but the Germans assured us that everything would be fine . . .

After the war broke out, we heard nothing from my father. We couldn't receive any financial aid from him. Nothing came through. It wasn't till way after the war ended that the Jewish organization HIAS helped us to come here. My father made sure, through them, that we were taken care of all the way to the United States. They took care of everything. All the paperwork. My father paid for the tickets, but HIAS arranged it all. We went to Warsaw for our passports, which HIAS also handled. We waited there about a week. It was a wonderful organization. All we brought was some clothing . . .

From Warsaw, we went to Danzig. Yes, we went to Danzig. Danzig was a free port after the war for all nations to be able to use it. We were in Danzig about a week. We were put up at motels, and they had various doctors and nurses that examined us there. And from Danzig we took a boat to London, England.

When we left Danzig for England, we had to pass a certain area where the mines had not been removed yet. And especially at my time, they had somebody at the front of the ship, the bow of the ship, standing and watching so we wouldn't hit.

In London, I remember seeing, it was in the papers, that the first [postwar] immigrants were coming through. And we got to the railroad station to take the train to Liverpool, and the [English] people just came out in droves, and brought baskets of fruit, candy. We were in London about six hours.

In Liverpool, we were put up in a hotel. In fact, it was in Liverpool that we saw the first black person. We were just amazed, you know. We just kept looking . . . Then we were taken care of by the steamship company. It was the Cunard Line. The boat

was the *Celtic*. And it took us eight days to get to the United States.

There was a dining room on ship, and there were about sixty Jewish families, mostly Polish, that came across, and they served kosher food. Everything was taken care of for the Jewish families . . . We had a wonderful captain who made sure that everything was right.

We were not in steerage. Me and my brother were in like a dormitory with bunk beds. The women separate. My sister was very sick on the boat the whole trip. She got a fever from seasickness, where she had to be attended by nurses and doctors practically twenty-four hours a day. We feared that she would not be able to make it, and that she might be turned back, but thank God she pulled through.

When we were told, on a Saturday morning, we would be passing the Statue of Liberty, we all lined the deck. The thrill of seeing that statue there. And the tears in everybody's eyes, which, as a child, got me the same feeling. It was more, not freedom from oppression, I think, but more freedom from want. So that was the biggest thrill, to see that statue there. And we continued into the pier in Manhattan, the Cunard Line pier in Manhattan. First-class passengers and second-class went through customs immediately.

We, after a while, were put on a ferry, and we were transported to Ellis Island and the Great Hall, which looked like a loft with benches. We put our belongings, whatever belongings we had, right near us, and we sat down on the benches, and we were hungry. I don't recall whether it was meals, or just sandwiches that were brought in for us . . . We couldn't be processed. It was Saturday afternoon, and all the doctors were gone. We had to wait until Monday morning. I was separated from my mother and my sister just at nighttime. My brother and I slept in bunks. No mattresses, just narrow three-tier bunk beds on taut springs.

The stay at Ellis Island was not bad. We wandered around until Monday morning. Then, we were segregated and we went through different rooms. And, of course, we were very scared about my sister, and the different tests, doctors in those rooms, that tested us. I recall in one room, the doctor says, "Your name." My mother answered for me. She says, "Larry." I recall that he told her he wanted me to answer my name to see if I could speak. And, of course, the thrill after we all passed through and my father waiting, and relatives of my father, waiting, in a large room where all the visitors gathered. He had already rented a three-bedroom apartment for us in Harlem, at 118th Street near Madison Avenue, one of those railroad flats.

My father, at that time, was foreman for the Ingersoll Watch factory. So we were not in want then. We were comfortable. Ingersoll eventually closed up, and he went into business for himself. He had an office in Manhattan on Nassau Street, watch repair, which he did mostly for trade people who had jewelry stores.

. . .

A few years ago, after the renovation, I went with my second wife and a couple friends of ours to Ellis Island because we had a plaque made with our family name. We got on the ferry, and it was a wonderful feeling. We went up to see the movie they show, and the person handling it asked who came through Ellis Island, and I raised my hand. She was saying how scared the people were, not knowing whether they were going to be accepted. She says, "How did you feel?" I said, "I had a wonderful time." [Laughs.] She couldn't understand it . . . Then, we went down to the Wall of Honor, and I looked, and I saw the plaque, and there was my name right on the wall. It's hard to describe that feeling.

Abraham Livshein

· · · · · · · · · · · ·

BORN JUNE 26, 1903
EMIGRATED 1921, AGE 18
PASSAGE ON THE *ALGERIA*

He was one of the rare immigrants who, nine years after his arrival, became an inspector for the Immigration and Naturalization Service at Ellis Island. Once an aspiring writer, he penned an unpublished book about his experiences as an immigration officer. Married since 1927, he lives with his Ukrainian wife, Rhona, in Long Island, New York. They have a son, a daughter, four grandchildren, and two great-grandsons.

The little town where I was born, Shershev, you will probably not find on any map. It was in the western part of the Russian Empire and, in 1903, there was no independent Polish government. In Yiddish my first name was Yankel. That's what they called me as a young boy. Yankel.

· · · · · · · · ·

I lived in Shershev for all my first eighteen years, with the exception of two and a half that I went to another city to study. The city was a well-known town, Brestlitovsk. In our little town there were no public schools. All the kids used to go to the Jewish school, called a *heder*.

I was the oldest one of six brothers and one sister. Unfortunately, there was one other sister who died . . . I was closest to my grandfather and grandmother on my father's side. I remember them well. My grandfather was a very strong, robust man with a nice, trimmed beard, very jolly good-natured. His occupation was that of a shingle maker—long, thin pieces of wood to cover the roof with. Most of the homes had shingles. About half of the town were Jews and half were gentiles, mostly peasants, who had their own fields and also had governors and so on. Some of their houses were covered with thatched straw, thatched roofs, but most of them had shingles. It was a very highly skilled job, and hard work, too.

My grandmother was not born in Shershev. She was betrothed to my grandfather through a *chatkan*, a matchmaker, from some other town. She came from a bigger town and kind of looked down upon the slovenly women in Shershev. She had a little better education, and she always dressed immaculately, even when she went shopping in the marketplace. She would dress, I remember, I could see her right now, in a dark dress, down to the heels, or maybe even the shoes, with a nice kerchief on her head. She always had a tiny gold watch pinned down to the left side of her breast on the dress, with a chain going to the right side. When she walked through the marketplace, she was admired, looked up to, and nobody could say no to her when she wanted something. She commanded a lot of respect.

When I was born, I was her first grandson. My parents had a store, a general store,

and my mother was always busy. She ran the store. My father didn't work in the store too much. He traveled to other cities to buy wholesale merchandise and bring it for our own store and also for other stores. My father was an unusually kind man, not very educated, but learned in the folk ways. So my mother was busy in the store, and my grandmother decided that she was going to raise me, and she did. I really didn't have much to do with my mother at all. For that matter, I didn't have much to do with my father. In fact, for the first three or four years of my life, I lived in my grandmother's house.

I hate to say, but I think I inherited a good deal of the uppitiness that she had. I do know that when I played with kids later on, I almost invariably was the leader . . . We were economically of the upper strata. Below us were the tailors and the shoemakers and the peddlers and the carpenters, who worked hard labor in construction. By education, the intellectuals were the top layer. Moneywise, they were not necessarily the top. Next came the merchants, us, and then came the workmen.

The gentiles, most of them, worked the land. They grew fields, and that was their income. They all had big gardens, too. Everyone had a tremendous garden with planted vegetables they used to sell. Some of them also used to work in wintertime. When there was nothing to do in the gardens or in the fields, they would work in the forests, felling trees and helping to ship the shingles. There was a big lumber industry where whole trunks of trees used to be shipped to countries that didn't have ample forests, like Germany. We had no railroads, we had no cars. An automobile I saw for the first time in 1917, and that was during the war. So they lumbered only in wintertime when there was snow. They would put the trunks on sleighs, and pull them by horses out of the woods to the nearest river that was not frozen, tie them together, and float them to Germany.

I was the oldest of seven children, but that was not the most important thing. The most important thing was that I had an education. Shershev had no school. They had a *heder* where they taught you the Torah, or to write Yiddish and Hebrew, the script, but that's it. They didn't teach you to write Russian, which was the language of the land. There never was, in our town, a normal school to teach children arithmetic, grammar, Russian, or anything else.

When I was eight years old, my father decided that he doesn't want me to grow up illiterate. I have an idea that my fancy grandmother had something to do with it, who was his mother; that Yankel, the little dear Yankel, should get an education. And the word spread, and six more boys, myself, and six other boys, who were prosperous, because school cost money in those days, decided we would be sent to Brestlitovsk, which was a big city, to attend a formal school. It was a big city with boulevards, with trees, beautiful shops, ladies who dressed with hats. It also happened to be a garrison city for the Russian army, so all the officers used to ride around in the beautiful carriages with the fancy ladies dressed in the latest Parisian styles, not Russian styles. They were Russian aristocracy, the officers. And the soldiers used to go marching through the streets. I attended school there for two and a half years, until the First World War broke out.

All I remember is that school gave me a love of literature. Education was the desire, the spiritual desire of every Jew. To become a rabbi was one of the highest achievements one could think of. Or, of course, to become a doctor, a teacher, or a philosopher, that was the highest. As a matter of fact, the highest title of honor in Yiddish and among the Jews is "rabbi," teacher. That is the highest honor you can give.

At the age of seventeen, without ever having heard an English word pronounced, I spoke and wrote English all by myself by studying a book called *Allendorf's Method*, printed in the United States. Books were something we hungered for. We would give away our food, everything that we had for a book, because we didn't have any. We used to scour the garrets to find old books that somebody threw out a hundred years ago, or something. I spent days and nights studying that book in front of a mirror by kerosene lamp. That book gave me not only a translation of the words, and told me not only how to form sentences, but how to pronounce the difficult sounds, like the "th" sound. My pronunciation was atrocious. But my written English was damn good for a self-taught young boy.

. . .

When World War I broke out, the first thing we had to give up was school. Then, a year or two after the war started, 1915 or '16, the Germans came in, and they issued strict orders. First of all, there was curfew. You couldn't go out at night at all. You had to observe certain regulations as far as cleanliness, such as sweeping the houses, keeping the outhouses clean.

Then they requisitioned. They put a tax on every peasant to give so much potatoes and so much milk. They went from peasant to peasant to find out what they had: how many cows, how many horses, and so on. They made a list of everybody's possessions and how much land they had, and how much it produced. And they had to give. Germany was not an agricultural country, so everybody was taxed a certain amount, and it was all shipped to Germany.

Also, whatever work the Germans needed to be done, they would just catch people in the street. They would catch women and clip off their hair. They clipped the Jewish men's beards, because there shouldn't be any lice. And they took me. I was fourteen years old when it happened. They took me in the middle of the street in the marketplace, put me on truck, shipped me off to the forest. Luckily there was somebody with me, people around there, that told them, "Tell his mother that he is going to work." I worked as a slave laborer for them for over a year until the Germans were driven out, until the end of the war.

It had an effect on me only in the sense that I realized what war is. I'll never forget a young whippersnapper, maybe eighteen or nineteen years old, who must have been some rich man's son, because most of the soldiers were older men, the younger ones were on the battlefield. I and a partner of mine were sawing a log in half. We had no experience. And the saws were at least six feet long, with a handle on each side, so you need two men.

We would saw it about a quarter of the way through, and then you just couldn't budge it because the sides were stuck. So this whippersnapper, this little bastard in the fancy uniform, dressed to kill in the forest, comes over and says, "I'm a policeman." And he slaps me in the head. "*Verdammt Jude!*" Meaning, "Damn Jew!" I get angry even now. I felt like killing him. I don't think I ever hated anybody as much as I hated this guy.

Another thing. When the Germans first came in, before the Russians departed, the people burned everything. They burned the crops, they burned the villages, they burned some houses, so as not to leave anything for the Germans, so there was tremendous poverty. Some of it was built up during the years the Germans had occupied. But once the Germans left, there was a scarcity of almost everything. A scarcity of food, scarcity of clothing. Nobody bought any clothing. Nobody saw any clothing. Scarcity of medicine. We had a druggist in town, but there

was nothing to resupply the medication. We didn't have a doctor in town.

Shortly after that, some miracle happened to us from a country called the United States of America. They organized ARA, American Relief Administration, to provide food for the devastated lands that suffered during the war. From nowhere, trucks came into our little town, laden with the kind of goods we never had in peacetime, all being given away free: beans and lentils, rice, flour, sugar, salt, barrels of herring, giving it away, preserving us from starvation. I cannot stop being moved emotionally, talking about it.

A town committee was set up to supervise the distribution. The committee made a list of the whole town population. Not much. Two thousand at the most. This committee made a list of the townspeople, how many children, how many adults, and what the conditions were, and decided by the volume. It was 1919, so I was sixteen years old. And being one of the so-called educated kids, I worked for them, but I didn't get paid any money. There was no money, so the workers would get an extra half-pound of this or that. It was a very big thing to take home, because there were so many mouths to feed.

The Jews and the gentiles got along in Shershev both before and after the war. They depended upon each other. The gentile peasants needed shovels and rakes and ploughs and horseshoes and fixing wagons and clothing and nice things, too: kerchiefs to dress up, and hair ribbons for young girls when they went to church on Sundays. The Jews needed them to sell their goods and to buy their produce; to buy the apples and the potatoes and the pears and plums they grew. So it was a mutual trade.

They were many like myself, and some of my friends, who were not really religious, but we observed the rules because we didn't want to hurt our parents, and, besides, we would get slapped in the face if we didn't observe it. But we were also the educated, elitist. We read Russian literature, and we sang Russian songs, and we knew about love from books. We were still kids. But we went with girls, and they had little groups where we would read together aloud and discuss things. It was a different generation altogether. My father was very tolerant, and he was very proud. I taught my younger brothers and sisters Russian. I mean, everybody was proud of the kids who could know Russian. It was a big achievement.

I came to America because of my maternal grandfather. He had already come to America several years before in 1901 or 1902. He had come here to earn money for a dowry, so he could marry off his four daughters. While he was here, he sent a steamship ticket for his only son to come, my uncle. But the only son was sickly, and my maternal grandmother didn't want to part with him. "Why is he going to America?," she said. "To work in a shop? He's sick." So, being her oldest grandson, I took his steamship ticket, and I came in his place.

I had to make about two dozen different kinds of papers: medical certificates, birth records, police records, statements from my parents that they have no objection to my travel; statements from the local authorities that I don't owe any money to anybody, etc. These had to be sent to the American consulate in Warsaw. Then the consul sent you an appointment when to appear for the hearing, and presumably, there you had to get the visa to America. In order to get the visa, you had to have an affidavit from a close relative in the United States who promised you would not become a public charge. My maternal grandfather sent it to me, I sent it to the consulate, and I had a pending appointment in Warsaw for my visa.

I was put on a horse and wagon in order to get to the railroad station, and literally the whole town came out to say good-bye. That

was the custom. It was somebody going to America, which was like going to heaven. They all followed the wagon, crying and blessing, until the driver got tired of this and whipped the horses, and off we went to Warsaw. I had made up in my mind that I would never come back.

I wore a suit made from a black cape my mother wore at her wedding. She had called the tailor, and he took measurements, and then made the big pronouncement he could make a suit for me, a pair of trousers and a small jacket. And that is what I wore on my way to America, nothing else. I had one shirt I wore, one other for the road, a change of socks, the shoes that I wore, and a cap. I think that's about all. Oh, I'm sorry, the most important thing, my books! Without the books I wouldn't budge. I could only take so many, the most important ones. I still have the books which I brought with me. [He is moved.]

I wanted to see the big capital city of Warsaw. I was never in any big city except Brestlitovsk, my little town. I had a relative there with whom I could stay briefly. I went to the American consulate for my visa appointment. I already had my Polish passport.

I'm in a little office with a Polish officer and a Yiddish interpreter. "Is this the affidavit of your grandfather?" the officer asks. The interpreter interprets immediately in Yiddish. And I, being a smart aleck, figured I'd show off my English. "Yes. This is my grandfather's affidavit." I could see the officer stiffen as if somebody hit him with something. He pushed the affidavit in front of me.

"Did you change this?" I took a look. A word was changed. Obviously the notary public made it. My grandfather didn't know how to write English. Instead of putting down *grandfather*, the notary put down *cousin*, and changed it later to *grandfather*. In other words, the degree of relationship may not have been strong enough. But the consul, seeing that I knew a little English, thought that I made the change.

He refused to give me a visa. I think it was the biggest blow I ever had in my life. He suggested I write back to my grandfather to send a new affidavit, and he gave me three months to get it. This was February 1921. I had until May. I couldn't stay in Warsaw.

So I had to travel back to Shershev—despite having promised myself that I would never return—undergo the departure business again, come back to Warsaw a second time, go to the consul. This time they didn't even look at the affidavit. I got the visa pronto, in a matter of ten minutes. Then I made my trip to America, by train to Danzig. Danzig was a free city at the time. It didn't belong [to] either Germany or Austria. In Danzig we underwent quarantine for fourteen days. We were put in isolation. We were inspected every day. We were given injections every day for fourteen days, everybody.

From Danzig, we went by small boat to Hull, England. From Hull, we took a train to Glasgow, Scotland and got the *Algeria*.

We arrived in New York a day or two before a new quota act went into effect. If I came two days later, I probably wouldn't have gotten in. Those are the vagaries of fate.

In those days the ship would drop anchor opposite Staten Island. There was a big Veterans hospital in Staten Island, and a U.S. Public Health Service doctor would come on board from the hospital. The ship doctor had to report any sicknesses that occurred en route, and any patients who were not well. That was very formal.

The Public Health Service doctor would take his report, and on the basis of the ship doctor's report, decide whether the ship should be quarantined. If a contagious disease was reported, tuberculosis or malaria, then the whole ship would be quarantined. This was the procedure.

While this was going on, immigration inspectors, like I would later become, started inspecting American citizens and first-class passengers from the steamship company manifest, which listed the passengers in alphabetical order. The passengers would line up in alphabetical order, assisted by the stewards, in front of the immigration officers at tables they set up in the main dining hall. One officer would have from A to E, another F to G and so on. American citizens, first class and second class, were inspected, and if okay, discharged by ferry to Manhattan.

Everyone else [third class, steerage, plus those suspected of ill health] remained on board until they were taken to Ellis Island by the inspectors on small INS ferryboats. As an inspector, you also dealt with immigrants who were here illegally, and who were caught. How they suffered! They either became legalized, or had to be deported. It was very tragic, most of them.

I, being a steerage passenger, was not privileged to be inspected on board ship the first day of arrival. We were taken to Ellis Island, and spent the night there. The following day we were inspected, and those who were admitted, which was most of us, were taken by the Ellis Island ferry to Battery Park in lower Manhattan, and let off.

It was June, nighttime, when I was let off, and a new night world to me. The mysterious Hudson River, with lights blinking all over. I never saw electric light. The only light we had was a kerosene lamp. But now there were red lights and green lights and bright lights, blinking, and little boats. But the most important thing, we couldn't get over it, there was flashing like giant handwriting in the sky: "Lipton's Coffee, Lipton's Tea, Lipton's Cocoa." That was a marvel I never even dreamt of.

I was turned over to HIAS [Hebrew Immigrant Aid Society]. They had representatives to help Jewish immigrants. One of them took me in tow to their building in lower Manhattan, and telephoned my uncle, who came to the place, and I was discharged to him.

I was in America!

I walked out on Longwood Avenue in the Bronx. That's where my uncle and aunt lived. My first day, I went to see the marvels of New York. I went by trolley to Battery Park and back. Trolleys, in and of themselves, were a miracle. I never saw one in my life. Longwood Avenue was not Fifth Avenue, but it had groceries and pushcarts and peddlers selling with their horses and a stationery store. The store was near the trolley. I saw a little red book that had a map of New York in it and the names of all the streets, twenty-five cents. I had twenty-five cents on me. That was my first purchase in the United States. The man who took the money was startled at the way I spoke. I told him I just arrived. He couldn't get over it. He said, "You like books?"

I said, "Do I like books? And how." He says, "You know there's a library here on Intervale Avenue, on 161st Street," and that was the first place I came to other than my aunt's house, and became a member. All in all it was a land of wonder . . .

My first job was as a grocery clerk, and the only reason I could get the job is because I knew enough English. I got fifteen dollars a week. I insisted on paying seven dollars to my aunt for room and board. She didn't want to take it. I didn't send it every week, but I put five dollars aside for my whole family in Poland. Lunches I didn't have to spend, because in the grocery store, I always made a sandwich. I also registered for evening school. I studied at night. I took Regents examinations.

By December 1924, I had all my courses requisite for entering college. I entered City College in the evenings and, in 1927, got a degree in accounting. I worked as a bookkeeper for the City of New York, and then, nine years after I arrived, in 1930, I became an inspector for the Immigration and Naturalization Service at Ellis Island.

David, Lois, and Alvin Garrett

. . . .

BORN JUNE 25, 1918; OCTOBER 1, 1922; FEBRUARY 22, 1925
EMIGRATED 1929, AGES 11, 7, AND 4
PASSAGE ON THE *AQUITANIA*

They came from Poland in 1929 and were detained at Ellis Island for six weeks. David, the oldest of four siblings, was physically present for this interview, but could not participate. Born legally deaf, he suffered spinal meningitis as a child, and at seventy-nine, his memory is virtually gone. Lois and Alvin live in New York; David and brother Philly (not present for this interview) live in Florida.

*L*OIS: There were four of us children. David and my brother Philly, who live in Florida, were born in a very tiny village called Odziwil. Alvin and I were born in Opcznie. Both towns were not far from Warsaw. My father and his father and his brothers were the town shopkeepers and merchants of Odziwil. They were mostly egg merchants.

We lived with our maternal grandparents in Opoczno. I don't remember my grandmother because she died shortly after I was born. I remember that we were poor people. We lived in the Jewish ghetto, in a two-room house. Still, I have pleasant memories. I remember summertime, swimming in the pond. And across from my grandparents' house were orchards, flower orchards. And my maternal grandfather, Grandpa Zeta, was a lovely man. He had a beard. Typical Orthodox Jewish beard. And he used to smoke. We were also living near my mother's sister's family, so it was a nice communal life.

We were very religious. I remember my grandfather going around and cleaning the whole house with a goose feather. There were rituals. The house had to be very clean and pure. If, for example, a meat knife was used for dairy, it was no longer kosher, but there was a way of cleansing that knife. You went outside and stuck it in the ground, and that cleansed the knife. There were a lot of superstitions involved. We were raised Orthodox.

My grandfather was a shoemaker, and people used to say, Zeta the *shiester*, Zeta the shoemaker. From what I was told, a shoemaker was the lowest class of occupation. But he was a lovely person. Even though I was young, I remember how lovely he was.

ALVIN: My father came here first. He wanted to go to either Palestine or the United States. He had applications made to both countries. He got the visa to the United States, and about a week or two after, we got the visa to Palestine, but he chose the United States because he had three aunts living here and because he felt it was the land of opportunity.

My father hated the anti-Semitism in Poland. I didn't see any anti-Semitism till I came to this country, to be honest. All I remember is what my mother told me about it. They had pogroms, and it was terrible. Every time there was something wrong, some sort of famine or some sort of reaction in Poland, they blamed the Jews for everything. It just got to my father so badly, he just wanted to get out of there, and he wanted his family out of there.

LOIS: He was also a Zionist at that time.

ALVIN: He was a Bundist. He wasn't a Zionist. A Bundist was like a socialist, and a Zionist was a Zionist. But he figured Palestine was going to have a socialist state, which eventually did happen. But he was looking for business opportunities, and to take care of his family. He came in 1927.

LOIS: Nineteen-twenty-six. He was here three years when we came.

ALVIN: He came in 1927. I beg to differ with her, but let's keep it that way.

LOIS: I had to be four or five years old when Father left. I remember we went from our town to his parents' hometown where he was born, Odziwil. We were in a wagon and I remember falling asleep and being covered in the wagon. I remember being traumatized that he was leaving, because, from what I was told, a lot of men didn't bring their families. But he said the one good thing about President Hoover was that he allowed people to bring their families on their first citizenship papers rather than having to wait five years. So as soon as that happened, he applied to bring his family.

ALVIN: My mother, during those three years while he was gone, took care of the four children. She did not go to work. My father sent money, and my grandfather took care of us.

LOIS: She always had help at home. It was very different for her when she came here because she no longer had her nieces and nephews who were always around to help with four children. As soon as she came here, she went to help my father in his business.

I remember when we decided to leave in 1929. We had to go to the American consulate in Warsaw, and my father, who was in America, was worried that they might not allow my brother David to come in because he was deaf. There was no problem apparently, but that was a fear that they had.

ALVIN: My father's fear was, in fact, he told us later on, that if they don't let David in, we would all go back. Imagine what could have happened to us with the Holocaust and all. As it turned out, it was held up because of me, not because of him.

LOIS: I don't remember what we brought. From Warsaw, we took the train to Danzig, and from Danzig we took a boat, a small vessel, to Liverpool. Then we waited in Liverpool in a dorm-type place, and took the *Aquitania*.

ALVIN: But before we left Liverpool, my brother David was mute, and my mother, who was a young thirty-five . . .

LOIS: She was thirty-six years old.

ALVIN: She was a thirty-six-year-old woman. Unfortunately, she had bad false teeth, and they cracked. And here she was, shaky because she was going to see her husband who she hadn't seen in two years, and she hasn't got teeth in her mouth. She went out on a snowy night with my David here. She had only ten dollars. It seems in England, like in Canada, the dentists do their own bridgework. They don't send it out. David, despite being deaf and unable to speak and only eleven years old, found her a dentist in Liverpool so she could have teeth. We all think our mother was handsome, and she wanted to greet her husband, who was a very handsome man. We came steerage.

LOIS: No, we didn't come steerage. We had a cabin for the whole family, but it was probably third class. It was small. I remember my mother being sick almost the whole trip.

ALVIN: I was a little over four and a half years old, but I think you're probably right. I remember somebody was laying on the bunk with a cold towel on her head. It must have been my mother.

LOIS: It wasn't me. [Laughs.] Whenever Mother had a headache, she'd put a wet cloth on her head. I think the trip lasted two weeks.

ALVIN: No.

LOIS: That's what Philly said. He said it was two weeks.

ALVIN: It didn't take two weeks. It took us about a week.

LOIS: That's what I thought. Maybe when Philly said two weeks he meant the whole trip from the time we left the hometown until we got to America.

ALVIN: Probably. But it was seven days.

LOIS: Anyway, when the boat docked, my father came on board before we were taken to Ellis Island because he was trying to get us off. I was so happy, because like any little girl I worshiped my father, and my father really was very handsome. He had blond hair and blue eyes and he was striking-looking. As a matter of fact, he had joined the theater here, you know, as a hobby. He was with the Jewish theater. And we were overjoyed. I mean, there was no question. I remember that very clearly. I remember the excitement. Do you remember that?

ALVIN: Sort of.

DAVID: I was ecstatic to see my father.

ALVIN: Speak louder. What did you say?

DAVID: I was ecstatic . . . I cried and all.

LOIS: Then, when we had to be detained, it was like a shock. They examined us on the boat and that's when they found that Alvin had a ringworm on his head, and that's why Papa couldn't take us directly from the boat home, and we were transported to Ellis Island.

ALVIN: The ringworm was considered very contagious at that time. Why they kept the rest of the family there six weeks I don't know. But they kept me at the hospital on Ellis Island.

LOIS: I remember going to see you in the hospital.

ALVIN: They came to see me every day. And the nurses were crazy about me because I was a . . .

LOIS: . . . Cute little boy. I remember being in the hospital running up and down in the wards, and every-body being good to me. I had a wonderful time. From the nurses, I learned how to speak English very quickly. By the time we left there, Alvin was speaking like a native American.

ALVIN: When I left Ellis Island people couldn't believe that I wasn't born American . . . The bad part was they took off my hair by electrolysis, and they told my mother, "Your son will never have hair again." And to this day I have a bald spot. My hair has been the same way for sixty years. It hasn't changed.

Women's ward, 1923

(NATIONAL PARK SERVICE: STATUE OF LIBERTY NATIONAL MONUMENT)

LOIS: They didn't have enough knowledge about ringworms at the time. So they used extreme methods.

ALVIN: The Ellis Island people were vicious to the immigrants. They weren't very nice to them.

LOIS: He had platinum-blond hair, which never came back. It came back light brown.

ALVIN: But I ate good. I helped people. There were no other children. I was in a ward with a bed and I was on the ladies' side, because I was too young to be on the men's side. I went over to all the patients, and I was making them laugh, and they all loved me. My poor father was laying in Manhattan on the Lower East Side, waiting for the family to come, and we couldn't come until the doctor said, "Okay, he's cured." It was a nice six weeks for me.

LOIS: He kept them entertained singing songs . . . We spent our first Thanksgiving in America at Ellis Island. So I think we must have had turkey for the first time . . .

As soon as we got permission to leave, my father took us on the ferry and then a cab to an apartment he had in Manhattan. As we were riding in the taxi, you know, Orthodox people don't ride on a Saturday, I said to my mother, "You know, we're riding on Saturday." So she said, "We're allowed to today."

We arrived on Saturday, and on Monday the next-door neighbor, along with my mother, took us to register us at the school; P.S. 19 on Fourteenth Street between First and Second Avenue, and the registrar named us. I was Loschell, I became Lois. He was Davnar, he became David. Phulen became Philly [Phillip], and Arden became Alvin. That's how we got our names. David went to [the] School for the Deaf on Nineteenth Street.

ALVIN: My father insisted that we retain our heritage. He insisted that we learn to read and write Yiddish. He said, "The English will come."

LOIS: We went to the Workmen's Circle School for Yiddish two or three times a week after school. Papa insisted that my mother speak Yiddish to us in the house, he said, "Because you'll never speak English perfectly anyway, and you want them to remember." But he himself would speak English to us. [Laughs.]

ALVIN: But my mother did go to night school to learn English.

LOIS: Well, she learned, because we all spoke. Within two or three months nobody knew we had been foreign-born . . .

My mother was helping my father sell eggs. He had rented space in front of a store on First Avenue where he sold eggs. He was an egg merchant. Eventually he went into an indoor business. But there was the elevated train running on First Avenue at that time.

ALVIN: It was called the Second Avenue El, which came down Second Avenue and turned east on Twenty-third Street and then south on First Avenue to Hanover Square in New York. The elevated train was running right above my father's stand. I remember when he was selling eggs, and the train came by, you couldn't hear what was transpiring because, "How much did you say?" [Laughs.] We had to put up with it. But after a while you didn't even realize the train was there.

I remember near Fourteenth Street, in our neighborhood there were a lot of Ukrainians and Italians, mostly Italians, and as boys, we used to play ball against the wall of the telephone building. [Gestures to David.] He protected me. All the Italian boys said, "Yeah, let's beat up the little Yid." And he used to fight for me. [To David.] You always fought for me.

LOIS: David was our protector. Right, David?

[David, who fades in and out, does not respond.]

ALVIN: He chased the Italian kids because I was a little frightened boy, but he was the one who protected me. So we got used to having these ethnic fights, and it was part of growing up in New York at the time.

LOIS: In the meantime, my mother missed her family. Luckily, her father died before Hitler got to Poland. Of course, when the war hit Poland in 1939, everybody vanished. It was a very sad time for my father and mother. My father, I think, even more so, because he lost both parents, his eight brothers and sisters, and all the extended families, even his grandparents. My father had a grandfather who was ninety-six years old. My mother used to tell me he wouldn't talk about it. He used to have nightmares about what happened to them.

ALVIN: From what I heard through relations of my father's, my father's father, my grandfather, and my father's brother were the two richest men in the town when the Nazis came in, and they hung them in the middle of the square. They asked the Poles who the richest merchants in town were, and they pointed . . . and hung them.

I think the saddest time that I remember was the fact that my mother wasn't in Europe when her father died. I remember the tears in her eyes. She sat shivah. I remember her sitting on a box here in America for a week, because her father died. After that, she became acclimated and liked America.

LOIS: I remember coming into the house and she didn't have the box yet. She had just gotten the letter, and she realized that her father had been dead a month, and so she was sitting on the floor. I said, "Mama, why are you sitting on the floor?" She looked at me, and I was probably about nine years old at the time, and she said, "Zeta died." I realized what had happened. And you're probably right. At that point, her closest tie to Poland was gone.

Isaac Bashevis Singer

. . . .

BORN JULY 14, 1904
EMIGRATED 1935, AGE 31
PASSAGE ON THE *CHAMPLAIN*

The son and grandson of rabbis, he studied at a rabbinical seminary in Warsaw (1920–27), before pursuing a career as a writer. He emigrated alone on a tourist visa to reunite with his older brother and literary mentor, Israel Singer. He went on to write over forty books—novels, plays, memoirs, short stories, and children's books—first in Yiddish, and then translated into English. He is best known for his novels and short stories, set in the Jewish ghettos of eastern Europe, such as The Family Moskat, The Manor, Satan in Goray, The Estate, The Magician of Lublin, *and* A Crown of Feathers and Other Stories. *He was the recipient of numerous literary awards including two National Book Awards (1970 and 1974). In 1978, he won the Nobel Prize for literature. He died in Miami on July 24, 1991.*

. . . .

I was brought up in Warsaw . . . which is not very much unlike New York. It is noisy, it is dirty. There is everything which a big city has, all the good sides and all the bad sides. So I wasn't really very much shocked when I came to this country, to New York, because we had the same thing there in a smaller way. But just the same, we all were brought up that America is almost like a different planet, and in a way I was very confused when I came here.

First of all, I did not know English. I hadn't studied any English there, so I was actually mute when I went to a bus or to a trolley car. I didn't know what to say. In addition, things looked to me very different. For example, when I looked into a drugstore and I saw that they served sandwiches there, I was bewildered because for us a drugstore was a most dignified place where one took off one's hat, and the idea that people sit there on little benches, and drink coffee, and smoke, looked to me almost sacrilege. Now, I know, that it was silly because there is nothing special about the drugstore . . .

In fact, so many things looked so different that I thought, in my heart, I will never be able to write about this country. And the truth is, for thirty years, I never dared to write anything about this country, but now I have been here in America longer than I had been in Poland and I would say that I have my deep roots also here. And I have learned, it is true, that I don't write about people born in this country, I write mostly about immigrants, but at least I dare to write about America.

There was anti-Semitism [in Warsaw], but I personally did not have much of this kind of experience, because I always lived among Jewish people, on the Jewish streets. First, I went to the synagogue or to the study house where I studied the Talmud, and there was no anti-Semitism there. Later, I was connected with the Yiddish writers for the Yiddish Writers Club, so although I knew that it existed and I read about it in the newspapers, I personally didn't have any trouble.

However, what you read in the newspapers is very much real, and you know that what happened to another man can the next day happen to you, so we were all afraid, especially in the '30s. Men from a pro-Fascist party, they were almost pro-Nazi, visited Poland, and we Jews knew that Poland was a very dangerous place for us. This was one of the reasons, or perhaps the main reason, why I wanted to get away from there. Also, my brother was here, who was a writer, many years older than I. I considered him my master, my teacher, and I wanted to be together with him.

I came by boat, a French boat called *Champlain*. I was told later that this boat was sunk during the war. It was quite an elegant, beautiful boat. As a matter of fact, the agent from whom I bought the ticket told me that if I would have waited another two weeks I could have gone with the *Normandy*, which made its maiden voyage, and this was considered among many people a great privilege to go on this first trip. But I felt that the ship would not add anything to my value. I came here the first of May 1935. I traveled tourist class, which was good enough for me.

I remember my arrival quite well. A man from the *Jewish Daily Forward* waited for me and also my brother, and they took me in a car. My first impression was New York is a city like all cities. It is not the planet Mars or Venus or Jupiter. When I saw the skyscrapers, I felt there was something unusual, but just the same, the Polish had already tried to build a skyscraper in Warsaw, a lower skyscraper, let's say. It had eighteen floors, but even this was big.

Many immigrants had this kind of feeling that America is so different that they really felt that they were coming into a different world, but I don't have to tell you that the world is actually the same. It only takes time until you learn the language and you get acquainted with people, you realize that human nature is everywhere the same. Although there are many differences, I would say that American people looked to me then, and they look to me now, more kind and more sincere and more ready to help people than the Europeans. But there is also a reason for this, because American people are richer and they are accustomed to immigrants. They are not clannish as the Europeans are, where people have fought for every inch of earth for generations. There are great differences, but there are also many, many things which are common to all people.

The first thing I saw from the ship was the Statue of Liberty, and it always made a great impression on me. Immigrants . . . I even heard about the Statue of Liberty when I was a small boy in Warsaw, when I went to *heder.* They spoke about this because there were many people in our neighborhood who could not read or write, and they had relatives in America, so they came to my mother that she should read their letters. And they all wrote about it, how they came to America, how they saw the Statue of Liberty, and they also wrote about Ellis Island, which they called the Island of Tears, and about all the troubles some of the immigrants had when they came. There was a great fear of this island because people were told that if the doctors find that someone is sick, or they think he is sick, they send him back.

So many immigrants, I remember, before they went to America, went to doctors to cure their eyes and all kinds of sicknesses which they suspected might hinder them of entering the United States. In my case, when I came to this country, they only asked me if I was a communist, and I said, "God forbid!"

. . .

A country where the great majority are immigrants is different than a country where people have been living for hundreds of years, but this doesn't mean that the difference makes a country of immigrants worse. It may be even the opposite, because people who come to another country, who are torn out from their homes, learn that things are not just as they thought. When you stay long at home, where you never leave your own country, you have the illusion that everything which happens in your country is hard, this is human nature. If you are accustomed to eating for breakfast, say, a roll and coffee, and you travel and see them eat corn flakes, you think that the world is going to pieces because you see that things can be so different. In a way, traveling is a lesson in tolerance. We learn by traveling and by immigrating . . .

But as far as literature is concerned, it is necessary that a man who writes should have roots somewhere. If, let's say, he has been traveling all his life, let's say like children of ambassadors, who one day they are in Spain, the next day in China, and the next year in Russia and so on, for such children writing would be very difficult, although we never know. If a person is really born with a talent, he may overcome all kinds of difficulties and still write, but as far as we know from the history of literature and from experience, it is a fact that being rooted is very important. Writing without roots is almost no literature—it becomes journalism.

It is possible to write and be alienated, but I will tell you, in a way we are all alienated. Every human being feels that he is a stranger on this planet. I don't think alienation is more a problem here than in any other country, because people who have been born here should feel at home. The reason for this talk about alienation is people who try to deny themselves—a man who says, "I am Jewish, but I am not Jewish, I am a Frenchman, but I don't want to be a Frenchman." People who try to assimilate to deny their roots are alienated. But, if you are frank and sincere, you say, I am so and so, my name is so and so, I speak this and this language, I am not ashamed of anything, such a person is able to feel at home anywhere. In other words, spiritually at home. It's the man who likes to put a mask on his face, who says that he is alienated, it is his own fault. I have heard this business about alienation from many Jewish writers who say, "I am not a Jew, I am not an American, or I am only half an American and half a Jew." If you are half of everything, you already don't belong. But if you do like I do, you say, "I'm hundred percent a Jew and I am also hundred percent an American, a naturalized American, but just the same an American," and you are not ashamed of anything, and you don't deny anything, and you don't change your name, and you don't change your language and your habits, then you are at home everywhere. It's only this fear, this desire, to mimic others which makes people feel like strangers.

. . .

My first year here I lived in Seagate in Brooklyn, and then in Manhattan on East Nineteenth Street, a furnished room, and I lived there for some time. Later on, when I married, I lived one year on Ocean Avenue in Brooklyn. And then I moved back to Manhattan, and I lived about twenty years on Central Park West, a few years on West Seventy-second Street, and now the Lower West Side near Union Square.

As a young man, I chose the neighborhoods because rent was cheaper. It was also natural to me to live more or less among my people. I wouldn't have gone, say, to Staten Island. I like to live in the middle of everything and not far from the public library on Forty-second Street. I would say I still like the West Side because there are more of my kind of people, the people who read the *Jewish Daily Forward* on the West Side than on the East Side. But the East Side is also

nice, I wouldn't mind having an apartment there, too. [Laughs.]

My happiest surprise about being here was when I once went into the subway, and I saw a sign in Yiddish that said you are not allowed to smoke. I said to myself, "Here, in this city?" In Poland, only the Jews had signs in Yiddish. The government never used the Yiddish language. Here, I saw people use the Yiddish language. I saw a lot of tolerance in this country, and I still keep seeing it. When I read the *New York Times*, I see that banks which advertised Christmas Savings Books now have Hanukkah Savings Books and Hanukkah candles in bank branches. There's no question about it. There's not another country I know of, so tolerant, and has such a feeling for strangers and for strange cultures as this country.

My parents never came to this country. To my parents, America was like another planet, you know. But my brother lived here, and I have a son who lives in Israel, but he came to visit me twice here. Once he stayed three years, so I would say I feel like an American. I am a member now of the National Institute of Arts and Letters, and the American Academy of Arts and Sciences. The Americans consider me one of them, and I consider the Americans my people.

I was very happy for many years in this country, but in later years, I feel that the wave of crime has taken such measures that it's just frightening. We have reached a degree now where we are afraid to walk in the streets of New York, and if this will go on, this state of affairs will destroy everything good which America has ever had. You can have a million good qualities, but if one is afraid to enter your home, then all the qualities are nothing. This is what is happening to this country. This state of affairs will destroy the entire image of America. People will not dream anymore about entering America. They will only dream about running away from it. I am sorry to have to say this.

Clara Rudder

· · · · · · · · · · · ·

BORN OCTOBER 7, 1910
EMIGRATED VIA BELGIUM, 1940, AGE 30
PASSAGE ON THE *NYASSA*

*She came from Galicia Blazowa, located in the lower Carpathian Mountains in
Poland. She learned English by reading* Gone with the Wind, *given to her by
a young doctor at Ellis Island, where she, her husband, and son were detained
for seven weeks. She lived in Far Rockaway, Kew Gardens, and finally settled
in a luxury apartment in Forest Hills, Queens, where she has lived for more than
thirty years. Her husband, a diamond merchant, left her well off. "If you hate,
you lose yourself," she said. "There's nothing left in this world after hate. I can't
hate. I have never been taught to hate. Even after pogroms, after all that
happened in our town, my father tried to explain . . . I was ten years old. I asked
that question 'Why?' There was no answer to it. There still isn't."*

It was a small farming village, maybe four or five hundred people. There was no railroad. Just one small street with stores, and one market where people came every Wednesday, to sell their greens, their vegetables, their cows, and also bought what they needed, like kerosene. You knew everybody in town, and most of the people who came knew everybody else. It was comfortable. There was a little brook, and we could go swimming there. There was lots of woods where we could go walking and playing.

My father and mother, they had a nice brick house, because before I was born in 1910, there was a big fire. The whole town burned down. They were all wooden houses. So when they rebuilt, they made brick houses. The house had four rooms, and a tremendous eat-in kitchen with a big iron stove for cooking and heating. Everything was heated with wood. There was lots of wood. We were surrounded by woods . . .

We lived with my grandma, also my father's sister, and her two-year-old child

my mother took care of. We were four children of our own, my two brothers, my sister, and me. I was the third in the row. My name in Poland was Chaja. Chaja is a Hebrew name. It means "animal," and *chaj* means life, so you could say "live animal," or if my husband wanted to tease me years later, he said a wild animal. [Laughs.] I didn't like that name. So when I became a citizen here I changed my name to Clara.

My father was born in Blazowa and lived there all his life. He had a store that sold pots and pans and iron parts to build stoves, because there was no electricity and no gas in Blazowa. He was a good man, I could talk to my father. He was a man mostly of learning. He studied a lot of Torah, a lot of Hebrew. The store was to make a living, but his major thing was to study. He was very religious, and my mother too, and my grandma.

My maiden name is Rudder, and historically, the Rudder's lived for four hundred years in Spain before coming to Poland. The king in Poland was Crul Sabieski [John

Sobieski]. He let the Jewish people come into Poland because he needed the commerce, and Jewish people were good at that. But we have no papers left. Everything was gone when my parents were killed by the Nazis. Nothing was left. When I was ten years old in 1920, Poland became a country. It was after the First World War, and I never forget that day because the pogroms came.

I remember it was a Saturday. All of the stores were closed because they were owned by Jewish people. One man came and knocked and knocked at the door. "I need to talk to your father." My father comes. The man says, ". . . I came to take your family to my house." My father says, "You know it's a Saturday. We are not going on the Sabbath to travel." He says, "They're going to come to this city. They're going to rob you. They decided, and I came to take you." My father thanked him.

That evening my father went to the synagogue, and Saturday night there was a ceremony where you light a candle and you say the Sabbath prayer . . . My father warned the congregation and said to take their silver Menorahs, all the silver, whatever they had, and put it up on the roof or in the attic, which they did, us too. Later that night, we started to hear shooting and my father said, "Take Grandma and go to our neighbor," a block away from us. He was a gentile, the organ player at the church. "He'll let you in, and Mother and I will lock up and we'll come."

When we came there, the organist's daughter opened the door and she says, "Our house is full, everybody came to us. But I can put you in the cow barn . . .," and we sat there until my father and mother came, the whole family . . .

When we returned in the morning the windows of our house were broken, glass all over everything. The doors were broken. They make a terrible mess. Nobody was killed and nobody was hurt, but they ruined the whole street, every store. They couldn't take sacks of flour or sugar. It was too heavy. So they put naphtha, petrol, over it to spoil it.

We were ashamed, we felt bad, because they didn't open our store. We were the only ones not touched. We couldn't figure out why. My father was a very honest person, and he treated the people very nicely, and I think that's why, or perhaps they didn't need pots and pans, who knows? We didn't know who was responsible. We knew they were young men with guns back from the war, and whenever there was something, they blamed the Jews . . . My mother took the biggest pots and cooked for the whole town. Every child in town we brought in, and my mother fed them. We helped all our neighbors to clean up and to straighten up. But for four weeks we didn't sleep at all.

Despite the help we gave, when I came to school, all the children said, "Get out of here!" I felt like nothing. And that day, I made up my mind that I wouldn't have a child in Poland. I lived in Blazowa till I was twenty. I wanted to leave. My mother didn't want to let me go. By then, I was a Zionist and wanted to go to Palestine. My mother said, "I'll die if you go to Palestine." It was very hard life there, and she says, "You're going to split rocks in Palestine. I did not bring up a child of mine to go and split rocks." I said, "Mother, I'll be a free person there." She couldn't understand it. I said to my father, "If you keep me here I will be an old maid because I'll never have a child here." That was my way of getting out.

I decided on Belgium instead. My older sister married a man who went to Belgium, and she lived in Antwerp since she was married. Then my oldest brother married his sweetheart and went there. So I said, "Now it's my time." My father said, ". . .You stay with us, because we need somebody here."

I said, "You should come with us there. There's no point for you to stay here. Sell the house, sell the business, and come." But they were very orthodox, and they didn't feel like going to a big town like Antwerp. They just felt we were born here, we lived our lives here, we'll die here.

I had already a boyfriend in Poland. This boyfriend of mine did not live in our town. He was about eighteen and a half. I met him because his older sister and her husband had a drugstore in our town, and his sister was very lonesome because they were not religious, and religious people did not accept the nonreligious Jewish people. But I became friendly with her, and I used to invite her for coffee to our house, and my mother was too good not to be nice to her. Then her brother came for a vacation and we met and we used to go out together during the summer. We became engaged, but he studied in Prague, in Czechoslovakia. He

studied there because Poland had a quota. Only 3 percent Jewish people could go to college. If you didn't make it, you had to go out of the country to study. So he studied in Prague.

I said, "I'm going to Belgium. I'm going to leave now and go to Belgium." He says, "Okay. I'll try to come to Brussels and study there."

But the university in Brussels did not accept him. He remained in Prague, and he said, "What are you going to do when I finish? Are we going to get together and go to Poland to live?" He wanted to go back. I said, "That's not for me. I will never go back to live in Poland. Either you come to Belgium, or we're going to go to Palestine." He said, "No. I have promised my parents that I'd come back." So I sent him back my ring, and I said, "Forget it."

In the meantime, I lived in Belgium with my sister for two and a half years. I worked

Orphan children with Jewish social workers at Ellis Island. Their parents were killed during the Russian pogroms of October 1906. They arrived on the S.S. Caronia *May 8, 1908.*

(NATIONAL PARK SERVICE: STATUE OF LIBERTY NATIONAL MONUMENT)

at my brother-in-law's office. I was an accountant, carried on the books, and that's where I met my husband, Paul.

We got engaged in 1936 and were married soon after. By 1940, the war was coming closer to Belgium, and I had a feeling that the Germans would have to go through Belgium to get to France. I kept on saying to Paul, "We have to leave." So we tried to go to Palestine. We couldn't get papers. I had cousins from Vienna who came to Belgium. They told us about the atrocities the Germans did to Austrian Jews. I said to Paul, [and] my sister, "We got to go to the United States." My sister said, "Take the children and you go. We'll come later." I said, "You come with me or I'm not going." By then, I had one child, my son was born. My sister had two children. I kept on crying and screaming and pleading with Paul to send money to the United States, to a relative so it will be safe . . .

One day Paul says, "A man said we can buy passports to Haiti." I said, "Go ahead. Buy it." So my sister, her husband and two children, my brother, and his wife and two children, plus us, we all got passports to Haiti. We hired a bus and went to France, because the French government said all diamond dealers were welcome. Paul was in the diamond business, my brother-in-law was in the diamond business, and my brother was in the diamond business. "We'll take you in." And they did take us in. But by the time we got there, the Germans came and we had nowhere to go.

We were caught in France in a small town not far from Dunkirk, and the Germans made us go back. We had to hire a man with a car. It was a Swiss man who took us back to Belgium, and we went back home.

A Paraguay attaché in Belgium said he would take us across France to Spain, and from Spain we could get to Portugal. My sister went first with her husband [and] two children, and she wrote me a letter in Polish.

She said, "Everything is fine, we are across the border. Take two valises and come . . ."

When it came to load the car, only one valise fit. So the other valise we left standing. I closed my apartment. I had this beautiful apartment. Paul and I were four years married, we had just organized our home the way we liked it. I don't want to talk about it . . .

I left everything. We went to Perpignan in France, on the Spanish border, but the Germans stood there, and they said, "You need an outgoing visa from France. You can't go out without a visa." We had to go back to Perpignan, stood in line, got the outgoing visa, called the driver. He says, "My car broke down. I can't take you, but I'm going to arrange for you to go by train." We were now two families, my brother with his wife and two children. We had $12,000 in money and diamonds with us . . . but the driver stole the money. He was carrying some [of] our belongings to the train and never came back. We only had a thousand dollars on us.

We went from Spain to Portugal, to Lisbon, and we stayed there about three months. We couldn't get a boat, we couldn't get a plane. Everybody was trying, and everybody wanted to go. My sister had already left to America about two months before. First we went to a hotel, but it was too expensive. So then we went into a boardinghouse, where it was cheaper.

One day, we found a boat that was going to leave in ten days. So we paid the passage, but the boat didn't leave. What happened, Germany invaded Greece. It was a Greek boat, so we couldn't go. We didn't have any more money. So we sent a telegram to my sister here. Paul had sent money to America, so they sent us money.

Finally, we got a berth on the *Nyassa* for seven people, four grownups and three children in one berth. It was a small boat. It must have been a cattle boat. They just put paint over it, and that was it. One meal I ate on that boat, the first night. And after that it was very hard. We traveled for twelve days. I couldn't eat. It was a nervous time. One day they said there were mines. Water mines. Another day a German boat passed by. We wondered whether we would ever get to America. I was thinking, "Survive the day." That's it. Nothing else mattered. To survive the day and survive the voyage. Nothing else. I didn't cry for what I lost. I didn't cry for what I haven't got, and I didn't care. To wash my face, to wash my hands, to keep the child going, and to be well. That's all.

We got to New York; we were so elated. We were so happy. We weren't screaming. The elation came from the heart. You could see it on the faces. That's all you could see. The faces of the people. They were in awe. It's like, we were safe. That's all there was. When we landed at Ellis Island, they said, "What do you want? You want something to eat?" I said, "I want a good glass of milk." That's all I wanted. The milk tasted like cream. It was delicious. [She is moved.] That's all I remember.

Ellis Island was a terrible letdown for us. We didn't expect to go there. I didn't know ever of the existence of Ellis Island. Why should they put us in jail? We didn't do anything wrong. Nothing we did. We had only one valise, nothing. I had a coat, a winter coat, made for myself, because we came in December. I felt like just lying down and screaming and crying. They just wouldn't let us off. We didn't know why. I didn't know a word of English. Neither did my husband. I spoke German, French, Flemish, Yiddish, Hebrew, and Polish, of course. Not one word of English. Nothing was explained to us, nothing.

There were maybe three to four hundred people in that big room all day from seven in the morning to seven at night. I had such a headache. I couldn't breathe. There were a lot of people from Belgium. A lot of Jewish people.

My husband slept with men in a separate room. Every morning, every evening at seven o'clock you had to take everything up with you and go upstairs. The beds were clean and nice. The rooms were clean. The women slept with their children separate, and we were about six beds in the room. All this didn't bother us because you felt it's only for a little while, it will get over. But then the days passed . . . I had two suits for my son, he was three years old, and they both were white linen. So every day I washed a suit, hang it up overnight, and every morning I put him in a clean suit. His underwear, everything. I had nothing to change. I wore a blouse and a skirt. I didn't care. It didn't matter . . .

We were seven weeks at Ellis Island before the mystery cleared up. What happened, my brother-in-law gave the money for our passage, for all seven of us, to a lawyer. The lawyer took the money and gave his check to the travel agent. The lawyer's check bounced. We didn't know it. Immigration finally said, "You didn't pay the passage," and we didn't know the telephone to my sister's, so we were in jail! We had to prove that we paid and, after that, they finally let us go . . .

Years later, we found out my mother and father were killed, all my cousins, the whole town. Until 1942, we still had mail from my mother and father. After '42, the Germans evacuated them, and they became refugees. I have a cousin who saw them in Auschwitz. They were put in the ovens. My husband, Paul—his whole family got killed; his father, mother, two sisters, a brother who was married with a wife and two daughters—they all got killed in Poland. He was the only survivor.

Sadie Gold
· · · · · · · · · · · ·

BORN DECEMBER 15, 1915
EMIGRATED 1952, AGE 36
PASSAGE ON THE *GENERAL STUART*

*One of seven children from a small Polish village, her entire family was
exterminated by the Nazis, with the exception of two brothers who settled in
France after the war and who are now gone. She spent five years in concentration
camps and another seven years in hospital sanatoriums after the war, before
immigrating here. Never married, she learned English at night school, until she
got her citizenship papers. During the day, until age fifty-six, she worked at a
pharmaceutical company in Philadelphia. Her credentials? She clerked in the
ghetto pharmacy at Auschwitz. Today she lives alone in south Florida on a
pension. Her memory is scattered at best, not just from old age, but from the
trauma and bitterness of a life experience that defies imagination.
"I lost my whole family," she said. "I'm the only one left."*

I didn't want to work no more. My
legs were swollen from the war. I was
tired. I had enough. While I was at the
pharmaceutical company, somebody said I
should be eligible to receive disability until
age sixty-five. So I applied to Berlin and got
disability checks. I decided to quit. I wanted
to read, to travel, to see the world. I went to
China, Japan, Hawaii, Scandinavia . . .

During my trip around the world, I went
back to Poland. I never even went to the city
where I was born and went to school. I went
to Poland to look for a child. I had an older
sister who had a little girl. The boy she
couldn't save because he was circumcised,
and the Germans looked. But the girl was
over a year. I thought, "Maybe my sister gave
the baby away." My brothers in France said,
"You always go with this in your mind. Go!"

I went to that village, smaller than a
village. I said, "Is there anybody I can talk
to?" So I went to an office there. They said
they were too young. I knew they wouldn't
know. I said, "Give me somebody who

would know." So they sent me to see a man
so handsome and so good-dressed in such a
village. I said, "Look, did you know, did you
hear maybe about the name?" Her name
was Leosha. He said, "Don't even look.
Don't even bother. They came one day with
trucks and they took all the Jews from all the
small villages . . ."

I went to Dresden, to Germany. To see
one of the camps, to confront it, to face it.
During the war, I was sent by myself to
Auschwitz, to Birkenau, to Stutthoff near
Danzig . . . about six, seven concentration
camps. When I came to the railroad station
in Dresden, it had become beautiful city.
Flowers in every window, clean, people are,
you know, well dressed. And I thought, how
could the Germans say they didn't see, they
didn't know? Didn't they see us going in
every city, going to work, how we looked?
I used to have to clean that railway station
in Dresden. [Laughs.]

I remember I was in Stutthoff near Danzig. You know what they did over there?

There was a gas chamber, too, and a crematorium, but they took ships with women and throw them in the sea. Every day. They killed all of them, all of them. I run away four times. But they always caught me. One time, they was supposed to kill me at eleven o'clock, but I don't know what happened . . .

I am Jewish, but I'm not religious. How can you believe? They used to take us out, three o'clock at night, and count us in the cold. The cold was worse than the hunger. It was so cold because it was near the ocean and it was winter. It was worse than hunger. When you are hungry you don't think about anything. Just how to eat. I used to stay three o'clock at night in the frost and cold, and think, "Where is God?" How can you believe in anything? The Germans killed a million and a half children. The children did something wrong? You know, to kill 6 million Jews, it's a whole world. If not for the Russians, we wouldn't have Jews. I'm talking mostly of the end of the war. The Russians were coming nearer and nearer, and Americans were not in a hurry. If they wouldn't be afraid that Russia will be first in Berlin, they would still be I don't know where.

The German people are guilty, too. They looked the other way. We were walking in their streets to clean, to work. How could they not see us? Now they say they didn't know. That's not true. My opinion is that it is not only Hitler, but it's the whole of Germany, all the folks in Germany. They all helped him. He would never be a Hitler. He would never do what he did if not for the people . . . I was there where he committed suicide, he and Eva Braun. I was there after the war, and I put my name. I took a nail, and I put my name. Even today on television, they start again. This can happen again. I say always that the whole war is their fault because it didn't take a year, it didn't take months, it took from 1933 to 1945. He came to Poland in '39 when the war broke out, but he did plenty from '33. He couldn't do this alone. And the whole world was quiet, nobody said anything. Everybody knew, but they didn't do anything. Nobody said anything . . .

At the end, I don't know how many of us were left, and the Germans put us on death march, they called it. We were five together. We walked out, and there were two Germans with pistols like this, and they saw us. They didn't do anything. They knew it's the end. And we were walking, and we went to a farm. We didn't have anywhere to sleep. It was already dark. The German farmer didn't let us stay. He said, "*Raus! Raus!*" But then a woman came, and she said, "Come, I take you." And she took us to her camp, a little house. And there were Ukrainians and Polacks. The commandant, he was a nice man, a hunchback. If he would come today, I give him my whole apartment, a German. He said to me, "Don't worry. You will sleep here. Go to the cellar . . ." and he brought old clothes, I slept on the floor, and I was there till the end of the war, when the planes came . . .

How many times did I lie on dead people? [Pauses.] When the Russians came and the Americans, they were crying, the soldiers, when they saw it. This high [gestures to the ceiling] with naked bodies. This will go to the rest of my days as long as I live. This cannot be forgotten . . .

The Russians, they took me straight to a hospital. They were nice, the doctors, the Russians. They said, "This is not for you. You are too sick to be in such a small hospital. You have to go to Prague, to a big hospital," and then they sent me to the American zone. And from there a sanatorium in Heidelberg, which was beautiful. I was there two or three years. I had TB. There was some sort of oil inside me. I had maybe seven, eight doctors inserting needles to get the oil out, but the oil got hard like a stone inside, so they couldn't do anything. But I didn't fight for my life. They were taking every day thousands of people. I said, "Well, the only thing is death, so what?" You don't have to live always. I have enough. After the war, nothing interested me. I didn't care anymore . . .

I was still sick. So they sent me over there to a sanatorium for two years in the mountains in France. And the doctor said, "You are all right." I went out in the street, and I said, "How can I be all right? I can't walk. I'm so weak." Nobody knew. I packed my little bag, and I went back to Heidelberg to the sanatorium, and I had an operation on my chest. They said to me, if I wait two years I can go straight to America. I had friends in New York and, at that time, everybody used to go to America because nobody wanted to stay in Europe. Besides, I didn't have anybody. Just these friends. So I waited more than two years, doctors said everything is okay, and I came in 1952.

There were eleven hundred people on the ship. I was on the ship eleven days. We left from Bremerhaven to Ellis Island . . .

I saw my friends who live in New York, they were waiting, but they couldn't see me. I saw them. The first day, they didn't give us nothing to drink, nothing to eat, the whole day. It was not a prison, but we were not free. Then days passed and I saw people leaving and I was staying. I send a note to the director of Ellis Island. I pushed under the door, so he came out and he said, "Who's Sadie Gold?" I said, "Me." I said, "I didn't come to America to stay in Ellis Island. I came to work, to live here." He said, "You want to go back?" I said, "Yes. I don't want to stay here." So he said, "I can only send you back to Germany where you came, because you are *stättelose*." *Stättelose* means I

don't belong to any country. Poland was not my country anymore, and Germany, certainly not.

I didn't belong to any country . . . We had a lawyer, we were only about eighteen people left from my boat. The rest all went. I wrote a letter the lawyer translated into English, because I didn't speak a word of English, and I sent it to Eleanor Roosevelt.

About ten o'clock one evening, a policewoman came who spoke Yiddish, and she said, "Who is Sadie Gold?" I said, "Me." "Come with me." She said there was a telephone call from Canada for me. I said, "I don't know anybody in Canada." But she connected me, and it was a girl that I worked with in the ghetto five years. I said, "How did you know where I was?"

She said, "Don't you know, today in the paper, the *New York Times*, I saw your name." Eleanor Roosevelt said, "If the immigrants are sick, we should send them to hospitals and heal them, and if they are well, they should go out and be free."

I was sent to Denver, Colorado, to the National Jewish Hospital, which is the best in the country. I was there six months and every month I gave sputum and blood and all. They checked that everything is okay. I was set to leave, when a social worker, she said, "Stay, and I'm going to give you a good job, and it's beautiful here." I liked it there and I didn't have anybody, so what's difference? She said, "There is a family here, they have two children. You speak French, German, Polish, and they want to learn foreign languages."

The very next day she came to me and said, "I have very bad news for you. Last night, a plane fell down on their house, and though nobody got killed, they have no house anymore . . . You are lucky."

9

· · · · · · · · · ·

Germany

(APPROXIMATELY 1.1 MILLION IMMIGRANTS, 1892–1954)

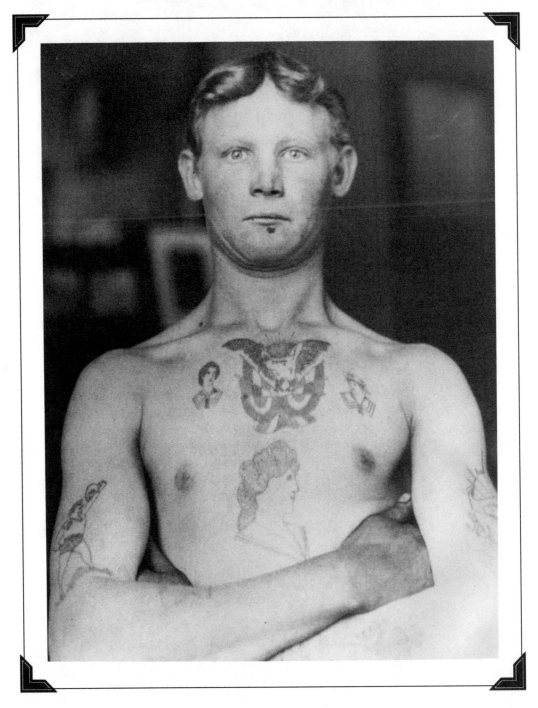

Tattooed German stowaway, May 1911

(NATIONAL PARK SERVICE: STATUE OF LIBERTY NATONAL MONUMENT)

· · · · · · · · ·

William Reinhart

. . . .

BORN JUNE 29, 1905
EMIGRATED 1910, AGE 4
PASSAGE ON THE *ROTTERDAM*

Born in Milan, Italy, he lived his first four years in Stuttgart, one of twelve children. In America, he worked his "way up from a lowly billing clerk to traffic manager of three divisions" of an international steamship company. Now ninety-two, he lives alone near Harrisburg, Pennsylvania, having lost his wife, Lisa, twenty-four years ago.

My father came here first. He was in the chemical-laboratory glassware industry. He was an engraver, and our family history in that business dates back to 1611. My two oldest brothers were both officers in the German army, and they told him about the imminence of World War I. They suggested to my father if he wanted to leave, now was the time. That was 1909. So my father came to this country to get a home for us and establish us. He was employed by a New York company which represented the parent company where he worked in Stuttgart.

We came the following year. My mother must have been a saint, because she had the courage to bring eight children by herself to America. Her voice was so soft. When she scolded you it hurt more than a physical punishment. We came over on the Hamburg-American Line vessel, the *Rotterdam*. We also left from the port of Rotterdam. She gathered us, and we got aboard ship. I was four years old. And that's the only European remembrance I have.

We had very bad weather crossing the Big Pond, as I got to call it in later years. And it took twenty-one days. I was the first one to get seasick, because we were cooped up. We had the lowest cabins in the ship. Two cabins. One for my mother and my three sisters. And one for my four brothers and me. I still can't fathom how we got along in such close quarters.

Then at some point, we docked, and they told me we were at Ellis Island. The Health Department came aboard, and we received vaccinations. We didn't know a word of English. Then we took a small ferry from Ellis Island to the Battery. As we got off the ferry, our father met us. And it was just overwhelming. We hadn't seen our father for more than a year, and I really got to know him that first day. It was both exciting and wonderful.

We walked up Broadway, our father and mother in [the] lead, and the eight little ducklings following behind. And I saw the big buildings. We didn't have big buildings in Germany. And what amazed me in New York, I saw a trolley car drawn by two horses. Then we got on an elevated subway train and, all of a sudden, we were in the sky. Here we were twenty-one days on the water, and now we were sailing through the sky with water underneath us, which was the East River. I know I never stopped crying until we came to ground level in Brooklyn. It was an immigrant German neighborhood, where my father had a cold-water flat on the third floor of an apartment building.

After we were here a short time, the landlord came one night with two big Tammany guys from the New York Democratic Party. They offered our father a proposition. If he would sign up to become a Democrat and guarantee that all his children would be Democrats, they would get him his citizenship papers within six months. At that time, you had to wait five years before you got your citizenship papers. And I just got up amongst all the family sitting at the dinner table. I said, "Father, don't you do that, because if anything happens, we'll be sent back to Germany." The Tammany men left. My father didn't accept their offer.

To this day, I vote Republican.

Ralph Becker

. . . .

BORN JANUARY 9, 1900
EMIGRATED 1925, AGE 25
PASSAGE ON THE *OHIO*

He was born and raised in the mountain village of Daaden. A large and solid man, he's lived in Schenectady, New York for seventy-seven years and worked for General Electric until retirement. "When I was nine or ten years old, I read The Leatherstocking Tales *by James Fenimore Cooper in German," he said. "I never dreamed that I would live practically a lifetime on that very soil."*

Daaden was actually a town where many of the people worked in the iron ore mines in the Siegenland, a very famous industrial area dating back to Celtic times. Siegen is the capital city of that district.

My father was a carpenter and cabinetmaker, and owned a shop. So was my mother's father and both of my grandfathers. After I was born, my father had contracted to do woodwork in an apartment house. But the mason was rather lax in putting in the windows and the doors. So my father helped out and got a bad cold, which led to pneumonia, and he died just three weeks after I was born. My father was thirty-six years old.

My mother was thirty-four at the time. In addition to me, she had two other sons. One seven, one five. So she could not operate the carpenter shop, even though there was a journeyman there to assist. The carpenter shop was on the farm where we lived. So after a family meeting it was decided that she would be able to earn money buying and selling milk and butter. But even this was extremely difficult for my mother with the kids. So she had the barn redone into a downstairs and an upstairs. We lived downstairs and she rented the upstairs to newlyweds. My grandmother moved in to help out. She did the cooking. Potatoes, carrots, green beans—vegetables we grew in our garden.

Of course, I always wanted to be a cabinetmaker. My oldest brother learned the cabinetmaking trade from [our] uncle. When he turned fourteen, my brother went to a distant city to work at a large furniture factory. He developed a lung disease from the sawdust, and so my mother said, "You're not going to learn the cabinetmaking trade. You have to learn another trade." And she had friends, and it was a small village so everybody knew everybody, and when I turned fourteen she asked the blacksmith if I could learn his trade. I didn't mind. This was the second major tragedy my mother had to face. So I agreed with her decision. And then she died soon after of pneumonia just like my father. Within a week she was gone. This was 1914.

So there I was a full waif, of course, and it was a tough experience. My mother knew she was going to die, so she had made arrangements. The furniture and things were sold; the cows left and the wagons were filled. And you're helpless then. You know that you're facing a life that many boys would not have to face if they still had their father and mother. [Laughs.] My grandmother had to move back to her old home and she lived four more years before she died at the end of the First World War.

My brother and I went to live with my mother's younger sister in Daaden. Same town. She had a fairly large house and four children; three boys and a girl. Her oldest boy was just a year younger than I, so I fitted well in that family. It was a very pleasant situation. My aunt and uncle lived at the end of the town. They had two huge, old linden trees. When you walked to their home, you walked between them as an entrance. And my uncle was a very good-natured man, and he let us build a tree house. So it was a pleasant surrounding for me, and I felt quickly at home there.

I worked in the blacksmith shop, one of three apprentices. But we also had many journeymen, one of whom was a Russian prisoner of war. He had been in his third year of service in Brestlitovsk in Russia, when he had to go to war. But he was caught and made a prisoner. He talked about his father, who had a steam mill, a steam-driven milling operation for wheat and flour, not far from Moscow. When the Bolshevik revolution started, every kulak, or person who owned property, had it confiscated, and [in] most cases they were shipped to Siberia. So I don't think our Russian friend ever saw his family again. But we did learn all sorts of Russian words, in most cases not very good ones! [Laughs.] The boss was paying his apprentices a small wage, enough that I could pay my room and board with my aunt. Of course, that left nothing for spending money, so we had to live very frugal.

At the blacksmith shop, we also sharpened the miners' drills. They used air hammers in the mine, and so we would get hundreds of them each day to sharpen. The next morning they would pick them up from various numbered bins. The miners would call for their numbers and put the drills in bundles and take them down in the mine, 1,800 feet deep, with short side-tunnels every forty feet toward the ore body. There was this endless hammering of drills. I remember the first spring after my mother died the sun shone so nicely through that window. I started to dream about the woods where my mother used to collect wildflowers, especially the "snowbells" which pushed through melting snow in the spring and had a delicate, bell-shaped flower and wonderful fragrance. I thought about that, hammering slowly, when all of a sudden the old boss came, and he knocked the hammer out of my hand, pulled the drill out of my other hand, and said, "We're not playing marbles here!" [Laughs.] That scared me to death, practically. And, of course, after that I was always on the job. Most of the miners were young fellows who died of lung sickness. The silicon dust blocked their lungs up, to the point they couldn't breathe anymore. So whether you were a carpenter or a miner, you met the same fate. So I was very happy in the blacksmith shop. There was little that could kill me there.

And then I was drafted into the army. It was 1917. I was seventeen years old, the age where I made good cannon fodder, as they used to say. [Laughs.] Then, one day, my uncle brought a telegram to the blacksmith shop, and said, "You don't have to go. You were deferred." I was deferred because they needed me to sharpen these drills and keep the miners going. I was also trained as an electrician so I could do repair work. And I did all of this for six years, long after the war ended. I continued living with my aunt and uncle.

By 1921, we started realizing what the Treaty of Versailles meant to Germany. After all, we were the losers of that war and so we lost tremendous territory. West Prussia went to Poland because the Poles wanted an outlet to the sea, so they took the Vistula River, which flowed past Danzig into the Baltic Sea. That was part of the cause of the Second World War. But not only that, we also lost a large portion of southeastern Germany we used to call Bohemia to Czechoslovakia. This is where Germany had all its coal, iron, and silver mines. And we lost Alsace-Lorraine. France demanded it back. It was territory they lost in the war against Germany in 1871. France also demanded back all the gold they sent to Germany and Chancellor Bismarck as reparations after that 1871 war.

All of a sudden, a terrible inflation started. At first, people didn't know what caused it. Suddenly, a loaf of bread tripled in price, as did butter, and the cost of living in general. People realized their money in the bank was worth less and less as inflation went rampant. The worst years were 1921, '22, '23, '24. It was so bad I remember hav-

ing a 10,000-mark note and the bank stamped across the front "hundred thousand." [Laughs.] It was like a joke.

In the meantime, I fell in love with the woman who would become my wife. I was twenty-two years old and you think of eventually getting married. But it was impossible to rent even a small apartment with two rooms, a kitchen, and a bedroom. We became discouraged. I started thinking about America.

There was a man in town that had lived in Kenosha, Wisconsin. He bought one of the nicest-looking homes in Daaden. And I heard that he also supplied people with money, dollars, to go to the United States, because we couldn't use our own mark. They wouldn't take the German mark for ship's passage. We had to have either pound sterling or dollars. So I asked to borrow money, but he declined. I offered him part of some land I inherited from my mother as a guarantee we would pay back the money. He refused. He said, "Why don't you sell me the entire parcel outright. You never will come back anyhow." And we consented to that.

We booked passage on the Royal Mail Line from Hamburg. Since we were emigrating, we thought it a good idea that we get married first, if nothing else so that we could sleep together on the boat. Then a telegram arrived from the ship's line that we couldn't go because the quota was filled. Germany, at that time, had more than 70,000 people trying to emigrate to the United States. So we had to stay. My wife lived with me in my old bachelor's quarters. [Laughs.] It was just a narrow bedroom, and a clothes closet, and a bed on my uncle's property. What could we do? We existed this way until 1925.

In the meantime, she became pregnant. You can't sleep with a beautiful woman night after night, and nothing happens. [Laughs.] When our daughter was born we got a letter from the American consul in Cologne. We had to go to there, the both of us, to get the visa. She was still in bed recovering from the pregnancy, but she said, "I'm going even if it costs my life."

It was an eighty-mile railroad trip. I bought first-class tickets so she wouldn't catch any draft or cold, because those early trains were full of labor people that got to work, and the doors were always open[ing] and closing. In Cologne, the railway station was almost directly in front of the consul so we didn't have to walk far. All the immigrants had to go the back way. You couldn't go in the front. And then they finally opened the door, and let us in. There was a long room with just plain benches, and we sat on the benches and waited for our number to be called. I said to my wife, "At this rate, we'll never get home tonight," because my wife had to breast-feed the baby. [Laughs.] Somehow we had to get home, so I said, "When the doctor comes again, I'm going to ask him whether he could take us first."

And he did. The doctor examined us, and we got our health certificates. I asked, "Do we need one for our baby?" And I showed him the health certificate they gave us at the birth.

"No," the doctor said, "that's no good."

"Well," I said, "couldn't you write one up?"

"Has she got all ten fingers? All ten toes?"

"Yes."

[Laughs.] He wrote up the health certificate. He charged us ten dollars each for ours and five dollars for the baby.

. . .

It was an English ship. We left from Hamburg in February, crossed the North Sea, and went to Southampton for several days for refueling. Then we crossed the English Channel and went to Cherbourg, France and from there the open ocean.

We hit a terrible storm and we both got so seasick. There was an old English nurse on board and she took care of the baby. She changed the baby and brought soup to my wife in our small cabin, but not to me. "No, no," she said to my wife. "He's a man. He can go up to the dining room." [Laughs.]

We could hear the waves thunder over the deck. In fact, it had knocked out the air circulation from the air vents. There was no such thing as air conditioning. It got terribly hot inside because it was a steam turbine boat. And we complained. "Well, this is a German-built boat!" they said. It was one of those boats that, according to the Versailles Treaty, was turned over to England. And this was the former München, or Munich. Either the Hamburg-America line or the Bremen-Lloyd. They called the ship *Ohio*.

The baby was eight weeks old when we brought her to New York. I'll never forget the first morning we stood on deck and looked at that Manhattan skyline. A fog came in, and they had to drop anchor. The sky was completely overcast and everything from the ship looked awful dreary and not very inviting at all. I had my arm around my wife, who held the baby in her arm. Neither of us could speak a word of English. [Laughs.] I had no prospects for a job. And here I was with a young family. It seemed as if even nature was against us.

They inspected our suitcases and we boarded a ferry which brought us to Ellis Island. We were separated immediately. I remember we walked up to a fairly high ramp and then into the examining rooms, and on top of the ramp was a man that checked your eyes and then, of course, we had to have enough papers—health certificate, birth certificate, marriage certificate, all in triplicate. And we had to leave that there. I went down the other side of the ramp and looked for my wife. She wasn't there. So I waited, full of anxiety because that was supposed to be our last examination. If we

Immigrant Aid Society officials, circa 1900

(NATIONAL PARK SERVICE: STATUE OF LIBERTY NATIONAL MONUMENT)

didn't pass, we had to go back. I waited about five minutes and she came down with the baby.

There was travelers' aid personnel galore! They spoke, of course, all languages, and I soon found the person that spoke German, and they sent a telegram to Schenectady and my wife's brother. The travelers' aid societies had a buffet of food. Great big bowls of oranges, bigger than we'd ever seen oranges before. And apple pies. There must have been other ships that had come in at the same time, because there was quite a commotion there. A tag was fastened on our outer clothing which said our destination—Schenectady, New York.

It took a few weeks, but I finally got a job at General Electric in the Induction Motor Division as a machinist. I started at fifty-five cents an hour. And I learned a few words of English. The operator that brought me in would say, "What do you call that?" Then he would proudly answer his own question, "Gears." But in the noise of a big machine shop, I wasn't sure whether he said "gears" or "deers"! [Laughs.] They both sounded alike. Naturally, we were called greenhorns. There was an awful lot of Germans working in that part of the shop, and they were quite helpful, even though we had a foreman that also was of German descent, and he more or less called me greenhorn. He didn't seem to want to help me much. But most of them were willing to help me.

But the difference between Germany and America I felt right off. The superintendent in the management office used to call me by my first name. They said, "Ralph!"— for Rolf. In Germany, they would never have called me by my first name, no matter

how well they knew me. Always Becker, not Ralph. And I thought, "Well, this is democracy. That is what democracy represents."

Rota Fichbach

. . . .

BORN MARCH 29, 1919
EMIGRATED 1926, AGE 7
PASSAGE ON THE S.S. *BALLIN*

She was an only child, raised in small towns east of Berlin. Her family was Protestant, though not religious. Once in America, she became a dental hygienist, nurses aide, married a German and had two children. Today, she lives in a suburb of New York with her husband and cherishes her three grandchildren.

We called my father Vati, and my mother, Mutti. She was Mutti to everybody. My father was a molder, a lighting technician. He skillfully learned this trade. At age fourteen they started you on a trade. So he always heard about America, and that was his dream even before he got married. And so my mother lived with this for seven years, knowing she had to leave her parents, because he wanted to come to America.

But he was not hasty. All his friends, all seven of them, came back from World War I and, one by one, went to America. The wives of these men were also friends of my mother. They were heartbroken that they were separated from my mother. They were writing and saying things like "[In] America you can get ahead. You can have everything you want, anything you can eat. You can get clothes cheaper, furniture cheaper. You can buy a whole house for—" I don't remember the amount, but they said it's just impossible to get that in Germany.

That you have to come, have to come. That's all we heard.

Well, the happy day came in 1926. My father says, "Okay, we go. I go first, and you come three months later. Let me get settled first. In case not, I come back again. However, on the word go, sell everything, and take care of everything and come in August." And that's what we did. Vati never saw his homeland again. He never went back. But he sent my mother and me.

Of course, my grandparents were heartbroken. My grandmother walked around. I remember her saying, "Here. Take this for Rota someday, and you take this." My grandfather picked up an ashtray. "Give this to Vati," he said. They went around the room grabbing things and telling them to pack it and take to America with them. It was heartbreaking. My mother often said, "We'll send for you." But they never came because my grandmother feared the water so. She said to my grandfather, "You go, I stay back." Of course, they didn't do that, so

. . . .

they never came. So it was letters and pack-ages back and forth. It was heartbreaking.

Vati came in April. He was writing us saying how I'll have my own bed and my own dresser and roller skates. That he al-ready bought a scooter for me. All that stuff I couldn't have in Germany. When I was a baby in Cochstedt they put me in a large bottom drawer. I had no crib or nothing. [As I grew] I slept on a pull-out sofa. I did not have my own bed. So I couldn't wait.

Mutti and I came in August as planned. She packed a huge trunk she got from my grandmother. Mutti was a dressmaker. She made my own clothes. So the trunk was filled with clothes including my teddy bear and my doll. That's all we had, plus two other bags. For the trip, Mutti made me a white satin dress with lace over it. That was supposed to be my party dress. Then I had skirts and tops with it. And everything had lavender. Why, I'll never know. She made me a lot of lavender dresses. In later years when we were in this country, my mother used to make sundresses for herself and me. We matched. People used to turn around and say, "Hey, look at that."

We took the train from Magdeburg to Hamburg. We left from Cuxhaven, which is the seaport [near] Hamburg. The ship was the S.S. *Ballin*. We spent eleven days on board ship. The first four days we were deathly sick, seasick, because we were down in the hold. The cheapest possible ticket. I was on the top berth, where I wanted to be. And as sick as my mother was, she used to put her legs up and bounce me up and down to humor me because I was so sick, and I wanted to die. I didn't want to live any more. Every day I would look for land. So they gave me *Schwarzbrot*. That's black bread, with wine. I was seven years old, and that did it. We ate in the dining room, and they had a green pea soup. I ate that like crazy. I think I had four bowls. I couldn't get over all the food that we could

have. And the games we played, shuffle-board, and I was just running. And people would say, "Is that the little girl that was so sick?" Because I no longer was sick.

Coming into New York Harbor, my mother said in German, "Soon you're going to see the Lady of Freedom." And I said, "What's that?" And she said, "That you're free here. You can do as you please. You can talk and say what you want. When you see that lady we're in America."

We were standing on deck looking, and finally we did see the Statue of Liberty. And my mother cried. She says, "Rota, we're in America. There's the big lady." I saw land. I couldn't get over seeing land. After that, I just wanted to see my father. "Where's Vati? Where's Vati?"

But we didn't see him right away. We had to go through examinations at Ellis Is-land, and my mother was nervous. She was afraid they would find something wrong with us, but we passed. "Rota," she said, "now we're going to see Vati." So sure enough we did, and he couldn't talk from crying. It was really something. And the next thing, he carried me and said, "Now we go to our house." He called it a house. And it was this six room cold-water railroad flat, they called it. "And you're going to have your own room." He told me about it and I was impatient. I couldn't wait. So now we took the subway, the fare was five cents, to Ridgewood, [in] Brooklyn, which was noted as a place where Germans settled. It was called Germantown. Vati had been three days in this country, and he got a job as a molder.

When he opened the door to the apart-ment, it was unbelievable. He had a table set with a vase and flowers, three cups, three bowls, three plates . . . There was a stove with a coffeepot on it, a soup pot, and two other pots. A pantry with shelves of canned food, and an icebox with real ice in it. And it was cold. I remember him opening it.

Well, I was just beside myself. And behind the table was a sofa. And then he said, "Rota, come here. Mutti." He showed us the bathroom, no longer an outhouse, it was a real bathroom, which we had in Magdeburg too, but not in Cochstedt or Aschersleben. And then I wanted to see my room. Sure enough, I had my own bed, my own dresser, and a lamp on it. And then my mother's room had a bigger bed with a dresser and a lamp on it, and then there was a front room, and it had a leather two-seat sofa and an extra chair, and a buffet with a lamp on it, and that was it. That was the house. I couldn't believe it. I fell asleep sound. When I woke up, I still couldn't believe it.

Bertha Stern

. . . .

BORN (IN THE U.S.) SEPTEMBER 23, 1915
EMIGRATED 1927, AGE 11
PASSAGE ON THE S.S. *DEUTSCHLAND*

She was born near Buffalo, New York, went to Germany when she was four years old, and returned through Ellis Island seven years later. She lived in Floral Park, New York, was married to an Irish merchant seaman captain for thirty-two years, before he died in 1970. They had two daughters. She remarried and moved to Tampa, Florida with a man who proposed saying, "I've known you for fifty-two years, and I don't want to live without you anymore." He died in 1990.

My mother met my father when he rented a room in a boardinghouse run by my grandmother. He was apprenticing in Bruchsal as a *Kaufman*, which is a salesman, and they fell in love. But in those days you didn't introduce your date to your parents until you were ready to get betrothed, and so nobody knew that they were going together. So one day they were walking. They saw his father and he took her across the street.

"Why do we have to cross the street?" she asked.

"I can't introduce you to my father," he said. But the real reason he did that was because she was from a poorer class than his parents, who were well-to-do.

My mother dumped him and went to America. The fare at that time was fifty-three dollars. My father finally got the courage to ask my mother to marry him and then found out she was in America. He was devastated. So he went to America, to Machias, New York, thirty miles outside Buffalo, where my mother's uncle lived. He was a preacher. And my uncle married them. Then the war came, and it was three years and the parents still didn't know anything about my father and mother being married and having three children. I do not remember anything about Machias except that my father was very ill with the William Osler blood disease, which ran in the family.

So after the war in 1919, they returned to Germany, to the town of Mannheim, near Heidelberg, and my grandfather graciously accepted my mother. She was a very pretty woman. But there was a shortage of apartments. Being the oldest child, I went with my father to his parents, who had a villa. And my mother went with the other two children to her home. I spoke not a word of German. So nobody could talk to me. And no one in my family was fluent in English, other than my father, who was ill.

There was a great deal of refinement in my father's parents' home. They were wealthy. They had a lovely villa, exquisitely furnished. My grandfather owned silver mines in Austria and an apartment building in Heidelberg with thirteen families. My grandmother read stories to me. She was a great storyteller. I remember the family got together on Sundays. We would play cootie, which is a dice game. And I had an aunt and she was theatrically inclined, and we would put on shows with us four kids. We had French doors. We opened them, pretending it was a stage, and we sang and danced. I remember that the menu was always potato salad and roast chicken, or as President Roosevelt later said, "a chicken in the pot every Sunday." The better people had chickens every Sunday, you see. My grandmother also baked a white bread, which not every family in Germany had and was usually considered a Sunday thing. Sundays you had white bread. During the week you had black bread. In the white bread she would knead little figures we could name, like a dog or a cat or a little boy or a little girl. And she would knead that at the table. And then she took her hairpin and made the eyes, and with a toothpick she made the little legs. And we could not just leave the table. We had to ask permission to be excused. And I thought that was absolutely a most cher-

ished memory for me, because I realize today, as an old great-grandmother, how valuable spending time is with your children, and this is what is lacking in the homes today. Courtesy, respect, honor. It's hard for me to believe. But it's now sixty-eight years since the last Sunday dinner.

By 1923, my father was more or less on his deathbed. I remember how my mother sent me at two o'clock in the morning across the street to a tavern to get ice to put on his head because he was delirious. I remember how cozy the tavern was, with nice little dark-wood booth-seats and pretty little lamps. And seeing how happy they all were, and then having to [come] home to this dismal contrast of a dying father. I remember the day he died. My mother told me to stand in front of the bed, that she had to go downstairs. There was a telephone on the wall, on the other side of the room from the bed, and the phone rang. I answered. And my father got up in his delirium, and fell in front of the bed. I never forgot that. I thought [gasps] that it's my fault, that I didn't hold him. But my God, I was seven years old. Just seven years old!

He died later that day. Before he did, he said to my mother, "If you ever have the opportunity, I would like for you to send the children back to the country where they were born." Strangely enough, some gentleman from Tampa, Florida came to Mannheim and visited my mother. She was four years a widow now and still a good-looking woman. And he influenced her. He said that he had a twenty-two-room house in Tampa, and that she should come. She could rent rooms, and have a better living for us children to get ahead in life, and so forth. So this gentleman started coming around on Sunday afternoons, and my goodness, he asked my mother to marry him. He was a bachelor, forty-eight years old, and he took my mother and four children and went to

Bremen and we caught the ship. The S.S. *Deutschland*.

I remember that I had an eye infection. I had little pimples in my eye. I remember that my eyes were all smeared up with Vaseline. And I had to wear glasses for a while. And I thought it was absolutely abominable the way the German doctor in Bremen treated people. I could just see how disgusted he was to look at us. And I felt really angry with

him that he should have that attitude, because a doctor is a very highly respected person in Germany. Although, from his perspective, some of those people were like pigs with pasty hair.

I remember how the foghorns tooted in the morning at Ellis Island. It was dawn when we came. And then my mother rushed us to the window, to see this magic statue standing there. Now we were going to go to heaven.

Harry Lehmann

. . . .

BORN FEBRUARY 28, 1929
EMIGRATED VIA SPAIN 1936, AGE 7
PASSAGE ON THE *NORMANDY*

*Born Heinz Lehmann, his name was changed to Harry at Ellis Island.
His family escaped Germany as the Nazi grip tightened. He grew up in
Chicago, where he still resides with Judith, his wife of forty-six years.
Of their three sons, two have Ph.D.s, the third became a lawyer. "I often
view my life," he said, "as having had a second chance."*

My father and mother owned a dairy store in Elberfeld, where I was born. My grandparents had started the business and turned it over to them. They sold cheese, bread, milk, everyday essentials. And they did very well, and we were happy. The town's one distinction was that it had a monorail which, in the early thirties, was very unique, one of the few monorails that existed. I had one sister, who was two years older than I. Her name was Lotte, but it was changed to Lois when she came here.

In 1935 things started to look quite bad. The Nazis were coming to power and sales-

men refused to sell to Jews. "It wouldn't look good," they told my parents. And our family was Jewish and quite religious. My parents ignored it for a time, and some months went by. And then one day one of their favorite salespeople came in wearing an SS uniform, and he said he had joined them and he thought he'd come in to show them the uniform. "The truth of the matter is that the Jewish people in this country really have to go," he said. "Now don't get me wrong, I like you. You're a customer of mine, but I'll give you some advice. If you're smart, you'll pack up your things and leave Germany."

Two months later, my parents left everything. In the middle of the night, they took my sister and I, and very apprehensively got on a train to Barcelona, Spain. Why they selected Barcelona, Spain, I don't know. We had no family there. We stayed about a year, living in a small apartment. I was six years old. The Spanish Revolution was going on in 1936, and I remember a lot of people running on rooftops, shooting at each other, and that was kind of scary. And my father, to survive during that time, sold whatever he was able to buy. He dealt in clothing, shoes. He was always a great believer in buying something at one price and selling it at a higher price. A true merchant. It was a period of struggle, and it's easy to understand how traumatic it must have been for them. Here they were, in their forties, uprooted from where they lived all their life, and suddenly they were in a new country with a different language, having to raise two children.

During the time we lived in Barcelona, it was my parents intention to eventually come to this country through my father's sister, who lived in Chicago. She had come here maybe ten years earlier. Her name was Regina. He was corresponding with her, trying to get the four of us to come to America. She was married. They were people of comfort. So my father assumed they were financially able to bring us over to this country. But what happened was, my father could only get a visa for one individual. So my parents decided that, between me and my sister, I should go because I was the youngest, a boy, and the future was greater for me. So it was decided that I would go alone to America and live with my aunt in Chicago. I had a positive image of America. My parents kept talking how it was a much better place to live, a land where you could do what you want. You didn't have to be afraid of people putting you in jail for saying the wrong things. It was always assumed that

they would come shortly after I left. As it turned out, it was two years later that the three of them came.

My father, reluctantly, of course, took me to Marseille, France by train. Just the two of us. He had made arrangements to put me on a German boat, and then my aunt would meet me in America. I remember the American consul office in Marseille where I was standing with my father talking to the doorman there. It was raining out, and my father had tears in his eyes, telling the doorman that he was going to put me on this German boat to America and that his sister would meet me in New York. But being a German boat he was very apprehensive of what could happen, and who knew if he would ever see me again. The doorman was listening to the story, and all of a sudden a couple walked over to my father and said, "We'd like to introduce ourselves. Our name is Beimel. I'm Arthur, and my wife is Miriam. And I couldn't help but overhear your conversation. We are completing a tour of Europe, and we leave in a couple of days for America on the *Normandy*, and we're Jewish. We own a dry cleaning plant in Chicago, and we would love to take your son and watch over him until he gets to America, and your sister meets him."

My father was delighted, but wary. He sent a wire to his sister in Chicago and asked her to verify that the Beimels were who they said they were. She wired back and said, "Yes, it is true, what they told you." And my father then felt comfortable in leaving me in the hands of this couple. He was crying when we parted. It was August of 1936.

The Beimels were absolutely wonderful people who never had children and, throughout my later life, kind of adopted me as their son and eventually came to my wedding. They spoke English and I spoke German and Spanish, so we had a communication problem. But I recall that even on the boat they were starting to teach me the

English language. Mr. Beimel said, "Go over and tell Mrs. Beimel that it's time for breakfast. Say, 'Time for breakfast.'" Those were my first English words.

When we arrived in America, my Aunt Regina assumed that the Beimels would get off the *Normandy* with me and come straight to Chicago. So she wasn't in New York when the ship arrived. I had to stay overnight alone at Ellis Island, and wait until my aunt came the next day, because the Beimels left. I didn't know what was happening. I really can't say it was trau-matic. I remember a boy coming up to me offering me some chewing gum, and I had never had chewing gum before, and I thought that was unique, and he said, "Don't swallow, it's not candy."

After my Aunt Regina met me, we stayed one night in New York at the Barbi-zon Plaza Hotel. I remember her calling down in the morning for breakfast, but rather than knocking on the door, they just flipped this trapdoor open at the base of the door and put the tray into the room, almost like a thing for a pet.

An immigrant boy on the job, December 11, 1924.

(NATIONAL PARK SERVICE: STATUE OF LIBERTY NATIONAL MONUMENT)

We took a train to Chicago. My aunt and uncle lived in a very nice apartment on Lake Shore Drive in Chicago. My uncle Benno was a wholesale egg broker and made a lot of money. He was also German. They had met in Europe, came here as newlyweds, and set up a whole new life. They helped my family considerably from the time that we arrived in this country.

The apartment building had a little grocery store inside the lobby where I worked after school. I always did something to make money. I mean, even at the age of eight, I was working and able to speak English. I had all kinds of different jobs, delivering groceries, working in a cleaning store. I always did something, and I enjoyed that.

I lived for two years with my aunt and uncle and it was very pleasant. I was closer to my aunt than I was to my uncle. My uncle was a very quiet sort of individual, and I can't even say that I had a great relationship with him. My aunt was a domineering, opinionated woman, but she was very loving, and she cared for me.

I had a difficult time adjusting to my parents and my sister once they came here. Leaving my aunt and uncle was traumatic for me. I didn't want to do that. At that age, when you spend two years with other members of the family, they kind of become your parents. And my aunt Regina loved me dearly. They also had no children. And thereafter she became like another mother to me.

There was more than a little resentment on my mother's part because of that. My mother never cared that much for my aunt Regina. And maybe resented the fact that she had some wealth and my parents had nothing when they came to this country. There was a definite clash there.

My parents and sister came to New York on the *Queen Mary*. My father got a job in Chicago with [the] Armour company as an egg candler. In those days, every egg was checked to see whether it was fresh, and the way you checked it was you took three or four eggs in your hand, twisted them around under a lightbulb, and if you saw a dark spot, then you knew that was a rotten egg and you pulled it out. I believe he told me he made eighteen dollars a week.

He stayed there until he decided to open up a little grocery store. But it wasn't an ordinary grocery store. It was a grocery store where he sold day-old breads and dented cans. My father learned quickly that there were places in Chicago where you could buy cases of foodstuff that insurance companies were stuck with as a result of train accidents, or just damaged goods from fires and things like that. "Insurance salvage," it was called. And he could buy those things cheap, and sell them cheap. My father's little grocery store attracted people from all different neighborhoods because he had these cans of Campbell's soup which were two cents a can less than what you would find at the A&P. And he had a big sign in his window that said, "For every dent you save a cent." And he loved that business. I worked in the store for a long time, my sister, too, along with my mother. And he'd come from the market. He used to be so proud of what he found. "Look at this!" Ten cases of some ridiculous thing. I said, "Papa, nobody'll buy this."

"But it's cheap! I only paid two cents a can. If we can get four cents a can, we'll make a lot of money on this." And he did.

My father had a great belief that a man should not only make a living, but that he should work for himself and not for other people. He did not encourage me to further my education. Most children say, "Oh, my parents just wanted me to get the best education possible." The truth is, after high school, my father wanted me to go into the store and forget about college. But, since all my friends were going to college, I went. After I graduated, I got a job with a large corporation, which my father thought was ridiculous because they paid you a straight salary, and he couldn't understand that anybody would work week after week getting the same amount of money. I remember it was fifty dollars a week that I made. And he said, "They give you fifty dollars a week, no matter whether you work hard or don't work hard—that's the amount that you get? That's not business." He said, "Business is buying something for a nickel and selling it for six cents. And if you came into my store, we could expand it, and we would do a lot more business." He was very disappointed that I chose not to take his route.

I have a great story. After World War II, my father found that a lot of the Germans here were looking for powdered milk, powdered eggs and flints used in lighters. There was a great demand for that. So my father went to salvage places and bought these things in bulk quantities, and the four of us, my mother and my father and my sister and I, would sit in the back of the store. We didn't live in the back of the store. We had a separate apartment. But we'd sit there, and we'd make up these individual one-pound bags of powdered eggs and powdered milk

and one hundred flints. We'd take a little spoon and take these bulk flints and count out a hundred with a spoon and wrap them up in paper. He bought this terrible old stuff, and we packaged it up. I mean, it was stuff that was laying around for a long time. I recall looking at some of this powdered milk, it had black things. And I said, "Papa, you can't sell this." But virtually all of my parents' family were killed in the Holocaust, so he said, "Put it in! Put the black dirt in. It gives it weight."

My father ran an ad in the German newspaper, saying, "We have special packages for your friends and family back in Germany, foodstuff packages." And he ran that ad in the Chicago German paper. It ran on Saturday. On Sunday morning there was a line a block long of German gentile customers coming to buy this stuff and send it over to their relatives in Germany. And he was so proud of that; that he got back at them by selling them this merchandise. He said he killed more Germans than the American army with the junk that he put in the powdered milk and the powdered eggs.

David Froelich

BORN JUNE 2, 1928
EMIGRATED 1939, AGE 11
PASSAGE ON THE *VEEDAM*

His family "were the Rockefellers of southern Germany." Stripped of their fortune by the Nazis, they escaped to America and started from scratch. He became a high school teacher and eventually immigrated to Israel with his wife and children. He is active in Israeli politics and has written a play about his life that he hopes to have produced. "I am German-Jewish, live in Israel, but I am first and foremost an American," he said. "If not for this country and the grace of God, I would have been exterminated along with the other 6 million, no doubt about it."

*I*was literally born with a silver spoon in my mouth. I grew up in Bad Mergentheim, forty-four kilometers south of Würzburg, where I was born. Bad Mergentheim was a picturesque, tranquil town surrounded by low wooded hills along the Tauber River, which flowed into the Rhine. It was a medieval town like so many towns in Germany. Initially, it was just a farmer's village, and then it became a very famous health resort which was the main industry. There was no other industry to speak of. During summers thousands of guests would arrive from all over Europe.

There were about sixty Jewish families in the town, all Orthodox. Most of them were merchants of one kind or another. My family was the wealthiest family. We were the Rockefellers of southern Germany. My family owned a large meat-packing plant and livestock business. The business was owned by my grandfather. The company was called David Froelich and Sons. David Froelich was my grandfather, after whom I'm named. My father was the oldest of twelve children. When my grandfather died in 1925, my father, who had married, became part-owner along with another brother.

My father was a typical German. Very strong-willed. Very dominant personality. Short in stature, he was built like a football player, a fullback. But he was very handsome and he had a heart of gold. He'd give you the shirt off his back. He served in the German army during the First World War and was rigidly trained. He was a very rigid man, very set in his ways. I worshiped the ground he walked on.

We were living in a fancy home on the edge of town. My father employed about sixty people in the slaughterhouse alone. And I was the boss's son. I was being trained to follow in his footsteps and one day take over the family business, when Hitler came along in 1933 and, of course, that changed everything.

By 1934, the business began to dwindle. My father used to half joke, "We had a big business with a small office, now we have a small business with a big office." There was a time when the Froelich name meant more than religion. Then the name meant less and the fact that we were Jews meant more. My father was the only one whose license to operate was renewed in '35 and '36. But in '37 it was not renewed, and at that point the business was forcibly taken away. It was sold for about one-tenth of its real value to a designated new owner, who was a member of the Nazi party and a former employee of my father. This man held onto the business until it went down the drain.

By now, we no longer lived in our fancy home. We were denied that. We lived in a rented home over a shoe store in the town square. My father recognized that in order to earn a living he had to have a trade. So he signed up for a butcher course in Munich, but he never was able to get to Munich. He got sick. He was laid up with a severe case of strep throat and fever. This was a few days before the first pogrom, called *Krystallnacht*, or Crystal Night, in November 1938.

Up until then, the Holocaust evolved slowly. The Jews were suffering much more in the large cities than in the small towns. But it was evolutionary, not revolutionary. It was a very gradual strangulation of Jewish life. Each day and each month and each year it got a little bit worse. For instance, the Nuremburg Laws, among other things, prohibited Jewish children from attending public school. So I attended a Jewish school at the edge of town that was part of a complex that had a synagogue, a monastery, courtyard, and the residence of the teacher. I was routinely beaten up on my way to school by members of the Hitler Youth. They were my peers, maybe a little bit older, and they were merciless. Children can be very cruel, more so than adults. They used to corner me and my friends and spit at us and taunt us and give us a licking. But there was no physical danger to adult Jews in Germany until *Krystallnacht*.

On the eve of *Krystallnacht*, we knew nothing. It wasn't until the next morning that a neighbor came hysterically to our door telling us that Jews were being rounded up, males only, age fourteen and over, presumably to be taken to Dachau, the concentration camp. I was not even ten years old. She also said the Nazis were burning down the synagogue complex.

I was at home. My father, who was sick in bed, asked my mother to find out what was going on. She asked the neighbor to babysit for my sisters and me. After my mother left, a Nazi officer about twenty-five years old came to our door, and I became hysterical. I knew why he came, and I ran to the kitchen and I began to cry. He was wearing the typical Nazi uniform and boots with cleats. *"Heil, Hitler,"* he said. He thought the neighbor was my mother. She said she's just a babysitter. He wanted to see my father.

"He's sick in bed."

"I want to see him."

And that's when I began to pray. I could hear the sound of his boots going up the stairs. He went to my father's bedside and asked him why he was sick. My father told him. The officer looked at the medicine, and he saw the name of the doctor, and he recognized that the doctor was a gentile and a member of the Nazi party, and he left my father alone.

When the officer left, the neighbor came, touched my shoulder and said, "You can relax. They didn't take your daddy."

I ran together with my buddies to the synagogue complex, and it was a horrible sight. The outer structures were still standing, but the insides were all burned out. We walked among the rumble, trying to salvage what we could.

As it turned out, when the officer returned to the police station he got chewed out by the SS, the *Gauleiter*. The SS officer called the doctor to verify he was gentile, and the doctor went out on a limb for my father. The doctor said, "This man is my patient. He is ill. Don't you dare touch him. If you do, I will call up Himmler myself."

Everybody knew that Himmler was the head of the SS. The doctor was bluffing, of course. He was not a personal friend of Himmler. But that frightened the officer away, otherwise my father would have been taken to Dachau. The doctor definitely saved my father's life. I later met him in Israel at a reunion of Holocaust survivors, but he since died.

My father recovered within a few days. He was the only Jewish man in our town who was not arrested. But the experience scared the living daylights out of him. And that's when he decided to come to America. He went to the American consulate in Stuttgart and asked for a quota number, because it was a quota system. And things went from bad to worse.

. . .

There was one particular person in our town who was the bully of the Hitler Youth. It was about a month before we left. My parents were studying English from a book and wanted me to return it to a teacher. We lived across the street from a Catholic church. I was walking through the churchyard carrying the book when this bully spotted me. He was about fourteen. And he never walked alone. He had an entourage. And he always wore his uniform. He always had a dagger with him. And he threw me against the outer wall of the church. He spit in my face, which was the traditional thing. Then he said, "Sing a Jewish song."

I did as I was told, because I was petrified. A crowd gathered, mostly kids, boys and girls, teenagers, preteens, and also adults, but they were further back. When he saw the book, he was ignorant of the fact that it was English. He only knew it wasn't German. He thought it was Hebrew. He said, "Read it."

"I can't."

"Read it or I'll kill you."

The kids started taunting, "Kill him! Kill him! Kill him!"

"Read it!"

"I can't!"

So he took his dagger and cut me across my neck. I saw blood. I got petrified. And the kids kept screaming, "Kill him! Kill him! Kill him!"

"Say your father is a bastard," he demanded.

I refused. He took his thumbs and began to choke me. I was standing, wearing Tyrol shorts, the leather Bavarian shorts. I fell to the ground that had sharp stones and lacerated my knee. I began to bleed. When this happened a policeman came by, and I started screaming, "Help me! Help me!" But he turned and walked away. Seeing this, the boy cut me again, this time on the arm and I passed out. Years later I was told this bully became a lawyer and an honorable citizen in Stuttgart. I don't know where in Stuttgart. I don't want to know. I wouldn't want to face him. I don't know what I'd do.

. . .

Five days after the outbreak of World War II in September 1939, we finally got our papers. It was for the five of us—my two sisters, me, and my parents. Our belongings were packed in the port of Bremerhaven. We packed five rooms, complete furnishings. My father had passage on a German liner. But at the last minute it was canceled by the Nazis, and we were stuck in Germany. In addition, we now had to have a special permit from the local authority to leave. Our belongings were supposedly sent to Rotterdam, but we never saw them again.

The day we got the permit, we said our good-byes and left immediately. The permit was a form of exit visa good for three days ending October 1, and not renewable. We were not allowed to take anything except one small suitcase for all of us.

My father asked the butcher, who was a friend of his, to drive us to Würzburg, where there was an express train. From there, we would go to Cologne, where he had a sister. And from Cologne, on to Holland. My father had faked papers to get into Holland.

We got to the butcher shop. My father said to a kid who worked there, "Take the suitcases, your boss is going to take us." The kid then went to the butcher, who was already afraid to help us to begin with, and said, "If you take these Jews, I'm going to report you to the Gestapo." You have to remember, not only had the war begun, but there was a complete blackout.

The kid came sneakingly out, and said, "I'm sorry, but he can't take you. Something came up."

We rode the horse and wagon to the edge of town and the local railroad station. We took the train to Würzburg, but we missed the connection to Cologne. So we had to wait. "I don't want to go to the waiting room," my father said. "Let's go to the track. I know where the train is waiting." My father used to travel a great deal by train all over Germany, so he knew. It was four o'clock in the morning. We went to the track and went into one of the compartments of the train until it left at six o'clock.

We got into Frankfurt. The train filled up with military personnel. They realized we were Jews and began to taunt us and curse us and spit at us. It was miserable. They made us stand until we finally got to Cologne. We took a taxi, a horse and carriage, to my father's sister's house. This was a

Saturday. The permit expired on Sunday, October 1. So we set the alarm clock Saturday night. There was one train leaving per day for the Dutch border, and that train was at 9:00 A.M. We were supposed to get up at six and we were an hour's travel from the station.

We overslept. My mother was hysterical. "We will never get out," she said. "The permit can't be renewed." My uncle, my father's sister's husband, who was a very pious man, said, "If it's God's will, you'll get out," or as we say in Yiddish, *"bashert."*

"I'll call the stationmaster," he said. "Maybe there's a second train."

"Nonsense," my father said, always the realist. "There is no second train."

My uncle called, and for some strange reason, there was a second train at two in the afternoon. Well, we rushed like hell to the station, got the train, and rolled to the Dutch border. There were a lot of people, mostly military. When we got to the last town in Germany, a border town called Kleve, there was nobody on the train but my family and one single man. We were in the first coach. He was in the rear. My father said, "I want to get into the station because we're not allowed to take any currency out. I'll wire all my money back to my sister."

My father went into the station. I saw three men come out. One in civilian clothes, one in a policeman's uniform, and one in the black SS uniform with a pistol. Within minutes the SS officer took the solo man off the train at gunpoint. My mother saw this and got very upset. "What are they going to do to Daddy?" I remember asking her.

The three men came to my mother. She was worried because in the suitcase my parents secretly hid their wedding bands in a jar of cold cream. We were supposed to surrender all silver and gold after *Krystallnacht.*

"Heil, Hitler!" he said. "May I see your passports?"

He looked at the passports.

"Why do you want to leave Germany?"

"You see why we're leaving."

He laughed sarcastically, then marked the passports with a big red *J*, and said, "That's a good idea."

"Do you want to look at our luggage?"

"That's not necessary," he said, and they walked off.

"I know why he was so nice," my mother said. "They arrested Father."

Just then, the train started pulling out, and no daddy. Out of the corner of my eye I spotted him. He was walking out of the station like nothing happened. He didn't know from anything. He saw the train in motion, and he ran after it, and jumped on. He looked at my mother who was white as a sheet. "What happened?" She opened her mouth, but nothing came out. He looked to me. "David, what happened?" But I, too, couldn't talk.

Within seconds, we were inside Holland. Hundreds of tanks, soldiers, all in black uniform. A Dutch security officer came on and said, *"Dach,"* which is Dutch for hello. He looked at our German passports. He saw we didn't speak Dutch and switched to German. He looked at my parents.

"You can relax now," he said. "You're free."

With that, we all began to bawl because the realization had sunk in that we had made it. We were free!

We rode the train to Nimwegen, which was the end of the line. It was Sunday afternoon, October 1, about 5:00 P.M., and we still had to face the Dutch authorities, who had a strict rule that allowed only transients to enter Holland. They did not accept anyone else. The trick for us was to get across the barrier where two guards were posted, one young, the other an older man about fifty. On the other side of the barrier was my father's cousin and a stranger, who was an agent of HIAS, the Jewish service organization, whose function was to see that we got across into Holland safely.

The younger guard asked for the ship's ticket, which was a fake passage. "I'm sorry," he said. "This boat has left already. You cannot come in." At this precise second the agent went into operation. He approached the older man. He whispered something into his ear, and they shook hands. I saw money. The older guard nudged the younger man, and said, "Hey, Karl, you're mistaken." And he showed him the money. "That boat was delayed. It's leaving tomorrow." The younger guard seized the money and said to my father, "I'm sorry, forgive me." And he opened the gate and let us through.

We took a train to Amsterdam. It was the time of the Jewish holiday Sukkoth and we went to a kosher restaurant. We were starved. We literally hadn't had meat in five years because there was no kosher meat available in Nazi Germany. Furthermore, everybody in Germany had to have rations and Jews had fewer rations than non-Jews. So we were subsisting on basics and our stomachs had shrunk. In fact, my sister Ruth had developed rickets because she was a baby, and she didn't get the proper vitamins. But the restaurant didn't have meat, so we ate roast duck, which is the greasiest, fattiest thing you can eat, and that night we were all sick.

The next day, my father went to the Dutch authorities and told them the truth. "We are here illegally," he said. "But we have no intention of staying. We have visas to come to the United States. I ask of you only one thing: grant us a transit visa for thirty days. I'll get passage on a liner and we'll be out of here." The official consented. "But if after thirty days you're still in Holland," he said, "we're shipping you back to Germany."

My father came back to the rooming house where we were staying singing and dancing, "We have thirty days' grace!" He went to the boat agent on a street where all of them were located. What he didn't realize was that every Tom, Dick, and Harry, had the same idea. There were literally hundreds and hundreds of people who were wanting to get out of Europe before the Nazis marched into the low countries. There was no room on the boats.

Well, one week went by, nothing. Two weeks went by. Three weeks went by. Still no passage. We were beginning to worry. We had seven days left. My father came home. "I got good news, and I got bad news," he said. "I got passage on a Dutch liner that's leaving from Antwerp. The bad news is we have to travel on the Sabbath." My father had pleaded with the authorities that the boat not move until after sundown. But the first law of Judaism is to preserve life.

We took the train to Antwerp. It was heavily guarded to make sure nobody jumped and stayed in Holland illegally. Every door had a guard. And we rumbled along, jam-packed, all Jews, all going to the same boat. We checked into a hotel near the port. The next morning we took a taxi and went to the port. We sat there for hours. Fifteen minutes before sundown they called us.

The name of the boat was *Veedam*, on the Dutch-American line. It was one of the smaller boats, but for an eleven-year-old, it was huge. My father saw the crush of humanity, because there were not only 750 booked passengers, but hundreds more who tried to stow illegally. Everybody smelled this was the last boat, which it was. "Let's make a human chain," my father said to us, "otherwise we're going to get separated." He told me to lead. I held the hand of my sister Leah, who was four. My mother held her other hand, and my father cradled Ruth in his arm with the suitcase.

We walked the gangplank, a huge crowd, and I became fascinated by the sight of a crane on the ship. I had never seen one before and got so impressed, I accidentally let go of Leah's hand. I turned around, and she was gone. They were gone. Consumed by the crowd.

The boat left the port. I started wandering around [the ship], asking people for the cabin, because I knew the cabin number, and everybody seemed to speak every language imaginable but German. In the course of my wandering, I literally bumped into my mother, who was hysterical. She didn't know whether I was on the boat or off the boat. She was so happy to see me she hugged and kissed me. But it was my fault, I shouldn't have let go.

My father, in the meantime, had a very unpleasant experience. There were stowaways in our cabin. They were Jews. And they refused to budge. It was them or us. So he went to the captain, and they had to be forcibly removed. My father cried, but there was nothing we could do.

The next morning I went up on deck, and people were vomiting from seasickness. I was better off than most. I was only seasick for a day or two. My mother was in bed throughout the journey. We were supposed to go to Southampton to pick up more passengers, but there were mines everywhere. The German U-boats were after us. They did not honor the Geneva Convention on neutrality. And so the captain SOS'ed a British destroyer for an escort. When the Germans saw the British come, they let us go. But before they did, they blew up a merchant vessel about half a mile away from us, and we were given SOS signals to pick up survivors, which we did. Then the destroyer guided us out to the Atlantic and open sea.

There was a massive storm. So the captain told us we were changing course. We were not going to America. We were going to Halifax, Nova Scotia. But within a day or two, icebergs were spotted. So we changed back to our original course, and the ship was battered. Our meals were given to us in our cabin. Two crew members were washed overboard. It was a horrible ride. Two people died of natural causes. We were supposed to be on the ocean seven days. We were on the ocean thirteen.

On November 10, at six in the morning, we finally made it into New York Harbor. I remember vividly being choked with emotion. I saw all these skyscrapers lit up. It was dark. It was wintertime. Little jewels, little twinkles, and the Statue of Liberty. Quite different than what I expected. To me, America was a land full of Indians. A wild country of cowboys and Indians. In fact, on my tenth birthday in Germany, I got a cowboy hat from my uncle in New York. I did not think they had civilized life here. I thought it would be like it was in 1492.

Immigration authorities came on board at Ellis Island. They were not very nice. They were all Irishmen. They spoke only English. They checked visas, calling people in alphabetical order. Then people were turned over to a health inspector. But my father didn't hear our name, so they said, "Wait till the end." He was petrified. All of us were. Because the boat was due to go to Boston to refuel, pick up food, and go back to Holland. We were afraid we were going to be stuck on the boat.

While this was happening, a lot of photographers came on board. I don't know why. But I recall this pretty young girl in her twenties with long black hair wearing an ankle-length dress taking cheesecake pictures. Years later, I found out it was the actress Hedy Lamarr.

My father had an uncle who had a brother-in-law who owned a famous fish restaurant at Times Square. He was like Toots Shor. He came on board and talked to the authorities. Once we got off the boat we were at Ellis Island no more than fifteen minutes. I remember taking a subway ride, which was alien and strange to me. I remember seeing Forty-second Street, and all the neon signs and all the hubbub, and that I didn't like it.

My father, always being the provider, was very concerned about the future, especially for a man who never had to work for anybody else in his life. Not only was he a boss, he was a millionaire. And now he had to start from scratch. He was forty-five years of age with three little kids, and he had no trade. He didn't know the language. He didn't know how to drive a car. He had no money. He was destitute. He lost everything.

We knew we were not going to stay in New York. This was already decided. Initially, we were taken to my uncle's apartment in Washington Heights in Manhattan. We stayed there for a week. My mother had a married brother and two married sisters, who had left Germany before us and relocated in St. Louis, Missouri. St. Louis had a large Jewish population. They owned a slaughterhouse, called Hunter Meat Packing, and my father got a job there. HIAS provided rail tickets to St. Louis, which I didn't like any more than New York. When we first arrived, I was crying that I wanted to go back to Germany, Nazis and all.

My father became a helper in the kosher department. He would verify that meat was kosher and put a seal on the wrapping. It was a very menial task. His English was scant, enough to do his job. He got ten dollars a week, but he made a living. In 1939 you could do that. We lived in a furnished apartment. And during the next nine years, my father transferred from one department to another in order to make more money. He took English lessons, [along with] my mother, and we moved into a larger, unfurnished apartment. Then he went into business for himself again. The meat business, of course. But it was never the same.

Heidi Reichmann

. . . .

BORN JUNE 9, 1907
EMIGRATED 1939, AGE 31
PASSAGE ON THE *FRANCONIA*

The older sister to three brothers, she was the daughter of a successful cattle dealer. She was raised on a farm in a conservative Jewish family. The farm was in the predominantly Catholic town of Reinheim, forty-four kilometers south of Frankfurt, where the Reichmann's had a homestead dating back to 1750. Though never married, she bore a son from a man who eventually died in the gas chambers at Dachau, though he wasn't Jewish. Today, she lives in Pennsylvania. "I live comfortable and everything," she said, "but something was taken away."

I moved to Frankfurt in 1927 when I was twenty years old. I lived in a residence for girls. This pleased my parents because they didn't have to worry, and I got a job in the office of a factory. I worked for the foreman, my boss, and we fell in love.

His name was Richard. Well, one Monday morning Richard came to work and you would think the roof had fallen in or something. I remember it was the 30th of January 1933, and the only thing he said was, "Hindenburg nominated Hitler." At the time, Richard also worked for a leftist underground newspaper. But the newspaper was closed the next day. And he went on the run until we both got arrested by the Gestapo. They blamed me for helping him although they never could prove that I did.

At the trial in Berlin, Richard was sentenced to two and a half years in prison. But after the prison time was over, they didn't release him. They sent him to Dachau, the concentration camp. I was sent to jail for one year as a political prisoner. I was pregnant with our child at the time. I gave birth to my son, Ernie, while I was in prison. Richard's mother picked him up from prison. We decided it would be best if he stays with her until I got out.

When I did, an uncle by marriage offered me to stay with his family in Frankfurt until I found a place of my own and found a job. To get a job at that time you had to go to the government employment office, so I knew I wouldn't get a job through them on account of being Jewish. I went there with apprehension. But the woman there was very nice and said, "Don't worry about anything. There is a Jewish agency. I know they're looking for people. You will find something."

I went to the Jewish agency, and I got a job in a nice company. But there were new laws in Germany, the Nuremberg Laws. One of them said if an employee was employed for more than six months, he or she could not be dismissed. But I was there less than six months, and being Jewish on top of it, was laid off. "You'd better look for something else," they said.

I didn't know what to do. All I knew was that there was no future in Germany for Jewish people. The stores had signs, "No Jews." I mean, you couldn't even buy anything. A friend of mine said, "Heidi, if you have to buy something for the baby, I'll buy it for you." Things like that. Ernie was four years old and too young for kindergarten. But it didn't matter. Kindergartens wouldn't accept Jewish children. So you had to find a Jewish kindergarten. There were also campaigns by the Gestapo, where we never knew what was going to happen. A friend of mine from prison used to call me in the office, hear my voice, and hang up. She just wanted to know if I was still around. But she didn't want to talk because the phone lines were tapped by the Gestapo.

Then I remembered that a friend of my mother's who lived in America once said to me, "Heidi, if you ever want to go to the States, I will help you."

So I wrote to her. She repeated the offer and I accepted. Richard was in Dachau, and I was torn about leaving him. I tried to see him so that maybe he could see the child, but it was denied. It wasn't possible, they said. And I never saw or heard from Richard again.

In the meantime, I went every day to the consulate in Stuttgart, because I had a hard time getting my papers on account of my prison record. But I finally got them. It was during the time of *Krystallnacht*. It was a Thursday morning. I had been taking private English lessons. I was going to my lesson with Ernie, when I saw the Gestapo arresting men who looked Jewish. Then, coming back from my lesson, I stopped off at a jeweler to get a watch that was being repaired, when the woman said, "All the synagogues are being burned."

The first thing I thought of were my parents. I packed a little suitcase and went with a streetcar to the railroad station. There were so many people in the streets and the streetcar went at a snail's pace. When I came to the railroad, the train I meant to leave on was gone. There was another train that would have gotten me to Reinheim at midnight but I was somehow afraid to take it. So through side streets I walked back to my place.

Early the next morning the doorbell rang downstairs. It was my parents. The Gestapo were rounding up Jewish men and my father needed a place to hide. And since only female Jewish people lived in my building, the Gestapo would pass it by. So my father was okay. The next day Ernie saw a synagogue burning and wanted to know why. So I explained to my son, "See, bad people have burned that building." I remember when we came to the States we passed a construction site. A building had been knocked down. So Ernie said, "Did the bad people also do this?"

I left without my parents. They didn't have their papers yet. In fact, everybody was trying to get out of Germany by that time. The hope was they would eventually emigrate to the States, which they did.

Ernie and I went by train from Frankfurt to Paris to Cherbourg, France. We had a compartment, my son and I. I would cover him with his blanket and he would fall asleep. Soon after we got on, two officials came to us, passport control. I gave the passports, and they disappeared with them. They came back, took a flashlight and checked our faces against the photo in the passports. A few hours later, another two officers came, customs control. "That's all we have," I said.

"Is there a camera in there?"

"No, there isn't."

A short time after that, two more officers came wearing different uniforms, but talking German. So I asked, "How many times do you check?"

"Madam, we are the French custom officials."

"We are in France?"

"*Oui, madam.*" [Laughs.] I was so relieved, and I dared to go outside.

I have no idea how we got to the boat in Cherbourg. I only know there was a small cabin for the two of us. Years later I found out that Enrico Fermi, the famous Italian scientist, was a passenger on that boat. My parents had paid for the trip. I didn't have money.

In the afternoons, I would give Ernie naps. He would sleep on deck in a deck chair covered with a blanket. I was busy writing letters. I had so many requests from friends to write to people or contact people to help them get out. So I had brought my typewriter and wrote letters whenever Ernie slept, or in the evening. People thought I was a journalist.

We arrived [in] New York the 2nd of January, a Monday. The inspectors were so busy. I answered their questions honestly. But he didn't like one of my answers, so he sent us to Ellis Island. We slept there two nights. They had metal beds, very high off the floor. Ernie fell out of one and got black and blue. I remember that. I also remember people making telephone calls from Ellis Island. I thought to myself, "Whom do they call? Who do they know?" That puzzled me.

My mother's friends, Max and Stella Goldman, came to meet us and vouch for us. Then they took us to Chinatown, to a Chinese restaurant. I had never eaten Chinese food before. And I saw the big buildings. I knew there would be big buildings. And I saw all the fire escapes, and I thought, "My, all the people here have balconies." [Laughs.]

. . .

I knew how to cook. People in Germany said if you know how to cook you'll find a job in no time. But I soon realized that cooking in Germany and cooking in the States is quite different. Different vegetables, different salad. And the terrible portions, big portions of meat. I said, do all people eat that much meat? The woman I worked for asked me to give her child a milkshake in the afternoons. I never had heard of a milkshake. I had seen chocolate milk at the Goldsmans'. So I mixed chocolate milk. "No, a milkshake," the woman said. So she showed me the appliances and how to make a milkshake. I didn't last a week at that job. [Laughs.]

Then I found out my family had cousins from Frankfurt who had settled in East Stroudsburg, Pennsylvania. They owned a kosher butcher shop there. And they invited us to visit. When we got to East Stroudsburg, my cousins were waiting for us. And it was beautiful. A small town in the Poconos with beautiful stores and farms. They asked us to stay permanently and I found a job in a boardinghouse as a domestic. But I couldn't keep Ernie there. There was a farm, Lord's Farm. And the Lords had children of their own and always took one or two children as boarders. So I went there and talked to Mrs. Lord and asked if she would take Ernie and she said yes. Ernie loved it there. I went to see him whenever I had a day off.

I became a citizen in 1944. I was working as a clerk at Gimbel's department store in Philadelphia. Ernie was still in East Stroudsberg. But I was an enemy alien because I had come from Germany. So when

I wanted to see Ernie in Pennsylvania, I needed a permit to go there.

I remember that year Franklin Roosevelt was campaigning for president in Philadelphia. And the youngest son of the founder, Ellis Gimbel, came to the store, which he frequently did. I worked at the soda fountain. And everybody liked to wait on Mr. Gimbel. All he ever had was a cup of coffee which cost five cents but, of course, nobody gave him a check. And it was raining on and off. Not hard, but it was raining. And Mr. Gimbel, who was [an] old man, was standing in front of the store watching Roosevelt in the parade. Somebody told him to come inside, and not stand in the rain, and he said, "If that man can sit in an open car in the rain, I can stand in the street in the rain also." [Laughs.]

I would never want to go back to Germany. Often you read about people who had immigrated to the States when they were young and wanted to go back to their country. I'm thinking in particular about a woman who left Italy. She was so anxious to go back to Italy, to see it. And after she had seen it, she was supposed to stay there for three weeks. After two weeks she said to her daughter, "Let's go home. I know now the United States is my home." I think I would feel the same way.

Molly Mendelsohn

· · · · · · · · ·

BORN APRIL 13, 1920
EMIGRATED 1940, AGE 19
PASSAGE ON THE *FAHNENDAM*

Born in the tiny village of Lichenroth, near Frankfurt, she was six years old when her family moved to Berlin. She lived there until 1940, then emigrated to America with her family when she was nineteen. Now seventy-seven, she lives in New York.

· · · · · · · ·

My father was a kosher butcher and he also was engaged in the synagogue and performed services. There was not much opportunity in this small village for him to be anything else. My mother was a very bright woman, although she had very little formal education. She had a very hard life bringing up five children. She had four girls and a boy. I was next to youngest. My brother was youngest. I remember that my mother baked her own challah for Friday night seder. In the village, all the Jewish families did. There was a village oven that was used by the villagers. There was a big trough and I remember my mother kneading that dough. And then we would go to the village oven, and the bread was formed, big, round, eggy bread. It was put on a wooden shovel which was shoved into that oven, which was heated by wood. And the bread had to last for either the week or the two weeks until your turn came to use the oven again.

The house was always crowded. We always had visitors for holidays. My father was a very generous person, [and] what little we had was shared. So we always were a big crowd, and we always had friends. My older sisters always had friends come over, so it was always a lively house.

In 1927, we moved to Berlin and my father opened a butcher shop. He did that until he died in 1934 at the age of fifty-two. It was a great loss. He died of stomach cancer. I remember his sickness. He hardly ever went for a checkup. He often complained about pressure on his stomach, but he didn't give it much thought and kept on working and then went to the hospital. He was in the hospital about two months before he died. And, of course, it was extremely difficult for my mother. But then my sisters Trudel and Selma were working as secretaries in an office, so they helped financially. My mother was close to her mother. After my father died, my grandmother came to live with us in Berlin.

[When] I was about thirteen, I became superreligious for a while. The reason was Hitler had come to power, and I was attending a German *Litzeum*, which is a high school for German girls. I had a scholarship for college, but after Hitler came, they took away the scholarships for Jewish children. So I went to a Jewish school, which was a very religious school. And I studied Hebrew. Unfortunately, I forgot everything now, but I really worked at it because all the young people at that time wanted to go to Palestine. My eldest sister, Trudel, had already left for Palestine when she was fourteen, so I wanted to go. She was five years older than me.

When I was fourteen I left school, and I felt I had to learn a trade because in Palestine you needed a trade. I learned how to sew. I took a job as a seamstress for a dressmaker who employed two or three people. In the meantime, I was communicating with Trudel by mail. And my mother was extremely unhappy about the idea that I wanted to go to Palestine, but I was determined. Still, as time went by I heard all kinds of horror stories and how the ships turned back, and then there were no more ships going.

When my sister, Selma, left for America in 1935, my mother decided she wanted to come, too. At that point, it was just my mother, my brother, my sister, and myself. But it took four years before we got our affidavits. There was a quota system, and we could not get out of Germany.

We were supposed to leave in September 1939. Then Germany invaded Poland and again we couldn't get out. We had to wait. But when the day of *Krystallnacht* came that fall, we were forced to move. The Nazis didn't allow Jewish families to live in our apartment building in Berlin anymore. We had a cousin in Frankfurt, a woman who was about sixty years old, and we went to live with her. It was a huge apartment in a bad area of the city.

Finally, in January 1940, we left Germany. My mother made all the arrangements. We could not take more than ten marks. We packed mainly clothing, tablecloths, linens, things like that. We were not allowed to take our furniture. But my mother insisted on taking our feather beds because in Germany we slept in very cold rooms. We didn't heat the bedrooms. We didn't have central heating, so we needed feather beds to stay warm. They're like heavy quilts. [Laughs.] And she took them.

We didn't actually carry it. It was shipped somehow. I remember it was wintertime. It was late January, freezing cold, and we went by train to Amsterdam. I remember the Nazi officials at the German border making slurs at us. "It's good that the Jews get out," one of them said. "Out with you!" And things like that.

Of course, it was a great thrill to get into Amsterdam, away from Hitler's Germany. I remember my mother had a friend in Amsterdam who picked us up from the train. From Amsterdam, we took a bus to Rotterdam. And I remember that the bus driver was very jolly. At one point, he stopped, got out of the bus, and he went to a store, and he showed us what he bought. Holland was a very different atmosphere than in Germany. We saw all the food in the stores, because by then there was strict rationing in Germany, especially for Jews. Jews were hardly allowed to buy any food.

We did not experience any physical violence. Because my father had died in '34, he wasn't picked up and put into a concentration camp like most Jewish men. Those who insisted on staying in Germany, like my grandmother, we never heard from again. I'm sure she was sent to a concentration camp.

From Rotterdam we went to Antwerp. We were not allowed out of the train. The train went right to the boat. It was a small Dutch liner called *Fahnendam*. There were a lot of other Jewish families on board and we were all very friendly, a lot of camaraderie, because we all were going to America for the same reason. And the Dutch crew was very nice. We enjoyed the trip. Of course, we were seasick most of the time because we were down in the hold, in steerage. It took about two weeks to get over here. The trip took so long because we went through the English Channel, and there was danger of mines, so they had to go very carefully. They stopped at night. Then at one point, the boat suddenly turned back and everybody was terribly worried. We thought we couldn't go to America. And the story was that a purser had committed suicide. He had jumped off the boat, and they had to go back and search for him, even though there was no hope.

I remember seeing the Statue of Liberty for the first time and it was the greatest thrill. It was a very clear, crisp cold day in February. And it was such a thrill that it's hard to describe. Everybody who was on the boat went to Ellis Island. We were there only a couple of hours. I don't remember much except that the immigration officials were smiling, laughing, being very friendly. Of course, we were searching for Selma, and then we saw her, and we hardly recognized her, she had gotten so Americanized. She had gotten very thin. She wore a lot of makeup, which we weren't used to in Germany. But we were thrilled to see her. She was thrilled to see us. She had gotten married in the interim and lived in a two-bedroom apartment in Astoria. I remember we all came to her place by cab, and we met her husband. He was a Fuller Brush salesman.

For my mother, it wasn't too happy an experience to be dependent on her oldest daughter and my brother-in-law and live in the crowded conditions. They kept us for a couple of weeks. My other sister Martha and I looked for jobs immediately. I had studied English in school, so I spoke it pretty well. But there were no jobs to be had, and both Martha and myself became maids in different households in Manhattan.

It was horrible. [Laughs.] I found a Jewish family who lived near Riverside Drive. But they were Polish Jews who hated the German Jews like poison. So I left there and became a domestic for somebody else taking care of a small child who cried all the time. I felt I was made for bigger and better things than that. I just wanted to find a job where I could go to school at night and finish my education.

I finally found something in a doctor's office answering phones, clerical work. The doctor was Jewish-German. But his wife was non-Jewish. And suddenly now I had to do the cleaning, which I thought I had gotten away from. They had no children, but whenever they went out at night I had to sit in their huge apartment, and take their phone messages. I hated all those jobs! [Laughs.]

Then my mother's brother came to America, via Cuba. He had a big business in Berlin. He had invented the first suitcase in which you could hang garments—suits, dresses. It was called Simpac, or garment bags. He had traveled to America on business. But things were so bad in Germany, it was the height of World War II, and he didn't dare go back. He started making these garment bags here. Being that I knew how to sew, whenever I had time off in my evenings from the doctor, I helped him make the first models on a little treadle machine. He started a factory, and I became an employee in that factory sewing these bags. That gave me the opportunity to go to school at night and pick up my education from where I left off. I got my high school diploma and went on to City College. Then I quit working for my uncle and got a job in an office at a publishing company until I got married in 1944. I had a daughter in 1946. I interrupted school after my daughter was born for quite a number of years.

. . .

In 1981, I had a tremendous desire to see Germany again. I went with a woman friend. We flew into Frankfurt, and we rented a Fiat. I wanted to see my little village, Lichenroth. And it was very emotional. I showed her the house where I had lived. The house had become the residence of the mayor of the town, so it had become a landmark. Village people are very curious, and they kept staring at us. We obviously looked very different than them. At one point, we had to stop the car where cows were crossing the road. [Laughs.] Some people came up to us, and we suddenly found ourselves surrounded by villagers. I explained who I was, and this old woman said, "I thought I recognized you, there's a family resemblance." And this man who had become mayor extended his hand and said, "Do you remember me? I'm the brother of Lena, your former maid." It was a wonderful experience. The villagers told me about the other Jewish families and how they all had left town. How there was just no way they could stay there during Hitler's time.

We went to Berlin. I saw the apartment house where I used to live. And I rang somebody's bell, the neighbor's bell. Our neighbor wasn't Jewish. And an old man came out and said, "We gave already." I tried to explain who I was. There was a woman standing behind him, and she said, "Father, she used to live next to us. It's Molly Mendelsohn!"

Friedrich Leipzig

BORN JANUARY 3, 1919
EMIGRATED 1941, AGE 22
PASSAGE ON THE *NAVEMAR*

Born and raised in Heidelberg, his was a middle-class Jewish family who lived comfortably until Hitler came along. His father was beaten to death by the Nazis in Dachau. His mother escaped to Palestine. His brother and sister escaped to New York where he lives today near his children and grandchildren.

I had a wonderful childhood. I lived in Heidelberg until I was fifteen. I had a brother and a sister in a house where we had just about everything you could hope for, all material wants. I was the youngest. It was a good-sized house, about nineteen, twenty rooms. And there were servants. I never really appreciated it until it was all gone, and it was too late. My father ran a tobacco factory on the outskirts of Heidelberg that he inherited from his father, and my mother ran the household. I had a nanny who I loved as much as my mother.

My father's business, M & F Leipzig, made cigars, smoke tobacco, pipe tobacco. I remember in the main square in Heidelberg there was, much to my embarrassment as a little boy, a sign that said in German, "Every Smoker With Good Taste Smokes Only Leipzig's Pipe Tobacco." [Laughs.] I didn't like to see my name on a neon sign. I thought it was tacky.

The tobacco was grown in Turkey and America. Once in a while I was allowed to go out to the factory and there were bales of tobacco my brother and I climbed over and the best ones smelled just wonderful, and those were usually the Virginia tobacco. [Laughs.] My mother never smoked. My father smoked a lot. My mother's family came from Bruchsal, a town about fifteen

miles from Heidelberg. Her father was also in the tobacco business, curing tobacco, and their marriage was arranged between the two fathers.

My father was strict and hard to get close with. My mother was always ready for a good joke or a good laugh. Full of wild ideas and unexpected things. My mother's family was less conventional. My mother's mother lived with us for a while after my grandfather died. My mother would pull tricks on my father. She would change her voice and call him up. Say my father just came back from a night out with the boys. She would call him at work the next day and say, "I'm so glad I found out where you are. Don't you remember the wonderful night we had together." My father didn't know a thing about it. She made it up. But he was embarrassed, so he went along with it, and she just teased him along and said, "Can I come visit you?" And he said, "All right." And she went over to visit him, and he knew, of course, that the whole thing was a joke. Those things went on quite a good deal.

. . .

By 1939, the atmosphere in Heidelberg had gotten pretty bad for Jews. People were paranoid. When they walked down the street, they looked over their shoulders to see who was following behind. And when all the grownups discussed whether or not we should leave the country, they took a bed pillow and covered the telephone because they thought the telephone was bugged. People were just getting paranoid. Everything was suspect. Not even your best friend was trustworthy anymore. Everybody was turned in, and you heard nothing but horror stories; especially about the famous *Krystallnacht*. That day, my father was rounded up and taken to Dachau, the concentration camp. When they let him out, my mother took him to a Catholic hospital. That was the only hospital that would take him. He was literally beaten, beaten in many different ways. He had broken bones. He had pneumonia. He was bruised all over his body to the extent his body was not able to sustain life anymore. And he died two days later.

My mother called me in Switzerland to tell me. I was at a boarding school at the time. I had been in Switzerland many times before as a child for different health reasons. I was a sickish child, and I was sent to a children's home in Otaboden once every year for a few weeks. But I was ultimately transferred to a Swiss boarding school because it was the only secure place I could be. It was a decision made by my parents. I enjoyed it tremendously. It was a school with students from all over the world. Their families had sent them there to be safe. You could hear almost any language you could think of. It's the only time I ever heard Spaniards and Italians talk to each other in their own language. When they don't understand each other they just raise their voices, and then they understand each other. [Laughs.] Most importantly, it was a place where my self-confidence was built up, and they knew how to do it. They challenged me. They gave me opportunities to prove myself. It's not that they praised me so much as they were very good at handling

children. The lady who was in charge of the place gave me a large amount of money one day and said, "Take it down to the post office and deposit it." She gave me instructions, and I thought it was a very difficult task. I was very young. I must have been about seven. I loved it there.

While this was going on, the SS came to our house and took everything from my mother. Furniture, jewelry, naturally. They even pulled the wedding ring off her finger, which bothered me very much. I didn't care if they took the furniture.

Another day, an SS man visited my mother and said, "Mrs. Leipzig, I'm not here to take anything away from you, but I have to tell you you must leave the country. I remember you from long ago. I know your family, and I want to do you a favor. You have to leave the country."

And she said, "I do?"

"Yes," he said. "You have to leave today." And she didn't know what she should do.

"I have a taxi," he said. "The driver will take you wherever you tell him, but you have to go."

So she packed a suitcase, as much as she could. And by that time my mother's mother was in Holland. She told the driver to drive to the Dutch border. The moment she crossed the border she heard Hitler give a speech over the car radio that Germany was invading Poland, that the war had officially started, and that all borders were sealed. So that man knew this was the last chance to get out. He had done a good deed.

My mother had no permission to stay in Holland. So she went to Palestine. She went there in a small boat. And she eventually died there. She wrote me detailed letters of what had happened. She wrote me letters from Holland, and she wrote me letters from Palestine, which later became Israel. I still have some of the letters, and I reread them occasionally. I'm now translating them for my kids to read.

After graduating [from] boarding school, I tried to get an immigration permit to come to America. My brother and my sister were already here. My brother came first, my sister a year later. I always wanted to come to the United States. The United States to me was a country full of miracles, and wonderful things that I had read in books that were really exciting and nice, and high-rise buildings. I read about the Pennsylvania Turnpike, a road that was dedicated for only automobiles without intersections. And things of that sort really impressed me, and I thought, that's a country where you can do almost anything you want to. While I was in Switzerland my brother and sister were writing me and telling me these things.

But I had a difficult time getting my immigration permit from the American consulate. There were too many people trying to come to the United States, more people than the quota permitted. If I had the money, I could have bribed my way; I would have been able to slip the right amount of money to the right person at the right moment and gotten my permit. But I was a young kid and I didn't have any money, so I was too naive to do that. And after a while the Swiss were trying to get rid of foreigners, Jews, anyway. They were a burden to them. I was taken to a labor camp for close to a year. It was a hard life. We were given shoes with wooden soles, which were very handy because we were draining a swamp area. And the wooden soles insulated us from the cold ground. I learned to work with my hands. We had to dig out stumps of trees so that the land could be used for agriculture. Switzerland suffered from a great lack of food. They were surrounded by Nazi-controlled countries. Hitler allowed as much food into Switzerland as he felt like. Switzerland was actually manufacturing weapons for Germany, and

that gave them a bargaining point, so they did get some food in.

After I got out, I worked illegally in Switzerland. Only Swiss natives were allowed to work. But I had to get some money somehow, so I worked for an architectural photographer in a darkroom, until the police found out and I quit. I asked the photographer what I should do, and he said, "Disappear." I remembered a farmer who had a hut high up in the mountains. So I stayed alone there for a couple of weeks. I rented it for one franc, or twenty cents a day. It was very primitive. The farmers used to drive their cows up there in summer, high into the mountains, tend them, and come down in fall.

My immigration permit finally came through. My brother had helped. Apparently he knew someone who knew someone on the House Foreign Affairs Committee. The committee inquired about my case by writing a letter to the consulate, and that's all it took.

Then came the real problem. How do I get out of Switzerland? It was surrounded by Nazi-occupied countries, except France, which was divided into occupied France and Vichy France. The Swiss government started negotiating with the German government to let trains go through occupied France into Vichy France, so they could get rid of some of the foreigners living in Switzerland. I went to Geneva and got on a guarded, sealed train. I was very uneasy about leaving Switzerland because I still felt secure there. But as we went through France the guards slowly disappeared. There were only a few guards left by the time we got to Spain. The train went along the Mediterranean at the foot of the Pyrenees, and there it stopped suddenly. No tracks. Spain was still suffering greatly from its civil war and had not been rebuilt at all. We took a bus from there through Barcelona to Sevilla, and from Sevilla to Cadiz, but there was no ship at

Cadiz, and we waited. I ran out of money, and it was desperate. I was staying in a hotel I couldn't really afford, but I stayed there anyway. Ernest Hemingway had been there a few days before. I stayed in his room.

I stayed in Cadiz about a month until we got news that the ship was coming to Sevilla. They provided transportation from Cadiz to Sevilla. And I rode the bus to Sevilla along a river, up and inland to the north. I spent my last night in Spain in a hotel. It was wonderful. I blew the last peso I had. I did not like Cadiz. But I enjoyed Sevilla, perhaps because I knew my ship was there, the *Navemar*. It had a black hull. And we left the next day downriver.

I was appalled how many people were waiting to get on board that ship. It was a freighter converted to handle a few passengers. But it had booked thirteen hundred. So accommodations were poor. We had triple decker bunks in the various holds. There were three freight holds for the thirteen hundred passengers. Not very good. The holds were left open for air, which was all right, except when it rained, then people got wet. But I didn't sleep down there. I slept in a lifeboat. I pulled back the tarp slightly and I sneaked in every night. That was much better. There were about eight kids all told who slept in that lifeboat.

I knew it was uncomfortable, and I didn't care. It was going to America! I couldn't understand why some people felt so bad about it. Some just couldn't stand it. Some people jumped overboard as time went on, and some became sick and died. It was a pretty horrible situation. We finally had to form our own ship's police to maintain order. I became a member. We could only eat in shifts because we were too many people to eat, and we had two meals a day. We had to take great care that people would eat just their two meals. There were some people who ate first shift, second shift, and third shift. And then the other people

couldn't get any meals at all, so that had to be regulated, and the ship's crew was unable to regulate that, so we succeeded in doing that. I also succeeded in meeting a very attractive girl from France with whom I got along very well. She wanted me to speak French, but my French wasn't that good. And she didn't want to speak English. So she spoke French and I answered her in English.

The trip took forty-seven days. It was a slow boat. [Laughs.] We went from Sevilla to Lisbon, where we stayed a whole week in the outer harbor. We had to take on food and some live cattle that were put on deck. We had waited so long, all of our American immigration permits had run out. So one day we were taken into Lisbon, also in shifts, one busload at a time, to the American consulate. The American officials in Lisbon were wonderful compared to those in Geneva. They were friendly and helpful, and I returned with a care package full of good food including canned sardines and a bottle of brandy, which was just heaven. In the end, I shared everything with the eight kids in the lifeboat.

We went on to Bermuda, because we were intercepted in the mid-Atlantic by a British frigate. In Bermuda all the women and children were taken off by the British and fed. We were allowed to take a bath, which was heaven. We only had cold, salt-water showers. From Bermuda, we went down to Havana, Cuba, and from there, up to New York.

We came to the outer harbor, and it was very exciting. Everybody rushed out on deck with the cattle to see the skyline of New York, and the Statue of Liberty. And then we stopped, dropped anchor. We were very disappointed. Somebody observed that we had raised the yellow flag, which meant we were being quarantined. The Public Health Service came on board in a launch and examined everybody. Alongside the launch was a press ship, and I noticed they were taking pictures with flash bulbs, and I couldn't understand why anyone would shoot flash in the middle of the day. I remember that clearly. This was September 1941.

My brother, who was in the U.S. Army, greeted me in uniform. He could come to the front of the dock because he was military. I was up on the top deck. I hadn't seen my brother in years and it felt good. I yelled down to him that I was running a fever. And that they told me to go to the hospital on Ellis Island. They wanted to find out why I was running a fever. I left my brother at the dock. That was very disappointing. I was taken in a launch to Ellis Island, and the hospital. There were a dozen others besides me, and a nurse checked off our names. She was sitting downstairs by the door. We were separated by sex. I was the only male.

Then we were sent upstairs [to] what looked like real beds. I hadn't seen a real bed for so long. And we were told we could take a shower, which was absolutely unbelievable, with real soap and warm water, unsalty. I was beginning to get in a much better mood already. We came out of our showers and we were sitting around the ward and suddenly somebody asked us, "Have you guys eaten yet?" And we said, "No." Even if we had eaten, we would have said no. We were starved. We were taken to a cafeteria. The concept of a cafeteria was new to me. I had seen something like it in movies, but never in reality. We were given stainless steel trays that had partitions in it, and we had to go from one station to the other, and they dished the food in. The women and I had ham, mashed potatoes, green peas. For dessert I had a pink strawberry ice cream bar that was unbelievably good. And so we sat and talked and ate all the food, and we didn't want to go away. Somebody from the cafe-

teria said, "Have you had enough, or would you like more?"

"Can we have more?" we asked.

"Sure, you can have as much as you want."

So we ate more. I went through the line five times. The doctor saw this and said to the cafeteria worker, "You're going to make these people sick. Don't give them any more food." Then we went to the wards, and I slept just heavenly.

The next morning we had breakfast, a very important event. [Laughs.] And then a man came by and said, "You may leave." I only had one suitcase plus a used piece of soap I stuck in my pocket, and a piece of sugar I swiped from the cafeteria. I went from the hospital and walked a long distance across this grassy area to the main building. There were three tables with immigration officials. I was told to wait until they called me.

It was my turn. They wanted to see my immigration permit, which thank God had been fixed properly in Lisbon. But my passport had run out. It was no longer valid. "If you want to renew your passport," they said, "you have to go back to Germany." Which I wasn't about to do. He stamped the permit, and said, "You may go."

It was wonderful. I stepped outside. It was a warm, breezy, summer day. I could see Manhattan. The high-rise buildings. The water was blue. Just heaven. I was taken by ferry to the mainland where my brother was waiting with a car and we drove at high speed up the West Side Highway to Yonkers.

. . .

One of the things that was hard understanding was the coins. In Europe, all coins have numbers that show what they're worth, but in America no coin has a number on it. Show me where a quarter says twenty-five, or where a dime says ten, or where a nickel says five. Nowhere.

The other problem was language. I knew some English—British English, and not very much.

About five months after I entered the United States I was drafted into the army. I was in basic training, and my drill sergeant yelled, "About face!" I had no idea what it meant. I knew "about" and "face," and I had no idea what he wanted me to do about my face. I looked right and left and I saw everybody turned around . . . But that's how I learned.

10

. . . .

Austria

(APPROXIMATELY 500,000 IMMIGRANTS, 1892–1954)

Cara Weichel

· · · · · · · · · · · ·

BORN JANUARY 23, 1896
EMIGRATED 1905, AGE 9
PASSAGE ON THE HAMBURG-AMERICAN LINE

*She lived a hard life in rural Austria. When she was eight years old her mother,
brother, and sister immigrated to the United States, but left her behind. She
became the indentured servant to a greedy, overbearing aunt. Free of her aunt's
clutches, she traveled to the United States alone, and was reunited with her
family. Today, she lives in a small apartment in New Jersey near her son.
"I have it good," she says now, "I am very grateful."*

We were very poor. The whole town was poor. There was no industry. The people were farmers. It was a Catholic town. But we were not religious. I vaguely remember attending church. And although we were farmers, we had no animals because we couldn't afford to feed them. The women would work in the field and dig potatoes, different things, they would plant. My mother, too. She was tall and thin and very smart, and on days when she didn't work the fields, she worked as a cashier in a grocery store owned by the mayor of the town. She washed our clothes with water from a well she got with a bucket.

We lived in one big room that was filled with nothing but beds. When my mother went to work, she would leave us there with my brother and my little sister. And she would make stuff for us to eat. And then we had a kitchen with a wood-burning stove. So we used to have to hunt for wood. Get wood. Because the winters were very bad, always cold. And the kitchen had sand on the floor.

I remember one time my sister was about two years old, and she was hungry. So she climbed up on a chair in the kitchen, and saw food. My mother had made a mixture of potatoes and flour and egg and rolled them up with bread crumbs, and that was supposed to be our food. Well, she picked it up, but the thing was too heavy for her and it dropped on the floor into the sand. The potato absorbed all the sand. So we had nothing to eat all day long.

My father came to America when I was very young, so I don't really know what he did. In America he worked in what they call a "lardy," a factory, in New Jersey. He lived in a boardinghouse. The landlords were a husband and wife and they were of the same nationality. And one day they said to him, "Martin, you need to get your wife and children over here. We'll lend you the money. And when your wife comes, she can work to help us get boarders in, and you can pay us back." So that's what he did.

I remember the day the ticket for passage came. It was fall, very cold, and my brother, my mother and I, were working the fields. We were all digging a hole to put the potatoes in for the winter. And the mailman came, and he's waving this thing because we were far back in the fields. We all ran to see what it was. My mother was so excited. It was the ticket from my father.

But I couldn't go because I had eczema all over my forehead. To this day I've always had some kind of dry skin problem. And, so [pauses] they left me there. My mother took my little sister who was now about four years old, and my younger brother who was nine. So she got a carriage—a horse and buggy, and they drove off. I remember running after that carriage screaming and screaming.

My heart was broken. Here they were going to America and they left me there with my aunt. I had no grandparents. My uncle, her husband, had already gone to America. And my aunt was not a very nice lady. And I sat down by the house sobbing and sobbing, and my mother had given me some money. My aunt came out and said, "Let me see what you've got in your hand." I showed her the money. "Give it to me," she said. "I'll put it away." [Laughs.] I never saw it again.

That was 1904. I came over about ten months later.

My aunt was very greedy. She used to take little babies in. The mothers would be out in the field. My aunt would strap the baby on my back, and I would have to go way out in the field. It wasn't close to the house. And I had to take the baby to the mother, so the mother could nurse the baby. And then I'd have to bring the baby back. Then I would go and get water from the fountain in the town square. It was more a well than a fountain. I was about nine years old.

It was not a very pleasant time. I was like the household help for my aunt so she didn't want to let me go. Sometimes my parents sent me money, say ten dollars, which was like a hundred dollars over there. And she would take it. She just wouldn't let me go.

Finally, the mayor saved me. He had gotten letters from my parents, and he went over to my aunt and said, "Now get her ready. She's going to go to America." My eczema had cleared. And we had a pair of shoes ordered for the trip, because we didn't wear shoes. We wore slippers. They called them *Pantoffel*. The mayor also brought over two dresses that belonged to his daughter. Nice dresses. Of course, he was wealthy. So he brought these two dresses so that I would have something to wear to come to America.

I brought nothing with me. I just had a little bag with all my papers that hung around my neck. I had to be very careful that I wouldn't lose it. And then he took me by horse and buggy to Germany. And he bought me a doll. To this day I love dolls. So I had the bag and the doll. [Laughs.] I was just glad I was going. That's all I remember.

When the mayor brought me to Germany, he put me on the train, and there was a young couple. So he asked them if they would look after me. And they did. They were nice. But I tell you [laughs], I was so afraid I would wet my pants on the train. That I remember so well. It was so important that I didn't do that. Because I used to wet my pants a lot, and I didn't have no panties to wet.

We rode the train for two days to Hamburg. I stayed there for two days in a hotel before we took the boat to America. It was August 1905. I was still the ward of this couple. They were also on the boat in second class on top. I was in steerage. There were no other children to play with. I remember being scared to go to the toilet because I thought a fish was going to come up and bite me.

I also remember people saying things like, "Oh, be careful. They'll steal everything on you. You have to be careful." So, of course, I wore brand new shoes and I never had new shoes before. So I thought, "Oh, they're going to steal my shoes." So I went to sleep with my shoes on. I was so afraid that they were going to steal my shoes. People in first class used to throw money and candy down to us. I don't remember the food, I don't remember eating. I slept on the bottom of a bunk bed. I don't know who slept on top. But that couple would see me every day. We would walk out on the deck because it was August. Beautiful weather. The trip took about ten days before we arrived at Ellis Island.

I don't remember seeing the Statue of Liberty. Nobody pointed it out to me. Or maybe they did, but it didn't mean anything to me. I remember the food—oatmeal and prunes, and the dining room and the tables like picnic tables and the benches and the sleeping quarters. Nothing was comfortable. They sent a telegram to my father, and he came the next day to get me. My mother couldn't come, she was still what they called a greenhorn. [Laughs.] She wouldn't know where to go. But my father knew.

It was the first time I ever saw him. And the officials would ask me questions, and then him questions trying to determine if he was, in fact, my father because I didn't remember him. And then I guess they were satisfied, and they let me go with him.

We took the ferry to Weehawken, New Jersey and then the trolley to Guttenberg, down the Palisades. The first thing my father did was buy me bananas. I had never had bananas, and I didn't like them. Then he showed me the machine where you put the penny in for the chewing gum. We never had chewing gum. And offered me a jelly doughnut from a brown bag he had. But I was leery about taking anything from him because I didn't remember him. He was a total stranger to me. But my father was very nice, very gentle. He was gentle to the day he died. He was never nasty. My mother was the domineering one.

When we arrived in Guttenberg my mother was there. The whole family. Everybody greeted me. The first thing I did was take off my shoes. For that alone, I was so happy. And I ran outside on the sidewalks, we never had sidewalks in Europe. And the sidewalks were hot. And I was jumping around. I was so happy.

Estelle Miller

. . . .

BORN FEBRUARY 28, 1896
EMIGRATED 1909, AGE 13
PASSAGE ON THE HAMBURG-AMERICAN LINE

She came from Austria in 1909 when she was thirteen years old. Today, she lives in Brooklyn, New York. Her two brothers and elder sister have long gone. "I've outlived everybody," she said.

I was born in the small village of Bilche Zlote. It was a very nice little town. It had a nice synagogue, a nice church. And there were about two thousand citizens living there and about, say, fifty Jewish people, Jewish families. They owned and ran many of the stores in town. And we lived a nice life. There was no anti-Semitism then.

We had good teachers in school. Jewish boys went to the Jewish school. Jewish girls went to the regular school. They started school when you were four, five years old. And it was pretty good.

The town was not industrial. It was farming. A farming town. We had a countess. She owned all the fields and she employed all the Christian people, all the non-Jews. The Jewish wouldn't work the field. She employed them [the Christians], and they produced very nice wheat and barley and fruit. We had fruit trees. Beautiful fruit trees: apple trees, cherry, plums. We had our own cow and our own chickens, I used to feed the chickens myself, and ducks. And I used to take the little ducks out when they were first born and they would swim beautifully with the mother. And it was a nice little town. We were more or less sorry to leave it.

But we had our own home. It was a nice little home. We had two beautiful rooms, and each room had a built-in oven. It was supposed to be for two tenants, but we were four children. It was a nice life, but a hard life because my father couldn't make a living. That's why we came to America. He was a true scholar. He was studying the Talmud, always with the Talmud learning and learning, and we couldn't get along. It was impossible. And here my sister and I were growing up, and my mother was worried she'll never have the money for us to get married. You needed money for a dowry. And my mother's brother, my uncle, was already in America. My uncle used to correspond with my mother. He advised her to come to America. So she began talking to my father that he should come to the United States, which he eventually did, in 1906, but my elder sister came first.

My uncle had been writing to my mother, saying how the children must be growing up. That they'd be better off in America than Austria. Then, when one of the families in the town decided to go to the United States, my older sister, who was fourteen years old, wanted to go with them, alone with them.

My grandfather, meantime, my mother's father, didn't want her or any of us to go to America—at least while he was living. He thought Americans were not observant, not kosher. "Even the stones in the sidewalks are not kosher," he would say. [Laughs.] It wasn't until after he died that my sister went. And she was terribly sorry she did.

She wasn't happy in America. She went to my uncle's house. He took her as a maid. He didn't even send her to school. He used her for the housework. She was miserable. She was in America for one year until my father came.

I remember the day he left. I was about ten years old. It was night and he was standing over us—me and my two younger brothers—and he thought I was sleeping. He was crying bitter tears. He left the next morning and I saw how broken up he was. He didn't want to leave. But my mother made him leave.

My mother always managed. She always made a decent living for herself. She used to deal in eggs. She used to buy them and store them and sell them. This was a good business. She would wake up at five o'clock in the morning and get the eggs. She also used to put windowpanes into windows when they were broken, and picture frames on pictures. The people in town bought a lot of religious pictures that needed framing. So she used to do that, and she did pretty good. My father used to help her too, but it wasn't enough to keep a family going. So she eventually sold the house and sold all the animals to come to America to join my father and my sister.

The day we left, I remember taking my mother's china bowl. It was an antique and my mother was afraid to pack it, so I carried it in my hands all the way to Hamburg,

Steerage deck of a steamship bound for New York in 1902

(NATIONAL PARK SERVICE: STATUE OF LIBERTY NATIONAL MONUMENT)

Germany. And when we came to Ellis Island the doctors were examining me, examining my eyes for glaucoma. I remember the doctor being rough with me. There was a lot of noise, and screaming and crying and, at one point, the door opened, and all of a sudden, a black man walked in.

I got so frightened. I never saw a black man before. I was so scared I dropped the antique china bowl, and it broke in pieces. My mother almost died. I almost killed myself.

We had gone by train from Austria to Hamburg. We slept overnight and then took the boat from Hamburg to New York and

Ellis Island. We traveled in steerage. It was my first time on a train or a boat. The whole experience was exciting for us, for me and my brothers. But it was bare. We had a bed to sleep, but the food was horrible. They fed you meat, but we didn't eat the meat. It wasn't kosher. My mother wouldn't allow it. Instead, she brought a lot of stuff, prepared food that we ate—cake, cookies, and whatnot. The trip lasted six days. And when we got to Ellis Island I remember somebody saying that it was the first time a boat made it in six days. When my older sister went, it lasted a month. She almost died on that boat.

We were seasick most of the time, sitting there in agony. I remember the passengers in first class. They used to look down at us and literally throw things to us; things they didn't want, things to eat. They'd throw it down to us. It was not a good trip. I had better trips going to Israel in 1940. [Laughs.]

When we arrived in New York Harbor, my brothers and I ran out to see the Statue of Liberty. But nobody knew what it was. One man said, "Don't you know? That's Columbus." [Laughs.] So we thought it was Columbus. For years I thought that.

Jake Kreider
. . . .

BORN MAY 5, 1899
EMIGRATED 1911, AGE 11
PASSAGE ON THE HAMBURG-AMERICAN LINE

He immigrated to America with his mother and younger sisters. His father had come before them. The family settled in Newark, New Jersey. Once here, the pressures of starting over turned his father into a mean-spirited and verbally abusive man, particularly to his mother. Jake went on to own and run a vegetable market and a delicatessen. Eventually, he became a salesman in the wholesale dry-cleaning business for more than fifty years. He had four sons from his first wife of forty-eight years. His second wife recently died after seventeen years of marriage. To this day, he harbors deep resentment toward his father. "I hated my father so badly," he said, "that I'm sorry, when I got to be fifteen or sixteen, I didn't kill him."

We had a big house. The biggest house in the town. My father owned a dance hall and a tavern, and made a living giving weddings, funerals, wakes, whatever it was. He had quite a good business. In the wintertime, there was a lake near us that used to freeze up, and he would cut these blocks and put the ice into our cellar so that we could keep the beer cool.

The house was on a county highway. There were trees all along the highway, and whenever anyone wanted to go to the city they had to take that highway. The city was Brochnic. The cemetery was also on that highway, and if there was a wake the townspeople—a mix of Jew and gentile, mostly gentile—would stop at our place after the funeral and get drunk. [Laughs.]

We had quite a big piece of property. We were very wealthy—for there, anyway. We had a maid and a gardener and a private teacher who taught us German, and Hebrew, and Polish. And we always had plenty of money. In fact, we had a china closet, and in this closet we had a little basket woven from grass. My father would put his money in that. He would dump it into that basket. And if my mother needed something from the grocery store, she would take some, and ask one of us to go to the store and take a penny for candy for ourselves. I had five sisters and three brothers, although one brother died of infantile paralysis when he was four years old. I was fifth in line.

We had an incident where gentile people were borrowing money from the Jews to send their children to college. They were supposed to pay them interest. They paid the interest with wheat and oats or whatever came off the field. They would put it in bags, and took it to the Jewish people, thinking all the time they were getting credit against the interest. When they found out they weren't, they complained to town hall that the Jews were taking these things under false pretenses, and a warrant was sworn out for their arrest. There were about seven of them. They were friends of my father's, although we weren't religious, and my father knew the head rabbi in town and went to see him. He told the rabbi that he wanted to hide his friends so they could not be served with a court summons. So it was decided that my father put them in a wagon and covered them with straw, hooked up a team of horses and he drove them someplace. He hid them.

In the meantime, he spoke to the court on their behalf. He said, "You know, if you're going to send these people to jail, you'll get nothing. Why don't you see if you can settle this thing?" So they did and they withdrew the charges. But somebody squealed that my father had harbored these guys, which was illegal. So the court said they would put out a summons for my father's arrest. To send him to jail.

He decided to run. To go to America. Somehow he got a visa. When they came to serve him, he had already left. He was already here. He took my two older brothers and two older sisters. That was in 1905. I stayed behind with my mother and three younger sisters. So it was the five of us. And I became the man of the house. I was six years old.

While my father was gone, we had a flood in town, and animals were floating—rats, mice, whatever. And our neighbors brought all their belongings to our house, Torahs, religious things, because our house wasn't flooded. Our house was built of concrete blocks, very thick walls, eighteen-inch walls. Most of theirs were made of log wood, and straw roofs. And so they brought everything over. Some of the people were sitting on our roof watching everything float by. It was really a disaster, it really was. I was about eight years old when this happened.

Then, around 1910, my mother wrote [my father] that the military were having maneuvers. That soldiers were staying at our house, putting their horses into our stables. That they were maneuvering with live ammunition, which meant there was going to be a war. And that's when we decided to sell everything. All our assets. We sold our property to our next-door neighbor, but not before the house, the entire estate, was burned down by the soldiers. So we moved in with my grandparents, my mother's parents, who lived in the nearby town of Chevre, before we came to America. My three sisters, my mother, and myself.

We packed a trunk and a bundle of things. My mother had a pair of boots made to order for my father. We brought that with us. I wore a special suit my mother had made to order for me. My mother took along a lot of dry fruits and things, so that we wouldn't have to eat the ship's food. Most of the time, people were fed hot dogs. She brought candlesticks, I remember, different things, but not too much. And the money. My mother had a money belt she carried with her.

We took the train to Bremen, Germany. We stayed there about a week. We had already been medically examined before we left Chevre. The papers were all taken care of. But our luggage was lost. The ship was on the Hamburg line so for some reason it was sent to Hamburg by accident. So I went to Hamburg by myself to locate the luggage while my mother stayed at the hotel with my younger sisters.

It was my first time out of Austria and I just remember how clean Germany was. Hamburg. The roads were very wide, nice and clean. The stores were beautiful. Nice window displays. The people were nice. You could see the students when they came out of the college. They would all swirl little canes, twirl them, and walk with a certain step. They behaved very nicely. I was eleven at the time.

When I returned to the hotel, I remember seeing a butcher shop and a midget salami in the window. So I bought it. I took it into the hotel and I was cutting it and I was eating it. Oh, was it delicious. Till this very day I can still taste what it was like. So the next day I went outside, I was wondering how come the salami tasted so good. I couldn't understand it. I looked up at the top of the store and there was a horse's head. They were selling horsemeat. [Laughs.] The salami was made of horsemeat.

At night my mother would take off her money belt and put it under my pillow be-fore we went to sleep. One night, about five o'clock in the morning people in the hotel start hollering, "Fire, fire, fire!" Everybody ran out of the rooms, including my mother. I didn't budge. I stayed there. And these guys came running in and out. They were looking under the pillows. They were stealing. When they came in, they took one look at me and I asked them in German, "What do you want? Get out!" And they left. My mother knew she could always depend on me. I was like the man of the house.

. . .

The ship ride to America was miserable. This was a German ship, and I spoke German so I got along, but I remember there were some Russian kids there, and they didn't like the Russians at all.

I used to do the shopping on the ship. Passengers would give me money and I would buy whatever they wanted from the canteen on the ship. Oranges, lemons, whatever they had. And then they would tip me. Tip me like crazy. Because they were nauseated. They were throwing up. They thought they were going to die. Money didn't mean a thing to them. I used to say, "Don't give me so much money." "Ah, what good is the money? I'm gonna die anyhow." They were so seasick they thought they were going to die.

I was so frightened, so disgusted. The people were all feeling lousy, scratching. They were dirty. They didn't get no attention. It was terrible. At least we had a shower in our room, we could shower, keep clean. When we got off the boat, got to Ellis Island, people were sitting on the benches scratching from the lice. They were loaded with lice. Ellis Island looked like a great barn with benches. We all sat on benches. Driven in there like a bunch of cattle.

It was about noon when we arrived. We were examined by the eye doctor, the medical doctor. And we all passed. But the ship was two days early, my father was supposed to meet us and there was no way of contacting him. "You'll have to lay on a bench and go to sleep," one of the officers said. I said, "That's not possible. This place is lousy. I can't take this. Why do we have to stay here? Why can't we go to my father?"

"Well," he said, "someone has to meet you. There has to be a certain amount of financial responsibility."

"What are you worrying about finances? We have plenty of money."

"What do you mean, you have plenty of money?"

"Yeah, we have plenty of money. My mother's got it in her money belt."

They took my mother with a nurse into a room. My mother undressed, and she took out the money belt, and they opened it up. [Laughs.] The officer took one look at it. He said, "Oh, my God, I haven't seen so much money in years!"

"You don't have to stay," he said. "You've got the money. You can take the ferry to New York."

So we packed up and left. We got to New York, but we had to get to Newark, New Jersey. So I tried to find someone who could speak German or Jewish or Polish. And what surprised me was seeing so many black people. In our country the only black people we knew were the Gypsies. And I was under the impression that's who they were, Gypsies. It didn't make sense to me to see so many black people.

Finally we found someone, got the directions. We took a trolley car to the Hudson tubes and Newark. And then another trolley to Springfield Avenue. We were a block and a half away from my father's house when we got out. A four-room house across the street from a livery stable where he worked. He was sitting on the front porch steps. And I recognized him, and I was delighted. But there was no affection from him. No real affection. Nothing. As though he saw us yesterday.

Samuel Silverman

· · · · · · · · · · · ·

BORN MARCH 7, 1898
EMIGRATED 1913, AGE 15
PASSAGE ON THE S.S. *IMPERATOR*

He came from a section of Austria-Hungary that is now Poland.
He went on to work for Harris and Company, a bicycle parts manufacturer. He
started as a floor sweeper; fifty-nine years later, he retired as vice president,
and now lives in Florida.

· · · · · · · ·

I lived in Tarnow until the age of fourteen. The town was half Jewish, half Roman Catholic, maybe sixty thousand people in all. Until about 1908, the town had no sewerage system, no water system, no electricity, no gas. For drinking water there used to be a water carrier who brought water from the city, from a pump in the middle of town. It was good drinking water and good for cooking, and you paid him so much a week or a month. But for washing, they used a pump. Most everybody had a pump there, but the water was not suitable for drinking, even if you boiled it.

I know the house I was born in because every time we would pass my mother would say, "You were born in this house." The only thing I remember about it were the oxygen tanks for my sister. She was two years younger. She died very young from pneumonia.

From there we moved to a house that belonged to my mother's parents that used to be a bakery, so there was a machine that was used to make matzo. My grandmother, once a year at Passover, would use the machine to make matzo for our seder dinner.

On the main street, the businesses were all Jewish, with names like Dobrofsky, Tchaikovsky, small shops. One would sell kerosene. Another sodas, or dry goods. But they were all Jewish businesses, and if it were a Saturday or a Jewish holiday, everything was closed and quiet because everyone was in shul. The only people you saw were the women prisoners. Twelve of them lined up on a Saturday morning with brooms, sweeping the street of horse droppings from the horses and wagons.

In school, books and writing paper were not provided like in America. You had to buy it yourself. So when classes started, the teacher would ask, "Can everybody buy a book?" And those who needed to borrow a book would stand up. So one day, about thirty kids stood up and I was among them. And the teacher said, "We only have twenty-eight books." So

one of the kids says, "Silverman doesn't need one. He's rich."

"How do you know?" the teacher asked.

"Well, every day he eats a roll, and sometimes it's got butter on it." So I was rich. [Laughs, then is moved.] I never forgot that. I was about eight years old, I guess.

My father was a tailor. In those days, there was no such thing as buying ready-made clothes, but my father did. What happened is when he made clothes to order he would only be paid after he did the work, and sometimes not even then. He would have to wait. But my father needed the money. So he created a wholesale business. Instead of making one suit at a time, he made several "for the rack," and then merchants would come and buy in bulk—eight, ten, or twelve suits. Complete suits. I mean, the jacket, the vest, and the trousers. He did the whole thing on premises. He had a big machine with a table that could cut twelve suits at a time; a big wheel with a knife. My father would lay out the patterns on the cloth, chalk it, and move the cloth into place to cut these suits. The buttonholes were done by hand. Everything was done by hand. We had about twenty-seven people working, between the men and the women.

Many of them lived out of town. So we had to give them Sabbath dinner on Friday night because there were no restaurants for them to go to, not that they could afford a restaurant anyway. So on Friday nights and Saturday afternoons after services, we had huge meals—anywheres from twelve to eighteen workers. My mother, who had a helper, used to serve fresh gefilte fish, chicken soup, meat, and so on. In between courses, to pass the time, we sang songs.

Tarnow was a commercial town. A factory town that manufactured ready-made clothing, like suits and felt hats, and employed thousands of people. Merchants would come [from] fifty or one hundred miles away to buy what we were selling. There was prosperity.

Then, in 1908, we had a terrible depression and my father left for America. There was a war going on in the Balkans that involved all the neighboring countries: Yugoslavia, Croatia, Montenegro, Bosnia, Slovenia. Austria was making war with all these little countries. Things got so bad, he just closed up shop and went to America, and left some money to my mother. We didn't have to go begging or anything, we always had something to eat. And he would send money from America.

I came to America on August 27, 1913 on the S.S. *Imperator* from Hamburg. My father was already here and the idea was that I come to America to help him, help the family. He had sent me a ticket to come later on in October on a new ship called the *Princess Augusta*. But I didn't want to go on a new ship after what had happened to the *Titanic* the year before. I wanted to go on an old ship. So I took the Imperator. I was in third class, not steerage. And I handled it all myself, made the changes, and so on. I went to the Hamburg-American Line and changed it over to that ship. I didn't have to pay extra, either.

On the ship, there were four in a cabin, two on bottom, two on top. There was one fellow in third class. He came with a violin and he used to play operatic pieces just to entertain us. The one I remember was "Tales of Hoffmann." And it was very nice, and he did a nice job.

When we arrived in New York Harbor, everybody, all the immigrants, went up to the top deck so we could see the Statue of Liberty, which we did. In fact, before we got into the harbor, we had to stop off at Sandy Hook to unload the mail. We didn't get into dock until maybe seven o'clock at night. Then, of course, the people that were American citizens came off first. They checked through customs and then foreigners with visas came in. The immigrants looking to stay permanently had to remain on the ship overnight before they were checked through Ellis Island.

So we stayed on the ship overnight. The next morning, we heard there was a fire on the ship the night before. The fire was in one of the boiler rooms, and one of the ship mates died of smoke asphyxiation.

I waited for my father, but he never came. I was upset because other people were leaving. And because I couldn't get off Ellis Island, because I didn't have enough money for them to let me off. In addition, I was not only an immigrant, I was a minor. But he came the next morning, a Friday. [He is moved.] We took an open trolley car up Broadway. It was summertime. It was August. Then we had to change for the Delancey Street trolley to go up to Rivington Street on the Lower East Side. There was a horse-driven car that took us to Cannon Street, so that my father could go to work to get a day's pay. He worked near the Williamsburg Bridge, where men were selling fish and all sorts of things. The men wore undershirts, which I never saw in Berlin. Not very appetizing. And they would shout, "Two for a nickel, three for a nickel." And my father took me up to the fifth floor of this tenement where we lived. And I remember standing by the window and looking down at the chaos on the street, men hollering in Yiddish, "Iceman, iceman." Then, my father went to work. When he came home, he washed up, and we went downstairs for a walk.

Lou Seigner

. . . .

BORN APRIL 27, 1900
EMIGRATED 1921, AGE 20
PASSAGE ON THE *RYNDAM*

He was the son of a powerful Austrian commandant, so he became a soldier. In
America, he became a furrier. Affable and funny, he now lives in New Jersey.

I was born in the city of Tarnow. My
father was a finance officer in the Austrian military and, [when I was] a
child, he was transferred from one city to
another. One year here, two years there. He
finally settled down in the town of Rudki
where he became the commandant, meaning the top military leader of the city and the
surrounding province, representing the Austrian government, the kaiser—the emperor.
He had a suite of three offices, the ground
floor of the governor's building. It was a
large, tall building. There were lots of girls
working on the various floors. They were
Catholic. You see, to me, what matters is the
race, whether it's Catholic or Jewish, or it's
a male or female. [Laughs.] We were Jewish,
but I am not religious. I don't speak Jewish.
My parents never spoke Jewish.

When I became seventeen, I decided I
would follow in my father's footsteps. They
didn't draft boys until they were eighteen,
but when I was seventeen, I volunteered. I
remember my father and I sitting before the
draft board being interviewed by a first lieutenant, a second lieutenant, and a military
doctor. "Yes, I want to become an officer, a
career officer like my father." And they
passed me. I went first to Tyrol in the Austrian Alps to learn to become a military
scout where you go from mountain to
mountain and post flags. Then I joined an

artillery regiment because it was stationed
in Vienna.

My mother was a lady. She met my
father when he was a young officer. A captain, I think. An officer of the rank of captain
has the privilege of having an orderly, a
military orderly to do housework, shine
shoes, do cleaning and so on. Now, because
the demand for manpower to feed the army
on the various fronts was the Serbian front,
the Italian front, the Russian front. So they
were only too glad to volunteer to be a
servant to the officer. Now, later on when
we became six, seven years, eight years old,
so my father, my mother became very ill.
We also had a few siblings who died. They
were born and they lived a few months or a
few years and they passed away.

My brother's name was Fritz. My sister
was four years older than I and her name
was Marie. And the younger sister was,
well, in German was Hermina. You would
pronounce it in English "Hermina."

I was very close with Fritz for things that
boys do. And I went skating with him.

Then one day, cossacks of the Russian
army invaded our province. The cossacks
were the elite of the Russian army. It was
1916 and the beginning of World War I. So
the major general of the Austrian army sent
a courier to my father to evacuate Rudki by
train and go to Hungary, with a platoon of
soldiers stationed on the outskirts of Rudki.

The platoon was under the command of my father, whenever he needed them because of insubordination by the gendarmes. At such times, he would send one of his assistants, the sergeant or corporal, who worked in my father's office, and who also served as my teachers, my private instructors. They taught me English. And that was important so that I could read the latest books and magazines my father purchased for me. They were written in English. I especially liked the ones about the Wild West. [Laughs.] The Indians, the buffalos, the cavalry. That's why I wanted to learn English.

The major general sent a train, a special train for us to go to Hungary. I remember one of the lieutenants packing our furniture and then putting our valuables on the train. The corporal and the sergeant who were in my father's office also went with us, and they took their motorcycle. [Laughs.] We were all in the last car. And when the train started to go, we saw from a distance the cossacks on their horses, galloping after the train and shooting. [Laughs.] But the conductor pushed it full throttle until we couldn't see them anymore.

We stayed in Hungary for about a year. My father became commandant of an ammunitions depot and had 250 soldiers assigned to him. Then, the Russian army, pressed on other fronts, were driven out of Austria by the Serbs, and we returned to Rudki. I remember the day we did. We found the building where we used to live, which was next to the governor's building where my father worked. It was destroyed. The entire building. My brother Fritz and I walked among the ruins. I was about sixteen. And I found torn pages of my Wild West magazines from the United States. I found Jack Carter and Sherlock Holmes books.

My father wanted to come to the United States because he had two older sisters living in New York. And then, he thought he'd be able to get a job and make a living. But he couldn't. He couldn't speak English. If you didn't know how to speak English, then you had to do menial work. So he wound up working in a factory. He came to America in 1919. I did not come with him. I came two years later. He stayed in New York with his older sister, who was my aunt Molly.

My brother remained in Romania because he was, he had a degree at the University of Bucharest. And my mother and both of my sisters went to Israel, immigrated to Israel, and they died there. I'm the only one remaining.

But I came to the United States before they went to Israel. I was in danger of being conscripted into the Romanian army. I was reaching the age of twenty, and they were drafting. So I just escaped to the United States. And my, I remember my mother running after, running after the bus when I was going to the boat—the *R-i-j-i-n-d-a-m* [*Ryndam*]. It was a Dutch ship. It was leaving from Rotterdam.

On the ship I used to jog a lot. I was handsome then. And I met these two girls, two sisters, and one of them had flashing eyes. She was about nineteen. The other was about seventeen. And I attached myself to them, and we became like family. Their mother used to fix my things when they were torn. They considered me like family. And then later, when we reached New York, we were supposed to go different places, males and females [laughs], because we had to be deloused for lice. We had to be scrubbed. [Laughs.] Showers under supervision, and so we separated. When we reunited, I kissed both of them good-bye, the two sisters, and their mother, and they left. We were supposed to be picked up by my father, but my father couldn't speak English, so my uncle came, my aunt Molly's husband. But the older one, Hilda, I think, wrote me letters for a whole year afterward. She and her sister went to Elizabeth, New Jersey, to their father. But my aunt Molly forbade me to answer the letters. She said, "You cannot become involved yet. You are too young." I felt very badly, but I had to agree, because even though I was twenty, I was like a kid. I'm still like a kid. [Laughs.]

My aunt Molly didn't have space for all of us. But she knew of a friend who had an extra room a block away. I was nearly twenty-one at the time. This friend was a bootlegger, and it was Prohibition. He gave me the room free of charge, with the proviso that he could store the cider that he made under my bed. [Laughs.]

Then, when the Romanian government, who participated in winning the war, joined the Allies and won the war, my father was entitled—as a commissioned officer—to get half pensions for life. So he came back in 1922 to Romania, after World War I, to get his half pension. And he remained there until he died in 1960.

I'm an American. I don't remember the languages. I don't know Polish. I don't know Romanian. I don't know German. I think in English. I dream in English. And that's why I didn't want to live with Aunt Molly, because with Aunt Molly I'd have to speak German.

Jack Weinstock

BORN JANUARY 18, 1914
EMIGRATED 1923, AGE 9
SHIP UNKNOWN

Now living in Rotterdam, New York, he came from Braunau Bemen,
Czechoslovakia, later to be Austria, then Germany, as a young boy.
Today he owns a house, two cars, has "a beautiful wife, three nice boys,
who all have terrific jobs. I am fortunate. America has been very good to me.
But you have to go after it to get it."

Well, it was during the time of the First World War. And, of course, after every war the victors get the spoils, and Czechoslovakia was broken up into Austria-Hungary, which later was absorbed by Germany.

I was born [in] Braunau Bemen. This is where my father's folks were, and my father's father was a butcher. He had his own meat-cutting place in Braunau.

My father was a tailor. And a very good tailor, if I may say so. He was a good-looking man. His hair never turned gray until the last year of his life. He would make suits for men. His customers were mainly in the city of Braunau because in Johannesburg the clothing was for farmers. Rough clothing. But every suit he made he made very meticulously, and it fit when he got through. He was a perfectionist. The type of man that wanted to be the boss. And if he said jump, you'd better jump, or else. [Laughs.] He was a good father, but very strict, very strict.

At one point he decided to move out of Braunau to a smaller town six miles away called Johannesburg—Austria, not Africa. It was a village of about 350 people three miles from the German border. We were Catholic. Most everyone was Catholic and very religious. People walked to church every Sunday. We lived in my aunt's house in the center of the village. And then, because of the war, we decided to come to America. My father's eldest brother came to America in 1915 on his own. He lived in Schenectady, New York. And eventually, he would send for one of the other siblings. My father had a family of nine brothers and sisters. So he contacted my father, "Why don't you come over for a visit?" My father's other brothers and sisters were already here. So in 1921 he decided to visit them, stay for a year and then come back. But that never happened. One year became two years and then he sent money for our passage to America, meaning my mother, my sister, my brother, and myself. I was the youngest.

I remember the day he left. I must have been about seven years old. It was sort of a sad day, and yet we were proud that he was able to go that far away. The way my uncles described it, America was a beautiful place. The streets virtually sparkled. Which they did, you know. They had the mica and everything in their crushed stone.

His first attempt at work here was with another tailor, but his brother convinced him otherwise. He was a butcher. He had his own market. His brother said, "Why don't you try that, Hugo? We'll find a little store and start your own meat market." Which he did. So he eventually had his own meat market. But he would never expand, like it's customary to do here, to a larger store. All he wanted was a small meat market, and that's what he had, a small one. My mother eventually worked there, too. In fact, I think she spent more time in that market than he did.

My mother meantime made a living by sewing. My father sent us money occasionally, which she used very carefully because it was at a minimum. So she did her sewing. And we managed. We had firewood from the forest, and we had berries and mushrooms and dried fruit, apples, and we picked cherries, which she canned. We didn't need a grocery store to speak of, except for the sugar and flour and some of the staple stuff. But the rest of the things we obtained ourselves. There was no suffering. I mean, we didn't know any different, so we didn't mind.

My father and mother had been writing letters back and forth. Then, one day, my father sent my mother a letter with money and said, "Sell the house, pack everything that you want, whatever you can get out, and come to America."

Well, we were exuberant because now we could see those streets in America. Everything was supposed to be beautiful in America. So my brother, sister, and I were very happy when we got that news.

So my mother sold the house. But whatever money she got from that she was not able to keep, because Austria at that time did not allow you to take money out of the country. We had just enough for the passage. My mother had a huge box made. I think it was about four-by-six-by-four, in which she packed our clothing, but mainly our featherbeds, because they were very important to my mother. She wanted things that were nice. Our clothing [was] in small suitcases.

We had quite a party when we left. We invited our friends, our neighbors, and, of course, my grandmother and grandfather on my mother's side. And we were allowed to have some strong drink. Schnapps [laughs] for a celebration. And I think that's the first time I ever got sick on alcohol. But it was also a time for sadness. My mother realized that she would never see her mother and father again. But the European trait is you go where your husband goes. So if he was going to America, that's where she went—with the family.

We took a train from Braunau to Prague. There, we had an examination. We were vaccinated. It was similar to the processing at Ellis Island.

When we got word that the boat was ready to sail, my mother went to settle the hotel bill, but she couldn't pay it. It was phenomenal. [Laughs.] So she went to the steamship company and stated her case. They said, "Not to worry, Mrs. Weinstock. We put you in here, we will take care of the bill." So from there they put us on the boat, in a small cabin, maybe ten-by-ten with two bunks, upper and lower, on either side, one for the girls and one for the boys, and that's all we had, just one bunk. There was no sink for washing. We had a common washroom at the end of the hall. We couldn't afford first class. But we had a main dining room on our deck [that] was terrific. The food was phenomenal. All the food you wanted to eat. This is where we were introduced to ice cream.

The first day was fine, but after we left the port, we were all sick for the rest of the trip. Eight days out of nine. It took nine days to go across the ocean. So here we had all this food, but we couldn't eat anything except oranges. It was tough for my mother being alone with three small children nine, eleven, and thirteen.

But on the way over we had to stop mid ocean. It was very foggy and, in fact, we were given lifejackets and told to go to our cabins and stay there unless you were told otherwise, because they anticipated possibly a wreck with another steamship. But that didn't happen.

It was still foggy when we got to New York Harbor, and I don't recall seeing the Statue of Liberty. At Ellis Island we were put into this large room with booths all around. And we were separated. The women on one side, the men on the other. It was an anxious moment for my brother and myself, my sister and mother, not being able to speak English, and they couldn't speak our language, German. So we were sort of up in the air. We were put into booths where various doctors examined you for disease. We felt like livestock. [Laughs.] They checked our lungs, our eyes, our throats, our entire body, because we were stripped naked. But we were fortunate. We passed fine and were reunited.

Word got to my father and his brother that the ship was supposed to come into port at a certain day, and it did not. So they were down there, I think two days, and it didn't show up, so they went back home. And when it did show up, there was no one there waiting for us. The mail was useless in terms of contacting my father because that would take a few days. And she had no money for the telephone. She wouldn't even know how to use a phone, much less know what the number was. So we waited, tagged with a card on our chest that said "Schenectady" and our names. And I remember my sister getting edgy. So to console her, my mother bought her a jar of hard candy and spent her last dime.

We didn't stay overnight. We left the same day. Someone directed us to a boat to New York. We were on our own. But at least we were put on land, solid land. I remember that. From New York we took a train to Schenectady. I don't know who paid for the tickets, because my mom was broke.

When we got to Schenectady, there was nobody waiting for us at the depot. So we got off the train and started walking and it was cold. It was October. And I was in short pants and we were carrying all this luggage. And then my mother heard a voice, "Fanny!" It was my uncle William. He was just coming from the beef house in his Ford truck. So he stopped, took us on board, and we went to his house. Again, we were lucky. [Laughs.] Otherwise we'd be stranded, probably still walking around in Schenectady.

Otto Preminger

BORN JULY 16, 1906
EMIGRATED 1935, AGE 29
PASSAGE ON THE *NORMANDY*

He abandoned a career as a lawyer to act and work in the Vienna theater and directed his first movie in 1931. He emigrated in 1935 to direct Libel *on Broadway, then moved to Hollywood, but quarreled with Darryl Zanuck, who prevented him from making movies. During World War II, with Zanuck away, he got to both act (playing Nazis, although he is Jewish) and direct, until he hit it big with* Laura *(1944). In the fifties, he became an independent producer/director, scoring considerable success with* Anatomy of a Murder *(1959) and* Exodus *(1960). Though most of his films were simply popular entertainment, two of them broke new ground:* The Moon Is Blue *(1953) for its use of what was then considered sexually explicit language ("virgin" and "pregnant"); and* The Man with the Golden Arm *(1957), the first movie to deal graphically with drug addiction. He died in 1986.*

I arrived here on the 21st of October 1935, and I came on a ship called the *Normandy* in the company of a theatrical producer who was very famous then, Gilbert Miller. He had asked me to direct a play called *Libel* on Broadway, after he heard I was coming here on a contract for Twentieth Century-Fox.

A man from Twentieth Century-Fox had come to Vienna. His name was Joseph M. Schenck. He was the chairman of the board, and he had heard about me at a very young age. I had made quite a career in Vienna. I had taken over the Viennese theater from Max Reinhardt when he retired in 1933. And that was a big thing because Max Reinhardt was the greatest Austrian theatrical director and producer of his time.

Mr. Schenck offered me a contract to go to Twentieth Century-Fox and I accepted it. I told him I needed six months to wind up my affairs in Vienna. And I was lucky enough in 1935 to come to this country. I had always dreamed about going to America since I was a little boy.

I arrived three years before the Nazis marched into Vienna. If they had found me I probably would have been killed or sent to a concentration camp like many of my friends. I still don't like to go to Vienna because there are too many sad memories.

I can also tell you an episode that will show you how coincidence takes part in our lives and in our futures. About a year or so before Mr. Schenck came, I got an offer from the State Theater in Vienna to become the head of the State Theater, and I accepted. A contract was to be prepared. I was only twenty-five or twenty-six years old. And the minister of Education invited me to his office. A huge office with beautiful antique furniture, and he was very polite. He said, "At last they are going to have a young man with new ideas at the head of the State Theater." And then he said, "Incidentally, I would feel very honored if you would permit me to be your sponsor when you convert to Catholicism."

And I looked at him. I am not religious, was not brought up religious. Still, without even thinking, I said, "But, your Excellency, I do not plan to convert to Catholicism." And he was very polite. He continued talking and I never heard of the contract again. Had I converted at that time to Catholicism, I would have still been in Vienna. I couldn't have left when Joseph Schenck made me the offer to go to Hollywood. I would have been there when Hitler arrived. And one thing about Hitler, a Jew, converted or not, remained a Jew. I probably would have met the same fate as all the other Jews.

So that incident changed my life.

. . .

I was born in Vienna. I went to school there. And my father was a very successful man. He was a prosecutor for the whole Austrian Empire. During the First World War, he went to the army and he was the prosecutor for the army in the most famous spy trials. After the First World War, he became a very successful lawyer. And by the fact that I was here, it was possible for me, in 1938 when the Nazis came, to help him. He came here on a visitor's visa with my mother, plus my brother, and his wife and child. They became citizens, thanks to the help of Tallulah Bankhead. She called me one day, she had heard my family had arrived. At the time there was a quota, an immigration quota, and the quota was filled. So she said, "I made a date with my father and my uncle for you in Washington tomorrow at eleven o'clock." Tallulah Bankhead's father and uncle were the Speaker of the House and a senator, respectively. I arrived there to find they brought a special bill before Congress for my parents and for my brother and his wife to become citizens. And they became citizens this way.

There is something very romantic about America when you grow up in Europe. You see, at that time the traffic between America and Europe was mostly one way. Only American tourists came to Vienna or to Austria or to Europe altogether because it was a very big thing for Europeans to make a trip to America. And I always wanted to see America. I read about it. I heard about it. I saw American films. And when I went to school I saw pictures of the tall buildings in New York. The highest building in Vienna was maybe eight floors.

There is no place I prefer to the United States. I go a lot to London and Paris. I might have been content with a summer house in the south of France, which is very pleasant. But, for living and being a citizen, I would not choose any other place. And the same thing is true about my children, I hope they will always be Americans and learn from me. They were born here. They should be proud . . .

I have never had any prejudices. On the contrary, I was a guest in the White House under every president except Eisenhower. There was Franklin D. Roosevelt, Truman. As a matter of fact about six or eight weeks after Nixon, for whom I did not vote and whom I didn't know, was inaugurated, I got a card that President and Mrs. Nixon request the presence of Mr. and Mrs. Preminger for dinner on such and such a day. And I called my wife and I said, "Somebody must be making a joke. Why should Nixon invite us to dinner?" And she said, "Are we going?" And I said, "Certainly, if the president of the United States invites us for dinner we are going." Besides, I said, I knew President Johnson very well, even when he was still a senator. I made a film in Washington and we saw each other quite often. It took him five years of being president until he invited us to a very dull state dinner for the prime minister of New Zealand. Here, Nixon invites us after six weeks, and she said, "Yes, but he is much more desperate for guests."

I was invited, as it turned out, because it was a birthday party for Duke Ellington, and he put us on the list. And I must say that Nixon in private life is a much different man. He is very easygoing, at least he was then, he probably isn't anymore—and charming. It was a very good party, one of the best parties I have seen at the White House.

Another time, I was in the White House with a play I had produced with Laurette Taylor. It was selected by Mrs. Roosevelt to be shown on Teddy Roosevelt's birthday in Washington. Afterwards, I was sitting at the table in the White House next to FDR. I was not even a citizen yet. I was not even in this country five years, but there I was sitting next to the president in the White House, which I think speaks for America, and how hospitable it is to immigrants.

Paula and Janice Kirschbaum
· · · · · · · · · · · · ·

BORN MAY 25, 1932 AND NOVEMBER 17, 1936
EMIGRATED 1939, AGES 7 AND 2
PASSAGE ON THE *BREMEN*

They came from Austria in 1939 with their mother and were detained at Ellis Island for ten days.

*P*AULA: My father was an electrical engineer. Dad was about six feet tall, originally from Bucharest. From Romania. He was a big man, and he had brown eyes and an increasing bald spot on the back of his head. It's strange. When we were young in Vienna, he was a very [she is moved] . . .

JANICE: Paula remembers him as a very gentle, loving man and after the experiences of the war he lost his family, he lost his friends. It took its toll on him. He was a sick man, physically and spiritually.

Financially, my father's family had some money, they even had a cook. My father used to love to tell the story of my mother's attempt at cooking. He liked dumplings. And he wanted to show her how to make them, so he took out a dinner napkin, quite large and and folded it and showed her how you make dumplings out of dough. Only she went into the kitchen and made a dumpling as big as the dinner napkin. [They laugh.] And he never let her live that down. I think the cook was kind of glad she didn't stay in the kitchen. So I guess you could say we lived a fairly comfortable life in Vienna.

PAULA: My father had a younger brother. He had come to the United States in the twenties. And my father could see what was coming in Europe and, being Jewish, he felt he had to leave. He left in 1938. That's all I remember. I think the idea was that he would send for my mother and the two of us. I don't know the circumstances. Eventually my mother said, "I think we'd better go." We were all with her parents at the time and I guess she got the necessary papers. I remember when it all came to an end; when the apartment in Vienna was broken up and the things were sent to storage in Switzerland. I remember the Nazis. They would say, "You can't take this. You can't take that," and inspected everything and then they sealed the trunks. I know other apartments in that building, people were selling things at auction. And we headed for Bremerhaven.

JANICE: It was a very difficult time for my mother. She was alone. My father was not there. She had two little children she was responsible for. By 1938, my father's grandparents had already gone back to Romania. I know it must have been very hard for my mother. She was very young. She was only twenty-nine.

PAULA: We took the car to Leipzig, the train station, and then we took the train to Bremen. My mother's brother went with us. I just remember at one point looking at my grandfather, my mother's father, and thinking, "I don't think I'll see him again." [She is moved.]

The Registry Room, or Great Hall, which had a daily capacity of 5,000 people, as seen here in 1903. The metal dividers were eliminated in 1911.

(NATIONAL PARK SERVICE: STATUE OF LIBERTY NATIONAL MONUMENT)

From Bremen, the boat went to Southampton, England and then the United States. We didn't travel first class, but we didn't travel steerage either. It must have been second class, or tourist class. We had a cabin. A tiny room. It had a cot, plus a top and bottom bunk. I think I was on the top.

I just remember we'd go on deck and every time we'd turn around there was somebody serving soup. The steward's soup and little sandwiches. All I remember is eating soup and sandwiches. [Laughs.]

When we were on the high seas Hitler had evidently marched into Poland. So this was September 1939. And when we approached New York Harbor, everybody went topside of course, and I just remember all of this anxiety because my mother was a German citizen. And the war had just broken out and she was considered an enemy alien, so they decided to detain her for what turned out to be ten days, until, my uncle—my father's brother—came to take us to his house in Leonia, New Jersey.

JANICE: Later, my mother said she never stopped crying. She said from the time the Coast Guard cutter came out to meet the ship and she was first interviewed by immigration officials until she finally got out of Ellis Island with my uncle, she said she never stopped crying. She said her face was as big as the moon and all red. She was scared to death that they were going to send us back.

PAULA: I remember the Great Hall. It was loaded with benches and, of course, you sat on the benches all day. There was really nothing else to do. You just sat on benches waiting for a number to be called. And they did have a playroom with toys that were old and shoddy, but it had an outdoor deck with views of the city and they would take small groups of children out for twenty minutes at a time, and I don't know why I thought of this, but it was almost as if they were guarding us from trying to escape from there.

Then at night they had dormitory rooms upstairs, and there were quite a few people in each room, and it had one bathroom, and we were in there. I can't stand the smell of Ivory Soap to this day. My mother always said that these people in the room with us never saw indoor plumbing so they shoved everything down the toilet, and the toilet overflowed and no one wanted to go into the bathroom. There was an inch of water on the floor. They locked the doors to the dormitory rooms at night with maybe ten people or fifteen adults plus children in each room. In the morning they'd open the door and yell in, "Time to get up," and you'd drag yourself down to eat something in the dining hall and then you went back to waiting. It was there I was first introduced to American bread and I hated it. [Laughs.] It had no resemblance to the rye bread we knew, and I remember a man sitting across from me at breakfast one morning, eating corn flakes, a new experience, and I was very suspicious. And he said, "Eat it. It's good for you."

I remember a group of people. Somebody said they were Gypsies. They were in one corner of the Great Hall, and it was a very large group, and the kids were always running around, and my sister spent most of the day sleeping because she didn't sleep at night. Janice was only two and a half. She had this doll clutched in her hand, and one day a little boy came and snatched it away and, of course, I was off and running and I caught up with him. He ran into this group. I grabbed it away from him and came back, and there was a woman sitting next to my mother, and she said, "Oh, you shouldn't have gone after him. You could have been hurt. They're Gypsies," and that was the extent of playing with other children.

One of the first impressions was going into a small room and having a man sit at a desk and scream at my mother, obviously in English. And she was crying and there was an interpreter and when he interpreted he was saying that my father was dead and my mother was lying. That she didn't come over here to join him. She came over here to spy for Germany, for Hitler, and, of course, that got me very, very upset. Later, she had to calm me down and told me father is alive. But they detained us for ten days as a result. In the meantime, my uncle visited us several times in the Great Hall and I think he talked to some people and got the thing cleared. And finally, yes, we were allowed to leave, to go to the United States. I think part of it was that we were going to Canada and we were not going to stay in this country, so they let us go.

We stayed at my uncle's house in Leonia, New Jersey for two, maybe three weeks. I don't know how my mother survived it. She was thrown into a house with her two children and my uncle's three children and my mother doesn't speak any English. On top of that, my uncle's wife was a divisive woman, who, if she saw any harmony at all, managed to destroy it. It was absolute chaos!

JANICE: My mother was never very willing to talk about any of this. All of this information we had to drag out of her and that's why a lot of the dates, I would ask her, "When did this happen?" and she wouldn't answer me, or she would talk about something else. It was a very painful period for her. I mean, she said good-bye to her parents and her sister, and I'm sure she had no idea if she would ever see them again.

PAULA: My uncle took us by train up to Boston. Then we got on an overnight ferry from Boston to Bar Harbour, Maine and then another one to Yarmouth, Nova Scotia. My uncle went all the way with us. The first words out of my mouth when I saw my father were, "Uncle Daddy!" He was a bit crushed. [They laugh.] We hadn't seen him for a long time. Then we went to a little town, where he lived, called Lunenburg and we stayed there for four years. It was a wonderful town to raise children.

JANICE: The people didn't care what religion you were. But you were supposed to follow something, and since the nearest temple was in Halifax, which was about seventy miles away, we obviously couldn't go to temple, so my father started sending us to the Anglican Sunday school there, more to fit in than because we were religious in any way. [They laugh.]

PAULA: We both wound up marrying Catholics, to add to the confusion. [She laughs.]

We picked up English at school and we'd come home and speak German to our mother. My mother would speak German to us.

We also had English lessons when we were in Vienna. I know my mother did, too. And I still have the book. It was *Grandpa and the Tiger.* [They laugh.] Someone used to come to the house. And I didn't pay too much attention of course. I must have been five or six. I wasn't that interested. And I don't really know how much my mother picked up. But she always learned her English from *True Romance* magazine up in Nova Scotia. [They laugh.]

Now you have to remember, the war had broken out. England was already at war with Germany. And, of course, here we were speaking German, and right away the kids at school got onto us. But just teasing. Not even nasty teasing. It wasn't that kind of town. The people there were very honest, salt-of-the-earth type.

JANICE: My mother said she knew a lot of widows there because the fishermen would go out to the Grand Banks and then they would hand fish from dories, and a lot of the dories never made it back to the mother ship, and a lot of men were lost at sea. And the reason that my father was working up there was, the way they dried the codfish was to lay it out on the docks, and Nova Scotia summers are notoriously uncertain. They can be very wet and foggy,

Serbian Gypsies having just arrived at Ellis Island, circa 1901.

(NATIONAL PARK SERVICE: STATUE OF LIBERTY NATIONAL MONUMENT)

and if that happened they would lose their entire catch. The fish would rot instead of dry, so they were trying to find a new way to dry the fish. And this was done in a factory, in this turbo-dryer that my father was plant engineer for.

PAULA: I think my father enjoyed the work. It was the uncertainty of what was going to happen after that job finished that ate at him. We moved down to Leonia, New Jersey in June 1943. My father went back to work for his brother until he died in 1952. After he died, my mother worked in a department store. Then she went to school,

became a beautician and wound up owning her own shop.

JANICE: She was very successful. Then when she couldn't do that anymore, she worked as a nurse's aide in a nursing home. And when she couldn't do that anymore, she worked in an office until she couldn't work anymore.

After the war was over she started taking trips to East Germany rather frequently. She'd go every two or three years. She would enter East Germany and each time she would ask them to put her visa on a separate piece of paper and not to stamp it

. . . .

into her passport because it was during the McCarthy era and she was afraid. This way she could just get rid of it and she would not have any vestige of having visited East Germany in her passport.

Mother died February 1988. But she was a very strong woman. She went through so much and she came through it. There was never a moment's hesitation. She always did what she had to do in the best way she could.

Part IV

. . . .

EASTERN EUROPE

The Bolshevik revolution of 1917 and the fall of the czar brought émigrés such as these Russian Cossacks to Ellis Island in 1919.

(NATIONAL PARK SERVICE: STATUE OF LIBERTY NATIONAL MONUMENT)

11

. . . .

Russia, Lithuania & the Ukraine

(APPROXIMATELY 750,000 IMMIGRANTS, 1892–1954)

Tessie Riegelman

. . . .

BORN DECEMBER 26, 1892
EMIGRATED 1905, AGE 12
SHIP UNKNOWN

*"I was born on the second candle," she said. "See, Hanukkah has eight candles.
I was born on the second . . ." in the village of Barafka, near Odessa. Later she
became a HIAS employee for seventeen years, several of them spent on site at
Ellis Island. Widowed after fifty-eight years of marriage to "a wonderful,
wonderful man," she has two children, two grandchildren, and two
great-grandchildren. Now 105 years old, she lives in northern New Jersey.
Though age has stolen much of her memory, she speaks with refreshing candor.*

My father, Max, was a scholar. He didn't do anything. He was tall, good-looking, scholarly, and observed his religion.

My grandmother had a store, and through that store we lived very nicely. I'll tell you, she was a very clever woman, very intellectual. People used to come to her for advice. Then she was bedridden, she was sick. She couldn't do anything. She lived with us. We all lived together. My four brothers and myself. I was the youngest. The only girl. I was spoiled. I was a spoiled brat. [Laughs.] I usually got what I wanted from my father. I was well attached to my father. My mother, too. We were an attached family. My father, in the house, he taught us how to read, how to write, you know, Jewish, Hebrew. There was no school.

My mother came from Constantine, in Russia, and her brothers were in the wine business. I don't know how my parents met. In those days, you know, it's arranged, especially with the Orthodox people. I assure you they didn't know each other before they were married.

My mother was lovely. She was kind of stout, and very devoted to all of us. She was a wonderful woman. She did the cooking. She used to make delicious fish, stews, and she used to bake . . .

We all came here together. At that time, the boys were growing up, and they were afraid of the army. We had some cousins here [in America], and they told us to come. Nobody thought about it, thought about America, until they started in about the army, and the possibility of being drafted.

We left from the port in Russia [does not remember the city]. [Coming to America] it was awful. The steerage. And, you know, crowded, immigrants. It took about four weeks. I don't remember getting sick. My mother didn't feel well. The boys made the best of it, my father. So we got here. A lot of people, the bunks. Didn't have nice beds . . .

When we got here everybody, you know, crowded up, that you couldn't see what's that. They would talk about the Statue of Liberty. We didn't know what it was. The statue, a big deal, you know. So what? . . .

. . . .

[At Ellis Island] they took us into a room. They examine us. Your eyes, especially, and they ask you questions. Have you had any disease? Were you sick? Were you this, were you that? If your answers are all right, they put you in another room until we were ready . . . Our cousins were there to accept us. My father's side. So we had no difficulty . . .

We came to their home, and stayed there for about a month. Then they helped get us an apartment. Ludlow and Delancey Street. New York, on the East Side. We stayed there for a number of years. Me and my brothers. We couldn't imagine that a place like this exists. The buildings at that time were different. They were high-rises. They were beautiful buildings, big office buildings.

My father got a job rolling cigars. He was a scholar and he didn't want to work, but he couldn't help it. He wasn't going to sit in the synagogue all day like he did in Europe, and my mother never worked . . .

How did I learn English? I went to school. The teacher knew I was an immigrant. She was very nice. And little by little I conquered it, like anybody else. All immigrants did the same thing. In those days, my God, immigrants were coming from all over. It was the height of immigration.

[Job with HIAS] I was ready for it. It was after World War I. I went to business school, and I learned, I became a stenographer. A typist. I knew somebody at HIAS, and they sent me in for an interview, and I got the job. Lovely people. And I stayed with them till the end of the First World War . . .

HIAS took care of all the Jewish immigrants, and we had an office in Manhattan. On East Broadway we had our building, the whole building. Our work was, the immigrants that came here, they didn't have anybody to take care of them, and the officials, some of them, wanted to send them back. Our work was to intervene and take the responsibility. So we used to take the immi-

grants to our building to shelter them and feed them, and try to locate jobs for them . . .

I was a stenographer at first. Then, in later years, I became a secretary. I had a nice boss. He liked me, I liked him, and he asked me if I would like a little change. Would I like to go to Ellis Island to work there for a while, see how I like it. So I said, "I'll try it." I went, and it was bedlam there. It was like a madhouse. But we had our office there, we had our manager there. And I saw that they really needed somebody there to help. We had to make out affidavits and type things and so on. So I stayed at Ellis Island a few years.

Immigrants used to come in crying and crying. My heart would break, and naturally you tried to do the best you could for them. Having been an immigrant, I knew what they're going through. I felt it. I was very considerate. I tried to be more considerate, and have sympathy, and tell them not to worry. The immigrants that came here, they all had their share of heartache. Some of them had trouble with their eyes, and inspectors wanted to send them back, and they did. That was sad, and that happened very often. There was always one or two that had glaucoma in their eyes, or some other kind of disease. They were put in different rooms . . .

There were a lot of organizations that had offices there. There was one, the Council of Jewish Women, that connected with us. A lot of the different countries had their offices there. At that time, HIAS had offices all over the United States, even in Japan . . .

I had to be on the boat by 8:30 A.M. It took about a half an hour to get over to the island. We used to say, "Good morning," to the Statue of Liberty. [Laughs.] We had a big staff. Every day we had immigrants coming in on different lines. We had to take their name, address, and what they could do. We were responsible for them. Then we had people from the HIAS take them there to [the main office on] East Broadway. My job was to register them, typing, make up their affidavits. There was a lot of affidavits. I was able to speak a little Yiddish at that time. I can't speak it now, and they had a cafeteria there for immigrants and the people who worked in the offices . . .

Then I got tired. I didn't like the idea of getting on the boat in the morning, coming back by boat in the evening. Hello, the Statue of Liberty, good-bye. So I told my boss I want to come back. He says, "All right, come right back." I worked for seventeen years.

My father stopped working when my mother took sick. They wanted to operate on her. She might have had cancer. But she absolutely refused to be operated. She was against it. My father wouldn't even consent. Neither would the children give consent. She was seventy-four when she passed away. Four years later, my father passed away. He was seventy-seven . . .

A couple of years ago, I come from Florida. I was in New York, and we went for an evening out for dinner on the boat, and saw the Statue of Liberty. All the years that I worked at Ellis Island, I saw the Statue of Liberty, and I got used to it, so it didn't mean anything. But let me tell you, I got such a feeling, such a kick, when I saw her right near me, because like my grandson at that time said, "Grandma, all your life you saw her." I said, "At the same time, when you see it right near you, you get such a kick, and such a feeling you have no idea."

Sonya Kevar

. . . .

BORN JANUARY 3, 1898
EMIGRATED FROM RUSSIA 1911, AGE 13
PASSAGE ON THE *LITHUANIA*

She was raised in the cold of Yasinoc, where her parents farmed and cut trees for lumber that was transported by river. She remembers seeing her father for the first time at Ellis Island. Widowed, she has three children, four grandchildren, five great-grandchildren, and lives in New York.

I grew up in Yasinoc. We had a farm. We had cattle. We had two horses. We had chickens, turkeys. Everything was nice. My mother used to sell butter and cheese and eggs. Everything we had was produced on the farm. I helped to take care of the cows when they were in the pasture. I really loved the life there. But, suddenly, my mother decided she didn't want to be a farm lady anymore. They talked it over, that he should go to America, and in 1906 he left for America, and he left us living in the city of Mglin. We lived there for five years, until we left to join my father.

We had to wait till my father sent us money to live on. I don't remember what he did [in America]. But every time he earned money he sent it. If he couldn't earn money, then we were out of luck. For food, potatoes was the main thing, and bread. We had vegetables, like borscht out of cabbage and borscht out of schav. We grew it on the farm, but in the city we had to buy it. Whatever my mother cooked was good to me. She made nice chicken broth and *timmus*. She was a good cook.

I was pretty, they told me. For five years I started to go to the village school, and I did pretty well. We learned writing and math and spelling, and they also took us to the Greek Orthodox church every morning to pray. I liked the way they prayed. I liked the Greek. I used to be able to read the Greek prayers, and now I forgot about it. My father could read and write well, but my mother not so.

After my father went to America in 1906, he was writing back to us and sending money. He wrote about the things he went through. Sometimes he has good times, other times he called it crisis. A crisis was he can't get a job and we can't have any money, and that's why he was sending us little bits of money. But when he got a job, and the crisis was over, he sent us more money. Then he saved up money for the tickets to get us over here. He wanted his family. It took five years for him to save up enough money to take us over.

My mother was happy about leaving Russia. She didn't like Russia. She didn't like all the happenings, the pogroms. I didn't live through the pogroms . . . I thought America would be wonderful. But when I came to America, I didn't like it. I wanted to go back and stay with my grandparents. My father was ready to send me back, but the war broke out. In 1913 the war started, so I couldn't go, then we forgot all about it . . .

I took my Russian books. My mother sold everything. She took some towels and sheets and tablecloths she made especially for the trip, but I don't have any of those. One of my sisters got it.

We left from the port of Lebow in Russia. We had to take a horse and wagon. A man drove us to Netchen and we took the railroad to Gomen, because we had to stop to examine our eyes before we got to the port. The doctor in Lebow found out that one of my brothers and I had something wrong with our eyes. Our eyes turned pinkish or reddish, and he said that's no good. The other two children were fine.

After a while my mother got disgusted and said, "Well, I'm going anyway. If they want to send you back, I'll take the two children to America, and you go back to your grandparents . . ." But they passed us. There was nothing wrong with our eyes.

We were on the boat for twenty-one days. It was the *Lithuania*. I didn't like it because we got seasick. We didn't enjoy it. We slept on bunks downstairs. We had to walk up steps to go to the first class of the boat. They were supposed to be the rich class. My father just sent us third-class tickets.

They had tables for eating, but we couldn't eat it because we kept throwing up. They didn't give us any medicine. They didn't even give us any eggs. Just some kind of meat and soups. I don't even know, because if I ate it, I threw up. It was my mother and the four of us. She was sick. But she didn't care. She just wanted to get to America.

We'd walk around on deck and try to see the waves, to look over the waves. I picked up my little sister. She wanted to see. I picked her up on the railing and then the boat turned and I almost lost her, and that was a terrible feeling. Thank God I held her tight, you know. [Laughs.] She's here. She's still here. Sometimes she tells me that she wishes I dropped her in. [Laughs.]

Before we got here, the boat stopped in England. Some people got off there, and some people got on. Apparently there was a leak. And everybody got excited and said that the boat is sinking. My mother got excited. She started to pray. I remember a sailor took a sheet, and stuffed it into the hole where the water was coming out, and the water stopped coming out, and I don't know what else they did to make the ship keep going for five more days because the boat was packed.

As a matter of fact, when they started out from the port in Lebow, after a few days another boat got stuck on a sandbar. So we had to pick up those passengers from the other boat. So we had a double load. It was really crowded.

We were at Ellis Island for three days before my father came. On the fourth day they called us, Max Kevar is here. My mother got happy, we all got happy. When he joined us, they looked us over again, checked to make sure he was our father. I couldn't recognize him. I kept looking at him and looking at him if this was . . . I eventually realized that it was . . . Five years had faded away, faded away. I couldn't imagine that, you know. He was dressed differently, too. He was dressed like an American. He wore regular shoes. In Russia, he always wore boots, seldom did he wear regular shoes, except to a party or to a wedding.

My mother was so happy to see him. She put her arms around him, and they were talking. My father was telling why he was late. But my mother did all the talking.

My father took us to the Bronx, 146th Street. The number of the house was 460 East 146th Street. It was a three-room apartment, well-furnished. One bedroom, a big kitchen, and a nice front room. That was the living room. We had gaslight, and we had a coal stove to cook on, and just gaslight. We didn't have a telephone. There were telephones, but we didn't have any.

The first thing I noticed that was different here was the air. I didn't like the smell of coal smoke. That was the one reason that I wanted to go back. The air was much fresher in Russia where I lived.

My father worked in a silk factory, but it wasn't well paid. He was looking for other work. Finally, he found a job at Borden's Milk Company, and he worked there for a long time until they found out he had high blood pressure, and they thought that he was too old, or too sick to work, and they fired him . . .

I was put into school immediately after we got here, and it was difficult. I didn't know what they were talking about. But, little by little, I got into it. Then when I got married, my children were going to school, and I used to help them. I was very good in math and spelling. Even English I was good. I was better than the American children.

My mother liked it better than being in Russia. She was happy to be in America. She had to do the cooking and the cleaning, and she had a newborn child. But she used to get help from her own children.

I also worked in the silk factory for a while, but then I got sick. Unfortunately, I got sick a lot. I had surgery on my neck, and I was unable to work and help for a long time. Then, shortly after I started work again, I met my husband and we got married. I was almost twenty-two, I think. My husband was born in Gomen, and he was also about the same age, and we had three wonderful children. I worked hard and sent my children to school. I wanted them to get a good education. My older daughter is here. Then I had a son, a genius. He was not quite nineteen years old when he graduated from college as a physicist, cum laude. Ten weeks later, he died in an automobile accident . . .

Jacob Lotsky

BORN SEPTEMBER 9, 1901
EMIGRATED FROM THE UKRAINE 1920, AGE 19
SHIP UNKNOWN

*"I was born in the small town of Ratne, near Lutsk, not far from Kovel,
which is in the Ukraine, but which is really near Brestlitovsk, an old Polish town
near the Polish border." He started out making twenty-five dollars a week in
a millinery in Chelsea, Massachusetts, and emerged from the depression with his
own trucking business that he ran until retirement. He married his first wife in
1923, and had a son and daughter. Widowed, he lives with his second
wife in North Miami Beach, Florida.*

It was a plain, ordinary town, little business stores, merchants. A lot of farms all around. There were no apartments, only small individual houses. Our house had three rooms, for my parents and my grandfather. I had three sisters and two brothers. Two sisters immigrated to the United States around 1912. I was a little kid. They were much older than me.

While I was growing up, it was at the time of the war, and my father worked for a rich farmer. The farmer was in charge. He had all the villages around for miles and miles, all around. It belonged to him, and the sharecroppers worked on the land. My father was the headman for this farmer. We called him a *poitz*. *Poitz* means he is the gentleman of all, a gentleman farmer. Then they made him the judge for the district, and what he said goes. My father worked for him. He took care of all his business, and he made a living.

When I was maybe fifteen or sixteen, we had a creamery. We had cows from this farmer, and we paid so much a year to rent the cows. We milked them, and made butter, cheese to sell. I took care of the farm and the creamery. I had two girls milking the cows, bringing in the milk. We had a little machine that divided the cream and the sour milk and we made butter, cheese. I lived a good life when I was a youngster.

I lived through Denikem Petruvla. Petruvla was the patriot of Ukraine. I saw killing. We were afraid for our lives. At that time, before the revolution, Germany was in the war with them, and after they left, the revolution started. My sisters send out papers to me that I should come to the United States, and tickets were on the way. The revolution started in Rovna, a town a little further away from us.

I was young. I wanted to do something. So I went to Rovna to enlist in the Red Army. I thought this was the only answer for Jews. Jews wouldn't be afraid of freedom, so I wanted to enlist in the army. I got a ride with somebody who was going there overnight by wagon.

I met one guy from my city. I knew him as a kid. I knew he was a crook, a gangster. He didn't care for nothing. I was from the better class. He had two guns on him. "It's freedom," he says. "You go in the store and take what you want. You could get all the women you want." I thought to myself, "If it's good for him, it won't be good for me."

So I turned back, and when I came to my mother, I say, "Good-bye, Mother. I'm going to America." I didn't have a penny to my name, and my mother couldn't give me a penny, either.

I was still waiting for my papers and tickets from my sisters, but I knew they were coming. I knew that. The revolution was already on. I figured I'll go to Warsaw. I'll go to the consul, and I'll ask him for the papers . . . But I didn't have no money to get to Warsaw. So I took down a wagon from the attic and I sold it, enough money to get me to Warsaw. I went out on the road and the Germans were evacuated. They were going home. I hitched a ride with them to Brestlitovsk, and I bought a ticket to Warsaw. When I came to Warsaw, I didn't have money, just a couple of rubles. I went in some hotel. There were a lot of people going to the United States.

They were running, and the Red Army was right in back of me, running. When I went to the consul to find out where my papers were, they said they haven't got it. I was stuck. I didn't have no money, no tickets, no papers. But they were evacuating the people from Warsaw, all the refugees in Russia to Danzig, Germany. So I went with them. I didn't need a ticket because the whole mob went and I went with them. I didn't have no luggage.

When we came to Danzig, what can I do? There was a man from the United States there, an agent. He came to help people come to the United States, and he was from the same city that my sister lived, Chelsea, near Boston. I told him the story where my sisters had lived there, and they shipped me the ticket, but it's lost on the way. And if he would give me a ticket and I'll pay him when I come to my sister. It so happened that my sister was married. She had a good married name, Ra-

banovich, and he knew them. He said, "Yes." But it took three or four weeks. We were there in barracks, all the refugees. And, by the way, I met my first wife there.

We waited for the steamship company. He told me, "When the ship comes, I'll give you the ticket and you'll go." My wife, she was a young girl and I was young, nineteen years old. She helped me out. We used to go out at night and she'd buy me a beer because I didn't have money. Same on the boat. I was strong, young. All the women were sick on the boat. We were traveling maybe three or four weeks. I was in a cabin, two or three to a cabin.

We went upstairs to the dining room. It was a place with long tables. It wasn't napkins and tablecloths. It was a long table, and they brought herring, potatoes, and there was a family there with kids, and the kids were so hungry, everybody was hungry. But the kids, they said to the mother, *"Momishu, hut, momishu."* *Momishu* is "Mama." They were grabbing the potatoes.

After suffering for three or four weeks, we came out on the deck and we saw tall buildings, the Statue of Liberty. At that time, somebody had to be responsible for you. My sister didn't know I was coming. If nobody's there, you had to have twenty-five dollars on you. I didn't have it.

So what happened was, there was this mother with a little girl, and I helped her out all the time. She says, "Yankel," — Yankel is my Yiddish name—"don't worry," she said. "As soon as my husband meets me, I'll get twenty-five dollars and I'll give to you."

I said, "Oh, you'll get all excited. You'll forget all about it." I was standing there worrying what to do. Then her name was called. Her husband was downstairs waiting for her. She gave me the twenty-five dollars.

How I came to Boston, I don't remember. I remember in New York I went in the underground train, and it was so light, I couldn't get over that. I was excited. But how I came to Boston I don't know. I imagine it was a representative from HIAS. I came to North Station. I went out in the street. They let me off.

Now, I can't speak English. I had to speak to find out how I was going to Chelsea. I went out, looked around, and I see the guy that sells papers, looks like a Jew. I went over to him and talked Yiddish. So he says, "You're going to Chelsea? Over there, the streetcar, you take."

So I went over to the conductor. I told him, "Chelsea Square. Chelsea, Chelsea." He says, "All right. Sit down." When we came into Chelsea Square, he says "Chelsea" to me, "move." I couldn't talk, and I couldn't understand. So I went off and I started walking. Broadway, the main street. I had the number and street where my sister lived. I knew it, but I didn't have it written down. How would you pronounce Jefferson Avenue? You would pronounce Jeffer-SON Street, right? So I said, "Jeffer-SON Street."

I asked some people and they just looked at me. They didn't know, they didn't understand. I went to another guy, until I found a guy that looked like a Jew. So he looks at me, "Jeffer-SON." He was an immigrant too, so he understood. He says in Yiddish, "Yes. I think it's way up in the hills." Chelsea had a big hill. I saw the street named Jefferson Avenue. I turned into the street and, my luck, 31 Jefferson Avenue—the "1" fell down. It was an older house, just the "3" on there. I said, "Well, it can't be 3. I need 31." Well, there was a little store there. I went in and I tell them, "Rabanovich." "Yeah," he says. "The third house." They knew the name, and they knew where.

Now my sister left me when I was a kid. She couldn't recognize me. I figured I'd surprise her. I'd tell her that I met her brother and I know about her brother and talked to him . . . I went in through the back entrance. It was a Friday night. My sister was cleaning the house and preparing for Shabbat. I knocked [on] the door, and she says, "Come in." I walk in. My mouth closed, and I couldn't talk, I was so excited. It maybe took five minutes. My sister looked at me, and I looked at her.

"Oh, Yankel!" she says.

. . .

To me, the United States was a golden medina. When I came to Chelsea, my second day, my sister took me to the library. It was a small library and Chelsea's a small town. I saw books, Jewish books, a whole shelf. I was so excited! All books, so much books, and all in Yiddish, because Yiddish books we couldn't have in Russia.

I remember I saw a policeman near the library, and I walked past him without being afraid. In Russia, when you saw police you were shivering, you were afraid they might find something on you. But over here, in Chelsea, I saw all this freedom. So naturally it was wonderful to live through. I started taking the streetcar to downtown Boston and getting acquainted. And we had, all immigrants, we had groups. We never went alone. It was a whole group. A Yiddish club, to discuss and read books. People got together, they played cards . . .

I stayed in Massachusetts until 1970, then I retired to Florida. I met my [second] wife here. I moved into a condo next door to her. She had her husband, I had my wife. My wife died first. Her husband died a year later. I needed a shoulder to cry on about my wife, so she had the shoulder for me, and after a while, we got married.

Betty Garoff

· · · · · · · · · · · ·

BORN DECEMBER 12, 1913
EMIGRATED FROM RUSSIA 1921, AGE 8
PASSAGE ON THE *CARMANIA*

*She came from Stansa Nigarela, a small village near Minsk, and grew up
during the turmoil of World War I. When she was eight years old, she saw her
father for the first time in the Great Hall at Ellis Island. She went on to marry a
doctor and "live a wonderful life." Widowed, she lives for the love of her
great-nieces and great-nephews, having never had children of her own.*

There were many farmhouses, but there was a railroad station within walking distance, and several of my uncles would give me money. We went to the railroad station to buy our candy and waved to the passengers. It was a happy moment because there were children around. I had grandparents, and we were warmly taken care of. I remember the house that we lived in. I remember during the wintertime we used to sleep on the side of the oven for warmth, and my grandparents used to do their baking in this big oven. It was a huge room. It was a large property. See, that was the style.

When I went back to Russia two years ago, and we were on the bus, I couldn't remember how the house looked. Now they were all painted green with the little flowers. I remarked to my roommate that it's quite possible that I lived in a similar house when I was in Russia as a child.

My father was a shoemaker. He was a craftsman. When we came to the United States I remember seeing the shoe forms, wooden shoe forms [molds], and he would make shoes for my mother. My father was in the garment trade here [U.S.]. Then he left that and went into business for himself and

he was a shoe repairman. My mother was a housewife . . .

My father left for America the year I was born to avoid going to the service. My mother was pregnant with me when he left. So he never saw me until I arrived at Ellis Island.

It was really rough on us. During the war years, to make a living, my mother illegally sold salt. I don't know where she got it. She had it under her clothes, and she would sell that to make the money, and that's how she supported us, my older brother and me. I remember my grandfather. He lived on the farm. My grandmother died during the influenza, and I don't remember her at all . . .

I must have been about four or five years old when the family became separated. The soldiers had come, and we were dispersed from the village entirely. Everyone went their own way. My brother and I were left behind. We got separated from my mother. Just Lou and I were together. Lou and I were very close. Lou was thirteen months older than me. We traveled during the night, and slept during the day hidden in barns, until a family who knew of my grandfather, they took in Lou and me as their grandchildren. They hid us. This particular gentile family took us in, and she really did save our lives.

When the soldiers came to look for us, we were hidden in a closet. She fed them [the soldiers] food and drinks until they were intoxicated.

They didn't find us, and they left. I can't remember how long we stayed. But it was after the war, and the village was taken back. Everyone started coming home, and then we found each other, and we were able to go home to our village. We went back to my grandfather's house. It was still there, and we were reunited with our mother.

In the meantime, mail was being sent back and forth to my father. He saved up enough money and he sent for us, and that took until 1921.

My father requested for us to come to the United States. It was time. The war was over, and he was lonely, and he wanted to bring the three of us. We got as far as Amsterdam. I remember my mother was constantly washing our hair for lice and keeping us clean. We were supposed to be leaving from there, but in the interim, my brother had an infected thumb from a nail and he couldn't pass the physical—we were deloused, examined—so we had to stay behind. He was hospitalized. I remember the hospital clearly. I remember it was a high building, and I was constantly running up and down the stairs, while my mother stayed with my brother Lou. And we had to wait until it healed.

We had a Russian visa. But it was for a particular date and particular ship. The infected finger delayed us, so we had to wait, and the earliest visa was through Poland. My mother applied for a Polish visa. She had relatives living in Warsaw. So we stayed with them in an apartment until we were permitted to travel.

This was the ghetto in Warsaw. I remember very well the gates. We had to stay inside. We couldn't leave after a certain hour. If we were outside of the gate and the gate was closed, we weren't permitted in.

So we always played near the gate so as to be within our living quarters.

When I made the trip to Russia two years ago, and one of our tour stops in Warsaw was the ghetto. [Pauses.] It was a terrible experience for me. I saw the marker, and a small square of grass. That was the reminder how that area was destroyed. [She is moved.] It really broke me up. Everything was destroyed, there was nothing left. I asked the guide who took us for this tour if they had any old pictures. I would have recognized it. He says, "Nothing." The entire city was destroyed. We saw a film, *The Destruction of Warsaw*. It was complete. I shudder when I think of how many people died . . .

The three of us were just looking forward to going to America to join our father. I don't know whether we stayed in Warsaw for weeks or months. I don't remember. But I think it was part of the summer because we didn't have any heavy clothes when we arrived in December of 1921 in the United States. My father immediately took us and bought us American clothes. He discarded all the European things that we brought with us. So we were gradually getting into the community.

We were in steerage, of course. It was just the three of us. My mother wouldn't leave us out of her sight. We were very close together, but there was nothing for us to do except childish things. Lou and I have always been very close. We slept in hammocks. Rows of hammocks. It wasn't private or luxurious. [Laughs.] Mostly we ate hard-boiled eggs, raw potatoes, and we got an occasional apple. I don't remember a dining room or anything. It was just a mass of people. And whatever you wore, and whatever you had, was with you. We didn't have any luggage or anything like that.

We arrived in cold, cold weather. But we were all elated. Seeing the Statue of Liberty. It was a thrilling moment to know that we arrived and would soon be on land. The trip was so long. The first time I saw the Lower East Side, immigrants were standing around metal drums, huge drums, and fire in it, and warming their hands, and I thought it was so dirty, so many people.

At Ellis Island I remember the huge room [where] we were sitting and waiting to be called. I remember a lot of activity going on. It was rushing, rushing. People were leaving. Some were staying behind. Everyone was eagerly awaiting the person who was going to meet them. It was emotional. I was bewildered. I never saw that many people after living in a little town, so it was exciting, when I think of it now.

The big moment, circa the late 1920s. In the Registry Room, or Great Hall, official interrogation of an alien that would determine his acceptance or rejection by the United States. The Immigration and Naturalization Service inspector (left) asked an average of thirty-two questions before passing judgment. The next stop was either the ferryboat to freedom, or detention and exclusion.

(NATIONAL PARK SERVICE: STATUE OF LIBERTY NATIONAL MONUMENT)

I could not speak a word of English. When I was registered in school, it was the registrar who gave me my American birth date, because we had no birth certificates. My mother guided us by holidays, and I was born six days before Hanukkah that year. We knew that Mama's birthday was the last day of Passover. That's the way we understood it.

The only thing I knew was that I was there alone, and that we would have to go back. Papa didn't come for us because we were the last ones left from our ship. Everyone else from our ship had gone. New passengers from new ships were coming in.

I was crying and I was telling my mother that I think we'll have to go back, Ma. Papa doesn't want us. We will have to return. They're not going to keep us here. Oh, I cried. I went to the lavatory and I was busy washing my handkerchief. At that moment, the name was called that my father was there for us.

Everybody became hysterical looking for me. Then we were called into another room. Again, we were questioned. I was thrilled. I was thrilled. This was the first time I saw my father. I couldn't take my eyes off him, because I knew that was my father. That was it. My mother said, "Stand up and show your father how tall you are." Well, I stood up. Lou didn't. He was very shy. Then a guard stood between us, so that we wouldn't give any signals. But my father saw how tall I was. It was a very special time. He was a very special man to me. My father was questioned, and then we were released, and we went to live with an aunt.

Like I said, he made us discard the clothes that we came in and he took me separately and he bought me an outfit for everything that was needed, and then he did the same for Lou, and he dressed my mother all in American clothes, and then he took us and registered us for school, the public school. He also got us an apartment, furnished. It was just a plain room. The toilet was outside. It was on a single floor. It was used by everyone.

I spoke Yiddish. [Laughs.] That was funny, because the teacher, I'm sure the teacher didn't know Yiddish, and the children helped. They asked me and I answered them until we were able to communicate. My aunt didn't speak much English either, so it was a little hard. But I fit right in. My mother went also to school. My mother really was amazing. She went to school, she learned English, she was able to write a letter. She read the newspaper. She got her own citizen papers. I admired her for that.

We lived on the Lower East Side a year and a half, and then my father went into business for himself in the Bronx: shoe repairing. He had a store with his brother, but then he went out for himself, and we moved to a much larger apartment. We had our own bathroom, we had a living room, a dining room. I remember a dining room, because that's where we ate when family got together. Then we moved to a much larger apartment, and I went to high school. I was married when I was twenty years old . . .

But it was my mama's letters that were most precious to me. After I got married I lived in Chicago, I lived in Massachusetts. I lived in many places. Lou lived in Florida. Mama used to write him letters in English. But her spelling was the way she said it. The only way you could have read her mail was reading it aloud.

It was hilarious. When we tried to spell the word it didn't make sense, but the phonetics were there. That was the beauty part of it. Me, I had help. I had teachers. I had friends who spoke English. My mother, she did it on her own. She was fabulous. Plus, she had two more children when she came to America. My sister Lillian. She's ten years younger than me. And Howard. He's fifteen years younger.

· · ·

My life turned out very well. My husband was a medical student. We did it the hard way, fifty-odd years ago. He went into the service. I followed him. He went overseas, I came home. He did his training, went out into private practice. We had a nice home. [She is moved.] He, too, died very young. We never had any children. [Pauses.]

But I enjoy my life, I do. It could have been worse. In many ways, it couldn't have been better. I have the love and respect of nieces, nephews. In fact, two of my nephews are married. So, you see, they are grown. They respect me, they love me, and I love them in return.

So the circle in a way is really full. Do I have regrets about coming to America? No! I would have been incinerated if I had stayed in the old country.

And I'm doing this [interview] for the next generation. For these young children who are growing up. I have twelve great-nieces and great-nephews. I'm sure that they will come to Ellis Island one day, and see our family name on the wall, and know what I have done today. They'll feel very proud. They'll know they had a good background, especially their great-grand-parents, both my mother and father.

Rita Seitzer

. . . .

BORN FEBRUARY 22, 1902
EMIGRATED FROM LITHUANIA 1921, AGE 19
SHIP UNKNOWN

She lived through the German occupation of Lithuania during World War I, having grown up in the Lithuania border town of Sveksna near Mamel, Germany. Her father died when she was not even ten. She emigrated with her mother and worked for her two brothers, who came to America several years before and started a factory in Harlem. Married in 1923, her husband is gone, but she has two daughters, four grandchildren and five great-grandchildren who "all turned out to be excellent, good people . . . If I had stayed in Lithuania, my life would have been entirely different. Maybe I wouldn't be alive now. I know my friends all got killed there by the Germans."

Sveksna was a very small town, and everybody knew one another, sort of like one family. We just grew up there. We didn't know any better. We had a school there. The school was a Russian school at that time. I don't know why, but that was a Russian school. My family had a

little business there. My father was always traveling, you know, bringing merchandise—piece goods, fabric, by the yard, he would sell.

I was the only girl. I had two brothers, and my two brothers had left for America. I was a youngster when they left. They were rabbinical [students]. They had no future in Lithuania, and they didn't want to go in the Russian army, so they skipped the border and they went to America. They were very young boys, eighteen, nineteen years old. Bennie and Max.

I lost my father as a very young girl. So I really hardly remember my father. He used to come home weekends. He was always traveling. I don't remember too much about my father. Who knew what sickness he had? There were very few doctors. Nobody knew anything. I don't know what he died of. I must have been about ten years old. I just remember him when he was very sick, just a few days before that I saw him. He was very much in pain, and it was very tragic. So I was left just with my mother. My brothers had gone to America.

My mother continued having that little store. She was the main business lady there. She was hardly ever home, you know. She was a good-natured person, a very good woman, a simple woman and she tried to help. I had a grandma living with us, my mother's mother, and she raised me. My mother and my grandma pampered me. I was spoiled. [Laughs.] I had all the privilege. There was nothing, nothing too much for me. Whatever my mother and grandmother could do, they did for me.

We had a nice little home. It was a wooden house, all on one floor. About four rooms, yes. It was a nice little house. We had a stove with wood, a wood stove, that would heat the house. We had to dry the wood first in order to make it burn. Light was by kerosene lamp. My grandmother did the cooking. Very simple food. It was meat, and a lot of potatoes so we could fill up. Potatoes was the main meal, and we had herring, a lot of soups. No vegetables. We didn't know of any vegetables. We had no garden. But my mother had a cow in the back for milk.

All the farmers used to come to the market on Thursday. And they'd bring their fruit, eggs, live chickens, and potatoes to sell for cash, then come into our store and buy our goods. A *schoctet* [rabbi] killed the chickens. My mother being a merchant, I think we fell in the better class of people.

I had a tutor who used to come and teach me German. German was a very important language there, because we were so connected with Germany. Everybody traveled to Germany, to Mamel, it's right on the border there. Most of them traveled there with a horse and buggy, and you showed your identification. For us, it was to get away. Germany had big stores and, you know, it was an enjoyment to be there.

Our little town was mostly Jewish. The Catholic Lithuanians lived on the outside of town. They were mostly farmers, and they used to come into town. We had a good relationship because the farmers bought from the merchants. There was no anti-Semitism. We only started feeling bad after the Germans came in 1914.

It was a bitter time in our lives, because we were afraid of the Germans. When they raided, everybody ran away from town, left everything, and we ran away outside on farms, and the Lithuanians accepted us. The Lithuanians kept us. We had some very good friends.

The Germans didn't bomb, but everybody was afraid of them, so most everybody ran away from town. When we got back weeks later, all the stores were opened and vandalized, including my mom's store. After we moved back, the Germans stayed quite a while there. We had soldiers living in our house. They occupied us and took over all the buildings, all the houses, and they stayed there.

We knew nothing of America growing up in Lithuania. We didn't know anything, because anybody that left from Lithuania in those years, nobody ever came back to tell us. But we thought it was wonderful. We knew it must be wonderful. Why else would everybody be going?

My brothers already came. My mother wanted to be with her boys. In those years, when you sent children to America, nobody ever saw them again. It was for life. Only through mail did you hear from your children, but some children forgot about their parents and never wrote. It was heartbreaking.

My mother sold the house and we bought the ship tickets. I remember being involved in getting the passports. It wasn't so easy to get. You had to travel to different towns. It took months and months to get with the stamps and with necessary papers.

We came with pillows and rolling pins and pots and pans and [laughs] it's a joke. When we came here, we never even used those. We had them in suitcases we bound with rope. I know we brought feathers, a lot of feathers.

We got as far as the German border with a horse and buggy, and we took the train to Hamburg. It was such an empty feeling to leave, you know. Everybody knew one another. It was, I remember, very sad. We came here July 21, 1921. It was very hot. It was just my mother and myself in a cabin. There was no delay, no medical exams in Hamburg. It wasn't a very big boat. It was all one class. It wasn't luxurious. I don't remember the name . . .

I remember Ellis Island. Coming to a strange, strange country, everybody's strange to you, even your own folks are strange when you come. I remember standing downstairs and looking up to the balcony. There were a lot of people standing and chewing. I was thinking to myself, "What is that? Is that a sickness here? They all keep chewing." Until I talked to my family later, they explained to me that this was chewing gum. Nobody's sick. [Laughs.]

They examined our eyes for trachoma, and if you had it, they would send you back.

That's the main thing they looked for is the eyes. They called us in a room and they checked our eyes. Everybody had to be checked . . .

We did not wait too long. We came in in the afternoon, and one of my brothers and my aunt, my father's sister, came to pick us up, and took us to my brother's apartment in Harlem, 117th Street between Fifth and Madison. It was a railroad apartment. You know, you come in, and everything is on one side of the house. And we stayed with him for a couple of years. He lived alone. He took the apartment before we came, so he could stay with us. I hate to say it, but that apartment was worse than what we had in our house in Lithuania. The neighborhood wasn't bad. Lots of immigrants, it was a Jewish neighborhood: 117th up till 125th. At that time, Harlem was a very populated, nice neighborhood.

My brothers were in business already. They had a factory. Two weeks later, I started there and worked with them. Just on the floor. I couldn't do anything. I didn't know how to sew, I didn't know how to do anything. In those years, there were so many immigrants that only the immigrants worked in the factories. It seemed to me they were all immigrants.

It took a little time to get used to it [America]. It took a little time to adjust myself. Many times I was lonesome. It felt lonesome; coming from a small town. I had a lot of friends in Lithuania. But I started night school to learn English. I came here in July and, of course, the school was closed during the summer. In the fall I started night school on 124th Street and Madison Avenue, not too far. I started to go to school every night. They were all Europeans, all foreigners, mostly adults. I went to work with my dictionary. During my lunch hour I used to sit and learn the words. I was determined to learn English. I met my husband in the factory. He was a worker there, and we married in 1923, maybe it was 1924. We had two daughters. He came from Poland. He came before I did, because he spoke English already.

My mother did not learn English. She never adjusted. She was an old-fashioned woman, and she never learned English. She just remained the same as she was. She practiced her religion. She just stayed with us and did the cooking. She never learned the language, so she just couldn't speak to anyone else but the family.

My mother felt badly when she came here. She was a very religious woman, and the boys did not observe the Jewish religion, and she saw they sort of changed. She wasn't happy about it, she couldn't help it,

but she made the best. It used to be she'd use two kinds of dishes. We were supposed to use kosher meat. We're not supposed to do anything on Saturday besides go to temple. She was very strict about these things.

It hurt her to see her children not to observe the old ways, but she never said anything. I know she was hurt, but she didn't try to change us. For instance, my brothers kept their business open on Saturdays, things like this. Maybe she realized that we were living in a different country, and we can't be the same as we were at home. But she wouldn't think about going back to Lithuania. No, no. Never. She had all her children here. America was now her home.

Sylvia Broter

. . . .

BORN AUGUST 14, 1911
EMIGRATED FROM RUSSIA 1922, AGE 10
SHIP UNKNOWN

She was born near the wheat fields of a tiny Russian farming village.
She was raised in Toledo, Ohio. Today, she lives in southern New Jersey.
"If you let everybody come into this country, you'd have too many people
coming in," she said. "People are sneaking across. They're risking
their lives to come here. It is wonderful."

My father came to this country in 1914 and, of course, he could speak no English at all. When he came to Ellis Island and he was asked what his name was, he did not know what the question was. Standing by another lady who had come with him on the ship, they said to her, "Is this your brother?" I guess he nodded, and they put "Brother." Eventually

the H was taken off and it was made into Broter. Then when he became a citizen he said he could have changed it back. "But," he said, "it's much easier to spell Broter than Zamarchovsky." That was my maiden name.

I was born August 14, 1911, possibly 1912 or even 1913. There were no birth certificates. However, my father had registered me in school as 1911.

When he was in Russia, my father worked for a wheat farmer as a bookkeeper. He was very educated in Hebrew and the Jewish religion. When he came here in 1914, he had been on the last ship coming to this country before communication was cut off. War was on, and the factories were booming. He got a job as a factory worker. And he made a good home for us, a two-family home that was in Toledo, Ohio.

When we arrived in 1922, however, he was a peddler, a horse-and-wagon peddler of clothing. He had gotten sick while he was working those years in the factory. TB was prevalent at that time, and although he was cured, he was much thinner and he was told not to work inside again. So when I came to this country he was peddling with a horse and wagon . . . All I can say is he was the most wonderful person in the world. He was a real saint, a real angel. Physically he was six feet. When he came to this country he said, "Six feet, two hundred pounds."

There had been a picture on our wall of him, and he had a beard. But when we received a picture in a letter after the war, he was bald and beardless, and thinner. Still, it was the most amazing, wonderful thing to know that I had a father who was in America and that he planned to take us out to this country.

. . .

In town, they were all Jews. Only the Christian people were living outside the town. They were in the country. We call that a *dorf*. Those were the farmer people. And I suppose that's one of the reasons why my father was working for a wheat farmer before he left.

I remember someone said, "Oh, my goodness, the soldiers are coming." They put me down in the cellar. It was completely black. I mean, I had no idea. I just know that the door was opened like a sewer thing, and I walked down, and I was scared. My mother said, "Don't be afraid, God is with you." And actually, even to this day, I don't have fear. I always feel that with God you don't have to be afraid . . .

My father came to America because of the pogroms, and, of course, the chance of coming to a land of liberty, and a chance to raise children in a good country, as my uncle had gone to America. My mother was very happy that he came to this country. At the time he left, there was no war yet. He planned on making a little money and bringing us out.

However, as I pieced things together later, some of the men never called for their families to come. After a while, they just forgot them. I was trying to figure out why my mother didn't mention more often about my dad being in America. So I figured maybe that was it. That, or perhaps you simply didn't tell the children many things that were going on. She sang me lovely lullabies, told me beautiful stories of the Bible, and so many of the truths that she said, I'm still quoting.

My father sent us letters, money. Once he sent us a letter with a picture of three men; two of them with whom he had stayed together in Toledo. It was very happy photo, a letter, and the attempt that he's going to make to get us out as soon as possible. I remember the excitement. I don't remember the letter. I remember the picture. I said [to my mother], "Which is my father?" Because to me they all looked pretty much alike. [Laughs.] At that time he was already bald-headed, thinner, and clean-shaven.

We could not get a visa in Russia even at that time. The only way to get out of eastern Europe was to go to Poland. So we sneaked across the border. I remember going on pebblestones, on a little stream of some kind, and then ending up in a house.

The next thing I knew, we were in Warsaw. A beautiful city. That was my first time in a big city, besides Kamenitz. My mother and I were the only two that left. I remember saying good-bye to my grandfather and to Aunt Freda. They hugged me, and kissed me, and said we should write.

We were nine months in Warsaw. Nine months waiting for the visa. We stayed with cousins. A lovely family there, a husband and wife, and a son and daughter. The Silvermans. Mr. Silverman had a boutique shop. He had all kinds of little dolls and lovely little Chinese things, little animals, bric-a-brac.

Everybody was poor, but nobody felt poverty. We were all the same. But there was no problem of money. I never felt hunger. I never felt I didn't have enough clothing. I never felt a lack. My dignity was there, just as with everybody else . . .

I couldn't read. My mother could read and write Yiddish, and that for women was something special. She could also read Hebrew. People used to come to my mother and ask to have her write a letter because they couldn't write . . .

The passport, the visa, was from Amsterdam, Holland. So we went from Poland to Holland, but I don't recall anything really until I was actually on the ship itself.

The boat. I remember the rocking. I remember we were in a cabin downstairs. There were two bunk beds for my mother and I to stay. As far as I know, she stayed the whole time in the cabin, but they used to go up and take a walk in the ship, see it rolling. I was the healthy one. I was the one who was able to give her things, you know. The boat was supposed to take two weeks, and instead it took three weeks because of a bad storm . . .

I remember this couple from Holland who were on our ship, and we were all standing in line to be examined by the doctor at Ellis Island. I remember how sorry I felt, their being so nice, when they looked at her thumb and it was black. The doctor consulted with somebody else and looked

again, and she was turned down. They had to go back. So both of them were taken out of the line to return home.

I remember it was a big, big room, lots of benches, a lot of people. As we were sitting there, they showed us a movie. It might have been Charlie Chaplin, a black-and-white movie, the first one I ever saw. That was really thrilling. And then somebody walked by, a black gentleman, and I had never seen a black person in my life. I didn't know what to think. Mother didn't know any more than I did, and I didn't ask too many questions. We just were doing our best. But we had problems because many people got off to go to New York.

We had to go on to Toledo, Ohio. There was not enough money for the train. There was supposed to have been a check sent to us for the train fare and it didn't come through. So a telegram was sent, and I remember Mother talking to somebody, and then we had to wait overnight. As far as I remember, we just stayed on the bench. We just slept on the bench. Nothing really bothered me, as long as Mother was with me, and it was an adventure. Nobody met us at Ellis Island. I just know my father met us in Toledo when we got off the train.

I was disappointed. I thought I was going to have a father with nice curly hair, a nice strong man, and here he was bald-headed and kind of stooped over, you know. He was a little disappointed, too, because my little sister wasn't with me, you know. But for my mother and father, it was a happy reunion. They kissed each other and I don't remember just how we got to the house, but it was a very lovely home. It was a nice section of the city then. He had bought a house. When he worked in the factory, he bought this two-family dwelling. We lived upstairs for a while. There were five rooms upstairs and six rooms downstairs, and the downstairs was rented. The backyard had two lovely rose bushes and a beautiful lilac bush. We had an apple tree and a walnut tree. When my sister was born—I have a sister born in this country—we moved downstairs, and then we rented the upstairs. There were two bedrooms. I had my own bedroom when we lived upstairs, and later downstairs I had my own bedroom, too. But when things became kind of bad . . . after 1929 the savings was all gone. Fortunately, FHA [Federal Housing Administration] let us keep the home, so we didn't lose the house, thank goodness. We had roomers. One bedroom was rented out, and my sister and I shared the living room.

We must have gotten here a month or two before Passover, because I was too late in the year for me to go to regular school. I didn't know a word of English. They had a special class for immigrants [after regular class]. There were, in fact, two little brothers, Chinese children, and myself. There were only the three of us. The rest of the class didn't bother much with us.

They'd give us little readings to learn the element of English, and also I would want to show off that I knew something, so I'd go to the blackboard and write down some of my math . . . But it was kind of a lost time in some ways, because they weren't doing that much for us, and it was okay, there was nothing else they could do.

They put me in the second grade, and you must realize, being ten, I was quite old. My clothes were rather old-fashioned. My dresses were a little too long, you know. So I had, for a long time, an inferiority complex. However, I studied hard, I had B's. I learned English as much as I could. I was a nice little rosy-cheeked child when I got here. Later, I became quite pale, and Mother took me to a Dr. Piliad. I don't know why I remember his name, a very nice doctor. In the 1920s, TB was a major problem, and he recommended that I go to a tuberculosis hospital out in the country. They took children from six to fourteen. If you had TB, you didn't go

there, because you could infect others, but if you were close to it, or if you were run down where you might get it, that's where you went.

And that's where I went for about fifteen months. When they told me I was well enough to go home, I wasn't happy. [Laughs.] We had all kinds of books to read. All the classics, *Five Little Peppers and How They Grew*, *The Secret Garden*, etc. We had three meals a day, balanced meals. On Wednesdays we had a movie. The Kiwanis Club came and showed us a movie in the school, black-and-white, of course. It was our treat. Also on Wednesday, for lunch we had ice cream.

I must have been there maybe six months or so when they started another program, and that was for posture. They had a lady, and she came to different schools. They would take pictures of you that came out black-and-white, silhouettes. And then your posture would be from A to D. None of the children were perfect. So if you were B, you were all right. I was a C. Then we were given exercises to take care of the posture. We also had to breathe in to a big glass bowl to see how much breath we could give, or the strength of our lungs. Sometime later, the same lady came back, the teacher came back, and again silhouettes were taken and I came out A. A lot of us came out A, but we knew how to stand up straight and take care of ourselves. So this was a big boost. Not only did it sort of assimilate me into American culture, but it gave me a great confidence.

We sang around the piano, all kinds of songs. The lady, Mother McLain, we called her—She was sixty, a heavy woman—she was just an angel. She would play backgammon with me, and sometimes I would beat her. I also made an extra grade. I made fourth and fifth grade in one year. So when I came back to my regular public school, I got right into the sixth grade. I was caught up.

But in high school I made a mistake by quitting school. A new store had opened in Toledo, a McCrory five-and-ten, and I got a summer job: ten dollars a week, forty-eight hours a week on my feet. When September came around, instead of going back to school I kept working for my folks, so I could help them out. Then, I spent about five years in night school to get my shorthand and typing. I got little jobs in offices. That's what I wanted to do—work in an office, but I got underpaid and overworked. I would give the two weeks' notice, and get my recommendation. I did not burn bridges. I always had a recommendation . . . I had a wonderful job at the Bender's corporation. I retired after twenty years. It has given me a wonderful hospitalization plan and prescription drugs . . . No question. It was a right decision of my father to come to this country and bring us out. Absolutely.

Esther Rosenbaum

· · · · · · · · · · · ·

BORN JULY 18, 1911
EMIGRATED FROM THE UKRAINE 1923, AGE 10
PASSAGE ON THE *BYRON*

She was born in Stancha Chesinifka, near Kiev, witnessed rape and plunder during the pogroms, and eventually settled with her family in the Bronx. Her husband of thirty-six years died in 1970. "I have two sons and five grandchildren," she said. "They all live here in New York. And I have seven nieces and nephews in Moscow, seventeen nieces and nephews in Israel, and six nieces and nephews in California."

*I*t was a small town with a railroad station. We were eight children, four boys and four girls. I wasn't the youngest. I had a younger brother. My parents had a grocery store next door to our apartment. They used to go shop in flea markets and stock the store.

The first bad experience was when we had to leave Chesinifka. I went to school and the older children went to school, too. Some of them worked. The oldest ones worked. But my brother Yasha was getting married, and my mother didn't want my Yasha to marry this woman. She was much older. There was no engagement. But my mother gave in and made a beautiful wedding for Yasha.

During the wedding someone came running in [with news] that a train of bandits came into town. The pogroms. I remember the pogroms like today, and I was so young. So what did my mother do? She made my sister-in-law take off her wedding dress, and she put on an old dress, and she hid them in a cellar because she was afraid they shouldn't seduce them, rape them. So she did, she sent them away. And the younger ones, we remained in the house. The pogroms did come in, a whole bunch of them. The minute they opened the door, "Where is the bride?" They heard it was a wedding. "We want the bride." My mother says, "We don't know where she is. She left. Go look for her." They got so angry they took a bunch of eggs, and they threw them at my mother's face. There were three musicians, and they took the musicians, we heard afterwards, and hung them. They took them to the train, and they hung them up on the train, the three musicians. I remember that. I can't remember what happened last week, but I remember that.

We had a horse and wagon. My mother put us all in the horse and wagon, covered us with straw, and went to our grandparents in Terlitza, about 200 miles away, a great distance at that time. I can't tell you how many hours it took us, but it was quite a ride there.

We came to our grandparents. It was an apartment, and we were a big family. We slept on the floor. My grandparents were delighted that we escaped injury. What happened? A week later we heard there was more bandits coming. I think they were all Polish bandits. They came into my grandparents' house. They looked and looked, and they saw a young woman, my aunt, in a bedroom, and I was in that bedroom, the next bed. I was sleeping with someone. I don't remember with whom. And they came in, six of them, six bandits came in. They walked into the room, and they started and chased out my uncle. They took my grandpa. They put him next to me. And they started to rape my aunt. I think she was about thirty years old. They were standing in line. I didn't know what was happening. I thought they were hitting her, because she was crying. I didn't know about rape. Anyway, six of them were raping her to death.

In the meantime, my mother heard they were raping my aunt, and she went for my sister Sophie, who was eighteen years old

and a beautiful young girl. And my mother cut Sophie's leg, made a rag from the blood, and put it between Sophie's legs with the blood so they wouldn't rape her. They got very angry. They threw a bunch of eggs at my sister, my mother. And they went out. They left. They didn't hurt anybody else.

So my mother again started to think, "What to do now?" She can't stay there anymore. So we got back into the horse-wagon, and rode to the border, the Russian border. We thought maybe somehow we'd be able to cross into Romania. We wanted to go to Bucharest in Romania. That was the nearest town from where we were. We had to pay someone, what you would call a contraband to take us across the border. We crossed, and we all landed on the Romanian side. I remember walking up to our knees in mud. I remember my father carrying my brother, he was five, six years old. Carried him on his back. We were put into a tiny room with about fifty people who had all paid this guy. Everybody paid this guy. And we were there overnight. Safe . . .

. . .

For two years, we lived in Bucharest until we got our visas [to America]. First my aunt and uncle, that was my father's sister and brother-in-law of my father's, sent one visa, first to my brother Max. He was fourteen years old or so, and my uncle wanted him to come first, he wanted him to work for him, see how it is. So my brother Max went to America first. My brother and sister, Yasha and Ludya, remained. They were already married. My sister and her husband went to Terlitza, the town where my grandparents lived. Yasha, his wife, and his two daughters, were in Moscow.

I came to America when I was ten years old. My uncle sent for us. We had the visas to go to America. My sister Tanya got sick with TB, so my mother had to stay behind to take care of her. Tanya eventually came, but we received a letter a couple of months later that Mother died in Bucharest.

We took a ship to America from the port in Constantinople. It was the Cunard Line, the ship *Byron*. I don't remember getting examined. There were five of us, including my father. The voyage was unbelievable. We traveled a whole month on this boat down in steerage, in the hold of the boat. It was awful. Everybody was stretched out. Everybody was sick, throwing up, stretched out on the deck, everybody. Nobody was able to eat. There was no food on the boat. We had three times a day sardines. When I came to this country, until a couple of years ago, I couldn't touch a sardine. We didn't think we'd be able to reach the United States. That's how bad it was.

My aunt and uncle met us at Ellis Island. My aunt, that's my father's sister and her husband. There we had to be examined. That I remember. We had to stay in line. I remember my aunt and uncle said, "My God, we've already been here about seven, eight hours. What's taking so long?"

Hundreds of people came in at the same time. Different ships came in at the same time, or earlier that morning. There was no help, there was no welfare. No one helped you here in America. This was 1923. You couldn't get help from anyone . . .

We went to my aunt and uncle's house in the Bronx. Eastern Avenue near 160th Street. I think we took the trolley. We stayed with my aunt and uncle for a couple of weeks, and then we got an apartment on the same block on Eastern Avenue.

I started school. My younger two brothers went to school with me. I had to be the homemaker, the house woman because my mother wasn't with us. I was the youngest, and my older two sisters had to go to work. I had to shop. I was the homemaker, the housekeeper. Don't forget, I was ten years old and I had to cook and clean for six

children plus Papa, seven. It was difficult, very difficult.

My uncle was in the banana business. So was my oldest brother Max, and my father. My father sold bananas at a little stand near a fruit store. That's how he made a living, so we couldn't go to high school and get much education. I finished elementary school and that's about it. My father was never able to buy me even a pair of new shoes . . .

When I was seventeen, eighteen, a woman came to see my father from the same town where my father came from. She came with her son. Her husband died or something, and someone suggested they get married. She was alone, Papa was alone, they should get married, and she was a nice woman. She was from Terlitza, right where my mother lived. She even knew my mother.

Papa and her got married, and I was delighted. I liked her. She took a burden off my hands. God, wow, it was a pleasure. I opened my eyes. I didn't have to do any work. He was happy with her, and I think they lived about ten years. Then Papa passed away, and she went to live with her son. We stayed in touch, and she died, too . . .

I had already gone to work at a factory where they manufacture embroidery. There was a friend of the family who came with us on the ship. And this friend, this man, had a factory, an embroidery factory in the Bronx. I only lived in the Bronx. I didn't live anywheres else. I came to the Bronx in 1923 and I lived there until my husband died in 1970.

The day I met my husband, I was taking a walk [with] a friend of mine. It was Fourth of July, and the two of us took a walk to Katonah Park, and there was my husband sitting there on the grass in the park with four more young men. His mother had died, he was sitting *shivah* for a week, and his brother and friends dragged him out of the house to cheer him up . . . His name was

Hymie. He was Polish, handsome, ambitious. He was in the plumbing business and later the real estate business. He did very well. We were married thirty-six years . . .

When Papa passed away I already had two little boys. Papa died at sixty-four in 1941. I loved my father very much, and he loved me, because I took care of him for many years, you know. And he was so happy the way I took care of the two little boys, so I was very close with Papa. When he passed away I was angry at the whole world. I don't know. Maybe because I wasn't close with Mama. I was ten years old when I left Mama. I don't remember. After his funeral, I felt, "If my papa can't come and have dinner here, have a cup of tea in my house, I don't want a kosher home." I started to take all the dishes and I mixed them all up, and I never kept a kosher home again. My husband didn't care. He wasn't that religious . . .

I've gone back to Russia five times. The first time I went back, it was in 1958 with my husband and he met my whole family there. They all came from Tashkent to greet us, with flowers, and they're all so happy. A reunion. But I didn't see my brother Yasha. So I started to cry, "Where is Yasha?" We parted in 1921. I hadn't seen him for thirty-seven years! "He's sick," someone said. "You'll see him . . ." That was on the way from the airport to the hotel. When we came to the hotel, my sister Ludja says, "Your brother is in jail. He was arrested and I don't think you'll be able to see him. But we can try . . ."

Yasha had worked in a store where they sell secondhand merchandise, and times were very bad. So what he did, about forty workers got together, and people would pay say five rubles for an item, and they would report three rubles and put two rubles in their pocket, and then all the guys would take their cut. But somebody squealed, probably a goy, because they were living it up. And the police came during the night, and arrested my brother, locked up the apartment, and kicked out my sister-in-law, who went to live with one of her two daughters in Moscow.

We always corresponded, and before he was arrested, I mean, he knew we were coming, and that I was trying to get permission to go and see Chesinifka, and the house where I was born. So he went to Chesinifka first. He told my sisters that he traveled by train to see the place where we lived. He didn't have a chance to write to us before we came. He said he couldn't find the house. He couldn't find anything. He wanted to save me the job to travel around to go see where we lived.

At the time, no one could see a prisoner held in Russia until the prisoner was sentenced—not even a mother, not a child. But we had hopes of speaking to a lawyer in Russia, and we spoke to a district attorney there. I started to cry and I begged him, "Please let me see him for five minutes . . ."

"I'm very sorry," he says. "No one can see him. Your family knows the rule, our Russian rules . . . You'll find out when he's sentenced. Maybe you'll come again. Anyway, he won't be in jail that long . . ."

"But we're going to go back to America soon . . ." and I cried my eyes out, my sister and I. Then he says to me, "I heard very bad rumors in your country that you hang colored people, you kill people." I said, "You just hear bad stories. We don't kill, we don't kill nobody." I didn't want him to ask me questions about America. I was interested to see my brother, and we walked out.

He was sentenced. My sister wrote to us, she didn't want to say Yasha was sentenced eight years, but she said, "The baby was eight years old yesterday." So we knew. Nineteen-fifty-eight, Russia was awful at that time.

Eight years later, I went back to Russia to see Yasha. My husband couldn't go away.

He was involved with things. So he says, "Take both your sisters, Sophie and Tanya, and go." Tanya had lost her husband, so she went. My sister Sophie had lost her husband and was never there before, so the three of us went to Russia.

Yasha met us at the airport. He came toward us. The first one he came to was me. He says in Yiddish, "*Oy,* my little sister." I said, "Yasha, I'm not anymore your little sister. I am a grandma, I am a Bubba."

He says, "In my eyes you're still my baby sister." And we both cried—cried like never before to see each other, and that he was released. It was a joy . . .

The last trip, 1993, my son and my granddaughter joined me to Russia. We had a wonderful time. And that was the last time. I'm not going there anymore, no more. I have my nieces and nephews in Moscow now, but they don't want to go to Israel. They want to come to America.

Isabel Belarsky

BORN JUNE 26, 1920
EMIGRATED FROM RUSSIA 1930, AGE 9
PASSAGE ON THE *AQUITANIA*

"Some people call me 'Belachka,'" she said. An only child, she spent her early childhood in Leningrad and Kreshopel in the Ukraine. Her father, Sidor Belarsky, was a famous Yiddish folksinger who sang in the opera houses of Leningrad, and later, in America, performed with several opera companies in Chicago, San Francisco, and Los Angeles. He opened the City Center in New York in 1944 with a performance in Tosca, *and later, sang with Arturo Toscanini and the NBC Symphony Orchestra in Beethoven's* Fidelio. *Now widowed, her life is devoted to keeping the memory of her father alive.*

In Leningrad it was an apartment house. They had six rooms. Each room had a family. One bathroom, but the bathroom wasn't a regular bathroom. It just had a bathtub, but we couldn't take baths because you had to get coal to heat it, and it was too expensive. So maybe once a month my father would stand in line, get some coal, heat up the water, and the three of us would take a bath. First I would go, then my mother and then my father, and they would carry me back to the room, to that one room.

I'm the only child so it was just Mama, Papa, and I. Papa was a student at the Leningrad Conservatory of Music. He was only twenty or twenty-one when I was born. His name at that time, it was Isidor Belarsky. Originally it was Isidor Livchitz. But he changed the name when I was born. I was named Isabel, or in Russian, the more endearing name, Belachka. So my father took the "Bela" in Belachka. Then, my mother's name was Clara, so my father made it "Belar." Then the "sky." Many Russian names

*Isabel Belarsky, shortly after arriving in America on
February 8, 1930. This picture was taken April 20,
1930, two months after her tenth birthday.*

(COURTESY OF ISABEL BELARSKY)

biggest room because I was the only child.
In the room was a baby grand piano, a little
bed for me, and a bed for my father's sister
who lived with us in that one room. Her
name was Eva. Eva Livchitz. She's in America now. She lives in San Jose, California.
She started to live with us when she was
about fourteen years old, because my
mother was very ill. My mother had a mis-
carriage in Kreshopel, and she had to be
taken out on a stretcher and stay in bed for
almost a year, so we needed someone to
take care of her and me.

So this aunt Eva came to stay with us to
take care of my mother and myself. We lived
in an apartment with six other families. We
were not related. Originally this was an

end with "sky." So it became "Isidor Belarsky." Then, after we came to America, to
simplify his name, and make it more of a
stage name, he changed Isidor to just Sidor.
Sidor Belarsky.

He was going to the conservatory for
about four years and he graduated the conservatory in Leningrad in 1929, just before
coming to America. He was in the opera
house and he was singing. He was a basso
cantato. My remembrance of the time,
maybe I was five years old, was of going to
hear all the operas in that big, beautiful
opera house—the Kirov—in Leningrad.

My mother had a lovely voice, but she
was a real mama. She took care of us. She
did the cooking. In Leningrad, we had the

*Nine-year-old Isabel Belarsky (left); her father,
Sidor Belarsky, who would become a famous opera
singer and composer and perform with Arturo
Toscanini; Isabel's mother, Clarunia (rear, left); and
Isabel's aunt Eva, in their Leningrad apartment,
November 1929.*

(COURTESY OF ISABEL BELARSKY)

apartment for one family. Then Mr. Stalin came into existence and he made everybody take a room. The original couple that were living there had their room. Their son-in-law and daughter lived in another room and then they rented out the other rooms. Each floor was like this. We were on the sixth floor. When this apartment was made into this community living they took off the front entrance where the elevator was so people had to walk up and they had to go through the kitchen into the apartment, and that's where the doorbell was.

Being an only child, I was spoiled by everybody and my parents were the only Jewish couple that lived there. And I used to run to each room because I could never be alone. I couldn't even sleep alone. I liked to be around people. One of the couples—her name was Pavla and his name was Ivan, and they had no children—and especially Pavla just adored me, but she was very religious. In those years, people still went to church. It wasn't completely prohibited. So she used to take me to church with her, and I would mimic her and go to all the ceremonies and Eastertime. The Russian Easter is called *Pasca*, and we used to color the eggs, and I would go at midnight with her, holding a little candle, because you had to look for Christ.

My mother was free about it, I mean, she didn't prohibit me from going. There was no temple in Leningrad anyway. My parents weren't fanatic, religious-type people. And I didn't know the difference until Pavla told me Easter morning when we were coloring the eggs. She would make a *babka*—an Easter cake—and put a little rose in the middle. She said, "Belachka, this is not your holiday. You're Jewish." I ran to my mother crying, "What does that mean?" But my mother was waiting for a time to explain it to me . . .

My father had a life of music and of students and they used to come to our one room, because he was the only one that was married with a child. So there was laughter,

Isabel Belarsky today

(COURTESY OF ISABEL BELARSKY)

and there was song, and the musicians would come. The only ones that complained was this Ivan. He complained about the electricity, because everybody paid a certain amount of money for the electricity.

Ivan used to come home from work and go to sleep and he didn't need the electricity and he would get drunk. He would get so drunk that Pavla and I would take off his boots in the kitchen and put him to bed. He would curse and he would yell at her that she had to, in the middle of the winter, run out and get him more liquor to drink. He used to cut the wire, because he didn't want to pay his share, so they were always fixing the wire. We were always in the dark.

. . .

My mother was from a town called Masckif-ska. She was an only child, too, and her father was in the same business as my grandpa. In fact, he was a competitor to my father's father and that's how they met. My grandfather, my mother's father, used to travel to Berlin, and he brought her a little fur coat and a piano. This was unheard of in those years to have a piano. When they were old enough, both my father and my mother were sent to Odessa to go to school, to *gymnasia,* which is like a high school, but it's a higher level high school than high school here. It was almost a college level. And that's where they actually met, my mother and father. My mother was educated. She was older than my father. Four years older.

When they met, my father was probably eighteen years old. My mother was twenty-two, an only child, beautiful and wealthy. But it was bad times. My father was arrested. All young men, especially Jews, were sent to the army. At that time, to be sent to the army was forever. This was at the start of World War I. And my mother was very much in love with him. They weren't married yet, but she went to the commissar to plead for his release. She was very beautiful, and this commissar, he liked the way she looked, and he said he will do it if she goes to bed with him, and she did.

You can imagine in a small town an only child to do this to save her boyfriend. He was more than a boyfriend. I mean, "boyfriend" sounds so flat. It's almost like a story from the classics. And he was released.

When my grandfather, my father's father, and the family found out that she gave life, she was adored by them all. This is something they never told me. I found out from Aunt Eva who came to America and she told me they all knew but they never told me. My father used to say, "Mama saved my life." My mother used to say she begged this man, she was kissing his boots . . . A child never realizes that parents could be in this position. So it never dawned upon me how she saved his life . . .

My parents were married in 1919. They were married in the woods actually because it was during the pogroms. And when my mother saved my father, my grandfather was modern enough, sophisticated enough, to say to his only son, "Isa, you have to marry Clarunia, otherwise she's lost." They got a rabbi, and the parents married off these two young people. My father couldn't have been more than nineteen and my mother, let's say she was twenty-three.

I was born in June of 1920 during the real pogroms. It was summer, so we were in Kreshopel at my grandparents'. And at that time, they had these *petruloffs*, a certain clan that would come through the town and burn the homes, and the Jewish people used to hide in the cellars. The cellars were equipped. They were deep enough, cold enough, they could bring food in there and save their lives. My grandparents on my mother's side were not saved. They were hiding and they were burned during one of these pogroms. I never knew them.

So during the middle of the night, my father's father had influence with the railroad people because he dealt with them and he was able to get us on a train to Odessa and that's why I was born in Odessa Hospital and my father brought my mother there. In that same hospital, Sholem Aleichem's grandson was born. His granddaughter is Bel Kaufman, who wrote *Up the Down Staircase,* about being a schoolteacher. Well, Sheldon, her brother was being born, and, when the nurse came to my mother, she said, "In the other room, Sholem Aleichem's grandson was born." That was a great event because Sholem Aleichem was the greatest Yiddish writer . . .

My memories of Kreshopel are vast, because they were merry times, good times, and the same way in Leningrad because [of] being an only child with so many families. I ate in everybody's room and I ran to everybody and then the experience of going to church, seeing Russian weddings, the Greek Orthodox, which is very festive, very grand, with the crowns, and the brides. My parents didn't feel that they kept me away just because we were Jewish. After I learned we were Jewish, it made very little difference. At Christmastime, one of the people would have a Christmas tree and I would go to sleep early the night before, because they would say Santa Claus is coming and I would get all kinds of gifts . . . I had the best of both worlds, you know. I had the Passover goodies and I had the Russian Easter goodies . . .

When my father was graduating in 1929, he had an uncle, my grandfather's brother, who lived in America. He was involved in the turkey business in Utah, and there was a commission made at that time in America to come to Russia to see a certain section, Birobidzhan. They thought they could bring poor American Jews to Birobidzhan as a resettlement. The commission was made up of, among others, this Benjamin Brown and Professor Harris of Brigham Young University, who were professors of agriculture. Benjamin Brown also came to see his brother Moishe Livchitz, so his original name was Benjamin Livchitz. He got the name Benjamin Brown because he came to America, maybe 1905, when he was a young boy, and he worked for a store and the store's name was Brown, so they used to say, "Here comes the Brown boy."

It was during summer, and Benjamin Brown came to see my grandfather, and we were all there. The whole clan. Brown brought along Professor Harris and we, as children, were so excited. We were running after these two Americans, and then they went back to Moscow, and my father went back. He was singing in the Moscow Opera and this [Professor] Harris, Franklin Harris,

heard him in the Moscow Opera, and liked what he heard. So it was a combination: Benjamin Brown had the money to bring us over, but Harris had the possibility of bringing him to teach at Brigham Young University.

It took almost a year to arrange. Harris went to the Russian government office and got us a six-month visa for us to come to America. Somehow or other, they allowed my mother and I to come along, which was rare. There was no immigration from Russia in 1930.

Before leaving Kreshopel, I remember staying up all night because the last time we took the train—two years before—the train derailed. I was seven years old, and we were heading back to Leningrad from Kreshopel, where we had spent the summer at my grandfather's house. The train was to leave at 2:00 A.M. to Leningrad, and they woke me up, and it was cold. My teeth used to chatter and the train stopped for two minutes because it wasn't a regular stop but my grandfather had influence, so the train stopped for us. We loaded the train with all these packages, these crated things of food . . . And then on to Leningrad, but the train derailed. There were 200 people killed. By miracle, only two cars remained unaffected, and we were in one of those two cars. It was September. It was late at night in the woods and cold. It gets terribly cold in the woods in September, and they made a bonfire from the remains of the train.

I slept in a compartment from one of the derailed cars. No lights. Nobody had any matches, the yelling and the screaming is still in my ears. My mother lost her voice for about a month. My father was injured slightly. We stayed in the woods the whole night until another train, a train full of cattle, brought us to the next town where they had doctors and nurses take care of the survivors.

This time, thankfully, we got the train to Leningrad without incident. It was a very emotional experience in Kreshopel in September 1929 before we left. Everybody came to see us, because they all realized that it was the last time they would ever see us again. And they never did. We stayed in Leningrad for three months waiting for the visa to America. The visa finally arrived in November 1929. All of my father's students and friends from Leningrad Conservatory came to see us off. They called my father "Isa," and their last words to him were, "Isa, take us out. Save us. Take us out of Russia . . ." And we went from Leningrad to Warsaw by train.

I remember in Berlin at the end of 1929, already there was a feeling the Jews were hated. I felt it. In fact, in Warsaw we were strip-searched before continuing our trip to Berlin and then Paris. For instance, my mother had a Persian coat. They stripped it to look for something. People were looking for diamonds, money, whatever. We had nothing. The only thing we had, my father had, was ten American dollars that Benjamin Brown sent us. That's all we were allowed to bring. That and a samovar. A brass samovar. Because Benjamin Brown said the only thing we should bring is a samovar. We went through customs in Warsaw and they said the samovar had to be crated. My father paid the ten dollars he had to crate the samovar, so we were without money now. Except my father stashed two dollar bills in my shoe, and when we were searched, in the nude, stripped, they didn't see those two dollars. When we arrived in Berlin, if Papa would stop and ask somebody for information, the Germans didn't want to have anything to do with us because we were Russian Jews. Luckily, my father knew of this pension [boardinghouse] in Berlin, so when we got off the train we took a taxi and told them to drive us to that pension and he figured that the people there would know him and they would pay for the taxi. When we arrived there, it was different people, but they paid for the taxi

and he sent a telegram to New York to Benjamin Brown to send money to us.

. . .

After we received the money, and after spending a week in Berlin, we took a train to Paris. We had some relatives there. My father, meantime, was hiding from the police, in that police shouldn't stop us, because there we had no passport, to stay in Paris. But how can you miss Paris? It's once in a lifetime. So we stayed nearly a month, and every night we were terribly frightened that somebody would ask for our passports. The three of us couldn't be one family. So I stayed with one family, with this Lucille Feldmann who I'm still friends with, and my parents stayed in the room with other relatives, poor people, but they gave whatever they could. We stayed that way in Paris until the boat left from Cherbourg, on the *Aquitania*, a beautiful ship. We were second class.

We had a cabin, and it was February, and it was cold. Most of the people on this ship stayed in their cabin the whole time because it was stormy. I don't think my mother was sick much, but my father and I were out a little bit. During the trip my father sang "Ramona." Do you know that song? [Begins to sing.] He sang it in Russian, and he even got a little prize in the big salon, and he was very popular after that.

I remember eating on the boat, and, especially, eating a banana. I didn't know what to do with this banana, never saw one before. But on the boat we met a man, an American Jew named Seltzer, who traveled often. He was in the costume jewelry business. He used to go to Japan and Europe to buy pearls, and he was coming back, and he befriended us. He taught us how to eat certain things. He was with us all the time until we arrived in New York on the Fourteenth Street Pier.

It was the morning of February 8, 1930, and this Mr. Seltzer says, "I'll go out and look for Benjamin Brown," because Brown had to have a bond to get us out, "and you stay where you are." We did, until there were only three people left on the *Aquitania*. And nobody to speak Russian. Talk about nervous! And we're sitting in the lounge, and nobody shows up. Finally, two o'clock in the morning, this Seltzer shows up with another man with this tall tale of his experience. He left the ship, and he was looking under the B's for Benjamin Brown, no Benjamin Brown. He had the telephone number of Benjamin Brown's business office in New York. He called up the office. "He's in Los Angeles marrying off his daughter . . ."

So they had to reach a certain Abe Shein in Peekskill, New York, and it was too late to reach him. The next day they brought us to Ellis Island, and it was frightening because it was February, wintertime, and the winds and the snow. In 1930 there were no immigrants. It was a criminal element who were detained there. My parents were beside themselves going through these halls. They had to go to court, to a judge and we were sitting there for hours. When it came time for us—court closed, four o'clock, and we stayed overnight. The sleeping arrangements were about forty beds in one room, without sheets or anything for women. Everytime we went any place we were counted back and forth. During the day they gave us ten minutes outside to get fresh air and then we were counted again. The eating, in their mess hall, was a big bowl of soup. To kill time in that big room, the men, who were being detained, did arts and crafts or playing cards. There was nobody to talk to. No children and no body of immigrants. We were the only ones. My father was cursing, yelling in Russian and carrying this crated samovar, which I still have in my living room. It's my treasure.

Finally, Abraham Shein from Peekskill came to Ellis Island with the money. I think a $500 bond. The judge didn't speak Russian but he knew German. He understood a little German. Yiddish sounds a little German. I remember the key question distinctly. The key question was, "If you have a chance to remain in America, would you?" My father made sure to say, "No," because we had to be back. We only had a six-month visa where he had to report to Brigham Young University, and so when we arrived back to Fourteenth Street Pier with this Abe Shein, we stayed the first night in the Union Square Hotel near Klein's department store.

I was thrilled to have the room in the Union Square Hotel because we had a private bath. We slept there that night until we got a room on Tenth Street and Second Avenue with a family. Then we lived in a bungalow colony in Peekskill with this Abe Shein until my father went to Utah. He was teaching at Brigham Young University in Provo, but only the summer session. We joined him. They extended the visa six months and then we had to go back to Russia. But my father knew somebody in Washington, D.C. from the Immigration Department and my father sang on the telephone to this person who gave permission for another six months; just by singing on the telephone. My father didn't even have to go there. So it was a year and a half we were here now, and then we had to go back again.

Now you have to understand, we're Jewish, Russian Jews, and we're dealing with Utah Mormons. They never saw a Russian Jew in their lives. But they were just wonderful beyond means, and somehow we managed to stay. In fact, some fifty years later they gave me a reception there at Brigham Young University and I've remained in touch with them to this day . . .

In 1932 we moved to Los Angeles and there I went to school four years until 1936. My father was teaching summertime in Utah, and the rest of the time singing as a soloist with the Los Angeles Symphony Orchestra under the direction of Artur Rodzinski. It was Rodzinski who changed my father's first name from Isidor to Sidor.

My parents loved it here. They never wanted to go back. In fact, they became almost anti-Russian. My father never saw his parents again. He died in 1975. The last fifteen years, I'm keeping his memory alive by reissuing some concert cassettes because I own the rights. I also have a scholarship, the Sidor Belarsky Scholarship, at the Elaine Kaufman Cultural Center in New York near Lincoln Center. He made about twenty-two albums of Yiddish folk songs and he is the most well known Yiddish folksinger in America.

12

· · · · · · · · · · ·

Greece

(APPROXIMATELY 518,000 IMMIGRANTS, 1892–1954)

Greek soldier, October 1911

(NATIONAL PARK SERVICE: STATUE OF LIBERTY NATIONAL MONUMENT)

• • • • • • • • •

Theodore Spako

BORN AUGUST 22, 1895
EMIGRATED 1911, AGE 16
PASSAGE ON THE *PATRIS*

*He came to America from a small Greek fishing village with twenty-five dollars
in his pocket. He settled in New Jersey. He started out shining shoes, and
became a salesman in the wholesale meat and coffee business. Now 102 years
old, he lives with his wife of seventy-one years in upstate New York.
They have two daughters, four grandchildren, and religious faith.
"Even now," he says, "I never miss a Sunday."*

The village I was born was Afede. I was raised in Volos. From Volos, I come to United States. Volos was fishing village. Boats coming in and out. Fishing boats. They had good schools, outstanding churches. Greek Orthodox churches. The ocean liners didn't go there, because the water not so deep.

My father didn't say to go to America or not go to America. He didn't say a word. He figured out that I make up my own mind. Although I was sixteen years old, I make up my own mind. My mother said, "Don't go, don't go. I already lost one son, I don't want to lose the other one."

We went to Pireaus, a port near Athens, and then we got the boat. We showed the papers and everything else, and we stayed, my father and I, three nights. And when the ocean liner come in, we were notified that the passengers are going on board. So my father and I, we walk, and we go in a rowboat because the ocean liner wouldn't get to the pier. And we get on the ocean liner. My father and I, we get up on the deck. Then my father, for the first time, expressed his opinion, how he felt. We shake hands, and he say, "Theo, I never say to you go or not go. I'm very proud that you make up your own mind to go to America. I know you're going to have a better life in America than we have here." Because there my father was a hardworking man, working day and night. He was in the fish business, in fishing boats with the nets. And then I left, and he was crying. He was crying. And you know how I felt when I left my home, my father and my mother? Terrible, terrible. That's how I felt. I was the first in my family to come to the United States.

I was third class, seventy-five dollars for the ticket. There was three in the cabin. I was on the bottom, a man named Gus on the top bunk and his father on top of me. I remember when they had soup all the floor was wet. I used to get on line and bring for Gus and his father. The father was too old. Gus was too fat. I'd tell the chef, "For three." Otherwise, to eat, men came around with a big basket on their back—fruit, bread. You stick hand in, you take. But the man was checking. So this Gus was a heavy eater. Eating, eating, eating. And he kept sticking his hand in there, and the man say, "Next time you put your hand in there you'll have scratches all over it." Gus didn't touch it no more.

We landed in New York after twenty-two days at sea. I remember we see Statue of Liberty. Gus ask me, "What's the statue?" And then we're looking at the statue, and his father say, "That's Christopher Columbus." And I put my two cents out. I say, "Listen, this don't look like Christopher Columbus. That's a lady there."

Everybody was hungry, and they started examinations on Ellis Island. I had twenty-five dollars in my pocket. I knew to bring money, otherwise they keep you there. They wouldn't let you go to shore without money. Because if you were hungry, you might steal. And I was alongside Gus, and I noticed he had a chalk mark on his back. I couldn't reach or see my back, so I asked him, "Do I have a chalk mark on the back?" So he looked, he say, "No." I say, "You've got one. Your father, too." And I'm thinking, either they go back to Greece or I go back to Greece. So what happened, the one with the chalk mark went back to Greece. Gus and his father had to go back. I don't know why.

I just thank God. To this day I pray, dear Lord, and thank God, that I was admitted to the United States, that they didn't put a chalk mark on my back.

James Karavolas

· · · · · · · · · · · ·

BORN MARCH 30, 1909
EMIGRATED 1915, AGE 6
SHIP UNKNOWN

His family of six escaped Turkish bombs and Turkish occupation immigrating to America in 1915. He started delivering newspapers. He ended up becoming a furrier. He has been married for fifty-four years to his Hungarian wife, Marsha, whom he met at a YMCA dance in Manhattan. They reside on Long Island. "The United States is God's country," he said.

I remember just faintly. I was five years old. The Turks captured the Greek ground, you understand. And I was born between there. But there was no birth certificates because there's war. It was during the clash between Turkey and Greece. And when the Turks were coming nearer to capture, I heard the airplanes and then the sound of whistling, horrible whistling. Boom! We ran for shelter in the basement. It was terrible. They were bombing in the backyards, big holes. It was amazing. Three, four, six big holes, you could put a car in.

And after they bombed the whole place, my father took me to the main street, and all the people that got killed, their bodies were piled up on the sidewalk. It was horrible. Blood all over. So my father says, "Well, there's no use staying here." And that was the opportunity to get the heck out. He had some money. He was a merchant man. He sold handkerchiefs, small things, buy and sell. If he didn't have no money, I wouldn't be here. [Laughs.] If you can't pay, you stay in Greece a lifetime.

He paid the boat for me, my mother, my sister, and two brothers. Six in all. We didn't take nothing. Empty. We were lucky to be on the ship. People were frightened for their lives. You make it, or you don't make it. This was 1915. We went from Athens by boat to the Italian coast, and they put us in the freight, the hold. [Laughs.] And we were lucky for that. We made it.

It was like a barn down there. They had only cots. "You ought to be happy you're getting out alive," someone said. So while we were going on the ocean, the captain had to zigzag because there were a lot of German submarines and torpedoes. Everybody in the ship was saying their prayers. Then there was rumors on ship that if you're not healthy, America wouldn't accept you. They're going to send you back where you come from. So everybody was praying to have their health, you know? My parents were worried. My mother clipped my hair to prevent the lice. Clipped it up completely.

Ellis Island didn't impress me at all. The memory is faint. My father had a buddy from Greece who came to the United States beforehand. He met us. My father spoke only Greek. His friend recommended the United Biscuit Company [for him] to work, and he got a job there. He didn't know English to talk. It was wicked, and it was hard. He was making an easy living in Greece. He was a merchant man, buy and sell. Here, it was a torture for him.

. . .

We first settled on the Lower West Side of Manhattan, Twenty-second Street, Hell's Kitchen. It was a tough neighborhood. A mixed neighborhood. Some blocks was just the Greek neighborhood. Another block was Italian neighborhood, Spanish neighborhood. I used to help the lamplighter on Twenty-second Street, and he used to go all the ways down to fourteenth Street to the river. And there was a market: vegetables, fruits, meat, poultry. That was the nerve center. I can still smell the vegetables. It was so nice. Milk was delivered by horse and wagon on cobblestone streets. Early in the morning, around four, five o'clock, you could hear the horses go click-clack, click-clack. Far away, echo. It was like a tune. It was so nice, sentimental. Now it's gone. [Laughs.] Macy's had the most beautiful horses. They took care of them. They delivered the merchandise. On Tenth, Eleventh, and Twelfth Streets was all stables. It was beautiful, but nothing stands still. It disappears.

School, I wasn't good at it, because I left school to help my parents. To survive. That was the tradition. Forget about the education.

My father had a cousin who married a Greek girl. Her father was a furrier. Through him I learned the furrier trade. So many years I worked, and I made a nice living. No hardship. My father always used to say, "Learn a trade, anything. You could make a living. If you're ordinary—no trade, nothing—you'll suffer."

One day my boss comes over, and he says, "How long you working here?" I says, "Twenty-seven years." He says, "How old are you now?" I says, "Seventy." He starts hollering, "Get the hell out of here." That hurt me terrific.

My daughter Stephanie, she became a teacher. It was a steady job, good pay. They dumped her. Downsizing, bad economy. She was divorced with a house, two kids, a mortgage to pay. The bank don't want to know nothing. So she went job hunting. She couldn't find anything. One of her girlfriends says, "There's a job in Sing-Sing, the prison." She took that job. I was hollering, "You're working with killers!" "But Daddy, I got to make a dollar regardless, like you always taught us." She has to not dress sexy, not to be attractive. And don't have personality. Just talk. Cold as ice. She's teaching school to killers trying to come back to civilian life. [Laughs.] The things we do for money.

Whenever my father used to go to different towns, countries, he used to get gold coins for my mother as a gift. And we had all different kinds of coins. My sister got all the coins. But she had no will. My stupid sister did not think of it. Then she died of cancer of the blood, and her husband got everything. But he's mean, you know? I had the nerve to ask him for the coins, my birthright. I says, "For the love of Pete, my sister left you so much money. Three hundred G's." He suggested I talk to his attorney. He kept the 300 G's, got my sister's house, remarried . . .

Money. It's been like a curse for me.

Doukenie Papandreos

BORN DECEMBER 12, 1905
EMIGRATED 1919, AGE 15
PASSAGE ON THE *KING ALEXANDER*

She was a Turkish subject, who left Greece when she was fifteen years old. In America, she wanted to become a doctor and return triumphantly to her homeland and her parents, having made something of herself. She did not become a doctor nor did she return to Greece, but she did make something of herself. "If God wants things to happen they will happen," she said. "If he doesn't, regardless how much you try, you won't be able to do it."

I don't know if I have to mention it, but my name "Doukenie" has a meaning. When the Turks kept Constantinople, my great-grandfather was one of the dukes. He was murdered. But his son escaped capture, and came to my town, and got married. Every family, if they had a boy, had to name the boy "Duke" as a commemoration. Being that my father only had two girls, instead of putting "Duke," they put "Duchess." And not to be afraid of Turks, they turned to "Doukenie," to further hide my origin. They used to tell the story that our family was from royalty, which, of course, isn't true.

I was born in Saranda Klisse, the name today is Kirk Klisse, which is northern Greece. The Turks, when they chased all the Greeks out of Saranda Klisse named it Kirk Klisse. This means church. The Turks are not very progressive. They didn't rebuild the town, or fix the town, or clean the town. It was ugly, really.

The life, the Greek life, was very horrible. We used to live all the time in fear. And many times they used to try to steal girls, rape the girls, and the Greeks are very religious, Orthodox Christian. The Turks are Islamic, Muhammadans. So always we lived in fear that they steal girls.

They used to do the same thing in our schools. The parents had to support the schools, because they wouldn't get any help from Turks. We used to carry wood to school in the wintertime to warm our rooms, but we had to learn. We had to have knowledge so that we would get out from slavery. Constantinople was the capital of Greece 600 years ago. The Greeks lost all Constantinople, and we became slaves under the Ottoman Empire. Always, our dream was that someday, maybe, the Greeks will recapture our towns, which were taken from us.

Our house, even when I went in 1968 to visit, remained in very good condition because two families lived there. It was a very large stone house—four bedrooms, kitchen, and a big yard with trees, fruit trees, in the middle of the property where we used to have dances. The Greeks celebrated name days. And they used to celebrate and have dances. Behind the house was a little river and more trees. But when I went back in 1968 all the trees were cut down by the Turks and used for wood. In fact, the house next door to my house was my uncle's. It was a beautiful house, and the mayor was living there. So I asked the mayor, "What happened to those beautiful trees and beautiful yards?" He said, "The Turks cut all the trees down."

The kitchen wasn't modern like they are here. It was a little stove heated by coal or wood or kerosene. The stoves we used to heat the rooms. We never had electricity in Turkey. The winters were very cold. I remember the snow many times was up to the door. It was a hard life.

My father helped his mother raise four children. She was widowed. She used to weave Turkish carpets. And when my father grew up, he wanted to go away. His mother, my grandmother, didn't want to lose him. In those days it wasn't so easy to separate from the family like today. So she wanted to see him married. And they used to match the girls. And my grandma found a good girl with a good family background, and they got married. But unfortunately,

within sixteen months she had appendicitis. In those days the whole town was four thousand people—Turks, Greeks, Jewish, and Bulgarians. We were mixed. There were only two doctors, but they couldn't operate. So she died from poison.

My father was desperate and, again, he wanted to get away. But my grandmother again said, "Please, don't go away. I lost your father. I'll be all alone." She found him another girl, and they got married. But she had TB. And in nine months, he lost his wife again. Then he said, "Mother, I don't think God wants me to be married. I want to get out." He had a beautiful voice and often sang at parties, so he said, "Either I will become a priest, or I will go to Russia." Many Greeks used to go to Russia or Bulgaria to make money before they came to America. He went to Russia, then back down to Bulgaria and started an outdoor roadside restaurant so he could be near my grandmother.

By that time my mother was married to a very rich fellow. She was a beautiful woman. She got married when she was eighteen years old. The husband was a horse trader, and he used to have guards travel with him because he used to carry a lot of money. They had been married nine months, when one of the guards cut his head off while he was sleeping, and stole the money. So they found his head at his feet. It was the tragedy of Kirk Klisse, a scandal.

A year or so later, when my father came back to visit his mother, he met the widow, fell in love and asked for her hand in marriage. This despite the fact she had two stepchildren from her previous husband. The problem was he was twenty-five years older than her. And mother said, "Let me think about it. Give me a week." And then she said, "I will marry you because I want children of my own." But now my father wasn't so sure. When he returned to Bulgaria he found out that his younger brother sold his business and took all the money. He came back and told my mother, "I don't think we will be able to marry, because I haven't got a penny." My mother said, "Don't worry. My father has left me plenty. Together we will become somebody," which they did. This was 1900, five years before I was born. My sister was born four years after me.

. . .

They worked very hard. My father started a vineyard and he used to send the wine to Constantinople. He was also sheriff of Kirk Klisse. So this permitted us to live more comfortably than others because he used to be friendly with the Turks as a Greek official.

But when the First World War started, it started from Bulgaria. And the Bulgarians marched into Kirk Klisse, drove out the Turks, and we thought the Bulgarians would remain there because they were Christian. We had hopes they would, so we could live a little bit better. We suffered a lot from Bulgarians, too. But they stayed only nine months. And then the Turks came back in 1916. I remember very well. I was eleven years old. We didn't have anything to eat. The Turks, when they used to sell us bread, they used to mix sand in it, just to kill us. They closed the schools. So my father, who was very intelligent and self-made, used to teach us at home for a few years until the schools reopened.

My father always wanted a boy. And we were only two little girls in the family. My father said it would be an honor to have a boy in the family, because the family will inherit the name. And the boy could [carry] responsibility. And many times I used to hear my father talk with my mother. "We have two beautiful girls," he would say. "If only we had a boy." And as young as I was, I used to feel for my father, and I used to tell him, "Don't worry, Dad. Someday I'll become your son, and I'm going to help you. Don't worry about the future."

Another thing used to hurt me. In those days they used to give *trousseaux* to get married, like a dowry, to get good boys and get their daughters married. My father was well established now. He owned two houses, and lots of land for the vineyard. When my father would take us to church every Sunday, his peers, Turkish men in the village would say, "Hey, Papandreos, your daughter is growing. She'll be good for my son. That big house on the vineyard is going to be mine." Then they would laugh. And we'd come out of church: "Hey, Papandreos! The little one is growing up nice . . ." That used to hurt me a lot. I used to say, "Dad, what will you do? You have two daughters, two houses—where will you and Mom live?" And he used to say, "Don't worry, dear. God gave me two girls. God will provide for everything. You just don't worry." I used to think at night, "Someday I will go to America and become somebody, so I can help my father."

Many times I used to visit my aunt. She wore false teeth. And my father didn't have false teeth. He didn't have money for that. After the war, father wasn't so rich like before. And I used to say, "Auntie, can I see your teeth? Because someday I'm going to buy teeth for my father." That's how much I loved him.

Finally, in 1918, a man came from America. He knocked at the door. I opened the door, and he said, "Where is your mother?" My mother had a brother in America who became lost or disappeared. I went after my mother. He said to her, "I brought you a letter from your brother." She opened the letter and found twenty-five dollars. In 1918, twenty-five dollars was a lot of money. She was so happy, not for the money, but being that her brother was alive.

So in a few days I wrote him a letter. Mother said to first thank my uncle for the money. Then I told him about my dream of coming to America. After you finish the high

One of the original photographs of the Statue of Liberty, taken in 1894 from a boat in New York Harbor. Construction of the Statue of Liberty was completed on October 28, 1886.

(NATIONAL PARK SERVICE: STATUE OF LIBERTY NATIONAL MONUMENT)

school in Kirk Klisse, you had to go to Constantinople to finish. So I wrote that father will never be able to afford to send me to Constantinople. To please bring me to America to finish my schooling, because I hear in America the schools are free. There we had to pay the teachers.

My uncle was a heavy gambler. I found out later, the same night he got the letter, he was playing poker with a man who was a boat agent. He sold boat tickets to America. My uncle said, "We'll play one round for my niece." And he won. He said, "We'll play another for the expenses." And he won.

A month later, I got a letter from my uncle with the ticket and I was so excited. My mother was happy for me. When my father came back from work, I said, "Father, I got the ticket to America." He said, "Never a child of mine will go away from my arms. I went to Russia, and I know what I went

through. I went to Bulgaria and I know what I went through. Child? Fifteen years old? Never!" For three days I begged him, saying, "Dad, trust me, trust me. Give me a chance."

Meanwhile, I heard that the family of a classmate of mine was going to America. Without saying anything to my father or mother I went to my friend's house, and I said to my friend's mother, Effie, "I heard you're going to America. Can you take me with you? I got my tickets, too." She agreed. My father agreed. "All right," he said, "as long as you're going with a family and not alone." And then he took me aside, gave me advice, and said, "I know you're going to be desperate. One thing I ask you. Don't ever dirty my forehead." Just like this. I can see him now. And then, "Don't ever let any man touch you. I raised two daughters and they are pure. I want them pure married. I'd rather see you drown than come back touched."

I said, "Dad, you have nothing to worry about. Just give me the chance to go."

The day me and that family got the train, the whole town was at the station to say good-bye with their handkerchiefs. I just looked at them, and I remember thinking, "Where am I going? What have I started?" But I asked God to give me the opportunity and here it was. I had to go through with it.

I took one small, old valise. One coat that I had, clothes, panties, and a few stockings. That's all. We went to Athens and then Piraeus. We were going to take the ship *Magalia Hellas,* or "Great Hellas," but something was wrong with the boat. It got replaced with a new boat called the *King Alexander.* But we had to wait forty days for it to arrive from Germany. We stayed in a miserable one-room, rundown hotel in Piraeus.

Meanwhile, my money finished. Effie said, "Write to your uncle to send you more money." But I didn't have the nerve to call. The man already sent so much money. So I asked Effie to lend me money, which she did.

The *King Alexander* was a beautiful boat. I slept with them in one room. There were four bunk beds. But Effie got very sick, and instead of second class, because she had money—me and the other three girls all moved to first class and a better cabin.

I remember playing mandolin. I used to go to the deck and play mandolin. One time I gave an impromptu concert.

After thirteen days, we finally came here and I was so happy that I was now in America. I saw the Statue of Liberty. And I said to myself, "Lady, you're beautiful. You opened your arms, and you get all the foreigners here. Give me a chance to prove that I am worth it, to do something, to become somebody in America." And always, while I was here, that statue was in my mind.

. . .

My dear, I saw tears on Ellis Island. I saw tears with happiness, but I also saw tears with pain. Many people had to wait, and they were living in an agony. Next to me was an Italian woman with three children, and one of the children got sick. Pneumonia, I think it was. The child was coughing. The mother was holding the child and singing. All of a sudden, a doctor and two nurses took the child away. The mother couldn't speak English. And they're talking to her in English. They were saying that the child had to go to the hospital. And they took the child from her arms, and the mother was crying, and I was crying with her, too. I was praying so hard for her, for me.

The guards were all Irish people, and they used to go, "Come on, come on." Like lambs to slaughter, we used to go upstairs to the rooms to sleep. One Sunday it was a beautiful day, but the pain was still in me. I couldn't enjoy nothing. I was afraid they were going to send me back. And I was dreaming that if they try to send me back, I'm going to fall into the river and die. I couldn't go back. I promised everybody that someday I'm going to come back as a doctor. Finally, the third day, my uncle came to take me.

My uncle didn't have a lot of money. We came by subway to his house in Astoria, Queens. Two rooms, no shower, no bathtub. All the houses looked the same. He took me next door to the neighbor, an old Turkish woman who was giving a Christmas party for her sons and their friends. It was Christmas week. My hair was down. Short hair. I wasn't dressed like an American girl. He opened the door and I saw one big table and eight boys. One boy saw me and said, "This spring chicken will be for me." Everybody started laughing. I was embarrassed because I thought something was wrong with me. I looked at them, and the lady said, "Shut up," which means "wine" in Turkish. And I thought, "Great, I have to live next to a drunk." In Greece, women didn't get drunk and didn't drink. When we were leaving I asked her, "Why did you ask for wine the minute I walked into the room?" She said, "Who ask wine?" I said, "I speak Turkish well. I know 'shut up' means 'wine.'" She said, "No. Shut up means keep quiet." So the first English words that I learned were: "This spring chicken will be for me."

Maria Tovas

· · · · · · · · · · · ·

BORN NOVEMBER 14, 1899
EMIGRATED 1920, AGE 20
PASSAGE ON THE *NEA HELLAS*

Her husband long gone, she lives alone in Boca Raton, Florida. "There's an expression in Greek that says, 'When person is feeling low, the Lord makes them high. And when a person is feeling high, the Lord makes them low.' [Laughs.] It sounds a lot better in Greek."

I remember everything. I was born in Acovos, a tiny mountain village where the snow never melts. And we would sit on the porch, and we see the mountains all around us. In the night we would see a light, somebody driving on the narrow roads to go to the cities. People were farmers. They had fields that produced lentils, wheat, corn, grapes, pears, all kind of fruits. My father had a store. He made saddles for the mules and the donkeys.

We were six children. Three brothers and three sisters. Both sets of grandparents, on my mother's side and father's side lived in the village. We had a little house with a fireplace, two rooms to one side, and then one large room where all the children slept in a row. At night we used to have pillow fights and my father would get angry. He was strict with his eyes. He would say, "Maria." I would look at him and he wouldn't move his eyes. Then I got hypnotized. I stopped. We never answered Father. We were not allowed.

In 1972 I went with my husband to see that village. My family still had the house. My sister lived there now, with her children. When I left I was twenty years old, and she was two years old, and now I was back after seventy years! We used to correspond. But now I couldn't find anything to talk with her about. We found nothing in common. She was talking different things and I wasn't interested. And then if I wanted to talk about America, she didn't understand anything. I left a little baby and I found an old lady.

I remember the time I saw my teacher knitting. I was interested in arts and crafts, but I didn't have the materials. So I went home and I pleaded my mother to give me a few pennies to go and buy the materials. I wanted to learn how to do it. My mother said, "Dear child, I don't have no money." Finally, my father went to the city and he bought me the needles and the fabric and my teacher taught me how to sew.

Then I said to my mother, I want to go see the city, which was at least a day's journey by horse and carriage through the mountains. "We don't have no money, my dear child. If you go there, you have to stay with somebody and pay money. We don't have no money."

Then, when I was about fourteen, I started to plead [with] my mother that I wanted to go to America. "No, no, no," she said. "You don't go to America. The girls go there get sick and they die."

"Not me!" I said. "I'm different!" [Laughs.]

. . .

My father came to the United States first in 1905. He was working on the railroad in Utah for fifty cents a week. He was writing my mother. One time he sent us a bank check for twenty-five dollars. My mother was so thrilled to get the check. She went to the city and came back with a little stuff.

"Mother, why didn't you get more?" I said.

"Honey, the money wasn't enough," she said.

"I thought father sent a check."

"He did. But the check was enough just for this."

"That father of ours," I said. "Why didn't he put more paper in the envelope?" [Laughs.] I didn't understand the concept of checks and money.

When my father left, my oldest brother went to the city and got a job. We didn't pay no rent. We had plenty to eat, food we preserved, saved from the fields. My father came back in 1909. Then in 1916 he took one brother back with him. In 1918, he took the other. In 1920, I came. At the time I thought America was going to be paradise. I thought it was going to be just like Cypress Gardens. [Laughs.]

"Now, my dear child," my mother said. "If you're going to America, don't let no one touch you. No touch! And don't forget, wherever you go, you have to live a good name." That was my mother's philosophy I still keep

inside me. People like her never went to school, but they were educated by life.

The boat left from Athens. My father took me to the train. The train started to go. My father was on the ground and he waved to me. I came with three girls from the same village. One girl had an uncle, and he was the village priest. He accompanied us to Athens. I spent a week in Athens trying to get a visa. My father paid for the boat ticket and gave me twenty-five dollars. The rule was you had to have minimum of twenty-five dollars cash to show at Ellis Island.

The trip lasted eighteen days, the four of us in one cabin. I didn't get sick, and I used to go to the front of the boat to see all the dolphins. The other girls stayed in the cabin seasick, moaning, complaining. They didn't like the food. The smell. The seasonings were different from the village. I must admit, I didn't like the food either. I just ate bread. Pita bread and cheese.

In the cafeteria at Ellis Island, I saw colored people for the first time in my life. They served us. I said to my girlfriends, "Look at that. It's a colored person. Look how dark they are!" [Laughs.]

We didn't stay overnight. We left the same day, all four of us, on a train to Lowell, Massachusetts. My brother met us and took us to his apartment. There were five boys staying in that apartment, plus him. At that time landlords didn't want to rent apartments to single boys because they ruined them. Each boy had a bed, no dresser, no nothing. One box underneath the bed to put the underwear.

I said to my brother, "This is America? Send me back to my mother," I cried. "What a stupid thing, a waste of money, coming to America." One of the boys, a cousin, saw me crying and said, "Maria, don't cry. Wait. After a year you won't remember your village or your mother."

"Don't tell me I won't remember my village or my mother!" [Laughs.]

Gradually I got used to it. I lived there for three years. I found a job in a fabric mill. Then I went home each night with food to cook for the boys, and then wash the dishes, and then wash the clothes. Each boy brought me his underwear to wash. "I didn't come here to wash them clothes," I said to my brother. "You better buy me a ticket home." "Oh," he said to me. "You know why you do that? Because you don't pay board." I'm still mad with my brother.

All my friends from the village, who I'm still friendly with to this day, had families in Lowell. One had an aunt, another had their mother and father. There was a big Greek population in Lowell. In fact, my husband was from the same village as me and he was in Lowell. I recognized him because he used to come to my father's saddle store. One time my father saw him and he said to his father, "You have a good-looking son." Then he said, "Listen, I have three daughters. Some day I want to make you my son-in-law."

Right away we got married and had a son. He was a good man, a good-looking man. My husband started a restaurant with my brothers in College Point on Long Island. I had a good life.

. . .

But America was not paradise. The minute I moved to Lowell and the apartment—after a couple of days, a couple of weeks, working in the factory, preparing my lunch every morning, washing the underwear of strangers every night, and slipping and sliding on the wintery streets—this was no paradise. This was suffering. But at that time I didn't know it was suffering because I said I wanted to come here.

Now I'm the happiest woman in the world, and I always said to my friends, "Kneel down and kiss the ground, and say, 'God bless America.'" I know the people here in Boca Raton. I don't want to go back home anymore. I don't find anybody. At my age they're all gone. The young people there are married, they have kids. I don't know them. I'm a stranger there. I'm happy here. So I want to die here. I said to the priest, I said, "Father, if you're going to build up the church, one thing you have to know. I'm going to die happy."

I remember in Acovos I used to like to go on the mules. And then all the girls, they used to say, "Maria, girls are not supposed to go on mules like a man." But I did anyway. I enjoyed life. Even now I enjoy life.

Christo Spanos

. . . .

BORN SEPTEMBER 25, 1910
EMIGRATED 1930, AGE 19
PASSAGE ON THE *SATURNIA*

He served in the U. S. Army, then opened, along with his two brothers, a twenty-four-hour coffee shop in Manhattan's theater district near the Hippodrome on West Forty-fourth Street. It was frequented by New York Ranger hockey stars, and Broadway celebrities such as Jackie Gleason, Gypsy Rose Lee,

. . . .

Lee J. Cobb, and Elia Kazan (he came through Ellis Island). "Kazan always
ordered the same breakfast: two boiled eggs, four minutes," he said. "Jimmy
Durante used to play the Hippodrome. Then, he used to come into our place.
He used to keep female company upstairs at the Algonquin Hotel. He'd come in,
'Christo, send your man up to the room. See what she wants. Send her food.
I'll pay you later'." Now eighty-seven he lives with his wife of forty years in a
New York suburb. They have three children and five grandchildren.

England was ruling Cyprus then. But they treated the Turks better than the Greeks. They took sides. Our village was small. There were Turks, but friendly Turks. There were no problems. My father was a priest. He came from a long line of priests dating back generations, and he used to go to the coffee house called *cafeneum*. It was like a club. See, the Greeks got to have the church, and the *cafeneum*. That's tradition.

My father was well respected. When he went into the *cafeneum*, everybody stood up. At the *cafeneum*, the men would get together and talk, and the Turks would give my father Turkish Delight, a powdered candy wrapped in paper, for the children. We called it *loukoumi*. I always had a pocket full of *loukoumi*. The police officers were mostly Turks. In the offices inside, mostly Turks. But the people weren't happy, Greek and Turkish. The people were poor. There was no running water. They revolted against the British. The British didn't build no highways. They didn't improve anything. They just took the tax money. They also took 10% of your crops. Your best crops. I used to call it *corgi*: the bribe for the government.

My father serviced the church and got donations, tips, but to pay his expenses, he farmed wheat, corn, carob vegetables. He also raised chickens and pigs, and he got someone to slaughter them. My father had helpers. He used to rent people. Laborers. It was a hard life. I had seven brothers and sisters—four sisters, three brothers. I was

third youngest. We were very close. Always close.

We used to go swimming. The ocean was not very far. The Mediterranean was beautiful. The sea was clean as can be. When you looked down you saw the fish next to you. No pollution. We take our lunch, our big lunch. A piece of bread, a few olives, an onion, some cheese and a tomato, a piece of cucumber. That's lunch. [Laughs.] And we go swimming. The sun was very strong. You needed an umbrella. If you don't, you get blisters all over you. The teacher, when I was [a] small one, took us to the beach. It was so hot, everybody got sick. There was no such thing as sunblock, or sun lotion, in those days.

We lived in a small house made of stone and dirt and stalk. No metal. It was cool inside in the summertime, and in the wintertime you light the stove, get together. There was no heating system, no electricity. The house was one big room. A square. With bedrooms upstairs.

When I was eleven years old, we moved into a monastery. It was called St. George a la Manu, near the small town of Limassol. From the monastery I used to commute about three miles with my donkey to school in a small village called Monagurli. [Laughs.] In the morning, I would feed the donkey, go to school, and ride my donkey back to the monastery. And the donkey was trained so good, nobody else could get on his back but me. I called him Sidara for his color. Black and white, mostly white.

In this monastery there were four or five monks. The monastery was a square wall made from dirt and manure piled up. They called it Copripia. One day, a shephard discovered some archeological cave nearby, dating back thousands of years. Inside the cave he found beautiful copper pots and a big pot of gold. So he returned his flock to the village with the idea of coming back and getting the gold. "Don't go in the cave," he said to one of the monks who saw him coming out. "There's no air in there. You might get sick."

But the monks suspected something, found the gold, and took it. They left the monastery, never to return. This shepherd went back to the cave, and, of course, the gold was gone. But he got those copper pots and he was happy.

The bishop meantime said to my father, "Bring your family to St. George Monastery. Nobody's there. You've got a big family. You can live there. Take care of it, and perform services." Because people were very religious. Every Sunday, every holiday, they went to the monastery and prayed and sang. It was beautiful.

Then, one of my sisters went to Cairo, Egypt to visit relatives because they said "we got a husband for you." In those days it was by introduction. See, the woman had to buy the husband. Her family would give a piece of land, a house, a vineyard, farm animals. They come to an agreement. The families sign. You had to have money to marry your daughter in those days.

My sister married, had children, and four years later returned to Limassol. The husband opened a sweet shop. He used to run a big confectionery store in Cairo, with imported items from Germany and England. And he asked me to help him. No money. Just volunteer. He was very good at what he did. But money? You're a relative. You don't get paid.

That was 1927. That year I make my application to come to the United States. My oldest brother had come here in 1926 and he sent me and my brother the proper papers to immigrate. While I wait, I worked for my sister's husband for three years at no pay; but he did buy me clothes, give me food. Like that.

Then in 1930, we left for America on the *Saturnia*. We left from the port of Limassol to Porsyte, and the American consul, to get our visas. I had my passport in my pocket. Then we went to Piraeus, Athens and finally Patras, where the *Saturnia* was. It was the sister ship to the *Volcania*. I just wanted to find a better world and get away from the British. [Laughs.] That was my motivation to leave. That, and the fact I was with my brother, so I wasn't alone. And my oldest brother was already in America. And everybody talked America. Go to America. Find the good life.

We had a cabin. We shared it with two strangers. Four to a cabin. After three days, I got so sick. I think it took us two weeks to come over. When we came into New York Harbor, everybody shouted, "Hey, get up! C'mon, see the Statue of Liberty! C'mon, see Manhattan! C'mon, see Ellis Island!" They knew, people who had been here before. They oriented us. I remember they were building the Empire State Building and Rockefeller Center. I remember all the newspapers they were handing out on the boat: *New York Journal, New York Post, Daily News, The Sun, New York Times, World Telegram, Telegraph*, a pile of papers, all for one city!

I spoke English enough to get along. I learned some from the British in Cyprus. But I wasn't fluent. They gave us examinations at Ellis Island. But we didn't mind it. We didn't care. The guards shout, "Hey, get over here! . . . Don't look there! . . . Get in line!" They watched you like cattle. But when you're young, you don't care. We didn't stay very long, half a day.

My older brother had somebody meet us. He lived in Manhattan on West Forty-fourth Street. It was like a Greek colony there. We went to South Ferry, put a nickel in and got the Ninth Avenue elevated trolley. We got off on Forty-second Street. We went to my brother's apartment. But it turns out, he was in the hospital having his appendix removed. So right away we went to see him. Of course, we were strangers, we hadn't seen each other in so many years. Then, right away, we went first to church, and then, next to the church, a *cafeneum*, and sat down and had a cup of coffee.

It was the Depression. There were bread lines out in the street. There was a bread line in Times Square. There was a bread line in Columbus Circle and on Fourteenth Street. There was a bread line or soup line everywhere. Stores went out of business. Business went out of business. Men sold apples,

five cents an apple on the street. Scotch ale, we used to call "beer ale," was ten cents a bottle.

Luckily, I got a job right away. I went to the employment agency on Sixth Avenue.

"What can you do?"

"What have you got?"

"A busboy job. Ever been a busboy?"

"Sure," I lied.

"Good. It pays sixteen dollars. You work twelve hours a day, seven days a week. It's called Excelsior Cafeteria at Yankee Stadium. You go there."

"Sixteen dollars a day?"

"No, sixteen dollars a week, and you've got to pay me my fee in advance."

"How can I pay in advance? I don't have any money. That's why I'm looking for a job."

"Fine, you can pay me when you get paid, providing you get me Babe Ruth's autograph. He takes his coffee at the Excelsior."

13

. . . .

Czechoslovakia

(APPROXIMATELY 170,000 IMMIGRANTS, 1892–1954)

Eastern European immigrants in a detention room, circa 1920

(NATIONAL PARK SERVICE: STATUE OF LIBERTY NATIONAL MONUMENT)

· · · · · · · · · ·

George Banovert

BORN APRIL 4, 1916
EMIGRATED 1922, AGE 6
PASSAGE ON THE *MANCHURIA*

*He was born in Dolna Suca, a remote farming village near the Moravian border.
He was named Juraj, after a Roman Catholic priest who "wanted to baptize
somebody with his name as a commemoration to himself." Juraj was later
changed to George when he passed through Ellis Island with his mother and
sister at the age of six in 1922. His father, who had arrived earlier that year
through Boston, was a menial laborer who came here "to seek his fortune,"
having been a laborer in a POW camp in Russia for more than one year.*

My mother, my sister, and I came with one trunk. In this trunk, besides everyday clothing—and I always marveled at what she considered her most valuable possessions—was an overstuffed feather quilt and pillows. I can vaguely remember her working by lamplight in the farmhouse in the evening, peeling off the goose feathers and duck feathers from the quills so they would not be coarse. The bedding was like her dowry, her contribution. Women were supposed to provide the pillows and the quilts. I remember sleeping under them.

I vaguely remember that we were driven by horse and carriage to the train station in Trencin, which was the main market town only a few kilometers from Dolna Suca. That's where my mother used to go to peddle wares or buy things—farm produce, chickens, ducks, geese, whatever. There was no market in Dolna Suca. Anything you wanted you had to go to Trencin, and that's where the railroad station was, and where we were driven to our departure.

We went to Hamburg. I think we stayed for a week. In those days things were done on a more leisurely time frame. There were no set schedules. You got there ahead of time and you waited for the vessel. In Hamburg, I remember seeing tricycle automobiles for the first time. I was always fascinated by the way those little things would scoot around. I remember running somewhere to buy a package of cookies. [Pauses.] We had to go through a physical. I remember going into a group shower. Both my mother and sister and I with other women. It was the children accompanied with their mothers. Apparently this was done by the shipping company to make sure they wouldn't have the burden of taking us on a return trip, in case we were refused entry to this country.

I remember walking on the gangplank to the boat. We traveled steerage, of course. I remember we had a room in the lower part of the vessel; enough room for my mother and sister and I to sleep. It was very hot and very noisy because we were apparently over the propeller shaft. Any time we were down there it was just thump, thump, thump. It was very uncomfortable. My mother, of course—along with everybody else—got seasick. She was seasick most of the way. But my older sister and I weren't seasick.

And so as a six-year-old who wasn't seasick I had the run of the main deck. I had a ball on the vessel, as far as I can recall. I would run around on the deck and try to keep from falling overboard. I would climb the mast. I must have really driven the deckhands crazy. One of the things that fascinated me–at the aft end of the vessel—was this huge section of gear, with teeth in it. It was the steering mechanism. I spent hours watching that thing for some reason. Of course, we weren't permitted to go up to the other decks. They were reserved for the first-class and second-class passengers. And so we were fed down in the hold. I remember eating this one kind of soup I had never tasted before and not liking it. It was like broth with small granular things floating in it. The soups we ate at home were real nice, thick hearty things you could chew on. [Laughs.]

We arrived in August. August 2, I believe. I think the trip lasted ten days. I recall as we started to approach the shore, we saw birds and things floating in the water. I wasn't aware of the Statue of Liberty. I don't know if anybody pointed it out. If they did, it didn't leave an impression, let's put it that way.

The rest is just a blur. I, we, everybody had their baggage collected, waiting to get off and onto the ferryboat to Ellis Island. Just one constant blur of activity. I do remember after we left Ellis Island, we got over to what I think was the Jersey Central Railroad Station, because my father was waiting there. We were all joyful. My sister spotted him first. She pointed him out to me because I did not remember him. I just remember that he greeted us, and there was hugging and kissing. And we went on a train, and then a bus, and he took us to this house where he had been living with this Slovak family in Newark.

Our first winter in this country was miserable. My father had found a cold-water flat with a wood stove, not too far from the place where he had been rooming. I can still remember my mother and father in the snow, cutting wood with a cross-cut saw in the yard. I don't know where he got the wood from, but they were big logs. I can remember running around picking up scraps of wood in the neighborhood and bringing them home for kindling for the fire. We tried to be self-sufficient. At that time there was no aid or public assistance. Even if it was offered I don't think my father would have taken it. He was poor, but he still had pride. And it was cold. That winter I caught the measles. I had just started kindergarten and I had to miss school for about a month.

But I can still recall my first Christmas tree. What an elaborate thing it was! There was a school assembly for Christmas. And all the children got down and sang Christmas carols, and it was just beautiful. Of course, we had trees in Czechoslovakia, in Dolna Suca. But they were little conifers with a couple of candles stuck on them. They celebrated Christmas very simply there. And so this was my first real, American, lit-up Christmas tree, with all the tinsel and all the electric lights and everything you could imagine. That left quite an impression on me.

The other was bigotry. It was an inhospitable neighborhood is all I can remember. There was a grumpy lady living next door who would not associate with us. The Germans ignored us. But I think the people who were the most bigoted to us were the Irish. They seemed to go out of their way to make life miserable for us. To them, we were the dumb Polacks. They had only two terms for any foreigner. You were either a dumb Polack or you were a dumb Hunky, meaning Hungarian. And there was no other distinction. After I became older and read a lot about the history of Ireland, it always amazed me how the Irish, who were so persecuted over the years, would not be more understanding or compassionate or considerate. Because they rode us unmercifully. I will always remember being abused by our so-called Irish neighbors.

Kate Janovich
. . . .

BORN MAY 30, 1916
EMIGRATED 1927, AGE 12
SHIP UNKNOWN

Born in Hust, Czechoslovakia, hers was a happy, but spartan life. Her mother
did the family laundry at a nearby river, bathrooms were outhouses and there
was no electricity. Her father, a Hebrew shochet *or kosher butcher, came to*
Chicago via Ellis Island to join his two sisters there when she was six years old.
Nearly seven years later, having attained citizenship and having provided money
by mail, he saved enough to send for his wife and four children who voyaged
fourteen days, plus a two-day holdover at Ellis Island. She studied social service
at Northwestern, married a Russian physician at twenty-three, had a son and
lived in Chicago most of her life. Today, she lives in Florida.

A year ago I went back to Czechoslovakia. Parts of the trip I had only a slight recollection. But I did go to Hust only to find it wasn't there anymore. There, I heard the stories about all the people who perished. You felt like you were walking on human lives wherever you went. It was very, very tough.

I can only tell you that as years have gone by, I keep saying how lucky I am to be in this wonderful country, really. I've seen all the freedom and all the educational things, and as I got older I said to myself, "How many people had these opportunities where I came from?" We forget what it was like. Here, for instance, grammar school and high school are free. In Europe you had to pay for that. And then when I heard all the terrible things that happened to people after I left I said, "It's only by the grace of God that I wasn't one of them." So I love this country without a question. Over the years, every time I've traveled out of the country, I come back and think, "Oh, it's so wonderful to be back."

Estelle Zeller
. . . .

BORN NOVEMBER 7, 1928
EMIGRATED 1952, AGE 23
PASSAGE ON THE *GRIPSHOLM*

She was born in Uzhorod, Czechoslovakia. At the age of fifteen, the Nazis
separated her from her family and she was put in concentration camps.

. . . .

*Today she leads a happy life with her husband of forty-four years, a retired
sergeant of the New York City police force; she is a former real estate broker.
A devout supporter of Israel, she has visited the country fourteen times and has
many friends there, many of them Holocaust survivors. "If you had told me in
1944 when I was in the ghetto, that one day I'd be living six months in
New Rochelle in a beautiful home, and six months in Florida, and have two
wonderful children, I would have never believed it."*

Uzhorod was a city with a large Jewish population and lots of schools. There were gymnasiums and high schools. It was a beautiful city, and all the children from the surrounding communities used to come to the railroad station every morning to attend the secondary schools. The people were wealthy, middle class and poor. We were, of course, Jewish. My father went to synagogue. He didn't smoke on the Sabbath, and we kept a kosher household. But we were also kind of modern. We weren't ultra-orthodox. The only time my mother attended synagogue were the high holy days.

My family had a bakery, a wholesale bakery, and there were five children in the family. Three boys, two girls. I was the oldest. All the children were very happy, because we had the basics. We had good food, and we had loving parents, and we certainly had a lot of friends. We always had household help for the hard work. And my parents definitely wanted to send us to schools and have as much education as we could.

The Germans occupied our city on November 10, 1938. The reason I remember the date so vividly is because my mother was giving birth in the house to the youngest child. And my father had to get the midwife, and there was shooting all over town while he went to get her. Anti-Semitism grew by the days. It became a police state and it was frightening. All the Jewish bakeries were denied licenses and if they weren't denied the license, they were de-

nied the allocation of flour. Without flour, we couldn't exist.

My father was put in the military service, so my mother had to take over the bakery and run the whole business. My mother was very smart. She was a tremendous businesswoman. She didn't have as much time to devote to her children. I was not as close to her as I was to my father. She was much more critical. Maybe she expected a lot more from me because I was the oldest, but I admired her.

By 1943, I was fifteen years old. My mother suggested that I hide. There were some Christian families we were close with, and they wanted to hide me and dye my hair and put a cross on my neck, but I refused. I refused because my father was in the service and I couldn't see myself letting my mother go with the four kids.

At the time, the Jews were being rounded up and put into one of two different ghettos surrounded by guards. One was a huge brick factory. The other was a huge lumberyard. The Jews were divided based on where you lived. We had to leave our house and all our possessions. We only took what we could carry to the ghetto. It was nonviolent. We just did what they told us. We went in like herds. They put us in cattle cars. I came to Auschwitz. I was separated from my mother, my sister, and my brothers at the railroad station. And I haven't seen them since.

I was in Auschwitz maybe six weeks because I was one of those that was going to be sent to Germany for labor. Young children and their mothers were in a different camp. The other inmates, mostly Polish-Jewish girls who were very hard, used to point at the big flames, and say, "That's where they are." So I had to accept the fact that that's what happened.

But somehow or another, when you are with a large group of people, you roll with the punches, and also, you suddenly become concerned about yourself. We were counted every morning, and we had to sleep in bunk beds like sardines. We had to sleep on the side, and everybody had to turn at the same time because there was very little space. I became friendly with two other women. They were maybe four years older than I. One of them was a house servant in one of my neighbor's houses and one was a neighbor's daughter. And they took charge of me because I was the youngest, and we were concerned that when the Nazis selected us to go to Germany that we should stick together. We were afraid to stand together, because then they would know we were friends and they would separate us. So we tried to be in different spots and sure enough we were all picked together. We were transported to a place called Gelsen-Kirchen in Germany. And they didn't have any facilities for us other than tents—huge tents for us to sleep in. And there were two thousand of us, all young women. They used us to unload brick from ships. We would make a human chain and pass the brick one to the other all day long until the tips of our fingers bled.

The first night was the biggest surprise of my life. Up to this point I was not exposed to the war. And the first night I went to sleep [she uses a tissue], the air raids went off, and there was bombing all over, and I was so scared that I ran to the two openings of the tent trying to see if I could escape, but it made no sense because there was no place to go. There was bombing every day, so the fright of the war was even worse than just being in a prison.

We were there a couple of months when some German dignitaries came. They were officers of Krupp, a big ammunitions factory. They lined up all two thousand of us, and picked out five hundred. Once again, my friends and I spread out in the hope they would pick us randomly. Of course, we had to stand in the nude because if they saw a pimple, any marks, or you were too heavy or too skinny, you weren't selected. So they picked five hundred. Sure enough, all three of us were together. And they took us to Essen, a large industrial city. I remember the street, Humboldt Strasse, and there were barracks, and for the first time, only a couple of girls were put in each room with regular beds, and it looked like this was going to be terrific.

What we didn't know was that Essen was the second target city to be bombed heavily after Berlin, and all the barracks burned down. In addition, there were some Russian prisoners adjoining our camp, and one of the bombs fell on their bunker, and killed them all. We ran to see if we could salvage some of the clothes. From this point on we had to be in a cellar that was all concrete. Water, from condensation, dripped all night on our blankets. So in the morning in the winter, you had to go out to be counted at five o'clock and take the wet blanket, which was actually our coat. We used to wrap it around us, and then take a belt and tie it around our neck like a cape. The Germans tried to rebuild the barracks, but each time they were two-thirds finished, new air raids came and it was down to the ground again.

Then I worked at Weilswork for seven, eight months. It was a huge ammunitions factory where they would take steel and put it in the ovens to harden. And I was working these ovens. You had to adjust the ovens for temperature, for gas, for air, and then the steel would be lowered by cranes and put into the ovens.

As a matter of fact, a strange incident happened to me recently. I know a girl who's been a member of my social club. I knew that she was a Holocaust survivor, but I never discussed anything with her. Then, one day, I saw her picture in the local newspaper, and when I read her story, I had goosebumps. I called her up. I said, "I see you were in Essen during the war and that you worked in Weilswork." I said, "What did you do there?" "Oh," she said, "I was on the crane lowering the steel into the ovens." I said, "Really. I was the girl at the ovens accepting the steel." We had known each other for three years and never knew.

We worked twelve-hour shifts. The biggest problem was winter. The Nazis used to put us on the streetcars, and there was snow on the ground. We had to walk from Humboldt Strasse to the factory, which was a very long walk. We had wooden soles on our shoes, and as you walk in snow a ball forms underneath your sole, so you couldn't walk. We would fall backwards, to the point where the SS had to use their bayonets to chop the snow off our shoes or else we couldn't even get to the factory. So that was one bad situation. The other was when we worked nights, and the air raids came. The Germans wouldn't let us into the bunker. So all the planes would be bombing and all the lights would be flickering and we would clutch each other tight because we didn't know what was going to happen. One time we were huddling in one corner of that room. The Germans were underground in their bunker. All of a sudden, a big radiator fell down from an air raid in the very place we were standing. Had we not been in that corner we would have all gotten killed.

So that was a very bad emotional thing, because you never knew. Many times we would come out of the factory and find planes shot down. When I got to Essen there

were many beautiful homes. When I left Essen, I don't think there was one building that wasn't hit. So it was a terrifying experience just to be part of the war.

I was in the concentration camps over a year. When the English started to get closer to Essen, the Germans packed us up and took us to Bergen-Belzen. They decided to take us out of Essen so we couldn't be liberated, but there were six girls who escaped. And, of course, the Germans were searching for them high and low. Four of those girls were from my hometown. Two of them I'm still in touch with. And, of course, they told me what happened to them. They went to a local cemetery and hid.

We got to Bergen-Belzen and they put us into one huge room, hundreds of us. All young. All women. We were there for a whole month, and there were guards standing all around, and they were giving us very inferior soup, because they didn't have much to eat themselves, and some bread, and the terrible thing was diarrhea. All these thousands of people who had no chance, I don't even remember if there were any latrines. We just walked out of the room, squatted down, and did our thing wherever it was comfortable. As a result, typhus was rampant. There were friends that I spoke to one minute and the next minute they were dead. So people were dying like flies. We had to pull their bodies by the hands and drag them out to this big mound of dead bodies. We spent our days exchanging recipes because when we spoke about food it sort of made us feel better, and the other occupation was picking lice out of our clothes. All day long we spread the seams of our clothes and then, of course, the lice were back the next hour.

. . .

We were liberated April 15, 1945. That day we suddenly noticed there were no guards. We couldn't believe that anything good could happen. And the next thing we knew we saw tanks and the English going through the camp. My lucky break was that I was with two girls whose fathers were in the United States, and these girls spoke English. I didn't. And they went over to one of the military men and said, "Look, we're still alive, we still feel good. Please get us out of here," because we were afraid of getting sick and dying. Everyone was raiding the kitchens and stealing canned food, whatever we found, like potatoes, and we would sit there baking potatoes. We would bake them for two minutes and eat it raw, and we would eat all that canned stuff, and the diarrhea was getting worse.

The English deloused us, cleaned us up, and put us into these makeshift hospitals they had set up. I started to run a fever, and they didn't know what was wrong with me. In the meantime, more of my friends died there. And after they sent me for X rays, they discovered that I had a spot on my lung. Those two other girls from Essen decided to go back to my hometown. They wanted to know if I would join them, and I said, "I'm not going back." Number one, I was thrown out of there. Number two, if I'm sick, I'm afraid I won't be able to get the care I need.

So they left. At that point I heard Sweden would take some of us. I hate to say this, but the United States only wanted you if you were well, and if you had private people guaranteeing that you wouldn't be a burden to the government. Sweden didn't care. So I wanted to go to Sweden. I remembered from my history class that the Swedes were nice people, and there was no war there, and it would give me a chance to heal.

We were taken to Lübeck, where we were deloused again. Then we took a ship to Malmö, which is a Swedish city on the southern border. We were put into a huge school that was converted into a quarantine, and for six weeks they wouldn't let us out because they had to double-check whether

anything was wrong with us. There were hundreds of us. Hundreds.

I was in fairly good health, despite my TB. But there were so many young girls that were so sick that they couldn't even eat. I would say, "Don't give it back. Just take it." I used to collect all the sandwiches from them and sit up all night eating. I gained thirteen pounds in one week.

I stayed there for six weeks, at which point they sent us to Karlstad, which is a city at the northern border, where they also made a hospital out of a school, strictly for TB. There was a very prominent doctor who had a sanitarium, and he came to oversee the treatment of us. The treatment was medication called pneumothorax. They would put a large needle in your rib cage, and pumped air to collapse the lung, to give it rest, which meant you were only using the good lung to give the bad one a chance to get better. And while I was on the stretcher waiting for my turn to go in for treatment, which I understood wasn't very pleasant, I received a phone call from a cousin of my mother who was in Sweden. I was afraid to take the phone but everyone was encouraging me. She said to me that her sister, who was not in the concentration camps because she married a Christian man long before the war, went to my hometown to look for her family and met my father. That he is alive, back home—and I cried. Maybe I was childish, but I said, "I don't want my father to know that I'm alive, because I'm going to die anyway." I was brought up with the idea that if someone had TB, they were dying. I remember if I knew someone had TB, I wouldn't even walk on the same side of the street.

Soon after, this very prominent doctor who was conducting my treatment went back to his sanitarium. I didn't know the other doctors, and I became a little bit concerned, because he took all the other sick people with him to that sanitarium. I wrote him a letter saying that I really would like to come to his sanitarium, and sure enough he wrote back and arranged for me to go. So I stayed in his Swedish sanitarium, which was beautiful, and I was getting the best treatment. I must have stayed there six months, at which point I was ready to go to a convalescent home, a place called Vickingshill outside of Stockholm. I was with a lot of other people and a lot of other friends, but I did not stay long. Since I was young, I was offered to go to a boarding school in Darlana in northern Sweden. It was called By'Kyrby, and it was a boarding school that was absolutely fabulous. We had all the subjects, plus languages including Hebrew and English. It was all Holocaust survivors, mostly girls. We had classes every day. I took courses in bookkeeping. We had a lot of extracurricular activities: classical music, all kinds of dances and games, and it was a very nice place to be. I must have been there two years. I became fluent in Swedish and English. And just before I was discharged, a lot of the girls went to Israel illegally, and I started to think about what I was going to do.

. . .

It was now 1948. I hadn't seen my father since 1943. He had come back to Uzhorod after the war, thinking that he was going to find his family, and then he found out that I was in Sweden and it didn't look like anyone else was coming back. He started to operate a bakery after the war, but when he saw that the Russians were coming in to take over, he decided to escape before they closed the borders or else he'd never get out. He lived in Germany, in a displaced person's camp, for three years until I arranged for him to join me in Sweden. He got a position in a bakery. I left the school and went to work as a bookkeeper in a large company called Asea, the equivalent of General Electric. My father remarried and moved to Stockholm. I asked to be transferred there, because Asea had offices in Stockholm and I did that until December 1951.

By this time, although I loved Sweden, I missed my roots. In Sweden, Jews were spread out. So my choice was either to completely assimilate and forget my roots, or go to Israel or the United States. I didn't go to Israel because I felt my health was not perfect, that Israel didn't need people to take care of. Israel needed people who could take care of it. And since I had family in the United States—my stepmother's brother, cousins—I chose United States.

I went to Göteborg, where I came on the ship, *Gripsholm*. It was New Year's Eve. I was wearing a beautiful dress. There was a great party on the ship and I was dancing and having a great time. Suddenly, I had terrible stomach pains and went back to my cabin. I had an attack of appendectomy. When they took the blood test they also discovered I had TB, and I decided to have the surgery on the ship. I understood that medical bills were very high in United States, that I'd better have it done on Swedish territory because it wouldn't cost me anything, and I had no money. And the fortunate part was that there was a passenger who was a doctor who was immigrating to the United States, and he assisted the ship's doctor, who never did surgery in his life.

But my greatest shock was when I came off the ship and wound up at Ellis Island. When you're young and you're alone and you have a lot of unknown things awaiting you, you really don't fall apart so fast. But it was a scary experience, because when I arrived at Ellis Island, I saw the same guard stands with guards I remembered at Bergen-Belzen. It brought back terrible memories, and I really didn't know what the outcome of my stay would be. I remember one day they took me to Staten Island from Ellis Island to a navy hospital where they pumped my stomach. They took a rubber tube and put it down into my stomach to get the juices, which they then injected into a rabbit or something, to test for bacteria. And so I had all these tests, and then X rays arrived from Sweden that I asked my father to send. Immigration officials reviewed them, let me go, and I was picked up. My stepmother, who had a brother who was close in age to me, picked me up. He and his wife lived in the Bronx in a fifth-floor walk-up. They came here a few years before. He barely spoke English. And I stayed with them . . . but I was very turned off by the Bronx. I saw clotheslines hanging, and cats running around garbage cans. Coming from a progressive country like Sweden that's so clean and so neat and everybody does the right thing, and then to come to the Bronx, well, let's just say it was an adjustment. But I didn't jump to conclusions. I was the one who wanted to be here and I was determined that things were going to be all right.

My father and his wife followed me. They came in May that same year. When they came, I rented a little apartment for us behind a butcher shop in Brooklyn. The butcher was my friend. My father didn't speak any English. But he had a trade, and being a baker was no problem. He worked for Ebbinger's Bakery in Brooklyn from the first moment on. He became a union member, and had absolutely no problem earning a living. My stepmother was a seamstress. She never really learned how to speak English, because she was a true Hungarian, and Hungarians have more difficulty learning a new language for some reason. But she got a job. She knew how to sew, and subsequently they moved to a much nicer apartment, and after that bought a two-family house. My father learned English, drove a car, and he loved it here.

I met my husband in June of '52. I was married in September. Of course, my father and my stepmother were at my wedding, and they were very pleased. The following

year, in August, I gave birth to Ruth. And then my second daughter was born nineteen months after that, Harriet. So my father had a tremendous amount of pleasure from these girls. He just absolutely adored them. And so he never spoke about his children, you know? He wasn't there when my mother and all the children were taken to the concentration camp. Sometimes I wish I would have asked him certain things. But you put it off, and put it off, and I guess if you don't want to cry, you don't want to talk about it. I was very close to him. My daughters were very close to him. [She is moved.] I get emotional. I lost him at age seventy of lung cancer.

I went back to Uzhorod in 1986. It was my husband and I, plus my stepmother's brother and his wife, the four of us. We went to Budapest to get a Russian visa so that I could visit my hometown. This was before glasnost and the openness. As I was getting closer, I didn't want to go but my husband insisted. He said, "I want to see your roots, I want to know where you came from." So the two of us went to the railroad station and got on this Russian train, which gave me the chills. I wanted to get off, but he just insisted. The KGB were searching the cabin. And I started to get very nervous. At the time, I had these nightmares that I went back to my hometown and the Russians wouldn't let me out. So here I found myself on the Russian express going back.

We arrived in Uzhorod. And I went to my school and the houses of my friends knowing that nobody came back and nobody's around. I went to my house. I met an old lady there and she didn't know who I was. And she started telling me this story about my father. How Mr. Zeller came back after the war, how he operated this bakery and then left, how he was going to try to get to the United States. Upon which I told her who I was and she broke down in tears. I came home and wound up with a nervous breakdown. I had to be under a doctor's care for six months.

This year, I have some friends that are going back, but I don't think I can go back.

My girls said that maybe one day they would like to go. If they still feel that way in a year or two, maybe I'll be ready. Maybe I'll feel different.

William Denovak

. . . .

BORN APRIL 24, 1921
EMIGRATED 1953, AGE 32
PASSAGE ON THE S.S. *UNITED STATES*

He was part of the last influx of immigrants to Ellis Island before it closed its doors in 1954. He arrived here with his wife via West Germany, in January 1953 during the height of the McCarthy era. Suspected of being communists, they were detained nearly four and a half months until their release in May 1953. They lived in New York briefly, then settled in Seattle, Washington and raised a family.

Before World War II, my family was sort of prominent in Prague. My grandfather was one of the founders of the National Theater. My father was a municipal officer, a magistrate. And my uncle was a staff officer of the gendarme.

My mother was at home. I mean, in those days women didn't work. I had two brothers who died of the Spanish flu at the end of World War I, so I was the only one that actually made it. I remained alone. I lived in this small family circle which included uncles and cousins. I lived in the same building on the same street for twenty-nine years. The building was a typical European brick apartment house. No elevator. We lived on the third floor. There was no central heating. That came later. I remember I used to run from the basement all the way up to the third floor with pails of coal. [Laughs.] But it was a stable life. You

always knew what was going to be the next day.

Then, in 1938, I was about seventeen, the politics started and Hitler's Germany began a partial mobilization against Czechoslovakia. I was at school. But I was brought up in a patriotic manner, so I finished my exams and immediately volunteered for the armed forces. I tried to get into the air force, the Czech air force, but wound up in the infantry in Malacky, a big garrison town. It was close to the Austrian-Hungarian border.

Then, the following year, there was a general mobilization and the German army invaded the rest of Czechoslovakia. I was transferred to border guard. Everything was in a hurry. There were fights, skirmishes, uprisings. There were German soldiers everywhere. All types of troops, from infantry and armed vehicles to SS. I remember the day Hitler came marching into Prague. I actually saw him. He was standing on the quai of the Vltava River, having come from Prague's main castle. But in the end, the country was occupied without major incident. We had surrendered.

So I went to work for one of my uncles, who owned a textile plant in the town of Nemecky Brod. Today it's called Havlickuv Brod. I was there just a couple of months when all of a sudden the Germans started to collect young people. I was about to be hauled off to Dresden, Germany with a couple of other Czechs, but we skipped the transport and went on our own to Berlin. A few months later, the Nazis tried to induct me into the German army very vigorously, and I resisted. Then Hitler said that he didn't want any Czechs in his armed services, so I was finally released, and I went back home to Prague.

I was put into forced labor. I worked in Prague as a riveter on a German airplane called the *Seabill*, a light bomber. In the meantime, all around me, people were being executed. One village, the village of Lidice, was totally exterminated.

I was transferred into forced labor again, this time in Germany. I worked at Schonebeck, which is very near Magdeburg. I worked at Junker's plant for Junker's aircraft. During this time, the heavy bombardment started. The air raids, I mean. First by British, then by American forces. And so it went on.

Two American bombing raids actually saved my skin. Because whenever they made a raid, the Americans synchronized the ins on the Gestapo, then backed it up and you could run. Well, I made a run. It was May of '45, the Russians were moving in and I was shot in my right hand by an SS trooper. But I was saved by the Russians who put me in some sort of medical facility. We greeted them as liberators.

I was in treatment for two or three months, got reactivated, even though my right hand was crippled, and went back into the Czechoslovak army, this time as a gunner, a cannoneer. I didn't want to go. I didn't care to become an officer. So in March of '46 I got out of the army and worked for an import/export firm and then Czechoslovak airlines because they were looking for people who were bilingual. I did that until 1950, when I was fired because of my political views, which I did not put forth diplomatically. [Laughs.] In fact, I was warned by the government and I was worried I was going to be arrested. So I managed to sneak across the border into West Germany, to Nuremburg, at Camp Balka, a refugee camp, and worked as an interrogator/translator for American intelligence which is where I met my wife.

She was a typist. We got married in Nuremburg in 1952. And we were looking for a place to go. We didn't want to stay and always be worried about the threat of war. We thought maybe we'd go to Australia or Canada, whoever would accept us. I was anxious to save my freedom. I could have spent ten, fifteen years in that refugee camp. But when President Truman enacted the Refugee Act into law we thought it would be easier to go to the United States.

But it wasn't that easy. There were whole examinations, and not just physical, but interrogations. We were interrogated for three days in Munich by IRO, the International Refugee Organization. Anyway, we finally got our passports and we left for Bremerhaven. On January 4, 1953 we sailed for five days on the S.S. *United States* to New York.

We had very good accommodations, but because we were immigrants the men slept separate from the women. My wife and I would meet at meals. Then about 600 miles off the coast of Ireland in a spot called Devil's Hole, the ship was hit by a hurricane. There was a big gash in the side of the boat and we had to sail at a forty-five-degree angle for a couple of days just to get through the storm. My wife got scared, we were all scared. So much for separate sleeping quarters. She stayed with me the rest of the trip.

In New York, a friend of mine was supposed to meet us at Ellis Island. He was from Czechoslovakia, too. He came to the United States the year before. He lived in New York.

We were taken off the boat and ferried to Ellis Island. And all of a sudden someone called us and said, "You stay here." I wasn't frightened, but I was thinking, "What's the problem?" Of course, I already spoke English, but nobody told us anything. And there we were, among all of these people who were being detained for one reason or another; people of all different races from ship stowaways to prostitutes from Cuba and Canada. And then, naturally, we were interrogated by immigration officers. They were posing all sorts of questions. So I told them my story. And all the time they were asking me about what was I doing in China.

China?

My wife was interrogated separately. When she rejoined me she said, "He kept asking me about what I was doing in China." I didn't understand it. The only thing I understood was that we were being detained and didn't know why.

They put us in married quarters. It was clean. Clean bedding, the food was good, no

A Board of Special Inquiry, 1906. From left, an Immigration and Naturalization Service administrator;
Robert Watchorn, an English immigrant who was then commissioner of Ellis Island; an interpreter;
two immigrants; and an INS inspector. Across the desk from Watchorn sits Augustus Sherman, a
confidential clerk later noted for his extensive photography work at Ellis Island.

(NATIONAL PARK SERVICE: STATUE OF LIBERTY NATIONAL MONUMENT)

complaints. But there was nothing to do. So we read newspapers and magazines, and played canasta and Czech cards. The only entertainment was one TV in the main hall. That's where I watched the inauguration of President Eisenhower.

We decided to work. In the morning I used to wash the walls of the main hall for fifty cents a day. My wife worked for a lady who was a social worker, typing. She earned a dollar a day.

We were never allowed out of the main building for any reason except to walk outside along the fence. That was it. Back and forth along the fence. And it was guarded. On the other side were all the newly arrived immigrants who were being detained, so we got friendly.

I remember one lady who was separated from her family because they found something in her lungs. She was awfully sad. There were Chinese and one guy from Cuba I used to talk with who was here illegally. There was a young couple, also Cuban, also illegal, who were interrogated and I thought deported, and then I saw them years later in the subway in New York and we talked. There were a lot of Cubans, in fact, all trying to escape the coming of Castro. I remember a guy from Malta named Frank Falcone who was with his sick mother—almost on her deathbed. An immigration officer accused him of being a deserter from the army in Malta or something. Frank said, "I don't care. Send me to the army, navy, whatever you want, my mother is dying. Here are my papers." And all of a sudden, one day they came in around four o'clock in the morning. Frank didn't even have a chance to get in touch with his lawyer. They put him and his mother on the boat, and they were deported. There was even one fellow who, due to poor health, traveled the high seas for one and a half years between New York and Casablanca, Southampton and New York, because no country would admit him.

Then one day a Czech couple arrived. My wife and I were walking the fence. And they, too, were detained. He called himself Fred Brown. His wife's name was Mira. So we got acquainted. We were keeping each other company. He used to work for Radio Free Europe in Vienna. And one day in the main hall he was reading some defunct magazine like *Colliers*, or something, and there was an article about his former boss at Radio Free Europe. All of a sudden he jumps up and says, "Mira, I know why we are here. They think we're communists!"

When they left Czechoslovakia a customs officer had come to their flat, checked their luggage, sealed it and took it. The same thing happened to us. But Fred still had printed matter from the archives of Radio Free Europe; communist newspapers and books and so forth. So the customs officer reported that Fred was a communist agent. [Laughs.] So he wrote to his boss, who eventually cleared him.

When this happened it struck me as to why they were asking us about China. While I was working for American intelligence in West Germany, there was a Catholic priest who was posing as a missionary from China. I was posing as his assistant who had come back with him. All of this was just a cover for intelligence reasons. But immigration officials somehow found out and took it literally.

I was furious, so I wrote a letter to President Eisenhower. I said that we came to this country legally after completing all that was required of us to get a visa. That nobody had the right to detain us without knowing why and put us into prison—because for us Ellis Island was a prison. I gave that letter to the friend who was supposed to meet us because I didn't trust immigration officials to mail it. He mailed it from Manhattan someplace.

Ten days later, we were cleared. When I saw the immigration officer for the last time, the letter was on top of his desk. So I asked him: "If we were good enough to leave now, how come we weren't good enough to leave in January?"; because this was nearly June. We had been detained four and a half months! And he said, "Just let sleeping dogs lie. I cleared you. You have just enough time to get the hell out of here. The ferry leaves for Manhattan in thirty minutes." [Laughs.] So we threw everything together and boarded the ferry. We were euphoric. I mean, it was such a funny feeling just standing there, you're slowly backing out, and Ellis Island disappearing behind us . . .

We got to South Battery Park pier, flagged a cab and went to Astoria where my friend lived. I worked for KLM at Idlewild Airport for two years before I was transferred to Seattle, Washington. But it was a tough adjustment. Seattle was not like New York. It was very provincial in a way. I don't want to use the term, but for some people I was considered a "white nigger." There were those who told me very plainly, "Get the hell out of here and go back to where you came from."

There were not that many Czechs in Seattle. But to tell you the truth, we didn't care to associate much with our own compatriots because you never knew who they were. You had to be very guarded and very cautious. You didn't know who you could trust. And after dealing with Nazis, and especially the Commies, you get paranoid. I used to have a hangup where if I was walking down a street I would subconsciously cross the street so I would always be in sight of the doors of the houses.

You have to understand something. With the Nazis, you had a foreign enemy, a clear adversary. But with the Commies, you never knew. You could have guys you grew up with and you couldn't trust them. That's what happened to my mother. After we arrived in America, I found out she was arrested for espionage or some ridiculous thing. But it was a Czech guy acting as a double agent who turned her in. She was in jail for years. When she was released in 1965, I brought her over, which was the last time I saw her. She came to visit us in Seattle. She died in 1968.

I don't know whatever happened to my father.

14

. . . .

Hungary
(APPROXIMATELY 165,000 IMMIGRANTS, 1892–1954)

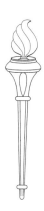

Photograph of Hungarian mother and daughters in 1906 in the Great Hall

(NATIONAL PARK SERVICE: STATUE OF LIBERTY NATIONAL MONUMENT)

Margaret Wertle

BORN APRIL 6, 1903
EMIGRATED 1910, AGE 7
PASSAGE ON THE *PRETORIA*

*She never knew her father, who disowned his family. The aunt she lived with
in Budapest neglected her and beat her. Her stepfather in America was an
abusive alcoholic, who was eventually sent to an insane asylum for raping a
fourteen-year-old girl in New Jersey. Today, she lives on the outskirts of Albany,
New York. Her husband is gone, but she has her children and grandchildren.
"I always felt that I had a guardian angel, because I was so Catholic," she said.
"And because I'm still living. I still pray."*

I was born in a small Budapest hospital near the Margit Bridge, so I was named Margit. When I came to America it was changed to Margaret. Mother was a cook for very wealthy people. She was a very outgoing person, although she never learned to read or write or go to school. She was born in Pustavom. *Pusta* means "pleasant valley." But the water was so bad that they drank wine for dinner.

My father was a locksmith. He had four children he never told my mother about, and to this day I don't know who he is or where he is. He must be dead, of course. My mother was shocked when he told her he had four children. She was pregnant with me at the time. Mother never thought it was important for her child to know her father, which was wrong. When I was a child, she never told me until I grew up. I don't even have a picture of him. It's very sad.

When I was three years old my mother went to America. She boarded me with my aunt and my grandmother. My family is of German descent. In school I learned Hungarian, but my grandmother couldn't understand me so I had to learn the German. So my aunt had to interpret my Hungarian to

German to my grandmother until I started school. My grandmother had a nice, big home there, because my grandfather was a carpenter.

But my aunt, my mother's sister, was in charge of me. She was an epileptic and very mean, especially when she'd start drinking wine. [Laughs.] My aunt was so mean to me because she never had a child. That's my theory.

My grandmother was wonderful. She walked with a cane. But she wasn't that old. She was in her late sixties when she died. I was five. I found her on the floor and I had to run to the neighbors. She was dead. She just closed her eyes and she was gone. I tried to shake her, she was gone. The priest and the altar boys came with their gowns on. They had the cross. And they walked all the way to the cemetery, me trotting on behind the coffin. I remember the women wore these little babushkas, and the little blouses and big skirts, because they wore petticoats in them days.

I was a lost child after she died. I used to walk up to the cemetery and cry, and it was very sad. How can you forget that? There was a dike nearby, a big body of water, and

I slipped in and almost drowned, and they pulled me out and pumped my stomach. And they took my clothes off and dried it because my aunt would have killed me after I got home. [Laughs.] Now I see my little grandchildren, how mischievous they are, and they get away with it, because here in America, you're not supposed to hit kids. But I got it good.

My mother came back to get me in 1910. I was seven. She had already gotten married that year to my stepfather. She had a job with very wealthy people in Passaic, New Jersey. My stepfather was the gardener and she was the cook. I remember the day she came. She stepped down from that carriage. She had a big hat on, a great big hat. And, of course, she wore a corset. She was quite well-endowed. And she saw me and started to cry. I was full of lice. I was dirty.

My aunt and my mother had such a big battle over me that I could cry today yet. Auntie was tearing me one way and my mother's tearing me the other way. [She is moved.] My aunt was so crazy. She thought my mother would never come back and get me. And she says, "You owe me money. You never paid for her." So the two women started fighting over me. My mother said, "You're going with me. I'm your mother." I had no brothers or sisters.

It was terrible. My mother had a doll cabinet. My aunt took this thing and smashed it on the floor. And I just ran out of there. It was just too much for me as a little girl. I didn't know what was going on. That had me so upset that I wet the bed for a long time because I was scared. My aunt should have been put away, believe me. My mother actually saved my life because she'd have killed me. My aunt beat me up terribly.

So my mother just grabbed me and took me. She had a suitcase of American clothes for me. She took me to a cousin, and there they gave me a bath and cleaned me up. My mother was so immaculate, so clean. I never

saw such a clean person. They took me to the doctor to see if I was all right. I was healthy, but I was a dirty little girl. [Laughs.] They had to scrub me, because my aunt never washed my hair or anything.

My mother took me by train to Bremen. It was April or May. We stayed in a hotel overnight. I remember Mother bought me a pair of shoes, because I didn't have any shoes. I was barefoot up to then, except some velvet shoes that you wore only on Sunday, see. But I ruined them on the boat. I remember I wore a skirt and a midi-blouse. It was white with stripes and stars on. Regular sailor outfit, with a pleated skirt. That's the one thing I remember. She always dressed me well.

We were in steerage, and she was so sick. She was too sick to even get up and walk around. I'd bring a big bowl, a wooden bowl with sauerkraut and pork, and she couldn't take that. Also don't forget, she was a lady. She worked for very fine people all her life as a cook. Not a cleaning woman, as a cook. The boat trip took three weeks. We were down in that hole for three weeks. We couldn't see nothing. My mother didn't eat.

When we got to America, we saw the Statue of Liberty and Mother said to me in German, "That means we are free." I remember her saying that. And I didn't know what she meant by being "free." I only learned that after. And to this day I think I'm a better American than a lot of them born here, because when I sing "God Bless America" I'm in tears. You see, I feel I've been very blessed to live to be over ninety and be healthy.

They put us in this cage at Ellis Island. Wire fence all around. All these people shoved in there. And I remember just holding on to that wire and looking around and looking to see the people. And all of a sudden I see a man coming with a straw hat, a caty, as they called it, and a red tie. I can see him yet. And he was a good-looking man, my stepfather, and he came with his boss, because you could not come in unless you had a sponsor.

Once we came to America, my mother's life changed because she then had to give up her cooking job to take care of me. My stepfather was Austrian. We lived in Passaic, New Jersey. There was a large German population there. And not only that, but all the men bunched together, in the same dance halls, in the same saloon for drinks. I saw a lot of drinking as a child.

We had a flat. No heat, the kitchen stove, that's all we had, and two bedrooms. No living room. We ate and lived in the kitchen until we went to bed at night. That's all we could afford. No electricity, just gaslight lamps on the wall.

Then we moved to Wisconsin when my stepfather was put in jail. He was a mean man. He was a drunk. He was an alcoholic. But my mother didn't know about his background. He was a good-looking man. She wanted a father for her child. And things gradually became worse. Once he threw beer in my mother's face at the dinner table because there was a little nick in the glass, and he threw it in her face, and she went after him, and they had a free-for-all. I went for the police. I used to have to get the neighbor lady to call the police. And he'd be put in jail again and get out again. And when he got out he was like a madman. Once he took a hammer and smashed up the stove. He threw things. So my mother would point me to get the cops. The last time it happened I got to the door and he grabbed me and I got the worst beating you ever saw for a little child. When I went to the neighbor lady, she said to the police, "You better get that guy out of here before he kills her." So he was put in jail again. But he also threatened to kill us when he got out.

So we went to Sheboygan, Wisconsin, where my mother had another sister. I was twelve. I was in fourth grade. We had been in America four years. Mother got my report card to take along to Wisconsin. She put me

on the farm, and then she made her own life, started over again, see. We left everything in New Jersey. We didn't take nothing except a trunk full of clothes. We had to get away, because he would have gotten out and done something terrible.

In fact, after we settled in Wisconsin we found out by mail that my stepfather molested a fourteen-year-old girl. He raped her. The mother of the girl had a gun, and she shot him. After she shot him, he landed in the hospital. Then he was put into an insane asylum and that's the last we heard of him.

. . .

Mother went out again to work for wealthy people. She lived in their homes. I lived with my aunt and uncle. The farm was right on Lake Michigan, and we could go swimming across the road. I used to walk one mile to school. I enjoyed it there. But we had no home of our own.

After mother saved a little money, she bought a house about thirty miles away from my aunt and uncle on Lake Michigan. She bought it for $500 and was able to make the payments by keeping boarders. It had four bedrooms upstairs, so she rented them out mostly to men who worked in the factory at Kohler, the faucet makers. One of those men became my stepfather, and he was a good man. But I had to sleep with my mother every night at that time, because she didn't want people to talk. There was a place where the men could go to shower.

As years went by, mother's hands got very crippled. And I had to help her comb her hair and braid her hair. She had a big head of blonde hair, and she'd put it around her head. It had little combs on this side. She was a pretty woman.

When I was fourteen I had to go to work. She took me out of school. I was in the seventh grade. That's all the education I had. I worked in a pea canning factory. I think [I] earned twenty dollars a week. I didn't like the job. I made bolts, threads on both sides of the rods that I put in, a little lathe. My boss said, "Don't you like your work?"

"No!" I said.

"Well, what do you like to do?"

"I like to cook," I said.

"Oh, you can cook?"

"Sure. I've been cooking since twelve."

He said, "Listen, we need a little girl like you." He went in the office, called his wife. She said, "Bring her out."

I came home, I said, "Ma, I'm quitting my job. I'm going to cook."

"You ain't going to get the money you're getting here. You're bringing home twenty dollars now." I would only be paid ten as a cook .

"I don't care," I said. "I'm old enough to go to work, and I can do what I want." I got real nasty. And the boss had a nice, big red car. I wanted the neighbors to see me with him. I was going on fifteen then. I was a young lady. And they took me in and I stayed there until I left and got married . . .

I was a lost kid. I prayed for God to help me all the time.

Marilyn Kovath
. . . .

BORN (IN THE U.S.) NOVEMBER 3, 1914
EMIGRATED 1921, AGE 7
PASSAGE ON THE *ADRIATIC*

She was born in Bethlehem, Pennsylvania and went to Hungary in 1920, stayed for one year and returned to the United States when she was seven years old. A college graduate and proud of it, she worked as a civil service employee most of her life and married a soldier, who was decorated for bravery. He died in 1986. She has three children, four grandchildren and still lives in Bethlehem near her younger sister, with whom she remains close. "We're true Americans. Even when I was a little girl I didn't want to go to Hungary, but we respected our parents and their background."

When I was six years old my mother and father decided to go and bring my sister Mary home from Hungary. Mary was two years old. They had earlier tried to bring her to the States, but then the war broke out and they couldn't get her over here. So they were preparing to go back to Hungary to pick Mary up and they thought maybe if they liked it they might stay.

I cried. I didn't want to go. My mother said, "You have to go. The whole family is going." I had tantrums. "I want to be an American," I kept saying. But we went.

For the trip, I remember my teacher gave me a book, *Br'er Rabbit*, and being thrilled with it. I remember the boat, getting on the boat, and getting lost the first hour we were on. I remember there was a movie star on board who was a cowboy and he taught me how to jump through hoops. I remember running everywhere.

We went first class. My father had worked for the American Wire and Steel Company, and they made barbed wire. And he was a very big fellow, and he had a big job, and he made big money. So I guess he had enough money to go first class.

My father used to sing a lot. I remember him always whistling or singing, and I did like that. He loved his church songs, and the Hungarian songs. [Sings in Hungarian.] My mother used to sing that all the time, too. The translation is, "Whoever loves their baby, no matter how it snows or rains, will find her. Even cross the bridges to find her."

It was not a very good trip because it was right after war. Somebody suggested we go to the Red Cross so we could pass from one country to another, and the Red Cross took us in boxcars. I remember it was at night we traveled, and they put us in these boxcars that had six bunks on top of each other, four sets of six. There were a lot of people going back to Hungary.

We lived in Hungary for a year before returning. We lived in a little house and storks would nestle up in the chimney. That was amazing to me, these big, long-legged birds. They'd go up into the chimneys and nestle. I remember we had five chickens and we had a horse. The horse's name was Munsey. I loved that horse! I used to take my dinner out there and feed him with my fork. It was a gorgeous horse. But every time he saw another horse he started acting up and got so excited, he'd get up on his hind legs and bluster. [Laughs.] So if we saw another horse coming we'd duck. My father was so mad, because he paid a lot of money for this horse. But we put up with it. And then he had to sell him without telling the new owner the real trouble with Munsey.

I remember we had a beautiful wagon, and on Sunday afternoons my father would take us for a ride, Munsey pulling. And Mary and I would take pillows and lay in the wagon in the back. And my mother had a mink coat. A beautiful long one. And she'd cover us with this. I remember going to visit my aunt Vilma. A lovely person, but she was huge. Fat. But she was a great baker. I remember going to little fairs, or *buchu* which means fair in Hungarian, where they sold these cakes that looked like hearts. If you liked someone, you bought them one of these Hungarian cakes and gave it to them like a valentine. It was beautiful. And, of course, there was Gypsy music, lots of Gypsies who played violins.

My mother was the one who really wanted to go back to America. My father liked to drink. He enjoyed going to the tavern and sitting there and just talking and having a wine or two, and my mother was at home alone, see. So she figured that's for the birds, and then she said, "I'm not staying. We're going back to America." And we did.

I remember the trip to Cherbourg on the train. First we stopped in Budapest. And my aunt Vilma brought us bread. It was huge. I'll never forget it. I remember staying at a hotel in Cherbourg, and there was a fort there. My father would take us for a walk on it, and it was laid out in brick, and you went up in a circle all the way up high, and then you could look out over the ocean.

My only memory of the boat ride back is looking down into steerage. The top of the boat was smaller, and you looked down into steerage, and the people looked like ants. And I caught lice because I'd run all over. And mother combed it out. I got rid of it. And then we landed in New York, and somehow we had difficulty with our luggage. That's how I remember we went to Ellis Island. But it was Christmas week, I remember. And I enjoyed Ellis Island. I ran. [Laughs.] I ran.

Evelyn Berkowitz

. . . .

BORN DECEMBER 2, 1909
EMIGRATED 1921, AGE 12
PASSAGE ON THE *MONGOLIA*

*One of nine children, she came to America with her parents after World War I
and settled in Braddock, Pennsylvania.*

I was born in Kochanovic. It was a very small farm town. It was only about three dirt streets. My dad moved there to get a job. He was working for businesspeople that had farms, and he was like the foreman. He was a short man, and had a good life until he went into the service. Then we had to struggle until we left for America. It was my parents, my five brothers and four sisters. Nine of us. I was second oldest. I don't remember any of my grandparents.

We had a one-story house. There were two rooms and like a summer kitchen in the center. It was a front room, a nice, large front room, and in the back we cooked. It was a nice, large room. We had beds there and a nice, long table with benches. But no water in the house. We had a well on the outside. No electricity, just gaslight lamps and candles. The house was heated by wood. There was a big oven. We used to bake in that, and then there was a stove for cooking. This house was not on the grounds of the farmer's property that my father worked for. It was separate. Up the street a little bit. We had our own cows, chickens, geese, and ducks. In back of the house there was a stable or barn.

My father fought with the Hungarians against the Russians for five years because he was captured. He was held prisoner by the Russians in Russia for about three years.

We didn't hear from him. At one point we got a card from the army, saying he was killed. He wore a heavy coat—when they were running in the woods, when they were fighting, it was too heavy, so he dropped it. Another man picked it up and was killed, and they found the name Berkowitz on it. So they thought it was my father. But my mother didn't know this until he was able to send a card from Russia and we knew that he was alive.

Everybody celebrated. We were just so happy to hear. After the war was over, he came home. One of my brothers was born while he was gone. He was already three years old. And my dad went over to my mother to touch her, my little brother said, "Don't touch my mother."

"But I'm your father."

"No. My father is in Russia. You're not my father. My father's in Russia." Because that's all he was told.

While Father was gone, it was very hard. Half the time we went hungry, and we went into the fields and picked the wheat that was left over, for mother to thresh out, and go to the mill and grind it, and make us some bread. And we had potatoes and stuff like that. We tried to get along. There was no work to go to work. There was nothing there for women to do. Just the fields. And there wasn't much to do.

During the war a lot of times we had to pack and run away because the Russians were coming in. I was very little, but I remember we packed up and went deeper into Hungary where there wasn't so much fighting. My mother had an uncle there. So we stayed with him for about three weeks. Then we came back and we didn't find anything. The cow was gone, the chickens, everything was gone. They left the furniture though. And we just went on with our life again.

My school was a block away, a large brick building. And when we came home we did chores. As little as we were, we had to help. Whatever needed to be done. I remember we had a beautiful river there right across the railroad, and we used to go there and go swimming and enjoy ourselves. When I finished the fifth grade, the Czechs took over after the World War I, and we had to go to Czechoslovakian school for two years, which I didn't like much. We also went to synagogue for services. There were maybe seven or eight Jewish families, all Slovak people. There was no anti-Semitism. We were very close with all the people there.

My mother had a brother in Braddock, Pennsylvania. So my uncle wrote my parents they should send two of the children to America and he would send them to school and raise us. My sister and I were the two oldest ones. My dad wrote him back. "If you want to see my children, you'll have to take all of us to America because I am not going to be separate from my children again. I was away from them for four years . . ."

In the next letter we received the tickets to come to America. I didn't know what to think about it. We were all excited that we were going on such a long trip. We took all the bedding, and some of the dishes. There was a lot of luggage.

We went to Prague. We spent a week in Prague waiting for papers to come through. From Prague we went to Rotterdam and we waited for three weeks for our ship. We were inspected thoroughly. The people with cash went through first. We stood in line, and they had to check out our hair, so they made excuses, "You have nits here," and "you have dandruff here, you can't go through." All kinds of excuses. At one point my mother got so angry, so disgusted, she cut off our hair. My oldest sister, Helena, said, "Mom, leave me some hair in front so when I put a cap on they'll think I have hair." She was thirteen years old. When Helena went through the line again he said, "You have dandruff here in front, you can't go through." So Mom cut that hair off, too. Helena began to cry. "Don't cry," my dad said. "When we get to America they have some kind of lotion they put on, and your hair will grow in no time." [Laughs.]

They gave us a cabin for the family with six bunks. We were in the third class. There was no extra room so my dad went down to steerage, but it was so bad down there, he came up and said, "I'm not going down there."

First of all, everybody got sick. It was rough seas. For five days I laid up. I didn't eat a thing. I was the worst. The little ones would throw up, and then they were all right. My brother came in eating a piece of bread from the lunchroom and he said, "Oh, this piece of bread tastes awful." Next thing, he starts throwing up. [Laughs.]

There were also rats on the boat. I was on the upper bunk, and there were pipes above. And the rats were just running back and forth on those pipes. One day, Dad hit one on the tail, and that thing was squeaking so far. After that we got relief, because usually when they get hurt they don't come back to that same spot. [Laughs.] It wasn't a nice boat.

Then a couple days out, the ship sprung a hole and water was coming in. In fact, we were walking around with our life jackets. They sent an SOS out, and told us another ship was coming to help us. But before that

The railroad ticket office in the main building, circa 1912

(NATIONAL PARK SERVICE: STATUE OF LIBERTY NATIONAL MONUMENT)

ship got to us, they fixed it, the hole, and we kept on going. In New York they reported in the paper that the *Mongolia* sunk, and all the people went down. When we got to New York, they couldn't believe it. They said we were found people, that the boat went down.

We arrived New York late December 1921. We were eleven days on ship. When we saw that Statue of Liberty, everybody started screaming and crying and hollering, they were just so happy to see it, to be in America. By this time I was feeling better and it was such a thrill to see it. Then for one week we waited in New York Harbor, because a lot of other ships had come in and we had to wait our turn.

Since we couldn't get to Ellis Island right away, relatives, whoever had relatives in New York, used to come with small boats right near us, and pull up on ropes food and stuff. Because they didn't feed us so well after

· · · · · · · · ·

we were there for a week. So the relatives used to send it up on a rope to the ship.

My mother meantime was nursing a baby. She didn't get the food that she needed. When we got off the ship onto the ferry, she passed out from hunger. But they brought her to, and she was okay after that. They gave her something, and she felt better.

When we got to Ellis Island they tried to open up all our luggage, but it was so cold the inspector couldn't do it. It had rope on it, and he couldn't open it, so they let us go through without it. It was freezing. When we got in the building we had to stand on line for questions, everybody separately. We didn't go through medical exams. Just questions they asked us. Name, date of birth, etc. Then, all of a sudden, we got a call over the loudspeaker for the Berkowitz family to come to one side. We got so scared that maybe something happened to somebody and we wouldn't be able to go through. Turned out it was a couple of my mother's aunts who came to meet us with some cousins. They brought pound cake and ice cream for us and sat us down on a bench. I remember those big benches in the big hall. And we looked at it, we couldn't put it to our mouths because we were still sick. We wanted something hot because it was cold, and here they give us ice cream. We couldn't eat it. Meanwhile, they left us there, and we just left the ice cream and the cake, everything melting on the bench. We didn't know what to do with it. And we had to wait a few hours for our train.

They had a station near Ellis Island. We didn't have to go to New York. And we got aboard the train. We rode all night, most of the night. We were supposed to go to my uncle who bought the boat/train tickets to Braddock, near East Pittsburgh. But that train wasn't going to stop in Braddock, just in East Pittsburgh. My uncles were waiting with a car in East Pittsburgh. We didn't know that. But the train stopped special for us to get off in Braddock. [Laughs.] So we got off, and there was nobody there to meet us because they were in East Pittsburgh. And it was cold, snow. There was one man at the station waiting for a family on the next train. So he came over and wanted to know what we were looking for. So my dad told him. None of us spoke a word of English. This man at the station was German. If you speak Jewish then you can understand German, and he understood what we were talking, so we were able to converse with him. He says, "I'll take you down." We went to my uncle's store in Braddock, a tailor shop. But the store was closed. So he told us which way to go and we're walking and walking in the snow and the cold. My dad was carrying the luggage, Helena and I holding on to the little ones, my mother was carrying the baby. We looked very immigrant, I would imagine. And we turned a corner and some children were coming home from school for lunch hour, and they started yelling "Greenhorns! Greenhorns!" and throwing snowballs at us. My dad got so angry. But then my mother's sister saw us through the window, and came running down.

It was a four-room apartment near the steel mills. A lot of eastern Europeans were working in the mills. It was a mixed neighborhood, not Jewish, although Braddock had two synagogues. The town was dirty, filthy, a big black box. We weren't used to that. We were used to clean. There was no toilet in the house. They had an outhouse with rats running around again. My mother started crying. She wanted to go back to Europe. But we had to live there for a few months until we moved to a better place.

My dad got a job right away in a steel mill. Thank God he started working right away. After he made a little money, he bought dairy cows, and we sold milk and dairy. Before we went to school we had to deliver the milk, all the children. We put the milk in milk bottles, then it was glass bottles.

After he bought the cows he said to my mother who was very unhappy, "I'll send you back with the younger children. I'll stay here with the older ones. We'll make money, and then we'll come back to you." But by that time she got used to it, and everything was okay.

My mother occupied herself. She bought geese, and we used to feed them special feed to get them nice and fat, because years ago that's what they used instead of beef fat. Goose fat was the best, healthiest fat at that time. And she used to sell it to people. She made a few dollars that way. And we helped her as little as we were. We babysat. Or we cleaned somebody else's apartment to make a few dollars. My mother picked up English after a while. She learned more than father. Eventually, all five of my brothers opened a beer garden, a tavern in Braddock.

I went back to visit Hungary in 1981. When we got in, my son-in-law drove into town. We passed what I thought was our old house. But everything looked so little. When you're a child everything looks big. We knocked on the door. But the man wouldn't let us in. He was afraid. He locked himself in, because it was a communist country. They weren't allowed to talk to strangers. So then we started walking down the street, and I said, "This must be it." I didn't recognize right away because they had made a fence. We didn't have a fence. I remember we had a strawberry tree that was gone. And some women came out in the yard, and they saw us looking around, and they started talking to me. I told them who I was and they remembered my name. And they said, "Oh, yeah, this was your house."

It was very emotional for me. I just lingered there for a little while and looked around. I couldn't believe my eyes that I was there.

Harriet Kovak

· · · · · · · · · · · ·

BORN MARCH 12, 1915
EMIGRATED 1948, AGE 33
PASSAGE ON THE *NORMANDIE*

Born and raised in Budapest, she took a vacation to America, met her husband, and decided to stay. "It was a beautiful marriage," she said. "I had a beautiful life with him. We had two beautiful children and a grandchild. Unfortunately, I lost him nine years ago."

After the war I was working as a file clerk for the American State Department in Budapest. I was a widow already. I lost my first husband during the Holocaust. He was deported and never came back. And at a certain point in 1947, I wanted to come to the United States for a two-week vacation. At the time, my sister and brother-in-law, who was American, were in Paris. They invited me to come with them to the United States.

I had a passport, but I had no American visa. To get an American visa you had to have an affidavit. There was no time for an affidavit. So I went to see the consul general, who I knew well. I told him my story. He was very nice. And he authorized the visa, without an affidavit, in my passport.

I left Budapest, and I went to Paris to meet my sister and my brother-in-law. When I got there they said, "Our plans have changed. We're not going to America." I had no money to go by myself. After my two weeks' vacation in Paris, I went back to Hungary and continued work.

But I still had that visa which was valid for one year for two weeks' stay in the United States. So in 1948, I decided to go. I went from Le Havre on the *Normandie*, a beautiful French boat. Six days later in June, I arrived at Ellis Island around six o'clock in the evening, but immigration officers didn't accept my visa because I had no affidavit. "You can't stay here," they said. "You have no affidavit."

I was scared to death. There were two other women who had similar visa problems, and one man who was a criminal. He was taken away. The two ladies were also scared to death. I almost fainted, because in Europe at that time the reputation of Ellis Island was terrible; that it's a dungeon and they beat people up. It was a horror even to hear the name.

I remember a woman, a matron, in a white robe with a big bunch of keys at her side coming toward me, and I was trembling. I didn't see the other ladies anymore. And this matron suddenly said, "Are you hungry?"

I said, "Yes, I am."

"The cafeteria is closed, but I can get you something."

I said to myself, "This is Ellis Island? They are so nice to me?"

"Eat whatever you want." And I did.

Then they let me make a phone call to a friend. I came here with only eighty dollars in my pocket. But because I did not have an affidavit, the immigration officer asked for a thousand dollars bail, which I didn't have. They were going to ship me back.

So I called this friend. She was an American girl who worked for the American Military Mission in Hungary. I had her phone number in New York. I told her my story, She said, "I will be there tomorrow morning."

The matron came back and guided me to a room where there were other women sleeping. She lifted up the cover of the bed and she looked at the sheet and said, "That's not clean." She changed the sheets, and said, "Would you like to have a shower? We have hot water." She showed me the bathroom. I had a shower. It was unbelievable. Where was this horrible Ellis Island?

I had a good night's sleep and the next morning, I had breakfast in the building that was the big hall. And naturally I was waiting for that friend to bail me out, and she was smart because she had her I.D. that she worked for the military mission, and I had my I.D. that I worked for the American State Department, so they reduced my bail to $500. She paid the $500 and I was able to leave. Afterwards, I paid her back, and I am still grateful to her.

During my two weeks here, I met my husband who was a very prominent lawyer. After I went back to Europe, I returned to America in December of '49 on a three-month visa. My husband and I married quickly, otherwise I couldn't have stayed here. We moved into a beautiful apartment on the Upper West Side of Manhattan.

According to immigration law, now that I was a U.S. citizen, I was supposed to be able to get that $500 back. But the law also said that if you marry an American citizen, you have to leave the country and come back. That was the law. But I couldn't leave the country. I was pregnant, and I had a very difficult pregnancy in the sense that the last three months I had to stay in bed if I didn't want to lose the child. The doctor didn't permit me to travel, not even to sit in a car, nothing.

So my husband, who was an excellent lawyer, asked for the $500 They didn't want to give it back to him. They said, "Your wife didn't leave the country. You don't get the money back." For my husband, it was not so much the $500, as the principle. Here a woman is pregnant, is going to have American children, cannot leave, which is justified by doctors, cannot move, and you don't give back the $500? So he sued the government. Not for the money, but out of principle. The lawsuit cost him thousands of dollars.

I went with him to Albany at least ten times. Finally, six years later, they said, "Okay, you're right." He got a letter that said he won the lawsuit. We were waiting for the $500. The money was supposed to be sent from the Treasury. At that point, my husband gave up. He said, "I had enough. I wanted to win the suit because I felt I was right. I wanted to make a precedent of law, which I did."

We never got back the $500.

15

· · · · · · · · · · ·

Romania

(APPROXIMATELY 155,000 IMMIGRANTS, 1892–1954)

Eastern European Gypsies being excluded or deported, circa 1907

(NATIONAL PARK SERVICE: STATUE OF LIBERTY NATIONAL MONUMENT)

Esther Gidiwicz

. . . .

BORN MARCH 5, 1900
EMIGRATED 1905, AGE 5
PASSAGE ON THE *ROTTERDAM*

*She grew up in the noise, hustle, and bustle of Norfolk Street on the Lower East Side,
during its immigrant heyday. She graduated from grammar school, got a job doing
trim work in a hat factory, and later married. Today, she lives in New Jersey.*

I do not remember the name of the town, what we used to call a *shtetl*, a little town. It was really a small village. We lived there until I was five years old.

There weren't any houses there. They were really more or less huts, and what I faintly remember, there were about three rooms and we all lived in the three rooms. The house was wood and my mother had a cow and made her own butter, milk, cheese. Stores were very far apart. They had to go to another village to go to a doctor, or to be in contact with other people. We had an outhouse and no running water. The well was quite a distance away, and I remember my mother saying, always coming to argue with my older brother, "Somebody has to go get a pail of water," and there was always a fuss in the house. The stove in the house was built in the wall, a big brick thing, and there was always something cooking on it.

My father came from the village we lived in. In those days, the marriages were just made. Somebody knew him, and somebody knew her, and she was an orphan, and he was working for some tailor, and he came to know her, and they got married. That was the way people got married in those days. My father was not handsome. But he idolized my mother, and we children grew up idolizing her. She was everything to us because it was Mother. He catered to her. She never used a harsh word, either. I was brought up with parents that suffered a lot in their youth, and when they got to this little village and they started living there, they appreciated each other and what they had. She was not a demanding person.

I had two brothers, and a sister, and I was the baby. My father, with an uncle of mine, heard about America. They heard it's a wonderful place, a lot of opportunities there. The living was so poor in Romania. There was no synagogue or temple. So my father and this uncle, having no money at all, figured they'd work their way through going to America. They had to wait until the butcher passed through the village, and they went with him in order to get transportation, and that's how they traveled, from one place to another, to eventually get to America. It was a miracle how they got here.

My father and uncle came here in 1902. They had passports. Another uncle of mine that was here in America previously, sent my father the passport, but no money, naturally. He came here and lived with this uncle, and got a job. My father became a furrier. He lived with my aunt and uncle who lived in four rooms on Houston Street on the Lower East Side, and I remember my father telling us he slept on the kitchen floor because they had other people staying there with them.

When my father started working, I re-member him telling us, at the end of the week they gave him his check. But he didn't know what that was, and he was ashamed to ask so as not to appear foolish. So he kept it. He thought it was a ticket of some kind and he waited about a month or so, and he wasn't getting any money. Finally, he asked somebody, and then he realized that piece of paper is really money. And that's how my father accumulated money.

Then, he sent for my oldest brother, who was about seventeen years old at the time. My brother was here for two years with my father. And my brother, too, lived with this aunt and uncle and he accumulated money. My brother worked in a factory that made skirts and jackets, tailoring.

The two of them worked very hard and they saved every penny they could, and they sent for my mother, my other brother, my sister, and I.

Almost everybody had somebody going to America. So we all had that in common. "Did you get a letter? Did you get a letter?" My mother couldn't read. So when she got a letter she would go to the butcher. He was the one that read the letter for her and he was the one that used to write. My father couldn't read too much either, but he had someone read the letters here for him and that's how they lived. We children had no schooling in Romania. Whatever education there was, was in Hebrew, so there was always an educated man in town that would come and give my brothers and sister lessons.

. . .

I didn't want to bring this up, but we didn't mingle with too many people. There were very few Jews there and nobody made friends with us. The butcher was Jewish, and there was another little store that was Jewish, just three or four. The rest were not Jewish people. They didn't argue with us. They got along enough to say "hello," but they didn't mingle with us. My mother told us a story where one time they were notified the cossacks were coming in, and she would take us children out into the woods. She'd take the pillows and the blankets, and stay there. She'd hear shooting and come back after it was over. The gentile people would say, "Where's your God now? Your God allows this?" and things like that.

My father worked for a man in town who was supposed to be like a constable. He was very lucky this constable gave him this job. My father must have been a very good tailor, because through this constable, if anybody annoyed my mother and us chil-dren, my father would tell him and that was that. Also, through this constable, we got food. Many times, when the constable had a party, or celebrated something, and he had leftovers, he'd give it to my father, and through this constable, we led a little eas-ier life.

My mother took her candlesticks to America. That was the main thing. She took along her samovar, and just the clothing we had and some bedding. I remember riding on this wagon to a certain cousin in a large town and that was the first time we saw real houses. We stayed with this cousin for about two days. I had an uncle there who was a politician, and through him, we were able to ride across the Belgian border, be-cause in those days people had to steal their way across.

. . .

Then we got to the seaport, Antwerp. We stayed there only for about a day or so. My mother was telling us this story: that when she went into the ladies' room, there were a lot of sinks and mirrors, you know, and the toilets on the side. And we children were standing by the mirrors. She came in and she saw us. She didn't see herself. She saw us in the mirror. She never saw a mirror before, and she thought we were there, and she started scolding us, "Come over here, . . ." and then she realized. She was very much embarrassed. My mother was a very sensitive person all the way through. If she made one mistake and people laughed, then she wouldn't say another word.

Anyhow, we got on ship. The *Rotterdam*. And we went steerage. I remember them taking us downstairs. I'd never seen a boat. There was a lot of beds, cots, and we all slept one alongside the other, and then there's a partition, then there's another large room. There were a lot of people, an awful lot of people, sleeping in one room together. The odor was awful. There were a lot of children, a lot of grownups, a lot of men, a lot of women. People didn't even talk to each other they were so miserable and we always huddled together and it was very, very hard, very bad.

I remember the food was so bad that many times my mother would say, "Don't eat it," or, "Eat a little." She herself was very sick. She was confined to her bed the whole trip, and we three kids were standing there around her. We were allowed to go out on the deck. People from upstairs, first class and second class, would look down on us, and

Immigrant dining hall in the dormitory and baggage building, where immigrants were detained for overnight stays, adjacent to the main building

(NATIONAL PARK SERVICE: STATUE OF LIBERTY NATIONAL MONUMENT)

they would feel sorry for us, and many times they would throw down an orange, or apples, or candy. We, the children, would all stand by and this one would catch this and this one would catch that. You were lucky to get something. Of course, being that my mother was sick, if it was an orange or a banana, we'd bring it into her. My mother never saw an orange or banana. None of us did.

The trip was very hard. We couldn't take a bath. On Friday nights, Jewish women light candles, and the first Friday night we were aboard ship there were Jewish women who lit their candles, which was a dangerous thing to do, and that infuriated the sailors. The sailors would all walk around blowing out the candles and they'd yell, *"Dumpke Juden!"* stupid Jews, which really was a terrible thing to do. But the whole voyage across was terrible. It must have been about two weeks.

Then, all of a sudden, we heard a big commotion and we came to America and everybody started yelling—they see the Statue of Liberty. We all ran upstairs and my mother got out of bed. We went upstairs and everybody started screaming and crying. We were kissing each other; people that didn't even know each other before were kissing and crying. Everybody was so excited to see America and the lady with her hand up, you know.

Then the ship came into port, and there was a doctor there that examined you. Examined mostly your hair, your head, your eyes. There were people who did not pass. At Ellis Island, they were put aside and had to go back.

It was a very big room. You were always with a lot of people. Everybody was pushing and shoving and we were examined again. My mother held us [with] her hands . . . They sent us to another large room and they had a meal for us. That room I remember distinctly because it was immense. To me it looked like it was everything; the whole world there. It had long tables and they gave us some kind of meat and we looked at my mother whether we can eat it, because it might not be kosher. My mother just smiled and said, "Eat it," because we didn't have a good piece of meat all the way through.

As we were eating, they were calling people who came to pick somebody up. And finally they called our name. We were there only a short time. In fact, we were in the middle of eating, when they called our name. We looked at my mother. Should we go, or should we eat? We went to this table, and a couple of men, they asked us our name. There was a big gate there and a lot of people . . .

My father and my brother was there, and an uncle of mine. I remember my father putting his arms around my mother and the two of them standing and crying and my father said to my mother, "You're in America now. You have nothing to be afraid of. Nothing at all." He explained to her that you could go out in the street and you could mingle with people. That's the first thing he said to her, and then we continued going.

I didn't want to go to my father. I didn't know him. He picked me up. I started to cry. I didn't want to go. I started kicking and crying. I didn't remember my father and it took me about a week before I really went to him. Finally, we got out of that building and looking around. I remember my mother saying, "So this is America. It's wonderful!" These big buildings, she never saw anything so big.

My father got a furnished apartment for us on Norfolk Street on the Lower East Side, three rooms on the fourth floor. We got on an elevator for the first time. We were in a different world. The apartment had a bedroom, a kitchen, and a dining room, and in the bedroom, we had a large mirror and my mother looked at it and she saw the same thing she saw in Europe, and she marveled at it. You can see your whole body. You could see what you're wearing. When my mother sat by the window, she looked out and saw people having lines of clothing, you know, wash, out—and she looked down and she says to my father, "In America, they have such big ladders that they climb up to hang the wash?" And, of course, people started laughing and that shut her up for a while.

I remember this distinctly. We were in the apartment and we had some company, and the religious Jewish people used to wear wigs and my mother wore a wig, and this cousin of mine who was Americanized . . . She came in and the first thing she did, she went over to my mother and took off her wig. My mother said, "Oh, my God! What are you doing to me?," and my cousin said, "In America you don't wear a wig. You can go just the way you want to go," and so on and so forth. It took us quite a while to get used to America.

. . .

Norfolk Street was very noisy, very crowded and everybody knew each other. The buildings were tenement houses, all about six stories high. The school was about two blocks away . . . We had running water. Cold water. No hot water. We had a coal stove. The apartment was lit by lamps for a short time, and after that they put in gas and we had gaslight, and I remember you had to buy these little mantles to put in, and every once in a while one of them would go bad and you had to buy another. In order to pay for the gas, you had a meter in the house. You used to put a quarter in the meter and that would allow you to use a certain amount of gas and when that went low you knew you had to put another quarter in. So my father always had a couple of quarters on the side.

For heat, we just had the coal stove. In the morning, we got dressed by the stove. The toilets were in the hall. Two tenants used one toilet and that was the way of life. My father was a hardworking man and he used to take work home at night. He used to make the linings for the fur coats. After supper, he'd work a little and then he'd go to bed. He'd get up about four o'clock in the morning and he had these linings all ready to work on. My sister and I, as young as we were, slept in the kitchen and he used to work in the kitchen so the light woke us up. Many times, we'd fall asleep again, but most times we'd sit up with him and my father would tell us stories of Europe and we'd thread the needle for him and he would make these linings.

My mother stayed in the house for about a week when we first came. She was afraid to go out and she wouldn't know how to mingle with people. And, of course, she loved America. The idea that she could be free . . . Still, my father kept saying, "You got to go down! You got to get used to this! There's a butcher downstairs. They're Jewish. There are Jewish people all around you!" She went down to do some marketing and the butcher was very nice to her, and she was so happy that they spoke to her. They spoke in her language. And she went back up one stairway and she didn't know how to get back to our apartment. She was too embarrassed to ask, because people laughed at her whenever she asked a question, you know. So she stood there.

Finally, she called out my sister's name. My sister's name in Jewish was "Sepa," and she stands there yelling "Sepa!" But my sister was told in America, you don't open the doors unless you know who is there and she didn't hear her anyhow. Well, one of the women in the building heard her and said, "You're on the third floor. You got to count your floors," and told her how to get upstairs.

After that, she used to go down and do her shopping every morning, got acquainted with the butcher, and the grocer, and was very glad. She learned how to do the washing here, the laundry, because in Europe, she went to the river to do the wash . . . A neighbor told her, "You can send your children to school. Why are they home? You're here already a month or so, . . ." and we still didn't go. So somebody took my sister. My brothers were too old, sixteen, seventeen. So my sister was the first one that went. She was about nine years old, and she came home and told us, the little sister can go, also. Me. My mother said, "No, you go for a couple of weeks and see what it is and then . . ." Because to my mother, it was like a miracle that her children could really go to school here.

Well, my sister went for about a month and she told her teacher that she's got a little sister home. "Well, bring her in, by all means." So my mother dressed me up fancy. Our clothing was given to us when we came to America by cousins of ours. I remember this distinctly. They sent me to kindergarten and the teacher asked me my name. I couldn't talk English then. We spoke Jewish in the house. So my sister said to me in Jewish, "Tell her your name." I said, "Esther." I said my name is Esther. So she said, "Esther what?" Well, the teacher had the hardest time, and my sister couldn't get the drift of it either, because she didn't know too much English . . .

My teacher's name was Mrs. Levine. I'll never forget that. She was the nicest person, and I remember that she put her arms around me and made me feel at ease, and when I came home and I told my mother how nice the teacher was—my mother was petrified: God knows what was going to happen to me there. At the same time [that] she was nervous, my mother kept saying, "It's the most wonderful thing in America that your child can go to school with gentile children, come home, her hair isn't torn, her dress isn't torn, she isn't beaten up, she comes home, walks with these children in the street . . ." To her, it was a miracle that nobody hit us, that nobody did anything to us . . .

My parents were very happy. They never wanted to go back. They didn't always have a lot of money, they struggled. But everything here was paradise. I lost a son two years ago, and my son always said that he worships his grandfather, my father. He always worshiped him. He always thought he was the most wonderful thing; to think that he had the foresight to come to America and that's how all of us felt. All us children, we always felt that way. No matter what hardships we go through here; you can complain about your presidents, it's still the best place in the world.

Gerald Wine

. . . .

BORN JUNE 18, 1904
EMIGRATED 1923, AGE 19
PASSAGE ON THE *PARIS*

He was born in the city of Vizhnitsa, part of the state of Bocovina, which became part of Romania by the time he left. Today, he spends a good part of his days

. . . .

reading the Talmud. "When you come before God Almighty, he ask you one question, 'What have you done with your life?' You must give him an answer. I wanted to make sure that I have done with my life the proper thing."

The town had a population of five thousand. It was in the heart of the Carpathian mountains. It was close to the boundary lines of Hungary, Poland, Romania, and it was surrounded with a rural Ukrainian population. But it was actually on the river Cheremosh. The river Cheremosh was a mountain river which flowed into the river Prut. The river Prut flowed into the river Dniester, and the river Dniester flowed into the Black Sea.

It was not an industrial city, it was a lumber city. From the Carpathian mountains, they would get the lumber, and let it float down all the way to Bessarabia.

The city itself was mostly Jewish. The population was separate from the Ukrainians. The Ukrainians had their own schooling, which dealt mostly with making different things from wood, and they had a special school for that, which had nothing to do with the Jewish population.

There was constantly fear of an outbreak of war because it was right during the Balkan War of 1912. It was a war atmosphere constantly. I attended Jewish school and German school. There was a patriotic feeling. We had to have the patriotic prayer every morning. But, in general, it was of enormous worry due to the constant fear that we didn't know when the war would start. My parents felt this fear more, but I participated. Every morning you didn't know that tomorrow . . . the Balkan War . . . they might throw in Austria any moment . . . We would read the papers . . . I listened to all the discussions every morning, and by listening to all the different discussions it more or less, as a young child, it left me with a certain knowledge, that [was] developed much further than any ordinary

American child. There was an antagonism between the Russians and the Ukrainians and the Austrians and Romanians; between Russian-speaking and German-speaking peoples.

The minute we left on a Saturday to go out in the country, those Ukrainian boys would see us, and there would be a fight right away. The Ukrainians were very poor. They would steal lunches from each other, because they didn't have enough to eat.

My father worked as a clerk in the sheriff's office. His job was that he would go up in the mountains to notify people when they had to go to the army. There was no mail there. My father came to America briefly in 1901, before I was born. He was looking for something, for a better world. When he came to America, he realized most Jews peddled because the Jewish population at that time had no trade. But he wasn't a peddler. He was an educated person. He was a musician. He composed as much as he could. His father, my grandfather, loved music, too. After one year, he went back to Romania. He kept on working in the sheriff's office all the way to the last day of 1914 and World War I.

My mother was a housewife. Her father, my grandfather, was the chief of police. He held this power there. The power of his was such that every year a commissioner would come to examine people to go to the army and stay in his place because there was no hotels. At the same time, the army took away the breadwinner from some of the people who needed the boys, and my grandfather wasn't very popular for that, but it had to be done. The peasants from the mountains weren't very happy. When my grandfather had to let them know, he always was armed.

My oldest brother was my mother's darling. My father wanted him to be a doctor, but he didn't have the ambition to be a doctor. He simply wanted a plain job. He was killed in the army, on the 21st of November 1916 on the Isonzo River in Italy. He is buried somewheres in the city of Ljubljana in Yugoslavia. My oldest sister, he wanted her to be an opera singer. She's ninety-two years old now, and lives with my niece in Wilmington, Delaware. She didn't have the voice to be an opera singer. Another sister, she wanted to be a piano teacher. My father was ambitious for his children, but you have to pay money for lessons. He didn't have it. He had a good heart, he wanted everything for us. On me, he gave up. I was the youngest one. My father was taken in the war in 1914. From the trenches he was sick, and he died in 1922.

From 1914 on, my whole life changed. Everything fell apart. Romania, we didn't know Romania. Our culture and everything was Austrian. And here we were confronted in a strange city, a strange culture. There was no more life for us. First, they took my brother away into the army. He was nineteen years old, and that was already a very hard knock for my mother. My father still worked for the Austrian government, but they knew any moment the battle will change to such an extent the Russians will come in and take over the city, and the end of Austrian rule, and it happened. That was the end. The Russians came in, they took whatever they wanted, because the battle was right next to the city.

I remember it well. There was a rumbling every night, a rumbling of the cannons being moved along the road, it was cobblestones. We heard the shooting. We were sitting in the school class. All of a sudden we heard explosions. Everybody was running here and running there. The parents were running after the children. The Russians were bombarding the railroad station. There was no battle in the city, but they knew they would march in the next morning, and it happened.

The Austrian army withdrew, people who had money traveled to Hungary. Those that didn't have enough money, or a wagon, would have to remain there and get the best donkeys. Terrible scared, terrible scared. The Russians marched in, they were crude, they were hungry, just like soldiers. They said to my mother, "Have you got something to eat?" And my mother said, "I haven't got anything." He says, "All right." He went out, ten minutes he came back, and he brought a sack of chickens, live chickens. He says, "Go ahead." He opened up the bag, and the chickens flew all over the house. He says, "Slaughter the chickens and feed us." My mother had never done it, she says, "I've never done it." He says, "If you are not going to slaughter the chickens, I'll slaughter you." He was wild. He was drunk. She says, "There's nothing I can do." My grandmother, my father's mother, was an old woman. She got so scared she became paralyzed out of fear.

After a while, the soldier quieted down. He says, "All right, just give us to drink." And he fell asleep, he was tired. My grandmother just sat there paralyzed, afraid to move. The place was full of soldiers, and they fell asleep, and we just sat there. We were able to move my grandmother downstairs where she slept, because she couldn't move.

In the morning, the soldier woke up. He was sober. He was entirely different. He was a different human being. He apologized and he went . . . I was ten years old. It hit a terrible nerve, terrible on my mind. I couldn't sleep. To this very moment, I still suffer. To this very moment I must take a Dolmain, a sleeping pill, otherwise I can't fall asleep.

All over the city, the soldiers went back and forth. The Russians won, the Austrians withdrew. Two weeks later, the Austrians won, the Russians withdrew. Two weeks later, the Russians won, the Austrians withdrew. And so it went back and forth. Once Austria was free for a few weeks, immediately they took my brother. We didn't hear nothing. My father was forty-five years old. They immediately took him in the army. My sister went in the army and joined the hospital. She became a nurse.

I was left with my two sisters and my mother. We had school for a few weeks. When the Russians withdrew, the school opened up. When the Russians advanced, the school closed up. Finally, it got to the point the military authorities told us, "You have to leave. There's going to be a big battle. We'll give you twenty-four hours."

"Where are we going to go?"

"We don't care," he said. "Everybody has to withdraw."

We packed whatever we could, and we started walking. Where could we walk? Up towards the Hungarian Mountains. They were the nearest one, there was no other way out. So we dragged ourselves. Sometimes we got a little break from the soldiers. At that time they still had covered wagons. There were no trucks. They gave us a little ride. It was dangerous. I was with my sisters and mother, and they were in danger of being raped by our own soldiers. But I did not understand, I was ten years old. Others took my mother and sisters. I could hear them scream. The soldiers held onto me, they clawed their nails in on me to make sure to hold onto me, and this scared me and they . . .

We traveled to a place we were safe. There were thousands of people from all over, refugees, and the Austrian government started distributing us to different places in Austria.

Our town was destroyed, so we lived in the country inside Germany among the peasants, for about a year's time, no education, nothing. But my father was released finally from the army because he couldn't serve anymore. He had rheumatism, he was a sick man, so they let him go. He was more dead than alive.

In September 1916, we went to Vienna. I immediately registered at school and Vienna was starvation, starvation, really starvation. There was nothing to eat. The authorities were able to scrape something together, which they gave us to eat. My mother would travel to the countryside to get from the peasants some kind of food; apples, she would cook it and made compote. And beets, Austria had an awful lot of beets . . .

But I got a big education. I did my homework in the opera house because it was warm. They had a system that every opera singer hired a club of boys who would applaud him after he got through singing. So little by little, being I came regular, one of about ten, fifteen boys, who would applaud.

. . .

After the war, I stayed in Vienna, and then the revolution started. Fascism began to come in. They called themselves, not Nazis. They called themselves *Haken-kreuzlers*. They started in Vienna. *Haken-kreuzler* was the beginning of the Fascist movement. Being a schoolboy, you know, we fought it, we were against it, because I belonged to the club of the Social Democratic Youth Committee. So there were always fights. Each one carried a knife. They were very dangerous. It was fascism all the way through. We had no chance. It was an awful revolution. They didn't listen to anybody. There was no police, there was no soldiers. People with armbands went around claiming they were guards. What they did actually was stealing and robbing. And for about two weeks there was fighting going on. Men on horses with sabers. They were slashing people. One was coming at me with a saber, but he couldn't hit me because I hid behind a mailbox. There was people, right in front of my eyes, fifteen people were killed. That was the end, that was the end.

We left there finally when the republic was broken up, each one was independent, and they told us we had no business to be in Vienna. We didn't feel like leaving Vienna. We had to go home, because the Romanian government told us if you didn't come back by a certain time, you lost your citizenship, and we went back, but we lost everything anyway. We lost our citizenship, we lost the house, we lost everything. When my father died in 1922, we had nothing.

Meanwhile, I grew up, and I was already groomed for the Romanian army. My grandmother said, "You're the only one that's left over. You will not be in the army if it's my last penny. You'll go to America."

My father's brother lived here. He came here first in 1910 or 1911, and then he took his family over. They were not very rich. They couldn't afford to send for us. Finally, when the war stopped, they were able to send us. They got money together to buy tickets for us to come to America.

I came with my older sister. Everybody came to the railroad station and they kept on telling to me, "As soon as you come to America," they said, "you save us. Work hard, save money, and take us over to America. That's our only chance . . ."

I just took one good suit. That's about all, one suit. My suitcase, there was nothing else to pack. The suit that I packed was sent to me from America from the Joint Distribution Committee. The Jewish societies collected old clothes and it happened to fit me.

Before I left I learned English. I was very well acquainted with American history. I loved American history. I knew about the Civil War, geography, the battles. I studied wars. I knew why there was a civil war, and the differences between the South and the North.

We went from Chernovtsy to Budapest. Then from Budapest to Vienna. From Vienna to Zurich. From Zurich to Paris. From Paris to Le Havre. We left to America from Le Havre. In Le Havre, we stopped for two weeks where they examined us. What scared me most, my tear sac was closed on my eye. They said they were not going to let me in America because it's a sickness [trachoma]. And, you know, people have a habit of scaring you. They examined me, they found me okay. They says it's up to the American doctor at the consulate. To my surprise, the doctor was joking with me. He took a look and he seen right away that a tear sac is not a sickness. In fact, he made a joke. He says, "It is Prohibition. Your name is Wine, you're not supposed to come in." But it took such a big load off me, you know, that it made me double-happy.

In Le Havre we had a concentration camp. Everybody was thrown together. They were from all over. We ate there, everything given us. We stood there, everybody was examined because America would not let anybody in unless the travel agency passes first. After they passed, then they let you in. They had women nurses, and I had to undress for them to examine me. And I fought like hell. I wouldn't let a woman see me, because I was brought up, according to the old tradition—a man does not undress himself in front of women. But I had to finally give in . . .

The boat was just like anything else. Small, third class, you know. From 1914 to 1923, we experienced such hardship, such everything, such hunger, nothing matters. You're hardened. You survive. You're a survivor. First of all, the language. We didn't understand the Romanian, and the Romanian treated us very bad because we were German nationalists. They had no use for us. They took away from us everything. My father's job was taken away, everything. Nothing.

I was looking forward to coming to America. I was very well acquainted with the Constitution, with the Civil War. I had an idea that America was a democracy. I could see for me a liberal life. I don't have to be afraid to come home at night from school or to carry a revolver or a rifle. But I also was thinking I am leaving my mother and one sister home, you know, and I will never see them again . . .

My older sister, she came with me and she cried constantly. Then she forgot about it. In less than a year here, she got married . . .

During the boat trip, passengers tried to find out what kind of disease the other one had in order to use it to scare them. That used to be the joke. People were really scared. After we arrived in New York, the desire to speak English was so intense. I said something in German, they bawled me out. "Stop talking German!" Because German was my language. They says, "You speak English. You're in America."

As soon as we went to Ellis Island, nobody picked us up. We got scared. It was packed with people. There was a table where a commissioner sat. He was a very nice man. He tried to get people to relax. He made jokes. He was very easygoing. And anybody that comes back from him came with a smile on their face because they were all scared, scared, scared.

So after I came on line, he asked me, you know, he examined me, he looked in my ears, and he made a joke. Then comes the question, "Who is picking you up?" "My cousin is supposed to pick us up but he didn't . . ." So we were sitting waiting. It was about ten o'clock. We kept on waiting and waiting and waiting. Finally, it was already late in the afternoon, so the official there said, "I'll tell you what we'll do. We'll put tickets on you. You take the boat, and go to Battery Park. In Battery Park, it might be that your cousin is late. He will recognize you, or you'll recognize him. I mean, some-

body will help you. We can't keep you here. We have no place for you to sleep . . ."

As soon as we arrived at Battery Park, my sister recognized my cousin, whom she hadn't seen since she was a kid. For some reason, you know, he was late. So he took us home in a car for the first time. He took us to Brownsville, Brooklyn. But I didn't stay. There was no room for me. The following night, I moved to the East Side in Manhattan. My aunt lived on East Ninth Street.

The question was money, money for my mother, to help her. My father was dead. I had to look for a job. I didn't know where. But I bought a Jewish paper, looked through the ads, they were looking for a machinist on Second Avenue. I was hired, fifteen dollars a week. Machine shop repairs. And it came lunch time. I didn't know a word. I pointed to a salami and there was bread, and I ate. I had a place to sleep. I worked there.

I slept at my aunt's who lived with some woman from my town, who came to America years ago. A simple old woman. She kept people living there because they knew her from the same town. So she charged me about eight dollars a week. She had like a railroad flat. I put my suitcase under the bed, you know. After a couple of weeks, I found myself a room in a boardinghouse with other young boys. The boarding room was on Clinton Street. They started taking me around. They went out, I went with them. All of us were immigrants. It was right in the territory of the Jewish gangsters down on Clinton and Delancey. Sunday I would go with the boys to Prospect Park. Every Saturday I would go to the Metropolitan Opera. I liked music. It didn't cost me anything. America, New York, gave me all the opportunity for culture, whatever there was. When I had a chance, I used to go to lectures at the Youth Education Alliance. There was a library down there, and I could write and read. I would go to different places, and little by little, I saved and I sent to my mother.

But it just happened that Congress passed a bill that set quotas for immigrants, and the biggest immigrant quotas were for Nordics, not for eastern Jews. So what happened, my mother and my younger sister couldn't come over. Imagine, from 1924, according to your quota, they had to wait till 1936 to be able to come to America. But I was able to get more money together, and in 1936, my mother came to America. My younger sister died in Europe.

My mother, I lived with her in Borough Park in Brooklyn, and she died in 1955 in Boston. She is buried in Everett, Massachusetts. My older sister is already ninety-six, and she is living in Wilmington . . .

In the workplace, in those days, it was mostly English. Anybody that didn't speak English was considered an ignorant, never mind what you spoke over there. Everybody spoke English here. Today, where I live in Borough Park, there's so many different nationalities, I think I'm in Singapore.

Carl Bellapp

. . . .

BORN NOVEMBER 27, 1913
EMIGRATED 1930, AGE 18
PASSAGE ON THE *CONTE GRANDE*

He was born and raised in Soroki, a Romanian border town near the Ukraine. His family emigrated in pairs; he came with his sister. "I came here when I was eighteen," he said. "The country has been good to me. America, I love you."

My father was a barber in Soroki. He had a pretty good-sized barbershop with three mirrors and himself and two employees. Eventually, one of my brothers became a partner. He also became a barber. So they had the two of them plus an employee, and it was rough making a living. We were a family of eight. Four brothers and four sisters. I was the one before the youngest.

My mother was a saint. She was one of the finest ladies anyone can have. Very honest, always giving of herself, feeding people who didn't have what to eat, which was very common in that part of the country. All in all, I worshiped her. Her children and

seeing everybody, and everybody getting along, was all she wanted in life.

Each one of the kids had a nickname. My nickname in Hebrew was "Urtza." *Urtza* means a treasure. She called me a treasure, and I was very proud of it . . .

We lived in a house that was rented. My father used to rent it from somebody who had the house next door to us. Soroki was in a valley near the river Niustru, which emptied into the Danube, and divided Soroki from Ukraine. The town on the opposite side of the river was called Zichinuvka.

Of course, we had no plumbing in the house. It was an outhouse with two partitions, which was pretty rough going out there in the wintertime, and we had some very cold winters. We also used to have a little pottie. If it was real cold, and you didn't have to go badly, you used the pot. By 1930, we had electricity that used to be cut off at midnight.

We did have some education. The highest education you were able to get in Soroki was high school. After that, you had to leave Soroki. It was impossible to support anybody living out of the city. My father hardly made ends meet to care of a family that size. First my eldest brother and sister came in 1918 or 1919 through a network of landsmen, or societies that helped people get out of Romania and placed in America. They settled in Pittsburgh. He was a barber like my father and got a job in a barbershop. She worked in an office.

Then, around 1927, my father and another brother of mine decided to leave for America. My father knew a landsman who had a barbershop on the Lower East Side in New York, so they didn't go to Pittsburgh. Between my father and my two brothers, they accumulated enough money to get me and my sister Nita here.

As the family immigrated to the United States, I was left with the role of breadwinner. It was just my mother, my three sisters, and myself, left. Everyone else—the older ones—were already in America. They came in twos, until it was my turn and my sister Nita. Later, my mother and my two sisters came, and that completed the family.

Nita and I went by horse and wagon to Bel'tsy, and then by train to Bucharest. There, HIAS—the Hebrew Immigrant Aid Society—met us and took charge of us. I remember a doctor examined me, and he found something wrong with my eyes. They kept me back for five days for treatments in the eye. It was a thing called "trachoma." Also in Bucharest, I met the woman who would become my wife, and her fam-

ily. They were a family of five, and also immigrating to America.

From Bucharest, we went, we took a long train ride through Yugoslavia. I remember we changed trains about midnight in Jimbolia, and it was dark, cold, nothing there. We had to take all the baggage from one side to the other, and it was a mess. With the second train, we went direct to Genoa, Italy. An American doctor examined us before we boarded the ship. My wife's family, the Bussen family, they were rejected. In three of them, they found something wrong with their eyes. They sent the whole caboodle back to Bucharest. I remember the Bussen family rented a little rowboat, and as my sister and I were leaving on the big ship, they on this small boat, and you can imagine tears galore on both sides. But fortunately, after they got treated, they got on another ship and they landed in Providence, Rhode Island and they got here. She knew where to contact me in New York at my father's . . .

The journey over took nine days. We were in steerage. Most of it was smooth. My sister was sick. I wasn't. The worst part was the language barrier. I couldn't talk to anyone. Most people spoke Italian. I met one man, he had a bottle of whiskey. He kept on taking more and more, and he offered some to me. I said, "I don't drink." He says, "I like it." I didn't know what "liking" means. He was an Armenian. He spoke English some. But it didn't do me any good because I didn't speak English. But with sign language, we got along better than most people . . .

Everybody got to one side of the ship to see the Statue of Liberty. There were howls and screams and, "America, I love you." Everybody in his own language. It was a celebration. It's very hard for me to tell it to you. Certain things in life you have to live. You have to live them to appreciate them, and we lived it, and boy, I appreciated it.

When my sister and I got to Ellis Island we were very suspicious. I imagine everybody else felt the same way. They put tags on us. My tag said, "E.I." Other tags said something else, because first-class and second-class passengers were let go at the dock on West Twenty-third Street in Manhattan. What is E.I.? Am I considered a criminal? Then I found out what E.I. stands for, "Ellis Island."

We stood on line to the inspector's booth. Of course, there was the language barrier again. I remember a fellow that spoke Yiddish, and I spoke to him in Yiddish because nobody knew Romanian . . .

We spent the better part of the day at Ellis Island before my father and my brother came, and they picked us up and took us off. We went to an apartment on East Eleventh Street on the corner of Avenue C. We stayed there about three months. It was a cold-water flat. I came here on December 20, which was quite cold. So the only way we got a little heat was, my father would make the stove in the kitchen. Also in the kitchen was an inside toilet. This was heaven . . .

About two years later, my mother and two sisters came. They were the last ones here. They flew in to Kennedy Airport . . .

Part V

SCANDINAVIA

16

· · · · · · · · · ·

Sweden, Denmark, Norway & Finland

(APPROXIMATELY 1.3 MILLION IMMIGRANTS, 1892–1954)

Caren Lundgren

. . . .

BORN APRIL 25, 1903
EMIGRATED FROM SWEDEN 1921, AGE 18
PASSAGE ON THE M.S. *STOCKHOLM*

*She was born in Mattmar, in the province of Jantlind. As a child, her
grandparents put her to work as a maid, leaving little time for her studies. Fed
up, she emigrated alone and became a cook in private homes.*

Mattmar was mostly farmers. My father worked in the mill there. He made boards out of lumber. But this was a really small town, and, of course, we went to school. We didn't start school until we were seven, and we went two years to a small school, and then four years to the regular school, but one year I skipped a grade, so I only went to school for five years. My school was one teacher for four classes, and one big room. We learned to read and write, that's for sure, and we had history and geography, and all that sort of thing.

I was the elder sister to three brothers. One brother died when he was eight. My mother let us play, because she was the oldest in her family, with an awful lot of children. There were twelve. And she had to work all the time, so she made up her mind that if she ever had children, she was going to let them have a real childhood. So we benefited from that.

We lived in a regular house. Everybody slept in the kitchen, and what we called the *skafferi*, like a little pantry, in the wintertime. [Laughs.] It was so cold. We had a bedroom alongside that, and then a room called a *salong*. That's where if you had company you went in there, but otherwise we never went into that room.

The kitchen had a wood stove, of course. It was the children's job to bring in wood and water. We had to pump. The pump was some distance away, because it belonged to my grandmother and grandfather who lived across the road. So the pump was on his property, so we brought water from there.

Mother made a lot of milk food; a lot of puddings and cereal twice a day, for breakfast and at night, and sandwiches, and then sometimes, even in the middle of the day, we had a pudding. Very little meat, because meat was too expensive. We couldn't afford that. Most of the time if you had meat, it would be meatballs or some meatloaf, something that you could stretch out. We ate a lot of fish because my father would go fishing, freshwater fish, so that was nice. And vegetables; of course, my mother had a little garden.

My grandparents lived across the road. My father's parents. My grandfather was wonderful. He made a little playhouse for me and he made skis for us, and he made little sleds, and he was really wonderful.

I finished schooling when I was twelve, and I wanted to be a teacher. You were confirmed when you were thirteen, which I was. Then, at eighteen, you could go into the *seminaria* so that was four years [away] still.

During those four years, I was sent to my other grandparents in Sundsvall. My mother's parents. It was on an island called Alna outside Mattmar. My grandfather was

. . . .

a tailor. He had his own tailoring business and he needed help. My youngest aunt was going to get married, so they needed to have somebody take her place. So that's where I was for four years before I came to this country.

Well, I wasn't happy there at all, because it wasn't like my own home. I was a grandchild there, but I slept in the kitchen just like a maid, and they were sitting in the bedroom, and never talked. They never spoke. So I mean, I was never happy those four years. Absolutely not.

I did housework, cleaning, really hard work, because my grandfather had his own business, and there was a house where the people sat who worked for him. I had to clean that all the time, morning and night. Clean his own office, and . . . [Laughs.] I was more than amazed that I never received a cent for it. Not a red cent. My grandmother was quite old even then, and she was good, but he was so terribly stingy. Oh! She never had any money for herself either.

I wish I never had to live those four years. That's the reason I came to this country, to get away. The thing was, I felt my parents were going to be ashamed of me, because I'd never pass, and they would have to be so ashamed of me, so I have to get out of it somehow. I didn't have any money, and my grandparents wouldn't give me any money. My parents didn't have any money.

I wanted to go to America because my grandmother, the one I lived with, was saying, "If I was a young girl, I'd go to America." I heard that, and she was always talking about that. "If I was a young girl, I'd go to America." I thought, "Well, that's one way to get out, [laughs] get out of this dilemma." Then I had to get permission from my parents because I was under age. My father gave in, but I never told my mother the reason why I came here.

I didn't know anything about America except I had three uncles living here. They wrote letters and they came home to visit,

too. I heard stories. Also, there was a lot of immigration when I was a child. I saw people immigrating to America. We used to go down to the train and watch the train. There was a train station where I lived in Mattmar. The people leaving had wreathes of flowers around their necks because that was the end. They would never see them again, you see? So those were funeral flowers practically, around their necks.

To come to America, I borrowed from my grandfather, the stingy one. He was not happy I was leaving, but he did not try to stop me. I went by train to Goteborg. But I was not alone. There was an old lady from the island and her younger son. They were coming over here, because she had all the rest of her family here. But they came second class, so I didn't see them on the boat. I only had enough money for third class.

Before I left Sweden, I had to go to a doctor and get a clean bill of health; that I had been vaccinated against smallpox. I remember on the ship they examined my head for lice. If you had lice, your hair came off. I saw some girls who were bald.

I had my father's trunk that he had when he was a young man. It was a square wooden box, painted blue and had a padlock on it. Instead of a suitcase, I had a basket, a square basket, and it was also painted blue and it also had a padlock on it. The ship ride was fine. I think it took seven days . . .

In New York, we spent three days on the boat because Ellis Island was filled up. It was the end of July . . . I remember I had a tag on. We walked [laughs] like cattle herded into this great big hall. They had tables there, and they asked you questions in English and, as I remember it, you had to have fifty dollars to show you weren't destitute, and there were different rooms. There were a lot of tan-colored rooms and netting to separate the room.

I was put into such a room. I didn't see anybody from the boat, and thought, "Oh, maybe I'm in the wrong place. I certainly can't belong in here," and I saw a black man. I'd never seen a black person in my whole life before that. [Laughs.] So I tried to walk out but, of course, I was pushed back. I guess I was in the right place all right.

But what happened was, I had the address to one of my uncles, and he was a single man, and he was not allowed to take me out because he was not married. So, luckily Pastor Haelandler, from the Swedish Seaman's Home, came to Ellis Island when the ship came in. He was supposed to be responsible for me, and I was out that same afternoon.

The pastor came and he took me and three or four girls that were on the boat to 5 Water Street, to Seaman's Home. We stayed there two weeks. It was for seamen when they came in, you know. It was a seaman's home, really. It was a nice little house.

I stayed in New York City, but most of the girls were going to different places. But if you had an address to a single man, and a single man came to meet you, he could not take you out, so you had to get married. The ceremony was at this house. The gentlemen would come, and the pastor would marry them there. If they didn't get married, they would go back, which would have happened to me, except my uncle came and got me from the Seaman's Home.

I went to an employment agency, and got a job as a kitchen maid in Glen Cove, Long Island. So I went from the Seaman's Home right to the job. The job was easy compared to what I was used to from home, plus I was getting paid! [Laughs.] I got fifty dollars a month. That was a lot of money.

The only other Swede, she was the cook. The rest of the help—one was English, one was Scottish, one was Finnish. The cook, she was a son-of-a-bitch. [Laughs.] She was impossible, too, because she was not a good cook. She had been a laundress all her life, and she started to cook, and she was nerv-

ous and didn't know what she was doing half of the time, and she took it out on me. She said in Swedish, "You're so stupid. You will never make it in this country. So the best thing that you can do is go back home." And, of course, I believed her!

I thought, "I guess I am dumb." My pillow was soaking wet in the morning. It was really terrible. She had to show me how to mop a floor and always told me I was stupid. That was all I heard all day long, and I only had two days off a month.

So on those two days I went back to the agency. I asked if they could do something because I was so unhappy. This was in August. "I'll try to get you another job," she said, "but wait another month because people come back from the country at the end of September . . ."

When I wrote home, I had to be so careful about getting tears on the paper. [Laughs.] I thought, "I can't go back and admit I'm so stupid." You know? I was saving my money to pay back my grandfather, and I did. He couldn't understand how I could make that kind of money in such a short time. He couldn't believe it. [Laughs.]

The employment agency got me another job as a kitchen maid, because most of the time, in those days, there were Swedish cooks. The rich families, they had Swedish cooks so they'd put you in as a kitchen maid. They sent me to 19 East Seventieth Street, to Dave and Ann Morris. The building had a doorman. I was ushered into a side room. Of course, I didn't speak any English. After two months, you don't speak any English. So the housekeeper had the cook come upstairs, because she was Swedish so she was going to speak to me, you see. And of course, she wasn't too pleased because here I'm eighteen years old, and at that time, they used to have three in the kitchen. There used to be a cook, second cook, and the kitchen maid. But the Morrises did away with the second cook. So they wanted a kitchen maid that was very experienced, that could take over as a second cook, and here was this eighteen-year-old girl, who couldn't speak a word of English! [Laughs.] So this cook, she was not too pleased, naturally. But I got the job all right, and she was wonderful to me! She really was.

I went back to Sweden in 1926, 1930. I went back several times. It got a lot smaller, it seemed. The things that seemed big got very small. I still have one brother over there. I don't think I'll go back anymore. Now, it's too difficult to travel when you get to my age . . .

Garth Svenson

· · · · · · · · · · · ·

BORN AUGUST 27, 1899
EMIGRATED FROM DENMARK 1923, AGE 24
SHIP UNKNOWN

He had a hard time adjusting to America and learning a new language. Made of rugged Danish stock, he is now ninety-eight, and lives in Connecticut with his daughter. "Someday when I come back, no matter what happens, I'm going to stay in that particular place that I was born," he said. "I wouldn't move. I found that out in life. I would never move from my birthplace, because when you do that you're making an awful mistake. You make it awful hard for yourself. I hate to think that every time I open my mouth, they know I'm a foreigner. I don't like that."

I lived in Copenhagen until I came to America. Even at that time, from a country of 4 million Danes, there was over a million living in Copenhagen. So that's a fourth of the people in the country living in one city. So you can imagine how congested it was with transportation, with buying things.

We were very poor, because we had bad things happen to us. I was not quite four when my father died. My mother had to go to work, and there was no work, and there certainly wasn't too much work for lonely ladies. There was no government help like they have today.

We were two, my sister and I. She was about seven years older than me. My mother got a job sewing ladies' underwear. My sister got a job in a soap factory. It was common for children to work in Denmark then.

My father had worked for a furrier. His job was to go to Sweden, Norway, or Finland and buy fur. He was a big man, and supposedly a rough man, because he was very husky and supposedly quite a man. On one his trips, he caught pneumonia. Then, before he realized it, he had double pneumonia [affects both lungs], and that was enough to kill him, as husky he was, and that was the ending of the Svensons. I was four, my sister Katie was eleven. Father was buried in a family grave, a three-tier grave. He was buried at Christmas, and because of that, us two kids, we never had no Christmas, because it made my mother so sad when it came to Christmas. She just wanted to get it over with, so I never had a Christmas, the feeling of Christmas. She never remarried.

We moved quite a few times, because after my father died, we were fairly low on income and just trying to have enough to eat. I remember we had to move in with my mother's mother, my grandmother. We lived with her for a couple of years, and then she went into this convalescent home. It was paid for by the government, and that's where she died.

The only fun, as kids, was playing in the streets, or there was a park not too far from our house. Once in a great while, we would [laughs] get a dime and go across the street to see a movie picture. The movies were just beginning . . .

My mother did not push education. There was always one thing that you had to choose. You could be a mason, or a cabinetmaker, carpenter, electrician, and so on. My sister Katie became a nurse. I should have been a mason or an electrician. Instead, when I was fourteen, my mother got a job for me as a gardener at a nursery, but I had to have a bicycle. My mother saved up the money, so I could get a bicycle and go to this particular nursery, which was about five miles outside of Copenhagen—Danish miles. They were a little longer than the American mile.

I became a gardener, because gardener was the only trade that would pay you the first year. Any other trade, they wouldn't pay you the first year, but the gardener would. I made two crowns a week, so it wasn't such a big deal. But it was a help to the household. I remember riding my bicycle wearing wooden shoes.

My sister didn't contribute because when you took up nursing, you had to live in the hospital. And living in the hospital there was no earnings, because room and board took up the earnings. In later years, once she finished her studies and became a nurse, she made money, and then she would help with the household. We were always short on money.

Later, I worked in a little factory that was resilvering cups and saucers and all sorts of things. I worked there in the afternoon as an errand boy. One day there was such a commotion outside the shop. They were telling me the war had just started, World War I. Of course, I didn't know anything about it. I was a kid. After maybe a week or two there were soldiers everywhere . . . We didn't feel that there was a war going on except after a few months, maybe a year, it became hard to get different things, and you had to have cards, like food stamps. Since my sister was grown, I was grown, and my mother was grown, we each got one card. Still, we were always short.

. . .

Motorcycles and cars, that's what really got me going on coming to the United States. Because to have a motorcycle or a car, at least at that time, was almost impossible. You had to be very well off in Denmark, and I think it was the same in most of Europe. I had no family here. But my cousin had a friend who went to the United States, and he was back to Denmark on a trip. He was going to be in Copenhagen a couple of months, and then go back to the United States. So I went with him.

My mother didn't like it too much, because it was another helper that had to leave. But she accepted it. I told her that just as soon as I could get a job, and earn some money, I would send her help, which I did. I sent her ten dollars a month, and that was a help.

So this friend of my cousin convinced me to come with him. He had been in California, and he met a girl who came from Hartford. She was on a trip to the different lodges, the Danish lodges in United States, and she had gone to this place in California where my friend was. They were talking, and the girl said, "If you ever get out East, come to Hartford." So that's where we were heading for. She gave him permission to use her family's address in Hartford.

When I applied for the boat ticket I was told to see a doctor. I remember there were three different shots that you were supposed to have, and I did.

Maybe I had two suits, in a suitcase. The night before I left, we had a few friends up for coffee and so on. When I was leaving, it was really with the understanding that I was going to come back within three years, just to see what it looked like to be in United States. Before this trip, I had been in Norway, and I had been in Sweden. I had been in Finland. I went all over Denmark. Norway is like Denmark is like Finland. I never went to Russia. That was my next step. But then I met this friend of my cousin, and we came to United States. Otherwise I would have probably gone to Russia.

We left Copenhagen by ferry. They called the ferry *Esbjerg*. It went to Liverpool, because at that time the Danish boat wasn't running. They had a Danish boat that went to the United States. We took a British boat from Liverpool. We came second class . . .

We came September 9, 1923. They told us to get up early in the morning so we would see the statue. We got in, and then they docked in New York City. They let first class and second class off, but they didn't take us because we had to go to Ellis Island to be inspected. I stuck to my friend because he spoke English, and he knew what was going on. Whatever he was doing, I would do the same thing.

We must have been fifty, sixty people left from the ship. We were all stripped where the doctors were . . . The doctors were a little rough at times, but they

couldn't help it. There were so many people that went through there in a day, it was unbelievable.

About four to five hours later, we went back to New York City and there was somebody there to accept us, so we could get on the right train to Hartford. That was already arranged. But once we got to Hartford we were on our own. The girl whose family lived in Hartford didn't know we were coming. This friend of my cousin's didn't say anything to the people that we were coming, and now it was getting dark. It must have been nine o'clock or so, and you don't come to people at that time unless they know you're coming, and they didn't.

So we headed for the Danish church in Hartford. We found the church, and from there the minister took us to a Danish lady that had a boardinghouse, and she took us in. She gave us something to eat, and she told the minister that she would see to it that we got to my friend's address. The address belonged to a Danish carpenter who was well known.

The next day, this carpenter came and got us, our suitcases. He took us both to Blue Hills Avenue, where there was a nursery. He thought maybe I could get a job there, because I was a gardener. But I couldn't afford to work there, because the pay was only two dollars a day. The room and board and transportation to this nursery would cost me more than two dollars a day. My friend, he was an electrician. He got a job at Hartford Electric Light working at the power plant.

But I did get a job. The Danish lady's husband was a foreman who worked in Bushnell Park, and he was supposed to get me a job in Bushnell. But somehow or other, there wasn't any opening. But there was at Cole's Park. So I could walk from the boardinghouse to the park. I got a job helping the caretaker make wood benches in a big carpentry shop in Cole's Park. But it wasn't a year-round job. In summer, I polished the face of stones for graves and grave monuments. It was a rough job, but I got enough to live on, and that's all that was necessary.

I stayed with the lady at the boardinghouse for about two years. She had seven or eight boarders, and they were all Danes except for one, who was Irish. Everything was new to me, and at certain times, not too inviting, because I would say something, and they would laugh, you know. [Laughs.] There were Danes there, but that was the same thing. Some Danes came from different sections in Denmark, and I had just as much trouble speaking to them as I had to the Americans, because of the different dialects and so on. But we got along. I eventually learned English just by being with people, and I think one winter I went to night school.

But I remember how frustrating it was not to be able to understand what people were saying. I'll tell you, if somebody would have said, "I'll give you the money, and you can take the boat back to Denmark," I would have done it, because you get so disgusted, and you don't feel good. It took me about a year before I conquered that.

In the meantime, I promised my mother I would send her money just as soon as I could afford it. I tried to send her about ten dollars a month, which at that time would pay for her house rent, and that was a great help for her. And then I managed to bring her over here for a visit in 1929, after the stock market crash.

By then, I had gotten a job with Hoffman Wallpaper in Hartford. They needed a warehouseman to take care of the warehouse. So I got a job there, and I got pretty good pay. And within a few months, I could save enough to send my mother a ticket. I started a home for her and I. I found an apartment on Zion Street in Hartford, near Trinity College. It was an apartment building where quite a few Danes were living. I thought it would be a good place. I only got two rooms and a kitchen there. I bought some furniture, and my mother had her bed, and I had a bed . . .

My mother loved it here. For starters, she didn't have to work. She worked all her life and I felt that I owed her that enjoyment. She came in the fall, 1929, and went back home the following April or May, before the summer, because she had heavy blood in her body. In the spring, when it started to get hot, her blood used to flare up, like she was almost on fire, so she went home . . .

Lisa and Laura Tollessen

· · · · · · · · · · · · ·

BORN JULY 21, 1917 AND JANUARY 17, 1919
EMIGRATED FROM NORWAY 1925 AND 1935, AGES 8 AND 6 (FIRST VOYAGE)
PASSAGE ON THE *BERGENSFJORD* (1925), *STAVANGERFJORD* (1935)

*Their parents came to America from Norway before the First World War,
and returned when the war ended. Their father, a merchant seaman, was
already in America when the sisters emigrated with their mother in 1925.*

· · · · · · · ·

Lisa celebrated her eighth birthday on the boat ride. After their mother's death in 1929, they returned with their father to Norway, lived there for five years, and returned in 1935.

LISA: My parents were here before the First World War, and my older sister was born here. This was before we were born. Then they all went back to Norway and we were born on the island of Hisoy Arendal. It's in the southern part of Norway. The town was actually on the mainland.

LAURA: As a young girl, I remember the island. Of course, we had a ferry to get over to town. It was an old sailing town and very historic.

LISA: We lived in a three-story house made of timber. Grandpa built that house.

LAURA: The house was built alongside a rock, so that's why it was three stories. My grandmother lived on the first floor. The third floor we lived with my mother. It was heated with wood stoves. All three stories had wood stoves . . .

I remember my brother Tom, he was fourteen, had to row to town to get the midwife. On his way back, it was so cold that there was a thin layer of ice on the fjord. When the midwife got there, he held me. The midwife just said, "Here, take her and go by the kitchen stove," and he held me first.

LISA: My mother had eleven children, but only four of us lived. Me, Laura, my sister Margaret, and my brother Tom, who was the oldest. I was second to youngest. Laura was the baby. Seven died. I don't remember any of that. It wasn't something my mother ever talked about. She was sick a lot, too, after we came over here. That's the reason she passed away. She had a heart attack four years after we came here. She was in and out of the hospital all the time. She suffered.

LAURA: Mother was very pretty. I mean, she was very Norwegian, she was very dark. She had dark hair, velvety brown eyes, and she was a very pretty lady, very good-natured, a lot of fun.

LISA: She was a wonderful mother. [She is moved.] I loved her very much. I never forgot when she died. We all tried to take care of her, help her, and do all we could. I was about ten years old.

My dad, on the other hand, was very strict. I remember fooling around as kids, and we got the worst whack in the behind, I never forgot, and we had to sit on a chair each and we weren't allowed to move. We didn't move for nothing. That was the way he was, but not a mean father. At the same time, he could be very happy-go-lucky. He loved life. He could sing and dance like nobody else. [Laughs.] He was one of the best fathers, I would say, anybody could have.

My mother was a very happy person, too. She had a lot of friends. She loved life. She loved people. They matched, I would say they matched very well as a couple . . .

We didn't see our father too much in Norway. I don't remember too much. I know he was home a couple of times. He was a merchant seaman. He was a chief engineer. So he was out two years at a time. But he wrote a lot. We didn't see too much of Dad until we came here . . .

LAURA: I just remember our parents called us the Katzenjammer Kids, because we were into all kinds of trouble.

LISA: We were. We were like twins.

LAURA: We were into everything.

LISA: We were together since we were little. We played a lot of ball. In summer, we'd go to the islands and swim. In winter, I remember one Christmas there was a wooden doll hanging on the tree. It wasn't a big doll. But my grandfather had carved it out, and that was supposed to be my Christmas present. I can still see that little doll hanging there. We didn't have much money. There was no radio . . .

We didn't start school there because they started school when you were seven, and we were waiting for the passage when our time came, so my mother couldn't start us in school. We didn't start school until we came over here, and we were excited, because we had always heard about how everything was so beautiful over here. We didn't know too much about it. But we wanted to come because we had a lot of family here. We had my sister, aunts, cousins, an uncle.

LAURA: My mother, of course, had to auction off everything, and we had to be vaccinated. I think that's why I don't remember the packing. I got very sick. I remember they put me in this room and every day all these people were carrying stuff out, and I was so sick. My arm was all swollen like that. [Gestures.] I had not one, but three vaccinations! I still have those marks from that. I never had vaccinations before. But I had to have it. You couldn't leave Norway, and come here, without that.

I remember saying good-bye to my grandfather. I remember my mother saying, "I'll never see this place again . . ." [She is moved.] [To Lisa] do you remember that? . . . Grandfather was sad to see us go. He wanted us to stay. My father was already in America and was waiting for us.

From Arendal we went by train along the coast to Oslo. There was no room on the train. Then, we got on the ship *Bergensfjord.* The passengers were all Norwegians. It was a Norwegian boat. There were people from our hometown, but you got acquainted with a lot of people. Met people from different places. And stayed friends with many of these people for years after we came over

here. My mother never lost contact with them.

I wasn't seasick. That's one thing. [Laughs.] I was on my own a lot because my mother was seasick, Lisa was seasick. My brother, of course, was in a different part of the ship, because he was together with another young fellow from our hometown. So he would play the harmonica and I would sing, and people used to give me change. But I gave the change to my brother. He said later that I kept him and his buddy in cigarettes. Once in a while they'd throw me a bar of candy . . .

LISA: I remember it was big and it was scary. But I remember good times on there because I had a birthday there. My eighth birthday. I'll never forget that big bowl of hard-boiled eggs. Eggs were very expensive, you know. We never had eggs. I guess that was the only thing mother could do to make it like a party. I remember Laura and I were up on deck, and I had gotten a red apple, a big red apple, and the two of us were singing. The two of us stood up and sang. Oh, we really had a party!

Somebody gave us a nickel and a penny. And then I remember we got ice cream, and that was something we had never had. I thought it was kind of cold to eat it. So I went down the cabin and I took the ice cream and I put it up in the porthole where there was sun coming in. My mother asked what I was doing. I said, "I got to make it warm, it's too cold. I can't eat it." She said, "You can't do that. It's going to melt. You got to eat it cold." Till this day I like soft ice cream. [Laughs.]

LAURA: We arrived in New York in July of 1925. I still wonder how did we get off the big ship and onto Ellis Island. My first experience here was when I saw my first black person. I had never seen a black person in my life. He was a heavy-set man, and he was whistling. I was trying to follow him. I was on one side of the fence, and I was trying to follow him and trying to whistle, imitate him. My father was just laughing. He thought this was something . . .

I remember the Great Hall downstairs, because we were sitting on one side and my father was with a lot of our family who came to welcome us. But it was no hardship or anything. We were all very happy . . .

I remember the first night in this country. I didn't want to sleep. I wanted to be with my mother, and not my father. I didn't want him around . . .

LISA: Like Laura, the first thing I saw was this big colored person. I'd never seen one before, and he was the happiest person. He was laughing. I was crying. My father, like she said, was standing there laughing his head off because I was screaming my head off. I never forgot that, and my cousins, who stood on the side with a big bunch of bananas which was something we never had in Norway. All I remember, I see that. My father and my cousins. I remembered my father. I had seen him in Norway, and he didn't seem strange at all. He was just his happy-go-lucky self, and I was just happy to see him . . .

Another thing is the Nordic people. They [INS inspectors] didn't hold us back for anything. I mean, all Scandinavians, not just Norwegians. We were known to be very truthful. We didn't harm people. And I think that was one of the things. We were very, you know, accepted.

We went to Brooklyn, an apartment. A couple of bedrooms, living room, kitchen. Just a regular American apartment, but with the old-fashioned, parquet wood floor. There was electricity and heat from large radiators. I think it was furnished. We didn't stay there too long, and shortly thereafter went to a different, but similar, apartment nearby. My father was a dock builder in Brooklyn. That's how we made a living.

LAURA: Of course, we started school in September. That was a big experience. My mother and father would have family over every weekend, and they would put on skits. We used to have a lot of fun with that—just the family together. So we had a very happy childhood, I would say.

LISA: We were so many. We had this one cousin, Carrie. She lived up in Yonkers, and we used to go there. I'll never forget the first Christmas [in America]. Her husband was Swedish. He used to make his own beer. They didn't have kids, so he loved us too much. We were the only young kids in the whole family, so the gifts, you wouldn't believe. I'll never forget these glass dolls we got. They were beautiful. They were unbelievable. We got so much presents. I'd never seen anything like that in my life. It was unbelievable.

Our father had this great big toolbox, and I was going to bed one night. He shut the light. I didn't see where I was going, and I was carrying the doll to take it with me to bed and I fell over the tool box and dropped my doll. I've never been so heartbroken in all my life. I had never had a doll like that, and a glass doll, and it couldn't be fixed . . .

LAURA: School was no problem because, the teacher would say, "Have your parents speak English to you so that you learn our language." Of course, we spoke Norwegian in the house. But we learned English very fast.

LISA: I learned just by going to school and playing outside with other children. It came little by little. Mother, I remember, saying that we had learned American [English] in about a month. We knew how to speak. My mother never did. She couldn't understand. She was always fighting with people, you know, to try to get them to understand her.

LAURA: It wasn't long after that my mother said, "Speak English so I can understand you." [Laughs.] I already started forgetting my Norwegian . . .

We went back to Norway October 4, 1930. Our mother had died in the interim—1929. Lisa, me, and my father went back, and we stayed for five years. We lived in the same house with my grandfather. He was still living. And then we went back to school over there, which was hard in the beginning.

LISA: In Norwegian, there are three more sounds to pronounce: They have "aw," "ir," and "ah." And that was very hard for us to learn. We wanted to go back to America. At the same time, we were happy in Norway. We had our friends. All our friends we had when we were little we had when we came back. Then, we returned to America in 1935 on the ocean liner, *Stavangerfjord . . .*

I've always loved Norway, and if things had worked out a little better, I would have been happy there. I mean, what I'm happy with now is that I have five wonderful children. They're my life. That's what I live for, and thirteen grandchildren, four great-grandchildren, and I got two more grandchildren on the way. So I'm happy. I've had a good life.

LAURA: Yes.

Murray, Isaac, and Adelle Youman

. . . .

BORN AUGUST 16, 1928; NOVEMBER 10, 1931; DECEMBER 19, 1935
EMIGRATED FROM FINLAND, 1940, AGES 11, 8, AND 4
PASSAGE ON THE S.S. *BERGENSFJORD*

Siblings, they came from Finland via Norway in 1940, and were detained at Ellis Island for six weeks before settling in Brooklyn, New York. They remain close to this day and live in the New York area.

ISAAC: I was born in Helsinki, Finland, and my sister, Adelle, was also born there.

MURRAY: I was born in Warsaw, Poland. My mother was there. My mother and father originally came from Poland. My father left for Finland. While he was in Finland she gave birth to me. Then I went to Finland. I was still a baby. My mother's name was Greta, and my father's name was Herman.

ADELLE: However, as they left one country to the other, their first names changed. In Poland they had other, first names. In Poland my mother's name was Grincha, which became Anglicized in Finland to Greta. And my father's name was Herschel, which became Anglicized when it went to Finland as Herman. The reason was the other names were Yiddish names and *shtetl* names in Poland. Finland, it's a Christian country, so you picked a Christian name, as was done in America very often; names were Anglicized.

My father, when he first met my mother, said, "She's the prettiest girl in town," and he wanted to marry her and really chased her for years and years. He was ten years older than her and she really didn't appreciate it. But as she grew up he was more [financially] comfortable than she, and in those times, you married for a lot of reasons, that [finances] being one of them.

MURRAY: My father started as a tailor. At fourteen years, he had his own shop with married men working for him. He was always a very hard worker, and he continued when he went to Finland and started his own business. This was a business that was first taken care of by his brother and him, and I understand other brothers came into it afterwards.

ISAAC: Yes. In Finland, my mother worked with my father in the factory. They had a men's clothing factory. Whether you want to consider it fortunate or unfortunate, we children were brought up basically by maids. My father was very [financially] comfortable in Finland. We basically didn't see very much of our parents.

ADELLE: Our apartment was in a three-story building and it had wood on the walls. It was an upper-middle-class apartment in those days, and they [parents] went to business every day. There were maids in the house that took care of us. It was an extended family. We had an uncle that lived with us, a grandmother that lived with us, two maids that lived with us. There must have been five or six bedrooms. You know, it was one of these old, large apartments. We were a noisy Yiddish family that spoke Yiddish as a primary language in Finland.

MURRAY: My grandmother, she got us started on the Yiddish. But actually, we were brought up in two religions. For example, at Christmas time we had a Christmas tree. My father used to put on a Santa Claus suit. You have to understand that we lived in a society that was 99.9 percent Lutheran. So we were a tremendous minority over there. We were unlike anything that you would expect to come out from over there, you know. We were very modern-thinking

and everything, yet we knew where our roots were.

In Finland, most Jews had their own businesses. There was one synagogue, and the fellow in charge was the only rabbi in the area. Of course, we'd go and pray, but outside we'd eat whatever we wanted to eat. We weren't very Orthodox. Of course, most of the Jewish people had dark hair, and the Finns were about as blond as they come. So you could see that there was a lot of intermarrying and things of that sort.

ADELLE: There were two thousand Jews in Helsinki in 1940. All of the children went to a Jewish school, us included. There was no religious persecution, not in Finland. People coexisted very well.

ISAAC: It's interesting, in 1962 when I returned to Finland, I visited Finland. I was thirty-one years old at the time. I had left when I was eight years old, and I never had a birth certificate. So I went back to Finland hoping to get my birth certificate. I went to the hospital and found that the hospital had been bombed during the Finnish-Russian War, and all records were destroyed. So I went back to my old school, and as I walked in the front door, the receptionist behind the desk took one look at me, and yelled out my name, "Isaac!" And this is after twenty-three years. I think my big ears were a dead giveaway. [Laughs.] But they did have records of my birth, and I got a copy from the school.

I remember the bomb shelters near school and a cemetery not far away. I remember hiding behind the tombstones. I figured when the trains came down to strafe they wouldn't get me that way. This was not World War II. This was the Finnish-Russian War.

MURRAY: Actually there were two Finnish-Russian Wars. We're talking about the first one. One day, they had an air raid, and they told us to go home. They wouldn't tell us why . . . Well, I went to the bookstore first. As I crossed the street, a bomb hit right near me. A trolley car completely blew up. All the people died on it. I somehow lived. I don't know how. I saw red all around me. I saw my father run into a building they had told us not to go into, to save somebody, come out, and sure enough, the building blew up right before our eyes. Well, that night we left Helsinki . . .

We were constantly living in the shadow of Russia. Although, when Finland was part of Russia, they treated the Finns better than they did the Russians. But living next to a country which could swallow you up in no time at all was scary. It was scary.

ADELLE: Later, in America, we played at air raid drills. During World War II, we really played at air raid drills.

ISAAC: Exactly. Being eight years old, I think it was more of a game really; this business of running and hiding behind in the basement. And hearing about the guy my father pulled out of a burning building who weighed considerably more than he did. These were all, it was almost like a game thing, you know. I don't think fear was amongst the very young. I think as you get older there's more fear because you know what you're getting into.

The air raids were daily. My father would be at the factory and my mother would maybe be home and we would be at school. Then one day, an air raid occurred, and there was no time for the family to reunite. My father had to find his own shelter, my mother hers. We found ours. Adelle was young then, so she was with her mother or with a maid. That was the biggest fear that my parents had, you know. They never knew if we had made it through the air raid or what. And from what I gather, when I spoke to my mother and father, this was a big fear.

ADELLE: You don't leave a country that has been very good to you for twelve years and go to another country where you don't know the language, unless you find

something so traumatic. I don't know if I would have left. I ask myself all the time.

As I get older, I realize how much courage it takes to leave a country; to leave the place where you were born, and spoke the language in very close quarters like Poland, and go to Finland, which to a Pole is like going to Siberia, and do very well, even become wealthy. Then, twelve years later, again have to leave for another country where you don't speak the language, where there's no money waiting for you, with papers that aren't terribly good. The older I get the braver I think they are. My father, in particular. We always said he made the big decisions and mother made the little ones.

MURRAY: My mother, she was easier to talk to than he was. A typical man of the times. Men in those days were very dominant. For example, even at night when we had our dinner, nobody would eat until Dad got home, and then we'd eat in the dining room. We never ate in the kitchen like they do over here. But he had a good heart. He tried to do everything within his power.

ISAAC: My mother was born in the wrong generation. If she had been born in the present generation, she would have been a genius. She had a super mathematical ability of adding columns of numbers together. She was very bright. She was the brains behind the family. When we came to the United States, neither my mother or father had much of an education, maybe to the second or third grade. They both spoke semifluently about seven languages, which is quite common in Europe, though. My mother went to night school and graduated from high school in the United States. She hungered for education.

In Poland, where they grew up, they didn't have the opportunities to be educated. In Finland, they were too busy making money. My father started night school with my mother, and after a short time, he quit. It was just too much for him. But my mother continued on, and got a high school diploma. She was very brilliant. She was really the brains behind my father; the book-keeper, the one that kept the accounts. My father had a knack of handling people. That was his thing. He was a bad businessman. He had an uncle who was a good business-man. This uncle could lie, he could cheat. He would never tell you what the price was. My father, if you asked him, he would tell you, you know. The people in the factory loved to work for him.

ADELLE: As with most women, she was the strength in the family. [They laugh.] Except, in those years, you weren't allowed to say so.

MURRAY: Things haven't changed. You have to understand we lived in a total man's world. She could say whatever he allowed to be said, okay. That's what it amounted to.

ISAAC: The truth is that my father didn't want to leave Finland. He loved Fin-land. My mother knew nothing of America, except that she had a married sister here working in the garment center.

ADELLE: She knew America was safe. She always said that, way back when they were in Poland. Rumors had gotten there that America was safe. There were no po-groms there. There were no wars.

MURRAY: In Finland, we had mixed reviews of America. We felt, from our stud-ies anyway, that Abraham Lincoln was the greatest president you had, okay? However, there was another thing, too. You have to remember that Finland hadn't had capital punishment since 1937. So when we read about America's electric chair, we sort of frowned on that. We felt it was barbaric. We didn't know America had so many ethnic groups. When I was in school in Finland, we once had a play where there was a black fellow. They had to paint him and put him in a grass skirt. I never realized what a black person was until I came here . . .

ISAAC: When we were children we were allowed to go to movies, but there were only two types of movies we could go to see. One was Shirley Temple, and the other one was Tarzan. To me a black person was a man with a hoop through his nose, carrying a spear, wearing a grass skirt. When we first went to Stockholm and I saw a black person in a suit carrying a briefcase, I was surprised. You know, it was really a big surprise. And when we came to the United States and we moved into Brooklyn and there was a park across the street. I remem-ber we went across the street and they had all these black kids playing there. My father rounded them all up and put us in the mid-dle, there must have been about fifty of them, and took a photograph of us. I mean, to us it was something very strange, some-thing different. We weren't raised with in-herent fears most New Yorkers had of the different ethnic races.

ADELLE: In 1940 and '45, you did what your parents asked you. We didn't discuss things as a family. Things that were bad were kept from you. Problems were talked about behind doors. Everything had to be quiet for the children and happy. Now, the whole family knows about every tragedy in every family. That's not how it was in America, in Finland, or any place in 1940, '42, '44. You went where your parents took you, that's all.

MURRAY: When we were going to school, you've got to understand. It's like seeing the Hitler Youth. We sat in school with our hands in front of us. You couldn't look at the girl that sat next to you. If you did the twitch, your hand would be hit. If you as much as spoke out, they'd tell your parents and you got another twitch. In other words, the parents had absolute control of the children. In school I think we had one kid once that failed something. They all looked at him like he was retarded. Maybe he had to go and see a doctor or something. It just wasn't done. Same thing at home.

ISAAC: We left Helsinki in a rush. The streets were full of glass from broken windows. I recall my father had to look for somebody who would take us out of Helsinki. He finally was able to buy somebody off, and they took us out, and eventually we got a train. I remember the train went north toward Sweden.

MURRAY: First we went to a little town north of Helsinki named Nummela. But there was no place to put us, so they put us up in a gym at the school. Picture that, they just put the bedding right on the gym floor, and we slept there. We heard that one boat had come across from Hango to Stockholm in Sweden. But they had bombed that boat, so Dad and Mom were afraid to take that boat across, although it was a very short trip. We took the train all the way up north to where the Bothnian Gulf closes up, and there's a town on the Finnish side called Tornio. We went from there to the Swedish side and took the train all the way down to Stockholm. We're talking about old trains, not trains that go the speed that we have today. We stayed in Stockholm. I don't remember how long, but it wasn't that long.

ISAAC: The train also stopped during air raids. Every time there was an air raid the train would stop.

MURRAY: That's right. You'd go back in the woods.

ISAAC: Everybody would have to get off the train and lay down in the snow. We had these white robes, so we'd be sort of covered up by this.

ADELLE: I have a story about the white fabric. You had to bring white fabric, and most people probably brought white blankets. But my father was in the clothing business, so we had bolts of beautiful white wool to take to America with us. Need I say, that until I was twelve years old, I had white winter coats.

ISAAC: And white dresses.

ADELLE: Of course, you didn't waste. I remember so well getting my first red coat at thirteen. I remember all the sterling silver that we brought from Finland. We had to have it all monogrammed with the family's initials to make sure nobody could say it was theirs.

MURRAY: In Stockholm, we stayed at a hotel. I still remember the name of the hotel. It was called Hotel Regina, that was right close to the palace. I understand that the hotel still exists. After a week or two in Stockholm, we finally took the train over to Oslo. There was a Norwegian line at that time that had the *Oslofjord*, the *Stavangerfjord*, and the *Bergensfjord*. The *Bergensfjord* was the ship we took from Oslo.

I remember going through the fjord into Bergen, and we stayed there maybe a day. Then we continued straight to America. They were trying to dodge the submarines. I remember something . . : that on the *Bergensfjord*'s next trip to America, they snuck all the gold out of Norway before the Germans came in.

ISAAC: As we went, we changed the flags, the colors on the ship, to German colors, English colors, Norwegian colors . . . I don't know if that fooled the submarines or not, but we made it. To avoid the mines and the subs, we also moved in a zigzag pattern. That's why it took longer for the ship to come from Norway to the United States. And on deck, there were continuous safety drills. They used to make us wear these orange vests.

MURRAY: I remember on the trip. We had a terrible hurricane. If you ever want to see Hell, take a boat in the middle of a hurricane in the middle of the Atlantic. I was so sick that they had to tie me outside of the ship to keep me from going overboard. I was watching waves that looked over a hundred feet high, the boat looked one-quarter of its size, you know. It was a terrible experience in itself.

ADELLE: We had first-class tickets because those were the only ones available. That's the only time we've ever been on a first-class ship. We did have good accommodations.

ISAAC: I remember the captain had us over and we ate meals with him many times. The sailors were very friendly with us and they sort of watched over us, and taught us some English.

MURRAY: On that boat there were three classes. First class, as my sister says, you ate pretty good—lobster, whatever. You ate good. Second class was down below a little bit. And, of course, there was tourist class, which was way on the bottom. We used to get movies, second-rate movies. The guys in the bottom didn't get no movie. This boat wasn't a big boat. It wasn't the *QE2*. It was about 11,000 tons.

ADELLE: My mother was afraid. She didn't know what would be waiting for her. She didn't know if they'd send her back. She knew she was going to New York with papers for Haiti. She didn't want to go to Haiti because the Polish quota for America was closed up. The Haitian quota obviously was not closed, and what we wanted to do was get out of Finland, and that's why we had papers to Haiti.

ISAAC: My father did have a bank account in the United States, as he had one in England, too. How much was in there I don't know. So it wasn't like he was coming to absolute nothingness. My mother had a sister in New York . . .

ADELLE: And they thought they would soon be back. That was their intention. That the war would be over in three months, and they'd go back. They could not believe that the war would last five years. In Finland, my father was privileged, a wealthy man. He sent us to private schools for our education, not public schools. Well, he came

here and became a garment center laborer for the rest of his life . . .

MURRAY: When I first saw it [Statue of Liberty] I had tears in my eyes, and do to this day when I get close to it.

ISAAC: The sailors told us a lot about it, and talked about the United States. Of course, the biggest disappointment I ever had was realizing that the streets of New York were not paved with gold, as the sailors told me. I really expected them to be. [Laughs.] The ship came into New York around Canal Street on the West Side pier, where the Norwegian-American Line used to land. Then we were taken to Ellis Island by tugboat.

ADELLE: They took us to Ellis Island because our papers weren't good. The only people that came in 1940 were if you had something wrong with your papers, or criminals, not for health reasons.

MURRAY: It was like a dormitory. We didn't have individual rooms. And we were separated from our parents. The little ones went with the mother.

ADELLE: Yes, Isaac and I went with my mother and grandmother, and Murray went with my father.

MURRAY: Everything was regimented. You ate when they wanted you. You had a lot of time where you got bored, so they did try to help us. They gave the children toys which they were able to keep. We looked forward to those times, you know. The dining room was like a prison dining room you'd see in the movies.

ISAAC: The main thing I remember is being outside and looking through this wire fencing and noticing the segregation where the Orientals were segregated from us, and they were almost like prisoners. They had to work. We sort of hung around and did nothing, but they really had to work. They were raking, cleaning, moving rocks, things like that. They were totally separated from everybody else, and I couldn't understand

Detention, 1904

(NATIONAL PARK SERVICE: STATUE OF LIBERTY NATIONAL MONUMENT)

• • • • • • • • •

why. Later on they said, "Well, there's a lot of diseases that come from the Orient. You have to be careful." I was eight years old. I didn't know about these things.

ADELLE: I was with my mother, you know, Heaven. She was frightened all the time. There were people that wanted to sell you things. She didn't like the idea Murray was separated from her, and she was afraid we'd be sent back.

I had been to Ellis Island several times before they did it over [in 1986], when my mother was still alive. One time, I says, "Ma, how about coming with me and my children. You could really show us everything." And she said, "In my life I'll never set foot there again." I mean, that, I think, says more than anything she ever said. She would never, ever come.

MURRAY: I had that same fear. I had tears in my eyes when . . .

ADELLE: Murray had trouble coming here again, too.

MURRAY: Yes, I had trouble coming here. I had a traumatic thing I can't understand in my head today, why a lot of people, and I see them coming through immigration, and by our standards, they don't come even close to us. I mean, here you're looking at three people that, children that came over here. Every one of us is a professional.

ADELLE: But that's America. That's not any of us. That's the America of the '40s and '50s.

ISAAC: That was the opportunity.

MURRAY: We came here speaking a very difficult language, harder than English even. The first thing we tried to do when we came here is learn how to speak English.

ISAAC: Yes. There were classes here for English. Of course, it was limited. The biggest class for speaking English was the class of hard knocks, growing up as a kid in Brooklyn. You know, "You dirty foreigner." "You greenhorn." They made fun of you and they fought with you. I remember going to

my mother and saying, "I don't want you to speak Finnish to me. Speak only English so I can learn how to speak English." As a result, I learned how to speak English with a great New York accent, and I forgot my Finnish.

ADELLE: The HIAS arranged for legal help that allowed us to come to America as tourists, but not to work, but to get off Ellis Island. In the meantime, people had visited us. My aunt used to come, and cousins came . . .

MURRAY: When we left, we were separated for about two weeks. Different relatives took us in until we could get a place to live.

ADELLE: Really?

MURRAY: Yes.

ISAAC: I didn't know that.

MURRAY: I stayed with Aunt Ruth, you both stayed with . . . Then, finally, Dad got an apartment on 2041 Pacific Street in Ocean Hill, Brooklyn. Now, of course, it's a pretty bad area.

ADELLE: We must have had twenty suitcases. I remember that.

MURRAY: Try thirty.

ISAAC: Half the ship must have been suitcases of ours.

ADELLE: There was a cousin living in that building, and he found the apartment.

MURRAY: Dad wanted a home across from a park. See, he remembered the way it was in Finland. What he didn't know was that park was a hell of a park. It taught us how to fight, not how to live with other people.

ADELLE: We learned English. We went to the New York City public schools.

MURRAY: And unlike a lot of the Russians who stay with their old language, we divorced ourselves completely to talking English. We wanted to learn how to be American, and we worked at it. We did not retain Finnish at all. When we couldn't talk to people in English, we would fill in with Yiddish. It was a Jewish neighborhood. It was a ghetto neighborhood. The very next street was Italian. A lot of Irish, Italians. On our street, a lot of American-born, second-generation Jews.

ISAAC: I think the only outcast I felt was having an accent, and they make fun of you.

ADELLE: We also dressed differently. I wore woolen woolies and no other girls did. And a white winter coat. I also had a little fur coat that Americans didn't have. And this did not go unnoticed. I remember well. We were dressed warm when they weren't. I hated it. They wore socks and I wore long, ugly woolen stockings. But we adjusted. My mother made it her business to adjust to America. She loved it.

MURRAY: She was a marvelous woman. Dad was like all the men from Europe at that time. He decided whether we needed it or not. Whatever he said, that's the way it was. So when Mom went to school, "I don't have to go to school. I'm a businessman. I'm the one who makes the money, not you." Right? So he wouldn't go to school to learn English. Then, when she got a diploma, he became a little jealous of her, you know. "Hey, you're my wife. You're not supposed to be smarter than me." We lived in a day when a woman was nothing. The man was everything.

ADELLE: But we all became Americans. My father always stayed a foreigner, always. My father would have gone back to Finland to live out his life. He tried to go back. My parents went back for a little while in 1948.

ISAAC: 1947 to 1954.

ADELLE: Yeah. He wanted to bring us back over there. My mother went to Finland and there were Russian soldiers all over the place and she said, "I can't bring my family back here."

ISAAC: My mother found her dream here in the United States.

MURRAY: She really felt that the schooling was good over here.

ISAAC: And she, they, had a lot more money. She worked in a bakery. She was the chief breadwinner for [a] long, long time. But we had no maids. She took care of her own children. She brought us up, and she loved it. She said, "This is the only way to live." All the money in the world didn't mean a thing if she was not happy with it. She was far happier in the United States. She thought it was the only place to raise children. I feel the same way. I've been traveling for many years now. I spent over ten years traveling with my family. My son was born in the Philippines. I've been offered some very good positions in various countries. But this is the only place to live. I honestly feel that Americans should travel outside the United States to realize what they have. They have a wonderful country here.

Part VI

WESTERN EUROPE

Aristocratic Dutch family, newly arrived and awaiting inspection in 1907

(NATIONAL PARK SERVICE: STATUE OF LIBERTY NATIONAL MONUMENT)

17

. . . .

France, Spain, Portugal
& the Netherlands

(APPROXIMATELY 1.1 MILLION IMMIGRANTS, 1892–1954)

Doris Fagendam

. . . .

BORN AUGUST 5, 1898
EMIGRATED FROM THE NETHERLANDS 1908, AGE 10
PASSAGE ON THE *ROTTERDAM*

Her father emigrated first in 1903, stayed for three years and then sent for the rest of the family. Hers is not a story of suffering. She lived a comfortable life in Holland. In America, she married a good man, had two children and became a schoolteacher and superintendent, working with retarded children. Today, she has five grandchildren, eight great-grandchildren and lives in New Jersey. "I've had a very good life all the way through," she said. "Of course, I had trials and tribulations. Who doesn't? But when I look back, I was very fortunate."

I lived the first ten years of my life in Friesland, which is a province in Holland. In fact, all of Holland at one time was Friesland. I went to school there, and we spoke Frisian. We spoke Frisian in the home. We spoke Dutch in school. But the minute we got into the play yard at recess time we'd speak Frisian again. The Frisian people are very proud of their heritage. They're good, honest people, known for their cleanliness, and in fact they have a right to be. They're stubborn.

We lived in a little village pronounced "yet" in Holland, but it's called Jet. It had just a few houses. And my father worked in a dairy there. I was one of six children, fourth from the oldest. There were three sisters older than I. Although after we came to America, my mother had twins, so we were a family of ten children.

My mother was the soul of goodness. She was kind, and always happy, even though she didn't always have everything to be happy about. She was just a wonderful mother and a wonderful cook. Buttermilk was a great thing in Holland, and my mother used to make soup with barley and buttermilk. She used the milk of a sheep, and that was just

wonderful. She'd serve it cold, or she'd heat it, and you'd eat it with syrup. And that was good, substantial food. But we also had plenty of meat and potatoes and vegetables.

Our house was part of a row of houses all made of brick. And that's one thing that startled me when I came to this country. I saw wooden houses. I had never seen anything but a brick house. We had brick steps going to the streets, which were all brick, and each person would clean their section of the street. People got on their hands and knees and scrubbed like you would a kitchen floor. No horse or wagon were permitted on the street. There were side streets for that, where the peddler would stop. And the children had nice places to play.

I can remember a beautiful home that stood on a little hill at the end of the street. His name was Tepstra. I think he was a doctor. And he had peacocks in his yard, and we, as children, just loved to watch those peacocks which were quite prevalent in Holland.

In the wintertime, we just skated. I can remember there was a long hall in our home, and there were a bunch of skates laying there. And as soon as we came home from school we'd go for those skates and go to the

May 12, 1908. Johanna Dykoff, forty, with her eleven children at Ellis Island.
They were bound for a farm in Loretta, Minnesota, where they would become laborers.
They came via the S.S. Noordam.

(NATIONAL PARK SERVICE: STATUE OF LIBERTY NATIONAL MONUMENT)

frozen canal across the street and go skating. When we came back, my mother would have a little piece of cake on the table for each of us. My mother liked to gossip with the neighbor. It was a very nice neighborhood and she knew we were safe. At night the men would go around these canals, fill in all the cracks, so that the ice would be smooth. [Laughs.] A friend told me it isn't that way anymore.

People used to do all their traveling on ice. They had horses and sleighs. Merchandise would go by sleigh, by canals. And they had tents all along the way, where they sold hot chocolate. They traveled from town to town. And then the peddlers would come up from the canals to the side streets and you could buy anything you wanted.

As I say, we had a good life, but my father saw better opportunities in America. He left when I was about five. To help out, my grandmother took one of my sisters, and in the house my mother always had a maid. She also had sisters not too far away. So she didn't do it all alone. She managed very well. No dire circumstances. We lived very comfortably.

At Christmas, gifts were exchanged on the fifth of December, that's Santa Claus Day. And all children looked forward to that. There was one big Christmas tree for the whole town and there was a Santa Claus who came at night to hand out little cookies the size of peppernuts. But we weren't supposed to see him. We celebrated Christmas in a religious way, although it didn't interfere with the gift-giving, and we weren't that religious. But we'd go to church and Sunday school. I can remember my mother taking us to church down a beautiful street that had trees that met overhead. It was lovely. And I remember in church they had little foot-stool warmers. It was a little square box with hot coal in it, and the women would put their feet on those little boxes to keep warm. My mother always had some peppermints with her, so she'd give each of us children a peppermint so we'd be quiet in church.

. . .

We came to America in September 1908. I looked forward to coming. The children did.

Immigrants leaving east wing of the main building for freedom, 1907

(NATIONAL PARK SERVICE: STATUE OF LIBERTY NATIONAL MONUMENT)

But I don't think my mother did. [Laughs.] She had to leave all her loved ones behind. I remember my little brother always saying, "Mom, when are we going to America?" And she'd say, in Frisian, "Oh, when a ship with money comes over." Then the next day he'd say in Frisian, "Mom, did the ship with money come over?" And she'd change the subject. But she knew it was best for the children. And she was always happy here. Later, she said she was glad she came.

There were not many others from our village who went to America. There was a neighbor of ours that went on the same ship we did. We came over on the *Rotterdam*, which was brand new, only its second voyage. And it took us nine days which was very quick for 1908. The older ships took much longer.

We had examinations as we entered the boat. We had two going, and another one when we got off the boat. I don't remember whether it was second or third class. But I do remember we were treated well, the food was good, and that the people in first class seemed to take pity on my mother with all her children.

I don't remember the Statue of Liberty. But I remember Ellis Island because they detained us there. When I see pictures of it now, it comes back that we were there. They detained my sister, who wore leg braces. She had polio as a child. My mother made her dresses a little longer, hoping they wouldn't notice, and they did. But my father could prove that she would not be a burden to the country if they admitted her. So we just stayed overnight. In fact, about a month after we were here, one of my sisters became ill, and the nurse came in and saw my other sister who was crippled, and said, "If you'll let us take this child to New York, we'll operate on her and it won't cost you anything." We couldn't imagine that, but they did. They took her. They operated on her. And she never wore braces again. She walked with a limp, but the braces were gone for good.

The best part about coming to America was seeing my father again. It was wonderful! He met us at Ellis Island and I remember him saying to me, "Compared to America, we're sort of a slow nation. You can't dawdle here. You have to step on it a little bit." And then we hopped on a trolley car. And everybody was in such a hurry. I just couldn't fathom that.

We went to Pleasantville, New York and stayed in a small house there until a house was ready for us in Briarcliff Manor, about a mile away. We loved Briarcliff Manor because it was country, and it was mountains, and Holland is as flat as a doornail. And we could pick apples for free, and wild roses. My mother would go up to the mountains and pick blackberries. We thought this was wonderful. My mother learned to make jam. She baked bread.

We went to Briarcliff Manor because my father worked at a dairy there. The same work he did in Holland. But it was also an affluent community, good families, this was Westchester. So there was no built-in prejudice because there were very few foreigners. When we went to school, we learned our ABC's and the other children treated us very nice because we were a novelty. They made a big fuss over us. For instance, when we first arrived we still wore our wooden shoes. I never wore regular shoes until I came here. So in a sense, we had a grand welcome to this country. We really did. And within a very short time we conquered the English language beautifully. My father spoke well. But in the home we spoke Frisian. My mother never conquered the English language completely. If we spoke to her in English, she'd answer us in Frisian. But she acclimated. We all did.

From my family, I'm the only one left. So when I'm alone, I think back. For instance, the other night I had a dream. And in my dream one of my sisters said, "Oh, Doris, come on in here. I have a surprise for you." And I walked into the house and there they were, all my brothers and sisters sitting around the table. I'm content and happy.

Anna Jordan

. . . .

BORN JUNE 12, 1909
EMIGRATED FROM FRANCE 1914, AGE 4
PASSAGE ON THE *POTSDAM*

An only child, she was born in Lyon and raised by her maternal grandmother. She came to America two months shy of her fifth birthday when her father decided to avoid the draft and the start of World War I. In America, she experienced an emotionally painful childhood, precipitated by the premature death of her mother. She eventually married a shoe repairman and raised four children. She has thirteen grandchildren and lives in Maine. "I have regrets," she said. "I regret I didn't ask my mother certain things. That I didn't learn more about her and about myself."

The war had started and I remember we had a big wall in front of the house in Lyon, my grandmother's house, and if we wanted to come outside, we had to put out a white flag because across the street the soldiers practiced shooting guns.

It was just my grandmother and I, my mother's mother. It was a two-tenant house. There were people living upstairs. My mother and father worked, and they put me with my grandmother, so that she would keep me during the day. I was the only child. I had a sister, but she died right off, when she was born. And my grandfather died years before that.

My father worked in a silk printing factory. He printed on silk. It was stencil work. The stencils were a frame. There were several frames, and he'd put it on the silk, and they would paint it. The silk would be used for dresses, scarves, tablecloths, etc.

My mother worked in a hospital. I remember seeing a picture of her in a white uniform. But otherwise she wore a jumper with a blouse, or a skirt and blouse. I never saw my mother in a dress, and I never saw my grandmother in a dress. It was a blouse and skirt, or a jumper. And always an apron, a white apron. It was always white. That I remember.

My mother had very long hair. She sat on her hair. And at that time, women put their hair in a bun on top of their head. But a lot of women didn't have much hair, so they had to wear an artificial piece. Well, my mother didn't need that. She had enough hair. She could make her own bun. So could my grandmother. I remember that.

My grandmother made a living growing and selling vegetables from her garden. She had a big garden. I remember it because I used to go in and eat the radishes. She said I could eat as many as I wanted. I liked my grandmother very much. She had a little cart with a mule attached, and she'd go to market. She'd leave me with the lady upstairs and her little girl. They would take care of me. I don't know where my parents lived. I presume it was nearby, because my father used to come over in the morning and have breakfast with my grandmother. And my grandmother had this rooster that used to drink coffee, and he'd get on the table and drink my father's coffee.

. . . .

My grandmother was very kind to me. She'd give in to me, buy me things, spoil me, like every grandmother does. [Laughs.] She was a wonderful cook. She used to make me my favorite, cream puffs. Sometimes she'd make it with whipped cream, other times she'd make it with regular French cream which is like custard.

I can't remember leaving my grandmother's house to go to the boat. The only thing I remember is my father coming one morning and saying to my grandmother that we were leaving. He said it was on account of the war. That he was going to be drafted, but by coming to America, he was exempt.

We boarded the ship *Potsdam*, on the eleventh day of April 1914 and got to New York on the 23rd of April. My passport says we left from Cagnes-sur-Mer, France. We traveled third class—my grandmother, my father, my mother, and me. Four of us.

I was all over the ship. I was almost five years old. I couldn't stay in one place at all. I'd go in the kitchen. I got friendly with the help, and I loved pickles. They had them in wooden barrels, so I'd reach in. I was eating pickles all the time. In the cabin, I don't remember beds, I remember hammocks. And for meals we ate at long tables with round containers to put the dishes in, so that when the boat went back and forth, the dishes wouldn't fly off the table. One day, they served me some milk, but I didn't like milk. So I took my glass, put it on another table, and found a bottle of wine and put it in its place. French people drank a lot of wine. All the people in the dining room laughed when I did that.

Then, one day, I saw this ladder. And I was always curious, so I started climbing the ladder to the top of the boat and the next thing I knew somebody grabbed me from behind and pulled me down. It was one of the sailors, and had I continued straight, I would have dropped right in the ocean.

I don't remember Ellis Island or the Statue of Liberty. The next thing I remember I was in kindergarten in Lodi, New Jersey and I couldn't speak English and I felt unwelcome. The other children teased me good. Once in a while, if I tried to say something, and I didn't say it right, they would laugh at me. And then I'd get mad, and I'd start to cry. I was the only immigrant child in my class in Lodi. The only one. Then we moved to Manhattan, to Broadway and 125th Street.

We lived real near the Hudson River. I used to go down there to see the rats. There were big rats down by the river. But also Red Cross boats that were coming in from the war transporting soldiers that got hurt. By this time I was going to public school in New York and my English was much better. But my father wasn't trying to improve his English, and my mother didn't care at all, neither did my grandmother.

We hadn't been living more than a year in New York when my mother died. I remember, when we lived in Lodi, my mother said to me, "*Ma petite fille,*" [my little girl] and then in French, "I won't always be with you." So I don't know if she had a feeling that she was going to die and leave me, but I remember that.

She died from influenza, from the epidemic that started during the war. People were dropping dead in the streets. I was nine years old when she died. But because we were Catholic, she could not be cremated. It went against the religion. But the U.S. government enforced a law that all people who died at that time had to be cremated because they didn't want to bury them. There were too many bodies. So my mother was cremated.

That left my grandmother, my father, and me. But my father and my grandmother didn't get along at all, so that made life unpleasant. And my grandmother liked her wine. But they had Prohibition at the time, and she could not get her wine. So she went back to France. But before she did, she said to me in French that she hated to leave me because "your father's alone now, and I fear what's going to happen to you with him."

We moved to Rutherford, New Jersey because the apartment in Manhattan was too big, too expensive, and Rutherford had a big French population. But then one day when I was thirteen I remember him coming and saying, "I have to leave you."

"What do you mean you have to leave me?"

"I've been offered a job, but it's far away, and I won't be able to see you for a long time."

I started crying, naturally, and said, "We'll write, won't we?"

"Yeah, we'll write."

He went to Sanford, Maine. I got boarded with friends of his, a family in Lodi, New Jersey who apparently had met us at Ellis Island when we first arrived here. Soon after, I came down with diphtheria. The doctor said, "Do you have your father's address?" I gave it to him. The doctor wrote to my father and told him, "You'd better come and get your daughter if you want her to live." It wasn't just the diphtheria, I was in a depressed state. I didn't care whether I lived or died.

When he came to me, he said, "What do you think about me getting married?" What did he want me to say? He planned to marry a Bohemian who didn't speak French or English. I forget what her language was. I always called him Papa. So I said, "Listen, Papa, you're old enough to know what you want. If you want to get married, go ahead. Get married. But I'll tell you one thing. She'll never boss me. She'll never touch me. My mother never touched me. If you want something done, tell me, and I'll do it. But I don't want her to tell me to do anything . . ."

I didn't get along with her at all. In order to talk to her, we had to translate each other. I was miserable. And then one day she started telling me what to do and I said, "No, I'm not going to do it." So she slapped me across the face. I turned around and slapped her back. I said, "My mother never touched me, and you're never going to touch me either."

She went and told my father what happened and he said to me, "This fight is between you two. Leave me out of it." He wouldn't take sides. But I thought he should take my side because he was my father and I was his daughter, and that I should come before her. But it wasn't like that.

Lara Bisset

· · · · · · · · · · ·

BORN SEPTEMBER 23, 1909
EMIGRATED FROM FRANCE 1920, AGE 10
PASSAGE ON THE *TOURAINE*

Though she was born in France, she came from a close-knit family of Russian stock. Today, she lives near her son, in Miami, Florida.

I came here from France in 1920 and settled in New Jersey, not too far from Ellis Island. But in all these years, I never bothered to see it again. I guess, like everybody else, when it's in your own backyard, you just don't go. There's always tomorrow. Then I started reading about the renovation in 1986 and I became intensely interested, except by that time I had moved to Florida. So on one of my visits to New Jersey in June of 1990, I decided to go to Ellis Island and I did. And I was absolutely taken aback by the wonderful things that were exhibited there, of such great interest to this country and to everybody living here. I noticed things that reminded me of our family history, particularly one exhibit on a wall illustrating the many Jewish people who had been murdered in Odessa in the year 1905, when the Cossacks in Russia went on a rampage and killed the Jews.

In the Jewish quarter of Odessa where my father and mother lived, the people posted sentinels to let the community know if the Cossacks were coming on horseback. What the Cossacks used to do was yank the men out of their homes and factories, line them up, and shoot them. The women and children were molested. The cossacks did this so that the men would flee across the border to Germany. The women and children were left behind with plans to reunite later, whenever the women could band together and cross the border.

The year 1905 struck me, because that's the year my mother and father escaped into Germany. And it just gave me chills. There were, according to a document in this exhibit, 574 killings in the month of October, which was the month they escaped. It was the most killings of any of the areas.

My father escaped first. My mother escaped a few days later when it was organized. All these women and children, as many as they could take, escorted by a few men, crossed the border in the snow. They knew when the guards had their post and they would time it so that they could escape when the guards weren't at the borders. My mother took with her in one wicker basket the family samovar with a tray underneath it, and in another wicker basket her six-

month-old child, my brother, whose name is Solomon. The snow was deep. The progress was going very slow.

Suddenly the baby, Solomon, began to cry. In desperation, one of the men, who was afraid that everybody would be endangered, took the wicker basket. He told everybody to go on, stop for nothing, just go. My mother stayed behind. She was not going to leave her baby behind, and everybody went forward. My mother was frozen up to the waist. Till the day she died, her legs were like two purple sticks. But Solomon survived. She was a courageous woman.

Once in Germany, my mother went to the appointed place, a hotel, where my father was waiting. They started to wander around, wondering where to settle. They didn't want to stay in Germany, so they went to Luxembourg, and they didn't like it. They went to Belgium and didn't like it, and they went to France and they loved it. My father had a brother in St.-Etienne, which is about an hour by train from Lyon. That's where my brother Maurice was born, and then I was born in 1909.

We certainly were poor, but we were helped by my uncle in St. Etienne. He owned a dry goods store there. My father had been a watchmaker, but the way they made their living was to buy up dry goods, go to country fairs they called *foires*, sell their goods, pack up, and come home. But when they came home they returned with fresh nuts, fresh fruit, fresh milk, fresh everything, and we had a really big party. Country bread! And we had this big kitchen in St.-Etienne with a tremendous table and everything got put on the table and we'd have a ball. But we were not allowed to leave a crumb. We were raised very frugally. You'd eat everything. Nothing got thrown out. My mother went along with my father to the fairs, so she had people take care of us. During summers, we were all parceled out to farms in the countryside, so they could do their business. She would find farmers who wanted to take in children at a price, sort of like children here go to camp. I remember milking a cow into a bowl and drinking it with all the foam on top.

France was a very happy time. School was a happy time. In St.-Etienne, the schools were either all girls or all boys. There were some Jews in the area. There was even a synagogue, but it was at the edge of town. Much closer was a beautiful Catholic church, a block away from where we lived. My mother sent us to the church. "You have to be exposed to religion," she said. "But just remember, you're Jewish and we don't believe in Jesus Christ as a god. We believe in him as a great scholar, a great man, but not as a god, and just remember that, but go."

She exposed us. And we'd go to midnight mass, and we'd go to Christmas mass with our neighbors. She did not go. But she had a little Bible and she prayed, in her own way, by herself. I still have that Bible. I remember during big storms she would take us to the huge window in the church, gather the three of us around, take out this little Bible, read from it and pray. [Laughs.]

I remember the living room had a very large fireplace. And this big urn my mother had brought from Russia. It was about a foot and a half in diameter. It used to hang on a chain over the fireplace. She'd make jellies in it, soups in it. And we'd sit and talk around the fire while she cooked.

I remember we had family outings, picnics in the park, where somebody always had an accordion, right? We'd take out the *saucisson* [sausage] from the straw basket, and slice it onto French peasant bread followed by fruit, a lot of fruit. It was a fun thing, because everybody talked and sang. There was a lot of singing. I remember that. It was a very happy time for us.

· · ·

But then, during the First World War, food became scarce. In fact, we had to go to the town hall to be weighed, and according to our weight was how much food was allotted to each person, adult and child. And with that you had to go in lines, to the bakery or the butcher. But if you were at the end of a line, sometimes you got nothing. Being Jewish, she did not allow pork in the house. And one day she was at the back of the line at the butcher, but all he had left was a ham. She had no choice. She bought the ham, a loaf of bread, made us sandwiches, and we ate it outdoors in a park.

After the war started in 1914, my father was away in the French Foreign Legion. He wanted to fight for France against the Germans and join the French army, but his citizenship papers were Russian, so he joined the Legion. My mother was left to cope with raising three children. I don't remember how long he was away, but it must have been a good while, because he was sent to Algeria for training. [Laughs.] I do know that the reason he returned was because Legion commanders noticed he was very nearsighted, and they were afraid he'd shoot the wrong troops, so they sent him home.

After he returned, my mother deviled the life out of him to go to America. "Let's go to America!" she'd say. My mother had family here. She had a sister and two brothers who had migrated from Russia through various countries and then settled in the United States. And she had always wanted to be with her family. Well, he resisted and resisted, but finally gave in. The war ended in 1918, and we finally came to America in 1920.

My mother packed three big bales she used for merchandise at the fairs. They were full of possessions. She brought the samovar, of course, the big urn, and clothing. One bale was devoted completely to my trousseau. A whole big bale, twice the size of a trunk and made out of wicker. She had engaged someone to hand-embroider my clothes with my initials. She had underwear, bed linens, handkerchiefs, everything with L.B. for Lara Bisset, and a design around it. But, as it turned out, the bale got lost or stolen in transport and we never recovered it. Somebody must have opened it, saw all those fine linens and things and could care less what the initials were.

We went to La Havre to get the boat, the *Touraine*. We stayed in Paris for two days because my parents wanted to see Paris, and then we went on to Le Havre and got on. It was the five of us, my parents and three children. We traveled with the last name of Bisset, even though in Russia my father's last name was Bissarov. What happened was, when my parents originally got to France, the clerk who wrote out the name decided to give it a French twist. It became Bisset. The clerk also changed my first name from Lara to Larie, to make it sound more French. And he gave me the middle name Sarah, after my mother. In the Jewish tradition, you

Immigrants awaiting inspection outside the main building in 1909

(NATIONAL PARK SERVICE: STATUE OF LIBERTY NATIONAL MONUMENT)

do not give the name of the mother to the child. But France is a Catholic country, so the name on my French birth certificate reads: Larie Sarah Bisset.

The departure was May 29, 1920. I don't remember our passage, except that it was dull, lengthy, and I thought it would never end. You don't see anything but water. Finally, when word got out that we were approaching land, everybody ran outdoors on deck. We were packed like sardines, gazing with such excitement and wonderment. I saw the Statue of Liberty. It was so impressive, so majestic, so meaningful. Freedom! Opportunity! And most of all, it linked to us, America and France, because we knew it was given to America by France. That I remember distinctly.

Then I remember getting off that boat like herds of cattle. Everybody pushing out onto the ferry that took us to Ellis Island. Suddenly the children were segregated and the parents were segregated and we couldn't understand this. Why were we at different tables for eating? Why were we in a different room than the adults? We just couldn't get over this.

I remember hordes of people. There were quite a few children and mothers, walking up those wide steps into the main building. I remember the darkness, the wooden benches, the poorly lit hall, the babies screaming, the children crying, adults crying. It was awful. It was a bad experience. There was so much commotion, so much sadness. Some families were being turned away because their papers weren't in order, or because they had some kind of an illness. The kids were running around mad, but it was so dimly lit. And lines, such long lines, and such impatience, and people waiting in line, carrying packages, whatever they brought off the boat with them. I remember looking for a place to lie down on one of those benches. There were people lying on the floor. I remember standing in line with my family until we reached the little cubbyhole where they took our papers. I remember the unhappiness of the people that couldn't stay. I mean, the crying and the sadness. The huddling together of these families that apparently were going to be sent back, or kept at Ellis Island for a few days. But we were all right. Our papers were in order.

We stayed overnight, and my mother's brother picked us up at Battery Park with a Model-T Ford. So there were five of us plus him. And we got into this car, and started for Wilmington, Delaware. [Laughs.] But in those days they didn't have the New Jersey Turnpike. So a three-hour ride today was more like six hours then. And I was so thirsty. But my uncle didn't speak French and we didn't speak English. The only common language we had was Yiddish, which became our secret language. "I've got to have a drink," I said to my mother. But I never got that drink. I was dying by the time we got to Wilmington. [Laughs.]

. . .

I remembered all of these things when I visited Ellis Island in 1990. I spent one whole day there by myself, and returned the following day to take pictures. Pictures of that 1905 exhibit, and the ferries and the statue and the Great Hall. I could hear the cries and the screams. I could see the sad faces. I could feel the crowds and the commotion. It all came back to me. In one exhibit I saw a photograph of the *Touraine*, the boat we came on.

I walked outside to the Wall of Honor and saw the names of the families immortalized that came through Ellis Island. And I suddenly realized, I'm the only one left now. I decided our family name deserved to be there, and got the forms to fill out.

I still have the samovar.

Eva and Juanita Quinones

· · · · · · · · · · · · · ·

BORN APRIL 27, 1903 AND OCTOBER 18, 1908
EMIGRATED FROM SPAIN VIA CUBA 1923, AGES 19 AND 13
PASSAGE ON THE *ESPERANZA*

*They are sisters from Bilela, Spain, near Madrid. They are part of a family of
six siblings. After their father died, the three youngest siblings were left behind
with relatives, and the sisters were taken to Cuba by their older brother and
mother to find work. After four years in Cuba, they immigrated to Newark,
New Jersey, and eight years later, they were finally able to bring the other three
siblings to America. Both sisters eventually married immigrant husbands from
Spain, who have since passed on. "Our kids went to school, to college,
everything," said Juanita. "Our kids, they got a better education than we did.
I'm proud of that."*

*E*VA: I never went to school over there
[Spain], never. They never sent me to
school because my father die very
young and left my mother with six children.
It was very bad for her. So her family, they
told her why don't you go to Cuba and take
the three oldest ones to a better life, and
leave the other [younger] ones, because
times were very bad, you know. A lot of
[Spanish] people went to Cuba . . .

JUANITA: See, my father die. Henry,
my oldest brother, was fifteen, Eva was
twelve, I was seven. Another [sibling] was
five, another three, and another one year
old. My mother, she got, you know, panicked, responsibility. My father got killed on
the train. He was looking out the window,
and the window fell right on his temple. I
was seven years old. He was a decorator,
painter—a contractor, nice. He made good
money. When he die on the train, we were
home in bed. Somebody, about midnight,
they're knocking on the door. It was a family
that lived close to the train. They tell mother
that my father die. Henry became the man
of the house. My mother panicked. She for-

got about us. You know, she wanted to die.
You know, with six children, and no
money . . . We were not close with my father's side of the family. They [the grandpar-
ents] had all died.

EVA: My mother was sweet, black
hair. She was educated. She could read and
write. But after my father died, she don't
even send the kids to school or anything. She
never sent me to school. All the other kids
in town went to school, but not us. She was
worrying and never was happy. Only when
she went to Cuba she started changing, you
know, because she got to work. She worked
as housekeeper in a wealthy household,
cooking. She was maid.

JUANITA: But she feel very bad about
leaving the three kids there. We went there
with the intention to bring them, too, after
a while. We went to Cuba with the intention
of setting up a whole new life, not going to
the United States.

I was happy to be going [to Cuba]. This
was right after World War I—1918, maybe.
But we didn't know anything about a war.
In the little towns you don't know anything.

· · · · · · · ·

We took a boat from Cadiz [in southern] Spain to Cuba.

EVA: We were down in the hold. It smelled. There was vomit. It took about nineteen days. They actually took livestock on the boat to feed the passengers. They killed the animals, the cows, pigs, every day. They killed the pig with a knife through the heart. About four men would hold the pig down. Then they burn the hair off the pig and clean it and cut out the ham . . .

JUANITA: We came with our cousins, they were sisters, and one, she had a little baby. She didn't give the breast [milk]. She went on the boat with only one can of milk. My mother said, "Oh, you got to get more milk. That's not enough." So after she started giving the baby all the [meat] food, the baby died on the boat from bad food. She [baby] got diarrhea. She was about eight months old . . .

When we got to Havana, the hotels—they call a *fonda*—everything was full, nothing. So a family that we knew, a friend of my mother's, let us stay with them for a few days in their house. That was nice.

EVA: My mother and I, we find a job. Because over there, even if they got [owned] a little store, they got servants. The wife don't do anything in Cuba at that time. They got two or three servants to do the housework, domestic work. This family we worked for, they were nice. The man was from Spain. He went to Cuba when he was a young boy. He had a deaf mother. And wherever she went, I have to stay with her, take care of her. We all slept there, ate there.

JUANITA: I didn't work, though. I was too young.

EVA: My brother, he got a nice job in Cuba at, like a country club. It was a good job for him. Then some friend [of his] wanted to go to America. He say, "Oh, come on, let's go to America. It's much better than here. Over there you don't do any work." So Henry came first . . .

JUANITA: . . . With the intention to later try to get us here, you know. So that's what happened. We lived in Cuba for four years. She didn't send me to school. I was in the house with her. I was a maid. For the Cubans, we were immigrants.

EVA: I hated it. In America, Henry got a job in Newark, New Jersey as a painter. He painted houses. He make a lot of money. That's what we knew about America, money is everywhere, you just scoop it right up. [They laugh.] Henry didn't send us no money to leave Cuba. My mother had it [saved] from working. But she also sent the money to Spain to take care of the [other three] kids. She suffered so much for the kids. I gave all my money, twenty-five dollars a month [to my mother]. That was a lot of money. I never got a penny. She take right away. I say, "Ma, don't send so much, because they got all the properties we got, you know, to take a lot of food there, and the house." But . . .

JUANITA: We left Cuba in September 1923. The boat trip to New York was seven days. We were in second class. We have a room with one on top of the other, bunk beds, you know. And my mother was on the bottom, and a lot of people talking . . . So we stayed overnight [at Ellis Island], and the next day, in the afternoon, we came here. My mother and us.

EVA: Oh! What a difference from Cuba. [Laughs.]

JUANITA: The big buildings, you know. And the subway. My brother came to the island. I was almost fourteen. But we were detained, I don't know why. I started to cry when he left. I want to go with him. I was afraid maybe they send us back to Cuba, you know. That's what we thought. We were detained for ten days.

EVA: Ellis Island was good. We eat. We eat in the big dining room. A lot of people. You got to be careful, because they take everything. If you look the other way, they grab your food, and you don't eat nothing. They [other immigrants] hog.

JUANITA: We kept our name tags on. Henry took us by train to a boardinghouse where he lived, on Madison Street in Newark. This was 1923. For me, I like it. To me, I was free, you know . . .

EVA: Freedom, yeah.

JUANITA: Because over there [Cuba], you stay in the house and you can't do what you want. I feel so free [here]. [They laugh.] We stayed there [Madison Street] for a week until we rented a house, two bedrooms, and the kitchen, dining room—that was everything. We had electric, and gaslight . . .

EVA: . . . And a toilet, and a sink in the kitchen. In Spain we went outside. [They laugh.] In Cuba, the rich people had. Newark had a big Spanish population. You hear Spanish people. But also a lot speaking Polish, German. You hear every language, a lot of languages . . .

The movies, I never liked them because I couldn't see the screen, and I tell my mother, I say, "How come you see the cars so far and I can't see?" She say, "Because you don't look right." She never took me to the doctor to have my eyes checked. I needed glasses so bad and I hated movies. I hated movies. She finally took me to the doctor, "I can't see the movies. I can't see anything." Even the people across the street, I don't recognize. A lot of people said, "Oh, she's so stuck, she don't even want to talk." When I got the glasses, I said, "Oh, my God."

JUANITA: I stayed home with my mother. She didn't send me to school. I went food shopping with her all the time . . .

EVA: I got a job because there were a lot of people from Spain, girls, and I got a job right away on Broadway sewing ladies' suits and clothing . . . So Henry and me worked. We were the breadwinners.

. . .

JUANITA: Then, after being in America three, maybe four months, two detectives came to our home one day [truant officers]. They told my mother that if I wasn't in school by Monday morning, we'd have to pay a $250 fine. And, you know, in those times, $250 was a lot of money. So I went to school. I didn't even know how to write my name.

EVA: Even me. I'm older than her. They told me, one time they come into the house and my mother say, "A man was just over here." She say, "You got to go to school in the night." They want you to learn English. And you know what my brother Henry say? He say, "In the night, only go the bad girls to school." This is how they [mother, brother] felt about women getting an education. Even when he came to this country, my brother was still thinking in these Old World sort of ways. So I'm the dope in the family.

JUANITA: Monday came, my brother took me to school. So I went. I didn't know what they were talking about. I went only two years to school, you know, and I didn't know nothing in Spanish, no math, nothing. They put me in a class with little kids, A-B-C. [Laughs.] It was hard on me. I didn't feel like staying there with these little kids. I was thirteen, nearly fourteen years old. I went to the third or fourth grade . . . I help my mother to get her American citizenship. That's how we brought the other kids from Spain [because of] her American citizenship. So I tried to teach her. If they ask, "What's your name? . . . How many kids do you have? . . . When did your husband die? . . . When did you leave Spain?" Things they were supposed to ask, and she was supposed to answer. I also teach her about the American flag, about the senators, representatives . . .

EVA: I learned English by talking with friends. [They laugh.] But where I worked, there was a lot of Spanish people, and talk only Spanish in the house. Henry learned English. He died about nine years ago. But he learned English. I mean, he went to school in Spain when our father was alive.

JUANITA: After four years in Cuba and eight over here, the rest of the family was finally brought over. Twelve years without seeing them. The kids were then twenty and eighteen and sixteen. After the whole family was together again, my mother was happy. Oh, she was happy. She was very happy. My brother took the truck to the boat.

EVA: We see the three together. By then, I was married and had a little girl. She was four years old. And she went with Henry with the truck and a couple of friends. Henry wrote Quinones on the truck so the three would know it was us. It had been twelve years. And we started calling [out], Henry started shouting, looking . . . and we find them. [That night] my mother, she make so much food. I can't believe it . . .

Juanita never wanted to go back to Spain, but I went three times. I went one time to my place and another time to my husband's, my husband's place. Things had gotten better. I went with my husband around two times to see his family, and then, well, after he died I didn't go anymore. I went with my daughter and her husband, to my birthplace. I didn't feel any deep emotion . . .

JUANITA: Rock-a-bye baby. How did mother used to sing it?

BOTH: [They sing.] *"Munequita linda, de cabellos de oro, de diente de perla, labios de ruby. Di me si le quieres, como yo te quiero, tanto como entonces, siempre hasta morir."* [Pretty doll with hair of gold, teeth like pearls, lips like rubies. Tell me if you love me like I love you always, until we die.]

Roberta Estobar

. . . .

BORN APRIL 12, 1917
EMIGRATED FROM BRAZIL VIA PORTUGAL 1925, AGE 8
PASSAGE ON THE S.S. *OLYMPIC*

Born in Brazil, she moved with her mother and father to Portugal at age five; three years later, they immigrated to America. Now widowed, she lives on Long Island. She has three children and four grandchildren.

I was born in Manaus, Brazil, the state of Amazonas, which is in the northern part, right under the equator, a thousand miles up the Amazon River. Manaus is the city where the opera house exists, and it was recently renovated and brought back to its one-time splendor and Caruso came from Europe, as well as other artists at that time, because it was a boomtown for rubber. My

grandfather had a rubber plantation. I guess that's why they were there.

My mother taught school to the children of the plantation workers, and they were of all ages. It was like a colony. School was held in the biggest building, but it still had a dirt floor and a tin roof. So it was very hot during the day and cold at night. My mother would be away all week teaching and then she'd come back. She was teaching where the workers were on the plantations, and it was all rubber trees and I guess dense forest, and she got bronchitis very bad which, later in life, turned out to be asthma.

I barely remember my grandmother's home. I was a sickly child. I had malaria, and they told me that I was going into a coma, and I had been treated with quinine, which in those days was all they had to treat malaria. So it was a case of just lying in bed, feverish. The fever would make me very hot and then very cold, up and down. So I really don't remember much about that [time].

My father also was coming down with malaria. So the doctor recommended that we all get out, because otherwise we would die. It was getting that critical. I was about four. And that's when we left and went to Portugal, and stayed there three years, and then came to the United States.

My father had sisters and brothers [in Brazil], but they all got scattered, and his parents died at a very early age. I mean, they died when he was six months old, and his older sister was just about eighteen or nineteen, and she married a man that came from Portugal, and took my father with them back to Portugal; he was raised there. Then my father returned to Brazil, when he was about eighteen. This brother-in-law of his, who was like a father [to him], and had raised him, had some kind of a business down there and sent my father back to take care of that.

I had the one brother, but he died when he was about three. He had pneumonia, and he died within two or three days. We were on vacation somewhere, and he got ill, so he died quickly. Otherwise, I was brought up alone, with the exception of Nazare. She was somebody who lived with us in Brazil, and came with us to Portugal. She was a black girl that my parents had taken in before I was born, and she was only about two years of age when they more or less adopted her, because her father was in jail and I don't

know where the mother was. But it was just an act of kindness. As she got older, in her teens, we taught her how to set a table or to do different things to help. She was with us while we were in Portugal, but then when we decided to come to America, my father heard that blacks and the white population did not mix, and she did not, certainly, live in the same house. My father and mother decided the best thing would be to send Nazare back to Brazil, and she was about eighteen, and they knew somebody there, and they sent her to live with a family. But she got pneumonia the following year, and passed away . . .

My mother's sister, Nilda, had married this fellow who was of Portuguese descent, and he was in Fall River, Massachusetts. He was down there in Manaus, I think. He was a great sportsman and he was sent by some zoo in America to catch snakes or something, and bring them back. I heard the story that one of his snakes had babies in my grandmother's basement. [Laughs.] That didn't make him too popular. But my mother's sister and he married, and came up to Massachusetts where he was from. Nilda was the first one that came up. My mother was the oldest of five girls and one brother in her family. And they all came up. Nilda married and came up first. Then another sister, and then a brother. Then my mother and father and me.

We all went to Massachusetts. Then we came down to Brooklyn, because my father couldn't find work in Fall River. We came to New York. We lived in Brooklyn. And then the last ones to come up was Grandma and the two other sisters.

My grandmother was left a widow at age thirty-five. My mother was sixteen, and she helped raise the others, and that's why she was teaching school. All the schooling I had was from my mother, and it was all in Portuguese. I could write my name and read and everything. It wasn't until I arrived in the United States that they [my parents] said I could count up to ten, and that was about all, I guess, my father hurriedly might have taught me on the boat coming over.

We went by boat from Brazil to Portugal first. I was very sick. My mother was nursing my father and I, because we both had malaria. So the trip from Brazil to Portugal was not very nice, and we gradually got over the malaria.

In Portugal, I remember my aunt's house, we didn't live with her, but I remember where we lived in the suburbs of it [the city Porto], and the church chimes, and my father and I would dance in the kitchen to those chimes. I remember because Portugal has a lot of vineyards, and the men would crush the grapes. I remember seeing them in those days. Now it's all done in mechanical ways. But then they would wash down the men's legs and feet and so on, put them in these big vats to crush the grapes with their feet, and I remember that.

I remember we had rabbits. We lived in the country, and my father traveled, I guess, a good two hours to get to work. He worked in the bank, because he had a background in office work and clerical work.

My aunt's house was grand. I would compare it to brownstones in New York City because it was brick, and it was in the city, and I remember it having a very big staircase. She was well to do, she had a cook, and a seamstress, even though she was a widow for many, many years. I never met her husband, who had already passed away. My father grew up in that house. He was educated in England, too, so they must have sent him away to school as well as being in Portugal.

Before we left [for America], I broke my leg at my aunt's house, because she had a big, above-the-ground goldfish pond. She had a nice backyard. And there was this big wheel you would turn and the water would go into this pond. I put my stomach on the handle of this wheel, and I went up and, of course, one of my legs got caught on the spoke, and I was thrown right down. I was lying in a pool of blood, and the cook came out, and then I remember going to the hospital in Porto. They took me by horse-drawn carriage because there were no cars to the hospital. I remember the doctor. I had panties on, and he slit the side of it, he had a little knife to cut, and I thought he was going to cut my leg with that; [laughs] not realizing what it was . . .

We decided to come to the United States because Nilda's husband, Daniel Days—his [last] name was Diaz, but they changed to Days, because the translation of Diaz is Days. He was writing to my father always urging him to come to the United States. But we had gone to Portugal because my father wanted to introduce his wife and child—me—to his sister, who had brought him up.

We didn't live with my aunt. We had a very small house. Maybe four rooms or something. It was a cement-block house, but it was in the suburbs. We had a big yard, and I remember we had rabbits that used to dig great big holes, and then my mother would have to put her hand way down there and grab this rabbit to come out.

After being there three years, my father realized that there was no future for him in Portugal. And since his brother-in-law, my mother's sister's husband, was writing to him all the time urging him to come to America, we decided, well, we'd better come. I think my father probably borrowed money from one of my aunt's friends, because I don't think my aunt was too anxious to have him leave. She thought that was the wrong move, leaving to go to a strange country.

My mother wasn't too happy about coming [to America], and my father's sister, because she had money and so on, looked upon the fact that my father married my mother, even though she was educated and so on in Brazil—she wasn't somebody that maybe his sister would have picked out. So from that point, there wasn't that much good feeling between my mother and the aunt; that he could have made a better marriage or something. In Portugal, I do remember, my aunt had very well-to-do friends, and we did visit somebody that was a countess on her estate, and my aunt had a seamstress who made dresses for my cousins and for me. We all had beautiful little dresses and we went to this estate for the day or whatever it was.

My father planned everything. He had the tickets well in advance of the whole trip, from the time we left Portugal and going right up the coast. We were in a cabin, not steerage. In fact, there was this fat fellow, Portuguese, too, and he started talking to my father on the boat. He said that he had paid much more for his passage than, I don't know if he was joking, than the three of us combined.

In New York, we went up on deck, and everybody was trying to get a glimpse, early in the morning, as soon as we were approaching. We had an exam by doctors there at the Ellis Island. They put some kind of a number outside our garment. Then I remember they gave me biscuits, and a small container of milk.

We arrived here in May, we were still in need of a coat. I don't think we had too much baggage with us. I don't remember any big trunk or anything like that.

We went to Fall River, Massachusetts because that's where my Aunt Nilda and her husband and son lived. We were there for four months, and my father was writing to different companies for jobs. I don't think there were five hundred Brazilians throughout the United States. When we were up in Fall River it was all Portuguese, not Brazilians, but, of course, it was the same language, and my father wanted my mother to pick up English as soon as possible, so he would say to her that she couldn't shop or go to the bodegas. So she shopped in the supermarkets that were strictly English-speaking. The whole idea was to learn English and, as I say, I knew how to count up to ten and that was it. But they said that within a few months after I attended school, playing with the children outside, and they only spoke English, I quickly picked up English.

My father couldn't find work up there because Fall River was a mill town and the industry there was factory work. So he then wrote to different companies in New York. The day he was to leave, he played the violin because he had violin lessons from the time he was eight until he was about seventeen or eighteen. So the day he was leaving with that violin under his arm to go to New York, a letter had come and gave him employment. I think it was Fraser & Company, Fulton Street, New York City. So he went to work there, and then after a few weeks, or a month or so, he sent for me and for my mother to come from Massachusetts to Brooklyn, where he found a room. It was a parlor room, and it had a two-burner stove, but very little [else]. My mother worked on Twelfth Street at the Ansonia Clock Company.

My father found this room in Mrs. Olsey's rooming house in Brooklyn, and that was at 389 Eighth Street, Brooklyn, and the school was right down the street. My father was always interested in getting close to, you know, convenience and school. One morning I insisted that it was eight-thirty and it was only seven-thirty and it was very cold and my father said, "No, it's not time yet." But I guess I was very, very anxious to go to school, having never attended school. So I went down there and everything was closed. The school had a great big iron fence around it. So I went back up the street because the house was about a half a block up, and I knocked on the door, and my father wouldn't let me in. You know, he was trying to teach me a lesson.

Mrs. Olsey more or less looked after me. She pulled me on a sled the first time I saw snow. One time I didn't feel well, Mrs. Olsey would put a hot-water bag on my stomach. She looked after me, and that's where we lived for a year. Every Friday we went to a movie, my father, mother, and I. On Ninth Street there was the Prospect Theater, and they had maybe five, six acts of vaudeville and probably more than one movie in those days. When we came out, there was a little tiny store where you could have a hot dog, or my father would buy me a Love Nest candy bar. So that was our beginning of life in the United States.

. . .

You had to be twenty-one years of age to vote, and when I became twenty-one I voted and gave my father's citizenship number, and that's all you needed. The fact that you were voting showed that you wanted to be an American. But what happened was some years after that, in fact, I was already on Long Island and I heard about some family, husband and wife and two children, and the wife was not born in this country, she was a foreigner, and I don't know if it was Cuba at the time of the revolution, but they gave clearance to the husband and two children, but not the wife. And I thought to myself, "That could happen to me."

So I decided I'd better go for my own papers, and I did. I applied, and I went right here in Mineola, 240 Old Country Road, Mineola, where I many years later went to work in that same building for the health department. But I went there and it didn't take more than a year or two after I applied for what they call a Certificate of Derivative Citizenship.

I feel that I'm very American, since I didn't attend school anywhere else, and I regret I don't know more the history of Brazil, but I certainly feel that I'm very much part of the American Dream. It certainly worked out for me. I'm very, very thankful my father did migrate to this country, because Brazil is a great country, and he'd always say, "Brazil is the land of the future." There's so much natural wealth there, but to get it out is something else, and there was always some drawback, whether it's politics or corruption, things just didn't work, you know?

I regret that I didn't go back to Manaus, where I was born. Because now, instead of rubber plantations, I'm told they have Sony and all these other different companies manufacturing computers and radios and all of this. It's a free-duty port on the Amazon River, so Manaus is now thriving again as a different kind of thing, and they restored the opera house, and I would love to see it . . .

Jose and Consuela Martinez

. . . .

BORN AUGUST 28, 1917 AND DECEMBER 2, 1921
EMIGRATED FROM PORTUGAL 1949, AGES 32 AND 28
PASSAGE ON THE *MARINE SHARP*

*They emigrated together as husband and wife, arriving at Ellis Island from
the Azores, Portugal. Today, they live in Massachusetts,
and enjoy their four grandchildren.*

. . . .

JOSE: I was born in St. Michael, Azores, Portugal. I came over here with my mother in 1919. My mother was a widow, and I was three and a half years old, something like that. We stayed over here for three or four years, and my mother go back with me when they had the Depression. There was no work. She was looking for work, so she went back to the island. Just me and my mother. I had no brothers or sisters. My father died when I was fourteen months old. So my last name is my mother's maiden name, Martinez.

CONSUELA: I was born in Taunton, Massachusetts, and we went back to the Azores when I was three years old; my father, mother, and two brothers. I was the middle child. I stayed in the Azores until I got married. Jose and me were in the same village, St. Michael. It was a fishing village, and people worked on the farms.

JOSE: I worked on the farms. They grew corn, wheat. That's what they did. All pasture. There was cows and everything. My father was a dairy farmer. After my father died, I don't know how we got along. My mother didn't work. I remember we lived without heat in the house, and it could be cold over there. I went to school to the third grade.

CONSUELA: I meet him around thirteen or fourteen. After school.

JOSE: She was a good-looking girl when she was young. A regular wedding . . . In those days, people went to America for three or four years and come back when they get a few dollars, you know. So I decided to do the same thing.

On the boat, we were in separate rooms. She came on one with the ladies. She was pregnant. I was in the other room. My boy stayed in her room, and I was in the other room with the men. And it was six days. We were in second class, in a cabin with four bunk beds . . . I remember the smells from the kitchen. I couldn't eat the food there. I

didn't like those smells. But I got bread. Before we came, I got some *linguista, chorizos,* you know. Sausages. I killed a pig before I came, so I brought some of them, already cooked, so that's what we eat. I used to go over there and get bread, come back to the room, bring some coffee, sausages with the bread and coffee, the three of us.

CONSUELA: I was throwing it all up.

JOSE: Every time she got up, she throws up . . . We got into New York on New Year's Eve, about three o'clock in the afternoon. It was Brooklyn on one side and New York on the other side. There was snow. Brooklyn was white. I never saw snow. I heard people say, "That's snow, that's snow!"

We came by train to Providence. When we got to Providence, they used to have another train from Providence to Taunton. When I got there so late there was no more train. So I got a telephone call from the family over here in Taunton, and they picked us up. It was two o'clock in the morning. They still had the lights for that Christmas. My English [laughs] was "Yes, yes" and "No, no." When I came on the train at night, you know, I see the cities, the lights in the cities and the towns, you know. Beautiful. We went to . . .

CONSUELA: My father's house. He was a fireman. He was already a citizen, I think.

JOSE: Yeah. We were there for a month until I got a job. I worked for a rubber company. I worked on the press making heels, rubber heels for shoes . . . The first year when we got here, it was wintertime with the clothes I brought from the old country. I said to my wife a few times, you know, "This is the last winter. Next winter we're going back to the old country." But, you know, you raise the kids, you have another girl . . . The first baby we had over here lived nine hours and she died. So we made another girl, and a little boy, and we kept staying, and soon we stopped thinking about going back no more. Now, I don't want to go back there no more.

I went to night school to learn English so I could get the immigrant's papers. I used to read the [news]papers and the books, but I don't understand what I was reading. It took me a long time because of the place I work, you know, my foreman was a Portuguese, and the people there was almost all Portuguese, so you never speak English. I came home and I speak Portuguese. My boy and my girl sometimes used to speak English to me, and I don't understand it. I used to say, "No, no. Speak in Portuguese." So I made them speak Portuguese . . .

Another thing is, see, I left my mother there [Azores]. My mother had no daughters, no boys, and she was a widow. I left her over there, so I thought about her. So

two years after I took American papers [citizenship], and we decided to stay, I called my mother and she came. We decided [to stay in America] because over here we lived better than we lived over there. We didn't live too bad over there. I had a house and piece of land, you know. But we couldn't save money over there. You lived day by day . . .

My mother wanted to work. I said no. She had to stay home and help with the kids, so that's what she did. She never worked here. When she came she was sixty-two, I think. She did not go through Ellis Island [the mother came in 1956, Ellis Island had closed], she came here by plane.

I worked in the heel factory in Stoughton for twenty-seven years. When the factory closed, I was still only fifty-seven. So I worked here in Taunton and two other places until I retired at sixty-two.

Part VII

. . . .

THE MIDDLE EAST

18

Syria, Armenia, Turkey & Palestine

(APPROXIMATELY 200,000 IMMIGRANTS, 1892–1954)

Osla Esen

· · · · · · · · · · · ·

BORN SEPTEMBER 1, 1903
EMIGRATED FROM TURKEY 1913, AGE 10
PASSAGE ON THE *ARGENTINA*

*In Angora, later renamed Ankara, she lived as a young child during the days of
the sultan and the Ottoman Empire, before Turkey was declared a republic in
1923 by Mustafa Kemal Ataturk. She grew up on the Lower East Side and in
Harlem. She completed grammar school at age fourteen, and went to work to
help support her family. She became a piece worker in a factory that
manufactured children's dresses. Her husband long since gone, she is now
ninety-four, and lives in Brooklyn, New York. "If I was going to be in Turkey,"
she said, "I wouldn't have gotten married. You had to have a lot of money to give
a dowry. Where would I get money for dowry? Over here, my husband didn't
want dowry. Here you work. You work together. You make it, that's it."*

During the Inquisition, Turkey opened its doors, and they took all the Jewish people in. They were very good to the Jewish people. My ancestors were Jewish. Some of them, during the Inquisition, went to Greece and other parts of the world, but my ancestors settled in Turkey. They're still there.

My father used to be a tinsmith. He used to solder lamps. There, we didn't have electricity. He used to make gasoline lamps, kerosene lamps. He used to make little lamps and sold them. He had a little bit of a store and people used to come from the outskirts, and buy those little things. Sometimes they used to bring things they had broken. My father used to solder it for them and that was his livelihood. The store was a little bit of nothing. Only my father could fit there. So I didn't go there that much. It was a hard life to make a living.

We weren't poor, but we got along. Things weren't that expensive then. We lived in two rooms. In one room we didn't have no beds. We slept on the floor—me,

my sister, and my two brothers. It was a wooden floor and they used to have carpets, beautiful Turkish carpets. We used to have mattresses and we all used to sleep in the same room with my parents.

My mother did the cooking, so I learned how to cook. We used to have lentils, beans, rice, all kinds of vegetables. We used to cook cow brains, lamb chops, *borek* [pastries stuffed with feta cheese and spinach], *doner* [thinly sliced lamb similar to the Greek *gyro*], *manta* [dumplings stuffed with chopped meat served in a garlic and yogurt sauce], and *patlican* [puréed eggplant]. In the summer, we used to get a lot of tomatoes and cook them for hours and hours and hours. We used to make delicious tomato paste. We used to bake bread, cookies, and boil eggs on Friday for Saturday, and make knishes to feed the children on Saturdays after they came from shul.

In Turkey, we were very religious, really Orthodox. All the Jewish lived within five, six blocks of each other. The Turkish Christians, the Islamic, were friendly to the Jews.

They were very good. They opened their doors. I remember there was a beautiful synagogue that had a curtain between the men and the women. There were screens so the men shouldn't look at the ladies, or the ladies don't look at the men. But you could see through.

In our house, the living room was a special room and we used to take off our shoes outside. We never went in the room with shoes. The few days before Passover, we used to eat in the courtyard. We couldn't eat in the room, God forbid there's going to be crumbs. Then, when the night of the holiday came, the families, one or two families, used to get together, relatives, and have a beautiful seder. The seder used to take maybe six hours, and the children used to fall asleep, and even the women were very tired from all the work and all the cleaning and cooking because on Saturdays they don't cook. They had to cook a few days before the holiday and it was a very nice holiday and the children, we used to get new clothes on Passover. My father's brother and nephews came, nieces from my mother's side. And both sets of grandparents. So we all used to get together.

As a child, I used to speak French fluently, now I don't speak it so well. For school, they used to bring teachers from Istanbul to teach us French. They used to travel two days by train from Istanbul. There was also a Greek school. Some Jewish people wanted to learn the language, so they also went to Greek school. We learned French and Turkish, but our language was Ladino. In the house we spoke Ladino, which is the Spanish from Spain. Outside, with the Turks, we had to speak Turkish.

. . .

My father came to America in May 1912. My mother had a sister here and they sent tickets for my father, so he came. He lived with my aunt and went to work in a battery factory. He used to solder batteries, Eveready batteries. The following year, 1913, he wanted the family to come to America. He borrowed some money from a friend and he sent tickets for us. We were five.

When it was time to leave Turkey, my mother sold all our possessions. I don't remember packing. We didn't have much to pack. Maybe she had a carpet, a couple of pillows, but the rest she sold. Then we took the train to Istanbul. My mother had two sisters there, so they got a room for us to stay until it was time to leave, like a rooming house. We stayed all in one room. My mother didn't have much money. And it just happened that we had to stay longer than we had to.

For the trip, my aunts gave my mother a jar of jelly to give to another sister in America who lived in the Harlem. My mother took it and then we boarded a boat. But it wasn't a regular big boat. It was a very small boat with chickens. Chickens all over. It was terrible . . . From there, we went to Patras, Greece to get the big boat and stayed almost two weeks. It was terrible. It was very bad because the boat was delayed. We went to a hotel . . . The day the boat arrived, my mother didn't have enough money to pay the fellow from the hotel. She begged to borrow money from some other people in the hotel who were also from Ankara, they lived on the same street, but they wouldn't give her. My mother started to cry. Everybody left for the boat. My mother and we children were the only ones left in the hotel. So she went to the owner. She said, "I only have this money here, what shall I do? They don't want to lend me no money. I can't stay here with my children." The man was very good. He was a Greek guy. He said, "Go in peace with your children to your husband . . ."

We were in steerage, all the way down. During the day we used to go on deck. The ones that weren't seasick, they enjoyed

Jewish immigrants on the Lower East Side in 1901

(NATIONAL PARK SERVICE: STATUE OF LIBERTY NATIONAL MONUMENT)

themselves. I didn't eat nothing on the boat. The only thing that kept me alive was garlic and bread. I couldn't keep anything in my stomach. I was throwing up all the time. As soon as my mother went on the boat, she took sick. She went into the hospital on the boat, and there were four kids. Who's going to take care of all the children? I could hardly take care of myself. There was another family from Ankara. They took care of the little ones. I took care of one of my brothers. They didn't get sick. My mother was in the hospital about a week and a half.

During that trip, we had a very big storm. It was awful. The boat was rocking and big fishes, sharks, they used to jump almost on the boat. People were afraid. Water was coming in the boat. And, you know, the Jewish people, when they're in a position like this, they always carried the matzo, the *afikomen* from Passover. They started to pray, and throw the matzo in the ocean to calm the sea. It calmed down very well and, thank God, we arrived at Ellis Island three weeks later.

The next thing I remember we were all sitting on the floor, in one corner of the main room, waiting for my father to come. He came with my aunt, the one from the Harlem. We kissed, and he gave us a banana which we didn't have in Turkey, and it was good.

We took a boat to the elevated trolley. My father already had prepared an apartment, two rooms on the Lower East Side; a bedroom and a living room. One-fifty Ludlow Street. That number I remember. Very Jewish neighborhood. Never see one Italian. There were a few synagogues. There was a Sephardic synagogue on Allen Street we used to go to. Very religious we were, same thing like in Turkey. No lights on Saturday, no shoes in the house, everything got to be just so.

I went to school on Ludlow Street. There was a school near the corner of Delancey and Ludlow. My mother had to take care of the four kids. My father was still working in the batteries. On Sundays, he used to go to shine shoes because my father didn't make much money, probably five, six dollars a week. He had to pay rent and the children and clothes. Clothes we didn't make. They were ready-made clothes, which was something new for us. Sometimes, at night, my parents used to enjoy themselves with friends. They used to get together, and they used to go buy a pitcher of beer, and they used to have a good time.

After Ludlow, we moved to Orchard Street. I think we got three rooms on Orchard Street, so we moved there. It was a busy street. They used to have pushcarts. They used to sell everything. Vegetables, dried beans, figs, lentils, pickles, rice. They were in barrels. But my mother couldn't speak English. At the beginning, she didn't know anything, so she would point. Eventually she and my father learned—mostly from the children, the streets, and they spoke pretty well. From there, we moved to Harlem where my aunt was on 110th Street. There were a lot of Sephardic in different blocks, some Italians, some Irish, but we all got along. We found rooms on 110th, and I started to go to a school on 113th, which is no longer there.

The thing I remember though, a month or two after we arrived, my father took us to Ellis Island to see the Statue of Liberty. The boat was only five cents. [Laughs.] We were impressed to see that beautiful statue. We went inside. We walked up. I remember staring out through her eyes to Manhattan in the distance.

Helen Saban

. . . .

BORN MAY 11, 1913
EMIGRATED FROM SYRIA 1920, AGE 7
SHIP UNKNOWN

She had two older brothers who had already left the house when she was born, so she grew up an only child. Her father came here first. In Jersey City she worked in her father's dry cleaning store, then a factory that manufactured clothing for infants, and got married. Today, she lives in Wayne, New Jersey. "The amazing thing, as far as I'm concerned," she said, "I have no remembrance of difficulty. It seemed like one morning I got up and I knew English."

. . . .

Aleppo, Syria is in northwestern Syria near the Euphrates River. Very mild, a beautiful climate. Compared to other towns in Syria, it was like a metropolis. There was a lot of trading back and forth. The caravans used to go through.

My mother and I lived with my grandmother and my grandfather. My father's parents. In fact, my grandfather looked just like my father. He was about seventy-eight, seventy-nine, had a big mustache, quite handsome. He was a tailor. My memory of him is mostly when I woke up in the morning. He's sitting at his table, a large table, and he's cutting fabric. I'd wake up to the sound of the scissors cutting the fabric. He was a very austere, severe guy, but he worked hard for his family. I mean, there was nothing else to do there, you just work hard for your family and keep the family together. We had a nice life, you know, we weren't poor or anything.

My father was a tailor, too, and he had an opportunity to come to the States, but he couldn't afford to bring my mother and myself, so he figured he'd come here first, save enough money, and then send for me and my mother. Well, that was in 1913, about a month after I was born. He had an uncle here who had a grocery store. He was a butcher in Union City. My father stayed with him for a while until he got a job at a factory—women's clothes, petticoats, skirts, etc., in West Hoboken, New Jersey.

By the time he got himself together, got a job, got some money, the war broke out, World War I. Travel stopped. There was no boats going back and forth, and they were separated, my mother and father. They were separated from that time until 1920, when we came. Seven years!

During those years, my mother stayed with her in-laws. Her parents lived nearby, but we always lived in my grandfather's house. Her side of the family was very joyful. They were musicians. My other grandfather used to play the violin. My mother had a pretty nice voice, and an uncle of mine used to play the "oud." It's a Middle Eastern instrument. Every Friday or Saturday night we'd have a party in the house. The neighbors would come in. Everybody would bring something, drink, play music, and dance. Both sides of the family got along great.

They used to send me to the Armenian school, Armenian Apostolic was the faith. The recollection I have is that we were taught French. We had to learn French there because it was French mandate. Syria was a French mandate at that time.

My mother didn't speak French, she spoke Arabic. She and her father were of Armenian descent, but having been in Syria for such a long time, they lost the Armenian tongue and they just spoke Arabic. I don't know why they left Armenia for Syria. I would imagine just to get away from the Turks. My father would write to her in Armenian, but of course she didn't know how to read Armenian, so she had it read by someone else to her. He would send money and we would save the money . . .

I remember particularly the day before we were going to leave for America, my grandmother was standing there cooking things for us to take with us. She thought we weren't going to eat on the boat, you know. She was very work-worn. After eight kids you could imagine. She was a very tired-looking woman. She was thin. Poor Grandma. She was crying and cooking, crying and cooking.

It was my mother, myself, and my uncle Leon, my father's brother. It was a long journey. We went by train from Aleppo to Beirut. Then in Beirut we took a boat to Egypt, and went on to Naples, Italy. We stayed on the boat overnight in Naples. I could see Mount Vesuvius. After that, we went to Milan and stayed there about three weeks in hotels. I forget why. Then we went to Paris, then Le Havre, then straight over here. It wasn't first class. There were a lot of people. They were a mixture.

I had pets, guinea pigs, three of them, that I brought with me. I don't know how we got away with it, but I had them. I remember my mother and my uncle Leon, they were getting tired of this ship food. The food was alien to them, you know. They hadn't eaten anything but Middle Eastern food all their life. So she decided to cook something of her own. I guess she had food-stuff. But the captain or somebody, came and said, "You can't have a fire." It was like a little Sterno fire, you know. And I remember the other people making a fuss over me, a seven-year-old kid. That's about all I remember from the boat.

I remember seeing the Statue of Liberty. It didn't mean much to me, but seeing the other people getting excited, it meant a lot to me. When I went visiting Ellis Island several months ago, I remembered the largeness of the place, and the stacks of beds. Just two stacks, but they seemed like three and four stacks, you know. And very plain, one iron bed on top of another.

My mother felt wonderful about coming here, but then again, she left her father, her sisters, her brothers, and her mother-in-law, who she grew to love. My grandmother loved my mother as much as she did her own children. My mother had mixed feelings about everything. And being that she didn't know English, my uncle Leon interpreted for her. Immigration officials asked her whether or not she spoke, read, and wrote Armenian. Uncle Leon said to her, "Say yes." She said, in Arabic, "But I don't know." He said, "You just say, 'yes.'" So she said, "Yes." They handed her a book in Armenian. She said to my uncle, "Now what do I do?" He says, in Arabic, of course, he said, "Open a page and recite the Lord's Prayer in Arabic." So she did. As soon as she did that, they passed her. [Laughs.]

My father couldn't pick us up the day we came, so we had to stay over. I was very excited. My whole thing was that I'm going to come and see my father. I don't think anything else mattered to me. I had never seen my father before, only pictures. He sent pictures once in a while, that's why I was able to recognize him when I saw him in the big hall. I remember seeing him from ten, fifteen feet. I pointed, "There's my father!" And, of course, I ran over to him, he picked me up and hugged me.

Then we went to New Jersey.

James Habjian

BORN (IN THE U.S.) MARCH 11, 1910
EMIGRATED FROM SYRIA 1920, AGE 10
PASSAGE ON THE S.S. *NIAGARA*

He never went to high school; he quit at age fourteen to make a living. His father was already dead. His mother was remarried, living in Syria. He started running errands and sweeping floors in a photo-engraving shop. He eventually bought the shop and worked there until retirement. He and Sera Tartunian (page 396) have been married for over sixty years and live happily in Franklin Square, New York. He is proud that all four of his children speak Armenian and graduated college. They have ten grandchildren. "I told Sera, 'It took about eight days to get here.' She says, 'Oh, it took two weeks.' I said, 'You came after me on a better ship than I did.' "

I was born in New York City. My parents and my grandparents, on my father's side, all lived in an apartment on East Twenty-fifth Street. Then, when I was three years old, we all went to Bulgaria. My grandparents stayed behind. And the reason we went was because my father made rugs for the Kasam Brothers Oriental Rug Corporation. They were Asia Minor Greeks. And there was a very scarce number of people that had knowledge of repairing rugs and weaving rugs like my father. So they decided to send him with his family to Bulgaria to open a factory, make rugs and send them back to the United States.

After we were there two or three years, he decided he was finished with rugs, enough rugs. But before returning to the United States, he wanted to go and see his sister and her five children in Bitlis, which is in far eastern Turkey near Diyarbakir. She was the only one left from his family, the Habjian family, who wasn't in the United States. By the time we went there in 1915, the massacre occurred.

I remember the day it started. It was on a Wednesday. And on Wednesday they did laundry there, and my mother wanted to help the maid that's working there, washing the clothes, when all the commotion came up. We looked out of the window, there were Turkish soldiers there, and they had brought my father close. I could see him from the window. Before you know it, my mother dressed me like a girl. She took my sister's dress and put it around me. I didn't know why she was doing that. But what happened, the soldiers came to the front gate, and said to everybody, "Come down."

We had men hiding upstairs, revolutionists, and they start to shoot at the soldiers. They knew they were going to get killed. They had no choice. So the Turkish commander shouts, "Let the ladies and the children come downstairs." So we all got out, it was two stories.

In the meantime, we had a man servant, his name was Kur Galo. He was an old man, seventy, maybe more. He used to take care of me, and he lived down in the cellar. So when this shooting happened, he stayed and hid there.

Once all the ladies and the kids came out, they had us line up against the wall. There were about three or four men upstairs in the house, and Kur Galo in the cellar. They started a fire. The fellows upstairs never came out, but Kur Galo came out. Now, I'm standing against the wall, one side my sister, my mother in the middle, and me. Kur Galo came out of the basement door with his hands up. He had his hands up, the old man, and the soldier just shot him. He fell down, he turned around, and he says, "Allah." He said, "God," in Turkish, and he died. I'll never forget this. The soldiers opened the gate and they all came in, and they took every little boy, my aunt's five children. See, my mother was smart. She had dressed me like a girl. So I was saved.

My mother said to the commanding officer, "We're Americans." So they took us to the police station. They put us in a compound, all the girls and ladies. No boys. I'm the only boy there. Now, people didn't know that I'm not girl. Five years old, I was. We stayed there maybe one or two days. We had no food. They had one soldier in the front of the door, the guard, so nobody could go out. We slept standing up or leaning against each other. There was no place to sleep. And it wasn't only Armenians. They had Christian Assyrians and Greeks.

My mother went over to the soldier, she said, "I'm going to leave one of my daughters here, I'll go see if I can fetch some bread and I'll bring it, I'll give you some, too." He agreed. She came back to me. She says to me, "As soon as I go out with your sister, you run out of the compound. He's not going to leave the door unattended and chase you." I was supposed to be a little girl. There were trees off in the distance. She says, "I'll hide behind the trees." My mother went with my sister.

I looked at the guy standing there, and I just shot out and ran, and I looked around and I see he's not chasing me, so I ran and my mother grabbed me, and she took us to a cousin of hers. I didn't know who they were. She knocked on the door, and the cousin, a lady said, "We have no men here." So my mother identified herself. "Please open the door. I have my two kids with me." The cousin opened the door and they hugged each other. This cousin had three men hiding up in the rafters so she was afraid of anybody knocking on the door.

Later on, we find out they had my father imprisoned in an armory. The Turkish doctor said, "I'll have you as a nurse. You work, you help to take care of the soldiers." Because a lot of soldiers were coming in wounded. The Turks were fighting the Russian army, the czar's army on the front, and the Turks had casualties. My father saved thirty Armenians, that man. Of course, that's how he got saved, because he saved those thirty Armenians. Then, one day, my mother got a permit for us, from a doctor that we knew, to go and see him. That was the last time I saw my father. Shortly thereafter we found out he died. How? I don't know.

The Turkish police took us from my cousin's, to a house filled with all these women, and every day I would look out the window, and they'd line up men against the wall, and they'd shoot them. You'd see them falling down. From the window, I saw soldiers raping the girls, I saw killings of the girls, but I didn't know what the hell they were doing. I didn't know what the hell it was. I was five, six years old.

Then, before you know it, six soldiers came and they arrested my mother. They said, "You people came from the United States. You have a lot of money. You must have buried it someplace." My mother says, "No, we didn't have no money. We didn't bury it . . ." They took her to the police station. She stayed there a couple of days, and then that doctor got her out. She came back to my cousin's house, what was left of it. And we stayed there until we left in 1916.

My mother had gotten friendly with this soldier who was getting discharged, and who helped us escape. He was Syrian and the other Turkish soldiers were mean to him, they mistreated him. So he was glad he was going to get discharged. So he made two square boxes. My sister and I sat in one, and my mother sat in the other one, and [he] draped them over a horse. The soldier, he was in uniform. And he took us from Bitlis, all the way south to Aleppo in Syria. Nobody touched us because this was a Turkish soldier, they saw he had his gun and a horse, the Turkish insignia on his horse, and all that.

We stayed in Aleppo nearly four years. I went to this horrible Arab school. I wanted to come back to America. But my mother wanted to stay, because that doctor from Bitlis had a house in Aleppo, and he proposed to her, and she decided to marry him. My mother was still young. You have to remember, my mother was not even fifteen years old when I was born.

I came with this young lady, a servant girl of the doctor's, who was engaged to an American soldier, a "doughboy," they called

*Christmas Eve, December 24, 1905, in the Registry Room. Commissioner Robert Watchorn (far right)
stands next to a missionary (to his right), who handed out Scripture in different languages.*

(NATIONAL PARK SERVICE: STATUE OF LIBERTY NATIONAL MONUMENT)

them in those days. He was a very nice young fellow. I was exactly ten years old.

We went by railroad to Beirut. Now Beirut, at that time, was part of Syria. In Beirut we went to live in an area where they had tents for Armenian refugees, on the grounds of an Armenian church. Everybody slept in tents. I slept on the ground. But I used to be afraid—they had rats there, big rats in the field. I used to be afraid of the rats.

We stayed there approximately four months, waiting for visas, and took a boat to Marseille. We stayed in Marseille about a week. Then we went to Le Havre. From Le Havre we took the S.S. *Niagara*. It was December 11, 1920, when we left.

The ship had one stack, and we were way down on the bottom. You had to go up three flights to go to the upper deck, the captain's area. I used to sneak in. Nearing the United States, the crew came down, and gave us beer. I never drank beer. They had to throw the bottles into the ocean because there was Prohibition.

The only other thing I remember were the bathrooms. I hated to go to the bathroom because you walk in the dirt. And the women, when they wanted to urinate, they used to hold their dress apart and urinate standing up like a man . . .

The ship arrived before Christmas of 1920. It anchored off Brooklyn. Everybody was going crazy, "*Artzan, artzan.*" *Artzan* is the Armenian word for statue. But I spoke Arabic. I didn't know what the hell they were shouting about. It didn't mean nothing. Nobody told me, mentioned about the freedom. I didn't know what the heck freedom was anyway, to tell you the truth.

We stayed on board one or two days and they took us in a small boat to Ellis Island. I remember they had a big Christmas tree there in the big building. I didn't know what Christmas was. I didn't know what a Christmas tree was. They had a gathering, a lot of people, and they sang Christmas songs.

I went on line for medical inspection. One immigration inspector and a doctor, through an Arabic interpreter, asked me where I was born. My passport had been lost. I was a very skinny ten-year-old boy. I showed him my immigration papers. But it didn't say where you're born. I said "I was born here."

"Where here?"

"New York City."

"What?"

"New York City."

"You're crazy. Get out of here!" And he started to chase me out, and my grandfather was standing nearby. When he saw me he wrapped his arms around me. Do you know what happened? You'd think somebody put a key in my mouth like this [gestures] and turned it: I started speaking Armenian. I forgot Arabic, honest to God.

I told the inspector and the doctor my story, that I really was an American. So the doctor finally said, "Oh, go ahead." He didn't even examine me . . .

My grandfather and I took the ferryboat to South Ferry, walked about a block, and took the elevated trolley—I had never seen a trolley, much less an elevated trolley—to Twenty-third Street. My grandparents lived on Twenty-fifth Street and Third Avenue, a typical old New York five-story building, a walk-up, the same building the whole family used to live. I thought [that] my grandfather owned the whole building. I didn't think this apartment, only a four-room apartment, was the only place that they lived. We had to walk up one flight, two flights . . . He lived on the fifth floor, the top floor. It was nighttime. My grandmother grabbed me and kissed me. "I've got to take and wash you," she said. Of course, I was happy. She took all the clothes off me. She gave me a good bath, rubdown.

When I went to the bathroom later on, worms came out of me. Worms, when you defecate, from God knows what the hell I was eating in Syria.

Sera Tartunian

. . . .

BORN APRIL 18, 1913
EMIGRATED FROM TURKEY 1922, AGE 9
PASSAGE ON THE *ACROPOLIS*

She is an Armenian born in Istanbul, and the wife of James Habjian. They have four children, all of whom went on to "marry non-Armenians," she said. "But that has never bothered me. I have never influenced them for who they were going to marry. Never . . . Even my oldest granddaughter; I'm not going to say she's Armenian, but she knows the background is there. That's all you can do."

My father was killed when I was seven, but let me go back. I was born near Uskudar, a town across the Bosporus from Istanbul. My father's family had two houses there, a big house and a little house, and we lived in the big house. He was a venereal doctor, a doctor for venereal diseases. My mother was a doll. She had three living sisters, and they all lived to a ripe old age. She lost two brothers in between. One had fallen into a *tonir*, and one had fallen out of a second-floor window when he was two years old.

When there was independence in Armenia, this was about 1918, after World War I, my father got a commission in Kars, in Armenia. My father, my mother, my younger sister, and I, we took everything you could imagine, furniture, too. We took a small boat, and the water in the Black Sea is very rough, and the only thing that we had to eat was just dry toast called galita. We went straight to Batumi, and from Batumi across Georgia to Kars, the most ridiculously old train rails you could possibly imagine. The rails had been used for transportation of the cattle and the horses, a most decrepit thing. Every few miles, they would stop and fix the track, and then go on again. I was about seven. My sister doesn't re-

member. She was eighteen months younger than I.

Kars was a very flat area. I remember an army truck picked us up there. And although it was a flat area, our house sat right on top of a mountain, a beautiful house. We lived very comfortable. The house was right next door to Protestant missionaries. It was an orphanage. See, my father was sent there to take care of the orphans. There were about three or four Armenian doctors and two American doctors, a Dr. White and a Dr. Fox.

I don't know how long we stayed there. History tells you exactly how long . . . when the Turks invaded.

One day, my father had gone to the hospital and we see his horse is back. At that time, they used to have someone who took care of the horses. When the horse came back by himself, my mother said, "There's something wrong." Later, my father came, completely bare, except for an army blanket wrapped around him. "Hurry, hurry!" he says to my mother, "Get some bread. We have to leave." Then he went to the kitchen window. There was a ravine, and a river, right across the street from where we lived. And it was very deep, maybe 200 feet. This river would be frozen the whole winter, and in the wintertime they would have Russian music, and they would ice skate to the music.

I saw my father pointing across the river at a lot of horses and soldiers running away. I saw this man holding onto the horse's tail, so he'd go along with the group. That was supposed to be the Armenian army that was fleeing, okay? You cannot blame them because they had no ammunition to fight. What else were they going to do?

What had happened was that the Turks had come. There was a small, narrow area of a road that led into Kars, and that is where they had entered. So my father said, "I have to go to the hospital." There were two hundred orphans in the hospital . . .

I have heard that a stray bullet came through the wall, or through the window, hit my father in the groin, and he told the other doctors, "You cannot save me. My bladder is punctured," and we never saw him again. But I do recall that one of the other doctors came back and said, "This is what has happened, and there's no sense in letting Marie," my mother's name, "going to see him, because it's useless, and then you'll be caught in the fire, in the crossfire." Anyway, he died. He was buried there.

We were taken by the missionaries. My mother saved an old bag with whatever valuables she had, and this went to the missionaries, where we were safe, fortunately, because the American flag was flying there. So the Turkish soldiers didn't get to us. They came to the fence. All the old houses had very high fences. The Turkish soldiers came to the fence, trying to get to us, and my mother threw this bag, with everything that she had in the world, and shouted, "Take it! And get out of here!"

They didn't touch us. I don't know how many days passed after that. I don't recall eating anything except a piece of a beet, and I remember a piece of meat that even my teeth could not break apart. We stayed with these missionaries, and one day I had to see what was happening outside. I heard noises. I look out, here's an army truck, and you know what they were putting into the army truck? The dead bodies of the orphans. The bodies were being thrown out the windows into a truck. I know that every one of those orphans were killed. I don't know how many, but I have heard two hundred. These were Armenian orphans.

Dr. White and Dr. Fox stayed with us at the mission. After a while, it was towards spring. I remember that, because the top of the mountains were still snowing, but there were flowers down slope. And we had a wagon. I don't know where the wagon came from, but we had a good clean horse, a strong horse. So both the husband and wife, Dr. and Mrs. White, and Dr. and Mrs. Fox, came with us. Most of the time I had to walk. My sister was small, and she couldn't walk through the snow. But the paths that the horses made, we followed. We stopped in different places with the animals, slept with the animals. And we got all the way down to Tiflis. From Tiflis we went to Batumi. In Batumi they put us on a boat to go back to Istanbul.

We stayed in Uskudar about two years, from 1920 to '22. I went to school there for seven or eight months. We learned both Armenian and French. A neighbor, an old man, he held our hands, me and my sister, and took us to school. My grandfather, my mother's father, would bring us home. My grandfather dealt in antiques. He was never wealthy, but he was well off.

Our house was made of wood. All the great old houses in Istanbul were made of wood and very large. It was exquisitely beautiful inside. We had three floors that led down to the Bosporus where the ships would dock. It was congested, but still very clean and very exclusive. When you went down the stairs into the kitchen, an enormous kitchen, there was a huge black oven, and a cistern, where you would extend things down on a rope if you wanted to keep the food cold. The kitchen led into a back-yard, a small area with chickens and a chicken coop, which then led further into an enormous garden with a center fountain and walnut trees, black plum trees, and green plum trees [limes] which they used in place of lemon, which was very expensive be-cause it had to be imported. We were living with my aunt, one of my mother's sisters. I was about eight years old.

I went to school until there was a fire, and the whole town burned, and there was no way of saving the house, and it was never rebuilt. That area was never rebuilt. I just remember that when it started burning, my grandfather was still alive at the time. He says, "Come, come, now! We have to go." They called them phaetons, they're wagons, they have one horse. We got onto that, and we just had to go away.

Because of the fire, we had to live else-where until we got our visas to come here. My mother had no choice. No Armenian would work in Istanbul. Not a doctor's wife. She had no choice. She had to work, so she had to come to America. I don't recall feeling scared. A child doesn't have fears as long as you have someone who is there for you, you know. You can't fear . . .

It was a Greek boat from Istanbul. It was a long trip. I was the only one who wasn't sick. My mother was sick constantly. It was first class. So our food was good, fancy things. We had bunks, two on one side. I don't know where my aunt stayed. She was with us. We were four—my mother, my sister, my aunt, and I. But even in first class, I remember there were a lot of roaches. It was not clean.

We crossed the Mediterranean and then Gibraltar. It was a very slow boat, rough water. We arrived in New York about a month later. At Ellis Island, I remember, we slept on cots. Two-level cots. And I was awed. I was awed at America. I was think-ing, "Well, my mother is free." That's all I was thinking. My mother was free. And, you know, it's funny. You feel a psychologi-cal feeling that just pushes you. Why should my mother have to go through this, a doc-tor's wife? It wasn't fair to her. I felt that from the beginning.

The first thing that they checked there—"Oh, you're coming from the Middle East?"—your eyes. They have to make sure, because there used to be an eye disease that came from the Middle East . . . We didn't have any problems. We didn't have to stay long.

My mother's uncle, my grandfather's brother, who lived in New York City, was the one in whose name we came, and we took the subway. Nobody had cars then. Everything was a surprise. Everything was just shocking.

My grand-uncle and his wife had a small apartment in New York. They had five rooms, and after two months my grand-un-cle's wife, whom I call aunt, came one day to my mother, and she said, "You know, I rent these rooms for five dollars." She says, "You can't stay here anymore." I think my aunt did.

But my mother, she had another sister who was married and lived in Massachu-setts. They were very generous, and said, "You're going to come here. Where else are you going to go?" So the three of us went to Lynn, Massachusetts, and we lived there. I finished high school there. After I finished high school, I said I would come to New York and continue my education. I went to Hunter College for two and a half years, but I was not matriculated. So I could not possi-bly do what I wanted to do, which was medicine. So I settled for writing, which I never pursued. I worked for a lot of places. My first job was stock girl in Bonwit Teller. My second job was Bergdorf Goodman, in dressmaking . . . Then I met him [James Habjian].

Gertrude Liebman
. . . .

BORN MAY 13, 1909
EMIGRATED FROM PALESTINE 1921, AGE 12
PASSAGE ON THE *RYNDAM*

*She lived through the Turkish occupation of Palestine during World War I,
and its eventual liberation by the British. Her father came to America in 1914 to
avoid enlistment in the Turkish army, then she and her family followed. In 1936,
she married a lawyer and Hebrew teacher, who has since passed on, but she
glows with pride for her son and daughter, both graduates of City College in
New York, and her four grandsons.*

*I*was born in the village of Montefiore Heiser, outside the old city of Jerusalem. *Heiser* means "house" in Yiddish. It was the first settlement outside the old walled city, built by Moses Montefiore, who was a great philanthropist.

Shortly after I was born, we moved more to the outskirts of the city. It was beginning to branch out, and they built a religious community called Shaare Hesed. *Shaare* stands for "gate," the Gate of Mercy, it was called, and there were rows of houses. Three, four rows. That was the whole community where we lived and where one of my cousins still lives in the house we were in.

It was a two-room house. Two beautiful rooms, made out of stone. In Jerusalem, all the homes were built of the native stones. There were only two rooms, and we were four children before my father left to the United States. He left because he was going to be drafted. He was eligible to go into the Turkish army, and none of the Jewish people wanted to join the Turkish army. Palestine was under the Ottoman Empire. I knew of at least one person who never came back from the Turkish army, the father of a friend—never heard from him again. So the Jewish people hid. My father hid in an attic.

We called it a *badin*. He hid in an attic for something like two months.

My grandfather, my mother's father, who was a very modern kind of person because he had already been in South Africa at the turn of the century, was a humanitarian, and he was interested in the Sephardim of Jerusalem. The Sephardics were neglected at that time. No one looked after them. No one saw to their health and their interests. My grandfather went to South Africa, raised money, and came back and established them in a home, what he called an old-age home, for the Sephardic Jews. He managed to work towards a passport for my father, and within a few months, my father was able to leave. This was in 1914. I was five years old.

My strongest memory of my father was at a seder at my grandparents' before he left. I always sang in my youth, and he always sang like a *hasen*. He didn't have too big a voice, and I accompanied him. I remember he showered me with compliments because I stayed up the whole night, I read the Haggadah all through the night and sang all the songs. At the end of the seder we sang all the Passover songs, and I sang them because I had a voice.

There were some very sad things. When my father left in 1914, we got one letter from him, and then everything stopped. No checks, no letters from my father. For three years we didn't hear, we didn't get anything. It was during the First World War. And my mother had to eke out a living for the four of us children, my older brother, a younger brother, a younger sister, and me. I was the oldest girl. I started attending a Hebrew school for girls. My kid sister, who was an infant at the time my father left, had a very unhealthy upbringing because there wasn't enough milk. My mother had no milk to nurse her with, and things were quite bad. I remember once I picked up an orange peel from the ground because the oranges there were so thick with peel. It was delicious. I was hungry.

My mother did a lot of things that an ordinary woman would be unable to do. She was a very strong person. For instance, there were many deserters at the time. The soldiers from the army who deserted would stop at our house because we faced an open field. My mother did a lot of things like baking bread, taking the bread to the Arab village of Emselabee, where she would sell her bread, and we'd have some money to buy what we needed. The soldiers who deserted would bring in blankets, army blankets. My mother would make coats out of them, sell them, and have some money for food. She was very resourceful in these things.

The Turks put the Jews in the front, the deserters would say. The Jewish people were placed in the front, and that's why they were killed off. That was one of the worst things. [Sighs.] I don't recall many things in those years because, you know, we were busy trying to live at the time. I used to pick off olives from the trees and eat them. Apricots were very prevalent, apricot trees. My mother would pick apricots and make jam. My kid brother would climb up—she would put it up on the top shelf,

but he would climb up, and I helped him to get to that jam jar, because it was so delicious. The pits of the apricots I saved in a bag, because someone said that if you rubbed an apricot pit you would get chewing gum. Well, I saved the pits for a long time. I got a whole bag full, until I tried one. I got no success with chewing gum, and I became disgusted, so I poured the whole bag into a hole in the garden—we had a little garden. And my mother used to wash the patio. It was all stone, beautiful Jerusalem stone. She would wash the stone, and the water would flow right into the pits, right into that garden. Well, by the time we left for America there was a tree, a little apricot tree. I remember I hated to leave it. When I came back twelve years later to visit Jerusalem, it was no longer there.

After three years, we started to get letters and some money from my father. It was after the war, everything was disrupted, and we needed clothes and so forth. The English came in through the Jaffa Gate, Lord Allenby on his white horse. It's not a fiction story. I remember it. He was riding on his white horse through that gate, and coming up what we call Jaffa Road. It was one of the most famous roads in Jerusalem. He rode up, and my mother had gotten us dressed in our Sabbath clothes, in the best things, because she knew that the English were coming into our city and that they won the war. The Turks were no longer there and that was a happy, happy occasion.

My father's letters were in Yiddish. He sent us pictures of what he looked like. This was in 1917 when the war was over, or almost over. It took another four years before he was able to bring us over here. He was in America a total of seven years without us.

In the meantime, there were skirmishes all along with the Arabs. We had a time of it. Once, when my mother went to sell bread to the Arabs, she went with a friend, she gave them the bread, and when it came to paying, one of the Arabs says to the other in Arabic, "Don't pay her. Here, stab her in the back." My mother understood because she knew Arabic. She dealt with them long enough to understand. So with her friend, they ran. Never mind the bread and the money, they ran, and they never went down to Emselabee again.

It was inevitable we would come to America. Leaving meant my father had to send us the proper papers. We traveled here on my father's citizenship papers. My father became a citizen because you had to wait five years . . .

By the time we finally decided to leave, my grandmother, my mother's mother, died, and that was a very sad occasion. She died before she was fifty. So we remained until after the memorial period was over . . .

The first thing we packed was a *periner*, a featherbed. That was very lucky because there was a train in Jerusalem to take us to Alexandria [Egypt], where the boat would be. We knew no other language but Yiddish, but we knew how to sign our names in English. We were taught that before we left. They said it was necessary to know how to sign your name, so that you don't put a cross.

When we got to Alexandria, there was no room for us. No berths [of] any kind. Even the deck was full. So they told us to wait three weeks before the next boat would come, and there would be room for us. We stayed at a nunnery, a church. There were no Jewish organizations at the time in Alexandria. Three weeks came, the boat came, and again there were no berths, but we got on deck with the featherbed, and my mother was also carrying a little trunk, which in Yiddish we called a *casden*. It was red, I remember. And on that trunk my mother still had some of those blankets, the army blankets, and that's where I slept. She got a deck chair for my kid sister, who was sick. She was sick throughout the trip. My

brothers were on the *periner*, the featherbed, and my mother laid her head on the trunk where I was lying. [Laughs.] It was a struggle. I think it took about eleven days for that trip to cross the Mediterranean at that time.

We ate herring, hard-boiled eggs, bread, and milk. Because we were kosher, we couldn't eat any of the meats they served in the dining room. We never ate in the dining room. We just sat at some bench where they gave us these foods.

The boat stopped in France first, Marseille. We got off the boat, and we took some kind of transportation to Cherbourg, because there we were supposed to take the boat to the United States. The U.S. Cunard Line, I remember. The five of us walked up the gangplank, and the next thing we knew, we were walking down the gangplank, with our baggage, back to port. They wouldn't let us on the boat. There was something wrong with my father's citizenship papers, they said.

Now we found ourselves stranded in a country, we didn't understand the language. Nobody understood our Yiddish. My mother started to yell at my older brother. She says, "Do something! Do something!" in Yiddish. Just then, a woman passed and understood the Yiddish, so she stopped and started to help us. She took us inside the terminal and introduced us to somebody in the Red Cross. They wired my father, sent back the information and waited for a reply. They put us in a nunnery. This woman! My mother always referred to her as the Angel of Heaven, because she was very helpful. She must have been a social worker. In later years, I worked for social workers all the time.

We left from Cherbourg on the *Ryndam* to New York. They did the examinations on the boat, and they suspected that my older brother had trachoma in his eyes, so they took us to Ellis Island, and we were quarantined. If you had trachoma you couldn't get into America.

I remember Ellis Island. The beds, we were placed on one of the floors with just cots. There were at least two dozen cots, if not more, and that's where we spent the night. But before we were bedded, my father came with a little tender boat. Of course, we hadn't seen him for seven years, so my mother introduced us from an arched window—when I think of Joe DiMaggio advertising his parents' trip, he stands in front of that arched window and talks about them—"This is your father, down below," she said. He was down on the tender boat, hoping to see us, hoping to take us off, but he wasn't able to until the next day. By then, it was discovered my brother didn't have trachoma.

My father had an apartment ready for us, a furnished apartment at 69 East Ninety-eighth Street in Manhattan. We walked up four flights to our apartment, and a neighbor came out to greet us. A wonderful woman. She was heavy, but she greeted us with such warmth, and she started to talk Yiddish.

"I'm going to help you," she said. "Whatever you want, I'm going to help you." And she remained our friend all the years.

It was strange at the beginning. We didn't know our father, and he was good to us to a point. He wasn't a wealthy man, but he could have made it a lot easier for us monetarily. He was used to living alone for so long, so it wasn't easy for him, either. He had become Americanized. He taught himself English, how to write. He read the Yiddish and English papers. My father was a *shochet*, a chicken slaughterer . . .

On the other hand, we were so glad to be in America, and live our lives, and live so differently, and get an education. My mother, when we finally got here, was told by that woman neighbor that school is compulsory here. You must send your children to school. Well, the very next day, my mother took us to the public school on Ninety-sixth Street and Lexington Avenue and we started our new life.

Jeanne, Molly, and Miriam Assidian

. . . .

BORN MARCH 27, 1908; JUNE 4, 1910; SEPTEMBER 12, 1912
EMIGRATED FROM TURKEY 1922, AGES 14, 12, AND 10
PASSAGE ON THE *KING ALEXANDER*

Daughters of a Christian minister, and Armenian by blood, all three sisters were raised in Smyrna, now called Dzmir, in eastern Turkey, and experienced, firsthand, the massacre of the Armenian people at the hands of the Ottoman Turks. They escaped to the United States as a family. They were detained at Ellis Island for two weeks. The sisters remain close to this day.

*J*EANNE: All three of us were born in the village of Zeitoon. Our father was the minister there.

MOLLY: Then we moved to Marash. I don't remember Zeitoon, but I remember Marash. It was mountainous, a beautiful place. In the summer, we had delicious grapes, all kinds of fruits, fig trees, and nut trees. We used to have many good times together, all three of us.

MIRIAM: Father was a very kindly, a very loving man. We always used to sit on his lap, all of us at one time, and he always put his arms around us, and showed a great deal of love to us. He was a very calm, very peaceful man.

JEANNE: Mother was a schoolteacher. She was quite strict with the girls. My father constantly kissed us and loved us, and my mother was a disciplinist. She loved us, but she also taught me many things, like sewing and crocheting and knitting. In Marash, our house was part of the church complex. The school was there for the children, and the church.

MOLLY: We have an older brother, Albert, who passed away, and of course, our younger brother, Vartan, he's the youngest, and he's a minister now, too.

MIRIAM: We didn't have any other family members. We didn't know any grandparents, aunts, uncles. There was just one cousin who lived with us. She was the only relative that we knew. She had no family. Her family had been massacred, and my father had taken her under his wing.

JEANNE: We were in Marash during the massacre of the Armenians by the Turks during the First World War. Many people were killed. We ran. There were fires and massacres. Friends of ours, their whole family was massacred while they were in their home. At the church, many people gathered there, and it was a miracle that some of us came out alive.

MOLLY: As a child, I think I was a very trusting and depending on whatever my father and mother said, so that I don't think I ever felt scared of things. But I know that while we were in our father's church there, the Turks were shooting at the church and shooting at us, and Father took us around

and said, "My dears, don't worry, we're all going to go to heaven together." Of course, thank goodness we were able to get out of that situation. And, of course, the Turks did a lot of cruel things, setting churches on fire . . .

MIRIAM: We escaped and went into a Catholic church, which was full of Armenians. There was hardly any room to move around. The Turks had surrounded this church, and they were starting to pour kerosene all over and set it on fire. But fortunately, an American missionary came by, and I don't know exactly what happened, but the Turks didn't light the fire, although you could hear screams coming from outside.

This massacre lasted about three weeks. After that, we had a few months of so-called peace before we left Marash to go to Smyrna, because Albert was there, the oldest brother, in college. So we went there to be with him, and then in a few months, we had another massacre over there.

JEANNE: Albert had another month to finish college, so my parents thought we would get him so that we could all go to America. We had our passports. We were in Smyrna about two months, I think, before we took our passage. The ship was at the shore. We had packed everything, ready to go. We were to board the ship on a Monday. But on Saturday, hell broke out. The Turks and the Greeks, this time, were fighting. They put practically the whole city of Smyrna on fire . . . Everybody was going towards shore. My father had us down in the basement, and, again, he was saying, "Don't worry. We are going to heaven." And, you know, he prayed. And my mother said, "Oh, no. Let's go upstairs, take your shoes off, and we will run for the American Girls College." We got there, and the Americans had sent sailors to take the missionaries to the shore, and we followed them through fire and bullets, and we got to the shore. Being my father was a minister, the missionaries knew him. We were put on an American battleship and, later on, transferred to a Greek freighter. And for three days, hungry, we arrived in Greece. We were there for a short period of time before we took our passage to America. We left everything. We had nothing but the clothes on our backs.

MOLLY: A good memory.

MIRIAM: Father would always say, "One day we're going to America." In our childish minds, we had equated America with heaven. So we just thought we were coming to heaven. After what we'd been through over there, America was heaven. So we all looked forward to coming.

MOLLY: After the burning of Smyrna, we were running away now.

MIRIAM: We had no passage money, but a missionary friend of my father sent us the money. We came steerage on the *King Alexander,* and I think it must have been Greek, but they served us spaghetti and macaroni the whole trip.

JEANNE: It was a Greek ship. We left from Pireaus. I think they had sent us enough money to go second class, but we couldn't get on, everybody was escaping, and my father was so anxious to get us here, we took steerage. One big room. There was a very bad storm, and we were way down in the bottom, and it was horrible . . .

MIRIAM: Too crowded. But every evening all the Armenians would gather in one little area, and we'd entertain ourselves. We'd sing. Somebody would recite a poem, and things like that. You know, we'd do that every evening to get together. I think we saw our first movie, a Charlie Chaplin movie, silent, of course. I think that was on the ship. I'd never seen it before.

JEANNE: We were detained at Ellis Island for two weeks, because my mother and father had problems with their eyes, and they took them into the hospital, and we were left to take care of ourselves. Except I had my older brother, Albert, to help out,

but at night he had to go with the men, so I took care of the three, my little brother and the two sisters. But it was very lonely without our parents for two weeks. We didn't see them at all. We knew that they were in the hospital, and that's about all.

MOLLY: I know that Jeanne went and got blankets and pillows and things like that for us for the night to sleep on. On very crazy-looking cots. It was not very comfortable, but we were all together. At least that was one great thing.

JEANNE: I was used to the responsibility. Being the oldest girl, my mother always made sure I did what was necessary. At night, when we were ready to retire, I would go to the door. They gave us a cake of soap, a towel, a blanket, a pillow, and I remember those cots that were one on top of each other. Bunk beds. During the day, there was not much to do. We talked, and we laughed. We were very good with each other, so I guess we passed the time that way. I don't remember physical exams. I don't remember that at all.

I remember the long tables in the dining hall. There were so many people, and the minute they opened the dining room door for everybody to go, they would grab at things, and if you weren't quick enough . . . children were left out. So Albert used to try to get something so that we could have it.

MIRIAM: But one thing I remember, at night, we'd be, the bunch of us, would be in a certain room, and the doctor would come in and say, "Anybody sick?" And we'd all say, "Everybody's sick." [They laugh.]

JEANNE: Finally they brought our parents, their eyes were all right, and we were allowed to go. And we went to Buffalo.

MIRIAM: Yes, directly to Buffalo.

JEANNE: We had an uncle there. We had never met our relatives. He was the first relative that we met. He was my mother's oldest brother. He had been in this country for a long time, and he's the one who sent some money for us to get here. As soon as we got there, he took all our clothes and burned them, and bought us new clothes. He was very good to us. I don't know how long we stayed in Buffalo.

MIRIAM: About a month, maybe two. For the first time there, we saw comic strips. Every Sunday morning Albert used to read the comics to us in English and, of course, translate it into Armenian. We'd laugh our heads off. The Katzenjammer Kids, Winnie Winkle. [They laugh.] And a bunch of others.

MOLLY: She knows them all. What struck me about the difference between America and Turkey was the cars. Literally. One day, we decided to go for a walk, and I think we were going to go to a movie. Of course, I had never crossed a street with cars coming back and forth, so I stepped out in the street freely, and a car came and hit me. But thank goodness, not to the extent where I needed to go to the hospital.

JEANNE: Well, we had never seen an airplane, never a telephone, never many things.

MOLLY: A can opener.

JEANNE: Many, many things were new to us. It was like coming into heaven. [They laugh.]

MIRIAM: Father was right!

MOLLY: But one thing we did feel is that we were able to communicate. You know, our parents were able to communicate, because they spoke English on the other side. We learned a little.

MIRIAM: Not much.

MOLLY: Not much. When I was in school, I had learned to say, "I feel so seeek." [They laugh.]

JEANNE: We spoke Turkish, we spoke Armenian, and English we learned enough that it didn't take us long to be able to understand when we came here.

MIRIAM: Not knowing the language was very difficult. When I started school here they put me in the third grade. And the children all stand up, and they look at the flag and sing "The Star-Spangled Banner." Well, I would listen to the words, and some of the words would sound to me like some words I knew in Turkish. So I would sing along with them, but sing my own words. I was in the sixth, seventh grade before I could speak the language.

As a result, the children wouldn't communicate with us too much. So, at recess time, Molly and I would each find three stones in the yard somewhere, and we knew how to juggle, so we'd stand there and juggle, and soon the whole class, at recess, was watching us juggle. [They laugh.]

JEANNE: From Buffalo, we moved to Philadelphia. My father became minister of this church, but the pay was very low. For quite a while, we lived by things that were given to us, you know, clothing, shoes, whatever it was. There was a day when we didn't have enough to eat, and the money was all gone, and, of course, Dad prayed. And he went out in a trolley, and there was some kind of an accident, and he hurt his hand. They gave him $200 or something, and he thought that was an answer to his prayers. [They laugh.] The church was also divided into two sections, and he headed one section, but the other section wanted nothing to do with him . . .

MIRIAM: I was going to say that this change was very difficult for Father, because in Marash where he was pastor, he was a very respected man. He found things quite different in this country regarding his position, in how he was treated. Criticisms, divisions, not enough pay. That sort of thing.

MOLLY: I think my mother liked being here, but it was very difficult for her, because there wasn't too much money coming in, so she sent us to work . . . But I think she was happy to be in America because it was freer. She had no worries as far as where our father was, where the children were. So she was happy.

MIRIAM: That's why we came to America, to be free.

JEANNE: We were a very close family. Every evening after dinner, we sat around in the living room. First, we would have a Bible reading and prayer, and then it was fun time. My father was just wonderful about giving us riddles and things to solve, and educational besides.

MIRIAM: They were happy for us, I think, more than for themselves, because their life was difficult here.

JEANNE: It was really wonderful being in a country like this, and that's all my dad and mom wanted anyway. If we stayed in Turkey, who knows?

MOLLY: We might have been killed.

MIRIAM: Probably.

JEANNE: We went through not one, but four, major conflicts. And through all that, many times I think to myself when I pray, I say, "God, we were no different than anybody else. But with all that, we came to this country as a whole family. We didn't lose one member of our family. All the five children, with parents, we got here, and it was a miracle. Thank you, Lord." I feel very good about that.

June Gusoff

BORN MAY 5, 1917
EMIGRATED FROM PALESTINE 1929, AGE 12
PASSAGE ON THE *ALIZA*

Born in Jerusalem, she was four years old when her father immigrated to America. She came six years later with her older brother. After graduating Morris High School in the Bronx, she worked in a factory sewing hooks and eyes on brassieres and corsets. She married in 1939, and still lives in the New York area. "I forget that I wasn't born here, until someone asks me where I was born," she said. "Someone will say, 'Were you born here?' I say, 'As a matter of fact, I wasn't.' And they're always surprised."

I never left Jerusalem. I left once to go on a trip for school. We went to Tel Aviv. But that was the only time until we came to America.

My earliest memory is of a house which was next to a huge field, and you could see nothing on the horizon. It was that big a field. I think it was a wheat field. Our house was the last house on the street, and it was right next to the field. And I remember playing in that field, and I remember all the flowers that grew there. They were cyclamens that grew among the rocks, and when the poppies were in bloom, it was a big, red field just full of poppies with other flowers interspersed.

I had two older brothers, an older sister, and a younger brother. We were five. I remember having a wonderful time. We had a lot of fun together. There was a lot of music and laughter in the house. In looking back, I realized that my mother had a very difficult time. She had five children to bring up alone. There was no indoor plumbing. There was no electricity. So I can just imagine what it was like, and I was a twin. I had a twin brother who died at about a year and a half. And she had another child after me, so it must have been very difficult for her. Of course, that was while my father was still there, but after he came, it was during the Depression and he wasn't making much money. He wasn't able to support us. So she had to earn money.

My mother took in boarders. For a while she was preparing food, and we would take it to the people she prepared meals for. It was a meals on wheels. We were the wheels. Then she opened a restaurant with an aunt and ran that for a while. But times were very hard for her, which I wasn't really aware of at the time. There was always food for me, and I was forever playing and having a good time . . . I realized we were not wealthy, but I think everyone was poor, everyone had a hard life because it was fairly primitive.

We lived in a two-story building, not enormous. I think we had maybe two bedrooms at most, but the rooms were large. Many times we slept on the floor. I don't think there were ever enough beds for all of us, but we were accustomed to it, and that's what it was like, so I never felt deprived in that way.

My mother was Puah. She was born in Palestine. My father was Schmuel, which was Samuel here. My oldest brother was Boaz, after him was Abraham. My sister was Tamar. My younger brother was Nehemiah. Nehemiah Gusoff is probably a name that might be familiar to some people because he's an actor under that name.

I remember my school and my teachers, and I was a member of the scouts. It was not Girl Scouts because there were boys in the troop. I remember many trips, hikes. I remember a camping trip with the scouts,

where we went into the woods and pitched tents. The first night was spent killing snakes with ammonia, because there were many snakes in the area where we pitched the tents, and I remember someone contrived a shower, it was a tin can and there was a stream and it was clear water that we could drink as well as bathe in, shower in. We slept out for what must have been a one-week trip. It was a long camping trip. I remember that very well. I remember having whooping cough, and I think my brother had whooping cough at the same time. And my mother took the two of us. I remember being wrapped up in a scarf around my neck and being taken to visit a friend in the "country," because Jerusalem was pretty much country then. But this was further out. The air was supposed to be better there. I have a clear memory of that. I have a memory of my sister having her tonsils out and getting a lot of ice cream, which I didn't get, and I remember being angry about that. [Laughs.] I remember my grandmother expecting grandchildren who lived in Egypt and they were coming to visit us, and so she brought chocolate to have for the visiting grandchildren. For some reason they didn't come, and we thought we'd get the chocolate, but we didn't. It went into a trunk to await their next visit, because sweets were hard to come by. A banana was a treat. I remember the most delicious fruits. We used to climb trees and eat apricots . . .

My mother was a good cook. We ate healthfully. We had hummus and many Sephardic-style dishes, because many of our neighbors were Sephardic. But we also used to get cod liver oil. That was not a pleasure. She'd go around with a teaspoon and a bottle of cod liver oil. Each one of us would get some, and she had wedges of orange to give, because the taste was so horrible. She knew about that. I remember we had trachoma very often because it was highly contagious. As soon as it cleared up we would catch it again. She had to go around and open our eyes every morning. Of course, first she had to open hers, because there was stuff oozing out of her eyes, too. So she would go around with cotton and boric acid, and wash our eyes so we could open them in the morning, because they were pasted together.

. . .

After World War I, the British were the victors, Palestine had been under Turkish rule up to that point. In fact, during the war my father was in the Turkish army, and he had been stationed in Damascus. He was teaching. He was not a soldier. He was teaching. He taught art, because he was an artist. He had studied art in Betsalel, the art school, which was established in Jerusalem not long before he was there, about ninety years ago.

Before he went into the army, he worked as a craftsman. He was a jeweler. In America, he worked as a jeweler. He made jewelry. But before that he had done a lot of metal work. He made plates, and metal pots with pictures on them, designs, decorations. He also taught in Betsalel. He taught filigree work, which is twisted silver wire work, which is still very common. In Israel they make a lot of jewelry that way.

My father remembered waking up in a dungeon with malaria. He was very ill. And the effects of that were with him all his life, because whenever he had a fever, it was severe, and he would have tremors with the fever. He was subject to bronchitis for most of his life.

My father wanted to come here for economic reasons. It was difficult to earn enough to support a large family, and he thought he'd do better here. Of course, he came here at a bad time and he didn't really do much better.

I came with my older sister and younger brother. My two oldest brothers came about a year before we did. It was just a matter of getting all the money together. So when there was enough for them, they came.

My mother had a brother who lived in New York, and he helped, he sent some money, and she also took a loan. She later was paying back the loan, which we had to take to make the journey.

I remember my last day in school and saying good-bye. I remember being photographed. I still have photographs, the photograph for the passport of the family together. We got the boat in Jaffa, outside Tel Aviv. I remember very vividly coming to Tel Aviv and staying with another uncle, my father's other brother, who had a hotel in Tel Aviv, and it was right near the beach. I remember playing on the beach with my brother and being excited, there were a bunch of dead fish on the beach, and we brought them to my aunt, thinking she could use them, and she chased us away.

We were in steerage, but there was first class on the boat. So they had cabins in the hold and we had a cabin. It was a French liner. I think it was its last voyage. I remember hearing that.

I was very excited. I had no idea of distances. I used to try to imagine how far away it was, because I was told it was far away, and it was difficult to imagine because the longest distance I had gone was to Tel Aviv up to that point. So it was hard to imagine. And we heard the stories, which we didn't believe. The streets were paved with gold. We did hear that. I didn't know what to expect.

I don't remember having luggage. We just had the clothes on our backs, nothing else. We left behind my grandmother, my mother's mother. She lived with us, but she didn't want to come with us. She was a religious woman, Orthodox, and felt she was near death and wanted to die in Israel.

At the last minute, my mother was not allowed on board because her trachoma became active. She was not allowed to come with us. So she got hold of everyone who boarded the ship and asked them to take care of us, and they did. It must have been very difficult for her. I don't remember being afraid to go without her, but I know it was hard for her to let us go alone, because my sister was about fourteen or fifteen and she was the oldest of my brother and I.

I remember I latched onto some gentleman, and wouldn't let go of him. It must have been hard for him because he was a young man, and there were young women on board the ship, and I hampered his style, I'm sure. I guess I was more fearful than I realized.

Despite this, we stopped at so many wonderful places. We stopped in Constantinople and Algiers and Madeira. We went through the Dardanelles and the Strait of Gibraltar. It was a long, long journey. It was fascinating, it was interesting, it was fun. We got off the ship only in Algiers and for just a short time. I remember walking through the city in an arcade, which was something new for me, with shops along the way. And it was during Passover. There was a seder on board the ship. We were asked whether we wanted to eat kosher or nonkosher food, and we said nonkosher because we were not kosher at home, but we had never had ham or pork. Whenever we sat down at the table, the kosher table would go "oink, oink" at our table. We ate mostly hard-boiled eggs.

In Constantinople, I was very impressed by divers, youngsters who were diving for coins in the Bosporus. And, in Madeira, I remember that someone bought a banana tree. It wasn't the whole tree, but a big branch with many bunches of bananas attached to it, and passed around, so we had lots of bananas. The banana merchants came right up to the ship.

I remember getting off the ship and coming into Ellis Island with my brother, because my sister was taken from us and put into quarantine in the hospital on Ellis Island

before we came into the big hall. When we did, it was just my brother and I, and I remember wondering how my father will ever find us in this place where there were so many people . . .

I didn't recognize him, but my brother did, and he was at least two years younger than I. My father recognized me because I had a broken tooth. I don't think he had gotten any photos of us. But he knew that I had fallen and broken a front tooth, and here I was with a half-tooth in front, so he knew it was I.

We slept, I don't remember how many nights. I remember a double-decker bed, the first time I've ever seen one. And I remember being taken outdoors to play. We were given games and toys. The only toys we had back home were wooden toys my father had made by hand. And I was very impressed with how white the bread was here. I guess we were given Wonder Bread. I thought it was just incredible that bread could be so white. But I had no idea how long we were here, or why we were here, or why we slept here. My only fear was that I might not ever be able to get together with my father, and that he wouldn't find us and we wouldn't find him.

My sister had to stay. After we left, she wasn't released yet. I guess she had to clear her trachoma, to cure it before she was released. So she came a few days after we left. My father picked us up, my brother and I, and took us to my uncle in Brooklyn, and then he came back and got my sister some days later. My mother came several months later.

We went by subway to Brooklyn and I remember being impressed by the subway. And he took us to my aunt and uncle, and there were four cousins, one of them my age, the others younger. And we stayed with them. I remember sleeping in this bed with all three of them. It was a two-bedroom apartment with a bathtub in the kitchen. We didn't stay there long. My father found an empty apartment, a cold-water flat, no steam heat, in Williamsburg, Brooklyn. My father was working as a jeweler.

It was odd being with my father, because I didn't know him. My father was a very handsome man and rather vain, dressed very well, sort of a ladies' man. He didn't know very much about children, because he had been away for so long without us. So I spoke very little. One of my older brothers, Abraham, and I had very few words. We were very quiet, silent. We only spoke when we were together. But when there were adults around, there was never a peep out of us.

When my mother came, it must have been very hard to be together again, and never having much privacy. I mean, we were seven people in this small apartment. Just two bedrooms. And, you know, Williamsburg was not a pretty place to come to after Jerusalem, which was a beautiful city, and it was sort of countrylike, and it was quiet, and the air was clear and fresh. This [Williamsburg] was a very noisy slum. We lived in a tenement building. So that transition was difficult for me.

I was very angry at being uprooted. The adjustment was difficult for me. I had to learn a new language. I was put into a grade with young children until I learned the language and arrived at my right grade for my age level. But I remember being angry at being uprooted. I didn't know the reason for it. In 1929, it was not one of the times when many immigrants came. We were the only ones who came from that part of the world. They were accustomed to eastern European immigrants. We were well-treated, but it was uncomfortable being with little children. I was as tall as the teacher. I was given the name June.

I remember being called upon to read aloud in class, and I was able to read rather quickly, but when I came to the word "colonel," I said, "Col-o-nel." Everyone laughed. But I didn't seem to have real difficulty in learning the language. I picked it up very quickly. I had my cousins, and I had made friends right away, and was out in the street playing very quickly.

My mother always thought she was the most fortunate of women, even though in looking back she had the most difficult life I could imagine. She was always singing, always cheerful. And she was certainly very happy to be reunited with my father. They were very much in love with each other. She was happy to be reunited and to have all her children with her. That was all she really needed. She felt just fortunate in having these wonderful children, as she put it.

I remember being lost, my father lost me in the subway the week we arrived, I think. He was taking us to the Bronx, or coming back from the Bronx, my brother and I. That was before my sister came and before my mother came. And we were at some busy station. It may have been Grand Central, Forty-second Street, and the train came and there was a big crowd, and everyone pushed into the train. My father just went in and my brother followed him, and I couldn't get in because people pushed me aside. I stayed on the platform and the door closed, and there I was on the platform alone, and that was a frightening experience. I had no idea the train could come back and get me. I didn't know what to do. I just wandered off. I started to cry. Some people gave me a token, which I didn't know what to do with, but someone finally took me to a token booth. They found someone who spoke Hebrew. I remembered the street where my uncle's house was. And this gentleman took me to a candy store, he owned the candy store, and gave me an ice cream sundae to eat and then took me by car, my first automobile ride, to Cooke Street, and he said, "You point out the house when you see it." And when we got near the house all the neighbors were out in the street looking for me. The police had been called. I'll never forget that.

19

Appendices

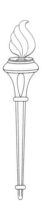

Immigration to the United States: 1892—1924

	Through Port of New York	Total U.S.
1892	445,987	579,663
1893	343,422	439,730
1894	219,046	285,631
1895	190,928	258,536
1896	263,709	343,267
1897	180,556	230,832
1898	178,748	229,299
1899	242,573	311,715
1900	341,712	448,572
1901	388,931	487,918
1902	493,262	648,743
1903	631,835	857,046
1904	606,019	812,870
1905	788,219	1,026,499
1906	880,036	1,100,735
1907	1,004,756	1,285,349
1908	585,970	782,870
1909	580,617	751,786
1910	786,094	1,041,570
1911	637,003	878,587
1912	605,151	838,172
1913	892,653	1,197,892
1914	878,052	1,218,480
1915	178,416	326,700
1916	141,390	298,826
1917	129,446	295,403
1918	28,867	110,618
1919	26,731	141,132
1920	225,206	430,001
1921	560,971	805,228
1922	209,778	309,556
1923	295,473	522,919
1924	315,587	706,896
Total	14,277,144 (71.4% of total)	20,003,041

(From June 15, 1897, to December 16, 1900, immigration through the Port of New York was handled at the barge office in Battery Park.)

Statistics based on *Annual Reports of the Commissioner General of Immigration*, 1892–1924, and data supplied by the U.S. Department of Justice, Immigration and Naturalization Service, Washington, D.C.

Immigration to the United States: 1925—54

	Through Port of New York	Total U.S.
1925	137,492	294,314
1926	149,289	304,488
1927	165,510	335,175
1928	157,887	307,255
1929	158,238	279,678
1930	147,982	241,700
1931	63,392	97,139
1932	21,500	35,576
1933	12,944	23,068
1934	17,574	29,470
1935	23,173	34,956
1936	23,434	36,329
1937	31,644	50,244
1938	44,846	67,395
1939	62,035	82,998
1940	48,408	70,756
1941	23,622	51,776
1942	10,173	28,781
1943	1,089	23,725
1944	1,075	28,551
1945	2,636	38,119
1946	52,050	108,721
1947	83,884	147,292
1948	104,665	170,570
1949	113,050	188,317
1950	166,849	249,187
1951	142,903	205,717
1952	183,222	265,520
1953	87,483	170,434
1954	98,813	208,177
Total	2,336,862 (56.0% of total)	4,175,428

Statistics based on data supplied by the U.S. Department of Justice, Immigration and Naturalization Service, Washington, D.C., and data found in *Annual Reports of the Commissioner General of Immigration*, 1925–32; Zeigler, *Immigration: An American Dilemma*, p. 17; and Bennett, *American Immigration Policies*, p. 332.

Famous Ellis Island Immigrants

(COMPILED BY BARRY MORENO)

. . . .

Immigrant	Native Land	Year	Occupation
Louis Adamic (1899–1951)	Slovenia	1913	Writer
Lucien Aigner (1901–)	Hungary/France	1939	Photo Journalist
Mary Antin (1881–1949)	Russia	1894	Writer
Isaac Asimov (1920–1992)	Russia	1923	Writer
Charles Atlas (1893–1972)	Italy	1903	Bodybuilder
Mischa Auer (1905–1967)	Russia	1920	Actor
Abraham Beame (1906–)	England	1906	Politician
Sidor Belarsky (1898–1975)	Russia	1930	Singer
Ludwig Bemelmans (1898–1962)	Italy	1912	Writer/Artist
Irving Berlin (1888–1989)	Russia	1893	Composer
Frank Capra (1897–1991)	Italy	1903	Director
Samuel Chotzinoff (1889–1964)	Russia	1895	Pianist
E. E. Clive (1883–1940)	Wales	1912	Actor
Claudette Colbert (1903–1996)	France	1912	Actor
Edward Corsi (1896–1965)	Italy	1907	Politician
Ricardo Cortez (1899–1977)	Austria	1903	Actor
Frank Costello (1893–1973)	Italy	1893	Gangster
Donald Crisp (1881–1974)	Scotland	1906	Actor
Xavier Cugat (1900–1990)	Spain/Cuba	1915	Musician
Karl Dane (1886–1934)	Denmark	1920	Actor
Al Dubin (1891–1945)	Switzerland	1896	Lyricist
David Dubinsky (1892–1982)	Poland	1911	Union Leader
Max Factor (1872–1936)	Russia	1906	Cosmetician
Edward Flanagan ((1886–1948)	Ireland	1904	Priest
Felix Frankfurter (1882–1965)	Austria	1894	Lawyer/Judge
Douglas Fraser (1916–)	Scotland	1922	Union Leader
Marcus Garvey (1887–1940)	Jamaica	1916	Ethnic Leader
Kahlil Gibran (1883–1931)	Lebanon	1895	Writer
Emma Goldman (1869–1940)	Russia	1919	Anarchist
Samuel Goldwyn (1882–1974)	Poland	1896	Producer
Arshile Gorky (1904–1948)	Armenia	1921	Painter
Bill Graham (1931–1991)	Germany	1941	Producer
Juano Hernandez (1898–1970)	Puerto Rico	1915	Actor
Jean Hersholt (1886–1956)	Denmark	1914	Actor
Joe Hill (1879–1915)	Sweden	1902	Activist/Writer
Sidney Hillman (1887–1946)	Lithuania	1907	Union Leader
Francis Hodur (1866–1953)	Poland	1893	Priest
Bob Hope (1903–)	England	1908	Actor

Immigrant	Native Land	Year	Occupation
Sol Hurok (1884–1974)	Ukraine	1906	Producer
Vincent Impellitteri (1900–1987)	Italy	1901	Politician
C. L. R. James (1901–1989)	Trinidad	1953	Historian
Al Jolson (1886–1950)	Lithuania	1894	Actor/Singer
Elia Kazan (1909–)	Turkey	1913	Director
Ruby Keeler (1909–1993)	Canada	1912	Dancer
John Kluge (1914–)	Germany	1922	Businessman
Simon Kuznets (1901–1985)	Ukraine	1922	Economist
Meyer Lansky (1902–1983)	Poland	1911	Gangster
Alfred Levitt (1894–)	Belarus	1911	Painter
Charles Luciano (1897–1962)	Italy	1906	Gangster
Bela Lugosi (1882–1956)	Hungary	1921	Actor
Mike Mazurki (1909–1990)	Ukraine	1915	Actor
Claude McKay (1890–1948)	Jamaica	1921	Poet
Antonio Moreno (1886–1967)	Spain	1902	Actor
Alan Mowbray (1896–1969)	England	1920	Actor
Philip Murray (1886–1952)	Scotland	1902	Union Leader
Pauline Newman (1894–1986)	Lithuania	1901	Union Leader
Louis Nizer (1902–1995)	England	1905	Lawyer
William O'Dwyer (1890–1964)	Ireland	1910	Politician
Warner Oland (1880–1938)	Sweden	1894	Actor
George Papashvily (1895–1973)	Georgia	1923	Writer
Frank Puglia (1892–1975)	Italy	1908	Actor
Gregory Ratoff (1897–1964)	Russia	1920	Actor
James Reston (1909–1995)	Scotland	1920	Journalist
Hyman G. Rickover (1898–1986)	Poland	1904	Admiral
Edward G. Robinson (1893–1973)	Romania	1903	Actor
Knute Rockne (1888–1931)	Norway	1893	Football Coach
Nicola Sacco (1891–1927)	Italy	1911	Anarchist
Ben Shahn (1898–1969)	Lithuania	1906	Painter
Igor Sikorsky (1889–1972)	Russia	1919	Inventor
Spyros Skouros (1893–1971)	Greece	1910	Producer
Lee Strasberg (1902–1982)	Austria	1909	Director
Jule Styne (1905–1994)	England	1912	Composer
Arthur Tracy (1899–)	Russia	1906	Singer/Actor
Baron von Trapp (1881–1948)	Austria	1938	Singer
Rudolph Valentino (1895–1926)	Italy	1913	Actor
Bartolomeo Vanzetti (1888–1927)	Italy	1911	Anarchist
George Voskovets (1905–1981)	Czechoslovakia	1951	Actor
Anzia Yezierska (1885–1970)	Russia	1901	Writer
George Zucco (1886–1960)	England	1913	Actor

Aliens Excluded from the United States by Cause: 1892–1954

Period	Total	Subversive or anarchistic	Criminals	Immoral classes	Mental or physical defectives	Likely to become public charges	Stowaways	Attempted entry without inspection or without proper documents	Contract laborers	Unable to read (over 16 years of age)	Other
1892–1900	22,515	—	65	89	1,309	15,070	—	—	5,792	—	190
1901–1910	108,211	10	1,681	1,277	24,425	63,311	—	—	12,991	—	4,516
1911–1920	178,109	27	4,353	4,824	42,129	90,045	1,904	—	15,417	5,083	14,327
1921–1930	189,307	9	2,082	1,281	11,044	37,175	8,447	94,084	6,274	8,202	20,709
1931–1940	68,217	5	1,261	253	1,530	12,519	2,126	47,858	1,235	258	1,172
1941–1950	30,263	60	1,134	80	1,021	1,072	3,182	22,441	219	108	946
1951–1954	13,678	197	1,184	117	661	120	244	10,530	9	9	607
Total	610,000	408	11,760	7,921	82,119	219,319	15,903	174,913	41,937	13,660	41,467

In 1941–1953 figures represent all exclusions at seaports and exclusions of aliens seeking entry for 30 days or longer at land ports. Bennett, *American Immigration Policies*, p. 339.

$\mathcal{P}_{ostscript}$

When the hardcover edition of this book was published in the fall of 1997, it included an appeal to readers for assistance in my long-time search to find my birth family. It was my hope that the wide distribution of this book would succeed where private efforts to uncover my past had failed. The following was published:

AUTHOR'S APPEAL

By writing this book, I hope I have helped you answer some of the questions you may have had regarding your parents, grandparents, or great-grandparents, and the enormous sacrifice they endured in coming to this country and in starting a new life.

Perhaps now you can help me. I am looking for my biological parents. I have never met them. It is ironic that I would feel the need, the spiritual pull, to write a book about Ellis Island, genealogy, and roots when I, myself, lack knowledge of my own past. Perhaps that is the reason.

The few details I know about my biological mother and father come from adoption papers I saw for the first time in the fall of 1996 when my (adoptive) father, long since divorced from my (adoptive) mother, was cleaning out his basement. Although I always knew I was adopted, the only proof of my past that I'd ever seen was a partial Xerox copy of my birth certificate—cut off at the part where information would be given about my biological parents.

I felt more than a little bit wary then, when I, as a grown man of forty, opened the old and frayed yellow manila envelope and discovered, for the first time, my true identity.

For starters, I learned what my real name was—Joseph Musselman. The papers said my mother's name was Martha Jeanette Musselman. My father's name was Charles W. Mehaffey. They apparently had one child between them. On my "complete" birth certificate where it asked, "How many OTHER children are now living?"—a number "1" was put. So I know I have, or had, a brother or sister.

But why was my last name Musselman and not Mehaffey? I read on. Although I was born February 14, 1956 at Doctor's Hospital in Cleveland, Ohio, Martha Musselman "obtained a final judgement of divorce in the Trial Justice Court of Anderson County, Tennessee, on June 15th, 1954." My parents, then, were already divorced when I came into this world. My father, according to the papers, "abandoned and deserted the said child and his mother prior to the birth." Why my mother wound up in Cleveland, Ohio I do not know.

Four days after my birth, my mother put me up for adoption and in a sworn affidavit, stated: "I feel it will be to the best interests of my child if he is adopted by these adopting parents who can give him the home, care and attention which I cannot give. I have done this of my own free will, without any duress or coercion and without any monetary consideration being paid therefor." These are the only words I have of my mother.

I was then placed under the foster care of a legal guardian, one Solomon Meyerson, residing at 1200 Marseille Drive, Miami Beach, Florida, while paperwork was being processed as to the "character and fitness" of my adopting parents, Robert and Renee Coan, who lived in Brooklyn, New York. Fifteen months later, in May 1957, I was released to their custody.

I have no information about Charles W. Mehaffey, except that the name Mehaffey, by genealogy, is Scotch-Irish and Protestant. My mother was Jewish. When I told this to an old Irish friend of mine he said, teasingly, "So, after all is said and done it turns out you're a McJew." . . .

If you, or anyone you know, has any information regarding Martha Jeanette Musselman, Charles W. Mehaffey, or the child they bore between them, please contact:

Facts On File, Inc.

11 Penn Plaza

New York, New York 10001-2006

or, e-mail: pmcoan@aol.com

Five months after publication, in March 1998, a reporter from the *Cleveland Plain Dealer* wrote an article about the book and my search, motivated by potential local interest in a Cleveland-born author. In the meantime, I had been working with a reknowned genealogist from Cleveland. Many facts were uncovered, but the story becomes too complicated, emotional, even bizarre—a panoply of twists and turns—for the space alotted here. Suffice it to say that endless e-mails and phone calls proved fruitless.

A few weeks after the article was published, it found its way into the hands of a retired social worker in Florida. That social worker, as it turned out, had not only once been best friends with my birth mother but was the first person to hold me in her arms after I was born in 1956—which is what she told me one day over the phone at my office, having contacted me through my book publisher.

I was stunned, particularly when she explained that she hadn't seen or spoken to my mother in nearly two decades and that as far as she knew, my mother, Martha Jeanette Musselman, was dead.

But she also had a son who was once a close friend of my brother (at this point I learned I had a brother), who had died accidentally in 1970 at the age of 18. He, the son, offered a crumb of information that saved the day. In his last conversation with my mother, he remembered the mention of her intention to move to Cincinnati, which is where I eventually found her—healthy, happy, and very much alive—grateful to God, as I am, for this second chance in life.

Her story, this story, of the stranger-than-fiction circumstances that led to the reuniting of a mother and her son after more than 42 years will be the subject of my next book.

My father's whereabouts are unknown.

Index

. . . .

. . . .